T0331696

Handbook of Research on Human Development in the Digital Age

Valerie C. Bryan
Florida Atlantic University, USA

Ann T. Musgrove
Florida Atlantic University, USA

Jillian R. Powers
Florida Atlantic University, USA

A volume in the Advances in Human and Social
Aspects of Technology (AHSAT) Book Series

Published in the United States of America by
    IGI Global
    Information Science Reference (an imprint of IGI Global)
    701 E. Chocolate Avenue
    Hershey PA, USA 17033
    Tel: 717-533-8845
    Fax: 717-533-8661
    E-mail: cust@igi-global.com
    Web site: http://www.igi-global.com

Library of Congress Cataloging-in-Publication Data

Names: Bryan, Valerie C., editor. | Musgrove, Ann T., 1956- editor. | Powers,
    Jillian R., 1972- editor.
Title: Handbook of research on human development in the digital age / Valerie
    C. Bryan, Ann T. Musgrove, and Jillian R. Powers, editors.
Description: Hershey : Information Science Reference, [2017]
Identifiers: LCCN 2017010367| ISBN 9781522528388 (hardcover) | ISBN
    9781522528395 (ebook)
Subjects: LCSH: Computer-assisted instruction--Psychological aspects. |
    Educational psychology. | Developmental psychology.
Classification: LCC LB1028.5 .H3164 2017 | DDC 371.33/4019--dc23 LC record available at https://lccn.loc.
gov/2017010367

This book is published in the IGI Global book series Advances in Human and Social Aspects of Technology (AHSAT)
(ISSN: 2328-1316; eISSN: 2328-1324)

British Cataloguing in Publication Data
A Cataloguing in Publication record for this book is available from the British Library.

For electronic access to this publication, please contact: eresources@igi-global.com.

Advances in Human and Social Aspects of Technology (AHSAT) Book Series

Ashish Dwivedi
The University of Hull, UK

ISSN:2328-1316
EISSN:2328-1324

MISSION

In recent years, the societal impact of technology has been noted as we become increasingly more connected and are presented with more digital tools and devices. With the popularity of digital devices such as cell phones and tablets, it is crucial to consider the implications of our digital dependence and the presence of technology in our everyday lives.

The **Advances in Human and Social Aspects of Technology (AHSAT) Book Series** seeks to explore the ways in which society and human beings have been affected by technology and how the technological revolution has changed the way we conduct our lives as well as our behavior. The AHSAT book series aims to publish the most cutting-edge research on human behavior and interaction with technology and the ways in which the digital age is changing society.

COVERAGE

- Computer-Mediated Communication
- Information ethics
- End-User Computing
- Technology and Social Change
- Cultural Influence of ICTs
- Gender and Technology
- Human Development and Technology
- ICTs and human empowerment
- Technoself
- Activism and ICTs

IGI Global is currently accepting manuscripts for publication within this series. To submit a proposal for a volume in this series, please contact our Acquisition Editors at Acquisitions@igi-global.com or visit: http://www.igi-global.com/publish/.

Titles in this Series

For a list of additional titles in this series, please visit: www.igi-global.com/book-series/advances-human-social-aspects-technology

Designing for Human-Machine Symbiosis Using the URANOS Model Emerging Research and Opportunities
Benjamin Hadorn (University of Fribourg, Switzerland)
Information Science Reference • ©2017 • 170pp • H/C (ISBN: 9781522518884) • US $125.00

Research Paradigms and Contemporary Perspectives on Human-Technology Interaction
Anabela Mesquita (School of Accounting and Administration of Porto, Polytechnic Institute of Porto, Portugal &
Algorithm Research Centre, Minho University, Portugal)
Information Science Reference • ©2017 • 366pp • H/C (ISBN: 9781522518686) • US $195.00

Solutions for High-Touch Communications in a High-Tech World
Michael A. Brown Sr. (Florida International University, USA)
Information Science Reference • ©2017 • 217pp • H/C (ISBN: 9781522518976) • US $185.00

Design Solutions for User-Centric Information Systems
Saqib Saeed (Imam Abdulrahman Bin Faisal University, Saudi Arabia) Yasser A. Bamarouf (Imam Abdulrahman
Bin Faisal University, Saudi Arabia) T. Ramayah (University Sains Malaysia, Malaysia) and Sardar Zafar Iqbal
(Imam Abdulrahman Bin Faisal University, Saudi Arabia)
Information Science Reference • ©2017 • 422pp • H/C (ISBN: 9781522519447) • US $215.00

Identity, Sexuality, and Relationships among Emerging Adults in the Digital Age
Michelle F. Wright (Masaryk University, Czech Republic)
Information Science Reference • ©2017 • 343pp • H/C (ISBN: 9781522518563) • US $185.00

Enriching Urban Spaces with Ambient Computing, the Internet of Things, and Smart City Design
Shin'ichi Konomi (University of Tokyo, Japan) and George Roussos (University of London, UK)
Engineering Science Reference • ©2017 • 323pp • H/C (ISBN: 9781522508274) • US $210.00

Handbook of Research on Individualism and Identity in the Globalized Digital Age
F. Sigmund Topor (Keio University, Japan)
Information Science Reference • ©2017 • 645pp • H/C (ISBN: 9781522505228) • US $295.00

Information Technology Integration for Socio-Economic Development
Titus Tossy (Mzumbe University, Tanzania)
Information Science Reference • ©2017 • 385pp • H/C (ISBN: 9781522505396) • US $200.00

701 East Chocolate Avenue, Hershey, PA 17033, USA
Tel: 717-533-8845 x100 • Fax: 717-533-8661
E-Mail: cust@igi-global.com • www.igi-global.com

Editorial Advisory Board

List of Contributors

Banner, Phylise / *Phylise Banner Consulting, USA* 1

Bird, Jennifer Lynne / *Florida Atlantic University, USA* 385

Brady, Michael P. / *Florida Atlantic University, USA* 281

Bryan, Valerie C. / *Florida Atlantic University, USA* 33

Buckner, Melody Jo / *University of Arizona, USA* 43

Deaton, Benjamin / *Anderson University, USA* 87

Deaton, Cynthia C. M. / *Clemson University, USA* 87

Duffy, Pamela Ann / *Des Moines University, USA* 258

Eleno-Orama, Maricris / *Tacoma Community College, USA & Western Oklahoma State College, USA* 205

Ellington, Linda Marie / *Southern New Hampshire University, USA* 449

Finnegan, Lisa A. / *Florida Atlantic University, USA* 235

Franck, Edwiygh / *The Greatest You Yet!, USA* 427

Frank, Eva M. / *Northern Illinois University, USA* 163

Goodrich, David / *Michigan State University, USA* 1

Gunder, Angela / *The University of Arizona, USA* 1

Herron, Josh / *Limestone College, USA* 87

Hugh-Pennie, Amoy Kito / *Hong Kong Association for Behavior Analysis, China* 330

Knott, Jessica L. / *Michigan State University, USA* 1

Lau, Bee Theng / *Swinburne University of Technology – Sarawak, Malaysia* 300

Lee, Gabrielle T. / *Michigan State University, USA* 330

Lowe, Jessica A. / *Florida Atlantic University, USA* 184

Loy, Jennifer / *University of Technology Sydney, Australia* 403

Luke, Nicole / *Brock University, Canada* 330

Melton, Robbie / *Tennessee Board of Regents, USA* 1

Miller-Rososhansky, Lori / *Children's Services Council of Palm Beach County, USA* 33

Mitchell, Jessica S. / *University of North Alabama, USA* 135

Musgrove, Ann T. / *Florida Atlantic University, USA* 184

Musgrove, Ann Terrill / *Florida Atlantic University, USA* 1

Novak, James I. / *Griffith University, Australia* 403

Ozdemir, Devrim / *Des Moines University, USA* 258

Park, Hye-Suk Lee / *KAVBA ABA Research Center, South Korea* 330

Powers, Jillian R. / *Florida Atlantic University, USA* 109,184

Preast, Vanessa / *Des Moines University, USA* 258

Randolph, Kathleen M. / *Florida Atlantic University, USA* 281

Ross, David B. / *Nova Southeastern University, USA* 205
Salah, Elizabeth Vultaggio / *Palm Beach County School District, USA* 205
Seamster, Christina L. / *Florida Atlantic University, USA* 66
Shah-Nelson, Clark / *University of Maryland, USA* 1
Tomsic, Frank / *Rush University, USA* 1
Win, Ko Min / *Swinburne University of Technology – Sarawak, Malaysia* 300
Wright, Michelle F. / *Pennsylvania State University, USA* 364

Table of Contents

Foreword xx

Preface xxii

Acknowledgment xxix

Section 1
Pedagogy and Andragogy

Chapter 1

Technology-Enhanced Exploratory Installations to Support Constructivist Professional
Development: The Technology Test Kitchen... 1
Ann Terrill Musgrove, Florida Atlantic University, USA
Angela Gunder, The University of Arizona, USA
Jessica L. Knott, Michigan State University, USA
Frank Tomsic, Rush University, USA
Phylise Banner, Phylise Banner Consulting, USA
Robbie Melton, Tennessee Board of Regents, USA
David Goodrich, Michigan State University, USA
Clark Shah-Nelson, University of Maryland, USA

Chapter 2

Use of Technology-Enabled Informal Learning in a Learning Organization 33
Lori Miller-Rososhansky, Children's Services Council of Palm Beach County, USA
Valerie C. Bryan, Florida Atlantic University, USA

Chapter 3

"Let Me Show You": An Application of Digital Storytelling for Reflective Assessment in Study
Abroad Programs 43
Melody Jo Buckner, University of Arizona, USA

Chapter 4

Distance Education in the K-12 Setting: How Are Virtual School Teachers Evaluated?.................... 66
Christina L. Seamster, Florida Atlantic University, USA

Chapter 5
Mobile Technology and Learning 87
    Benjamin Deaton, Anderson University, USA
    Josh Herron, Limestone College, USA
    Cynthia C. M. Deaton, Clemson University, USA

Chapter 6
Parochial School Teachers Instructional Use of the Interactive Whiteboard 109
    Jillian R. Powers, Florida Atlantic University, USA

Chapter 7
Self-Efficacy and Persistence in a Digital Writing Classroom: A Case Study of Fifth-Grade
Boys 135
    Jessica S. Mitchell, University of North Alabama, USA

Chapter 8
Healthcare Education: Integrating Simulation Technologies 163
    Eva M. Frank, Northern Illinois University, USA

Section 2
Diverse Populations

Chapter 9
Technology Shaping Education in Rural Communities 184
    Jillian R. Powers, Florida Atlantic University, USA
    Ann T. Musgrove, Florida Atlantic University, USA
    Jessica A. Lowe, Florida Atlantic University, USA

Chapter 10
The Aging and Technological Society: Learning Our Way Through the Decades 205
    David B. Ross, Nova Southeastern University, USA
    Maricris Eleno-Orama, Tacoma Community College, USA & Western Oklahoma State
        College, USA
    Elizabeth Vultaggio Salah, Palm Beach County School District, USA

Chapter 11
The Impact of Technology on the Teaching and Learning Process 235
    Lisa A. Finnegan, Florida Atlantic University, USA

Chapter 12
Systematic Approach for Improving Accessibility and Usability in Online Courses 258
    Devrim Ozdemir, Des Moines University, USA
    Vanessa Preast, Des Moines University, USA
    Pamela Ann Duffy, Des Moines University, USA

Chapter 13
Evolution of Covert Coaching as an Evidence-Based Practice in Professional Development and
Preparation of Teachers..281
    Kathleen M. Randolph, Florida Atlantic University, USA
    Michael P. Brady, Florida Atlantic University, USA

Chapter 14
Differentiated Animated Social Stories to Enhance Social Skills Acquisition of Children With
Autism Spectrum Disorder 300
    Bee Theng Lau, Swinburne University of Technology – Sarawak, Malaysia
    Ko Min Win, Swinburne University of Technology – Sarawak, Malaysia

Chapter 15
Applied Behavior Analysis as a Teaching Technology..330
    Amoy Kito Hugh-Pennie, Hong Kong Association for Behavior Analysis, China
    Hye-Suk Lee Park, KAVBA ABA Research Center, South Korea
    Nicole Luke, Brock University, Canada
    Gabrielle T. Lee, Michigan State University, USA

Section 3
Theoretical and Experiential Perspectives

Chapter 16
Youths and Cyberbullying: Description, Theories, and Recommendations......................................364
    Michelle F. Wright, Pennsylvania State University, USA

Chapter 17
Constantly Connected: Managing Stress in Today's Technological Times..385
    Jennifer Lynne Bird, Florida Atlantic University, USA

Chapter 18
Digital Technologies and 4D Customized Design: Challenging Conventions With Responsive
Design 403
    James I. Novak, Griffith University, Australia
    Jennifer Loy, University of Technology Sydney, Australia

Chapter 19
Distributed Work Environments: The Impact of Technology in the Workplace 427
    Edwiygh Franck, The Greatest You Yet!, USA

Chapter 20
Cognitive Investment Into the Interaction Society...449
    Linda Marie Ellington, Southern New Hampshire University, USA

Compilation of References 461

About the Contributors 513

Index...522

Detailed Table of Contents

Foreword xx

Preface xxii

Acknowledgment xxix

Section 1
Pedagogy and Andragogy

Chapter 1

Technology-Enhanced Exploratory Installations to Support Constructivist Professional
Development: The Technology Test Kitchen 1

Ann Terrill Musgrove, Florida Atlantic University, USA
Angela Gunder, The University of Arizona, USA
Jessica L. Knott, Michigan State University, USA
Frank Tomsic, Rush University, USA
Phylise Banner, Phylise Banner Consulting, USA
Robbie Melton, Tennessee Board of Regents, USA
David Goodrich, Michigan State University, USA
Clark Shah-Nelson, University of Maryland, USA

The growth in technology tools and their uses continues to grow at an exponential pace. Whether it is for personal or professional use technology is everywhere, and it is ubiquitous. It is changing the way we seek knowledge, interact with information, and process the world around us to construct our learning pathways. Technology has made it simple for us to be consumers of information, but how do we evaluate and synthesize this information to construct meaning and create value? The technology test kitchen is a curated and managed makerspace designed for exploratory installation where novices and experts engage in deep, meaningful, constructive uses of technology for teaching and learning. The goal of the test kitchen is acquisition of "native-expert" use of technology in support of authentic learning, engendering deeper levels of technological fluency within a constructivist professional development experience.

Chapter 2
Use of Technology-Enabled Informal Learning in a Learning Organization 33
    Lori Miller-Rososhansky, Children's Services Council of Palm Beach County, USA
    Valerie C. Bryan, Florida Atlantic University, USA

This chapter explores how an organization created to inform members became an online learning organization. Using technology, the organization continued to support the professionals as they evolved in their individual careers and within the organization. Best practices arose to better inform the members and to expand communities of practice (CoPs). Members meaningfully engaged in the learning organization, in their avocations, and their vocations. This mix-method study, with over a 118 Association for Talent Development (ATD) professionals, addressed how the ATD could continue to support professionals in our evolving technological society. The study allowed the ATD professionals themselves to identify how they could help the organization and its' members to advance the organization by using technology, informal learning and research-based learning to improve the membership organization roles. The study highlighted how important informal learning, professional development, modeling, and identifying best practices, are to an organization's growth and the professionals' growth.

Chapter 3
"Let Me Show You": An Application of Digital Storytelling for Reflective Assessment in Study
Abroad Programs 43
    Melody Jo Buckner, University of Arizona, USA

Criticism has been prevalent around the academic rigor of coursework within study abroad programs. Stakeholders of the study abroad experience are taking a closer look at student learning outcomes from these programs. This critique suggests that more attention be given to the development of innovative and meaningful assessment practices being implemented into these programs in order for students to demonstrate their learning outcomes. The purpose of this study was to investigate the affordances of digital storytelling as a response to this critique. The focus of this study was to implement a digital storytelling assignment in four summer study abroad programs led by university faculty. Over the course of four summers (2011 – 2014), digital storytelling was implemented to help students reflect upon what they learned and through this reflective process demonstrate the knowledge they gained. This article discusses the findings of digital storytelling as a reflective assessment practice in study abroad programs.

Chapter 4
Distance Education in the K-12 Setting: How Are Virtual School Teachers Evaluated? 66
    Christina L. Seamster, Florida Atlantic University, USA

The evolution of technology over the last century has in many ways changed how teachers teach today. From kindergarten through twelfth grade, students are now able to complete 100% of their schooling online. If novel teaching practices have been established as a result of technology advancements, tools which align with those teaching practices must be produced in order to ensure continued student success. The purpose of this chapter is two-fold; to review teacher practices in K-12 distance education today and to discuss the field of education's need for research in measuring K-12 virtual school teacher effectiveness. The chapter begins with an overview of the history of distance education, followed by an examination of virtual school teacher pedagogy, a brief review of measuring K-12 teacher performance in the traditional and virtual school settings, and a synopsis of current tools for evaluating K-12 virtual school teacher effectiveness. The chapter closes with solutions and recommendation for future research.

Chapter 5

Mobile Technology and Learning 87

    Benjamin Deaton, Anderson University, USA

    Josh Herron, Limestone College, USA

    Cynthia C. M. Deaton, Clemson University, USA

With an awareness of the unique characteristics of an increasingly mobile world and referencing socio-material mobile learning frameworks, this chapter will provide an overview of the initial stages and growth of mobile learning. The authors also discuss university initiatives to support mobile learning, and examine the implications of mobile technologies for teaching and learning. Additionally, the chapter will introduce a case study detailing the Mobile Learning Innovation at Anderson University (SC) and highlight its impact on the teaching and learning culture on its campus.

Chapter 6

Parochial School Teachers Instructional Use of the Interactive Whiteboard 109

    Jillian R. Powers, Florida Atlantic University, USA

This chapter presents findings from a study that utilized Davis' (1989) Technology Acceptance Model (TAM) to investigate K-8 teachers' instructional usage of the interactive whiteboard (IWB). Through surveying 145 teachers and 40 administrators of the Lutheran Church Missouri Synod schools, the researcher used multiple regression and moderator analyses to examine whether the TAM model helped explain teachers' reported teacher-centered and student-centered instructional IWB use. The results of the study indicated two variables adapted from the TAM, teachers' perceived usefulness (PU) and perceived ease of use (PEOU) of the IWB, contributed to the prediction of teacher-centered instructional usage, and PU contributed to the prediction of student-centered instructional usage. Moderator analysis indicated the variable for teachers' technological pedagogical content knowledge of the IWB moderated the relationships between PEOU of the IWB and each teacher and student-centered instructional usage, as well as between PU of the IWB and teacher-centered instructional usage.

Chapter 7

Self-Efficacy and Persistence in a Digital Writing Classroom: A Case Study of Fifth-Grade
Boys 135

    Jessica S. Mitchell, University of North Alabama, USA

Utilizing a New Literacies perspective, the purpose of this qualitative case study was to explore the digital writing experiences of one classroom of fifth-grade boys. Research questions for this study included the following: (1) What features of the digital writing environment impact student expressions of confidence in their abilities as writers? (2) How do expressions of confidence align with performance for students who are the least persistent in digital writing tasks? (3) How do expressions of confidence align with performance for students who are the most persistent in digital writing tasks? Through an embedded analysis, eight confidence features were identified. Compared against a holistic analysis of individual focal student experiences, this chapter provides two student vignettes to illustrate the differences between high-persisting and low-persisting students in a digital writing classroom.

Chapter 8
Healthcare Education: Integrating Simulation Technologies 163
    Eva M. Frank, Northern Illinois University, USA

The integration of technology into the education and continuous professional education of allied health professionals is evolving. Integrating simulation as an authentic instructional modality has changed how clinicians learn and practice the clinical knowledge, skills, and abilities they are required to be competent in to ensure patient safety. A lot of advances have been made in the utilization of simulation in various domains. Continuing medical education is such a domain, and this chapter will briefly describe the history of simulation, present simulation as an authentic instructional activity, examine education trends of using simulation-based learning, highlight two applicable theoretical frameworks, and present a case study that effectively utilized simulation as an authentic instructional strategy and assessment during a continuing medical education course for athletic trainers.

Section 2
Diverse Populations

Chapter 9
Technology Shaping Education in Rural Communities 184
    Jillian R. Powers, Florida Atlantic University, USA
    Ann T. Musgrove, Florida Atlantic University, USA
    Jessica A. Lowe, Florida Atlantic University, USA

This chapter examines how technology has shaped the teaching and learning process for individuals residing in rural areas. Research on the history and unique needs of rural communities and the impact of technology in these areas is discussed. Educational experiences of students across all grade levels, from early childhood though post-secondary education, is examined. Examples of innovative and creative uses educational technologies in distance and face-to-face settings are described from the perspective of rural teachers and students.

Chapter 10
The Aging and Technological Society: Learning Our Way Through the Decades 205
    David B. Ross, Nova Southeastern University, USA
    Maricris Eleno-Orama, Tacoma Community College, USA & Western Oklahoma State
        College, USA
    Elizabeth Vultaggio Salah, Palm Beach County School District, USA

This chapter provides information and support for researchers, family, and medical providers concerning how technology can improve the quality of life for older adults while remain independent as they age in place at home or a community. In examining the available research, the researchers did find continuous developments in Gerontechnology to be beneficial as the aging population is rapidly increasing worldwide. There is increased recognition of the advancement in technology to help the aging in areas of autonomy, socialization, and mental and physical wellbeing. This chapter covered areas of change, independence with a better quality of life, technological devices/adoptions, generational differences and learning with technologies, and university-based retirement communities. This chapter concludes with suggestions for future development in accessibility of technology-based educational programs and the Internet, how to infuse technology to advance the older adults' independence and quality of life, and how older adults are adapting to living in life span communities.

Chapter 11

The Impact of Technology on the Teaching and Learning Process 235
Lisa A. Finnegan, Florida Atlantic University, USA

The teaching and learning process of traditionally run classrooms will need to change to meet up with the requirements under the reauthorization of the Elementary and Secondary Education Act as the Every Student Succeeds Act (ESSA). Under the ESSA, the infusion of the Universal Design for Learning (UDL) framework into the teaching and learning environment sets the stage so that instruction and assessment support all levels of learners. Along with UDL, ESSA supports the inclusion of technology-rich learning environments to prepare students for 21st century problem-solving and critical thinking skills. Critical to preparing students comes an understanding of who the 21st century learners are. The current teaching and learning process involving the use of technology continues to hold students back as passive observers of content. Merging technology and the UDL framework in the classroom will be an avenue to meeting the learning needs and wants of 21st century students.

Chapter 12

Systematic Approach for Improving Accessibility and Usability in Online Courses 258
Devrim Ozdemir, Des Moines University, USA
Vanessa Preast, Des Moines University, USA
Pamela Ann Duffy, Des Moines University, USA

The purpose of this chapter is to provide a systematic approach for improving accessibility and usability in online courses. Accessibility and usability are of particular importance to provide equal human development opportunities to those who have various disabilities in the digital age. The authors developed a systematic approach as a result of a comprehensive accessibility and usability review process of an actual online course. The review involved a team-based collaborative approach. The team consisted of an accessibility professional, an instructional design coordinator, and a course instructor who collaborated to perform the thorough examination process. The presented model is of particular importance to improve accessibility and usability of online courses, which in turn enhances the quality of human development for disabled learners.

Chapter 13

Evolution of Covert Coaching as an Evidence-Based Practice in Professional Development and
Preparation of Teachers 281
Kathleen M. Randolph, Florida Atlantic University, USA
Michael P. Brady, Florida Atlantic University, USA

There is a tradition of coaching in many fields that prepares and improves performance among professionals. Coaching practices evolved over time, with several technological applications developed to improve the coaching process. An application gaining attention as an evidence-based practice is the use of wireless communication systems in which coaching statements are delivered to individuals while they engage in work. In education this has been called Bug-in-Ear coaching or Covert Audio Coaching, and has demonstrated its efficacy as a coaching intervention with teachers, families, and individuals with developmental disabilities. In this chapter the evolution of coaching across disciplines is summarized and specific applications that hold promise as an evidence-based practice for the professional development and preparation of teachers are described. This chapter summarizes 22 studies which support covert coaching as an evidence-based practice. Covert coaching enables immediate feedback without interrupting the participants, and provides opportunities for immediate error correction.

Chapter 14

Differentiated Animated Social Stories to Enhance Social Skills Acquisition of Children With
Autism Spectrum Disorder 300

Bee Theng Lau, Swinburne University of Technology – Sarawak, Malaysia
Ko Min Win, Swinburne University of Technology – Sarawak, Malaysia

This study developed a web-based social skills intervention system accessible via a tablet/laptop computer which combines differentiated instructions, social stories, multimedia, and animations. This creates an interactive learning environment which (1) allows children to learn social skills repeatedly and pervasively; and (2) promotes teacher/caretaker-parent collaborations to boost the ASD children's social skills acquisition as, a simple logon to the portal enables parents/ caretakers and teachers to view the media prepared by others; track and reinforce the skills a child has learnt at home/ in school, and add his/her social stories which others can view. The prototype evaluation and observation of voluntary participants from the special education school who were treated with differentiated animated social stories demonstrates that digital-based differentiated social story interventions have made the learning of social skills more interactive, appealing and effective compared to the traditional social skill tools.

Chapter 15

Applied Behavior Analysis as a Teaching Technology 330

Amoy Kito Hugh-Pennie, Hong Kong Association for Behavior Analysis, China
Hye-Suk Lee Park, KAVBA ABA Research Center, South Korea
Nicole Luke, Brock University, Canada
Gabrielle T. Lee, Michigan State University, USA

Applied behavior analysis is known as an effective way to address the needs of people with autism spectrum disorders. The layperson may also associate behavior analysis with forensic psychology through their experience of crime dramas such as Criminal Minds: Behavior Analysis Unit. However accurate or simplified these portrayals they are a very narrow view of the larger field of behavioral science. Behavior analysis has a host of applications in the real world. Some of these applications include but are certainly not limited to the determination of social policies, advertising, policing, animal training, business practices, diet and exercise regimens and education. In this chapter the authors will focus on how applied behavior analysis can be used as a teaching technology from the behavioral and educational literature that has the potential to help lead the way out of the educational crisis faced in the United States of America and abroad.

Section 3
Theoretical and Experiential Perspectives

Chapter 16

Youths and Cyberbullying: Description, Theories, and Recommendations 364

Michelle F. Wright, Pennsylvania State University, USA

Youths are immersed in a digitally connected world, where blogs, social networking sites, watching videos, and instant messaging tools are a normal part of their lives. Many of these youths cannot remember a time in which electronic technologies were not embedded within their lives. Electronic technologies afford a variety of opportunities for youths, but there are also risks associated with such use, such as cyberbullying. This chapter draws on research from around the world to explain the nature, extent, causes, and consequences of cyberbullying. This chapter concludes with a solutions and recommendation section, emphasizing the need for cyberbullying to be considered a global concern.

Chapter 17
Constantly Connected: Managing Stress in Today's Technological Times 385
  Jennifer Lynne Bird, Florida Atlantic University, USA

As society has transitioned from landlines to iPhones, people find themselves connected to their mobile devices 24/7. While the advantages of new technologies have led to constant availability, it has also led to additional stress and disconnection. For example, how many times have you seen a group of people out to dinner but they are all looking at their phones and not at each other? The problem is not the technology; instead, people need better coping strategies to deal with stress and the constant flood of information. This chapter will address the health consequences of stress and provide suggestions for how people can deal with stress in their lives. It will also illustrate the need for connection and the value of people being their authentic selves instead of portraying an image for social media.

Chapter 18
Digital Technologies and 4D Customized Design: Challenging Conventions With Responsive
Design 403
  James I. Novak, Griffith University, Australia
  Jennifer Loy, University of Technology Sydney, Australia

Digital design tools are rapidly changing and blurring the boundaries between design disciplines. By extension, the relationship between humans and products is also changing, to the point where opportunities are emerging for products that can co-evolve with their human users over time. This chapter highlights how these '4D products' respond to the vision laid out three decades ago for ubiquitous computing, and have the potential to enhance human experiences by creating more seamless human-centered relationships with technology. These developments are examined in context with broader shifts in sociocultural and environmental concerns, as well as similar developments being researched in Responsive Architecture, 4D printing and systems designed to empower individuals during the design process through interactive, parametric model platforms. Technology is fundamentally changing the way designers create physical products, and new understandings are needed to positively guide these changes.

Chapter 19
Distributed Work Environments: The Impact of Technology in the Workplace 427
  Edwiygh Franck, The Greatest You Yet!, USA

Technology is making the traditional workplace obsolete. Companies are taking advantage of the myriads of digital resources available to make their processes leaner, cut costs and have a larger presence in the global market through the concept of distributed work environment. In this chapter, the author provides an overview of the distributed work environment, as well as the impact it has on the human condition in the workplace. Although this technology driven work concept can be beneficial, companies have to ensure that it is the right business model for them and their employees. The author looks at different factors that companies need to consider in deciding to adopt a distributed work environment model. Several companies, over 125 of them, have successfully implemented the concept and the author shares some examples on how they were able to achieve success and employee satisfaction.

Chapter 20

Cognitive Investment Into the Interaction Society..449
Linda Marie Ellington, Southern New Hampshire University, USA

There is a cascade of interest in the topic of interactive time and space. and it might may be useful to align our cognitive investment that contributes to the operational goals of our thinking, our beliefs, and reactions to the phase of co-evolution of the human with the interaction society. If we want to build a rich understanding of how our mental assets influence involvement into this unique society, we need to be able to make a case for the crucial role of framing how the digital intergalactic transforms individuals and society. The mode of interactions may not be instruments of cognitive evolution, but the how of weaving together different perspectives of human development and engagement with cutting-edge interaction technology may be a significant player in the new cyborg society order.

Compilation of References 461

About the Contributors 513

Index 522

Foreword

The increasing proliferation of emerging smart technologies innovations of 'The Internet of Everything' (IoE) has undoubtedly, impacted human growth and development, in terms of how we now communicate (global networks), how we educate (create, teach, learn, access and delivery of digital content), how we operate (technology enabled smart homes, schools, and communities), how we care for ourselves (telemedicine, fitness and wellness medical wearable devices), how we conduct business (online shopping, banking), how we produce products and our productivity (word processing, processing of more products in less time, 3D printing, digital multimedia), how we entertain (digital music, gamification, online sports, mixed VR/AR reality), our safety and protection (online privacy, cybersecurity, and anti-cyberbullying) and most importantly, our interpersonal and social relationships (cultural exchanges, social media, online dating, and social networks). We are now living in a world that due to the rapid growth of technology is interconnected with everything and everyone.

Observing these technological transformations within my forty-five years of serving in various educational positions as a PreK-12 regular teacher, special education administrator, college professor, technologist, student service coordinator, distance education director, instructional designer, faculty trainer, curriculum specialist, program evaluator, author, researcher, international presenter, and twenty years of experience in higher education administration, I (like other educators) am in dire need of research regarding the educational implications, effectiveness of, and best practices for implementing these emerging technologies. Thus, I found that this book not only addresses those noted issues in an in-depth format but also presents possible use cases, noted challenges and barriers for adoption (ADA, digital divide, digital addictions) and workforce impact.

This book is also timely due to the latest technological innovations in the last three years regarding online delivery, virtual learning spaces, maker-space, global communication tools, digital content, and mobile technology. Whereas, the significance of this of this book is to assist educators and researchers in addressing the effectiveness of emerging digital technologies and standards for appropriate use in enhancing teaching, improving learning, increasing student retention, outcomes, graduation completion, and successful workforce obtainment. Furthermore, what I appreciate most about this collection of articles is that the information is designed with enough details for the reader to replicate or customize the methodologies to address one's campus strategic educational goals and faculty and students' needs. In addition, the research studies are presented for the reader to engage in a reflective assessment of current digital technologies in enhancing educational growth and workforce development.

Most noteworthy, this team of experts and experienced educational technology authors, provide a personal in-depth perspective of how technology has transformed our schools, workplace, community, health, welfare, businesses, and most importantly our social interactions. These authors provide personal insight and case studies to help the reader understand the issues, to acknowledge the trends, and to identify areas of needs for strategic planning. Not to mention that I have personally observed, presented, and published with several of the noted authors regarding the transformation of technology, serving on technology evaluation teams, digital content instructional curriculum support, and the effectiveness of emerging technology for teaching, learning, student success, and workforce preparedness for a digital world.

I highly recommend this book for addressing the relationship of human growth and development and the impact it has in the digital age.

I commend the authors for their efforts in tackling these issues and their willingness to mentor and invite others to contribute to this body of knowledge.

Robbie K. Melton
Tennessee Board of Regents, USA
February 27, 2017

Preface

We are currently living in an age of rapidly advancing technology that continually changes how we go about our daily lives. Technology affects us across different cultures and at all points of the lifespan, transforming how we interact, develop, work, and play. Ubiquitous technologies have made it possible for such transformations to take place anywhere at any time with a host of devices. The implications as to how these innovations are shaping the human experience are profound. The impact of technology is pervasive and permeates into the core of our daily lives on both a personal and professional basis.

In our current world, having access to information and knowing how to use that information has become an integral part of being an educated citizen. Knowledge is a dynamic, living thing. Everything from the way we work or play to the way we manage the ebb and flow of our daily lives is being changed drastically and at warp speed by technology. Individuals possessing the skills necessary for employment, to be self-sufficient, and to maintain a quality of life, are essential if our communities are to remain vibrant. (Bryan, 2006, p. 11)

The objective of this book is to examine the impact technology is having on the human development across a diverse group of disciplines. Chapters from scholars and practitioners from a variety of backgrounds, nationalities, and expertise document research, theories, and best practices that explore how technology is shaping the human experience at all levels.

Chapters examine how current and emerging technologies have changed the way we act and conduct our daily lives. Some of the questions examined in this book include:

1. In what ways does technology impact the exchanges between our learning partners in multiple disciplines?
2. How have interaction patterns altered how we process information and collaborate, and what impact will these changes have on the varied populations we serve?
3. What are products that will be produced (i.e., wearable devices, accessible equipment for the disabled, 3D printing, crowd sourced applications, smart machines, etc.) and what impact will these products have on education needed or new careers that have not been thought of yet?
4. How will information be delivered related to health, education, communication, economics, etc., and what type of career skills will be needed to harness the information?
5. Will collaborations across disciplines and across nations increase or become more divided by those who control the technology and the information?

6.   Who will be equipped to offer educational services to our digitally savvy children? Who will train these teachers or educators or guides on the side?

7.   How long will our aging population continue to work and what new careers will they spawn?

8.   With more women entering the world workforce with access to mobile technologies, what (if any) impact will they make on the health, education, law, business, medicine, and service sectors?

9.   Can technology encourage a global cultural exchange more now than we have ever known before?

10. When you can access people around the world anytime, where will the boundaries be drawn for how you interact?

11. Are there adverse technological impacts (such as a new kind of cyber-crime) for those working in the "cloud", less active youth and adults that are consumed by staying connected, health issues created because of "cyber-stress", etc.?

12. What impact, if any, will technology have on sustainability of business practices across the globe?

Not all these questions can be addressed in one book, but as you explore the topics think of the questions that need to be asked as we continue to move into the technological era and explore our new technologically enhanced world.

ORGANIZATION OF THE BOOK

This book is organized into three sections that examine the impact of technology with different lenses. The first looks at the material from a learner theory perspective of *Pedagogy and Andragogy*. The second lens focuses on how technology plays a specific role in serving *Diverse Populations*. The third allows the reader to see the impact of technology through various *Theoretical and Experiential Perspectives*.

Pedagogy and Andragogy

If we teach today as we taught yesterday, we rob our children of tomorrow. – John Dewey (1944, p. 167)

The first section of this book, "Pedagogy and Andragogy," illustrates how learning can evolve from *pedagogy learning model* to the andragogy learning model. Pedagogy (Whitmyer, 1999), the art and science of helping children to learn, is teacher-directed instruction and generally assumes the student is in a submissive role and needs the teacher's instructions in order for them to learn. The result is a teaching and learning situation that actively promotes dependency on the instructor (Knowles, 1984a). In pedagogy, the teacher decides what the content will be, how it will be organized and transmitted, and what the most effective method will be to accomplish that. For those reasons, pedagogy is generally viewed as more passive and more teacher-directed.

The *andragogy learning model* assumes that, as people mature:

- His or her self-concept moves from that of a dependent personality toward one of a self-directing human being.
- That he or she, as an adult, has accumulated a growing reservoir of experience, which is a rich resource for learning.
- The readiness of an adult to learn is closely related to the development task of his or her social role.

- There is a change in time perspective as people mature from future application of knowledge to immediacy of application. Thus an adult is more problem-centered than subject-centered in learning (Knowles, 1980, pp. 44-45).
- The most potent motivations are internal rather than external (Knowles & Associates, 1984, p. 12).
- Adults need to know why the need to learn something (Knowles, 1984b).

In the first chapter, "Technology-Enhanced Exploratory Installations to Support Constructivist Professional Development: The Technology Test Kitchen," Ann Musgrove and seven of her colleagues describe a unique model for technology professional development called the Technology Test Kitchen (TTK). The TTK is a makerspace designed as an exploratory installation where learners engage in deep, hands-on, constructive uses of innovative and emerging technologies. The chapter explores the background of both the space and effective practice of exploratory installations, present pedagogical challenges and issues addressed by this solution, and highlights the vision, theoretical foundations, history, and philosophy of the space more commonly referred to as the TTK.

In the second chapter, "Use of Technology-Enabled Informal Learning in a Learning Organization," Lori Miller-Rososhansky and Valerie Bryan explore how an organization created to inform members can become an online learning organization through non-formal, informal learning, and formal research-based learning. The organization, using technology, continues to support the professionals as they evolve in their individual careers and within the organization. As with many organizations, best practices arise to better inform the members and to expand communities of practice (CoPs) that meaningfully engage the members in the learning organization in their avocations and their vocations.

Chapter three, "'Let Me Show You': An Application of Digital Storytelling for Reflective Assessment in Study Abroad Programs," by Melody Jo Buckner presents a study that investigated the affordances of digital storytelling as a response to the critique of the academic rigor of coursework within study abroad programs. This chapter also discusses the findings of digital storytelling as a reflective assessment practice in study abroad programs.

Next, Christina Seamster shifts the focus to current trends in technology and K-12 education in her chapter titled "Distance Education in the K-12 Setting: How Are Virtual School Teachers Evaluated?" The chapter begins by reviewing the history of distance education, virtual school teacher pedagogy, and the role of a virtual school teacher. Next, research-based best practices for K-12 virtual school settings are examined. Finally, the author provides an overview of tools available for evaluating virtual school teacher effectiveness and discusses the work that needs to continue in the field of evaluating virtual school teacher effectiveness.

In Chapter 5, "Mobile Technology and Learning," Benjamin Deaton, Josh Herron and Cynthia Deaton provide an overview of the initial stages and growth of mobile learning. The authors also discuss university initiatives to support mobile learning, and examine the implications of mobile technologies for teaching and learning. Additionally, the chapter includes a case study detailing the Mobile Learning Innovation at Anderson University which highlights its impact on the teaching and learning culture on its campus.

In Chapter 6, a study of "Parochial School Teachers' Instructional Use of the Interactive Whiteboard," is presented by Jillian Powers. The study used the Technology Acceptance Model (TAM) to investigate K-8 teachers' instructional usage of the interactive whiteboard (IWB) (Davis, 1989). A survey of educators from Lutheran Church Missouri Synod schools was used to gather data, and the researcher used multiple regression and moderator analyses to examine whether the TAM model helped explain teachers' reported instructional IWB use.

Next, in Chapter 7, Jessica Mitchell details a qualitative study titled "Self-Efficacy and Persistence in a Digital Writing Classroom: A Case Study of Fifth-Grade Boys." The qualitative case study sought to explore the digital writing experiences of a single classroom of fifth-grade boys utilizing a New Literacies perspective. The chapter presents the findings of the study, and provides two student vignettes to illustrate the differences between high-persisting and low-persisting students in a digital writing classroom.

Chapter 8, "Healthcare Education: Integrating Simulation Technologies," by Eva Frank explores the use of simulation as an authentic instructional strategy during the continuing education of health care professionals. The chapter includes a discussion of the history of simulation, types of simulators, and trends in using simulation in education. The author also presents a case study of a continuing education course that used simulation to teach certified athletic trainers how to conduct a comprehensive cardiovascular screening.

Diverse Populations

The marvelous richness of human experience would lose something of rewarding joy if there were no limitations to overcome. The hilltop hour would not be half so wonderful if there were no dark valleys to traverse. – Helen Keller

The second section of this book, "Diverse Populations," shares information regarding how technology is being used to lessen the boundaries between people using technologies. Technology is providing myriad of new ways to help diverse populations. A quick internet search will yield many apps available to people with a variety of challenges. These apps include help for individuals with speech disorders, visual impairment, deafness or hard of hearing and autism, just to name a few. The technology of 3-D printers are being used to create a variety of custom orthotics. In many cases this is an attempt to establish social justice in the communities that previous may have lacked equality and solidarity. Many of the chapters address diverse populations that may have had less access to technology due to location, cultural lines, age cohorts, learning differences, disabilities, or lack of social skills. The chapters illustrate that one person at a time can be empowered to become the best they can be, while also becoming an ambassador of change in their own community.

Chapter 9, "Technology Shaping Education in Rural Communities," by Jillian Powers, Ann Musgrove, and Jessica Lowe paints a picture of how technology has shaped the teaching and learning process for individuals residing in rural areas. The authors discuss the unique educational challenges rural communities face and describe ways that technology is making new educational opportunities possible for learners in rural areas. The example of a one to one computing initiative in a rural Florida school district is presented.

Chapter 10, "The Aging and Technological Society: Learning Our Way Through the Decades," by Davis Ross, Maricris Eleno-Orama, and Elizabeth Vultaggio Salah, examines how technology is changing the lives of older individuals. The chapter provides information regarding how technology can improve the quality of life for older adults. Topics the authors explore include: how people handle change, remaining independent with a better quality of life, technological devices and their adoption, generational differences in technology, learning and technologies, and university-based retirement communities.

Next, in Chapter 11, "The Impact of Technology on the Teaching and Learning Process: Maximizing Learning for 21st Century Students," Lisa Finnegan examines ways technology has changed the teaching and learning process. The author explains how the Universal Design for Learning framework and technology integration are changing teaching, learning, assessment, and curriculum to benefit all students, including those with learning differences.

In Chapter 12, Devrim Ozdemir, Vanessa Preast, and Pamela Ann Duffy discuss "Systematic Approach for Improving Accessibility and Usability in Online Courses." The chapter describes a process for how to design online courses so that they are accessible and usable for all students, including those with disabilities. The chapter offers education stakeholders, such as compliance officers, learning management system administrators, faculty development personnel, course instructors, multimedia development specialists, instructional designers, and program administrators, a systematic process that can be applied in a broad range on online courses.

In Chapter 13, "Evolution of Covert Coaching as an Evidence-Based Practice in Professional Development and Preparation of Teachers," Kathleen Randolph and Michael Brady examine how covert coaching can advance the lives of individuals with developmental disabilities with the help of discreet wireless communication technologies. The chapter summarizes research that supports covert coaching as an evidence-based practice and offers guidelines for covert coaching with these various electronic technologies.

The next chapter, "Differentiated Animated Social Stories to Enhance Social Skills Acquisition of Children With Autism Spectrum Disorder," by Bee Theng Lau and Ko Min Win, presents a study that evaluated a web-based social skills intervention system and the behavioral responses of autistic children in Malaysia. The system was accessible via a tablet/laptop computer that combined differentiated instructions, social stories, multimedia, and animations. The researchers found that the digital-based differentiated animated social stories made the learning of social skills more interactive, appealing and effective compared to the traditional social skill tools.

In Chapter 15, "Applied Behavior Analysis as a Teaching Technology," Amoy Kito Hugh-Pennie, Hye-Suk Lee Park, Nicole Luke, and Gabrielle Lee describe effective ways to address the needs of people with autism spectrum disorders. In the chapter, the authors review the behavioral and educational literature, review the behavioral and educational literature, describe how to use applied behavior analysis as a teaching technology, and present practical classroom scenarios.

Theoretical and Experiential Perspectives

We always live at the time we live and not at some other time, and only by extracting at each present time the full meaning of each present experience are we prepared for doing the same thing in the future.
– John Dewey (1938, p. 51)

The third section of this book, "Theoretical and Experiential Perspectives," focuses on how technology changes the way we look at the foundations of learning. The study of educational theory and how we learn has its roots in ancient philosophy, with psychologists joining the discussion and in more recent times (in the 1800s). When educators explore learning theory it involves many different elements focusing on the process, as well as the goal, and all the variable in between. Skinner's (1968) behavioral theories of learning focused on the final result of learning using the variables of positive reinforcement, punishment and negative reinforcing, but not on the process of learning. Piaget's theory of cognitive development in children explored developmental stages describing new experiences as assimilation and adding knowledge to existing knowledge as accommodation. His theory addresses the process and divides learning into readiness levels by a child's age. Vygotsky (1980) contributions were late to arrive in the western world but he also described the process of learning including scaffolding and the zone of proximal development. Dewey (1916), considered more a philosopher than a learning theorist, explored learning as a reform movement and suggested social activism and cultural change. Perhaps the most relevant theory on technology and its impact on learning for this book is the TPACK framework of Mishra and Koehler (2006). The TPACK framework looks at the intersection of the three areas, Technology Knowledge (TK), Content Knowledge (CK) and Pedagogical Knowledge (PK). All three elements TK, CK, and PK need to be considered as variables when teaching and learning with technology.

Chapter 16, "Youths and Cyberbullying: Description, Theories, and Recommendations," by Michelle Wright, describes the growing problem of cyberbullying. The chapter draws on research to explain the nature, extent, causes, and consequences of cyberbullying among youths in elementary, middle, and high schools. The literature reviewed comes from a variety of disciplines, including psychology, sociology, education, social work, communication studies, gender studies, and computer science. The author concludes by offering solutions and recommendations, stressing the need for cyberbullying to be considered a global concern.

Next, in Chapter 17, "Constantly Connected: Managing Stress in Today's Technological Times," Jennifer Lynne Bird explores how living in an age in which individuals are connected to mobile devices 24/7 impacts health and well-being. The chapter is presented in the form of a narrative and examines different dimensions of this topic, including the author's temporary technology fast, stress in college students, and research from the disciplines of medicine and education that provide the theory behind the practice of stress management. The author also provides suggestions for how people can deal with stress in their lives.

In Chapter 18, "Digital Technologies and 4D Customized Design: Challenging Conventions With Responsive Design," James I Novak and Jennifer Loy explain how these '4D products' have the potential to enhance human experiences. In doing so, the chapter explores how the relationships between humans and products is changing, discusses the changing roles of designers, and presents examples of 4D products. The authors highlight ways in which 4D products have the potential to enhance human experiences by creating more seamless human-centered relationships with technology.

Chapter 19, "Distributed Work Environments: The Impact of Technology in the Workplace," by Edwiygh Franck, examines the impact that technology is having on the workplace. This includes the use of digital resources that make processes leaner while simultaneously cutting costs and expanding global presence in the market. The chapter describes the concept of the distributed work environment and discusses different factors that companies should consider in deciding whether to adopt the model. The author also shares examples of companies that were able to achieve success and employee satisfaction using the model.

Finally, in chapter 20, "Cognitive Investment Into the Interaction Society," Linda Ellington provides a perspective of a technological view point with an individual and social aspect of users who invest cognitive time and space into an interaction society. The chapter is grouped into three areas: (a) how immersion into the digital space may impact cognitive experiences; (b) how to understand the impact interaction technologies have on centrality of beliefs; and (c) how to gain a heightened understanding of the impact this phenomenon has on individuals (self) in a society. The author presents each of three areas along with a short preface of the scope and perspective taken from a literature review.

The authors hope that our research and scholarly studies add insight as we are all immersed in the new world of ubiquitous technology.

REFERENCES

Bryan, V. C. (2006). Impact of technology in community education: Its applications and effects. *Community Education Journal*, *30*(2/3), 10.

Dewey, J. (1938). *Experience and education*. New York, NY: Macmillan.

Dewey, J. (1944). *Democracy and education: An introduction to the philosophy of education*. New York: Macmillan.

Knowles, M. (1984a). *Andragogy in action*. San Francisco, CA: Jossey-Bass.

Knowles, M. (1984b). *The adult learner: A neglected species*. Houston, TX: Gulf Publishing.

Knowles, M. S. (1980). *The modern practice of adult education*. Englewood Cliffs, NJ: Prentice Hall Regents.

Knowles, M. S. et al. (1984). *Andragogy in action*. San Francisco, CA: The Jossey-Bass.

Mishra, P., & Koehler, M. (2006). Technological pedagogical content knowledge: A framework for teacher knowledge. *Teachers College Record*, *108*(6), 1017–1054. doi:10.1111/j.1467-9620.2006.00684.x

Skinner, B. F. (1968). *The technology of teaching*. New York: Aplleton-Century-Crofts.

Vygotsky, L. S. (1980). *Mind in society: The development of higher psychological processes*. Harvard university press.

Whitmyer, C. (1999). *Andragogy verses pedagogy*. San Francisco, CA: FutureU Press.

Acknowledgment

The editors would like to acknowledge the help of all the people involved in this project and, more specifically, to the authors and reviewers that took part in the review process. Without their support, this book would not have become a reality.

First, the editors would like to thank each one of the authors for their contributions. Our sincere gratitude goes to the chapter's authors who contributed their time and expertise to this book.

Second, the editors wish to acknowledge the valuable contributions of the Editorial Review Board member. Throughout the review process, their efforts were critical to the improvement of quality, coherence, and content presentation of chapters. Many of the authors also served as reviewers; we highly appreciate their double task.

A special thank you to Zachary Musgrove for his assistance with the figures and images.

Valerie C. Bryan
Florida Atlantic University, USA

Ann T. Musgrove
Florida Atlantic University, USA

Jillian R. Powers
Florida Atlantic University, USA

Section 1
Pedagogy and Andragogy

Chapter 1
Technology–Enhanced Exploratory Installations to Support Constructivist Professional Development:
The Technology Test Kitchen

Ann Terrill Musgrove
Florida Atlantic University, USA

Angela Gunder
The University of Arizona, USA

Jessica L. Knott
Michigan State University, USA

Frank Tomsic
Rush University, USA

Phylise Banner
Phylise Banner Consulting, USA

Robbie Melton
Tennessee Board of Regents, USA

David Goodrich
Michigan State University, USA

Clark Shah-Nelson
University of Maryland, USA

ABSTRACT

The growth in technology tools and their uses continues to grow at an exponential pace. Whether it is for personal or professional use technology is everywhere, and it is ubiquitous. It is changing the way we seek knowledge, interact with information, and process the world around us to construct our learning pathways. Technology has made it simple for us to be consumers of information, but how do we evaluate and synthesize this information to construct meaning and create value? The technology test kitchen is a curated and managed makerspace designed for exploratory installation where novices and experts engage in deep, meaningful, constructive uses of technology for teaching and learning. The goal of the test kitchen is acquisition of "native-expert" use of technology in support of authentic learning, engendering deeper levels of technological fluency within a constructivist professional development experience.

DOI: 10.4018/978-1-5225-2838-8.ch001

INTRODUCTION

Technology is pervasive. At home, at work, at play - it's everywhere, and it is changing everything. It is changing the way we seek knowledge, interact with information, and process the world around us to construct our learning pathways. Technology has made it simple for us to be consumers of information, but how do we evaluate and synthesize this information to construct meaning and create value?

Imagine trying to make Play-Doh at home as a tool for teaching and learning. Only a few years ago, we learned how to make Play-Doh with a recipe shared by a friend. "Here", they'd say, handing over a piece of paper, "it's easy to make, and it will save you some time and money." Today, a quick internet search will yield not only myriad choices of recipe options, but also hundreds of uses, user reviews, and comments. We focus not on a single right way to make Play-Doh, instead, we the right recipe for our needs.

It is with the sharing spirit of the Play-Doh recipe that the Technology Test Kitchen (TTK) was created - a place where we share technology-enhanced recipes for effective practice in an open, collaborative makerspace that focuses on options and solutions, and that embrace the philosophy of pedagogy before technology. The TTK is an exploratory installation of 21st century learning, where constructivist learning and collaboration come to life.

This chapter will explore the background of both the space and effective practice of exploratory installations, present pedagogical challenges and issues addressed by this solution, and highlight the vision, theoretical foundations, history, and philosophy of the space more commonly referred to as the Technology Test Kitchen (TTK). Recipe books and resources are available to freely share at http://www.technologytestkitchen.org/

BACKGROUND

A recent study by the Pew Research Center on lifelong learning and technology (Horrigan, 2016) found that despite the availability of digital technology and all of the resources that accompany it, more learners choose to pursue knowledge in physical settings than online. Moreover, the study found that the majority of adult learners seeking *professional* learning opportunities participate in learning activities in a *work-related* venue rather than on the Internet. The need for professional lifelong learning is well established with well over half of employed adults looking for training or coursework to learn, improve or maintain job skills in the last year. This research demonstrates that technology installations like the TTK are the preferred method for learners that want or need more professional learning opportunities. Learners are seeking face-to-face opportunities to increase professional technology knowledge. The TTK creates what Falk and Dierking (2002) identified as a free-choice learning space. Free-choice learning is a type of lifelong learning that is self-directed, voluntary, and guided by individual needs and interests

Understanding how learning occurs is a complicated theoretical construct. Why some approaches and techniques are more effective than others is still a cause for some debate. In the twentieth century several major learning theories have been posited on how the process of learning occurs. These theories fall into three major categories: behaviorism, cognitivism and constructivism. Early learning theories focused on behaviorism and observation of end result of learning. Behaviorism has solid contributions to the puzzle of learning, but does not explain the process of learning and only focuses on the end result. Cognitivism can be traced back to the early twentieth century and explores the learning process, and the works of Edward Chase Tolman, Jean Piaget, Lev Vygotsky, Jerome Bruner, and German Gestalt psychologists were instrumental in engendering the dramatic shift from behaviorism to cognitive theories (Yilmaz, 2011). The cognitive school views (1) learning as an active process "involving the acquisition or reorganization of the cognitive structures through which humans process and store information" and (2) the learner as an active participant in the process of knowledge acquisition and integration (Good & Brophy 1977; Merriam & Caffarella 1999).

Constructivism is a branch of cognitivism. Although both the cognitivism theory and the constructivist theory have some similarities there are some marked differences. "Both cognitivists and constructivists view the learner as being actively involved in the learning process, yet the constructivists look at the learner as more than just an active processor of information; the learner elaborates upon and interprets the given information" (Duffy & Jonassen, 1992). Whereas in cognitivism learners have their knowledge built by someone else, an expert whose job it is to convey as best as possible the mental construct that describes the objects being studied," in constructivism learners build their own meaning from new knowledge that they help construct (Leonard, 2002).

Although the learner can discover and process learning alone, learners may learn more effectively collaboration facilitated by an expert. The TTK is intentionally created with consideration of learning theory and creates an interactive, exploratory space where individuals have support to create new knowledge. Chef Frank Tomsic shares his reflection on the Quest for fluency in the use of technology for learner-centered learning in appendix 1.

Adult learning theory is another important consideration when creating the TTK environment. Malcolm Knowles is known for his research on adult learning termed andragogy. His four principles of andragogy (1984) are a natural fit for adults exploring authentic technology solutions. Knowles' first principle asserts that adults need to be involved in the planning and evaluation of their instruction. The TTK is an open and flexible space where adult learners share ideas, solutions, and are encouraged to pose the questions that are meaningful to their situations. It is a collaborative atmosphere where various diverse expertises, experiences, and ideas are shared. The second principle embraces the adult learner's experience, including mistakes, to provide a foundation for the learning activities. Conversations in the TTK build on the experimental and expanding nature of technology. The third principle asserts that adults are most interested in learning subjects that have immediate relevance and impact to their job or personal life. Whether it is a YouTube video to try and fix your broken washer or your supervisor giving you a never before assigned task, technology is often the first step in discovering the solution. Lastly, adult learning is problem-centered rather than content-oriented. Solving problems, both large and small, are part of everyday life, and while we expect technology to help, sometimes it is part of the problem as well.

The TTK is set up in the spirit and layout of a makerspace. Just as the kitchen is the heart of the home the library is the heart of the campus and community. Academic and public libraries are embracing makerspaces. Maker education is a branch of constructivist philosophy that views learning as a highly personal endeavors requiring the student, rather than the teacher, to initiate the learning process (Kurti, Kurti & Fleming, 2014). In these learning spaces arises an ideal constructivist environment, where the line between learner and instructor becomes blurred. In maker education, it is imperative that the process remain learner-driven rather than teacher-driven. At some level, maker education is a grassroots reaction against one-size-fits-all education designed for mass, warehouse-style instruction. Educational makerspaces do not need to be overly complicated or formidable. However, it is imperative to keep in mind the mantra of "pedagogy before technology" because no amount of bright, shiny new technology can take the place of inspiration. It is inspiration that is a direct result of the experience created by the space.

One of the most important considerations in the educational makerspace environment is how to invite curiosity. The TTK is inviting and open without pressure to endorse one product over another; rather, to play and explore. We may not yet thoroughly understand the power of play, but an effective educational makerspace will engage students through the medium of playfulness because it works. Maker spaces encourage what most of society calls "failure," because in reality, it is simply the first or second or third step toward success. The path to success is paved with failures (Kurti, Kurti & Fleming, 2014).

MAIN FOCUS OF THE CHAPTER

Issues, Controversies, and Problems

We are living in a world increasingly dominated by digital technology, and to engage digital learners we must embrace the language and culture of that world. Too often we try to acquire the skills, knowledge, and importantly, the culture of the emerging digital world through learning modalities that do not provide the proficiency educators require to function as "natives" of that culture. Much ongoing professional development for educators occurs in the classroom or through conference attendance (Horrigan, 2016) where the dominant learning modality is likely passive lecture. Through those passive learning experiences, we may learn *about* technology and learning, but we may never develop a fluency for its use to engage real-world learning for our students who are natives of ubiquitous knowledge, connectivity, and social influence.

Disconnect in Learning Philosophies and Teaching Pedagogies

The literature encompassing best practices in teaching with technology highlights the fact that there is no single accepted pedagogy for technology-enhanced teaching and learning. Further, articles and frameworks focused on quality and best practices in teaching instruct faculty to incorporate active learning, peer learning, and interactivity into learning spaces, both online and face-to-face (Crawford-Ferre & Weist, 2012). The literature surrounding how faculty learn and develop, however, focuses more on the skills they need than how they can obtain them. This disconnect is what the Technology Test Kitchen aims to address.

Austin and Sorcinelli (2013) said that "as higher education institutions incorporate online and blended learning, even highly experienced faculty members, as well as those new to the profession, face new challenges, as well as fresh opportunities for their pedagogical practice; teaching online is not the same as teaching face-to-face (p. 87)." Faculty members wishing to incorporate technology must not only learn how to use the technologies themselves, but how those unique technologies work within their personal teaching and professional goals and the teaching and professional goals of their institutions as a whole. Increasingly, faculty take roles beyond teaching and research, advising students, designing both online and physical learning spaces, performing user experience research, and the assessment of both student learning and the effectiveness of spaces and processes (Keengwe & Kidd, 2010; Major, 2010; Wilson & Stacey, 2010; Baran, Correia & Thompson, 2011; Knott, 2015).

Neumann (2009) said "although central to their work and careers, professors' scholarly learning is a 'black box' in the public's understanding of what it means to be a professor and to engage in academic work" (p.2). Technology integration, especially in fully online and blended courses, requires broad reimagination of the nature and definition of academic work. While they must expand and extend their subject matter knowledge across the span of their career, faculty must also reach beyond disciplinary borders to recontextualize content and engage in a different kind of learning in order to be successful with technology (Neumann, 2009).

As adult learners, faculty members engage in the learning process fluidly, incorporating what they learn with their pre-existing knowledge (Knott, 2015). Opportunities for self-direction and collaboration are important to learning and transfer, and measurable learning toward the goal of improving their practice must be evident (Gayle et al., 2008; Harasim, 1995; Sorcinelli, Austin, Eddy, & Beech, 2006; Tabata & Johnsrud, 2008). For many, outcomes must be observed before they are incorporated as practice. To this end, the Technology Test Kitchen model aims to move faculty away from the "black box" and toward a more open model of learning, allowing for an open, hands-on space where faculty can begin to engage in this reimagining of their academic identities. It provides a safe space for the vulnerability of learning, and a network of supportive peers with whom to learn.

SOLUTIONS AND RECOMMENDATIONS

History of the Technology Test Kitchen

The concept of the Technology Test Kitchen was initially conceived during a debrief meeting at the conclusion of the 2013 Sloan-C International Conference on Online Learning. Appendix 1 contains more details about the origins of the TTK by Chef Phylise Banner. The discussion concerned the disconnect between the concepts that were being presented at the conference (student-centered, active learning) and the methodologies being employed to teach them (lecture presentations). The planners identified that, in addition to the pedagogical disconnect, there also existed among many participants a disconnect in effective technology use to support active learning. Over a series of conversations, the planners looked to the emerging maker-spaces and traditional crafting methodologies as models for engaging learners. They determined that participants needed a venue whose primary outcome would be to facilitate the discovery and use technology tools, and with the guidance of a learning technologist, to emerge with new thinking for using such tools to support student-centered, active learning.

The appellation *Technology Test Kitchen* came about as a way to honor key characteristics to support its mission. The TTK space was intended to be friendly, open, and familiar to participants. Rather than the cold sterility often associated with technology, the kitchen metaphor connotes friends, family, and a place to meet and commune. Also, key to this concept was to make the kitchen a place to experiment, be messy, and try new things. From the beginning, the test kitchen would be a place where experimentation is embraced, where resources would be abundant, and where mistakes would be encouraged.

To bring the TTK to life, the planners reached out to their peer communities and colleagues to find like-minded collaborators who would be willing to take a chance and experiment with ways of bringing technology-facilitated learning to a makerspace.

The initial TTK installation took place at the Online Learning Consortium Blended Learning Conference in Denver, Colorado in 2014. To bring the installation to life, a diverse group of educators and technologists -- each one a "chef" -- were invited to bring their own unique flavor to the TTK.

Each chef brings their own personality to the kitchen, supporting learning through inquiry and action. These chefs were volunteers from academic institutions around the world, with expertise in instructional design and technology. At each installation of the TTK, the chefs serve as facilitators, standing side by side with participants to model and guide effective practice. As the TTK has evolved, the core chef team has grown to include experts from industry, academia, and government.

Since every TTK installation is considered a new opportunity to evolve and innovate the space, a new leadership team is designated to design and drive the spirit of the installation. This conscious change in leadership spices up the kitchen, enabling novel expression alongside innovation and change.

Structure and Components of the Space

Spaces that are designed with active learning in mind are often intentionally open, loud, perceivably chaotic, transparent and easily accessible. One of the chief advantages is that these spaces allow for more metaphorical "collisions" to take place enabling participants to pause, peruse, discover and then share in what each is finding in their exploratory process.

It is for these reasons that the placement of TTK instances have been and will be intentionally situated in high-traffic, high-visibility areas, rather than tucked away in an opaque corner. Similarly, the placement of chairs and tables along with electronic components tend to deemphasize a center of attention where a presenter would transmit knowledge, but are carefully placed in ways that orient participants toward each-other as collaborators in the participatory sharing of knowledge and experiences together. In appendix 1 Chef Angela Gibson discusses the TTK as an intentional spaces for reflection and experimentation.

Although core learning principles guide the design decisions of the structure, location and components within, they are intentionally not overly prescriptive of outcomes. Again, this is done to allow the experiences, knowledge, contexts and characteristics of each individual chef and participant to guide in the intended shared discoveries behind the architectural design decisions.

Finally, the layout of the space also promotes resources and stations that can be utilized to sprint toward rapid prototypes. These might be as simple as an iterated idea in conversation or as complex as a mental model generated using a whiteboard, tactile object or even digital representation. In turn, these learning intervention prototypes can be tested on-site with educators who share common interests in promoting good teaching and learning practices while thoughtfully utilizing technologies in the process.

Informal and Formal Learning Spaces

In the spirit of active learning strategies that work to weave the best of both formal and informal learning into one cohesive experience, the TTK design has promoted the natural oscillations between the two and even mixtures of both. For instance, there are portions of the space designated for modeling and sharing together in more of a formally prepared learning experience. There are other spaces designed around less formal and more spontaneous ideation. Together, these spaces are well suited for integrating both formal and informal situations that enhance the small group cohesion needed to cultivate solutions around shared challenges in each individual's unique learning environments. Appendix 1 contains Chef Clark Shah-Nelson's reflection on meaningful professional development in a conference setting.

Connection to Learning beyond Space

Imagining that each person who comes through the space would have a complete cognitive experience centered around design thinking, experimenting with educational technology between conference sessions or even during more formally facilitated sessions within the TTK is ambitious to say the least. Because of this, both the formal aspects and informal aspects of the space and plans for it are a flexible spectrum ranging from brief exposures to longer lasting and in-depth conversations. In either case, materials are made readily available digitally with short URLs in order to be a launching point for future exploration and findings.

One manifestation of this intentionality is found within the dedicated reflection spaces most recently in the form of digital reflection booths. Here individuals or groups are informally prompted to reflect on one or more questions as they relate to experiences in the TTK itself or at the conference overall. The reflective spaces generate artifacts and are intended to extend beyond the walls and timeframes of the conference itself into ongoing conversations throughout a lifetime or beyond.

Usage of Cooking Metaphors

The naming of the TTK itself was also intentionally drawing on culinary arts as metaphor for understanding the more formal instructional and informal exploratory natures of its existence. For instance, the term "chefs" are used to describe the creative, dedicated group of volunteers who engage with participants throughout the TTK experience. The chefs interact with learners within the space through active inquiry and hands-on demonstrations. Just as a chef would inspire others to innovate in the kitchen, the TTK chefs work to facilitate learners through the process of exploring technology for pedagogical solutions, knowing full well that there is no fixed right or wrong recipe for success.

Similarly, the term "recipes" is used to describe the documentation of steps used in the implementation of a technology-enhanced pedagogical solution. Much like how good recipes are shared from kitchen to kitchen over time and across cultures, it is intended that these pedagogical recipes are shared with a similar kind of openness to encourage creativity from classroom to classroom and across organizations. In this way, prior to the conference and during it chefs are tasked with taking some of the more meaningful pedagogical solutions they've seen or implemented in their own work and articulating them as a simple, step-by-step guide for others to adapt in their own contexts.

These recipes weave in culinary metaphors, listing tools as "ingredients" and writing the procedural narrative to look like a recipe. The recipes themselves are gathered, organized, printed and laminated and have been made available for participants to take with them. This is the case both in print and as digital files. Sometimes they are made available as individual sheets as needed. The work needed to create the recipes is often collaborative, using collaborative documents to prepare the recipes to format the individual recipes into a cohesive look and feel. Also designed "Create Your Own Recipe" cards have been made available where participants could document their live interactions with chefs and colleagues in the space as tangible, usable recipes.

Recipe for Creating Your Own Similar Space

As an example of what one of these recipes might look like, we are providing a recommended "recipe" for cooking a similar kind of space in the context of your own conference or faculty development offering. As with any recipe, remember that these are based on our own experiences and findings, and experimenting is encouraged. In the spirit of the TTK, we only ask that you share your own findings to the community of chefs to improve on the recommendations going forward.

Ingredients:

- Multiple perspectives
- Openness and collaboration
- Items, materials and devices that people will want to fiddle and play with
- Recording equipment for reflection prompts
- Collaborative planning tools such as Google Drive and open eMeeting tools for the organizational piece
- Intentional Ambiguity in Structure and Scheduled Learning Moments
- An intense intent to shift the locus of learning control to students
- Commitment to creating a community of inquiry where mastery is demonstrated in some artifact
- Reflection on the achievement

Directions:

1. Involve multiple perspectives in the planning and facilitation, and find ways to reward them for the significant amount of time that they will put into the space
2. Be open to the fact that the space will change over time, particularly with the changes in the people who are planning it
3. Work closely with the folks that control the space where you will setup the exploratory installations
   a. Make them your best friends and communicate ideas for setup as clearly as possible, especially the crazy ideas
   b. Create open space to capture and develop moonshot ideas for ways to innovate in the space
   c. Document the process, to include successes and considerations for future iterations
   d. Dole out tasks and keep people on track
   e. Manage the logistical information and the scheduling pieces
4. When scheduling, leave ample time for reflection and conversation amongst participants - fight the desire to overschedule
   a. Create quiet spaces and quiet downtime
   b. Connections to online collaborative tools and social media where people can continue to unpack big ideas
5. If you plan to have live demos occurring in the space, fight the urge to make them presentational
   a. Select your chefs carefully, making sure that they will take the role as guide more than presenter
   b. Consider having a synchronous "open house" where you meet with your chefs and discuss the ways in which they will make their demo hands-on and participant-focused
6. Be prepared for culture shock
   a. Participants are used to coming into the space and simply grabbing something to go
   b. Be ready to explain that the value add is what they will create in the space and not what has been created already (i.e. printed recipes, gadgets)
   c. Be ready to explain to outsiders seeking to understand the space that when people are most actively engaged, it may look chaotic or even like not is being directed by a "rock star" at the front of the room.
   d. Be supportive of necessary discomfort
      I. Include the process of simple exploration an intended learning outcome

        II.   Explain that although seemingly messy from the outside, there is a place of creation in chaos

7.   The technology is not there to "pitch" but to spark conversations

    a.   Try to find items, materials and devices that people will want to fiddle and play with so as to spark their curiosity and creativity

    b.   Note that you do not need to know how to use everything that you have available to play with. Learning alongside participants is key part of the exploratory installation.

    c.   We've also had great success with chefs working alongside of educators who have never had the chance to work with ubiquitous tools

        I.   We're helping them in a comfortable, safe space without making them feel like they are behind the curve

        II.   High touch, just-in-time personalized training (Jones, 2001) at its best

    d.   Resist the urge to spend the contact time explaining how the technology works - focus on discussing challenges and barriers to education, and then ask questions about how the technology might help to support an effective solution

Additional Resources:

- Appendix 2 contains sample recipes from the TTK
- Further OLC TTK recipes from 2015 in Google Drive at tinyurl.com/jgmscpp
- Recipe Books and other resources can be found at http://www.technologytestkitchen.org/

Emerging Technology

Joy and passion for experiential learning through facilitated technology are what bring the TTK to life. As technology evolves, so does the focus of inquiry and exploration in the TTK. The showcase of the latest innovations in educational and workforce emerging technologies and innovations is a key component of the physical space. Beyond serving participants learning about technology, the space supports technology developers and companies receiving direct feedback on ways to make their materials and services more accessible, affordable, and customizable for educators looking to adopt their products.

With each passing iteration of the TTK, the technology incorporated into the space is a reflection of the most promising tools available to support engaged and active learning in the classroom. In recent years, emerging technology related to the Internet of Things (IoT) and the Internet of Everything (IoE) have played a key role in the hands-on, live demos held within the TTK, particularly the interconnectedness of educators, students and devices within the evolution of teaching and learning spaces. Master Chef, Robbie Melton from the Tennessee Board of Regents, curates the collection and the "IOE" Showcases of smart devices, gadgets, tools, wearables, and emerging technology of mixed reality for TTK. Indeed, these smart connected "edugadgets", devices, and tools are quickly redefining how we teach and train, as well as how we acquire and process information. Additionally, IoT devices provide real-time, on-demand data that may assist in determining the effectiveness of our methodologies and practices in meeting our desired learning outcomes. The IoE can bring together people, process, data, and things to make networked connections more relevant and valuable than ever before — turning information into actions that create new capabilities, richer experiences, and unprecedented economic opportunity for businesses, individuals, and countries.

In terms of the types of IoT and IoE innovations presented in the space, here are some examples of the types of devices and technologies featured in previous installations of the TTK:

- **Bodies:** Many people will wear devices that let them connect to the Internet and will give them feedback on their activities, health, medical, and fitness. They will also monitor others (their children or employees, for instance) who are also wearing sensors, or moving in and out of places that have sensors. TTK has showcased such connected devices as iHealth Products, baby monitoring devices, health tattoos, medical jewelry, mobile apps for health and fitness.
- **Homes:** People will be able to control nearly everything remotely, from how their residences are heated and cooled to how often their gardens are watered. Homes will also have sensors that warn about everything from prowlers to broken water pipes. TTK has showcased innovations for connected homes from devices such as a smart egg carton, smart utensils dishes, and pots/pans, programmed lights, sensor furniture, bedding monitors, smart toilets and related bathroom accessories, and smart flooring.
- **Communities:** Embedded devices and smartphone apps will enable more efficient transportation and give readouts on pollution levels. "Smart systems" might deliver electricity and water more efficiently and warn about infrastructure problems as referenced by Verizon Connected City. TTK has showcased various products as iAg, Nest, iDevices, Beacons, iMother, and even smart pet devices.
- **Goods and services:** Factories and supply chains will have sensors and readers that more precisely track materials to speed up and smooth out the manufacture and distribution of goods. TTK has showcased wearables products such as sensor smart clothing, shoes, jewelry, accessories, workforce smart tools and medical sensors and tracking devices
- **Environment:** There will be real-time readings from fields, forests, oceans, and cities about pollution levels, soil moisture, and resource extraction that allow for closer monitoring of problems. TTK has showcased mobile tracking tools, smartphone apps, and smart workforce tools.
- **Sports:** There will be sensor sport equipment that will provide real-time data regarding one's performance. TTK has showcased smart sport equipment such as iFish and wearables such as sensor basketball, soccer ball, bats, golf clubs, and fitness clothes that will monitor one's physical fitness from heart rate to muscle performance.
- **Entertainment:** The format of TTK provides an opportunity for participants to play and explore the latest in educational gaming including virtual and augmented realities, holograms, and online team games.

As these "things" add capabilities like context awareness, increased processing power, and energy independence, and as more people and new types of information are connected, we will quickly enter the Internet of Everything (IoE) — a network of networks where billions of connections create unprecedented opportunities as well as new risks. With this new interconnectedness come a series of new considerations and challenges that educators must work to address. "The realities of this data-drenched world raise substantial concerns about privacy and people's abilities to control their own lives. If everyday activities are monitored and people are generating informational outputs, the level of profiling and targeting will grow and amplify social, economic, and political struggles" (Anderson, 2014).

Paul Saffo, Managing Director of Discern Analytics (2014) notes that, "Most of our devices will be communicating on our behalf—they will be interacting with the physical and virtual worlds more than interacting with us. The devices are going to disappear into what we wear and/or carry. The devices will also become robustly inter-networked. The biggest shift is a strong move away from a single do-everything device to multiple devices with overlapping functions and, above all, an inter-relationship with our other devices." Whereas, Tanya Roscorla (2014) shares that, "A world flooded with a sea of data from every connected device on the planet -- devices found in and on human bodies, in homes, around communities, in products, and in the natural environment. And these devices on the Internet of Things are sharing information constantly with the promise of making people's lives better."

Laurel Papworth (2015) social media educator, explains that, "Every part of our life will be quantifiable, and eternal, and we will answer to the community for our decisions. For example, skipping the gym will have your gym shoes auto tweet (equivalent) to the peer-to-peer health insurance network that will decide to degrade your premiums". Therefore, many expect that a major driver of the Internet of Things will be incentives to try to get people to change their behavior—maybe to purchase a good, maybe to act in a more healthy or safe manner, maybe work differently, maybe to use public goods and services in more efficient ways.

With these considerations looming on the horizon, it is with exploratory installations such as the Technology Test Kitchen that educators have the ability to both learn about these emerging innovations, but also allow participants hands-on exploration and evaluation of these items in order to assist in determining their value, potential and limitations within education, training and professional development. Chef Jessica Knott discusses the malleability of the constructivist learning environment in appendix 1. Participants are able to touch, try and experiment with these items prior to their full development, and sometimes even prior to major commercial marketing of products, giving educators a forum for addressing the educational impact and needs for IoT as feedback to developers and companies. It is important to note that the demonstrations on emerging innovations within the space are not intended to be events for advocating, promoting, or sponsoring products. Rather, they are in support of a community of inquiry where educators ask questions and experiment in order to help create and test effective practices related to technologies for teaching and learning.

Evolution of the TTK

While each iteration of the Technology Test Kitchen has several unifying elements, it also embraces the need to evolve, as new chefs share their own experience and flavor. With the underlying concept and philosophy of constructivist exploration in mind, planners and chefs iterate on the layout, themes, technologies, topics, recipes, and specifics of how participants will interact with chefs, explore stations, and engage in presentations.

The layouts of various test kitchens at conferences have varied slightly from iteration to iteration, as planners attempt to optimize the ability for participants to flow through the kitchen, explore tools and technologies, and engage in conversations about pedagogy and technologies with chefs. At the first test kitchen in Denver, Colorado, the layout included a green screen station with an iPad tablet on a tripod, a long table with chairs and laptops, a long table full of high tech gadgets and devices, a primary video screen, a small table with a demonstration of a Leap Motion Controller, and several tall standing tables with laminated recipes in the key categories of collaboration, audio, video, communication, presentation and mobile technologies. Succeeding test kitchens have each had variations on those key themes and categories, as well as tweaked the layout to try new ways to engage with participants. Figure 1 illustrates two samples of the layouts that have been used.

Figure 1. Sample test kitchen layouts

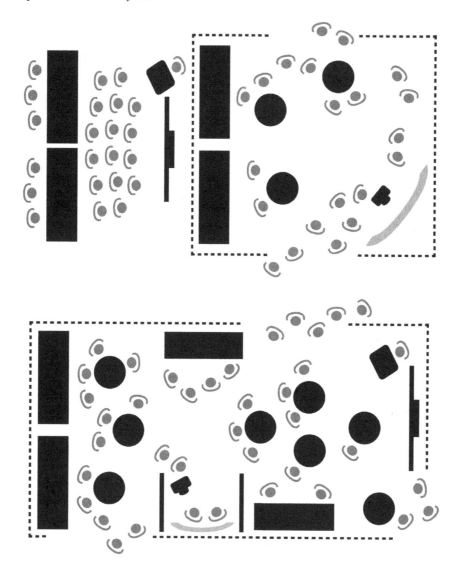

In addition to layouts, one other TTK area that has gone through some significant trial and change is in presentations/demos. In order to feature some specific recipes and applications, demonstrations were added to the third iteration of the test kitchen, at OLC's ET4ONLINE event in April, 2015, Dallas, Texas. The presentations were solicited via a call for proposals (CFP), along with a new track, entitled Innovative Tools and Media, which were then vetted by the track chair, Angela Gunder and test kitchen chair, Jessica Knott. In succeeding test kitchens, demos were scheduled and promoted along with the other main conference sessions, and held in a space alongside the test kitchen, where participants could easily sit and participate in a presentation or interact with chefs and peruse recipes and tools. At the Online Learning Consortium's International Conference later that same year in October, 2015, in Orlando, Florida, Ann Musgrove was the track chair for the TTK and Angela Gunder served as the co-chair. Building on the popularity of the TTK at the request of OLC every conference session included a demonstration in the TTK space. However, presentations were not always found to be as interactive as hoped, so there are changes planned for the 2016 OLC Accelerate (formerly named the Online Learning Consortium's International Conference). This iteration will feature small booths for 2-3 person demos called "chef's tables." These "chef's tables" are meant for participants to converse with 3-4 people in a casual, constructivist way, developing "recipes" for the people on the fly. This change is quite similar to the very first TTK, and helps personalize the experience for participants.

Other features include a "Walk and Talk", where once a day a chef leads a small group of participants for a walk around the Exhibit Hall, where a pedagogical challenge is discussed by the group, along with a digital reflection booth where individuals or groups will be prompted to share their reflections on the TTK experience.

Voices from the Test Kitchen

Hallmark to the experience of implementing a technology-enhanced exploratory installation is the weaving together of diverse perspectives and strategies amongst a growing group of volunteers. Indeed, a critical key to understanding the format and structure of the space is hearing of it described by the many people who helped to establish each installation, and support its evolution over time. Each narrative, found in appendix 1, was the product of an open-ended call for reflections that encompassed the ubiquitous challenges in education, the need for a space such as the TTK, and the individual interactions experienced as designers and facilitators of the space. Phylise Banner posed the following questions to each of the participants who completed narratives:

- What does the Test Kitchen experience mean to you?
- What did you learn?
- What did you share?
- What was inspiring?
- What was missing?

This collection, found in appendix 1, highlights the personal findings and reflections of several chefs from past Technology Test Kitchens, intentionally presented in plain language as a means of better illustrating the tapestry of interpretations of the space.

Benefits

Being an active participant in a learning event shapes knowledge creation and deep integration. It allows the learner to craft their own approach to acquiring knowledge and skill. Add a guide to that active learning event, and the acquisition of knowledge and skill become situated and framed within the context of applied effective practice.

The expertise of the chefs in the kitchen is to guide the discovery of new solutions, ideas, and designs for teaching and learning with technology, in a space where failure is an option, and iteration is encouraged. The exploratory installation approach of the TTK brings active participation to the forefront. The space itself draws in learners and inspires them to wander and explore -- to touch and to play with things, and to talk with people. The space inspires learners to create their own learning experience, and to choose how much exploration and conversation they want or need.

Creating a space where learning happens organically allows learners to move away from the lecture style to a participatory mode where they can engage higher order thinking, solve personally meaningful challenges and contextualize solutions within a community of inquiry. The TTK scaffolds learners to higher levels of proficiency within active, student-centered learning facilitated by technology.

The TTK augments the traditional lecture-style conference session by providing a place to enact the theory, research, and applied effective practices shared in those sessions. In the traditional lecture-style session, a presenter may model theories and ideas on a topic, but attendees have little opportunity to personalize the information for their own needs. Because there is no practice, the concepts remain external and formal. Bringing these concepts to the TTK allows learners to assimilate, personalize, and actualize theories and ideas, and bring them alive within their learning schemas.

Considerations

To be sure, the design and development of a space such as the Technology Test Kitchen requires a great deal of effort, planning and collaborative work to pull off successfully. Designers of the space must consider not only the technological components and the scheduling of formal and informal learning experiences, but also the spatial requirements in order to establish an open community of inquiry and exploration.

Though technology itself is not the main focus of the space, the sourcing and vetting of emerging technology is a critical consideration for those creating their own TTK. Typically, those tasked as chefs in the space will contribute devices that they are currently using in support of innovative teaching and learning experiences. Additionally, some exploratory installations leverage technology donations from companies seeking opportunities to put off-market and newly-released products in the hands of educators. It is important to ensure that these donations of technology are both rooted in pedagogy, and not serving as a sale promotion for the companies, so as to ensure the authenticity and unbiased interactions that are key to the analysis and adoption of technology solutions. Lastly, and most importantly, the space must support participants incorporating their own devices into the mix, allowing individuals to engage with emerging technology in correlation to their own laptops, tablets and mobile devices.

As previously mentioned with regards to the layout and location of the space, one must ensure that the flow of participants is supported by the situation of the space itself. Additionally, the space should be established in a high-traffic, high-visibility area so as to encourage informal exploration and repeat visits. Ideally, in a conference environment, planners should consider building the TTK in an exhibit hall or similar space where participants are prone to wander and peruse at a casual pace. In order to facilitate the many points of engagement within the space, those helming the space will need to ensure ample volunteers to help guide visitors through the entire experience. Participants well-versed in the conference culture of briefly interacting with exhibitors long enough to receive a bit of knowledge and a free takeaway may be taken aback by the exploratory installation which asks them to interact in a novel way. As such, another consideration to those planning similar spaces is the culture shift required of chefs and participants accustomed to passive learning experiences. Mitigating the habit to simply engage in sit-and-get presentations takes a group of dedicated personnel willing to engage each participant, especially those who are hesitant, in open, honest dialogue about pedagogical challenges and technological interventions.

Valuing the power of the space entails a deep appreciation of the time commitment of the individuals assisting with the planning and implementation of the space, particularly with its evolution over time. As conferences assemble planning committees to run the various aspects of the event, there should be set plans in place to dedicate personnel to the exploratory installation. From recruiting and training chefs, to building schedules and featured engagement opportunities, to ensuring that audio-visual and technology logistics are carefully handled, having a team of volunteers focused on the smooth operation of the space is an essential consideration. Additionally, documentation of the time and space commitments of each instance of the space can help to ameliorate future planning considerations, and help individuals in expanding the reach of the installation by passing the torch to future collaborators and participants.

Though prior iterations of the TTK have been focused on adult learners seeking professional development experiences in a conference environment, a final consideration would be expanding the audience to include learners of all ages. In that the space is inherently malleable and adaptable, the format described here might be easily adapted to new formats so as to address different populations of stakeholders. This, of course, would entail careful planning to ensure the same spirit of exploration in the hopes of supporting native fluency of technology.

FUTURE RESEARCH DIRECTIONS

Until now, our data collection has been largely quantitative, focused descriptive and demographic data. Qualitative data gathered has been largely anecdotal, and used to inform future designs for Test Kitchen installations. Moving forward, we have developed a plan to research the Technology Test Kitchen experience more purposefully.

First, we will incorporate on-site surveys. We have developed a short, two question on-site survey that can be administered to individuals attending the test kitchen. The questions asked include "What is your biggest teaching challenge?" and, in a ten point scale "Rate your comfort level with tackling ambiguous, or undefined problems." We will use this data to inform future recipes and topics to explore with participants.

Next, we will expand the literature review of faculty learning spaces included in this chapter. We hope to explore the research question "How do faculty learn what they need to know in regard to technology and teaching?" in a methodological literature review of existing faculty learning experiences. We hypothesize that the knowledge we gain from this endeavor will help us expand our knowledge of the gap that exists between what we, as practitioners and faculty, tell other practitioners and faculty they should do, and the ways in which we teach them to do that.

Lifelong learning is an important part of not only work-related development, but personal development as well (Horrigan, 2016). As we seek future research directions for the Technology Test Kitchen model, we look toward entities of informal learning. Questions we would like to explore include what are the long term retention and change benefits of concepts learned in the kitchen vs. more formal or traditional faculty development? What are optimal ways to provide recipes and maintain them over time? How can the test kitchen concept best be implemented in community centers, libraries, senior centers, places of worship, prisons or other learning spaces in our society?

CONCLUSION

Living within any construct it can be difficult to evaluate and synthesize reality regardless of the topic-- whether banal or meaningful. Due to our limited individual ability to process information, it can be exhausting to constantly track "where" we are and what trajectory we are taking. For much of history, it has been only in hindsight that humans have been able to evaluate and contextualize the gestalt of times and experiences as it would take vast amounts of time for individuals to process, document, share, reflect and learn. Computing technologies, however, have fundamentally transformed learning not only through *availability* of information and expert knowledge, but also by increasing access to the shared processing of experiences. Sharing and collaborating over distance, language, or culture, humans can now synthesize myriad perspectives and coalesce deeper and richer understanding, which is fundamental to constructivist learning.

The TTK brings into reality the learning theories and behaviors related to student-centered constructivist learning that we reference in our work as 21st century educators. By creating a safe, exploratory installation with passionate teaching and learning professionals serving as guides, the TTK offers a solution to faculty professional development by modeling the active practice of integrating technology into teaching and learning. As technology and pedagogy evolve, so will the TTK.

REFERENCES

Anderson, J., & Rainie, L. (2014). The Internet of things will thrive by 2025. *Pew Research Internet Project, 14*. Retrieved from http://www.pewinternet.org/2014/05/14/internet-of-things/

Baran, E., Correia, A., & Thompson, A. (2013). Tracing successful online teaching in higher education: Voices of Exemplary Online Teachers. *Teachers College Record, 115*(3), 1–41.

Crawford-Ferre, H. G., & Wiest, L. R. (2012). Effective online instruction in higher education. *Quarterly Review of Distance Education, 13*(1), 11.

Duffy, T. M., & Jonassen, D. H. (Eds.). (1992). *Constructivism and the technology of instruction: A conversation.* Lawrence Erlbaum Associates.

Falk, J. H., & Dierking, L. D. (2002). *Lessons without limit: How free-choice learning is transforming education.* Walnut Creek, CA: AltaMira Press.

Gayle, B. M., Randall, N., Langley, L., & Preiss, R. (2013). Faculty learning processes: A model for moving from scholarly teaching to the scholarship of teaching and learning. *Teaching and Learning Inquiry: The ISSOTL Journal, 1*(1), 81–93. doi:10.20343/teachlearninqu.1.1.81

Good, T. L., & Brophy, J. E. (1977). *Educational psychology: A realistic approach.* New York: Holt, Rinehart and Winston.

Harasim, L. M. (Ed.). (1995). *Learning Networks: A Field Guide to Teaching and Learning Online.* MIT press.

Horrigan, J. B. (2016). *Lifelong learning and technology.* Retrieved from http://www.leadinglearning. com/podcast-episode-34-lifelong-learning-and-technology-john-horrigan/

Keengwe, J., & Kidd, T. T. (2010). Towards best practices in online learning and teaching in higher education. *Journal of Online Learning and Teaching, 6*(2), 533.

Knott, J. L. (2015). *Online teaching and faculty learning: The role of hypermedia in online course design.* Retrieved from ProQuest Digital Dissertations. (AAT 3688361)

Knowles, M. S. (1984). *The adult learner: A neglected species* (3rd ed.). Houston, TX: Gulf Pub. Co., Book Division.

Kurti, R. S., Kurti, D. L., & Fleming, L. (2014). The philosophy of educational makerspaces: Part 1 of making an educational makerspace. *Teacher Librarian, 41,* 8.

Leonard, D. C. (2002). *Learning theories, A to Z.* Westport, CT: Oryx Press.

Major, C. H. (2010). Do virtual professor's dream of electric students? University faculty experiences with online distance education. *Teachers College Record, 112*(8), 2154–2208.

Merriam, S. B., Caffarella, R. S. & NetLibrary, I. (1999). *Learning in adulthood a comprehensive guide* (2nd ed.). San Francisco: Jossey-Bass Publishers.

Neumann, A. (2009). *Professing to learn: Creating tenured lives and careers in the American research university (No. 475).* JHU Press.

Papworth, L. (2015). *The internet of things: 11 experts on business opportunities.* Retrieved from http://arkenea.com/blog/internet-of-things-business-opportunities/

Rivera, J., & Meulen, R. (2014, March 19). *Gartner says the internet of things will transform the data center.* Retrieved July 26, 2016, from http://www.gartner.com/newsroom/id/2684616

Roscorla, T. (2016). *Where the internet of things could take society by 2025.* Retrieved from http://www.centerdigitaled.com/news/Where-the-Internet-of-Things-Could-Take-Society-by-2025-.html

Saffo, P. (2014, March). *Elon Pew future of the internet survey report: 2025 and the internet of things.* Retrieved from http://www.elon.edu/eweb/imagining/surveys/2014_survey/2025_Internet_of_Things.xhtml

Sorcinelli, M., Austin, A., Eddy, P., & Beach, A. L. (2006). *Creating the future of faculty development: learning from the past, understanding the present.* Boston, MA: Anker Publishing Co.

Yilmaz, K. (2011). The cognitive perspective on learning: Its theoretical underpinnings and implications for classroom practices. *The Clearing House: A Journal of Educational Strategies, Issues and Ideas, 84*(5), 204–212. doi:10.1080/00098655.2011.568989

KEY TERMS AND DEFINITIONS

Context Awareness: An attribute of devices and applications identified as nodes within the Internet of Things (IoT) whereby these nodes are able to determine where they are physically located and their proximity to other nodes.

Digital Reflections: An activity frequently scheduled within the Technology Test Kitchen where visitors are encouraged to use a dedicated space within the area to record a reflection on video. These reflections are sometimes guided by provided reflections or facilitated by an interviewer, sometimes a chef in the TTK.

EduGadgets: Emerging technology with advanced capabilities to both collect, track and provide data to users on when and how they are being used.

Exploratory Installation: A dedicated space for interacting, testing and assessing the value and uses of emerging technology in the creation of meaningful pedagogical solutions and interventions. The space, most critically, consists of dedicated volunteers supporting participants in their explorations, in addition to technology and tools for reflection and documentation.

Green Screen Booth: A space designated for recording subjects in real time using chroma key technology that takes their video and layers an alternative image in the background of the subject(s). Frequently, within the TTK, participants will record digital reflections using a mounted recording device within a green screen booth.

Internet of Things (IoT): A diverse collection of devices and objects of a multitude of sizes and purposes that are all connected through the exchange of data. Each device serves as a node that can communicate with other nodes, to include affecting the way that they operate.

Live Demo Space: A dedicated space within the Technology Test Kitchen for scheduled, synchronous presentations of effective practices and pedagogical applications of technology. The sessions, though led by a presenter, are rooted in the same hands-on, constructivist spirit as the informal demos held in the TTK.

Makerspace: A constructivist space where participants interact with resources and each other to brainstorm, strategize and create solutions to challenges presented to the group. Quite often, these spaces feature specific technology used to support the prototyping of objects that support the formulation of effective practices and applicable interventions for the aforementioned challenges.

Technology Test Kitchen: An exploratory installation featuring meaningful, constructive uses of technology for teaching and learning and support in the form of tools and guides, as well as designated volunteers.

APPENDIX 1

The voices of some of the many chefs of the Technology Test Kitchen on why it was created and the philosophy of the learning space.

Phylise Banner, Phylise Banner Consulting, on the Origins of the Technology Test Kitchen

Sitting in the back of a conference presentation session on active, constructivist teaching and learning, Frank Tomsic and I commented on the irony of sitting in a room being lectured at while learning about active learning. When the presentation ended, Frank and I turned our energies into a design session where we created an ideal learning space -- a hands-on, guided exploratory installation where learners could interact with seasoned experts. We would focus on teaching and learning with technology, and create a space where these seasoned experts could share their passion for pedagogy and innovative solutions to the issues that faculty, students, administrators and instructional designers face every day. Two years later, after sitting through another round of conference presentation sessions on active learning (yes, they were still lecturing) we brought our exploratory installation concept to the Online Learning Consortium conference planning committee in a debrief meeting.

"We can't keep lecturing about active learning!" we exclaimed.

"We need to model our own effective practices!" we added.

"We need a maker-space, a test kitchen of some sort!" we kept going.

"Who will bring this to life?" they asked.

"We will" we replied.

They trusted us to design and create this exploratory installation, and we made the Technology Test Kitchen happen. We made it happen thanks to countless hours from volunteer chefs and conference staff. Thanks to brilliant individuals who were willing to risk failure in order to bring this active learning experience to life.

When I tell this story, I usually say that Frank and I called the craziest people we knew to help us bring the Test Kitchen to life. It's not that they are crazy, it's that they are passionate. Passionate about teaching and learning with any and everything they can get their hands on -- research, effective practice, tools, technologies, apps, toys, games, and candy (always candy).

I knew that we had succeeded in our first installation in 2014 that it was all worth it, when a man walked up to me in the Test Kitchen and pointed to a table and said, "I need to learn how to use that". He was pointing to our Audio Technologies area, and I asked him questions related to audio tools, and what he was working on that we could explore together. He responded "No, I need to learn how to use a laptop. My dean gave me one and I don't know how to use it".

We worked together to bring him up to speed on the laptop, and then he roved over to the green screen and created a video to send to his dean. Right there on the spot. Technology Test Kitchen success. We had created an active learning space where someone was not afraid to walk up and ask anything -- even the simplest thing.

The Technology Test Kitchen is the actualization of our ideal learning space. We will continue to take risks in support of sharing our passions, and inspire others to fall in love with experimentation, evolution, play, and the integration of technology into teaching and learning.

Jessica Knott, Learning Design Manager at Michigan State University, on the Malleability of the Constructivist Learning Environment

What would education look like if it was customizable? Would we have the LMS landscape we have today? What would the tenure process look like? Would we groan about "having" to go to a professional development workshop or fill out another feedback form that said our needs weren't met?

The Technology Test Kitchen is hard. It's hard because these practices are so ingrained in how we live and work that we, as a society, have almost forgotten how to explore. We fear open acknowledgement of our skill gaps. We may not even know where to start, and saying so is difficult. We're afraid to fail. In every test kitchen we see people come in, look around, look for instructions, not find them, and leave. Which is to be expected. What we also see, however, is that those same people often hang out and watch for a while, see us playing with new teaching tools or ideas, and slowly re-engage. "What is this?" Welcome! This is the Technology Test Kitchen. Spend a little time here, and you'll see it's not as hard as it feels.

A few years ago, a group of inquisitive educators began to wonder: Could a space be created where people could ask any question they had and work with others to answer it? Could we share possibilities with them, while not influencing their pedagogical decisions? Could we have a space where we could just be and just try? We think the answer is "yes." We offer guidance, but not answers. We'll show you examples, but ask you to question them. We'll introduce you to technology and say "just try it." What should I do? "Just try it."

Learning is evolutionary. It is active. It is social. It is inquisitive. It is impervious to failure. It is open, and flexible, and ever changing. It is fluid. It can be uncomfortable. We relish that discomfort, and encourage it. We learn something new from each other, and from you, every time we have the opportunity to work in a test kitchen environment. The "we" changes and grows, keeping skills and perspectives fresh. The "you" becomes "we" and ownership is shared in the knowledge created. The recipes are only the beginning. The true value is in the collective whole.

Angela Gunder, Associate Director of Digital Learning and Instructional Design at The University of Arizona, on the Systematic Challenge of Maintaining Digital Literacy

Educators face a befuddling paradox - the ubiquity of technological innovation seemingly stands in stark opposition to the demand for them to meet established outcomes with dwindling support (both in the form of funding and time). While many choose to evaluate the paradox itself, what has become more telling is the landscape of the players themselves and where they fall in their approach to ameliorating the situation. For sure, some turn to more comfortable methods of teaching and learning, mitigating the lack of support by reverting to the easiest, but quite often least-effective, approaches. Others, however, see the paradox as simply a puzzle waiting to be cracked open and solved, more an invigorating opportunity than a debilitating problem. Better still, they inherently understand that the most satisfying solutions come from unpacking challenges in a collaborative context, and their passion for bringing in other likeminded folk is what drives their practice.

The concept of the Technology Test Kitchen was born of the minds of these puzzle solvers, innovators and collaborators. Breaking down the silos and separations present in much of academia, they immediately spotted an opportunity to reframe professional development as a hands-on, experiential process and a community of inquiry. In spaces where educators purportedly gathered to cogitate, experiment and play, they noticed that the deliverable was actually static, one-to-many presentations with little to no interaction. They were compelled to action to bring a more profound kind of professional development into the spotlight. And more than anything else, these innovators formulated an approach for bridging the ever-expanding gap between tried-and-true teaching methods and the unique needs of the current populations of learners.

The Technology Test Kitchen, with its rotating cast of players, is malleable, iterative and adaptive. At its best, it is messy - a feature that is inherent in all learning spaces constructed to best meet the differentiated needs of the learners present. Participants are individually empowered by the fact that they are all called to be creators of knowledge, actively contributing to the hacking of the concept of professional development as we know it. For a space with technology in the name, the commodity has never been the tools, but rather the interpersonal connections and ideation that occurs through the practice of inquiry and assessment.

Ann Musgrove, Assistant Professor of Instructional Design at Florida Atlantic University, on the Importance of Collaborative Creativity

Let's not talk about it - let's do it. It may begin with a question or just a sense of curiosity. There are always new tools, but do they help me and my learners? Technology seems to amplify your options and runs to extremes that can create wonderful solutions or barriers from hell. In the TTK we explore together and learn from each other's successes and mistakes.

The test kitchen is a fun, playful, collaborative space to explore solutions. We discuss possibilities and share experiences always with a focus on pedagogy before technology.

This space is authentic and practical you'll leave with new ideas, a renewed sense of possibilities, and probably some new collaborative friends.

Good conversations start in the kitchen but continue beyond its boundaries.

Clark Shah-Nelson, Assistant Dean, Instructional Design and Technology at University of Maryland School of Social Work, on Meaningful Professional Development

As a conference attendee, I have experienced many non-interactive presentations, many not quite on the mark and some that get the wheels spinning, but do not lead to in depth conversations as I rush off to the next set of umpteen sessions from which to choose. Naturally, I have cruised through the vendor zone, looking for some interesting new tools and swag to bring home to my kids. I've also gotten seemingly endless sales phone calls and emails when I returned to my home campus. But rarely have I had time to really experiment with tools, toys and ideas, or have in depth conversations with instructional designers or technologists about solving educational problems.

As an educator, I have experienced the limitations to time and access to professional development seminars that were interesting, but quickly forgotten and unimplemented when I got back to my classroom the next day. Some of these were just too hands-off, too passive, and others far too hands-on - waiting and waiting for someone in the group who couldn't find the right button or couldn't catch up to the others. I've also experienced not having enough time, being too bogged down to find time to explore new tools and techniques, and simply not having access to some of the newest, latest and greatest educational technologies.

As a Technology Test Kitchen chef, I have had in depth conversations about real educator problems, ideas, tools and techniques. I have seen the light bulb go on as an instructor realized a new way she could use a synchronous meeting tool in her debate class. I've seen many an instructor get to take as much time as she wanted to explore using a green screen with an inexpensive app on an iPad to record her own content to flip her class, and take home a slew of classroom technology activity ideas. I've seen an instructor set up a Twitter account and compose her first tweet, as well as take home ideas for using Twitter in any classroom to enhance student interaction and feedback. Some visitors to the test kitchen aren't sure what it is at first - because there's no sales pitch, nothing to sell. I've seen some visitors visibly relax and take their time to look around, explore and try some new things when the realized this. The TTK provides a space, a time, and the resources for exploration, experimentation, in depth conversations, problem-solving, innovation, and connection.

Angela Gibson, Professor American Public University System, on Intentional Spaces for Reflection and Experimentation

The Test Kitchen allows for the real-time application of learning. At conferences there can be an overwhelming amount of information offered and, at times, bombarded, at an attendee. There is little time to reflect and internalize, let alone test out, the new knowledge and if not stored in some way could be easily lost.

By providing a location where from beginning to end of the conference there is a staff of knowledgeable practitioners to work with interested and inquiring attendees, a safe space for learning and testing is created. Situated in a prime location where there is heavy traffic through the conference, those who didn't intend to stop by the place are drawn in by the energy, the activity, and the welcome greetings from staff. Offering one on one connections, staff are able to identify needs of the learner and also encourage them to physically put hands on technology. Those interested take away a tangible product in the recipe book full of simple steps to try out technology - physical equipment and online tools - to take home with them through a link or code to access on demand. Professional development and real-time learning in action!

Denise Malloy, Assistant Professor at Southwest Tennessee Community College, on the Open Collaboration between Chefs and Participants

The kitchen appears to have something that inspires everyone. My experience in the Technology Test Kitchen is sous-chef to Executive Chef, Dr. Robbie K. Melton. Thanks to Phylise Banner and Frank Tomsic who thought of this very innovative and interactive, must see/must touch session event, the Technology Test Kitchen has become a favorite staple of OLC. A participant since the Orlando OLC conference in 2014, I have witnessed session attendance in the kitchen grow as people bring others back with them to see what the chefs have cooking in the kitchen.

The Test Kitchen is engaging, encourages attendees participation, and ever captivating. Chef Melton always has a new recipe of gadgets to show and to let people have a taste of what is new, emerging and cutting edge. Attendees FaceTime, Periscope, text message, and tweet to share what she has brewing, and the responses of people getting a taste of whatever technology is wowing the crowd the moment she is presenting.

My job as sous-chef is assisting her, informing patrons in our portion of the restaurant about cutting-edge educational technology useful in pedagogy throughout K-12, higher education and workforce development. What we show is hot and happening and something for every educator to see! One just never knows what recipes will be laying around to pick up and try.

John Vivolo, Director of Online and Virtual Learning at New York University, on Experimentation in Education

I will admit that I am spoiled when it comes to resources and technology. I am eternally grateful that my school supplies my unit with a generous budget for equipment and other resources. However, when I first started teaching online, I also remember having no resources and no training in online pedagogy and technology (this was about 14 years ago). The time between my early years of "no resources" to my current "wealth of resources" was actually one of my favorite times as an instructor and instructional designer. I took this time to research and experiment with new technology and learning methods; as a result, I often felt like a chef in a kitchen experimenting (for good or bad).

During an OLC conference in Denver, I presented at the Test Kitchen for the first. This brought me back to those moments of trial and error. Here were people from schools from around the country (and world) and they were all showcasing exciting and often unique technologies. After being a guest chef for a few Test Kitchens, I realize that exchanging ideas and showcasing my own ideas remain one of the highlights of those conferences (even more than the presentations).

During two specific Test Kitchens, I had the pleasure of showcasing my schools Live Virtual Learning set-up. This was the ability to live stream on-campus sessions to remote students. As a result, on-campus and online students can learn together in a live environment. A unique technology, but often a rather sensitive one, it sometimes feels like it was put together with bubblegum and duct tape. It was a pleasure to talk with other people who were also interested in doing something similar. The exchange of ideas in that informal setting, allowed me to return with ideas for improvement (or at least providing stronger duct tape).

The Test Kitchen inspired me to continue to experiment with new ideas and not to give up on new technologies. The Test Kitchen reminds me of my own kitchen when cooking a Sunday family dinner: a mess to an outsider, but upon entering, an enjoyable place of creation and chaos.

Dave Goodrich, Learning Designer at Michigan State University, on the Participatory Nature of the Learning Environment

There are bleachers and there are the playing fields.

There are church benches and there are soup kitchens.

There are office cubicles and there are labs.

The TTK is not a place to sit and absorb. It is a place to connect, try new things and explore new discoveries. I like to think of the Technology Test Kitchen like that of an incubator of all the best stuff about an educational technology conference. First there are the keynotes, plenary sessions, workshops, poster sessions and breakout sessions, but then there is the really good stuff. I'm talking about the stuff that happens in between the formal events of a good conference. I'm talking about those conversations that happen in the hallway between the sessions. Or the networking and sharing of ideas that happen as a result of a good keynote or informational session. I'm talking about those moments when you are running between sessions and quickly trying to synthesize all of the great ideas, links, quotes, contacts and practices that you are trying to take in like trying to drink from a firehose.

The Technology Test Kitchen is not a place that talks about only the stuff that has worked in the past, it is a place to practice the new and emerging ideas that ask the big "what if" questions around our largest challenges in education. It is a space to dream big and then create models on the spot of what those dreams might look like in the classrooms of tomorrow. The TTK is a place to get your hands dirty and aim for the moon. It is a place to try new things and to fail faster so that the potential learning from a conference can breathe and grow rather than get shoved into a backpack from one session to the next. It is the loud and messy place where the good ingredients of one idea get tried with the fresh ingredients of another to unveil something entirely new and innovative that hadn't been thought of before.

Frank Tomsic, Director, McCormick Educational Technology Center at Rush University Medical Center, on the Quest for fluency in the use of technology for learner-centered learning

When children learn a language, they develop a deep, intuitive, native sense and "feel" for its meaning. The language and underlying culture are intrinsically tied to the learner. They acquire a deep personal sense of connection with the language that is difficult to break. However, many second language learners never develop the deep connections that bring them to the highly proficient, intuitive level of the native learner. They remain in a state of a non-native foreigner struggling to make sense.

Does a sense of native expertise exist in culture and language or in other domains?

If the analogy of language acquisition applies to other domains, then many learners exist and function, but they certainly do not feel the deep personal comfort or understanding of a "native" expert. Perhaps time is too limited to gain that deeply meaningful, generative connection, or perhaps it is the manner in which we engage the learner that has constrained us.

Is the depth of learning based on the age of the learner, the experiences of the learner, or the authenticity of the environment in which the learning happens? These are the questions that a group of educators discussed when struggling with the disconnects between our learning philosophies and how we engaged educator participants in professional development in the uses of technology for student-centered, active learning. Indeed, our philosophies informed us that we were engaging professional development participants poorly, and therefore could not expect to deeply affect their proficiency in the use of technology to create student-centered, authentic learning experiences. Further, participant use of technology in pursuit of learning interventions indicated that they were indeed non-natives struggling to make sense of the culture and language of technology and authentic learning. We needed a new modality of engagement that could engender native use of technology to more authentically engage learners regardless of the domain.

The TTK is not intended to be a lecture hall, but a curated and managed maker-space-inspired culture where novices and experts engage together in deep, meaningful, constructive use of technology, and where the ultimate goal is acquisition of native-expert use of technology in support of authentic learning. It is our construct and our metaphor for a better way to learn.

Robbie Melton, Associate Vice Chancellor for Emerging Technologies for the Tennessee Board of Regents, for the Educational and Workforce Possibilities and Challenges of The Internet of Everything (IOE) and Mixed Reality (VR/AR/Holograms) Technologies

The proliferating presence of devices, tools, gadgets, wearables, and even toys that are connected to the Internet provide new possibilities, as well as challenges for education and the workforce. By the year 2020, it is predicted that more than 50 billion connected devices will be on the Internet. These smart devices offer 'on-time – real-time' data regarding how these technologies are performing, our usages of these technologies, our location, and time on task. Thus, this opens up new ways to plan, implement, and evaluate how we teach, how students' learn, and how we perform in the workforce. You can expect some type of innovation every 90 days. So how can educators keep up, as well as, try out these emerging technologies? The TTK addresses these type of questions and situations by providing a showcase of the latest innovations impacting teaching, learning, and training. Participants can test out these smart technologies and provide feedback regarding possibilities and challenges. Case in point example of a device showcased at TTK: The IOE Smart Pacifier that tracks your baby's health and fever.

APPENDIX 2

Examples from 2015 Online Learning Consortium International Conference Technology Test Kitchen Recipe Book.

Quick and Dirty ePortfolios with Blendspace

You know what they say about giving a man a fish - the same goes for the classroom. The merits of creating ePortfolios are numerous, but a chief benefit is the support of student autonomy over the learning process. This recipe leverages the versatile web-based presentational tool, Blendspace, to allow users to create cohesive collections of resources into a playable, embeddable format. Each tile can hold video, images, files (such as PDFs, PowerPoint decks, Word docs, etc.), text, and quizzes - either your own or safely sourced from the web. The presentations are collaborative, allowing embedded comments, likes and feedback. The yummiest part is that Blendspace is free, and presentations can be linked together for a class, or created as standalone ePortfolios.

Cooking (Prep) Time:

- 1 hour (or less, depending on whether you've got all of your ingredients)

Ingredients:

- A free Blendspace account (https://www.blendspace.com/register)
- An assortment of items to combine into a presentations (images, links to web pages, videos on Dropbox or Google Drive, PowerPoint slides, Word docs, PDFs)

Directions:

1. Login to Blendspace: https://www.blendspace.com/login
2. Click on New Lesson to create a new Blendspace.
3. Using the toolbar on the right side of the screen, choose an element to add to the first tile in your Blendspace. You can choose from the following:
   a. a YouTube link - this video will play directly from within the presentation
   b. an image or website on Google*
   c. an image on Flickr*
   d. a video on Educreations or Gooru
   e. a link to any URL
   f. an uploaded file or embed code
   g. a file on your Dropbox account
   h. a file on your Google Drive account
4. To add that element to your Blendspace, simply drag and drop it into a tile on the left.
5. Give your tile a title by clicking on the first text line directly to the right of the slide number. Add additional annotations and comments to the tile on the second line next to the slide number. Click Done to return to the tile.
6. Both the title and the comment will appear for users when they play your Blendspace.
7. Reorder tiles by hovering over the center of the tile, and dragging and dropping it to your preferred location.

8. Add new tiles before a particular tile by hovering over the left side of the tile and clicking on the + icon that appears.
9. Turn a blank tile into a freeform text box by clicking on the Add Text button.
10. Turn a blank tile into a multiple choice quiz question by clicking on the Add Quiz button.
11. Change the size and color of the tiles with the Templates and Themes buttons on the top-left corner of the window.
12. When you are finished assembling your Blendspace, click on the Share button to:
    a. Grab a shareable link or embed code
    b. Share the lesson with any linked class accounts that you have created
    c. Share on social media or email
    d. Set the privacy settings for the lesson
    e. Set co-authors to allow multiple people to work collaboratively on the Blendspace
13. You and your users can hit Play to view the Blendspace:
    a. The full content of the tile will load on the left, to include playable videos and fully embedded, working websites
    b. Your comments will appear to the right of the tile, along with a comment box for viewers to leave responses
    c. Users can navigate through the tiles using the left and right arrows that appear when you hover over each side of the tile OR by using the small tiles located in the bottom-right corner of the screen
    d. To leave the presentation, click the x on the top-right.
14. From the Home screen, access additional information about your Blendspace, to include:
    a. The number of views,
    b. The average amount of time users spent on each slide
    c. Quiz results Comments
    d. Likes/dislikes, and
    e. Help requests

* No copyrights are harmed when using Blendspace. The files are embedded and linked into your presentation, retaining the original copyright of the author and protecting the intellectual property rights. Epic win!

Serving Suggestions:

Let your students cook it up! Have each person collect their work throughout the semester into a single Blendspace that is shared with you and their peers. They can then present their work at the end of the semester, either synchronously by playing it and explaining each resource, or asynchronously using the annotation feature. Include audio explanations by embedding links to audio in the comment area using a free recorder such as Vocaroo (http://vocaroo.com/).

Give your tiles some extra sizzle by importing your own images as title slides, overviews, agendas and additional information. Use a free layout program such as Canva (https://www.canva.com/), Haiku Deck (https://www.haikudeck.com/) or PicMonkey (http://www.picmonkey.com/) to create stunning slides, infographics and visuals to beautify your Blendspace. Time to turn that delicious dish over - it's gonna burn! Use Blendspace flip your lessons and get students cooking with the material before your contact hours to allow them to engage with the material more fully.

Additional Resources:

- Getting Started Creating Lessons in Blendspace https://www.youtube.com/watch?v=aQ_Mg3lSoew
- Flipping the Classroom Using Blendspace
- https://www.youtube.com/watch?v=D_5x3MW3p7A

Engage Students in Q&A with PeerWise

Peer learning and peer assessment are powerful tools to engage students and deepen learning through interaction. PeerWise is a freely available web-based peer learning tool which invites students to create & share their own multiple choice assessment questions regarding content in your class. They then answer, evaluate, and discuss each others' questions and answers. Participants can earn badges, get on leaderboards, make changes based on discussion and feedback, and deeply engage with the content of the unit. Meanwhile, the instructor can monitor questions and answers, comment, and see analytics about student participation, accuracy, badges earned, leaderboards, etc.

Directions:

1. Make sure your syllabus and/or class grading scheme includes a percentage for peer Q&A participation for a portion of your course. For example, you could make this worth 15-20% of the course grade. Be sure to elaborate on your expectations for participation: how many questions & answers are expected? Any bonus points for those who earn certain badges or get on leaderboards?
2. Pick a lecture, chapter, unit, or module for which you'd like students to engage in writing their own questions and answers. The topic could be most anything, but the questions will need to be multiple choice. You could also generally use PeerWise throughout the entire course, across all units or modules.
3. Go to https://peerwise.cs.auckland.ac.nz and type in the first few characters of your institution and then select it and click Go. If your institution is not in the system, email peerwise@cs.auckland. ac.nz to ask to have it set up.
4. If it's your first time, click to register a new account. NOTE: accounts are specific to the institution on PeerWise. It is possible to have a separate user account for different institutions. It will tell you which institution you are registering this account for at the top. As you register, choose an instructor account. You will receive an email with a verification code and instructions to proceed. You will then receive an email - within 24 hours (all the way from New Zealand!), from someone at PeerWise with your instructor account information and credentials.
5. Once you have that set up, you can enter PeerWise and "create a new course."
6. Next comes a screen with a Course ID and a box to enter a list of "unique student identifiers". These will be used for students to sign in and create their own accounts. Student identifiers could be last name, student ID #, first initial last name, or something like that. When a student registers

(or joins a course) with PeerWise, they must enter the Course ID and one of the "identifier" values on this list.

7. Click "Update Identifier List and Prompt"
8. On the right, click "View instructions for students"
9. Copy and paste the text in the box, and email it or post as an announcement in your course to students. It contains very specific links and instructions for them to set up their accounts and get started. Be sure to tell them specifically what their unique identifier is.
10. Ok, now you've got it all set up, and it's time to give it a whirl! You might want to also create an instruction sheet for students to get started beyond setting up the account:
11. After login, you will see a list of courses available. Click to enter the course.

Start by Writing Your Own Questions:

1. Choose "Your Questions" then click "Create New Question"
2. Enter a question and the possible answers (aka Alternatives)
3. Click "Select" next to the correct answer
4. Provide an explanation, and/or info for more information or review
5. Topics: you can select relevant topics or add them. This is a handy way to differentiate between units, modules, topics, etc.
6. Click to "Show a Preview" or "Save a Draft"
7. If everything looks good, click "Save Question"
8. At any time, go back to the main menu, and look for unanswered questions by other students. Answer them. Rate them! Discuss them! Look at the difficulty ratings, overall ratings, comments and help requests.

Instructors:

You can then go to the Administration to deal with anything related to this course in PeerWise: change settings, add students, change identifiers, browse questions, see scores, leaderboards, badges earned, usage charts, import/export questions, and so on. Use the analytics you have defined in your syllabus to assess student participation - or have them do self-assessment. Enjoy! You have just engaged your students even further in your learning community!

Additional Resources:

https://twitter.com/peerwise
    http://www.peerwise-community.org
    https://twitter.com/peerwise

Cooking with Padlet

Padlet is a website that lets you easily create a webpage called a wall where you can upload images, text, and video. It's like an online bulletin board or poster. Sharing the wall with other learners is where the magic begins. It's a creative process you can facilitate or have learners create their own walls. You can sign up for a free account or work without an account. There are a variety of privacy options or it can be totally public. Padlet generates a simple web link, embed code and CR code for the wall.

Ingredients:

- Computer, tablet or smartphone
- http://padlet.com/

Directions:

1. View tutorial for instructions and ideas for teachers using padlet (http://education.fcps.org/trt/padlet)
2. Add text, images, and videos about a topic and have students add to the wall.
3. Create walls to explore topics with your learners.
4. Have learners create walls to expand on topics or introduce themselves to the learning community.

Additional Resources:

http://ctreichler.wikispaces.com/Padlet#x-Padlet in Action
http://www.educationworld.com/a_tech/using-padlet-in-the-classroom.shtml

Create a Study Aide Using Google Forms and Autocrat

Ingredients:

- Google Form
- Google Form response spreadsheet
- Google Doc
- Gmail (NOTE: Gmail is an invisible need. Google installation must have it for this to work, but you will not configure Gmail in these instructions.)

Directions:

1. Create a folder for this study guide, in which you save all of the files you create.
2. Create your Google Form study guide. This may look like a sample test or exam,
3. or even a series of "think about it" questions, with text answers.
4. Go to the spreadsheet that will collect the answers for your form. You can find this by clicking Responses, then View Responses. When the spreadsheet opens, click Add-ons, then Get add-ons. When the script gallery opens, search for, and install Autocrat.
5. Now, take some time to think about design. I found this blog link very useful when I was deciding how to use AutoCrat in my work.

6. When you have everything ready, click Add-ons, then autoCrat, then Launch. You will be walked through the process.
7. After you have configured AutoCrat, make sure you fill out the form to make sure that the report it spits out looks like you expect, and will be useful to your students. Additional support resources are included below.

NOTE: Autocrat is built on the premise that Form responses will be piped into the document template via mail merge tags that look like this: <<mail merge tag>>

- What would you want the message you send to your students to say?
- What feedback would you want to give them for each question? You might want to tell
- them what they answered, then give them some background. Right? Start experimenting
- with designing your memo now.

Additional Resources:

http://cloudlab.newvisions.org/add-ons/autocrat

Creating Caption Files in Camtasia for Accessibility

Camtasia Studio is a purchased application. You can create captions using Camtasia Studio. As you begin, it is recommended to use the built-in Speech-to-text tool to generate automatic captions, then later editing the caption file for inaccuracies. This feature is only available in Camtasia Studio for PC.

Directions:

1. Open Camtasia and start a new project.
   a. To begin using STT, click on More along the bottom of the screen.
   b. Next, select Captions from the drop down menu.
   c. From here, click on the Speech-to-text button as shown below. This will automatically add captions to your video.
   d. Tips for Generating Accurate Speech-to-text Captions
   e. Consider using the voice training module in order to get higher accuracy when using STT. However, keep in mind that the voice training module will only work with one voice profile at a time.
   f. To do this, click on Tools located at the top of the screen. From the drop down menu, hover over Speech. Click on Improve speech-to-text.
   g. A new window should pop up like the one shown below. Under the section titled Train your computer to understand your voice, click on the Start voice training link.
   h. Another window should pop up, click Next. This should begin the voice training process as shown below. Follow the steps by reading the text given out loud.
   i. Once the training process is finished, your computer should better understand your personal way of speaking which will help improve accuracy when captioning.

2. Editing captions to correct inaccuracies using Camtasia
   a. If your caption is more than two lines long, split your caption into multiple captions consisting of two lines or less. This will prevent the system from cutting off the captions along the left and right sides of the video player.
   b. Three line captions must be split as shown below:
   c. Two line captions are the goal as shown below:
   d. Creating Two Line Captions
   e. To create two line captions, begin by finding the caption you want to split.
   f. 1. select that caption by clicking on it, and moving the waveform cursor over the center of the caption.
   g. 2. Once this is done you can click on the split button.
   h. Your caption will be duplicated in each section of the split video. Pick a good spot to make the split to ensure readability.
3. Exporting Your Captions: once you are finished captioning your video, click the export captions button and save it as an .srt file.

Additional Resources:

http://discover.techsmith.com/try-camtasia

Chapter 2
Use of Technology-Enabled Informal Learning in a Learning Organization

Lori Miller-Rososhansky
Children's Services Council of Palm Beach County, USA

Valerie C. Bryan
Florida Atlantic University, USA

ABSTRACT

This chapter explores how an organization created to inform members became an online learning organization. Using technology, the organization continued to support the professionals as they evolved in their individual careers and within the organization. Best practices arose to better inform the members and to expand communities of practice (CoPs). Members meaningfully engaged in the learning organization, in their avocations, and their vocations. This mix-method study, with over a 118 Association for Talent Development (ATD) professionals, addressed how the ATD could continue to support professionals in our evolving technological society. The study allowed the ATD professionals themselves to identify how they could help the organization and its' members to advance the organization by using technology, informal learning and research-based learning to improve the membership organization roles. The study highlighted how important informal learning, professional development, modeling, and identifying best practices, are to an organization's growth and the professionals' growth.

INTRODUCTION

As information continues to expand, it is essential that all organizations find means to assist their members to remain current and informed in order for the members to remain current and to expand their competencies. This engagement is especially true for member organizations where the members are at great distances from the host organization. In these situations, the travel necessary to share the information needed to advance may not be possible due to costs, distance involved, or varied schedules of the individuals involved. The Association of Talent Development, formerly known as the American Society

DOI: 10.4018/978-1-5225-2838-8.ch002

for Training and Development (ASTD), is a professional membership organization that helps its members develop skills and knowledge needed to lead organizations throughout the world in both face-to-face and using technology-enabled formats. As of 2013, ATD has over 41,000 members from over 126 countries. The ATD also has local chapters to enhance involvement and increase the level of presence.

The purpose of ATD is to "create a world that works better" (Association for Talent Development, 2017, p. 1) and its mission is to "empower professionals to develop talent in the workplace" (Association for Talent Development, 2017, p. 1). To do this the Association provides research, books, webcasts, events and educational programs. For those that can attend the association it also offers international events where its membership can view the "latest trends and best practices for designing, delivering, implementing and measuring learning programs" (Association for Talent Development, 2017a, p. 1).

The members are professionals that may become part of the "Communities of Practice" (Association for Talent Development, 2017b, p.1) under a host of titles: career development, global human resources development, government, healthcare, human capital, learning and development, learning technologies, management, sales enablement, science of learning or senior leaders and executives (Association for Talent Development, 2017b, p.1-4). There is a competency model where members may become credentialed through a competency-based model and become a Certified Professional in Learning and Performance (CPLP) by demonstrated competencies in 10 areas:

change management, performance improvement, instructional design, training delivery, learning technologies, evaluating learning impact, managing learning programs, integrated talent management, coaching, and knowledge management (Miller, 2015), p. 27)

These communities of practice (CoPs) exist across the USA and many countries who are actively involved in ATD. One such community is in the southern part of the USA and was the location for the study that will follow.

Background

According to the ATD (2015) report, "Bridging the Skills Gap: Workforce Development is Everyone's Business", there are jobs in the USA and beyond that are not being filled because the technology is constantly changing the view of the workplace and people are not being trained fast enough to fill the slots that are available creating a "skills gap" (ATD, 2015, p. 7). According to ATD study "people in the know," the talent development professionals, say that:

- 56% of the current workforce's skills "do not match changes in the company strategies, goals, markets or business models" (ATD, 2015, p. 7);
- When promoting internal people for select jobs, 48% of them "lack a requisite skill" (ATD, 2015, p. 7) and for 45% of "certain types of jobs there are too few candidates" (ATD, 2015, p. 7).

The workforce is changing, and at such an exponential rate, organizations like ATD have to become more proactive and address how to provide adequate training and talent development to the changing workforce and prevent what appears to be a skills gap. It is also essential that organizations like ATD devise new ways to reach the varied generations and manage a new workforce that is growing more and more to be a virtual workforce. New collaborative environments need to be created to allow for generational preferences in training, receiving information, etc., between the Veterans (1928-1945), Baby Boomers (1946-1964), Generation X (1965-1979), Millennials (1980-1994) and the Net Generation(1995-Now) [Note: numbers represent years of births of that group]. Each generation listed brings its own set of problems for the organization to address from the lack of technology skills to the lack of communication regarding how to use a common language.

Advances in technology have increased the tension between what strategies will best work to alleviate the barriers between the learners, the organizations and the skills sets needed. We need to create a better 'widget' that has universal application:

Distance learning has contributed to the large-scale breaking down of barriers that have, in the past, distinguished and separated adult learning cultures into categories labeled formal, non-formal, and informal. The globalization factors responsible for the rapid increase of open and distance learning have contributed to the breakdown of learning's neat compartments into a more homogenous type of life-wide learning (Conrad, 2008, p. 3).

For most people in the varied industries, work organizations and educational operations, informal learning appears to be a very significant way to acquire and develop work-related skills and competencies that are valid, reliable and cost effective. Informal learning is viewed as unstructured and self-directed and allows the learner to find his or her 'right path'. "The product of the individual learner and the social context of interaction … without a high degree of structure" (Lin & Lee, 2014, p. 127-8).

MAIN FOCUS OF THE CHAPTER

Issues, Controversies, Problems

In 1975, Malcom Knowles described adult informal learning as:

… learning in which individuals take the initiative, with or without the help of others, in diagnosing their learning needs, formulating their learning goals, identifying human and material resources for learning, choosing and implementing appropriate learning strategies, and evaluating learning outcomes (Knowles, 1975, p. 18).

In support of these assumptions, Miller (2015) states "Because of the critical importance of informal learning, educational leaders must explore methods of supporting it in a way which enables the adult learner to become more effective in acquiring, analyzing, and sharing this knowledge" (p. 10). This process is important in formal learning, but it is absolutely essential in technology-based (or online) informal learning, because the facilitator is not always present and the learner must structure the learning for himself or herself and be more self-directed in his or her learning process.

In its broadest meaning, 'self-directed learning' describes a process by which individuals take the initiative, with or without the assistance of others, in diagnosing their learning needs, formulating learning goals, identify human and material resources for learning, choosing and implement appropriate learning strategies, and evaluating learning outcomes (Knowles, 1975, p. 18).

This self-directed learning process is exactly what is needed in many workplaces today that are separated in time and distance from their corporate headquarters or their learning institutions. Individuals in these working environments are called upon to create their own strategies for solving problems and accomplishing work goals, often with support coming from an internet connections or an online community of practice of like-minded employees or learners. The learner alone, or with his or her 'community', makes a decision as to what needs to be done, how it needs to be done, when it needs to be done, and how the results will be measured. In many situations, the members of the ATD are called upon to function in such a collaborative environment. For the above reasons, the purpose statement of this study specifically addressed the "technology-based informal learning":

The purpose of the mixed methods study in this case was to determine the meaning of the effect of technology-based informal learning on the role of the Association for Talent Development (ATD) for its members with an online presence (Miller, 2015, p. 4).

The researcher found it essential to ask the following research questions:

1. What are the perceptions of ATD members regarding the effect of technology-based informal learning on the role of ATD?
2. How do ATD members utilize technology for informal learning?
3. Are there factors such as gender, age, ethnicity, educational level, or length of time in the field that predict a member's likelihood to utilize technology for informal learning?
4. Are there certain ATD competency areas for which informal learning is preferred over non-formal or formal learning? (Miller, 2015, p. 4-5)

Please note that to do so, several iterations were conducted to analyze the results.

Survey and/or interview questions were analyzed using quantitative research (multiple regression) (Aliaga & Gunderson, 2000) in combination with responses to select survey questions (Questions 2-6 that addressed gender, age, ethnicity, highest education degree, and years in talent development) to predict usage of technology for the *informal learning*. Qualitative analysis with codes and themes were used to address 10 of the questions. Descriptive statistics was used to address five of the questions.

The target population was determined using both purposeful and snowball sampling of workplace learning and performance improvement professionals. The individuals selected because they utilized technology to access the ATD webpages and groups. An a priori G-Power test determined the sample size with an effect size of 0.3, an alpha of 0.05 and a power of 0.95, yielding the need for 111 participants. One-hundred and eighteen responses were received from the ATD members and analyzed.

In addition, 14 participants were interviewed using an 18 question online survey yielding qualitative data to deepen the understanding of the data and the experience of the participants (Creswell, 1998; Maxwell, 2004). and triangulated with data from the surveys to check for validity. Open-ended questions as well as closed questions were used to "solicit perspectives regarding the effects of social learning via technology on membership organization" (Miller, 2015, p. 40). Coding categories were used to sort descriptive data. Both reliability and validity were checked.

SOLUTIONS AND RECOMMENDATIONS

Multiple regression showed there was no one demographic variable which had a p-value less than 0.05 and could predict the dependent variable of technology use, so the null hypothesis failed to be rejected. All the respondents used informal learning and half of the respondents indicated that they always use informal learning as a resource (see figure 1).

Figure 1. Responses to the survey question: How often do you use informal learning as a resource when you need to learn something? (Miller, 2015, p.50)

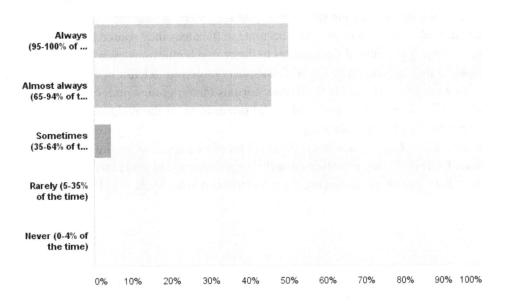

Figure 2. Responses to survey question: How often do you use informal learning as a first resource when you need to learn something? (Miller, 2015, p.51)

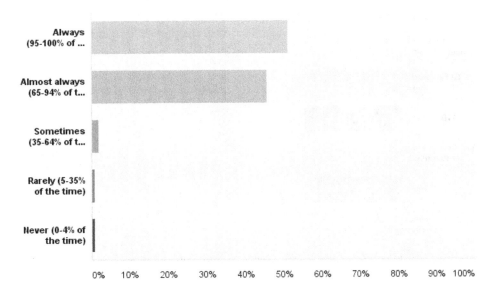

When asked *How often do you use informal learning as a first resource when you need to learn something?,* individuals indicated they are using informal learning, and generally as their first choice (see figure 2*).

The ATD respondents also indicated that ATD was the leading choice for them to get relevant information via informal learning, but many identify a number of online choices for getting relevant information as noted in Figure 3.

The participants are clearly comfortable with finding what they need to do their jobs. Many of the interviewees later reflected that they feel comfortable sourcing their own answers and in some cases no longer find the need for formal courses to address their needs. The ATD respondents did indicate that they used the informal networks as a convenience to find information and contact with other colleagues is afforded by technology. Overall the respondents felt they were getting the answers they needed and felt the on-demand information was generally accurate in the areas they sourced (see figure 3).

There was variability in some of the answers to the research questions even though not statistically significant. Table 1 indicates that how the ATD members preferred to learn in different areas in different ways. There was also some difference in how various ethnic groups preferred to learn, but again, not statistically so. The majority of participants did prefer to learn the ATD competencies informally followed by *nonformal* and *formal* learning.

Note that regardless of the competency, the ATD member prefers to use informal learning at least 50% of the time. There is also the possibility that this first choice could lead to the nonformal and formal learning if the ATD member did not secure the information that he or she was looking for initially (see figure 4).

Figure 3. Responses to survey question: What ATD related online groups are you a member of or visit to access content related to ATD?(Miller, 2015, p. 52)

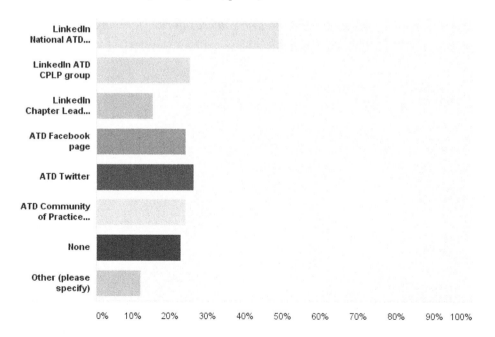

Figure 4. Learning preference for ATD competencies (Miller, 2015, p. 58)

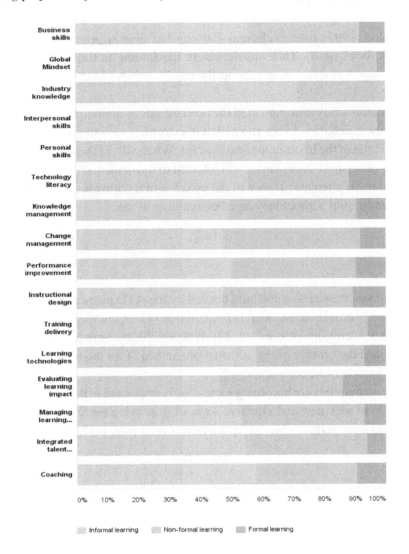

As Marsick and Volpe (1999) state, "Informal learning has always been the most pervasive type of learning in the workplace" (p. 3). That was definitely the finding in this ATD study. The participants in this study also expressed the need for information to be convenient, easy to access on-demand, and easily searchable. *Virtual collaboration* was viewed as something needed by the ATD members. This study also supports Conrad's (2008) view: "Virtual collaboration is promoted as one of the ways that workplace leaders can leverage workplace knowledge into results" (p.12). The members of the organization can become the creators and the brokers of the information created.

ATD and its members must not become one more of the "education and training systems (that) were built for another era" (National Center on Education and Economy, 2007, p. 8). ATD must continue to embrace change and allow input from its members as change agents to chart its future directions into the global economy.

FUTURE RESEARCH DIRECTIONS

As Marsick and Volpe (1999) state, "informal learning has always been the most pervasive type of learning in the workplace" (p. 3). That was definitely the finding in this ATD study. Will this trend continue? How can the informal learning support the nonformal and formal learning of the workplaces of the ATD members?

The participants in this study also expressed the need for information to be convenient, easy to access on-demand, and easily searchable. As we all know it is extremely easy to get lost in the virtual environment and return with little of the information searched for. What will ATD continue to do to insure that its virtual body remains accessible, informative, and relevant to its members? Will ATD remain responsive to changes suggested by its clientele? How will the increase in worldwide members alter ATD's way of responding to its membership without language becoming an issue?

CONCLUSION

Virtual collaboration was viewed as something needed by the ATD members. This study also supports Conrad's (2008) view: "virtual collaboration is promoted as one of the ways that workplace leaders can leverage workplace knowledge into results" (p. 12). Is it possible that members of this organization can become the creators and the brokers of the information created? Can the members of this organization leverage knowledge for other like organizations?

Virtual learning communities are becoming increasingly important in the knowledge economy. ATD members may be able to seek new and effective ways of improving performance in the workplace by meeting in a virtual space at a time, place and pace to suit their busy professional lives.

REFERENCES

Aliaga, M., & Gunderson, B. (2000). *Interactive statistics*. Saddle River, NJ: Prentice Hall.

Association for Talent Development. (2017a). *Together we create a world that works better*. Retrieved from https://www.td.org/About

Association for Talent Development. (2017b). *Why ATD 2017?* Retrieved from http://www.atdconference.org/?_ga=1.36520672.1906492158.1488225871

Association for Talent Development. (2015). *Bridging the skills gap: Workforce development is everyone's business*. Alexandria, VA: ATD Public Policy.

Association for Talent Development. (2017c). *Communities of practice*. Retrieved from https://www.td.org/Communities-of-Practice

Conrad, D. (2008). From community to community of practice: Exploring the connection of online learners to informal learning in the workplace. *American Journal of Distance Education, 22*(1), 3–23. doi:10.1080/08923640701713414

Creswell, J. W. (1998). *Qualitative inquiry and research design: Choosing among five traditions*. Thousand Oaks, CA: Sage Publications.

Knowles, M. (1975). *Self-directed learning: A guide for learners and teachers*. Cambridge, UK: Prentice Hall.

Lin, Y., & Lee, P. (2014). Informal learning: Theory and applied. *International Journal of Business and Commerce, 3*(5), 127–134.

Marsick, V., & Volpe, M. (1999). The nature and need for informal learning. *Advances in Developing Human Resources, 1*(1), 1–10. doi:10.1177/152342239900100302

Maxwell, J. A. (1996). *Qualitative research design: An interactive approach*. Thousand Oaks, CA: Sage Publications.

Miller, L. (2015). *The perceived impact of technology-based informal learning on membership organizations* (Order No. 10154967). Available from ProQuest Dissertations & Theses Global. (1818521179)

National Center on Education and the Economy. (2007). *Tough choices or tough times: Executive summary*. Retrieved from http://www.skillscommission.org/pdf/exec_sum/ToughChoices_EXECSUM.pdf

Palloff, R. M., & Pratt, K. (1999). *Building learning communities in cyberspace: Effective strategies for the online classroom*. San Francisco, CA: Jossey-Bass.

Senge, P. (1990). *The fifth discipline*. New York, NY: Doubleday/Currency Publishing.

Wenger, E. (1998). *Communities of practice: Learning, meaning, and identity*. Cambridge, UK: Cambridge University Press. doi:10.1017/CBO9780511803932

KEY TERMS AND DEFINITIONS

Association for Talent Development (ATD): Professional membership organization dedicated to individuals in the field of workplace learning and development, formerly known as the American Society for Training and Development (ASTD). ATD provides learning opportunities, set standards, identify best practices, and allows members to network with other professionals who share their interests.

Community of Practice (CoP): "Groups of people who share a concern, a set of problems, or a passion about a topic, and who deepen their knowledge and expertise in this area by interacting on an ongoing basis" (Wenger, 1998, p. 4).

Formal Learning: Learning that is intentional, organized, and structured. Most often formal learning occurs within an institution and includes learning objectives, expected outcomes, and credits leading to a degree or certification.

Informal Learning: Learning which is unstructured and self-directed.

Learning Organization: An organization where "people continually expand their capacity to create the results they truly desire, where new and expansive patterns of thinking are nurtured, where collective aspiration is set free, and where people are continually learning how to learn together" (Senge, 1990, p. 3).

Membership Organization: Any organization that you apply to or sign up to join or subscribe to. As a member, you may have to pay a membership fee.

Non-formal Learning: Learning which may or may not be intentional. It is organized but not necessarily structured. No formal credits are earned by attendance.

Self-directed Learning: "In its broadest meaning, 'self-directed learning' describes a process by which individuals take the initiative, with our without the assistance of others, in diagnosing their learning needs, formulating learning goals, identify human and material resources for learning, choosing and implement appropriate learning strategies, and evaluating learning outcomes." (Knowles, 1975, p. 18)

Technology-based or Online Informal Learning: Unstructured learning offered through some means of technology.

Transformative Learning Process: "Learning based on reflection and on the interpretation of the experiences, ideas, and assumptions gained through prior learning … rooted in the meaning-making process that is central to constructivism … a major feature of the online classroom" (Palloff & Pratt, 1999, p. 129).

Chapter 3
"Let Me Show You":
An Application of Digital Storytelling for Reflective Assessment in Study Abroad Programs

Melody Jo Buckner
University of Arizona, USA

ABSTRACT

Criticism has been prevalent around the academic rigor of coursework within study abroad programs. Stakeholders of the study abroad experience are taking a closer look at student learning outcomes from these programs. This critique suggests that more attention be given to the development of innovative and meaningful assessment practices being implemented into these programs in order for students to demonstrate their learning outcomes. The purpose of this study was to investigate the affordances of digital storytelling as a response to this critique. The focus of this study was to implement a digital storytelling assignment in four summer study abroad programs led by university faculty. Over the course of four summers (2011 – 2014), digital storytelling was implemented to help students reflect upon what they learned and through this reflective process demonstrate the knowledge they gained. This article discusses the findings of digital storytelling as a reflective assessment practice in study abroad programs.

INTRODUCTION

Reflection is the process of stepping back from an experience to ponder, carefully and persistently, its meaning to the self through the development of inferences; learning is the creation of meaning from past or current events that serves as a guide for future behaviour. - M. W. Daudelin

We are living in a world of chaotic change that is evolving exponentially where we find ourselves literally drowning in a sea of information. There now exists a global environment where citizens are being challenged to think creatively, become cooperative problem solvers, and effective communicators. People need to know how to interact, engage, and collaborate with others from multiple cultures using

DOI: 10.4018/978-1-5225-2838-8.ch003

various types of technology. They also need to be able to match left-brain analytical skills with right-brain creative, innovative skills to be competitive and successful in today's global market (Pink, 2006). Is our educational system preparing our students to become productive well rounded global citizens? And how are our students demonstrating in authentic ways what they are learning in diverse educational environments?

In the United States, we measure educational success based upon assessments where students are asked to recall facts taught to them in classrooms using an industrial-age model of instruction, where students sit in rows, listen to instructors, memorize facts and demonstrate their knowledge based on these high stake testing. As an educational system, we should have advanced past the information-age model, where information is readily available through technology to the conceptual age model of teaching and learning, in which students discover concepts and ideas through exploration, critical thinking and demonstration of knowledge with authentic artifacts that have meaning for students. Today's students are primarily assessed in ways that draw only on the left-brain analytical proficiencies, rather than also tapping into the right-brain creative abilities. Why is there a need for a more engaging and creative type of assessment? The main answer is accountability. Students are working to achieve something, in this case a grade, course credit, or a degree, so there is a need to make sure they have met certain defined standards before the award can be granted. It is usually easy and more convenient to administer a high-stakes objective assessment to a mass audience on left-brain analytic proficiencies. However, it is more difficult to assess students on right-brain creative abilities, as these are more subjective to evaluate.

Today's students are what we define as digital natives. Their natural world revolves around a digital environment. Digital storytelling used as a modality for reflective assement could be a more authenic form of reflection over the more traditional practice of essay writing. Narratives expressed through the technological modality of digital storytelling can be a mechanism used to effectively assess not only right-brain creative abilities, but also the left-brain analytical proficiencies. Further, a focus on narratives exposes learning processes often ignored when designing research on a narrow range of cognitive skills (McEwan, 1995). For this article, *digital storytelling* is defined as a modern method for expanding upon traditional storytelling techniques including narratives through a variety of digital modalities including digital photography and videography. The audience can be engaged in a passive way through just watching a video or in an interactive way through commentary, discussions, or social media after watching the video (Ohler, 2013). Therefore, the research study discussed in this article investigated, the potential use of digital storytelling as an effective assessment method for students to demonstrate both personal and academic learning outcomes. The theoretical framework used for this research was constructivism, how students learn or the way knowledge is assembled in ones' own mind. Through reflection students construct the meaning of their learning and *demonstrate* their outcomes with digital storytelling technological modality and techniques.

The study applied a qualitative approach for researching and collecting data from students participating in summer study abroad programs in Italy, Mexico and Rwanda held over four summers June 2010 to Aug 2014. The students were between the ages of 18 and 25 who were currently attending an institute of higher learning and were taking a faculty-led summer study abroad course for academic credit. The instruments used for this study were surveys, field observations, interviews, and the student's final digital stories. The research questions explored the influence of digital storytelling on the learning experience and the impact of demonstrating learning outcomes through digital storytelling. The findings from this study confirmed that reflection on learning and the creation of a digital story to demonstrate what was learned was is an effective method for engaging students and assessing their learning progress. Based upon these findings, digital storytelling can be utilized to engage students in a creative process as well as demonstrate learning outcomes, and support the idea of constructivism.

This article will start with a review of the literature about assessment practices and digital storytelling. The next section examines the research questions and theoretical framework used in the study. It is followed by an outline of the qualitative method utilized for the research. Next the results are discussed, along with a discussion about the study. Finally, implications and recommendations are made based upon the findings of the research study.

Literature Review

Daniel Pink (2006) points out that there is a major shift happening in the world today as we move from the information age to the conceptual age. According to Pink in the conceptual age, it will be vital for students to utilize new ways to "created artistic and emotional beauty, to detect patterns and opportunities, to craft a satisfying narrative, and to combine seemingly unrelated ideas into a novel invention… to empathize, the understand the subtleties of human interaction, to find joy in one's self and elicit it to others" (p. 51). Traditional storytelling, which employs the modalities of oral narration, the written word, or illustrations, is part of the foundations of the new literacies movement (Street, 2003). Digital storytelling expands upon these modalities by adding multimedia techniques, such as voice recording, digital photography, or video production. As educators we need to utilize these types of authentic assessment methods which allow our students to demonstrate their learning in a conceptual age way.

In reviewing assessment practices, there is a need to go back to our ancestral roots and explore ways we first began to learn, retain, and pass on wisdom. Collaborative, interactive narratives have been an entertaining and engaging way for people from cultures all over the world to express their experiences and give meaning to those experiences through telling their stories. From the beginning of time narratives were designed to teach, inspire, bring people together, or to pass along wisdom from one generation to another. Storytelling is a human trait that is universal, present and recognizable across cultures and epochs (Alexander & Levine, 2008). There is power in using narratives or personal storytelling to convey or demonstrate knowledge. Through the process of storytelling, meaning is constructed, knowledge is retained and the ability to pass along wisdom is enabled.

Narratives and Storytelling

Narratives historically have been the way in which humans pass on the knowledge of the world around them and were our first true assessment of learning. Stories in fact, help the people and the culture to survive and thrive in a hostile environment.

Storytelling was the first form of education. In the book, *Wisdom Sits in Places – Landscape and Language Among the Western Apache*, Keith Basso (1996) quotes a bit of wisdom from one of the elders Nick Thompson, "That is what we know about our stories. They go to work on your mind and make you think about your life…" (p. 58). Stories do work on your mind and make you think deeper. Stories help you define yourself, where you come from and what you know.

Gary Witherspoon (1977) in the book, *Language and Art in the Navajo Universe* asserts that when listening to and telling stories, it is important to remember that human beings actually create the world within which they live, think, speak, and act. "And even though they occupy the same globe, they traverse very different worlds" (p. 3). Through the telling of stories and creation of art, humans relate to one another. With language, man has the ability to express himself actively, creatively, and become a powerful part of his universe. "If he is void of language, then he is impotent, ignorant, isolated and static" (p. 62). Our language and our stories become a vital piece of who we are, where we come from and ultimately assist in pointing us to where we are going in this life.

According to McEwan (1995) narratives are a basic fundamental human capacity and the role of narratives in education clearly merits our attention. Narrative is an extended language configured in a way that embodies life. It has a rhythm springing from the patterns of human life and interaction. There is a structural symmetry between the content and human existence. It helps to remember, that knowledge has been gained within the context of someone's life and as a product of that person's inquiry. In focusing on narratives in the framework of education we can explore on how to build it into the curriculum and make it an integral part of the teaching and learning experience.

Bruner (1990) describes two types of narrative structures. The first is a summation of human consciousness, which relates to the growth of knowledge or the discovery of ideas gathered through the deployment of human projects and practices. The other is an individual consciousness, which are stories of an individual's educational growth and development. Throughout our lives we tend to naturally create narratives to give coherence and meaning to the whole lived experience (Bruner, 1990). These narratives of lived experiences represent constructed knowledge, not just the conveyance of information. Narratives allow us to put ideas into our own words, so we can make meaning of them. As we begin to learn, we are forming our own unique narratives. Narratives give us a way of expressing our ways of knowing by helping to organize and communicate our own personal experiences. If we start to understand that the central focus of narrative is to create human meaning making and formation of identity, then we can grasp the significance of narrative in education. With this in mind, narratives can play a vital role in helping to construct the future of the curriculum, the process of learning and ways to inform the practice of teaching (McEwan, 1995).

In his book, *Narrative schooling: Experiential learning and the transformation of American education*, Hopkins (1994) proposes a narrative schooling grounded in the philosophy of John Dewey. Dewey (1938) stated that education is a continuing restructuring of the learner's experience with the process taking into account personal meaning and social context. Basically, the content being presented needs to connect with the learner's prior experience and the learner must have opportunities to actively engage with the content based on their own personal lived experience (Dewey, 1938). Hopkins advances on Dewey's ideas by adding the narrative process through which the learner demonstrates meaning of their experiences and content. He writes, "Narrative is the indispensable process through which emplotment and meaning attribution flow..." (p. 10).

Narrative as Pedagogy

One educational arena that has explored narrative pedagogy is the field of nursing as this discipline relies heavily on case studies to both teach and assess principles of care and medical decision making. Diekelmann (2003) discovered over the course of a 15-year study with teachers, students, and clinicians that how nursing practice is being learned is as important as what is being learned. She found the use of narrative pedagogy, in which teachers and students share and interpret their lived experiences to gather collective wisdom in order to address existing challenges, was an effective practice. Bringing together both teachers and students to learn from each other's perspectives was useful in this educational environment. She found that when multi-perspective thinking is enacted, new possibilities open up for teaching and learning in both the classroom and in clinical situations.

There were two themes that emerged from the Diekelmann study, the first was "Thinking as Questioning: Preserving Perspectival Openness" and, the second was "Practicing Thinking: Preserving Fallibility and Uncertainty." In the first theme, students were not asked to specifically answer questions, but to persistently explore the meaning and significance of the practice. They were to explore and expose the underlying assumptions embedded in the experience. Through this exploration the teachers and students collaborate in new ways that preserve perspectival openness. In the second theme, thinking shifts from being a means to an end into cycles of interpretation. In this situation, uncertainty and fallibility are preserved. Students are not "told", but "guided" into thinking and learning difference content and practices. Through sharing of various viewpoints about how to solve a problem, students think through a situation and go beyond the problem to become deeper thinkers. This helps students learn the importance of generating many perspectives in order to understand a situation and see the complexity and uncertainty of each situation. By using narrative pedagogy to help students think differently, profoundly, and perhaps collaboratively they create a deeper meaning and understanding of the situation. This assists them in being able to tell their story or achieve the learning outcomes of the experience.

Traditional storytelling and narratives have proven to be a fundamental structure of human meaning making. The narrative gives us an epistemological perspective that we can understand and relate to on many levels. As an example, which is easier to remember a list of facts or those facts woven into a story that ties them together for deep meaning? To go even further, which is more intriguing or engaging for the listener or learner, the list or the story? Then take a deeper step and ponder another level of engaging the listen by adding a new way of delivering the story through the multimodal dimension of digital storytelling.

Digital Storytelling

Digital storytelling revolves around the art of telling a story through the use of digital media (examples are images, audio and video). The story needs to have a theme or topic coming from a particular point of view or perspective and possess meaning within the framework. The stories are usually under five minutes and include a variety of uses including personal experiences, historical events, meaningful content or instructions on a particular subject.

Digital storytelling roots go back to the 1990's when Dana Atchley first coined the term as he was experimenting with the use of multimedia elements in the workshops he offered at the American Film Institute on storytelling performances (Robin, 2006). Dana Atchley, Joe Lambert, and Nina Mullen started the San Francisco Digital Media Center, which evolved into the Center for Digital Storytelling, a non-profit, community art organization in Berkley, California. Joe Lambert (2010) created "The Digital Storytelling Cookbook" from his experience with the Center for Digital Storytelling. This Cookbook constructs seven elements into a rubric, so that students would have guidelines in which to create their stories. The seven elements include: a point of view, a dramatic question, emotional content, visual, sound, economy and pace.

Within the College of Education at the University of Houston there is a group exploring ways in which digital storytelling can be used for educational purposes. The Educational Uses of Digital Storytelling website was created almost ten years ago and has evolved into a resource for educators and students interested in integrating digital storytelling into educational activities. Over the years Bernard Robin, the professor who leads the educational uses of digital storytelling website has researched this area and discovered that it creates a strong foundation for many 21ˢᵗ Century literacies including:

- **Digital Literacy**: The ability to discuss issues, gather information and seek help,
- **Global Literacy**: The ability to create messages from a global perspective,
- **Technology Literacy**: The ability to use computers and other technologies,
- **Visual Literacy**: The ability to communicate through visual images, and
- **Information Literacy**: The ability to find, evaluate and synthesize information (Robin, 2006).

When a student participates in the digital storytelling process the following skills can be developed: research, writing, organization, technology, presentation, interview, interpersonal, problem solving and assessment. However, Robin (2006) also points out challenges with creating digital stories. Some of these challenges include: trouble formulating an educationally sound story, access to technology tools necessary to create a digital story, issues of copyright and intellectual property of others, and time factor to learn all the elements that go into digital storytelling.

Research Question and Theoretical Framework

To address the issue of earning academic credit for knowledge obtained during a learning experience the focus of this research asked the question: "What does digital storytelling offer as an assessment instrument and model for demonstrating expected learning outcomes for study abroad programs?" This study investigated the use of digital storytelling as a required project in four study abroad programs. The digital storytelling project was designed to form a meaningful assessment practice for student, by allowing them to create and tell a story of their own learning experience. The method was to engage the students during the learning process through the creation of content based upon their unique knowledge acquisition.

Constructivism (McDrury, 2003) is one of the theoretical framework used for this study which views learning as a process, or a way of making sense of knowledge through the addition and synthesizing of new information within an existing knowledge structure. Chaille and Britian (1991) describe constructivism in the following way:

The learner is actively constructing knowledge rather than passively taking in information. Learners come to the educational setting with many different experiences, ideas and approaches to learning. Learners do not acquire knowledge that is transmitted to them: rather, they construct knowledge through their intellectual activity and make it their own (p. 11).

Reflection and storytelling in concert are ways in which students can construct their knowledge of events or content. They reflect upon their new learning and bring their own unique stories not only from the current information, but merged with knowledge of their past experiences. This idea points to the funds of knowledge theory (Gonzales, Moll, & Amanti, 2005) whereby historical accumulated- and cultural-developed knowledge is essential for individual functioning and well-being. The student's own distinctive background can be as critical or influential to the learning experience as the academic content being acquired.

In socio-cultural constructivism there is more emphasis on the communication processes with the influence of social factors helping to construct the knowledge. Vygotsky (1978) stressed the importance of language and dialogue in the social contexts of learning when constructing knowledge. He recognized the importance of assisted and unassisted learning within the zone of proximal development (ZPD). ZPD is that area of learning where a student can problem solve independently to a certain point, but needs some guidance or collaboration from others to make it to the next level.

Digital storytelling aligns with the Vygotskian perspective, as the learning process is social and collaborative. It also values the prior experience of the student and promotes a reflective dialogue in which meaning is constructed. One aspect of Vygotsky's thinking that relates to the digital story paradigm is the importance of culturally situated learning that stresses educational interactions are influenced by the surrounding culture. Everyone is affected by the interaction of his or her own social, historical, ideological, and cultural contexts. These factors, along with a reflective process, inform and guide how we go about constructing our world.

In framing the digital storytelling process within the socio-cultural aspect of constructivism the idea of *dialogue* is central to the learning process and influenced by the cultural context. This is not just a simple contextual framework, but also one that includes process and the complex issue of surrounding influences including the role of discourse (McDrury, 2003). The learning process for effective digital storytelling includes a meaningful experience, a reflective process, making the experience relevant and a dialogue that promotes deeper thinking.

Noel Entwistle (2001) divides learning into two separate levels. There is surface learning, which is just the reproduction of knowledge to cope with certain requirements verses deep learning, which is transformative learning where students understand ideas for themselves. This becomes a significant theoretical framework for the digital storytelling process as it engages students to dive deeper into the meaning of their experience through the construction of storytelling around their own knowledge.

The other theoretical framework used for this research was supported by Kolb's model of experiential learning. With this model learning is connected to the ways in which a student processes and reflects upon those experiences. The learner gains knowledge in two ways: grasping or perceiving the knowledge, and then by transforming or processing the knowledge (Kolb, 1984). The digital storytelling project gives the learner a mechanism from which to accomplish both of these connections to knowledge. For learners to effectively demonstrate their learning outcomes they must first have a concrete experience, and then reflect upon the experience before conveying that experience to others through the digital story.

Kolb takes a holistic approach by combining both cognitive and behavioral theories together to emphasize how experiences including cognitions, environmental factors and emotions influence the learning process (Kolb, Boyatzis & Mainemelis, 2000). This mode of learning is portrayed as a cycle with the following elements. For grasping the experience there is the *Concrete Experience* and *Abstract Conceptualization*, while transforming the experience has *Reflective Observation* and *Active Experimentation*. Within this cycle, a person has a concrete experience thus providing the information to serve as a basis for reflection. These reflections help the person to form abstract concepts, and then these concepts assist in developing new beliefs or ideas, which the person then actively tests. Through these tests the person gathers information and the process begins all over again.

There are many connections from this theory to the digital storytelling process. Digital stories are the product of experiential learning. The student has a unique experience, for example an event that takes place during their time studying abroad. Through a reflective practice, the student forms a story around the event and in the process forms an abstract concept of what they learned from the event. In this case, the creation and sharing of the digital story moves the student to the active experimentation phase, where the discussion can assist the student in moving deeper into learning from the event. The cycle can continue as the student watches and comment on other student's digital stories who participated on the same study abroad program. Students can relate to the other stories, but expand their thinking about the same experience as it is viewed from a different lens or perspective.

This theory provides a framework for research with digital storytelling as an assessment practice. The process of digital storytelling allows for students to construct and demonstrate their knowledge through their own experience with the use of multiliteracies including writing a script, taking digital photos or videos, and recording their voice. The practice of digital storytelling could help to transform learning and assessment practices in the educational system as it moves more into alignment with the needs of students as they prepare to function in a digital world. James Gee (2013) expresses this view in his book, *The Anti-Education Era*, when he says, "Getting smart is now a 24/7 enterprise because intelligence comes from cultivating our lives and all our experiences in the service of learning and growth. Digital media today can make learning in and out of school engaging, social and life enhancing."(p. 215).

Methods

The choice of conducting a qualitative study for this research was based on the nature of what was being explored. The strength of the qualitative study is providing data that is subjective, descriptive, and gives a snapshot of a particular population. In this instance, the population was relatively small and the outcomes were based upon student and faculty perceptions of a specific intervention, the digital storytelling project in framing the demonstration of learning outcomes. The study was conducted to gain understanding of the students' feelings, impressions and viewpoint of the digital storytelling project as a reflective tool for the demonstration of learning outcomes. The qualitative approach was the most applicable choice for this research as the behavior of students was collected through field observation, interviews, and gathering of artifacts. The faculty members were also interviewed to gain their insight about the effectiveness of the digital storytelling project.

The target populations for this study were college students between the ages of 18 and 25 who were currently attending an institute of higher learning and were taking a faculty-led summer study abroad course for academic credit. However, the study abroad programs were not limited to this population of students. For example, there was one Ph.D. student who participated in the study who was in her forties and a few other students in their late twenties.

The digital storytelling project was constructed as a reflective assessment assignment to assist students in demonstrating what they had learned during their study abroad experience. This was not a slide show of the trip with a narrative of the events that took place, but rather a deeper reflection about the student's total experience. One way the project was framed for students was to consider this question, "If an employer were to ask you about what you learned on your study abroad experience, what story would you tell?" Table 1 shows the program goals, learning objectives and assessment methods used in the four programs.

The requirements of the digital story were given to the students in a rubric format. When constructing the rubric for this study several resources were considered. The Digital Storytelling Cookbook by Joe Lambert (2010), which contains the seven elements of digital storytelling, was the major framework. Other resources taken into consideration were the 21st century literacies taken from the University of Houston College of Education website, The Educational Uses of Digital Storytelling. Finally, Jason Ohler (2013) insights into the use of digital storytelling were helpful in framing the rubric for assessment purposes in this study. The rubric has six elements:

Table 1. Study abroad program's learning goals, objectives and assessments

Goals	Objectives	Assessment
Verano Mexico		
• To become familiar with cultural and historical origins of Mexico as a context for observing and participating in the Mexican education system. • To become familiar with the teaching, learning and management strategies used in school or clinical setting.	1. Gain a broad knowledge base of the similarities and differences among students in general and special education programs in México. 2. Observe different types of curricular materials, activities, and strategies for children and adults in academic, clinical, and non-academic settings. 3. Identify, observe, and record different classroom management strategies and routines. 4. Determine, identify, observe, and record what type of supplemental and support services are available for the population and settings in which you are observing. 5. Obtain information regarding federal laws, and practice and identify similarities and differences across the continuum of services including general education, inclusion or resource (USAER), and self- contained (CAM) classrooms and other clinical settings.	• Daily Journals • Weekly Discussions • Final Project • Written Summary • Digital Storytelling • Oral Presentation
Vivir Mexico		
• Flexible topic seminar for undergraduate students across several domains in the field of Mexican American Studies • To become familiar with topics on Mexican American issues.	1. To conduct research on the possible topics: border studies; economics of international exchange; migration; Mexican education system; society and culture of Mexico; language variation in Mexican and Mexican American communities; labor. 2. To exchange the research results through discussions, reports and papers.	• Discussion Post • 3 Written Exams • Curriculum Development & Delivery Report • Digital Storytelling • Commercial
Rwanda Africa		
• To experience and understand the dynamics of primate social relationships. • To think critically and learn scientific methodology. • To gain global competency by working in remote locations.	1. Have proficiency in the use of basic scientific methods and instruments for collecting primate behavioral data. 2. Be able to design and carry out a basic observational field research project 3. Be knowledgeable about the relationship between local ecology and primate social behavior 4. Understand human family/social systems in the broader primate comparative perspective 5. Have an improved familiarity with the cultures and peoples of Rwanda	• Presentations • Primate Profile • Journal • Digital Storytelling
Verona, Italy		
• To introduce the Mediterranean dietary patterns. • To discuss epidemiologic studies of the Mediterranean diet. • Recognize this diet pattern as an Intangible Cultural Heritage of Italy, Greece, Spain and Morocco.	1. Provide students with information about the health benefits of foods associated with a Mediterranean diet and for the prevention of chronic diseases. 2. Review and discuss the influence of bioactive compounds present in Mediterranean foods on metabolic pathways. 3. Provide students with an opportunity to learn about the food industry in Northern Italy, and dietary patterns of the Mediterranean area. 4. Acquire hands-on experience with food preparation supervised by local food instructors. 5. Experience the cultural diversity of Italy and influence of Mediterranean culture.	• 3 Exams • Paper • Digital Storytelling

1.	The *purpose* of the story is transparent to the viewers and a clear focus is maintained throughout the story,

2.	A progressive story flow that starts with a *dramatic question* capturing your audience's attention, has a clear plot and a resolution at the end of the story,

3. The gift of your *voice* achieved by having clear and consistent audible sound attained though good pitch, tone, and timing that connects with the audience,
4. *Emotional* content including a soundtrack if appropriate, that is apparent throughout the narration of your story,
5. A point of view through *content* creation that expresses your opinion, personal reflection, and learning outcomes of your experience,
6. The *economy* of the story in terms of language, pacing and maintaining the attention of the audience.

This rubric was merged with the specific discipline's learning objectives and used to assess the digital stories. Both the learning objectives and the storytelling rubric were given to the students at the beginning of the study abroad program. The introduction of these two elements were a major factor in the creation of successful digital stories. For when students know what they are to be learning and also know how they will be asked to demonstrate their knowledge there is less stress and more opportunity for successful outcomes. Assessment in this particular educational experience was a reflective exercise allowing student to go deeper into how the learning objectives become a personal journey. Table 2 was the rubric used for assessment of the digital stories in this research study.

The data was collected through several mechanisms including: an electronic survey before the study abroad trip, observations by the researcher during the trip, paper surveys, interviews after the trip from both students and faculty, and the collection of the digital story artifacts by students participating in the study. The surveys were given to the students before and after the study abroad trip and were compared to determine the differences or similarities in the perception and actual process of the digital storytelling project. The faculty were interviewed after each summer session for insights about the assessment process. The digital stories obtained through the project were reviewed and evaluated based upon the rubric and the learning outcomes of the course. The observations and interviews were converted into a transcript, then coded and analyzed for emerging themes.

Various methods were incorporated to check validity and credibility during the analysis phase of the research. All of the following procedures were utilized throughout the data analysis phase. The first procedure used was prolonged engagement. In this case, the researcher has been involved with the digital storytelling project for the four years. During the fourth summer the researcher was in the field observing the implementation of the digital storytelling project in two of the programs participating in the study. Another procedure was a member check, whereby the researcher shared the data and the interpretation of the data with the participants for verification of accuracy. Triangulation was used, as the researcher gathered data from a variety of sources including: 1) survey tools and interviews, 2) observations, and 3) collection of the digital storytelling artifacts created by the students.

Results

This study set out to determine if the methodology of digital storytelling was an effective assessment tool by answering the question, "What does digital storytelling offer as an assessment instrument and model for demonstrating expected learning outcomes for study abroad programs?" There were several themes that arose during the analysis phase of the research to assist in answering this question. The themes discussed in this section were: 1) reflections, journals and scripts, 2) instructor and peer reviews, 3) role of a rubric, 4) multimodal assessment, and 5) traditional assessment versus digital storytelling assessment.

Table 2. Storytelling rubric

Category	Excellent	Good	Satisfactory	Needs Improvement
Purpose 20 points	Establishes a purpose early on and maintains a **clear focus throughout**. (20 pts.)	Establishes a purpose and maintains **focus for most** of the story. (15 pts.)	There are a **few lapses in focus**, but the purpose is fairly clear. (10 pts.)	It is **difficult to figure out the focus** and purpose of the story. (5 pts.)
Dramatic Question 20 points	Story has a clear beginning, middle and end. Plot is **well developed** by setting up a conflict/dramatic question in the beginning that holds the viewer's attention throughout and ends with a resolution. (20 pts.)	Story has a beginning, middle and end. Plot is **moderately developed** with a conflict/question that sustains viewer attention throughout the majority the story and ends in a resolution. (15pts.)	Story has a clear beginning, middle and end. Plot is **minimally developed.** Has minimally interesting conflict/resolution. (10 pts.)	Story resembles picture slide show that **lacks plot, conflict or resolution.** (5 pts.)
Voice 15 points	Employs **one's own voice** to narrate the story and connect with the audience. Voice quality is clear and consistently audible throughout the story. Pace and rhythm is appropriate to the story line and holds audience attention. (15 pts.)	Voice quality is **clear and consistently audible** throughout the presentation. Pace and rhythm is appropriate to the story line and holds audience attention. (10 pts.)	Voice quality is **clear and audible** throughout most of the presentation. Pace is at times too fast or too slow to fit the story line and sustain audience attention. (7 pts.)	Voice quality is not **always clear.** Pace is consistently too fast or too slow. Does not employ proper pitch, timbre and intonation to connect with audience and sustain interest. (3 pts.)
Soundtrack, Emotion/Tone 15 points	Music, if used, is **evokes** the emotion of the story line and enhances the story. The emotion of the story is conveyed **effectively** through voice narration and images. (15 pts.)	Music, if used, is **appropriate** to the emotion of the story line and enhances the story. The emotion of the story is **moderately** conveyed through voice narration and images. (10 pts.)	Music, if used, is **adequate** to the emotion of the story line and enhances the story. The emotion of the story is **somewhat** conveyed through voice narration and images. (7 pts.)	Music, if used, **overshadows** the story. Emotion of the story line is **not satisfactorily** conveyed via either music or voice. (3 pts.)
Personal Reflection 15 points	Content clearly reflects your experience, the stages and learning outcome and **effectively** demonstrates personal and professional growth. (15 pts.)	Content clearly reflects your experience, the stages and learning outcome and demonstrates a **moderate** degree of personal and professional growth. (10 pts.)	Content conveys your experience and the scope of your learning outcomes to a **minimal** degree. Content demonstrates a minimal amount of personal or professional growth. (7 pts.)	Content does not clearly explain your learning outcomes and **does not demonstrate** any personal or professional growth. (3 pts.)
Economy 15 points	**Conscious use of economizing** of language for proper pacing of story and maintenance of audience attention. The length of the story is appropriate (15 pts.)	**Moderately good economical** use of language for proper pacing of story. The length of the story is appropriate. (10 pts.)	Pace of presentation is a **little too rapid or too slow.** The length of the story is not appropriate. (7 pts.)	Pacing of story is **too fast or too slow to maintain** audience attention. The length of the story is not appropriate. (3 pts.)

Reflections, Journals and Scripts

Reflections were one of the key factors in helping students to demonstrate their learning outcomes through the digital storytelling project. The reflection process assisted students to recall not only their personal experiences, but also their learning journey. One student made this statement about the reflection process:

Figure 1. Monica's digital story (Cotreras, 2014)

It (the digital storytelling project) really helped me to reflect on everything we did and [SIC] asked myself, "What was the real intention behind this trip? Why did we go to the museum? Why did we volunteer at Resplandor?" It is more than just busy work, there is a certain meaning behind it, and so that is what the digital storytelling project made me think about. – Monica, 2014

In her digital story, Monica was deeply reflective about her personal learning journey. She talks about the history and culture of Mexico and the indigenous past she saw all around her. She relates what she is learning about Mexico into her own identity. She says that being in Mexico helped to fill a void in her identity. In the closing statement of her story she says, "I found a City so rich in culture whose humbleness has greeted me with open arms." Monica's digital story helped her to demonstrate several of the topics that were outlined in the learning objectives and go even a step further by relating them to her own personal growth and identity. Monica's digital story is shown in Figure 1.

Journal writing was another factor that proved to be an effective means for students to reflect upon their learning experiences. Some students were natural journal writers, while others needed prompts and points. Here are two comments from students, the first student did not use prompts for reflection writing, while the second student had prompts provided each day:

I journal when I travel, because when you get back from a trip you immediately start forgetting every-thing. So if you don't do things like this you are going to forget all the little things and eventually the big things. It was nice to put pictures to the story, because with the pictures it jogs your memory. You remember exactly what was happening when this photo was taken. – Melissa, 2014

...the journals were a good way for us to remember things. We were instructed to write down significant things and go back to remember. I did not go back and look at every entry, but I did write every day

until the day we got back to the United States. It is a good part of the reflection process to be able to go back and look at a daily journal. I think it is a good match to journal every day and then reflect upon your writing for the digital story...you need to be held accountable for what you are learning every day. Some people tried to go back and remember what had happened in previous days and it was hard for them. – Tiffany, 2014

Keeping a journal about a learning experience can be beneficial to the creation of the digital storytelling project especially if the story is going to be used to demonstrate outcomes of the learning experience.

Another factor that was not as critical, but proved to be helpful in assessment was script writing for the digital storytelling project. The first two summers the digital storytelling was administered, a graduate student who traveled with the students reviewed the scripts. The next two summers the scripts were not reviewed. This was part of lifting the restrictive nature of the project that students complained about early in the research. It was found that most students in all programs studied did write a loose script even when it was not reviewed. Here are some comments from students who did script writing:

I had so much to say that I had to write out my script and edit it a couple of times and find just the right words. This improved my writing skills. – Monica, 2014

I actually did write a script. My writing part took less time than the visual compilation. I really wanted to choose the pictures that were my favorite or captured a specific moment or sparked a memory. – Jen, 2013

The hardest part for me was the script and making it more story like. We have this style of writing that students do, where we write everything in a certain way, so it was hard for me to make this more informal like you are telling someone a story. – Sky, 2014

Next are comments from some students who did not write a script:

I did not write a script, I just took chunks out of my journal...I am not going to say this or I am going to change this and sort of modifying the script. – Genesis, 2014

I did not write a script for this project, I was just talking off of my passion. I knew what I wanted to talk about, but I did a lot of takes (on the recordings). – Jimaral, 2014

In reviewing the digital stories, there was no obvious change in the quality of digital storytelling based upon the requirement of script writing, however it was apparent when students did not put time into reflecting about their study abroad experience. The digital storytelling became more of a vacation slide show presentation, instead of a reflective story about what they experienced. Take a look at several digital stories at: http://www.melodybuckner.com/#!digital-stories-03/c1uud to compare. Monica wrote out a script, while Jimaral talked of his passion. While Jimaral's story has a causal familiar feel to the presentation, almost like he is right in the room with you, Monica's story goes much deeper into her transformative experience on the study abroad trip.

Instructor and Peer Reviews

Sharing was perceived as a positive part of the digital storytelling project, however access and usability were major factors in the success of this aspect of the learning experience. The students in this study wanted to share their project, not only with the other students who participated on the study abroad, but with their family, friends, and even potential employers.

It would have been nice to see what my peers had to say and learning from their own VoiceThread. – Ana, 2011

I would definitely like to receive comments and if everyone else was doing it and if I thought they would read my comments, then I would definitely comment on things. – Lauren, 2013

I would be open to anyone's comments because it makes the story more worthwhile and interesting to listen to other people's viewpoints. – Jimaral, 2014

I would like to hear what others are thinking about and it is interesting to hear from their perspective and voice or read what they wrote because everyone thinks about things differently and has a different take on stuff. – Melissa, 2014

Students were very open to receiving comments on their stories from the instructor and even willing to receive and make comments on their peer's stories. This is an important factor in assessment as research has proven that feedback is perceived as having a powerful influence on learning, if it is used to enhance the learning experience. (Hattie & Timperley, 2007). Here are some comments from students about feedback:

I think feedback from both Dr. Fletcher and my peers would have been good, but especially feedback from Dr. Fletcher...I think it would have been neat if we could have posted it on a particular place and everybody had posted there and then if we could get feedback from somebody either the instructor or peers. – Sheri, 2014

I would definitely like to receive comments and if everyone else was doing it and if I thought they would read my comments, then I would definitely comment on things. – Lauren, 2013

I would be open to anyone's comments because it makes the story more worthwhile and interesting to listen to other people's viewpoints. – Jimaral, 2014

I would like to hear what others are thinking about and it is interesting to hear from their perspective and voice or read what they wrote because everyone thinks about things differently and has a different take on stuff. – Melissa, 2014

However, there were several reasons peer feedback did not happen with the digital storytelling project. The main reasons dealt with access and usability issues in both the VoiceThread application and the learning management system used in the course. The students created their stories in VoiceThread, a free application available on the Internet. In order for students to share a VoiceThread presentation, a box must be checked to share and allow others to comment, and then they need to generate a link that is shared with others. The students must copy this link and distribute it to anyone they want to view their presentation. This process proved to be confusing and time consuming for students. They got frustrated and just put the link in the learning management dropbox area for the faculty to view and grade. Therefore, it did not get distributed among their peers.

A solution did arise during the summer of 2014 that helped to eliminate the accessibility issue. One study abroad group decided to post their digital story links on the course Facebook page. Here were some of the comments from this innovative solution:

We all posted to Facebook and were watching each other's digital stories and commenting. – Rebecca, 2014

It makes more sense to share the VoiceThread on Facebook, where people can find it easily...people are kind of lazy. – Jenna, 2014

I posted it on Facebook to our little group, because they sort of knew what it was about, but I did not post it to everyone I knew. – Genesis, 2014

Adding the digital story to a social media site that the course was using for communication proved to be an excellent resolution to the accessibility issue. The usability problem with VoiceThread can be addressed with training before the students leave the country or through specific directions on how to share the presentation.

Role of a Rubric

The role of a rubric plays a critical role in the assessment of a project. It also provides transparency to students about the standards from which they will be evaluated. This type of creative project can enhance the learning experience for students, however restrictions can hinder both the creative and learning process. During the first two summers of the digital storytelling project, the focus was more on the rubric and the assessment than it was on the reflection of the authentic learning that was taking place in the study abroad experience. It was a forced effort to make students tell the story of achieved learning outcomes, rather than letting the students weave their own unique learning experience through storytelling. Here is a comment that reflects the feeling of the students from the first two summers:

...how it (digital storytelling project) was brought up and it was very restricting, like I did not really have a lot of options...it being so restrictive kind of takes a toll on you. I can't be as creative as I want to be. I can't really share the things, because the people are looking for certain, specific things...The focus was on diversity and the things you had done or things you were contributing to rather than your overall experience...You don't put limits on them and more restrictions because that is in a way telling them this is how I want you to do it. Grading effected the enjoyment of the assignment. – Ana, 2011

However, when the rubric was administered as a guide, the comments were very different:

...you are out of your comfort zone and you are learning so much...it is a different type of knowledge.... it is good to know initially when you go into it that there are expectations about the product you are going to have to produce at the end and be thinking about it. All of us were thinking about it and taking pictures and reflecting on things that were happening in the moment. – Rebecca, 2014

The assessment rubric did not change from the summer of 2011 to 2014, however the perception of how it was being administered shifted from directing students to what they must include in the digital storytelling project to guiding students through the exploration of their own storytelling of their unique study abroad experience. One comment from a faculty lead supports this idea:

In regards to the field study, the language and experiences that are shared in the personal narratives show their expertise through the new vocabulary to express their thoughts in this discipline. The vocabulary comes up spontaneously, so I don't use it as a formal assessment, because I don't want to spoil the favor of the assignment by putting this vocabulary as a requirement. It is a bonus for me to see them demonstrate their knowledge without being a formal requirement. – Netzin, 2014

In this instance, the digital storytelling project can assist faculty in assessing what students have learned through an authentic meaning of acquired language and explanation of the experience. For Netzin's program, the students demonstrated many of the learning outcomes through their digital stories. To view the learning outcomes and the stories, go to: http://www.melodybuckner.com/#!digital-stories-04/c1x1a.

Overall the rubric proved to be a helpful guide in assisting students through the various components of the digital storytelling project. It should to be noted that when the rubric was used in a restrictive manner the students were frustrated and felt their creativity was limited. However, when the rubric was used as a guide, then students were aware of what was expected from them and creativity flourished rather than be diminished.

Traditional or Digital Storytelling Assessment

In this study, digital storytelling was not used as a replacement to the traditional assessment rather it was used as an addition. Students were still required to perform either oral presentations or submit written reports depending on the study abroad program. This was a positive factor as the researcher could ask the students to compare the different type of assessments.

Two opinions surfaced when discussing oral presentation versus digital storytelling. The first was that an oral presentation allows the speaker to feed off of or react to the energy of the audience and some people thrive in front of a crowd. Whereas the digital story gives the speaker time to process and redo the presentation to get it "just right" and is much better for those who are not comfortable speaking in front of a group. Here are some comments that speak to this:

The digital story is not like a PowerPoint standing at the front of the class presenting your stuff. It was cool to kind of make it your own...The digital story gave me more room to think over what I wanted to do and put it all together. Whereas when you give a presentation you are put on the spot and for me that is hard to do. I need time to process things through and put it together, so that is what I liked about storytelling. – Kendra, 2014

The digital storytelling experience is very intimate so doing an oral presentation would not be very appropriate or comfortable. So the digital storytelling process allows for you to be comfortable, as you are by yourself. Other people are going to see it but you get to use your discretion of what you put into it. So I do think it is a very good format.... and an oral report can kind of be boring. A lot of people do not do oral reports well...you are just sitting there watching or you are the person up there wishing that it was over. – Rebecca, 2014

I would prefer giving a live presentation over digital storytelling, because of having the real audience. Speaking in front of people that you know you can have an impact on...that you are having a non-verbal conversation with and they are thinking things over in their minds. And the way you speak to them is so different versus just speaking to yourself. You receive feedback from the audience and adjust your message accordingly versus just creating it yourself and recording it. It is more lively, because there is this real interaction going on. – Summer, 2014

The digital storytelling project is great for students who work that need the flexibility. Increased distribution is great verses getting it one time in a classroom. So when the class is done it is over and nobody is ever going to look at again. It gets tossed in the trash and I just spend 10 hours putting together this great presentation and it is done forever. – Melissa, 2014

The most common opinions on the paper verses the digital story was the longevity and sharing aspect of these modalities. Students talked about how they would share a digital story with others and would even enjoy looking back at it, However, they would not do this with a written paper. It also appeared to be a more creative outlet for expression of reflection than a standard written assessment. Here are some of the comments generated around this theme:

The digital storytelling project is something that I would enjoy coming back to watching. I would be much more likely to look at throughout the years and have it be something special to me than a paper. I would file a paper away and maybe read it once or twice but it would not be as enjoyable as hearing myself talk about the experience when it is fresh in my mind and having pictures there to guide me through the story. – Lauren, 2013

The digital story forces you to reflect a little bit more and to go a little bit deeper than you would in a paper. And papers tend to be boring and we have all written so many of them. I think you approach the digital story with a little more exuberance and energy because it is something that you have not tackled before. It is a new challenge, where as a paper is something you have done before. There is a certain novelty to it. – Rebecca, 2014

The digital story is like a story...rarely in the academic world do you get the opportunity to say what you really want to say. In most of my classes it is write a paper on this subject and you might not even have an interest in that topic. The digital storytelling really allows you to take ownership of your education. It was like here is an assignment and you make it what you want it to be...there was so much liberty in it and that is what I loved about it. – Monica, 2014

It made me think about telling my own story in my own voice and captivating people that way than just the typical writing. It makes you think about how you are conveying your thoughts more because you are actually speaking it and have the emotion behind it. – Jenna, 2014

The faculty also had positive comments regarding the written assessment verse the digital storytelling project:

Visual literacy, learning and technology have really taken off and students are more engaged and motivated to be able to tell their story and to share with others. It is a solid reminder that the ability to share with others is easier than sending a paper...it is a short clip that demonstrates what they have learned and experienced more powerfully than they could ever do in a written format.... It creates a sense of perspective that can become very personal that would not normally happen in a paper or presentation. – Dr. Fletcher, Verano Mexico

The digital storytelling project was fun for the students and they were able to engage other people. They also have something that is a little more permanent or more of a record of what they actually did than showing someone what they wrote. They can show their family. – Dr. Ruiz, Vivir Mexico

These comments aid in demonstrating that the digital storytelling project adds a depth and dimension that traditional assessment lacks. The project engages the students to engage with the assignment, show it outside of the course and come back to re-experience it in the future. These are not traits that happen with a traditional oral presentation or written report. Through the use of media, the assessment becomes more personal and meaningful to the students and faculty. Dr. Fletcher's comment reaffirms the power of the digital story:

I think it is the sign of the times. This is one way for students to demonstrate what they have learned during their study abroad experience.... It gives me a snapshot of what they internalized and learned. It is one of the most effective assessment tools I used.

DISCUSSION

Once the students returned from their study abroad learning experience they were asked to take a short survey and talk to the researcher about their experience with the digital storytelling project. Figure 2 contains the results from the short survey.

Most students had a positive perception of the digital storytelling project. They preferred a creative tool for a reflective project to the traditional assignment, although a few expressed that it was not as academically rigorous as writing a paper. The technology for creating the digital story did not pose a problem for most students, but there were some discussions about being driven to just one application, instead of allowing for choice. Overall, students did find the reflective process that happened due to the nature of the digital storytelling project had a positive impact upon their learning experience.

This suggests that digital storytelling can be a valuable, and perhaps a transformative tool for a broad range of curricula, and discipline based content. Storytelling can be a powerful mechanism for teaching and learning as stories help make meaning out of our experiences (Bruner, 1990). These experiences in

Figure 2. Student survey results

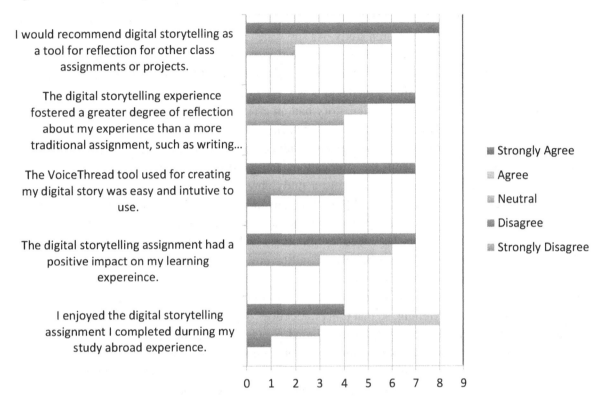

turn are the key to transformative learning. Stories can also help students build strong connections to former knowledge and improve memory (Schank, 1990). Parker Palmer states that teaching and learning spaces should honor the "little stories" of students, while telling the "big stories" of the discipline (Palmer, 1998). Digital storytelling provides this learning space by empowering students with the opportunity to express themselves in a variety of media. One great feature of digital storytelling is that with a little bit of guidance and creativity anyone can create their "little story" and make it available for the world to see, hear and learn from.

Implications and Recommendations

The main implications that were drawn from this research include not only assessment practices, but reflection for deeper learning for students living in a digital world. First and foremost, these modern students between the ages of 18 and 25 who were currently attending an institute of higher learning and were taking a faculty-led summer study abroad course for academic credit need an assessment mechanism to motivate them to reflect fully upon their study abroad experience. Without this mechanism, no matter the modality, students will not take the time and effort to reflect about their experiences and lose the opportunity for learning to take place. Offering a digital solution for assessment over a traditional one inspires students to dive into their creativity energy to produce a multimodal artifact that can be shared with the world. This ties into Kolb's (1984) model of experiential learning where students grasp and perceive knowledge through transforming and processing knowledge.

To give an example of this implication of the reflective process affecting a student is the story of Ana. Ana was on the Verano Mexico study abroad program in 2010 and then agreed to be interviewed four years later in 2014 for this research study. As she watched the piece she had produced four summers ago, she said, "I am such a different person than I was back then." She had created an in depth reflective story about her experience in Mexico, but as she watched it four years later, she was able to reflect about who she was, what she learned and how she has developed into the person she is today. It was a powerful moment for her. The digital story had an effect upon Ana more than an oral report or paper would have because of the multimodal elements. Her story complete with photos and voice made a larger impact than just words on a piece of paper or text on a PowerPoint slide.

From an assessment point of view, the implications are that digital story is an effective method for demonstrating not only learning outcomes from a study abroad program, but the personal growth of the students as they travel and experience different people and cultures. The digital storytelling project should not be the only means of assessing students, but it is an assessment that will continue to effect students, as it is an artifact that can be shared it with others and viewed later in life.

The major recommendations for the digital storytelling project to be taken from a pilot research study to a full practice assessment include several ideas. It is important to work with students both before and after the study abroad trip in teaching them to be comfortable with the technology. It is also crucial to teach students the art of storytelling, so that this project does not become a glorified slide show of their study abroad trip. Journaling during the study abroad trip and prompting students with questions to answer every day was an effective method for helping students to form their digital stories.

Two lessons learned that were unexpected during this research was agency and accessibility. Students need to have a sense of agency when it comes to learning. This was evident in giving them a choice about what they used to create the digital stories. The choice or lack of choice got in the way of the creativity. Once students were able to choose their own modality there were less complains and better products. In terms of sharing stories among their peers, it was found that when students were forced to go to a place that is not as accessible or "clunky", they just don't go and share or make comments. However, when students are allowed to share in spaces that are familiar and easy to navigate, comments and conversations grew.

The digital storytelling project was a successful assignment that was used for both assessment and for students to reflect on their personal growth. It is recommended that the digital storytelling project be expanded to other study abroad programs and that more studies be conducted as this research evolves into an effective practice for reflection of learning.

The digital storytelling project also demonstrated that it was an effective reflective media tool that inspires creative students to demonstrate their learning outcomes. It is not a total replacement for other methods of assessment, but it is an additive tool allowing students to create their own stories about their unique learning experiences. The lessons learned around the implementation of the digital storytelling project can be helpful for educators interested in pursuing a similar project.

It is recommended that the digital storytelling project be extended to more study abroad programs and even to other learning environments, including service learning projects or the traditional classroom where constructivism is an integral part of the learning environment. It is also suggested that more research be conducted with digital storytelling and other methods of knowledge acquisition to validate the effectiveness of demonstrating learning outcomes.

REFERENCES

Alexander, B., & Levine, A. (2008, November 1). Web 2.0 Storytelling: Emergence of a New Genre. *EDUCAUSE Review*, *43*, 6.

Basso, K. H. (1996). *Wisdom sits in places: Landscape and language among the Western Apache*. Albuquerque, NM: University of New Mexico Press.

Bruner, J. (1990). *Acts of meaning*. Cambridge, MA: Harvard University Press.

Chaille, C., & Britain, L. (1991). *The young child as a scientist: A constructivist approach to early childhood science education*. New York: HarperCollins.

Cotreras, M. (2014). *Digital story from vivir Mexico study abroad*. Retrieved from YouTube: https://www.youtube.com/watch?v=mdQeEwahcxo

Daudelin, M. W. (1996). Learning from experience through reflection. *Organizational Dynamics*, *24*(3), 36–49. doi:10.1016/S0090-2616(96)90004-2

Dewey, J. (1938). *Experience and education*. New York: Macmillan.

Diekelmann, N. L. (2003). *Teaching the practitioners of care: New pedagogies for the health professions*. Madison, WI: University of Wisconsin Press.

Entwistle, N. (2001, July 1). Styles of learning and approaches to studying in higher education. *Kybernetes*, *30*(5/6), 593–603. doi:10.1108/03684920110391823

Gee, J. P. (2013). *The anti-education era: creating smarter students through digital learning*. Palgrave Macmillian.

González, N., Moll, L., & Amanti, C. (2005). *Funds of Knowledge: Theorizing Practices in Households, Communities, and Classrooms*. Lawrence Erlbaum Associates, Publishers.

Hattie, J., & Timperley, J. (2007). The Power of Feedback. *Review of Educational Research*, *77*(1), 81–112. doi:10.3102/003465430298487

Hopkins, R. L. (1994). *Narrative schooling: Experiential learning and the transformation of American education*. New York: Teachers College Press.

Kolb, D. A. (1984). *Experiential learning: Experience as the source of learning and development*. Prentice-Hall.

Kolb, D. A., Boyatzis, R. E., & Mainemelis, C. (2000). Experiential Learning Theory: Previous Research and New Directions. In Perspectives on cognitive, learning, and thinking styles. Lawrence Erlbaum.

Lambert, J. (2010). *The Digital Storytelling Cookbook*. Digital Diner Press.

McDrury, J., & Alterio, M. (2003). *Learning through storytelling in higher education: Using reflection & experience to improve learning*. London: Kogan Page.

McEwan, H., & Egan, K. (1995). *Narrative in teaching, learning, and research*. New York: Teachers College Press.

Ohler, J. (2013). *Digital storytelling in the classroom: New media pathways to literacy, learning, and creativity*. Thousand Oaks, CA: Corwin Press. doi:10.4135/9781452277479

Palmer, P. J. (1998). *The Courage To Teach: Exploring the Inner Landscape of a Teacher's Life*. San Francisco, CA: Jossey-Bass.

Pink, D. H. (2006). *A Whole New Mind*. New York: Riverhead Books.

Robin, B. (2006). The Educational Uses of Digital Storytelling. In *Proceedings of Society for Information Technology & Teacher Education International Conference 2006* (pp. 709-716). Chesapeake, VA: AACE. Retrieved April 20, 2010 from http://www.editlib.org/p/22129

Schank, R. (1990). *Tell me a story: Narrative and intelligence*. Evanston, IL: Northwestern University Press.

Street, B. (2003). Current issues in comparative education. New York, NY: Teachers College, Columbia University.

Vygotsky, L. S., & Cole, M. (1978). *Mind in society: The development of higher psychological processes*. Cambridge, MA: Harvard University Press.

Witherspoon, G. (1977). *Language and art in the Navajo universe*. Ann Arbor, MI: University of Michigan Press. doi:10.3998/mpub.9705

KEY TERMS AND DEFINITIONS

Assessment Practices: The systematic gathering of information about student learning and the factors that affect learning, taking into consideration the resources, time, and expertise available for improving learning.

Constructivism: A theory that implies people construct their own knowledge by interacting with their own unique socio-cultural environment.

Digital Literacy: The ability to use electronic equipment to understand, filter, and validate material in various modalities in a strategical way to evaluate information, collaborate, produce, share content and/or achieve academic, professional, or personal goals.

Digital Natives: People who were born or were very young during the growth of the digital age. There is a lot of discourse revolving around this term as some people are referred to as digital immigrants. I personally refer to digital natives as those people who do not recall at time when personal electronics were not a part of their natural world.

Digital Storytelling: A modern method for expanding upon traditional storytelling techniques through a variety of digital modalities including digital photography, audio techniques and videography.

Experiential Learning: Learning that allows people to construct their own understanding and knowledge of the world through experience and reflection of those experiences to form deeper levels of knowing.

Learning Outcomes: Specific goals or objectives that students will be able to prove they know based upon demonstration of expertise, skills, attitudes or values once they have completed or participated in an instructional or transformative experience.

Study Abroad: Academic programs typically established by a university allowing students to pursue educational opportunities outside of their native countries.

Traditional Storytelling Techniques: An established or customary practice of sharing knowledge, interpreting experiences, or passing on the collective wisdom of the culture to others through the techniques of oral narration, written word, or illustrations. Not all, but most stories feature a beginning, middle, and end.

Chapter 4

Distance Education in the K–12 Setting:
How Are Virtual School Teachers Evaluated?

Christina L. Seamster
Florida Atlantic University, USA

ABSTRACT

The evolution of technology over the last century has in many ways changed how teachers teach today. From kindergarten through twelfth grade, students are now able to complete 100% of their schooling online. If novel teaching practices have been established as a result of technology advancements, tools which align with those teaching practices must be produced in order to ensure continued student success. The purpose of this chapter is two-fold; to review teacher practices in K-12 distance education today and to discuss the field of education's need for research in measuring K-12 virtual school teacher effectiveness. The chapter begins with an overview of the history of distance education, followed by an examination of virtual school teacher pedagogy, a brief review of measuring K-12 teacher performance in the traditional and virtual school settings, and a synopsis of current tools for evaluating K-12 virtual school teacher effectiveness. The chapter closes with solutions and recommendation for future research.

INTRODUCTION

Today students as young as five years old are beginning their formal education online. This means that young students are not in the same physical space as their teacher-something that would not be possible in today's world without technology advancements. With increased blended and online learning opportunities for all students, it is more important than ever to recognize effective teaching practices in the online environment. Moreover, virtual and blended schools continue to grow exponentially which results in an increased need of trained, and highly qualified virtual school educators. The eldest and most prevalent state-funded online school in the nation, experienced a 45% increase from the 2011-2012 school year to the 2012-2013 school year and the 5-year growth forecast from 2009-2013 was 1,197% (Watson,

DOI: 10.4018/978-1-5225-2838-8.ch004

Murin, Vashaw, Gemin, & Rapp, 2013). The speed in which virtual schools continue to grow supports that teacher education programs and local schools must be proactive in determining how to evaluate virtual school teacher effectiveness to ensure that the influx of students receive high quality instruction. Today, "hundreds of thousands of students are attending full-time online schools that provide their entire education" (Gemin, Pape, Vashaw, & Watson, 2015, p. 12). The purpose of this chapter is to discuss current virtual school teacher practices within the full time K-12 setting as well as current methods of evaluating virtual school teacher effectiveness. This chapter presents possible solutions for transforming evaluation techniques to ensure that they align with virtual school teacher practices.

The chapter begins by reviewing the history of distance education and virtual school teacher pedagogy. It continues to explain the role of a virtual school teacher then gives an overview of best practices in the virtual setting according to research in the K-12 online arena. Finally, an overview of tools available to aid in evaluating virtual school teacher effectiveness and the work that needs to continue in the field of evaluating virtual school teacher effectiveness is explored.

BACKGROUND

Accurately measuring successful teacher practices is essential to ensuring student success. Teacher effectiveness influences student learning at a higher level than any other school variable, including class size, school size, after-school program quality, or the school itself (Darling-Hammond, 2006; MET Project, 2010). Using daily practice, identified characteristics, and student performance measures, as means of teacher assessment, a complete view of effective virtual school teachers can be accurately reflected (Rice, 2012). According to Ferdig (2010), virtual school teachers are a driving factor in student success in the online setting. Therefore, research has established the importance of effective teachers in both in person and distance settings.

The 1970's marked the beginning of states working to "regulate learning and teaching by requiring outcomes and attaching incentives to their attainment" (Fuhrman, Cohen, & Mosher, 2007, p. 65). The National Assessment of Educational Progress (NAEP) reported that African American and Hispanic students achieved higher tests scores after tying incentives to outcomes (Cohen, Moffitt, and Goldin (2007). Subsequently, policy was implemented to influence classroom practices and standards-based reform was born in the mid-1980's, which, according to Fuhrman et al. (2007) resulted in higher levels of accountability efforts for schools and teachers. Ultimately, policies such as No Child Left Behind (NCLB, 2002) and Goals 2000 (U.S. Department of Education, 1993) were enacted. School Choice, where public funds are used to fund privately run schools, became a way to replace failing schools. In 2010, Race to the Top (The White House, 2010) was implemented to entice states through funding to further implement teacher accountability practices including linking student test scores to teacher evaluations (Gemin, Pape, Vashaw, & Watson, 2015). As an increasing education option and with today's reform efforts focused on using student data to rate teacher effectiveness, the quality of full time virtual schools and their impact student learning, must be investigated.

Concerns in regards to instructional quality in distance education can be traced back to correspondence education. Through such alternate methods of instruction, students received instruction without attending a class in a physical building (Russell, 2004). Critics of online learning often point out limitations of delivery technologies and often wish to duplicate the practices of a traditional classroom teacher (Larreamendy-Joerns & Leinhardt, 2006). Currently, measuring virtual school teacher effectiveness can be problematic because empirical research is geared toward determining the success of the technology rather than measuring specific teaching practices (Larreamendy-Joerns & Leinhardt, 2006).

Current literature is limited in the amount of research which examines the qualities of effective virtual school educators. The majority of the present-day research is faulty in that it is "rooted in face-to face content, not focused on content areas, built upon a post-secondary audience, or fails to use data from the teachers themselves to triangulate findings" (DiPietro, Ferdig, Black, & Preston, 2008, p.10). Moreover, the National Education Policy Center recommends using "emerging research to create effective and comprehensive teacher evaluation rubrics" (Molnar, 2014, p. 50). The K-12 virtual school setting lacks a tool designed explicitly for measuring the effective practices of virtual school teachers. There are times when tools designed for traditional school settings are being used to assess the unmatched tasks of the virtual educator.

ONLINE TEACHING PRACTICES AND EVALUATION TECHNIQUES IN THE K-12 SETTING

As previously mentioned, full time virtual school education lacks a measurement tool which accurately measures effective virtual teacher practices (Molnar, 2014). K-12 virtual school teachers have skillsets that are related to teachers in a traditional K-12 environment, yet they achieve results through means which are exclusive to the online K-12 educator (DiPietro et al., 2008). In order to develop an effective K-12 virtual school teacher evaluation device, it is important to first outline the means by which K-12 virtual school teachers provide instruction to their students but let's review the history of distance learning.

History of Distance Education

Before reviewing virtual school teacher practices and virtual school teacher evaluation methods, it is important to understand the history behind virtual education. "Virtual schools can be seen as a variant of distance education" (Russell, 2004). Distance education transpires when a student and an instructor participate in knowledge transfer in separate physical locations (Rice, 2012; Russell, 2004; Schlosser & Simonson, 2006; Schoenholtz-Read & Rudestam, 2002).

Correspondence Education

In 1833 a Swedish newspaper advertised correspondence education which enabled students to learn through newspaper communication. This marked the onset of correspondence learning (Russell, 2004; Schlosser & Simonson, 2006). Mail was the technology of the time and it enabled students to learn outside of the traditional school environment. Thus, correspondence education was an alternate means of schooling where students could learn without attending a bricks and mortar school building (Russell, 2004). Early examples of correspondence education include Isaac Pitman's short hand instruction and Ticknor's Boston-based society (Russell (2004); Schlosser & Simonson, 2006). Notably, in 1890, the University of Chicago hired 125 teachers who taught 3,000 students material from 350 courses (Russell, 2004). Similar to the demographic of today's virtual school students, correspondence education served students who lived rural areas, moved often, suffered from health issues or had difficulty fitting in socially in traditional school settings (Russell, 2004).

Radio and Television

The development of radio and television technology supported the next wave of distance education methods. In the 1920's, an audio element to distance instruction was implemented as universities began constructing radio stations for educational purposes (Russell, 2004; Schlosser & Simonson, 2006). Audio recording was a common method for teaching students without sight and also for instructing students in the area of language (Schlosser & Simonson, 2006). Continuing advancements in television technology lead to teaching programs at the University of Iowa, Purdue University, and Kansas State College in the 1930's. College credit courses were offered through broadcast television as early as the 1950's. Satellite technology contributed to educational television offerings in the 1960's (Schlosser & Simonson, 2006).

Two-way Communication and Fiber Optics

Two-way communication afforded students the ability to interact virtually with their instructors in a synchronous manner. K-12 schools began to embark on network communication practices in the early 1980's. The Learning Circles program launched by the InterCultural Learning Network (ICLN) is an example of early network communication practices where students wrote to one another internationally to form a joint classroom newsletter. As a result of the program, students increased their writing skills and motivation to write when writing for an audience of peers (Harasim, 2000). The late 1980's and early 1990's introduced fiber optic communication capabilities which fostered excellent quality live audio and video transfer where students could both see and hear one another from a distance instantly (Schlosser & Simonson, 2006).

World Wide Web

Perhaps the biggest technology advancement to help spread distance education occurred in 1992. Virtual schools have emerged from the onset of the World Wide Web and distance education (Russell, 2004). Not surprisingly, the invention of the World Wide Web introduced distance education to an increased number of students. (Harasim, 2000). This resulted in a paradigm shift in teaching and learning. Harasim (2000) reports that instructors had to learn new methods for teaching in an online setting. Harasim (2000) found that lectures are not the most effective practice in teaching students online. "Students would not participate, and long virtual silences ensued. Eventually, the faculty adopted group learning activities, such as discussions, and history was made" (Harasim, 2000, p. 52). "As distance learning evolved with the advance of the Internet, online courses were developed for Advanced Placement students, or to provide college preparatory courses that were not available in rural or inner-city schools" (Gemin et al., 2015, p. 10). Thanks to online learning in the postsecondary setting, development of online learning for children of traditional school age was more widely accepted (Gemin et al., 2015). Today, hundreds of thousands of students across the United States are enrolled in full time public schools which provide 100% of a student's formal education online. Students attend virtual schools full time for various reasons including medical or behavior concerns, scheduling conflicts due to arts or sports, and academic distress (Gemin et al., 2015).

This section gave a brief overview of the history of distance education. While most educators perceive distance education as a new endeavor, it has experienced growth and change for over a century (Schlosser & Simonson, 2006). Distance education has evolved over time with the help of technology from correspondence education to virtual education where students and teachers are the constants. The next section of this chapter will discuss K-12 virtual school teacher pedagogy.

K-12 Virtual School Teacher Pedagogy

"When practitioners or discipline specialists use a signature pedagogy, they sign on to a tradition" (Ciccone, 2009, p. xv). In other words, a signature pedagogy is a way of teaching that is passed down across multiple generations within a field or practice. The definition of pedagogical practices in K-12 education in the virtual setting has many limitations including: the age of formal K-12 virtual education, it's propensity to be teacher directed, the availability of reliable content on the Internet, and technology access.

According to Shulman (2005), in order for a field to have a signature pedagogy, the field or content area must be well established. Virtual education, especially at the K-12 grade levels, is a relatively novel concept. Gurung, Chick, and Haynie (2009) state, in regards to signature pedagogy in computer science, "it is too early to predict the exact form of that pedagogy, but it will focus on student learning and increasing student engagement" (p. 255). He continues to predict that "it will be applicable to the rapidly changing technology with which our students are living and learning" (Gurung et al., 2009, p. 255). Evolving technologies and increasing student achievement are common themes in virtual education and computer science education. In the coming decades, as technology integration evolves and matures, a signature pedagogy will arise that reflects the signature pedagogy of the technology field. Currently, in the field of virtual education, it is difficult to say "it's always been done this way" (Shulman, 2005, p. 55).

The invention of the World Wide Web has afforded students with new learning opportunities. "The Internet has opened up a world of learning beyond the formal classroom, offering people opportunities to develop their own personal learning environments" (Farkas, 2012, p. 83). Students can more easily than ever select the topics of their interest to learn. To align with this shift in available information, educators should be urged to develop student centered classrooms where students can broaden their knowledge based on their interests and findings in order to keep students motivated. However, "teaching is still largely focused on the transmission of knowledge from instructor to student" (Farkas, 2012, p. 84). Some "online learning management systems replicate these models with a focus on faculty content delivery rather than student participation. Learning Management Systems (LMS) that have incorporated participatory technologies like blogs and wikis have primarily included those as add-ons" (Farkas, 2012, p. 84). A shift in pedagogical practices needs must occur in order to reflect student discovery of knowledge rather than focusing on teacher delivery of information.

Another criticism of virtual education is the extent to which virtual school teachers can ensure student academic integrity due to an enormous amount of material available on the Internet. Students are encouraged to seek knowledge outside of the virtual school curriculum but they need direction on how to choose the best content online. At times, virtual school teachers find it problematic and labor intensive to sort through a colossal amount of material on the Internet in order to provide direction and support for student discovery. As a result, "teachers are left to determine appropriateness based on context-specific qualities and personal preferences, not necessarily taking into consideration the best for the concept and audience" (Mardis, ElBasri, Norton, & Newsum, 2012, p. 73)." It is necessary for virtual school teachers to possess the ability to evaluate student knowledge remotely and to implement and enforce policies which ensure student academic integrity.

The effectiveness of online learning decreases when digital resources are unavailable. Students cannot interact with the curriculum or their teachers in the virtual setting without access to technology. It is important for all students to have access to a working computer and the Internet. In a traditional classroom, students without technology are provided various opportunities for learning new material such as: working in centers, reading books or engaging in class discussion. Without access to technology in a typical classroom setting, only technology integration would suffer. However, in the virtual setting, the books are online, discussions take place over the Internet and hands on manipulatives are simulated. Therefore virtual school teachers must also ensure that students have access to the necessary technology tools for learning.

While the pedagogical practices of virtual school teachers have some similarities to teaching students in a face to face environment, there are clear differences. The degree to which effective technology integration affects student success in the virtual environment is a marked pedagogical difference. Students and teachers are brought together through technology mediums online. Virtual school teachers must understand how to integrate technology in the K-12 environment to ensure that students lead discussions, students are learning the material with fidelity, and students have adequate technology access.

The next section of this chapter focuses on the role of the K-12 virtual school teacher including an overview on instructional practices and managing the learning environment. Specifics will be shared in terms of how virtual school teachers work with students on a daily basis. The section ends with an overview of the importance of understanding how to effectively operate a Learning Management System to ensure student academic integrity.

Role of the K-12 Virtual School Teacher

Before evaluating an online teacher's performance, it is important to understand the expectations of an online educator. What does the day of an online K-12 instructor look like? Similar to traditional school teachers, online educators strive to increase student achievement through daily instruction. The difference is that online educators reach their students with digital tools to provide instruction and manage student learning.

Instruction

Comparable to face to face instruction, teaching online involves student interaction with both the teacher and the content (Rice, 2012). Rice asserts that effective virtual school teachers bring their content knowledge and personal teaching experiences when teaching online. Having prior experience teaching students in person provides a foundation teaching students online (DiPietro et al., 2008; Garrison, 2011; Rice, 2012). Technology tools such as the telephone, instant messaging, video conferencing, and threaded discussions assist virtual school teachers in facilitating instruction and interaction from a distance (Rice, 2012). Without these tools, online instructors would not have the capability to provide flexible, individualized instruction to meet the needs of all students virtually (Rice, 2012).

According to research on effective virtual school teacher instruction, in order to effectively integrate technology tools to engage student learners teachers must facilitate student learning rather than delivering information to students in a direct instruction format (Dipietro, 2010; Rice, 2012). This is especially important since virtual school teachers are not in the same physical location as their students. Through organizing and responding to discussion posts, facilitating discussion in teleconferencing sessions, and providing feedback on student work, virtual educators must make feedback relevant to student interests to encourage students to continuously think and reflect during the learning process (Rice, 2012). It is equally important for teachers to teach virtual school students to take an active role in their learning. Distance learning permits students to create learning opportunities in a manner that relates to their interests and learning styles (Mallinen, 2001).

Instructional practices of K-12 virtual school teachers also include ensuring that mentors and Learning Coaches are equipped to assist younger students in person (Rice, 2012). Young students enrolled in a full time virtual school are directed through daily lessons with a mentor or Learning Coach (often times a parent) in person in each day. As such, virtual school teachers must maintain constant communication with the student's mentor or Learning Coach to ensure the curriculum is executed with fidelity and that the student is the required state standards (Rice, 2012). Working with a mentor in the virtual setting can also provide a source of motivation and encouragement for the student (DiPietro, 2010). Virtual school teachers have a duty to communicate accurately and maintain positive working relationships with the student's mentor in order to make certain that the student adequately performs (Black, DiPietro, Ferdig, & Polling, 2009).

Yet another important role of the virtual school teacher is to ensure that students have opportunities for social interaction (Millet, 2012). Research shows that student learning increases when students interact with their peers (DiPietro, 2010; Rice, 2012). Online teachers afford students interactive opportunities through Live Lesson sessions which allow students to synchronously log in and interact with other students using chat pods, web cams, and microphones. The Live Lesson environment allows students to discuss content area material and get to know their distant peers (Rice, 2012). Synchronous discussion forums are not perfect and can include the following barriers: nonparticipation, technology glitches, student misbehavior, inappropriate language, or lack of participant ability to type in the chat pod. As a result, virtual school teachers must be able to effectively problem solve and proactively help students to engage learners while not physically present when these issues occur (Rice, 2012).

Because virtual school teachers are not physically present in a school building, it is important for virtual school teachers themselves to be socially present (Edwards, Perry, & Janzen, 2011; Garrison, 2011). Students in the K-12 environment thrive when they realize that their teacher cares about their success and is regularly reviewing their progress. Rice says that an effective way to bolster social presence is through forming a close relationship with both the student and their Learning Coach (2012). Ways to build a relationship with each family include actively listening and interviewing the family to determine the student's goals and previous educational experiences. This will also assist in increasing student motivation and ultimately increase student success (Rice, 2012). A strong social presence is characterized through frequent interaction with students and their Learning Coaches. The online teacher will get to "know their online students better than they knew their students in traditional classrooms" (Southern Regional Education Board [SREB], 2003, p. 2).

Manage Student Learning

K-12 virtual school teachers use a Learning Management System or an LMS to manage each student's learning environment from a distance. An LMS encompasses all of the tools which are essential to manage student learning including: curriculum, assignments, grades, calendars, and communication avenues (International Association for K-12 Online Learning [iNACOL], 2011a). The LMS is typically a closed system which only allows relevant stakeholders such as teachers, students, mentors, and school administrators to access student information any time, making online learning flexible. Virtual school teachers must have a thorough knowledge of how to operate the LMS in order to meet the needs of their students (Rice, 2012).

One feature of a Learning Management System is that it allows teachers to monitor student activity or participation instantly. For example, virtual school teachers have the capability to decipher when students login to complete course work, how long it took the student to complete their work, as well the level of student understanding. This is one way that teachers are able to track student engagement to confirm student course completions and to ensure that state attendance requirements are being met (Locke, Ableidinger, Hassel, & Barrett, 2014; Rice, 2012). "A tight relationship is found between the documentation of student attainment, the teacher-student-parent conference and the use of VLE [Virtual Learning Environment] tools, all constituting a network of aligned interests in assessment" (Johannesen, 2013, p. 302).

Virtual school teachers also monitor student progress and assign personalized and specific written feedback in the student's grade book. Based on the performance observed in the student grade book, virtual school teachers utilize synchronous instruction through web-conferencing tools and/or the telephone to verify learning and provide tailored instruction. Based on the results of the synchronous contact, the teacher determines the student's individualized instructional path. As an added accountability measure, virtual school teachers must ensure that the student has demonstrated mastery of the subject material with fidelity (SREB, 2003). If the teacher is unable to verify student knowledge demonstrated in the LMS coursework, the teacher has a responsibility to override the student's grade to match the student's ability demonstrated synchronously in the presence of the teacher (Rice, 2012).

K-12 Virtual School Research on Best Practices

The majority of research on online learning is piloted at the higher education level. "The temptation may be to attempt to apply or adapt findings from studies of K–12 classroom learning or adult distance learning, but K–12 distance education is fundamentally unique" (Cavanaugh, Gillan, Kromrey, Hess, & Blomeyer, 2004). Cavanaugh et al. (2004) points out that adult learners necessitate less supervision, motivation, scaffolding, and often do not involve methods which encourage cognitive growth. Another important finding of the student is that children as young learners do not have the vast variety of prior experiences to build upon. As a result children require more hands on learning opportunities and an entirely new bank of instructional strategies in order to learn adequately. (Cavanaugh et al., 2004). This chapter seeks to present full time K-12 virtual school teacher practices and evaluation techniques for measuring effectiveness. As a result, the studies reviewed in the following section exclude research in virtual school best practices at the post-secondary level.

The U.S. Department of Education conducted an assessment of evidence-based practices in online learning in 2009 (Means, Toyama, Murphy, Bakia, & Jones, 2009). The meta-analysis reviewed empirical studies between 1996 to 2008 according to the following criteria: "(a) contrasted an online to a face-to-face condition, (b) measured student learning outcomes, (c) used a rigorous research design, and (d) provided adequate information to calculate an effect size" (Means et al., 2009, p. 50). The study originally targeted studies published between 1996 and 2006 however the researchers extended the search to 2008 after yielding zero studies occurring in the K–12 setting from 1996-2006. Increasing the search resulted in five pertinent studies concerning online learning practices in the K-12 arena. The researchers caution against generalizing the results to the K-12 setting since most studies concerned higher educa-

Table 1. Research on teacher practices in the K-12 online environment (Seamster, 2016, p. 23)

	DiPietro, Ferdig, Black, & Preston (2008)	DiPietro (2010)
Title	Best Practices in Teaching K-12 Online: Lessons Learned from Michigan Virtual School Teachers	Virtual School Pedagogy: The Instructional Practices of K-12 Virtual School Teachers
Research Questions/ Purpose	To understand the practices of successful virtual school teachers.	Explores virtual educators' perceptions of their instructional roles in order to understand strategies that will support teacher pedagogy, technology, and content.
Methods	Interviews, grounded theory: coding data, constant comparative method, theoretical sampling, data synthesis.	Analysis of 16 interviews using grounded theory.
Literature Review/ Context	There is a lack of literature on the perspective of virtual school educators' pedagogical beliefs. Most of the literature is centered on traditional school content pedagogy.	Constructivist framework. Understanding pedagogy is important to the field of virtual education to increase teacher effectiveness.
Results	Identified possible "best practices" for virtual educators, which can now be tested including 12 general characteristics, 2 classroom management strategies, and 23 pedagogical strategies.	Five themes emerged: connecting with students, fluid practice, engaging students with the content, managing the course, and supporting student success.
Conclusion	Future research in online classroom management is needed. A framework for online certification will help promote a standardized model for K-12 virtual education.	The research facilitates an understanding of instructional practices used by online educators that are relevant for preparing future online educators and as well as those currently in practice.

tion locations (Means et al., 2009). The findings of the meta-analysis indicated that there was a lack of empirical research on K-12 evidence-based practices in the virtual setting.

Table 1 provides a summary of two studies which contribute to research specific to determining effective instructional practices for virtual educators in the K-12 setting. Both studies assert that there is a plethora of research on teachers' perspectives of effective instructional strategies in the traditional school setting but there is a need for further research in regards to effective teaching strategies in the virtual setting. While these studies were conducted at two isolated virtual schools, shared instructional practices have materialized including the importance of effective communication skills, providing student support, and making learning meaningful for students.

DiPietro et al. (2008) conducted a qualitative study entitled *Best Practices in Teaching K-12 Online: Lessons Learned from Michigan Virtual School Teachers* which included 16 highly qualified virtual school teachers from Michigan Virtual School (MVS). The study sought to identify the best practices of virtual school teachers in the K-12 setting. The Director of Quality Services, the Executive Director of the Virtual School, and the Instructional Manager at MVS first reviewed teachers' prior evaluations and subsequently selected the participants based on the following boundaries: hold teacher certification, obtain highly qualified status in their field and have at least 3 years of teaching experience in the virtual setting. Participants were interviewed using Adobe Connect, a tool that allows for synchronous verbal communication and live presentations through the use of the Internet. Data were coded using a comparative method using grounded theory. The researchers triangulated data with observation notes taken by the researcher during the interviews, the actual interview responses, and research references from the field. The results included twelve characteristics, two classroom management strategies, and twenty-three pedagogical strategies. The general characteristics of effective Michigan Virtual school teachers from the study included:

- Going the extra mile to support student learning
- Having basic technology skills, taking an interest in learning new technologies
- Exhibiting flexibility with time
- Understanding learning styles of their students
- Motivating students through social presence
- Being organized
- Self-reflectiveness of practice
- Displaying extensive content area knowledge
- Recognizing the importance of course pacing
- Working to extend content and technological knowledge
- Supporting opportunities offered by virtual high schools
- Implement strategies to address inappropriate behavior and monitor students' communication to Identify students needing assistance in personal crises

DiPietro et al., (2008) found the following pedagogical strategy categories to align with effective virtual school teachers in the K-12 setting:

- Engaging students with content
- Making course meaningful for students
- Providing support
- Communication
- Community

The study echoes the literature in saying that "Little research exists to address best practices of virtual school teaching in the K-12 context" (DiPietro et al., 2008, pg. 27). Finally, the study indicated that a lack of inquiry on the Technological Pedagogical Content Knowledge (TPACK) model was a possible limitation of the study.

A separate study which was related to virtual school teacher effectiveness was conducted in 2009 by Archambault and Crippen. Specifically, they examined Technological Pedagogical Content Knowledge (TPACK) among K-12 online teachers in the United States. "TPACK involves an understanding of the complexity of relationships among students, teachers, content, technologies, and practices" (Archambault & Crippen, 2009, p. 73). The researchers believed that understanding the connections between students, teachers, content, and technologies would contribute to an augmented understanding of virtual school teacher practices. Using the Tailored Design survey methodology, the researchers sent a web-based survey to 1,795 online teachers throughout the United States in a nonrandom and purposeful approach which resulted in 596 responses representative of 25 states (Archambault & Crippen, 2009). Prior to sending out the survey, to increase validity, the researchers conducted a pilot survey at a local K-12 online school. The participant's responses were analyzed using both descriptive and inferential statistics. The study's results indicated that the virtual school teacher participants had the most confidence in their ability to teach and in their content area knowledge. The survey results indicated that the teachers believed that they were proficient in using technology but not as proficient in the content pedagogy (Archambault & Crippen, 2009). The study's results are not generalizable to all virtual school teachers; however it is useful to distinguish that the participants from this study were more comfortable with content pedagogy than they were in the area of technological content pedagogy. As a result, virtual school teachers may benefit from additional professional development in incorporating technology successfully into their content area material online (Archambault & Crippen, 2009).

This section highlighted some of the literature on best practices in the K-12 virtual setting. The next section describes the importance of measuring virtual school teacher performance based on student achievement. There is research to support that little information in known in regards to the virtual school teacher practices which directly impact student achievement the most.

Measuring K-12 Teacher Performance

As a result of No Child Left Behind's (2002) implementation, the U.S. Department of Education has been holding states accountable for improving teacher quality. The President and CEO of iNACOL, Susan Patrick, reported a total of 50,000 K-12 virtual school student enrollments in the year 2000. In 2011, she stated that K-12 virtual school student enrollment climbed to 4 million students (Patrick, 2012). Based on the quantity of students enrolled in K-12 virtual education during the onset of NCLB in the early 2,000's, and in reviewing the research on virtual school teacher evaluation processes, it is evident that teacher evaluation measures were not intended for measuring virtual school teacher success. The field of online learning in the K-12 arena continues to grow and there is currently limited research on virtual school teacher practices or measuring virtual school teacher effectiveness (DiPietro et al., 2008), this section will briefly discuss evaluating teacher performance in the traditional school setting in addition to reviewing research studies focusing specifically on virtual school teacher evaluation.

Traditional School Setting

The Measures of Effective Teaching (MET) Project (2010), was established on the notion that today's teacher evaluation systems used nationwide are not generating outcomes which are successful in closing the achievement gap. The report continues to say that current evaluation practices do not provide the adequate necessary for teacher improvement. In addition, it reports that test scores alone do not successfully measure teacher performance since there are various factors which effect student test scores such as the learner's current level of performance (MET Project, 2010). This is mostly because current state assessments are geared towards measuring grade level proficiency which does not account for student growth for those students who either are performing at or below grade level standards (Darling-Hammond, 2010; MET Project, 2010).

In 2010, the MET Project recognized the need for a technique for evaluating teacher effectiveness beyond student test scores and they instituted a study in response. Over 3,000 volunteers across six school districts agreed to participate. The following indicators for measuring student achievement resulted from the (MET Project, 2010) research:

- Student achievement gains on assessments
- Classroom observations and teacher reflections
- Teachers' pedagogical content knowledge
- Student perceptions of the classroom instructional environment
- Teachers' perceptions of working conditions and instructional support at their schools

The MET Project's key findings indicate that effective teaching is measurable; balanced weights across the evaluation tools indicate multiple aspects of effective teaching, and the addition of a second observer rises reliability (MET Project, 2010). In an unrelated yet similar report, Darling-Hammond (2010) discusses a comparable method for measuring teacher effectiveness. "Performance assessments that measure what teachers actually do in the classroom, and which have been found to be related to later teacher effectiveness, are a much more potent tool for evaluating teachers' competence and readiness" (Darling-Hammond, 2010, p. 2). Similar to one component of the TPACK model for measuring a teacher's perceived ability to teach with technology, the MET Project (2013) collected data on measuring a teacher's Content Knowledge for Teaching (CKT) to evaluate a teacher's knowledge of how students acquire math and English Language Arts concepts: "The teachers with higher CKT scores did seem to have somewhat higher scores on two subject-based classroom observation instruments: the Mathematical Quality of Instruction (MQI) and the Protocol for Language Arts Teacher Observations" (p. 15).

Charlotte Danielson is also a current researcher that has studied the field of measuring teacher effectiveness and has developed a tool for identifying student achievement as a result of teaching practices. Danielson's (2007) *Enhancing Professional Practice: A Framework for Teaching* measures student learning as it related to teacher instruction. A modified version of Danielson' framework was developed into an evaluation tool to review K-12 virtual teacher' synchronous instructional strategies throughout the state of Florida (Florida Virtual School, 2015). While the adapted framework assists in providing feedback to K-12 virtual school teachers on their synchronous instructional strategies, it does not take into account all of the daily tasks of virtual school teachers. Danielson's (2007) framework enables teachers to improve their instructional practices through identifying areas needing improvement during formal classroom observations where the focus is on locating evidence of student learning as a result of teacher instruction.

Virtual Setting

This chapter seeks to identify virtual school teacher practices and the evaluation tools which effectively measure an increase in student performance as a result of K-12 said virtual school teacher practices from the literature. Using the best practices of K-12 virtual school teachers from the characteristics and strategies derived from DiPietro et al.'s 2008 study entitled *Best Practices in Teaching K-12 Online: Lessons Learned from Michigan Virtual School Teachers,* Black et al. (2009) administered a survey to K-12 virtual school teachers. The survey was validated through implementing Dillman's methods for question design in combination with executing a content matter expert. The pedagogical and general characteristic questions was presented through the use of a five-point Likert scale and all demographic questions were open ended (Black et al., 2009). Finally the questions regarding professional development asked the participants to rank order their answers. Data were first coded using Microsoft Excel and then the researchers utilized Cronbach's alpha and descriptive statistics for analyzing results (Black et al., 2009).

The results of the study specify that the participants favored having an interest in technology, having an online presence, and monitoring student progress closely as best practices in K-12 virtual school teaching profession (Black et al., 2009). In addition, the virtual school teachers surveyed in the study publicized interest in learning more about technology based skills, new methods of locating and evaluating resources to implement with their students and content based technology integration (Black et al., 2009). The researchers report consistency with the universal features that emerged from the sample size and as a result feel comfortable generalizing the results to other virtual school populations (Black et al., 2009).

Research on evaluating teacher effectiveness in the virtual setting is limited (Black et al., 2009; Cavanaugh et al., 2004). According to Rice (2012):

Learners participate in discussions, take exams, work on projects, and give presentations. These same strategies and tools exist in the online environment. You will exchange verbal discussions or text-based discussions using live chat or threaded forums, for example. Your overhead projector might be exchanged for an electronic presentation tool or a Web conferencing tool (p. 42)

Instructional strategies are frequently similar when teaching K-12 students online or in person, it is the technology tools and the means in which students are reached that makes up the difference. (Rice, 2012). Distance education and online learning have advanced immensely over the last hundred years. Technology integrated instruction is continually progressing, teachers and students remain constant. Great teacher are the most influential factors of student achievement (MET Project, 2010). As a result, the key to ensure student growth and continuous success is safeguarding teacher quality (Darling-Hammond, 2010). Because virtual school teachers reach their students through technology tools, it is vital to constantly evaluate and keep in mind the daily tasks of K-12 virtual school teachers as well as the characteristics of K-12 virtual school teachers with high student performance metrics in order to adequately measure K-12 virtual school teacher performance. Traditional classroom observations involving teacher based direct instruction are a major component in measuring their effectiveness. Virtual school teachers' instruction looks different and so should their evaluation techniques. K-12 virtual school teachers work with students individually through web conferencing, email correspondence, interacting and communicating with Learning Coaches over the phone (Rice, 2012). As a result, original techniques for evaluating virtual school teacher performance which mirror their daily instructional practices are necessary (Borja, 2005; DiPietro et al., 2008). "While the evidence based teacher evaluation practices are growing in traditional classrooms, little is known about how to evaluate teachers in a virtual setting" (Molnar, 2014, p. 23).

The next section of this chapter displays current tools that can be implementing when measuring the success of K-12 distance educators. While established organizations have put together rubrics, standards and recommendations for online learning, substantial research on the specific virtual school teacher practices which directly correlate to increased student performance must be explored. It is important to note that there is evidence to support student success in the online environment. However, there is limited information in terms of how to adequately measure virtual school teacher performance which directly relates to student achievement.

Current Tools for Evaluating K-12 Virtual School Teacher Effectiveness

In order to effectively measure the success of online teachers, an accurate reflection of student achievement must be obtained. Understanding how students of all ages learn online goes hand in hand with understanding effective virtual school teacher practices. A teacher's success must be measured by the results of their students. The following section provides an overview of national standards and recommendations for online learning as well as a model for teaching with technology. While the information presented by these organizations directly relates to teaching in the virtual environment, little research has been conducted to align the stated practices to student performance measures in the virtual setting.

National Standards and Recommendations for Online Learning

The following organizations have developed standards and recommendations concerning online educational practices: the International Association for K-12 Online Learning (iNACOL), the National Education Association (NEA), the Southern Regional Education Board (SREB), and the International Society for Technology in Education (ISTE) (Rice, 2012). Rice asserts that each of the organizations identify the importance of virtual school teacher proficiency in basic technology skills including: word processing, managing an LMS and effectively utilizing communication tools. According to Rice, the organizations each reflect the importance of teachers holding certification in their state and content areas. SREB states, "the teacher meets the core professional-teaching standards established by state licensing agency" (SREB, 2003) and Standard A in the National Standards for Quality Online Teaching lists "The online teacher knows and understands the subject area and age group they are teaching" as an indicator for effective online instructors (iNACOL, 2011b, p. 5). Table 2 summarizes the five common characteristics of effective virtual school teacher practices found across the four establishments.

Table 2. Organizations defining teaching standards for virtual education (Seamster, 2016, p. 30)

Characteristics	National Standards for Quality Teaching Online (iNACOL, 2011a)	International Society for Technology in Education Standards-Teachers (ISTE, 2008)	Guide to Teaching Online Courses (NEA, 2006)	Essential Principles of High-Quality Online Teaching (SREB, 2003)
Technology Skills	"The online teacher knows and understands critical digital literacies and 21st century skills" (p. 16).	"Demonstrate fluency in technology systems and the transfer of current knowledge to new technologies and situations" (p. 1).	"[Online teachers] are prepared well to use modern information, communication, and learning tools" (p. 9).	"The teacher has the prerequisite site technology skills to teach online" (p. 3).
Teaching Credentials	"The online teacher knows and understands the subject area and age group they are teaching" (p. 4).	"Teachers use their knowledge of subject matter, teaching and learning, and technology to facilitate experiences that advance student learning" (p. 1).	"Online teachers should maintain licenses, credentials and other documentation that arm school leaders with necessary evidence of their qualifications. They must maintain a valid state or national teaching license for the level, audience, and content of their assignment" (p. 9).	"The teacher has the necessary academic credentials in the field in which he or she is teaching" (p. 3).
Teacher as Facilitator	"The online teacher knows and understands the process for facilitating, monitoring, and establishing expectations for appropriate interaction among students." Facilitate and inspire student learning and creativity" (p.6).	"Facilitate and inspire student learning and creativity" (p. 1).	"[Online Teachers] foster community-building virtually and facilitate collaborative learning" (p. 10).	"The teacher promotes student participation and interaction" (p. 5).
Communication Skills	"The online teacher knows and understands the importance of interaction in an online course and the role of varied communication tools in supporting interaction" (p. 5).	"Communicate relevant information and ideas effectively to students, parents, and peers using a variety of digital age media and formats" (p. 2).	"[Online teachers] are effective in written communications" (p. 10).	"The teacher demonstrates high-quality written-communications skills" (p. 4)
Legal/Ethical Standards	"The online teacher knows and understands the responsibilities of digital citizenship and techniques to facilitate student investigations of the legal and ethical issues related to technology and society" (p. 9).	"Advocate, model, and teach safe, legal, and ethical use of digital information and technology, including respect for copyright, intellectual property, and the appropriate documentation of sources" (p. 2).	NA	"The teacher monitors students to ensure academic honesty" (p. 6).

Technological Pedagogical Content Knowledge (TPACK)

Shulman states that in determining teacher effectiveness, a teacher's content area knowledge is as vital as their pedagogical knowledge (1986). As a result, he developed the notion of Pedagogical Content Knowledge or PCK. PCK declares that effective teachers implement both content and pedagogy simultaneously, by embodying "the aspects of content most germane to its teachability" (Shulman, 1986, p. 9). Teachers who effectively integrate PCK comprehend how to implement content in a manner that is reachable by their students (Shulman, 1986).

In online schools, students and teachers are separated by distance; this proper technology integration is also vital in terms of adequate virtual school teacher instructional practices. Punya Mishra and Matthew J. Koehler's (2006) Technological Pedagogical Content Knowledge (TPACK) highlights teacher knowledge across the three knowledge bases, from Shulman's PCK model: Content Knowledge (CK), Pedagogy Knowledge (PK) and Pedagogical Content Knowledge (PCK) in addition to Technology (TK). Technological Pedagogical and Content Knowledge emphasizes new knowledge across each domain, which form four additional knowledge bases which are essential in teaching through technology. The innovative knowledge bases include: Pedagogical Content Knowledge (PCK), Technological Content Knowledge (TCK), Technological Pedagogical Knowledge (TPK), and the intersection of all three circles, Technological Pedagogical and Content Knowledge (TPACK) (Mishra & Koehler, 2006).

The TPACK model can aid in deciphering a virtual school teacher's ability to teach with technology. Using the TPACK model, teachers are able view their skills and abilities within the individual domains: content knowledge, pedagogical knowledge, technological knowledge or to determine how they fair in terms of integrating technology across each domain such as: technological content knowledge, technological pedagogical knowledge or technological pedagogical content knowledge. Ideally, virtual school teachers practice effective practices in teaching their students with technological pedagogical and content knowledge or TPACK.

SOLUTIONS, RECOMMENDATIONS AND FUTURE RESEARCH

Thanks to the evolution of technology, distance education has changed drastically from the days of correspondence learning. Students can now learn from a distance interactively with live virtual school teachers. Since the onset of the digital age has changed the way that teachers teacher forever, particularly in the online environment, a new teacher evaluation system must be established to ensure that the most effective means for educating students online continue to evolve.

Virtual school teachers in the K-12 setting must be evaluated based on student performance as a result of virtual school teacher practices. The practices which lead to improved student knowledge must be studied in depth in order to grasp a full understanding of effective virtual school teacher pedagogical practices. Currently, the research available suggests that daily virtual school teacher practices include:

- Augmenting the standard skills required of typical K-12 teachers with the ability to teach through technology in the virtual setting.
- Implementing technology in such a way that students actively participate in online lessons.
- Actively communicate student progress in an honest and relevant manner with the student, their parents, and their learning coach.

- Proactively ensure active student participation in the subject matter material.
- Being flexible
- Having extensive content area knowledge
- Building a community of learners
- Monitoring student progress and provide individualized interventions
- Upholding high academic integrity standards
- Ensuring that students, parents and learning coaches abide by the school's honor code
- Teaching digital citizenship and what it means to respect copyright and documenting sources appropriately

The virtual environment is in desperate need for a tool that measures virtual school teacher effectiveness to ensure continued growth and success for virtual school students. The first step is to research additional data which reflect the teaching practices that most impact student learning in the virtual setting so that an evaluation tool that matches the tasks of full time virtual school teachers coupled with student performance indicators can be established. Continued research on the pedagogical practices of virtual school teachers in the areas of using technology tools, evaluating student needs, collaborating, and providing individualized instruction should also be explored. As a result, further research to define evaluating student performance in the online environment should be reconnoitered. Since the purpose of teaching is to increase student knowledge, virtual school teacher evaluations should measure the extent to which the teacher's practices increase student performance. Ideally, the practices that most impact student learning will occur most often in the virtual environment. Using the current research on best practices in K-12 online education, a large scale study similar to the MET Project should be conducted across national full time virtual school schools to determine which teacher practices most impact student learning online.

According to Darling-Hammond (2014), "Teachers and school leaders should be involved in developing, implementing, and monitoring the [evaluation] system to ensure that it reflects good teaching well, that it operates effectively, that it is tied to useful learning opportunities for teachers, and that it produces valid results" (p. 12). As an incentive to increase teacher buy-in and to enable teachers to make instructional decisions on the practices that most impact student learning, teachers ought to be a part of constructing teacher assessment rubrics and an integral part of the evaluation process (Darling-Hammond, 2014). Thus creating a teacher evaluation model which integrates teacher perceptions and input on common practices would involve teachers in the teacher assessment process and also contribute to continuous virtual school teacher improvement.

The information presented in this chapter is relevant to current full time virtual school teachers, virtual school leaders, state education departments, and curriculum designers in the K-12 setting. Virtual school teachers and those interested in teaching in the virtual environment gain an understanding of teaching practices exhibited. Current virtual school teachers would benefit from reflecting on the impact that the instructional practices presented in this chapter have on their students, seeking out professional development opportunities in implementing each practice into their online classroom, and collecting student performance data to determine if their students' performance increases as a result of applying each standard. Virtual school leaders may find this information helpful in planning for professional development. Additionally, school leaders could use the best practices highlighted in this chapter as a starting point in determining which practices most positively impact student learning. Currently, most states across the nation do not require additional coursework or certification areas for teachers to teach online other that holding current state certification in their content area. Student performance data should be used as a guideline for establishing virtual school teacher certification modules in K-12 virtual environment.

Finally this information is also relevant for current instructional designers and curriculum design teams working in the K-12 virtual environment. The pedagogical practices found throughout this chapter are important to consider when planning and implementing courses for full time virtual school teachers and students in the K-12 setting. Virtual school curriculum writers should understand the best practices in reaching students through technology tools. Specifically, virtual school teachers' pedagogical practices which include collaboration and evaluating student needs to individualize instruction must be considered throughout the course design process. In conclusion, instructional designers would benefit from having a knowledge base in creating flexible courses which align with the needs of teachers, students and their Learning Coaches. K-12 virtual school courses are not meant to be the same for each learner, they must be flexible in order to meet the individualized needs of each student.

CONCLUSION

Over the last century, developments in technology have made advancements in distance education possible. Students in grades K-12 now have the ability to attend school online full time. This chapter gave an overview of K-12 distance education today and discussed the field of education's need for in depth research on measuring K-12 virtual school teacher effectiveness. If novel teaching practices have been established as a result of advanced technology, tools to measure teacher effectiveness must also be established to ensure continued student success. The chapter also included an overview of the history of distance education, examined virtual school teacher pedagogy, discussed measuring K-12 teacher performance in the traditional and virtual school settings, and went on to display a need for updated tools aimed towards evaluating K-12 virtual school teacher effectiveness. Finally, the chapter offered solutions and recommendation for future research in designing virtual school teacher evaluation tools.

Some pedagogical practices of online teachers in the K-12 setting are similar to teaching students in the traditional environment. Both virtual and traditional school teachers must be content area experts and they typically use similar instructional techniques to teach students. The main difference is that distance learning requires an additional skill set. Teachers in the online environment must able be equipped to integrate technology both to reach students as well as to ensure that students are completing their assignments with fidelity.

The best practices in K-12 distance learning differ from adult distance learning. Adult learners are by nature more independent and also come with background knowledge and experiences. Children are more likely to need scaffolding and hands on learning opportunities. Therefore, best practices in the K-12 online environment are not the same as best practices in online learning for adults.

The research on measuring virtual school teacher performance in the K-12 setting is restricted in terms of the number of research studies conducted (Black et al., 2009; Cavanaugh et al., 2004). Black et al., (2009) found that liking technology, creating an online presence and constantly reviewing student progress were best practices in the K-12 virtual school setting. These results were found to be generalizable to a wide range of K-12 virtual school teachers. Overall, the teachers surveyed expressed an interest in developing their technology skills (Black et al., 2009)

In reviewing the current tools available for measuring K-12 virtual school teacher effectiveness it is important to keep in mind that teacher success must be determined based directly on how it impacts student learning. Virtual school teachers' instruction looks different and so should virtual school teacher evaluation techniques. K-12 virtual school teachers do not teach adults and they do not teach in person. As the field of K-12 distance learning evolves, continuous research must take place to ensure that the development of virtual school students and teachers continue to progress as well.

REFERENCES

Archambault, L. M., & Crippen, K. (2009). Examining TPACK among K-12 online distance educators in the United States. *Contemporary Issues in Technology & Teacher Education, 9*(1), 71–88.

Black, E., DiPietro, M., Ferdig, R., & Polling, N. (2009). Developing a survey to measure best practices of K-12 online instructors. *Online Journal of Distance Learning Administration, 12*(1).

Borja, R. R. (2005). Evaluating online teachers is largely a virtual task. *Education Week, 24*(44), 8.

Cavanaugh, C., Gillan, K. J., Kromrey, J., Hess, M., & Blomeyer, R. (2004). *The effects of distance education on K-12 student outcomes: A meta-analysis.* Naperville, IL: Learning Point Associates/North Central Regional Educational Laboratory. Retrieved from ERIC database. (ED489533)

Ciccone, A. A. (2009). Foreward. In R. Gurung, N. Chick, & A. Haynie (Eds.), *Exploring signature pedagogies: Approaches to teaching disciplinary habits of mind* (pp. xi–xvi). Sterling, VA: StylusPublishing.

Cohen, D. K., Moffitt, S. L., & Goldin, S. (2007). Chapter four. In S. Fuhrman, D. Cohen, & F. Mosher (Eds.), *The state of education policy research* (pp. 63–83). Mahwah, NJ: Academic Press.

Danielson, C. (2007). *Enhancing professional practice: A framework for teaching.* Alexandria, VA: Association for Supervision and Curriculum Development.

Darling-Hammond, L. (2006). *Powerful teacher education: Lessons from exemplary programs.* San Francisco, CA: Jossey-Bass.

Darling-Hammond, L. (2010). *Evaluating teacher effectiveness: How teacher performance assessments can measure and improve teaching.* Retrieved from https://edpolicy.stanford.edu/sites/default/files/publications/evaluating-teacher-effectiveness_0.pdf

Darling-Hammond, L. (2014). One piece of the whole: Teacher evaluation as part of a comprehensive system for teaching and learning. *American Educator, 38*(1), 4–13.

DiPietro, M. (2010). Virtual school pedagogy: The instructional practices of K-12 virtual school teachers. *Journal of Educational Computing Research, 42*(3), 327–354. doi:10.2190/EC.42.3.e

DiPietro, M., Ferdig, R. E., Black, E. W., & Preston, M. (2008). Best practices in teaching K-12 online: Lessons learned from Michigan virtual school teachers. *Journal of Interactive Online Learning, 9*(3), 10–35.

Edwards, M., Perry, B., & Janzen, K. (2011). The making of an exemplary online educator. *Distance Education, 32*(1), 101–118. doi:10.1080/01587919.2011.565499

Farkas, M. (2012). Participatory technologies, pedagogy 2.0 and information literacy. *Library Hi Tech*, *30*(1), 82–94.

Ferdig, R. E. (2010). *Continuous quality improvement through professional development for online K-12 instructors*. Retrieved from http://www.mivu.org/Portals/0/RPT_PD_Ferdig_Final.pdf

Florida Virtual School. (2015). *Florida Virtual School instructional evaluation plan*. Retrieved from https://flvs.net/docs/default-source/district/flvs-instructor-evaluation-plan.pdf?sfvrsn=8

Fuhrman, S., Cohen, D., & Mosher, F. (2007). *The state of education policy research*. Mahwah, NJ: Erlbaum.

Gemin, B., Pape, L., Vashaw, L., & Watson, J. (2015). *Keeping pace with K-12 digital learning*. Durango, CO: Evergreen Education Group.

Gurung, R. A. R., Chick, N. L., & Haynie, A. (2009). *Exploring signature pedagogies: Approaches to teaching disciplinary habits of mind*. Sterling, VA: Stylus Publishing.

Harasim, L. (2000). Shift happens: Online education as a new paradigm in learning. *The Internet and Higher Education*, *3*(1), 41–61. doi:10.1016/S1096-7516(00)00032-4

International Association for K-12 Online Learning. (2011a). *The online learning definitions project*. Retrieved from http://www.inacol.org/resource/the-online-learning-definitions-project/

International Association for K-12 Online Learning. (2011b). *iNACOL national standards for quality online teaching (v2)*. Retrieved from http://www.inacol.org/resource/inacol-national-standards-for-quality-online-teaching-v2/

Larreamendy-Joerns, J., & Leinhardt, G. (2006). Going the distance with online education. *Review of Educational Research*, *76*(4), 567–605. doi:10.3102/00346543076004567

Locke, G., Ableidinger, J., Hassel, B. C., & Barrett, S. K. (2014). *Virtual schools: Assessing progress and accountability: Final report of study findings*. Retrieved from https://www.charterschoolcenter.org/sites/default/files/Virtual%20Schools%20Accountability%20Report.pdf

Mallinen, S. (2001). Teacher effectiveness and online learning. In J. Stephenson (Ed.), *Teaching & learning online: Pedagogies for new technologies* (pp. 139–149). London, UK: Kogan Page.

Mardis, M., ElBasri, T., Norton, S., & Newsum, J. (2012). The digital lives of U.S. teachers: A research synthesis and trends to watch. *School Libraries Worldwide*, *18*(1), 70–86.

Means, B., Toyama, Y., Murphy, R., Bakia, M., & Jones, K. (2009). *Evaluation of evidence based practices in online learning: A meta-analysis and review of online learning studies*. Retrieved from https://www2.ed.gov/rschstat/eval/tech/evidence-based-practices/finalreport.pdf

MET Project. (2010). *Working with teachers to develop fair and reliable measures of effective teaching*. Retrieved from https://docs.gatesfoundation.org/Documents/met-framing-paper.pdf

MET Project. (2013). *Ensuring fair and reliable measures of effective teaching: Culminating findings for the MET project's three-year study*. Retrieved from http://www.edweek.org/media/17teach-met1.pdf

Millet, J. A. (2012). *Virtual learning in K-12 education: Successful instructional practices and school strategies* (Doctoral dissertation). Available from ProQuest Dissertations and Theses database. (UMI No. 3497822)

Mishra, P., & Koehler, M. (2006). Technological pedagogical content knowledge: A framework for teacher knowledge. *Teachers College Record, 108*(6), 1017–1054. doi:10.1111/j.1467-9620.2006.00684.x

Molnar, A. (Ed.). (2014). *Virtual schools in the U.S. 2014: Politics, performance, policy, and research evidence.* Retrieved from http://nepc.colorado.edu/files/virtual-2014-all-final.pdf

No, C. L. B. (2002). (NCLB) Act of 2001, Pub. L. No. 107-110, § 115. *Stat,* 1425.

Patrick, S. (2012). Forward. In K. Rice (Ed.), *Making the move to K-12 online teaching: Research-based strategies and practices* (pp. ix–xi). Boston, MA: Pearson.

Rice, K. (2012). *Making the move to K-12 online teaching: Research-based strategies and practices.* Boston, MA: Pearson.

Russell, G. (2004). Virtual schools: A critical view. In C. Cavanaugh (Ed.), *Development and management of virtual schools: Issues and trends* (pp. 1–25). Hershey, PA: Information Science Pub. doi:10.4018/978-1-59140-154-4.ch001

Schlosser, L. A., & Simonson, M. R. (2006). *Distance education: Definition and glossary of terms.* Greenwich, CT: IAP.

Schoenholtz-Read, J., & Rudestam, K. E. (2002). *Handbook of online learning: Innovations in higher education and corporate training.* Thousand Oaks, CA: Sage.

Seamster, C. L. (2016). *Approaching Authentic Assessment: Using Virtual School Teachers' Expertise to Develop an Understanding of Full Time K-8 Virtual School Teacher Practices* (Doctoral dissertation). Retrieved from ProQuest Dissertations and Theses database.

Shulman, L. S. (2005). Signature pedagogies in the professions. *Daedalus, 134*(3), 52–59. doi:10.1162/0011526054622015

Southern Regional Education Board. (2003). *Essential principles of high-quality online teaching: Guideline for evaluating K-12 online teachers.* Retrieved from http://info.sreb.org/programs/edtech/pubs/PDF/Essential_Principles.pdf

The White House. (2010). *Race to the Top.* Retrieved from https://www.whitehouse.gov/issues/education/k-12/race-to-the-top

U.S. Department of Education. (1993). *Goals 2000, educate America: Building capacity: Higher education and Goals 2000.* Washington, DC: U.S. Dept. of Education.

Watson, J., Murin, A., Vashaw, L., Gemin, B., & Rapp, C. (2013). *Keeping pace with K-12 online and blended learning.* Durango, CO: Evergreen Education Group.

KEY TERMS AND DEFINITIONS

Digital Citizenship: Acting responsibly in the virtual environment through using technology appropriately.

Full Time Online Students: Students that receive all of their courses in a distance learning environment. Full-time online students do not attend traditional schools.

Full Time Virtual School Teacher: An instructor that teaches students for the entire duration of a school day and/or individual that is not an adjunct.

Learning Coach: An adult who works with a virtual school student and the student's teacher, in most cases from the student's home, to ensure that the student's academic needs are met.

Learning Management System (LMS): A technology platform accessible from the World Wide Web which allows teachers and students to conduct all day to day learning activities including interacting, monitoring student achievement, and completing assignments both synchronously and asynchronously from a distance.

Live Lesson: A synchronous form of interaction where students are connected with one another and their teacher through a tool such as Adobe Connect or Blackboard Collaborate.

Online/Distance Learning: "Delivers instruction and content primarily over the Internet. Used interchangeably with Virtual learning, Cyber learning, e-learning. Students can participate in online learning through one course (supplemental), or a fully online school or program" (Ferdig & Kennedy, 2014, p. 4).

Chapter 5
Mobile Technology and Learning

Benjamin Deaton
Anderson University, USA

Josh Herron
Limestone College, USA

Cynthia C. M. Deaton
Clemson University, USA

ABSTRACT

With an awareness of the unique characteristics of an increasingly mobile world and referencing socio-material mobile learning frameworks, this chapter will provide an overview of the initial stages and growth of mobile learning. The authors also discuss university initiatives to support mobile learning, and examine the implications of mobile technologies for teaching and learning. Additionally, the chapter will introduce a case study detailing the Mobile Learning Innovation at Anderson University (SC) and highlight its impact on the teaching and learning culture on its campus.

INTRODUCTION

Mobile technology is receiving growing attention in education just as it has in other realms of society—from media to business to healthcare. Educators and researchers have to critically examine its impact from a perspective that considers equally the social and material aspects of a mobile learning environment. Undoubtedly, the growth in the numbers of mobile device users changed the manner in which we communicate, access, and discern information (Pew Research Center, 2012).

As referenced, the integration of mobile technology in a number of aspects of our lives is becoming commonplace. Although such devices have been around for quite some time, including the Personal Digital Assistant (PDA) and flip phones, smartphones and tablets have picked up even more attention due to their increasing functionality and capabilities. A Pew Research Center report (Anderson, 2015) notes that almost 70% of US adults own a cell phone, double from just four years ago. Too, tablet owner-

DOI: 10.4018/978-1-5225-2838-8.ch005

ship has almost reached 50% of US adults while sales of laptops and desktops have slowed or declined (Anderson, 2015).

In 2016, Benedict Evans, co-founder of the venture capital firm Andreessen Horowitz, posted an updated presentation titled "Mobile is Eating the World" as part of an annual review on the role of mobile devices in society and business. Evans notes that mobile has scale in the technology industry that is unprecedented with smartphones and tablets at almost half of the consumer electronics industry. In fact, half of all online traffic in the United States occurs through a mobile app (Evans, 2016). With mobile dominating the technology industry and impacting a number of industries (e.g., in e-commerce since half of browsing and a third of purchasing occurs on a mobile device), we must examine the role that mobile devices will play in learning as a unique digital medium than tethered computing devices such as laptops and desktops.

The mobile society described in the previous paragraph has made an impact on teaching and learning, too. EDUCAUSE, an organization dedicated to advancing higher education through information technology, recently released findings from a multi-year study that found device ownership at a high and trending higher but the full potential was yet to be realized (Chen, Seilhamer, Bennett, & Bauer, 2015). The researchers identified the main mobile learning issue as not one of device ownership but of effective use and practices by students and instructors. They urge continued research in the emerging area and that faculty and students need comprehensive support to effectively use the devices to improve teaching and learning. Researchers and institutions have been doing just that as outlined in the two parts of this chapter. The first part of this chapter examines the initial developments and ongoing research concerning mobile learning, and the second part details mobile learning initiatives at a variety of higher education institutions.

MOBILE LEARNING FRAMEWORKS

The field of educational studies increasingly includes research on the integration of technology, developing into areas of study such as learning sciences or digital media and learning. This shift in educational studies that many are terming a socio-material framework has included an equal focus on the individual student and the technology, not prioritizing one over the other (Fenwick, Edwards, & Sawchuk, 2012). Mobile devices, in particular, play a role in this type of research and on educational practices as they either spur a change in mobile-friendly practices or traditional practices are impacted negatively by the use of devices.

Much of the early research on mobile learning stemmed from the field of computer science. Thus, much of it focused on hardware and software, competing with the educational studies frameworks of focusing on the individual student. From these competing techno-centric and student-centric frameworks, new theoretical and pedagogical frameworks are emerging that take into account the unique implications of mobile technology based on a socio-material framework that recognizes the symmetry between the student and the device.

One spurring factor for the creation of mobile learning studies was the realization that mobile technology is unique from stationary devices. A seminal mobile learning researcher, Yeonjeong Park (2011) noted the unique attributes and affordances of mobile devices in education. Further, in her essay "Mobile Learning: New Approach, New Theory," Helen Crompton (2013) argues for an m-learning theory to account for the differences from what she describes as tethered learning. Crompton compares traditional learning, conventional tethered e-learning, and m-learning using various learning attributes to note the unique characteristics of mobile. She then outlines criteria for m-learning based on previous literature, notes how theories of m-learning often connect with existing theories, and concludes with four emerging themes from her analysis – context, connectivity, time, and personalization. These are starting points when considering the unique characteristics of mobile learning and the development or revision of m-learning theories and research methods.

Specifically, research in the area of mobile learning has increased significantly since 2001 with numerous countries contributing. One hundred and twenty two papers were published from 2006 through 2011 (54 in 2010 alone) compared to just 32 from 2001 through 2005 (Hwang & Tsai, 2011). Gwo-Jen Hwang and Chin-Chung Tsai (2011) also noted that the increase in mobile learning research should encourage interested researchers and educators to participate in the area of study considering its rise in interest. In a meta-analysis of 164 research studies on mobile learning from 2003 to 2010, Wen-Hsiung Wu et al. (2012) identified that most research in this area focuses on evaluating effects of and designing systems for mobile learning. Interestingly, both Hwang and Tais (2011) and Wu et al. (2012) found that there was more mobile learning taking place in higher education institutions than in primary or secondary schools.

The first major book as it relates to education was *Mobile Learning: A Handbook for Educators and Trainers* in 2005 by Agnes Kukulska-Hulme and John Traxler. However, in 2010, Pachler, Bachmair, and Cook were still seeking to be the first to develop a conceptual and theoretical framework for mobile learning in *Mobile Learning: Structures, Agency, Practices*. This continual search for effective theoretical and pedagogical frameworks has not satisfied many mobile learning researchers.

Clark Quinn's 2011 *The Mobile Academy: mLearning for Higher Education* was the first major text to examine mobile learning as it relates to higher education, which is the context for this chapter. Routledge produced a *Handbook for Mobile Learning* in 2013, giving credence to the establishment of the area of study. There has been no settled definition of mobile learning, but a working definition for mobile learning based from these works might be the use of portable devices in anytime, anywhere learning situations, including consumption and creation of content, typically in the form of tablets and smartphones, with laptops not yet having the "portability and ubiquity" to be considered part of this definition (Pachler et al., 2010).

Earlier research in mobile learning focused more on the devices and productivity with works such as Clark Quinn's (2011) *Designing mLearning: Tapping into the Mobile Revolution for Organizational Performance* and Gary Woodill's (2010) *The Mobile Learning Edge: Tools and Technologies for Developing your Teams* highlighting these aspects. Quinn's (2011) *The Mobile Academy: mLearning for Higher Education* even begins with a detailed discussion of devices. He highlights the differences in construction and capabilities of PDAs, phones, and tablets. He even maps out the connectivity, input, output, and sensing aspects of each device. The processing power and platforms receive attention as well. This type of information can still be helpful but was most needed in the infancy of mobile learning. As the capabilities of mobile devices become standardized, more researchers and teachers begin examining the role that the devices play within a learning environment rather than focusing on the devices.

Mobile learning researchers are realizing that it is not mainly about the technology – though the material aspect should not be ignored. John Traxler (2009) notes that mobile learning is really about a mobile conception of society than it is about learning or mobile. Thus, the use of socio-material research methods plays an important role in analyzing the impact that mobile devices have on pedagogy as it is not just about the technology (as classic computer science frameworks suggest) and it not just about the student (as classic educational frameworks suggest). Socio-material studies within education "explore ways that human and non-human materialities combine to produce particular purposes and particular effects in education. They examine the messy textures woven through different kinds of networks – and the resulting ambivalences – that intersect in pedagogical processes" (Fenwick and Landri, 2012). Examining mobile devices fit within this framework fits well.

This socio-cultural framework for analyzing mobile learning has been specifically referenced by a few researchers, including Norbert Pachler, Ben Bachmair, and John Cook (2013) in "Sociocultural Ecological Framework for M-Learning." They label their framework as a complex consisting of structures, agency, and cultural practices. For Pachler et al. (2013), mobile learning involves a paradigm shift where learning's context is just as important as its content. The authors argue that appropriation is central to their framework. They are especially interested in the shifting literacy practices brought on by mobile devices, by which they mean the reading and production of cultural acts that interpret and shape the world for us.

Another study that emphasizes socio-material methods in mobile learning is Louise Mifsud's (2014) "Mobile Learning and the Socio-Materiality Classroom Practices." She uses Bruno Latour's (1993) Actor-Network Theory and also spatial theories to examine mobile learning as an embedded classroom practice. Mifsud suggests that many mobile learning practices conflict with and that educators and researchers should consider the socio-materiality aspects of a mobile society to determine if and how they should redefine classroom practices. Thus, mobile technology is not just a device one can bring into the classroom without consideration of its impact on the established classroom practices; either the classroom practices have to adjust to a mobile learning environment or we end up with bans on mobile devices because they conflict with established practices (which is often the case).

Mifsud (2014) use of Latour's (1993) Actor-Network Theory focuses on the symmetry and equal capabilities of humans and nonhumans as they create a network and impact one another. Mifsud and others are building on the fact that the introduction of a mobile device impacts the network, or what Bruno Latour terms the collective, a description for the associations of humans and nonhumans.

Because of the criticism that ANT receives for aspects such as giving agency to non-humans, Mifsud (2014) also makes use of Estrid Sørensen's (2009) concepts of space and spatiality. Sørensen identifies how regions in the space of a classroom impact educational practices. For example, he notes that the blackboard space in a classroom is typically one where the instructor resides and that when students are at that space, it gains attention. Thus, the relations between the students and technology in a classroom is impacted by the space of the classroom, too. Using a socio-material approach to designing a classroom experience involves analyzing the movement and relations as well as the process of knowledge making that stems from agency (Mifsud, 2014). These theoretical and research methods play a role in developing a mobile learning pedagogical framework that takes into account the socio-material aspect of mobile learning.

With the analysis of the socio-material aspect of mobile devices on educational practices comes the need for research on how best to do design a mobile learning environment by developing pedagogical frameworks. The first question for many may be about the benefits of mobile learning. In a 2016 study, Sung, Chang, and Liu found a positive correlation with the use of mobile devices in education over the use of stationary devices for certain activities. Their research signals the potential for mobile learning but also suggests that continually refining pedagogical frameworks for mobile learning is necessary. In fact, Sung et al. (2016) argue for further instructional design development to help fully realize the potential of mobile learning. However, several mobile learning pedagogical frameworks have been devised over the last fifteen years in addition to general educational technology integration frameworks.

Figure 1. Mishra and Koehler's TPACK model (Mishra & Koehler, 2006)

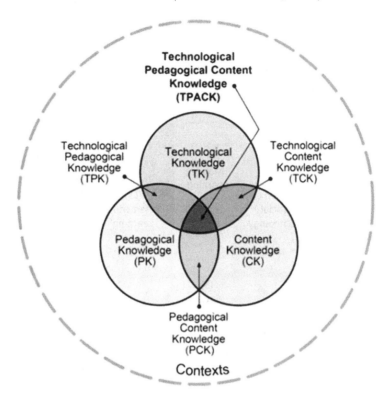

Much of mobile learning pedagogy has depended on these educational technology frameworks or models that were not specifically designed for mobile. One prominent educational technology integration model is the Technological Pedagogical Content Knowledge (TPACK) model developed by Punya Mishra and Matthew Koehler (2006). When the TPACK model was fully developed in 2006 to accommodate technology in pedagogical considerations (pieces of the framework been added on since 1986), it was considered groundbreaking as it gave instructors a language to discuss the integration of technology (Hunter, 2015). TPACK highlights seven components and their relationships as shown in Figure 1. TPACK allows teachers a framework to integrate technology while recognizing the complexities and context of each aspect of teaching and learning environments.

Another model for the integration of technology is Ruben Puentedura's (2014) Substitution, Augmentation, Modification, Redefinition (SAMR) model, which suggests a progression of adoption in educational technology (Hunter, 2015). The SAMR model is not based in as much research as the TPACK model, but it receives a good deal of attention from educational technologists in that it helps set enhancement and justification levels for the integration of technology along the SAMR continuum. TPACK, SAMR, and the derivative frameworks—such as Jane Hunter's (2015) High Possibility Classrooms (HPC)—incorporate context but are designed for all of educational technology. Thus, they form an important background do not address the specific characteristics of mobile learning.

Even before Sung et al.'s 2016 article suggested creating new mobile learning pedagogical frameworks, a 2009 report noted that the borrowed frameworks would no longer suffice considering mobile is not just a delivery system buy impacts knowledge processes that occur through multiple contexts and interaction

Figure 2. Koole's FRAME model (Koole, 2009)

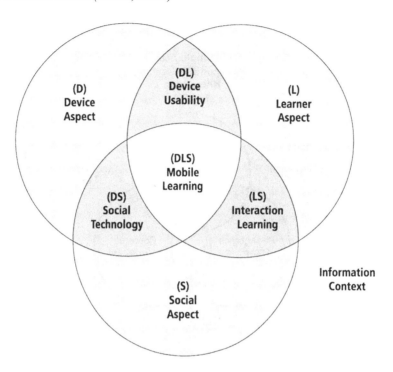

of people and technology. Giasemi Vavoula and Mike Sharples (2009) thus set out to create one of the first mobile learning pedagogical frameworks, the M3 evaluation framework for mobile learning. The M3 framework is a divides the evaluation of mobile learning into the micro-level, which is focused on usability; the meso-level, focused on the experience; and the macro-level, focused on the organizational context. This framework was designed to emphasize experience-centered over technology-centered development, and the researchers suggested that extension to this framework would be necessary, which others continue to do.

In the same year, Marguerite Koole (2009) was also working on a framework for mobile learning in that would become part of the foundation of the field. She developed the Framework for the Rational Analysis of Mobile Education (FRAME) to describe the mobile learning process as the meeting of technologies, human capacities, and social interaction. Relatedly, the three main aspects of the FRAME model include the device aspect, the learning aspect, and the social aspect; these three aspects overlap to form the Device Usability Intersection, the Social Technology Intersection, and the Interaction Learning Intersection as labeled in Figure 2.

A third 2009 mobile learning framework that receives attention from scholars is a three-part representation of engagement, presence, and flexibility in mobile learning and teaching environments. Danaher, Gururajan, and Hafeez-Baig (2009) note that the three parts are of equal importance and must each be included. They break down the concepts of presence and flexibility even further. The notion of presence stems from research from Garrison, Anderson, and Archer's (2000) Community of Inquiry framework and includes interactions by students with the content, with fellow students, and with the instructor in the mobile learning and teaching environment. Flexibility in a mobile learning environment builds upon research related to increasing flexibility in the educational process to promote access and multiple ways of learning; Danaher et al. (2009) identify flexibility in learning, teaching, and assessment activities and encourage the use of information communication technology tools to afford flexibility.

In 2011, Yeonjeong Park noted Koole's (2009) FRAME model but suggested that earlier work in the area lacked an emphasis on pedagogy. Transactional distance theory (TDD) emphasizes the role of the cognitive space between instructor and learner as opposed to just the geographic space as discussed in distance education (Moore, 1993). Using TDD and incorporating the individual and social aspects of learning, Park (2011) identifies four types of mobile learning: two high transactional distance types, socialized and individualized m-learning. There are also socialized and individualized m-learning as low transactional distance types. While her framework might be considered more of a classification, she intends for it to be used by faculty and designers for more effective mobile learning design, thus serving as a pedagogical framework.

In 2012, Kearney, Schuck, Burden, and Aubusson extended Koole's (2009) FRAME model by drawing on the socio-material aspects. Kearney et al.'s also note that their framework builds upon Danaher et al.'s (2009) model by making pedagogy more of a central concern. The Kearney framework emphasizes personalization, authenticity, and collaboration as distinctive features of a mobile learning. As noted in Figure 3, the use of time-space is the foundation for their model since these are often the constraints for traditional learning that mobile learning has a chance to transcend. The notion of personalization makes use of motivational and socio-cultural theories to emphasize the possibility of increased customization (or choice) and agency for learners. Their notion of authenticity espouses a model where students simulate the context of an authentic activity and where students are actually situated in an authentic environment to practice skills. Finally, collaboration stems from the idea that knowledge is created and negotiated in a social context. Thus, students have spaces for conversation and interaction with the instructor (including feedback) and one another. Too, students are able to share data files, including those created on the devices in the moment.

Figure 3. The Kearney framework (Kearney et al., 2012)

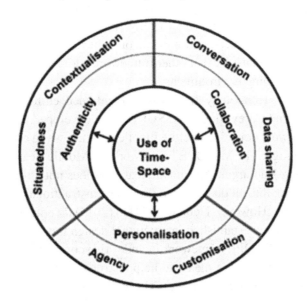

In 2013, Martin and Ertzberger developed a mobile learning framework based on "here and now learning" or situated learning, an educational theory introduced in 1991 by Jean Lave and Etienne Wenger in their book *Situated Learning*. Martin and Ertzberger's (2013) three-part framework incorporates the mobile dimension and its capabilities, including geospatial technologies, mobile search, use of camera, and social networking (p. 77). The three parts consist of engaging students in the context, authentic activities, and informal learning. In a study where these principles were applied, the researchers found that mobile learning allows for engaged, authentic, and informal learning opportunities.

Also in 2013, Ge et al. (2013) published a study titled "Three-Dimension Design for Mobile Learning" that recounts the experience of the Oklahoma University College of Nursing's implementation of a mobile learning initiative. The faculty and staff used traditional instructional design methods at first, including ADDIE, but also developed a new framework. The three dimensions of their framework include the pedagogical dimension, design dimension, and technological dimension. The pedagogical dimension is considered the most essential. In it, one considers how to create an authentic learning environment that makes use of social constructivism. In the design dimension, learning is contextualized through the design and sequencing of activities as well as screen design. Finally, in the technological dimension, issues concerning the user-interface, platform, and implementation are considered. The authors argue that their framework fills the gap of earlier literature coherently and systematically, which they argue is lacking from other mobile learning design frameworks.

Dyson, Andrews, Smith, and Wallace's (2013) "Toward a Holistic Framework for Ethical Mobile Learning" is unique in that it emphasizes an aspect of mobile learning that they suggest others have not. Although one component of Dennan and Hao's (2014) M-COPE framework includes ethics, Dyson et al. (2014) offer a full treatment of that aspect. As a starting point, they identified ethical concerns that prompted the need for the framework. Many of the considerations would be found in tethered learning environments, but since mobile learning often occurs outside the classroom, there are more ethical issues and situations to consider. While many educators seek to ban devices to minimize the risk of such issue, Dyson et al. (2013) note that educators are held to a higher standard that "harm minimization" and that bans on the use of devices are actually unethical considering the benefits that could be afforded to all types of students and the lack of critical awareness into the role that such technology plays in students' personal lives. Thus, they incorporate these aspects into their framework. The important principles laid out in the "Holistic Framework for Ethical M-Learning" include Enhanced Learner Agency, Responsibility, Involvement of All Stakeholders, and a Focus on Ethical Behavior (Dyson et al., 2013). This ethical framework adds items to consider that other frameworks do not and supports a positive view on the management of mobile learning environments.

Similar to the educational technology frameworks mentioned earlier, most instructional design models, e.g., ADDIE, Dick and Carey Model, ASSURE, were developed to take into account different learning contexts, but these were conceived before mobile learning was a concept. In their 2014 article "Intentionally Mobile Pedagogy: The M-COPE Framework for Mobile Learning in Higher Education," Vanessa Dennen and Shuang Hao argue that mobile learning does not alter the essence of instruction as it is just a delivery medium; thus, it does not require a new instructional design model since existing approaches remain appropriate. However, Dennan and Hao (2014) do note that there should be a mobile learning framework to accompany established instructional design models.

Dennan and Hao's (2014) M-COPE framework includes five components: Mobile, Conditions, Outcomes, Pedagogy, and Ethics, which are meant to help instructors and developers design learning for mobile or incorporate mobile into existing activities. The mobile component of the framework encourages faculty to examine why they are incorporating a mobile device and to what extent it is mobile dependent. Conditions to consider using the framework include student readiness, suitability, and time. Dennan and Hao (2014) also purposefully emphasize outcomes, including unintended ones, over objectives, and they argue most of the literature suggests mobile learning supports lower order cognitive skills despite evidence that mobile learning also supports higher order skills. The pedagogy dimension of M-COPE encourages an examination of the paradigms and learning theories that the instructor is operating within as it shapes the integration of mobile devices. Finally, Dennan and Hao (2014) include consideration of ethics, including issues of device ownership and the potential expectation for constant engagement. The M-COPE framework provides prompts for educators to consider fully the mobile learning context. It not only helps to decide how best to implement mobile learning, but it also encourages knowing if and why using mobile devices for instruction is best suited.

Most recently, in 2015, Jessica Levene and Hooli Seabury analyzed research on the evaluation of mobile learning to develop their own framework. Specifically, Levene and Seabury (2015) make use of Koole's (2009) FRAME model and Moore's Transactional Distance Theory. Using themes of student achievement comparisons, usability, and student attitudes/perceptions, Levene and Seabury (2015) developed three implications for the design of mobile learning environments: (1) Use Student Perception and Attitudes to Inform Design, (2) Usability and Access to Content, and (3) Aligned with Pedagogy. In using student perception and attitudes to inform design, Levene and Seabury make use of needs analysis and iterative nature of instructional design. In considering usability and access to content, the researchers mainly identify the need for content tailored to mobile devices down to the use of the buttons on the devices as part of the activity. Finally, Levene and Seabury (2015) agree with other frameworks in encouraging designers to make use of foundational theories and pedagogies to design mobile learning rather than focusing on the tools. These considerations by faculty and designers help ensure the effectiveness and sustainability of mobile learning for institutions.

The mobile learning pedagogical frameworks that scholars and teachers have been developing over the last almost-two decades recognize that technological devices and learners have symmetrical roles in the educational process, and that mobile devices in particular have unique characteristics when measuring impact and designing learning. Neither a technology-centric nor a student-centric framework for mobile learning provides a holistic perspective on mobile learning environments. Since mobile learning is still developing from a combination of disciplines—from computer science to educational studies—there is still work to be done to ensure the unique characteristics of mobile devices and the socio-material network are all fully taken into consideration.

Mobile Learning Initiatives

The second part of the chapter discusses existing one to one (1:1) mobile learning programs in higher education environments. 1:1 programs are those that provide or require all of their students to have a common device from one manufacturer (e.g., Apple, Microsoft, or Google). The design and implementation of 1:1 programs have taken on multiple forms throughout the higher education landscape. They range from campus-wide to program specific initiatives. Below, example models are highlighted from a variety of institutions. Additionally, an in-depth case study of Anderson University's (SC) Mobile Learning Initiative (MLI) is provided.

Abilene Christian University

Abilene Christian University (Texas) was a pioneer in the adoption and exploration of 1:1 in higher education. Beginning in 2008, ACU started providing its students and faculty members with mobile devices. The institution has used iPod Touches, iPhones, and iPads as part of that strategy. Their 1:1 program was "built upon the theory that humans learn best when they are in community – collaborating with others in a learning environment without boundaries" (ACU, n.d.). One of their primary goals was to create a connected community of learners and use technology as a means for enabling the community's development. As of Fall 2016, ACU's 1:1 program continues with each student having an iPad.

Seton Hill University

Seton Hill University (Pennsylvania) is another pioneer in mobile learning. Seton Hill holds the distinction of being the first university in the world to provide all of its students and faculty with iPads in 2010. At the same time, Seton Hill also provides its students with MacBooks, which means that Seton Hill is a 2:1 institution (2 devices per student). To support its initiative, Seton Hill provides several professional development opportunities to its faculty members ranging from workshops to intensive one on one support with an instructional designer to intensive year-long programs. Each of these opportunities is designed to provide the appropriate levels of support at the right time to serve a wide range of faculty needs and interests.

Lynn University

Lynn University (Florida) is another institution that provides all of its students and faculty with an iPad. Lynn's approach is slightly different than most institutions offering 1:1 programs in that their use of mobile devices is more closely tied to the deployment and delivery of curriculum. That is, a significant amount of Lynn's undergraduate curriculum (textbooks, resources, assessment, etc.) is delivered through tools and software only available on the iPad. In specific cases, Lynn has developed complete degree programs that use iPads to facilitate the delivery of the entire curriculum (Lynn University, n.d.).

University of Cincinnati – College of Nursing

The University of Cincinnati's College of Nursing began its mobile learning program in 2013. Their program required that all Bachelor of Science Nursing and Doctor of Nursing Practice students and faculty members have iPads. As part of its initiative, all entry level courses in the Nursing program were rebuilt using iBooks to provide digital textbooks to its students. The platform also enabled the College of Nursing to provide current reference materials to all its students in digital form. Another distinct advantage of a common device as identified by the College of Nursing is that the iPad provides a common device for students to capture video of field and clinical experiences that allows for formative assessment and additional feedback and support from faculty members.

Each of the programs described above have been national leaders in mobile learning. While they have all taken different approaches to mobile learning, each has continued to support and implement their mobile learning programs after several years. Their choice to persist illustrates both their commitment to and belief in mobile learning as a viable, sustainable direction in supporting higher education.

In the following section, an in-depth case study of another initiative, the Mobile Learning Initiative at Anderson University (SC) is presented.

MOBILE LEARNING AT ANDERSON UNIVERSITY (SC)

Anderson University is private comprehensive, liberal arts institution in South Carolina with a total enrollment of 3400 students. Since 2010 Anderson has been wholly committed to be an institution dedicated to innovation in teaching and learning. To achieve that goal, it set forth on a path to use mobile learning as a catalyst for realizing that change.

Foundations of Anderson's Mobile Learning Initiative

Anderson's President and Senior Leadership team first began developing and exploring the idea of a mobile learning initiative in 2009. In 2010, they developed a planning committee with faculty and administrative stakeholders from across the institution. That committee developed a comprehensive plan for implementing and funding what would become their Mobile Learning Initiative (MLI) during the 2010-2011 academic year. That plan was presented to and approved by both the President and the Board of Trust and fully funded for the 2011-2012 academic year. One of the primary reasons the institution was able to move so quickly in formulating a plan was due largely to the inclusion of the input and voice of Anderson's faculty members. They, not the administration, were the drivers and builders of the framework of the MLI. The administration, in turn, was fully committed to providing the resources, infrastructure, and personnel in making that vision a reality.

One of the key recommendations that was approved by the administration was to adopt a common platform and device for the initiative. Based on research and in communicating with other institutions, the planning committee felt the decision to deploy the MLI using a common device would provide several benefits. First, it would provide everyone with a device with the same capabilities and would make accessible a universal set of tools and software. Secondly, it would ease the burden on Information Technology in trying to support a wide-range of devices. Third, faculty and student training efforts would be able to be focused around a common platform. The device that was selected was the iPad.

With the aspiration of making the MLI viable for years to come, several components of Anderson's operations had to be engaged and provided with continual support. Those areas include: infrastructure, leadership, teaching and learning innovation, and faculty development. Each of those realms is discussed in detail below. Finally, the case study closes with evidence of success for the MLI.

Infrastructure and Deployment Model

In order to make the MLI a reality, significant investments in infrastructure were required. When the MLI began, less than 10% of learning spaces were equipped with Wi-Fi access. By Fall 2011, just over 50% had Wi-Fi access and by the beginning of the Fall 2012 semester, 100% of all learning spaces had Wi-Fi access through the introduction of a campus-wide fiber-optic network. Another major change in infrastructure was in bandwidth as well. When the MLI started, external bandwidth to the institution was doubled. Less than two years later, bandwidth received another 250% increase. In total, bandwidth increased 500% to accommodate the amount of utilization of mobile device and network traffic on the network. For institutions considering a mobile learning initiative on their campus, they should be cognizant of network needs and the hardware required to support traffic loads. For example, the number of wireless access points required to handle the amount of devices in learning and residential spaces has increased 10% to 20% each year after the initial deployment.

Like the scaled infrastructure upgrades that occurred on campus, the roll-out of devices to students was scaled as well over three academic years. This approach enabled the university to be measured in the program's deployment and nimble in addressing challenges (e.g., network and bandwidth issues, technological support, and faculty development). In the first year, only freshman and freshman transfer students received iPads. In year two incoming freshman and freshman and sophomore transfers received devices. In year three all students received iPads as part of the initiative. Each year thereafter (2014 – present) all students and transfer students to Anderson have received an iPad upon their arrival to campus. Unlike the student rollout, all faculty members received an iPad at the at the start of the MLI.

Leadership

As noted above the success of the MLI is dependent upon visionary leaders across campus. Principal drivers of that vision have been the Provost's Office and the Center for Innovation for Digital Learning (CIDL). The primary role of the Provost and his team is to ensure that funding and personnel are maintained and expanded from the instruction. The CIDL is charged with keeping momentum for the MLI, spurring innovation, providing ongoing professional development experiences, and supporting faculty members and students. Lastly, long-term sustainability of the MLI is fueled by Anderson's faculty members. The university's vision for the MLI and for technology is to be a leading, entrepreneurial innovator. In order to make that happen, faculty members were empowered to bring that vision into existence. Faculty members at Anderson have responded to and seized upon that opportunity to design and deliver learning opportunities that reflect the types of experiences they want to provide to students.

Teaching and Learning Innovation

From the beginning, the MLI has always been an endeavor solely focused on the goal of enhancing the teaching and learning experience rather than one about technological advancement. Anderson has used a targeted approach to assure that goal has been met. In its earliest days and for the first two years of the initiative, specific courses were targeted for redesign. The MLI began modestly with the redesign of six courses that were redeveloped by six different faculty members. By working with a small set of courses and faculty members, the initiative was able to provide early successes that could be made visible and shared across the institution. This approach also enabled supporting units on campus to identify the needs in supporting the MLI as it would be scaled. In the following sections, we share some of the findings in three key academic areas: student learning, instructional practices, and curriculum design.

Student Learning

Anderson University views learning as a personalized experience that should foster inquiry, personal growth, and curiosity. Anderson faculty members have adopted this view and make significant efforts to design learning experiences that support that vision. Students enrolled in courses developed through the "Mobile Learning Teachers Fellow" program use their iPads in numerous capacities to support their learning. Students across all of Anderson's Colleges and Schools use a wide range of apps to create, present, collaborate, and communicate among the entire class and with their instructors. Below, we highlight some of the outcomes on student learning those efforts have produced.

In "Biology I" students work in small groups to develop stop-frame videos to demonstrate and strengthen their understanding of cellular processes. Thus, students in Biology are enabled to creatively produce content that supports knowledge development and demonstrates their understanding. In the course "Introduction to Hebrew", the entire class uses a collaborative whiteboard app to strengthen their knowledge of the language and their ability to analyze and interpret texts.

In Anderson's teacher preparation program, teacher candidates capture video of themselves teaching on their iPads during their field placement. Capturing video allows teacher candidates to analyze their teaching individually and with their faculty mentors and peers. This process enables teacher candidates to better identify the areas and issues of practice they are doing well and those that should be refined.

Anderson's chemistry courses have made significant changes throughout several of their courses and degree programs. In addition to the creation of a state-of-the-art Biochemistry Lab, the Chemistry faculty has integrated iPads throughout the entire course sequence. Students also use a wide range of apps to support knowledge development and critical thinking. For example, students use apps to conduct stoichiometry, model and analyze compounds, and conduct virtual experiments. Students also use their iPads as essential tools in their lab experiments and their reporting. They, for instance, use their iPads to develop models and capture images and video that are integrated into their web-based digital lab notebooks. The notebooks can be shared with other students as well as the instructor.

While just a few examples of the MLI's impact on student learning were highlighted above, the effects of our efforts have been widespread across campus. Students are using their devices in all areas to conduct research and communicate with their peers and instructors to strengthen their learning. Haley, a senior elementary education major noted that the iPad allows "relevant learning and active engagement [to take] place" in the classroom. Students also indicated that the integration of technology helped their development of skills for their future professions.

Instructional Practices

Designing a learning environment is an intricate process. Since the beginning of the MLI, faculty members have met that challenge directly. Through the professional development activities provided by the CIDL, which are highlighted in the Ongoing Professional Learning chapter, faculty have been encouraged to focus on using the iPad to support learner-centered classrooms that foster inquiry, collaboration, and formative assessment. Nearly 100% of all faculty members have participated in training through one of the many options available to them.

Through the formal training provided by the CIDL's Mobile Learning Teaching Fellows program, faculty members are asked to design their courses through the 5E Inquiry-based learning model (Engage, Explore, Explain, Elaborate, and Evaluate). Adopting this instructional approach, which was founded in scientific inquiry, focuses course design efforts on learner-centered classrooms and purposefully choosing and selecting technology to support and enhance the learning experience. Through this approach that focuses on explicitly identifying course goals, instructors are able to design lessons that support students in meeting those goals and using technology to support student learning.

Curriculum Design

As faculty members have become more comfortable with and adept in integrating the iPad and technology into their individual classes, the impact on curricula across the campus is becoming more pervasive. Curricular change is initiated by individual departments and colleges and supported by the CIDL. The purpose of the institutional support is to help programs realize their visions for innovation and change.

As part of Anderson University's Mobile Learning Initiative, faculty from the English Department redesigned the English 101 & 102 sequence in the summer of 2013. This sequence of general education courses impacts all incoming freshmen at the institution. Beginning in fall 2013, the professors piloted the use of an electronic portfolio web application to facilitate process writing pedagogy in first-year composition courses. Through the success of that pilot, a broader implementation was launched in fall 2014. The course sequence redesign focused on the use of a web-based, electronic portfolio (ePortfolio) for active pedagogical purposes rather than archival purposes. The ePortfolio, designed around process writing pedagogy, allows students to compose, collaborate, revise, and compile their work digitally, all in one location. Using the web application on the iPad, students are able to do this work anywhere. With a streamlined process of submitting, peer reviewing, editing, and receiving feedback, the ePortfolio approach has transformed the learning experience for first-year composition students. The experience for instructors has been enhanced, too, by the option to have students electronically compose and peer review in class and the ability to offer enriched assessment by having access to all stages of the writing process for each student.

Faculty Development

As a whole, a strong commitment to professional learning for faculty members at Anderson is central to the values of the institution. The primary tenet of faculty development at the institution is to enable and empower faculty by provide them with a wide range of opportunities that lead to the development of exceptional learning experiences. The Center for Innovation and Digital Learning (CIDL) is the unit tasked with providing professional development opportunities related to the MLI at Anderson. When the MLI began, the CIDL had one instructional designer, but that team has grown to a team of six full-time employees providing services in instructional design, media development, and faculty development (see Figure 4). The CIDL provides numerous professional development experiences that range from just-in-time support to seminars and workshops to intensive year-long programs. Below, the signature programs offered by the CIDL are briefly discussed.

MLI Teaching Fellows

The Teaching Fellows program was the initial professional development offering from the CIDL. It is an internally funded competitive grant program focused on the development or redesign of courses to promote active, engaged learning with the purposeful integration of technology. The Teaching Fellows participate in a weeklong summer workshop that emphasizes sound pedagogical and instructional design processes. The result of that workshop is a redesigned course that will is deployed in the following academic year. Additionally, the CIDL provides ongoing and technological support while the course is being delivered. In its first year (2011) six faculty members completed the program. Since then another 50 faculty members have completed the program and several have participated in multiple years. In total

Figure 4. CIDL structure and operations

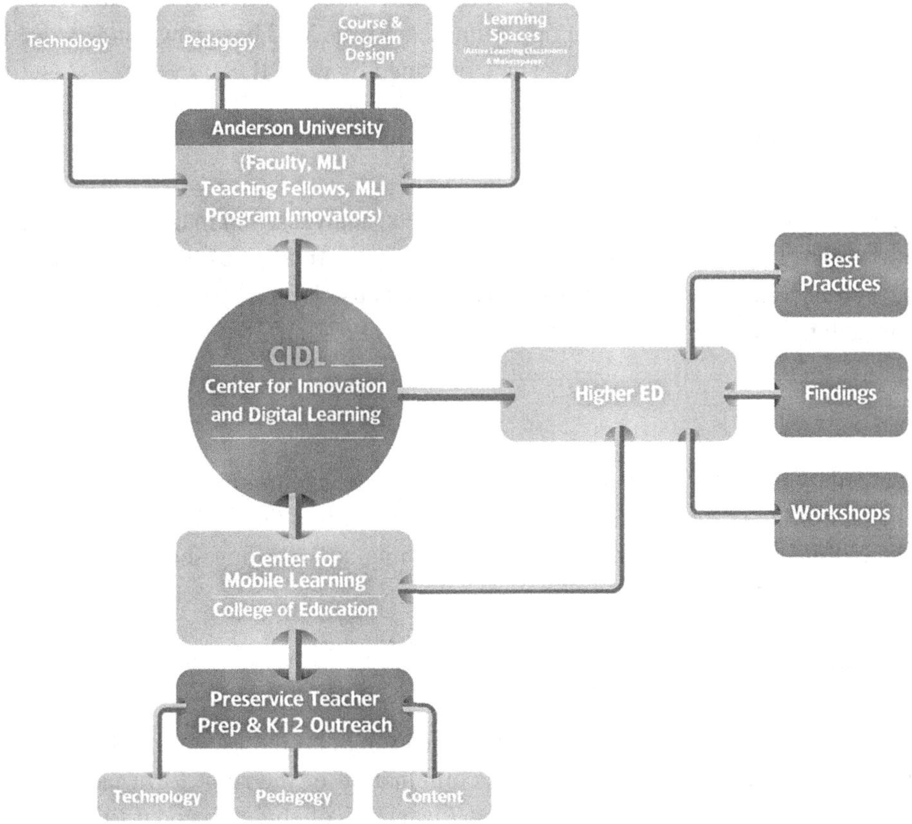

over 70 courses have been redesigned or developed through this program to intentionally integrate iPads and a large number of other technologies into their curricula.

MLI Program Innovators

In 2014 the CIDL introduced its second major program to support the MLI. The Program innovators tract supports teaching and learning projects that are broader and/or are not tied directly to an individual course. Program innovators are charged with utilizing technology in a manner that makes it a central component, or partner, in the learning experience. The response for the Program Innovators tract has been tremendous from Anderson's faculty members. Faculty members and faculty teams have been tackling key areas such as college affordability and accessibility with several projects related to textbook development or the adoption of Open Educational Resources (OER). Other projects include the creation of a multidisciplinary Undergraduate Laboratory for Scientific Computing and Modeling and the complete reshaping of the curricula in biology and chemistry. Other projects include the development of technology-enhanced makerspaces and a college developing its own professional development team and program. While not all of these projects are directly related to the use of iPads, their existence has become possible because of the MLI and its impact on the culture of teaching and learning at Anderson.

In addition to the teaching fellows and program innovators tracts, the CIDL provides a number of other opportunities including a workshop series that offers fifteen to twenty offerings per year, faculty learning communities, and numerous other opportunities. As the MLI has grown and evolved since 2011 so too has the professional development offerings provided by the CIDL.

Evidence of Success

As part of the MLI, Anderson University regularly collects, analyzes, and makes use of data for continuous improvement. The CIDL works across and within the institution to design assessments that measure both the impact of the MLI as a whole as well as narrowly focused research projects that examine courses redesigned through the Mobile Learning Teaching Fellows Program.

Quantitative

Surveys developed by the CIDL are conducted bi-annually – to incoming freshmen in the fall and to all students at the end of the academic year. The survey data informs the CIDL of trends in how students are using their mobile devices and what aspects of teaching and learning should be targeted for future professional development experiences.

Institutional Data

Students and faculty have been committed to mobile learning and the use of the iPad since the start of the MLI. The data indicate that the iPad has the combination of the right form factor, computational power, and battery life to support mobile learning. Over 70% of students noted that they believed the iPad is a better learning technology than a smartphone. Student use of the iPad to support learning has also remained consistent since the start of the MLI with at least 75% of students communicating that they use the iPad three or more days per week for academic purposes. Over 70% of students have also noted that the iPad is an effective tool for supporting learning and teaching. Our students' primary wish is that the iPad was even more integrated throughout the curricula. However, even in courses that do not intentionally integrate mobile learning, 70% of students regularly use their iPads throughout those courses indicating the students have naturally integrated the iPad into their personal learning experience.

Equipping all of our undergraduate students has had a tremendous impact on our students. Greater than 80% of all students indicated that having access to an iPad at all times impacted them positively in four key areas:

1. Gaining access to more material, content, and resources (86%)
2. Enabling interaction with other students (84%)
3. Enabling interaction with their instructors (85%), and
4. Increasing the range of content and skills they were knowledgeable about (82%).

Those data indicate that the MLI is expanding our students' access to and varieties of content, supporting the MLI's objectives of increasing engagement and interaction inside and outside of the classroom, and preparing twenty-first century learners for twenty-first century skills.

Table 1. Introduction to Religion: student performance

	Original Course (n=116)	Redesigned Course (n=58)
Average: Test 1	81.8	85.9
Test 1 A's	36.8%	40.7%
Test 1 DF Rate	24.1%	10.2%
Average: Final Grade	80.7	83.2
Final A's	37.0%	43.1%
Final DF Rate	14.7%	6.9%

Course Specific Data

Each faculty member participating in the Mobile Learning Teaching Fellows program conducts an individual, course-specific research study. These individual studies have a great deal of variance in size, scope, and research focus. This section will briefly discuss a select group of studies that examined the impact of mobile learning on student performance.

The "Introduction to Religion" course, a general education course that all undergraduate students take, was transformed from a traditional lecture-based course to a flipped classroom in order to increase active learning in the classroom. To achieve that goal, faculty member developed a comprehensive set of mini-lectures that students would view outside of the classroom on their iPads before class meetings. By providing the lecture component outside of the classroom, he was able to integrate an interactive eText for classroom use and design engaging, learner-centered activities for class meetings. The students strongly indicated (96%) that the iPad improved their learning. The student performance data, which is shown in the Table 1, showed that significant gains were made in student performance as well. The instructor was able to maintain course rigor, avoid grade inflation, and still witness gains in student performance. The data also indicated that the course redesign and the integration of the iPad reduced the rate of students receiving Ds and Fs (DF Rate). Since the successful redesign of this course, the curriculum he developed has been rolled out to all sections of the course, which has a direct impact on over 700 students per academic year.

Two faculty members in biology and chemistry have also been active with the MLI. One of their most significant efforts was to redesign the "Biology I" course that all biology and biochemistry majors take. Their goal was simple – to provide students with access to the best tools and methods for students to learn science. To accomplish that goal, they made use of several tools, which included digital microscopy tools that broadcasts images to student iPads in real time for annotation and analysis. They also wanted to increase student ownership of learning in the "Biology I" lab. To accomplish that goal, they designed activities that focused on student creativity and creation. To support students' understanding of basic cellular processes that are foundational to understanding biology (e.g., mitosis and meiosis), their students collaboratively developed stop-frame videos of those processes. The data indicated that their approach had a positive impact on student understanding of cellular processes. Even though students have previously encountered mitosis and meiosis multiple times in their K-12 careers, they did not have a strong understanding of the processes. Based on pre- and post-test data, the students' development of stop-frame videos coupled with course discussion had a significant impact on students' development of knowledge (see Table 2).

Table 2. Biology 1 student performance from stop-motion animation intervention

	Pre-test	**Post-test**
Average Correct Responses	1.21	7.44
Median	1	8
Range	0-7	3-10
SD	1.44	2.21
Correct responses on cellular processes questions	31.7%	90.2%

Qualitative

The use of qualitative data is also a cornerstone of our evidence gathering efforts for the MLI. Our student surveys allow our students to respond to open ended questions and share how the use of mobile devices has impacted their learning experience and how it prepares them for their future endeavors.

When asked to identify the greatest benefits of having the iPad in the classroom, the most common responses by students were the themes of access, convenience, interactivity and connectedness, research, and notes. In regards to access, students almost universally appreciate the ability to access content and course materials and access to each other anytime and anywhere. Students also indicated that iPads supported interaction and engagement in the classroom. Steven, a first-year pre-business major, highlighted both of those themes by stating that the iPad provides "[e]asier access to information and a collectively enhanced learning experience". Kristen, a senior elementary education major, noted that the iPad provides "easy access to information online" and enables her and her peers "to create projects and work with apps that we incorporate in our job settings." These sentiments as well as many similar experiences identified by other students indicate that the introduction of mobile devices across our campus provided access to learning and collaboration that have exceeded our expectations.

Students also appreciate the convenience of the iPad both in terms of access as well as its lightweight form factor and battery life. Students also indicated that the device helped them develop and maintain connections with peers, professors, and the institution. Community development inside and outside of the classroom is an overarching goal of the institution, and the iPad is one way in which that goal is realized. Freshman student Truman noted that having an iPad made the classroom "[m]ore interactive than just listening. I feel more connected to the class." Similarly, second-year nursing major Lauren stated, "I feel more connected with classmates and professors." For classroom use, the most common applications are through research, which include just-in-time and intensive research, and taking, accessing, and sharing course notes and materials. Kristen, a junior Special Education major, captured this sentiment, noting that the "iPad is useful for and annotating articles and presentations for research and reference."

Revisiting the "Biology I" study from above, focus group interviews revealed two common themes that encouraged the use of iPads in the classroom (Deaton, Deaton, Ivankovic, & Norris, 2013). First, allowing students to self-initiate how and when iPads are used in the classroom is valuable in regards to how they are able to organize their learning experience. Student-initiated use of iPads in the course promoted self-regulation and student ownership of the course materials. Teacher-encouraged uses (e.g., using ProScopes and web-based sharing of materials) provided the students with models for using the iPad to support learning. The professor-encouraged uses of the devices provided students with relevant apps for learning and practice with skills for using the devices during the learning experience. From the "Biology I" study, beliefs about the use of iPads for learning emerged. Students noted that using the iPad led to better understanding. One student noted, "We were able to be creative." Another stated, "We were able to make a movie to show our understanding." These student statements indicate that students enjoyed being engaged in the learning process and appreciated the ability to be creative, even in a Biology lab.

Summary

The MLI at Anderson has led to a transformation across its campus. Its most important impact, by design, is a change in the culture of teaching and learning. The faculty members are adaptive and willing to take risks in the design and delivery of their courses. In turn, students have been provided with engaging classroom experiences that ask them to be engaged participants inside and outside of the classroom. The integration of mobile devices and other emerging technologies has become a common and expected part of normal classroom activities, whether that be collecting and analyzing information and data, communicating inside and outside of the classroom, or developing media for course projects. The integration and use of iPads and technology in the classroom has become part of the fabric of the Anderson University learning experience.

CONCLUSION

As detailed throughout this chapter, there are several frameworks and models available to institutions to pursue mobile learning. As evidenced in the schools pursuing such a venture, several factors must be accounted for. At the heart of any successful mobile learning initiative is an institution-wide commitment that is aligned with the mission and a pursuit to enhance the learning experience. Simply providing technology to students and faculty members without purpose will inevitably lead to the demise of the initiative. Another factor that must be addressed is a commitment to professional development and ongoing support. Without that commitment institutions will have difficulty in developing and maintaining any momentum. Lastly, empower faculty and, when possible, students to be leaders in the initiative from the conception, development, and deployment phases. Ultimately, faculty members will be the hands to carry out the such an initiative and will either be its strongest champions or detractors.

REFERENCES

Anderson, M. (2015, October 29). Technology device ownership: 2015. *Pew Research Center: Internet, Science, and Technology*. Retrieved from http://www.pewinternet.org/2015/10/29/technology-device-ownership-2015/

Chen, B., Seilhamer, R., Bennett, L., & Bauer, S. (2015, June 22). Students' mobile learning practices in higher education: A multi-year study. *EDUCAUSE Review*. Retrieved from http://er.educause.edu/articles/2015/6/students-mobile-learning-practices-in-higher-education-a-multiyear-study

Crompton, H. (2013). Mobile learning: New approach, new theory. In Z. L. Berge & L. Y. Muilenburg (Eds.), *Handbook of Mobile Learning*. New York: Routledge.

Danaher, P., Gururajan, R., & Hafeez-Baig, A. (2009). Transforming the practice of mobile learning: Promoting pedagogical innovation through educational principles and strategies that work. In *Innovative Mobile Learning: Techniques and Strategies*. Hershey, PA: IGA Global. doi:10.4018/978-1-60566-062-2.ch002

Deaton, C. M., Deaton, B., Ivankovic, D., & Norris, F. A. (2013). Creating stop-motion videos with iPads to support students understanding of cell processes: "Because you have to know what youre talking about to be able to do it. *Journal of Digital Learning in Teacher Education*, *30*(2), 25–31. doi:10.1080/21532974.2013.10784729

Dennen, V. P., & Hao, S. (2014). Intentionally mobile pedagogy: The M-COPE framework for mobile learning in higher education. *Technology, Pedagogy and Education*, *23*(3), 397–419. doi:10.1080/1475939X.2014.943278

Dyson, L. E., Andrews, T., Smyth, R., & Wallace, R. (2013). Toward a holistic framework for ethical mobile learning. In Z. L. Berge & L. Y. Muilenburg (Eds.), *Handbook of Mobile Learning*. New York: Routledge.

Evans, B. (2016, March 29). *Mobile is eating the world*. Retrieved from http://ben-evans.com/benedictevans/2016/3/29/presentation-mobile-ate-the-world

Fenwick, T., Edwards, R., & Sawchuk, P. (2012). *Emerging approaches to educational research: Tracing the socio-material*. New York: Routledge.

Fenwick, T., & Landri, P. (2012). Materialities, textures and pedagogies: Sociomaterial assemblages in education. *Pedagogy, Culture & Society*, *20*(1), 1–7. doi:10.1080/14681366.2012.649421

Garrison, D. R., Anderson, T., & Archer, W. (2000). Critical inquiry in a text-based environment: Computer conferencing in higher education. *The Internet and Higher Education*, *2*(2-3), 87–105. doi:10.1016/S1096-7516(00)00016-6

Ge, X., Huang, D., Zhang, H., & Bowers, B. (2013). Three-dimension design for mobile learning. In Z. L. Berge & L. Y. Muilenburg (Eds.), *Handbook of Mobile Learning*. New York: Routledge.

Hunter, J. (2015). *Technology integration and high possibility classrooms: Building from TPACK*. New York: Routledge.

Hwang, G., & Tsai, C. (2011). Research trends in mobile and ubiquitous learning: A review of publications in selected journals from 2001 to 2010. *British Journal of Educational Technology*, *42*(1).

iLynn: College reimagined. (n. d.). Retrieved June 28, 2016 from http://www.lynn.edu/ilynn

Kearney, M., Schuck, S., Burden, K., & Aubusson, P. (2012). Viewing mobile learning from a pedagogical perspective. *Research in Learning Technology*, 20.

Koole, M. (2009). A model for framing mobile learning. In M. Ally (Ed.), *Mobile Learning: Transforming the Delivery Of Education And Training*. Edmonton: Athabasca University Governing Council.

Kukulska-Hulme, A., & Traxler, J. J. (Eds.). (2005). Mobile learning: A handbook for educators and trainers. New York: Routledge.

Latour, B. (1993). *We Have Never Been Modern* (C. Porter, Trans.). Cambridge, MA: Harvard University Press.

Lave, J., & Wenger, E. (1991). *Situated learning: Legitimate peripheral participation*. New York: Cambridge University Press. doi:10.1017/CBO9780511815355

Levene, J., & Seabury, H. (2015). Evaluation of mobile learning: Current research and implications for instructional designers. *TechTrends*, *59*(6), 46–52. doi:10.1007/s11528-015-0904-4

Martin, F., & Ertzberger, J. (2013). Here and now mobile learning: An experimental study on the use of mobile technology. *Computers & Education*, *68*, 76–85. doi:10.1016/j.compedu.2013.04.021

Mifsud, L. (2014). Mobile learning and the socio-materiality of classroom practices. *Learning, Media and Technology*, *39*(1), 142–149. doi:10.1080/17439884.2013.817420

Mishra, P., & Koehler, M. (2006). Technological pedagogical content knowledge: A framework for teacher knowledge. *Teachers College Record*, *108*(6), 1017–1054. doi:10.1111/j.1467-9620.2006.00684.x

Mobile Learning at ACU. (n.d.). Retrieved June 28, 2016 from http://www.acu.edu/technology/mobile-learning/

Moore, M. (1993). Theory of transactional distance. In D. Keegan (Ed.), *Theoretical Principles of Distance Education*. New York: Routledge.

Pachler, N., Bachmair, B., & Cook, J. (2010). *Mobile learning: Structures, agency, practices*. New York: Springer. doi:10.1007/978-1-4419-0585-7

Pachler, N., Bachmair, B., & Cook, J. (2013). Sociocultural ecological framework for m-learning. In Z. L. Berge & L. Y. Muilenburg (Eds.), *Handbook of Mobile Learning*. New York: Routledge.

Park, Y. (2011). A pedagogical framework for mobile learning: Categorizing educational applications of mobile technologies into four types. *International Review of Research in Open and Distance Learning*, *12*(2), 78–102. doi:10.19173/irrodl.v12i2.791

Puentedura, R. (2014). *SAMR: A contextualized introduction*. Retrieved May 3, 2016, from http://hippasus.com/rrpweblog

Quinn, C. N. (2011). *Designing mLearning: Tapping into the mobile revolution for organizational performance*. San Francisco: Pfeiffer.

Quinn, C. N. (2011). *The mobile academy: mLearning for higher education*. San Francisco: Jossey-Bass.

Sørensen, E. (2009). *Materiality of learning, technology and knowledge in educational practice*. New York: Cambridge University Press. doi:10.1017/CBO9780511576362

Sung, Y., Chang, K., & Liu, T. (2016, March). The effects of integrating mobile devices with teaching and learning on students learning performance: A meta-analysis and research synthesis. *Computers & Education*, *94*, 252–275. doi:10.1016/j.compedu.2015.11.008

Traxler, J. (2009). Current state of mobile learning. In M. Ally (Ed.), *Mobile Learning Transforming the Delivery of Education and Training*. Edmonton: Athabasca University Press.

Vavoula, G., & Sharples, M. (2009). Meeting the challenges in evaluating mobile learning: A 3-level evaluation framework. *International Journal of Mobile and Blended Learning*, *1*(2), 54–75. doi:10.4018/jmbl.2009040104

Woodill, G. (2010). *The mobile learning edge: Tools and technologies for developing your teams*. New York: McGraw-Hill.

Wu, W. H., Wu, Y. C., Chen, C. Y., Kao, H. Y., Lin, C. H., & Huang, S. H. (2012). Review of trends from mobile learning studies: A meta- analysis. *Computers & Education*, *59*(2), 817–827. doi:10.1016/j.compedu.2012.03.016

KEY TERMS AND DEFINITIONS

Flipped Classroom: An instructional method that involves moving lecture content outside of the classroom and using active learning techniques during class time.

Instructional Design: The design of learning experiences guided by educational theories and best practices.

Mobile Learning: The purposeful application of mobile devices in teaching and learning, also called mLearning.

Situated learning: The use of authentic environments and activities during the learning process.

Socio-Materiality: An awareness of the equal impact of social (human) and material (non-human) effects.

Transactional Distance: The cognitive space between instructor and learner as opposed to just the geographic space.

Ubiquitous Learning: The concept of anytime, anywhere learning that transcends formal and informal environments.

Chapter 6
Parochial School Teachers Instructional Use of the Interactive Whiteboard

Jillian R. Powers
Florida Atlantic University, USA

ABSTRACT

This chapter presents findings from a study that utilized Davis' (1989) Technology Acceptance Model (TAM) to investigate K-8 teachers' instructional usage of the interactive whiteboard (IWB). Through surveying 145 teachers and 40 administrators of the Lutheran Church Missouri Synod schools, the researcher used multiple regression and moderator analyses to examine whether the TAM model helped explain teachers' reported teacher-centered and student-centered instructional IWB use. The results of the study indicated two variables adapted from the TAM, teachers' perceived usefulness (PU) and perceived ease of use (PEOU) of the IWB, contributed to the prediction of teacher-centered instructional usage, and PU contributed to the prediction of student-centered instructional usage. Moderator analysis indicated the variable for teachers' technological pedagogical content knowledge of the IWB moderated the relationships between PEOU of the IWB and each teacher and student-centered instructional usage, as well as between PU of the IWB and teacher-centered instructional usage.

INTRODUCTION

Our society is evolving at rapid pace, challenging individuals and organizations to incorporate new technological tools into existing practice. Over the past decade, the interactive whiteboard (IWB) is a tool that has proven to be is valuable in teaching and learning (de Koster, Volman, & Kuiper, 2013). The body of literature on classroom IWB use suggests that the tool has the potential to foster positive learning outcomes in contexts from early childhood to the secondary level (Winzenried, Dalgarno, & Tinkler, 2010). According to Lee (2010), the IWB has had a powerful impact on transforming teaching from a traditional paper-based format to a digital mode.

DOI: 10.4018/978-1-5225-2838-8.ch006

However, research suggests that teachers do not necessarily utilize the technology that is available to them for instruction as they do for other purposes (Dorsen, Gibbs, Guerrero, & McDevitt, 2004). Specifically, Dorsen et al. (2004) wrote:

Schools may have all of the latest technological resources and systems in place so that students and faculty might have convenient access to this technology. The crucial factor in the digital divide equation is whether these tools are being used and how effectively they are being used in instructional settings. (p. 305)

If teacher utilization of available instructional technology tools is essential to closing this digital divide, naturally the question as to what motivates teachers to use instructional technology arises.

This chapter reports on a study that investigated a unique subset of teachers in the United States teaching in parochial schools within the Lutheran Church Missouri Synod. Specifically, the study that examined teachers' reported instructional usage of a popular form of instructional technology, the interactive whiteboard (IWB), and teacher reported variables identified in the research literature as factors influencing teachers' technology use. Understanding the extent to which teachers in this distinct parochial school setting adopted the IWB can help school leaders gain insight into how teachers adapt to a technologically advancing classroom.

Background

This study examined instructional interactive whiteboard use of a distinct group of kindergarten through 8th grade teachers working in The Lutheran Church Missouri Synod (LCMS) schools. For the purpose of brevity, such teachers will be referred to as K-8 teachers. The LCMS schools are the largest group of Protestant schools in the world (Pekari, 2011). There were 2,343 LCMS schools in the United States during the 2011-2012 school year, including 1,376 early childhood centers, 879 elementary schools, and 88 high schools, altogether which enrolled a total of 229,571 students (Cochran, 2012). That year, the racial background of students enrolled in U.S. LCMS schools was 82% White, 7% Black, 5% Hispanic, 3% Asian, and 3% other. The religious affiliation of enrolled students was reported to be 34% LCMS, 3% other Lutheran, 36% non-Lutheran, and 17% unchurched (Cochran, 2012). Schools serving kindergarten through 8th grade students within the LCMS system are referred to as elementary schools (Cochran, 2012). A national survey of LCMS schools during the 2011-2012 school year found that the average elementary school enrolled 110 students, employed 8 teachers, and had a student to full time teacher ratio of 14:1 (Cochran, 2012).

Lutheran school teachers vary in their religious affiliation and may be designated as rostered LCMS, which refers to teachers who were synodically trained in a LCMS teacher education program, or non-rostered, which refers to teachers who were not synodically trained. During the 2011-2012 school year 6,000 LCMS teachers were synodically trained LCMS rostered teachers. The religious affiliation of the remainder of the teachers was 5,500 non-rostered LCMS, 3,800 non-rostered non-LCMS, and 2,700 non-rostered from an unidentified affiliation (Cochran, 2012).

Many Lutheran schools educate students on a lower budget than public schools. The average per pupil expenditure at LCMS elementary schools in the U.S. for the 2011-2012 school year was $6,325 (Cochran, 2012). Salaries for teachers with a bachelor's degree averaged $33,132 in the 2011-2012 school year and $38,672 for a master's degree (Cochran, 2012). Sources of funding included congregation budget (20%),

Figure 1. Refined technology acceptance model (Adapted from Davis & Venkatesh, 1996, p. 20)

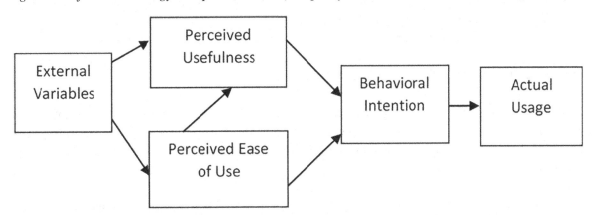

tuition and fees (67%), and other (13%) (Cochran, 2012). In contrast, public elementary and secondary schools spent an average of $10,297 per pupil and $49,630 on teacher base salaries for the 2007 – 2008 school year (National Center for Education Statistics, 2011). Understanding K-8 teachers' instructional usage of the IWB may help school leaders to better understand how technology is shaping the landscape of parochial education in the U.S., but may also offer a good example of teachers' technology integration within the constraints of limited financial resources.

THEORETICAL FRAMEWORK

The present study utilized the Technology Acceptance Model (TAM) as a theoretical lens for examining teachers' usage of the IWB as an instructional tool. The TAM has been used as a framework examining technology usage among a wide variety of technologies, users, and settings. The TAM was developed by researchers at IBM in the mid-1980s to evaluate the market potential of emerging computer-based applications (Davis & Venkatesh, 1996). The TAM posits that two fundamental variables, perceived usefulness (PU) and perceived ease of use (PEOU) influence one's behavioral intention (BI) to use a technology, and that BI influences actual system usage of the technology (Bogazzi, 2007, p. 244). Davis (1989) described PU as "the degree to which a person believes that using a particular system would enhance his or her job performance" and PEOU as "the degree to which a person believes that using a particular system would be free of effort" (Davis, 1989, p. 320). Davis, Bogazzi, and Warshaw (1989) also theorized that external variables specific to a given setting "provide the bridge between the internal beliefs, attitudes and intentions represented in the TAM and the various individual differences, situational constraints, and managerially controllable interventions impinging on behavior" (Davis et al., 1989, p. 998). Examples of external variables may include user support consultants, training, documentation, and educational programs concerning the merits a given system (Davis, 1989). The TAM has been refined via several TAM studies, and was depicted by Davis and Venkatesh (1996) as shown in Figure 1.

According to Davis and Venkatesh (1996), "TAM has proven to be among the most effective models in the information systems literature for predicting user acceptance and usage behavior" (p. 21). Researchers have used the model to study government employees acceptance of e-mail and word processing (Burton-Jones & Hubona, 2006), college students' Internet usage (Alshare & Alkhateeb, 2008), and teachers' acceptance of web-based learning (Gong, Xu, & Yu, 2004). The TAM has been found to explain up to 40% of behavioral intention to use and 30% of actual systems usage (Burton-Jones & Hubona, 2006). It is for these reasons that the TAM was used as a theoretical framework for the current study.

Study Purpose and Research Questions

The purpose of this chapter is to present a research study examined whether the Technology Acceptance Model (TAM) (Davis, 1989) helped predict K-8 Lutheran school teachers' (K-8 teachers) reported instructional usage of the interactive whiteboard (IWB). Specifically the following research questions were asked:

1. To what degree do K-8 teachers' perceived ease of use of the IWB and perceived usefulness of the IWB predict their reported instructional IWB usage?
2. Is the relationship between K-8 teachers' perceived ease of use of the IWB and their reported instructional IWB usage moderated by teacher and organizational variables?
3. Is the relationship between K-8 teachers' perceived usefulness of the IWB and their reported instructional IWB usage moderated by teacher and organizational variables?

The study aimed to help inform school leaders and policymakers about the technology adoption process as it pertains to K-8 teachers and the factors that influence teachers' instructional IWB use.

LITERATURE REVIEW

In order to develop a list of possible external variables that may influence the relationship between teachers' perceived usefulness, perceived ease of use and instructional IWB use, the researcher conducted a review of the literature on both classroom IWB usage and the usage of instructional technologies in general. In the section that follows, the results of this literature review are presented, beginning with an examination of the factors influencing teachers overall technology usage.

Factors Influencing Teachers' Technology Usage

Research suggests that both teacher and organizational characteristics need to be examined in order to understand the variables associated with teachers' instructional technology use (O'Dwyer, Russell, & Bebell, 2004). For example, O'Dwyer et al. (2004) analyzed data from the *Use, Support, and Effect of Instructional Technology* (USEIT) study, examining 22 school districts in Massachusetts and conducted hierarchical linear modeling of several teacher and school district factors and teacher technology use. Specifically, four types of technology use were examined: (a) teachers' use of technology for delivering instruction, (b) teacher-directed student use of technology during class time, (c) teacher-directed student use of technology to create products, and (d) teachers' use of technology for class preparation (O'Dwyer et al., 2004). The results indicated that most of the variability in each type of teachers' computer use existed within the schools, and a significant proportion existed between schools (O'Dwyer et al., 2004). The study revealed that much of the within school variance was explained by individual teacher characteristics, such as pedagogical beliefs and computer confidence.

Table 1. Teacher characteristics associated with teachers' technology usage

	Gender	Teaching Experience	Computer Experience	Computer Confidence
Findings	• Female teachers reported using computers for instructional purposes significantly more than male teachers (Wozney et al., 2006) • Male teachers were more likely to use computers in school settings (Mathews & Guarino, 2000). • Male teachers reported using computers for communicative, analytic, expansive, and creative purposes significantly more than female teachers (Wozney et al., 2006).	• Years of teaching experience was not statistically different among teachers who were deemed high and low technology integrators (Mueller et al., 2008) • Teachers with more years of teaching experience were more likely to use technology in school settings (Mathews & Guarino, 2000). • When asked, "Do you integrate technology into your lesson plans whenever possible?" 46.3% of teachers with less than 5 years of experience responded "yes", compared to 73.8% with 6 to 10 years, and 60.9% with over 11 years (Hernandez-Ramos, 2005).	• Computer experience was found to be a significant predictor of teachers' classroom computer use (Hermans et al., 2008). • Teachers' self-reported use of computers at home and at school yielded strong coefficients via multivariate analysis (Mueller et al., 2008). • The greatest predictor of teachers' classroom technology usage was found to be the amount of time teachers used computers for personal use outside of teaching (Wozney et al., 2006).	• A higher level of teacher confidence using technology was associated with increased use for delivering instruction (O'Dwyer et al., 2004). • Teachers' self-reported computer ability was found to be a predictor of classroom computer use (Mathews & Guarino, 2000). • The following survey item predicted a meaningful proportion of the variance in teachers' technology use: computer technology in the classroom "Is effective because I believe I can implement it successfully" (Wozney et al., 2006, p. 190).

Teacher Characteristics

Numerous scholars have studied how teacher characteristics influence teachers' classroom technology usage. Some of the factors that have been explored include gender (Mathews & Guarino, 2000; Norris, Sullivan, Poirot, & Soloway, 2003; Wozney, Venkatesh, & Abrami, 2006), years of teaching experience (Hernandez-Ramos, 2005; Mathews & Guarino, 2000; Mueller, Wood, Willoughby, Ross, & Specht, 2008), teachers' computer experience (Hermans, Tondeur, Van Braak, & Valcke, 2008, Mueller et al., 2008; Wozney et al. 2006), and computer confidence (Mathews & Guarino, 2000; O'Dwyer et al., 2004; Wozney et al., 2006). The matrix in Table 1 summarizes the research literature on key teacher characteristics associated with teachers' usage and adoption of instructional technology.

The matrix illustrates how different teaching and technology backgrounds as well as unalterable characteristics such as gender may shape teachers instructional technology use.

Technological Pedagogical Content Knowledge

Scholars have also suggested that a teacher's knowledge of how to teach specific subject matter is plays a role in instructional effectiveness. Shulman (1986) posited that teachers need more than knowledge of subject matter and pedagogical strategies to be effective. He contended that three forms of teacher knowledge were essential: content knowledge, pedagogical knowledge, and pedagogical content knowledge (PCK). Pedagogical content knowledge refers to a teacher's understanding of which pedagogical strategies effectively represent the subject in a comprehensible way, combined with an understanding of what makes it easy or difficult for students of different ages to learn specific subject matter (Shulman, 1986). According to Schulman, teachers who possess the relevant PCK are able "to transform the content knowledge he or she possesses into forms that are pedagogically powerful and yet adaptive to the variations in ability and background presented by students" (Shulman, 1986, p. 15).

Since Shulman's (1986) landmark theory, scholars have considered how PCK relates to how to effectively teach with technological tools in the classroom. Mishra and Koehler (2006) offered a framework of technological pedagogical content knowledge (TPACK) for understanding this process. Specifically, Mishra and Koehler (2006) refer to TPACK as:

Knowledge of the existence, components, and capabilities of various technologies as they are used in teaching and learning settings, and conversely, knowing how teaching might change as the result of using particular technologies. (p. 1028)

Mishra and Koehler (2006) contended that TPACK lies at the intersection of three forms of teacher knowledge: (a) pedagogical content knowledge (PCK), (b) technological content knowledge (TCK), and (c) technological pedagogical knowledge (TPK). The framework serves as a lens for understanding the role that different types of knowledge play in classroom technology integration (Harris, Mishra, & Koehler, 2009).

Organizational Factors

The body of literature on teachers' technology use also examined ways that organizational factors influence teachers' technology usage. O'Dwyer et al. (2004) noted, "although the majority of variability in each use [of technology] exists among teachers within schools, a significant proportion of the variability lies between schools" (p. 12). Hermans et al. (2008) confirmed these findings in an investigation of teachers' beliefs and the use of computers in the classroom. In the study, 18% of the variance in teachers' classroom technology use was explained by school level factors. As a result, the researchers suggested that further study of "specific school conditions and school culture variables" is warranted (Hermans et al., 2008, p. 1507).

Table 2. Organizational characteristics associated with teachers' technology usage

	Findings by Organizational Characteristic
School Technology Support	• Franklin (2007), found that that personnel support was associated with teachers' classroom computer use. • Sandholtz et al. (1997) reported that the quality of school technology support was an important factor to encourage teachers to change their technology-related teaching practices.
Access and Availability of Technology	• Franklin (2007), found that that access and availability were associated with teachers' classroom computer use.
Administrators Pressure to Use Technology	• O'Dwyer et al.'s (2004) found that teachers' perceived administrative pressure to use technology and the availability of technology were significant predictors of teachers' use of technology for delivering instruction. • Franklin (2007) found that incentives influenced teachers' use of technology in the classroom.
Principal Technology PD	• Research conducted by Dawson and Rakes (2003) found a significant difference between groups of principals receiving the fewest hours of technology training and those receiving the most hours. • Dawson and Rakes (2003) found that principals that received training based on basic computer applications and operations, significantly differed from those receiving training on technology integration, with the latter group exhibiting higher levels of classroom computer integration in their school.
School Size and Grade Level	• Dawson and Rakes (2003) found no significant differences in technology integration between schools grouped by size or grade level.

Several studies examined the relationship between a variety of organizational factors and teachers' use of technology in the classroom (Dawson & Rakes, 2003; Franklin, 2007; O'Dwyer et al., 2004; Sandholtz, Ringstaff, & Dwyer, 1997). The matrix in Table 2 summarizes the research literature on key organizational characteristics associated with teachers' usage and adoption of instructional technology.

As noted in Table 2, organizational characteristics accounted for a significant amount of the differences in teachers' technology use, and therefore are important to consider when examining teachers' adoption and usage of instructional technology.

Professional Development

According to Means (2008), "teachers feel uncomfortable introducing something into their classrooms that they cannot use proficiently themselves" (p. 130). This statement is consistent with the research on teachers' adoption of instructional technologies and professional development (PD). The research literature in the area indicates that both the quantity and the quality of technology-related PD are factors associated with teachers' instructional technology use (Mueller et al., 2008; O'Dwyer et al., 2004; Vannatta & Fordham, 2004; Watson, 2006; Wells, 2007). It is important to note that factors such as the quantity of PD taken are teacher PD characteristics, whereas availability, variety, quality, and the duration of the training program are organizational. The matrix in Table 3 summarizes the research literature on technology PD and teachers' usage and adoption of instructional technology organized by whether the variable is a teacher or organized characteristic.

Table 3. Teacher and organizational technology PD characteristics associated with teachers' technology usage

	Teacher Characteristics
Technology PD Quantity	• Vannatta and Fordham (2004) found that the amount of teacher-reported technology training was a strong predictor of classroom technology use. • Mueller et al. (2008) found that teacher-reported number of technology workshops attended was positively associated with elementary teachers' level of technology integration in the classroom.
	Organizational Characteristics
Variety of Available Technology PD	• O'Dwyer et al. (2004) found a positive significant relationship between teacher-reported variety of available technology-related PD and the variable teachers' use of technology for delivering instruction.
Durations of Technology PD	• Analysis of data collected about 389 teachers before, immediately after, and six years following training demonstrated that teachers' technology self-efficacy gains from the PD endured six years after the training (Watson, 2006). • In the same study, Watson (2006) also found that participants who had engaged in follow-up technology training possessed greater self-efficacy in integrating the Internet into their curriculum than those that did not.
Quality of Technology PD	• O'Dwyer et al. (2004) found that teacher-reported poor PD was a significant obstacle for teachers' use of technology for delivering instruction. • Wells (2007) found that the following key design elements of PD promoted change in teachers' instructional technology practices: (a) duration of process, including both contact hours and span of time (b) learner oriented, specifically focusing on content, theory, and pedagogy rather than technology skills in isolation, (c) engagement, particularly with the technology, (d) collaborative, or teachers working with instructional leaders and each other, and (e) support, both technical and pedagogical over the long term.

In sum, these findings demonstrate that both teacher characteristics such as the quantity of technology PD as well as organizational characteristics such as the variety, duration, and quality of the PD offered are important variables to consider in the study of teachers' technology usage.

Research on Teachers' IWB Usage

Research on the use of the IWB by teachers indicates that the tool has been adopted by teachers more readily than other forms of instructional technologies (Bennett & Lockyer, 2008; Lee, 2010; Winzenried et al., 2010). For example, Winzenried, Dalgarno, and Tinkler (2010) conducted case studies of six primary and secondary teachers in two rural Australian schools. The research focused on teachers' perspectives on the impact of the IWB on their teaching practice. The researchers found that in all of the cases teachers were enthusiastic, able to grow and evolve in their IWB teaching practices, and perceived improvements in student engagement associated with the IWB (Winzenried et al., 2010). Similarly, Bennett and Lockyer (2008) examined four Australian teachers' IWB usage and discovered that all of the observed teachers found the IWB easy to use and were able to readily integrate it into instruction.

Another line of inquiry in the research literature on teachers' IWB usage is the diversity of ways in which teachers use the IWB as an instructional and motivational tool. Winzenried et al. (2010) found that the SMART Notebook software provided with SMART Board brand IWBs was the most common application used by the primary teachers studied. The teachers mainly used the presentation and interactive elements, and a few of the teachers mentioned that they had used the software to create their own SMART Notebook resources (Winzenried et al., 2010). The researchers also found that primary grade teachers sometimes used their IWBs as a motivational reward by allowing students to play on it after finishing their work (Winzenried et al., 2010). On the other hand, the secondary teachers Winzenried et al. (2010) studied regularly used their IWBs to show PowerPoint presentations, both teacher and student developed, and to present Internet resources such as informational web pages, Google Maps, and YouTube videos.

Other research seeks to explain the various types of IWB usage among teachers by proposing stages or levels of IWB use. For example, Kennewell (2006) proposed four categories of IWB use for teachers which are as follows: (a) the Consultant, who uses the IWB for providing information, such as prepared questions and answers or ad hoc internet searching; (b) the Organizer, who uses the IWB for structured, but unpredictable activities, such as games; (c) the Facilitator, who use the IWB with even looser structure and focuses on activities involving choice; and (d) the Repository, who uses the IWB to enable students' ideas to be recorded for later revisiting, reflection, and revision. Kennewell's (2006) framework may help researchers understand how teachers grow in their repertoire of instructional practices with the IWB.

Summary

The current section of this chapter summarized the research on factors associated with teachers' usage of technology in the classroom. The influence of teacher characteristics, including gender, teaching experience, computer experience, computer confidence, TPACK, and technology professional development were examined. In addition, the research on how teachers use the IWB as an instructional tool was discussed. The review of this literature helped the research identify possible external variables that might help explain teachers' PU and PEOU and actual technology usage as posited by the TAM.

METHODOLOGY

Population and Sample

As noted earlier, educators from Lutheran Church Missouri Synod (LCMS) schools were the population of study presented in this chapter. LCMS schools represent the second largest group of parochial schools in the world. In 2012, there were 849 LCMS schools serving students in Prekindergarten through 8th grade in the United States (Cochran, 2012). In the spring of 2013, 361 K-8 teachers and 40 administrators in 40 LCMS schools across the South, Midwest, and Southwest of the United States were surveyed. A total of 28 (70%) of administrators responded to the administrator survey and 155 teachers (42.9%) of responded to the teacher survey. It should be noted that only teachers from schools with 50% or more of K-8 classrooms equipped with IWBs were included in the study.

Teacher Survey

The teacher survey gathered teacher self-reported data on teacher demographic and background characteristics, TAM components (PU, PEOU, and instructional IWB sage), and teacher and organizational characteristics from the literature review that were deemed to be possible external variables in the TAM

Table 4. Items measured in the teacher survey

Item Category	Items Included
Demographic and Background Characteristics	• gender (1 item) • grade level/s taught (1 item) • subject/s taught (1 item) • teaching experience (1 item) • highest degree completed (1 item) • IWB availability (1 item) • IWB type (1 item)
TAM Components	IWB instructional usage • TCIU (4 items) o TCIU use of web-based content during instruction o TCIU use of presentation software during instruction o TCIU use of electronic pens during instruction o TCIU use of IWB software tools during instruction • SCIU (4 items) o SCIU use of web-based content during instruction o SCIU use of presentation software during instruction o SCIU use of electronic pens during instruction o SCIU use of IWB software tools during instruction • Perceived usefulness of the IWB (3 items) • Perceived ease of use of the IWB (3 items)
Teacher and Organizational Characteristics	• Teacher Characteristic o computer experience (1 item) o IWB experience (1 item) o quantity of IWB PD (1 item) o IWB TPACK (4 items) • Organizational Characteristics o IWB planning time (1 item) o organization IWB PD (2 items) o IWB technical support (2 items)

model. In order to distinguish between ways the IWB is used during instruction both teacher-centered instructional usage (TCIU) and student-centered instructional usage of the IWB (SCIU) were measured. Teacher-centered instructional usage of the IWB was defined as "instruction during which the teacher controls the IWB and student-centered instructional usage refers to instruction during which students were provided with opportunities to interact with the IWB (Powers, 2014). A summary of the items measured in the teacher survey are presented in Table 4.

With permission, the TAM components included in the survey were adapted from those used by Davis' (1989). Teachers' reported TPACK of the IWB were measured using four items adapted from Schmidt et al. (2009.)

Administrator Survey

The administrator survey collected data regarding organizational variables, including the number of K-8 IWBs in the school. Data regarding the total number of IWBs, the number of K-8 IWBs in classrooms by grade level, and the number of K-8 classrooms was gathered by asking participants to provide the total number for each of the aforementioned items. This information was used to determine the concentration of K-8 IWBs in each school and to calculate the K-8 teacher survey response rate.

The administrator survey also gathered information regarding administrators' emphasis on technology. This information enabled the researcher to examine whether a school administrator's emphasis on technology served as an external variable in the relationship between PU and PEOU, and instructional usage of the IWB. Administrators were asked to indicate their level of agreement with three items that were used to construct this measure: (a) using technology to improve classroom instruction is important in my vision as a school leader, (b) increasing teacher proficiency in the use of technology is important in my vision as a school leader, and (c) allocating financial resources dedicated to technology in the school budget is important in my vision as a school leader. The items used a 5 point Likert-scale ranging from "strongly agree" and "strongly disagree" as endpoints. The responses to each item were assigned a point value of 5, 4, 3, 2 and 1 respectively. Then, the points for each of these items for each respondent were summed to obtain a single resultant score for administrator reported emphasis on technology.

Validity and Reliability

This study described in this chapter addressed the issues of validity and reliability in the following ways. A pilot teacher survey instrument was modified based on participant feedback. The pilot instrument was reviewed by two K-8 teachers and an instructional technologist and examined for face validity and item clarity. Content validity of the teacher survey was addressed for a number of measures because they were adapted from existing published instruments. Also, the administrator survey was reviewed by two school administrators and examined for face validity and to ensure the items were clear and accurate. The reliability of each of the instruments may be influenced by each respondents' motivation and memory when answering the questions.

Data Analysis

The survey data was entered in to a statistical software package for analysis purposes. Items that were part of a construct were summed to obtain a resultant single score. Cronbach's alphas were calculated to provide an overall measure of reliability for variables constructed from multiple items. The results of the survey were then summarized by reporting descriptive statistics for each of the quantitative measures.

Next, a series of regression analyses were conducted to answer the research questions posed by the study. In order to differentiate between usage that involved teacher-centered and student-centered interaction with the IWB during instruction, teacher-centered instructional usage of the IWB served as the dependent variable in the first series of regressions (Series 1), and then the regressions were repeated with student-centered instructional usage of the IWB serving as the dependent variable (Series 2). The first model in each series was a simple linear model, which addressed research question 1, and hence determine whether PU and PEOU were significant predictors of instructional usage of the IWB. The remaining regression models used product terms to examine possible moderating effects of teacher and organizational variables on the relationship between perceived ease of use and perceived usefulness of the IWB and both types of instructional IWB usage. These moderator analyses were used to answer research questions 2 and 3. Research questions 2 and 3 included three predictor variables in each model (i.e., PU or PEOU of the IWB, a moderator variable, and a product term). The level of significance for each of the regression models was set at an alpha of .05.

RESULTS

Administrator Survey Participants

A total of 40 administrators were surveyed, 28 (65%) responded to the survey, 15 (54%) via paper and 13 (46%) were electronic format. Two items on the questionnaire were used to verify the concentration of IWBs for K-8 teachers in each school: (a) "How many classrooms do you have in your school in each of the following grade levels?" and (b) "How many IWBs do you have in classrooms in each of the following grade levels or K-8 enrichment classrooms?" The concentration of IWBs in each school was calculated by dividing the total number of K-8 classrooms with IWBs by the total number of K-8 classrooms. The results confirmed that 100% of the schools participating in the study met the criteria of having a concentration of IWBs that was 50% or greater. This was not surprising because prior to administering the survey, the researcher contacted school administrators by e-mail and telephone to confirm that the schools had IWBs on campus.

Administrators were also asked to indicate their level of agreement with three items regarding their level of emphasis on technology in their school. The items were measured using a 5 point Likert-type scale ranging from "strongly agree" to "strongly disagree." The three items were, (a) Using technology to improve classroom instruction is important in my vision as a school leader, (b) Increasing teacher proficiency in the use of technology is important in my vision as a school leader, and (c) Allocating financial resources dedicated to technology in the school budget is important in my vision as a school leader. A total of 2 administrators indicated that they "agree" to each of the aforementioned items. The remainder of the responses to each of the items measuring administrator emphasis on technology were "strongly agree."

Teacher Survey Participants

A total of 361 teacher surveys were sent, 230 of which were sent in paper and 131 of which were electronic. A total of 109 (47.3%) of the teachers returned paper surveys and 46 (35.1%) responded to electronic surveys. Descriptive statistics were used to paint a picture of the respondents' demographic and background characteristics. These results are summarized in Table 5.

The grade levels taught by the teachers in the study are summarized in Table 6, the teachers represented every grade level of interest in the study from kindergarten through 8th grade, with a greater percentage of teachers representing the upper grades (6 through 8).

Table 5. Descriptive statistics of the teacher survey participants

Variable	Descriptive Statistics
Highest degree completed	• 1.3% of respondents had attained an associate's degree, 66.5% a bachelor's, and 32.3% a master's
Gender	• 15.5% of the responding K-8 teachers indicated that their gender was male and 84.5% responded female
Teaching experience	• Teachers reported teaching for as few as 1 and as many as 47 years, for an average of 17.6 years (SD =11.68)
IWB Access	• A total of 137 (88.4%) participants indicated, "I have an IWB in the classroom in which I primarily teach," 5 (3.2%) indicated, "I have access to an IWB in a shared classroom," 2 (1.3%) indicated " I have access to a mobile IWB that I can bring to my classroom," 7 (4.5%) indicated " I do not have access to an IWB in my classroom," 2 (1.3%) indicated, "I prefer not to answer," and 2 (1.3%) indicated "other"
IWB Type	• A total of 106 (68.4%) participants indicated that they had a SMART Board, 17 (11.0%) a Promethean Board, 18 (11.6%) a Mimio, and some teachers described other brands of IWBs that included 2 (1.3%) Eno and 12 (7.7%) Mobi.
Subject Taught	• The majority of teachers taught core subjects including Religion (73.5%), Reading/Literature (70.3%), Language Arts/English (67.7%), Mathematics (74.8%), Science (64.5%), and Social Studies/History (65.2%). Some participants taught enrichment subjects, which included Computers/Technology (21.9%), Physical Education (15.5%), Art (34.2%), Music (11.6%), and Foreign Language (3.9%).

Table 6. Descriptive statistics for teachers' grade level taught of teacher survey participants (Powers, 2014)

Subject	Frequency	Percent
Kindergarten	26	16.8
1st Grade	32	20.6
2nd Grade	31	20.0
3rd Grade	35	22.6
4th Grade	33	21.3
5th Grade	39	25.2
6th Grade	62	40.0
7th Grade	63	40.6
8th Grade	62	40.0

Participants Included in the Regression Analyses

Only K-8 teachers who reported having access to an IWB in a classroom in which they taught were included in the quantitative analyses. Therefore, only K-8 teachers reporting access to a SMART Board, Promethean Board, Mimio, or Eno Board were included. A total of 143 participants met this criteria. Those K-8 teachers reporting access to a Mobi interactive tablet were not included because the device did not fit the definition of an IWB as set forth in this study.

Method of Summing Variables

In order to handle the issue of missing data, the sums of all scale variables were calculated by estimating them from the mean of the variables used in their construction. In order to do so, all items were required to be measured on the same scale. The researcher specified the number of variables that were allowed to be missing in order for the target variable to be computed. With the exception of the variable K-8 teachers' technological pedagogical content knowledge of the IWB, the rationale for which will be described later, all summed variables were set at the *X-1* criteria for inclusion in the calculation. That is, the sum of a given target variable was only calculated if a total of *X-1* variables were reported. If less than *X-1* of the variables were observed, the target variable was coded system missing. Finally, for those variables that met the *X-1* criteria, the sum of the target variable was calculated by multiplying the mean of the variables from the scale by *X-1*.

Description of the Variables

Scores for teacher-centered and student-centered instructional usage of the IWB were computed by summing teachers' responses to four teacher survey items. As noted earlier, teacher-centered instructional usage was measured with four items: (a) "I demonstrate web-based content," (b) "I present content using PowerPoint or other presentation software," (c) "I use electronic pens," and (d) "I use IWB software tools (i.e. SMART Notebook, Promethean ActivOffice, MimioStudio)." For student-centered instructional usage, the four teacher survey items were: (a) "My students interact with web-based content," (b) "My students interact with presentation software," (c)" My students use electronic pens," and (d) "My students use IWB software tools." Cronbach's alphas were calculated to provide an overall measure of reliability for the set of variables. Descriptive statistics and Cronbach's alphas for K-8 teachers reported teacher-centered and student-centered instructional usage of the IWB are presented in Table 7.

Scores for the variables K-8 teachers' perceived ease of use of the IWB and perceived usefulness of the IWB were computed by summing responses to three teacher survey items. For K-8 teachers' perceived

Table 7. Descriptive statistics for K-8 teachers' reported teacher-centered and student-centered Instructional usage of the IWB (Powers, 2014)

Variable	N	Min	Max	Mean	Standard Deviation	Cronbach's Alpha
Teacher-centered instructional usage of the IWB	140	4.00	20.00	14.52	3.50	.668
Student-centered instructional usage of the IWB	132	4.00	20.00	12.51	3.58	.740

Table 8. Descriptive statistics for K-8 teachers' reported perceived ease of use perceived usefulness of the IWB (Powers, 2014)

Variable	N	Min	Max	Mean	Standard Deviation	Cronbach's Alpha
Perceived ease of use of the IWB	142	4.00	15.00	11.03	2.69	.890
Perceived usefulness of the IWB	142	4.00	15.00	12.28	2.59	.947

ease of use of the IWB, the three items included: (a) "Learning to operate the IWB is easy for me," (b) "I find it easy to get the IWB to do what I want it to do," and (c) "I find the IWB to be flexible to interact with." For K-8 teachers' perceived usefulness of the IWB, the three items were: (a) "Using the IWB increases my productivity," (b) "Using the IWB enhances my instructional effectiveness," and (c) "I find the IWB useful in my teaching." Again, Cronbach's alphas were calculated to provide an overall measure of reliability for the set of items. Descriptive statistics and Cronbach's alphas for K-8 teachers reported perceived ease of use of the IWB and perceived usefulness of the IWB are presented in Table 8.

Calculation of Moderator Terms

Research questions 2 through 3 sought to determine whether certain teacher or organizational variables moderated the relationship between K-8 teachers' instructional usage of the IWB and each perceived ease of use of the IWB and perceived usefulness of the IWB. In order to calculate the necessary moderator terms, sums for the teacher and organizational variables that were measured using more than one survey item had to first be computed.

Teacher Variables Computed

Three teacher survey items were summed to calculate the variable K-8 teachers' reported quantity of technology professional development. The items were measured on a four point scale ("0 hours," "1-20 hours," "21-60 hours," and "more than 60 hours") and included: (a) "IWB training," (b) "Other computer software/hardware training," and (c) "Methods of integrating technology into the classroom."

The variable K-8 teachers' reported TPACK of the IWB was measured with four teacher survey items: (a) "I can teach lessons that combine mathematics, the IWB and teaching approaches," (b) "I can teach lessons that combine literacy, the IWB and teaching approaches," (c) "I can teach lessons that combine science, the IWB and teaching approaches," and (d) "I can teach lessons that combine social studies, the IWB and teaching approaches." The sum of K-8 teachers' reported TPACK of the IWB was obtained by calculating the mean of the four items and then multiplying by three. The rationale for multiplying by three, and therefore not following the *N-1* criteria that was set in summing all other variables was due to the unique nature and meaning of this variable. This was because K-8 teachers' reported TPACK of the IWB in mathematics, literacy, science, or social studies only mattered if a teacher was actually teaching that subject. Elementary teachers often team-teach, or focus on just a few subjects. Middle school teachers may only teach one subject. Therefore, possessing technological pedagogical content knowledge of the IWB in all subjects is not applicable for all teachers. At the same time, it was necessary to compute comparable values in the summing procedure. As a result, the researcher opted to multiply the mean by three to produce comparable sums. This solved the problem of potentially excluding teachers for whom possessing TPACK in only one subject was applicable to them.

Organizational Variables Computed

Two teacher survey items were used to measure the organizational variables K-8 teachers' reported IWB professional development opportunities and K-8 teachers' reported IWB technical support at their school. The items asked participants describe the level of quality and availability of IWB professional development opportunities and IWB technical support at their school. The items were measured on a Likert-type scale ranging from extremely high to extremely low. The variables K-8 teachers' reported IWB professional development opportunities and K-8 teachers' reported IWB technical support were computed by summing the survey items used to measure each.

Finally, the variable administrator reported emphasis on technology was computed by summing responses to three items from the administrator survey. On the survey, administrators were asked to indicate their level of agreement with each of the following statements: (a) "Using technology to improve classroom instruction is important in my vision as a school leader," (b) "Increasing teacher proficiency in the use of technology is important in my vision as a school leader," and (c) "Allocating financial resources dedicated to technology in the school budget is important in my vision as a school leader."

Cronbach's alphas were calculated for all of the teacher and organizational variables that were computed to provide an overall measure of reliability for the set of variables and are presented in Table 9.

Table 9. Descriptive statistics for teacher and organizational variables (Powers, 2014)

Variable	N	Min	Max	Mean	Standard Deviation	Cronbach's Alpha
Teacher Variables						
K-8 teachers' reported computer experience	143	1.00	4.00	2.42	1.04	NA*
K-8 teachers' reported IWB experience	135	2.00	4.00	3.79	0.46	NA
K-8 teachers' reported quantity of technology professional development	143	3.00	12.00	8.70	1.46	.683
K-8 teachers' reported technological pedagogical content knowledge of the IWB	137	6.67	20.00	17.03	2.83	.751
Organizational Variables						
K-8 teachers' reported IWB professional development opportunities	127	2.00	10.00	5.99	1.88	.794
K-8 teachers' reported time to plan for IWB use	139	1.00	5.00	2.93	1.06	NA
K-8 teachers' reported IWB technical support	139	2.00	10.00	6.39	1.95	.859
Administrator reported emphasis on technology	116	11.00	15.00	14.72	.80	.793

* NA indicates a variable that was comprised of only one survey item and the calculation of a Cronbach's was not applicable.

Research Question 1

Multiple regression was conducted to address research question 1, "To what degree do K-8 teachers' perceived ease of use of the IWB and perceived usefulness of the IWB predict their reported instructional IWB usage?" In the Series 1 regression for research question 1, K-8 teachers' reported teacher-centered instructional usage of the IWB served as the criterion variable and the predictor variables entered into the analysis were K-8 teachers' perceived ease of use of the IWB and perceived usefulness of the IWB.

Table 10 lists the results of the Series 1 regression that indicated K-8 teachers' perceived ease of use of the IWB and perceived usefulness of the IWB contributed to the prediction of teacher-centered instructional usage of the IWB. The model summary showed that the squared multiple correlation was 0.374, indicating that 37.4% of the variance in the criterion variable was explained by the model, adjusted $R^2 = 0.364$, F (2, 139) = 40.848, p =.001. The effects of multicollinearity appear to have been minimal because collinearity diagnostics for each predictor yielded a VIF of less than 10. Since p was less than alpha the null hypotheses were rejected. As shown in Table 10, the results of multiple regression analysis showed that both K-8 teachers' perceived ease of use of the IWB (p =.015) and perceived usefulness of the IWB (p =.001) accounted for a significant amount of variability in the criterion variable teacher-centered instructional usage of the IWB.

In the Series 2 regression for research question 1, K-8 teacher reported student-centered instructional usage of the IWB served as the criterion variable and the predictor variables entered into the analysis were again K-8 teachers' perceived ease of use of the IWB and perceived usefulness of the IWB.

Table 11 presents the results, which indicated that K-8 teachers' perceived usefulness of the IWB contributed to the prediction of teacher reported student-centered instructional usage. However, the results indicated that K-8 teachers' perceived ease of use of the IWB did not make a significant contribution to the model. The model summary yielded a squared multiple correlation coefficient of 0.237, indicating that 23.7% of the variance in the criterion variable was explained by the model, adjusted $R^2 = 0.225$, F (2, 131) = 20.056, p =.001. The effects of multicollinearity appeared to have been minimal because

Table 10. Regression analysis for predictor variables teachers' perceived ease of use and perceived usefulness of the IWB and the criterion variable teachers' reported teacher-centered instructional usage of the IWB (Powers, 2014)

Predictor	B	Std. Error	Beta	t	p	VIF
Perceived ease of use of the IWB	.307	.124	.237	2.475	.015	2.002
Perceived usefulness of the IWB	.566	.129	.420	4.394	.001	2.002

Table 11. Regression analysis for predictor variables teachers' perceived ease of use and perceived usefulness of the IWB and the criterion variable teachers' reported student-centered instructional usage of the IWB (Powers, 2014)

Predictor	B	Std. Error	Beta	t	p	VIF
Perceived ease of use of the IWB	.073	.147	.056	.501	.618	2.109
Perceived usefulness of the IWB	.602	.131	.445	3.984	.000	2.109

collinearity diagnostics yielded a VIF of less than 10. Since p was less than alpha the null hypothesis was rejected. As shown in Table 11, the results of multiple regression analysis showed that K-8 teachers' perceived ease of use of the IWB was not significant in the model (p =.618), but perceived usefulness of the IWB (p =.000) did account for a significant amount of variability in the criterion variable student-centered instructional usage of the IWB.

Research Question 2

A series of moderator analyses were conducted to address research question 2, "Is the relationship between K-8 teachers' perceived ease of use of the IWB and their reported instructional IWB usage moderated by teacher and organizational variables?" Therefore, in each moderator analysis, the question as to whether a particular teacher or organizational variable changed the relationship between instructional usage of the IWB and K-8 teachers perceived ease of use of the IWB was investigated.

The teacher variables examined in this study were K-8 teachers' reported computer experience, reported IWB experience, reported quantity of technology professional development, and reported technological pedagogical content knowledge of the IWB. The organizational variables examined in this study were K-8 teachers' reported IWB professional development opportunities at their school, K-8 teachers' reported IWB technical support at their school, K-8 teachers' reported time to plan for IWB use at their school, and administrator reported emphasis on technology at the school. In order to create moderator terms to include in the regression analyses, each of the teacher and organizational variables were multiplied by K-8 teachers' perceived ease of use of the IWB.

In each Series 1 regression model for research question 2, K-8 teachers' reported teacher-centered instructional usage served as the criterion variable and the predictor variables were K-8 teachers' perceived ease of use of the IWB (PEOUIWB), the moderator variable, and the product of ease of use and the moderator variable. A total of eight multiple regression analyses were conducted to explore the question as to whether the relationship between K-8 teachers' perceived ease of use of the IWB and teacher-centered instructional usage were moderated by teacher or organizational variables.

In the Series 1 regressions, the VIF for each of the moderators examined, with the exception of administrator's emphasis on technology, was less than 10. A significant finding was observed in just one of the moderator analyses. The Beta associated with the product term K-8 teachers' perceived ease of use of the IWB * reported TPACK of the IWB was.609 and significant (p =.001). Therefore, K-8 teachers' reported TPACK of the IWB moderated the relationship between K-8 teachers' perceived ease of use of the IWB and teacher-centered instructional usage of the IWB. The effects of multicollinearity appear to have been controlled for because collinearity diagnostics yielded a VIF less than 10 (5.697). Since the Beta was positive the correlation between K-8 teachers' reported TPACK of the IWB and reported teacher-centered instructional usage becomes more positive as perceived ease of use of the IWB increases. The results of the Series 1 regressions are presented in Table 12.

For the Series 2 regressions for research question 2 the variable K-8 teachers' reported student-centered instructional usage served as the criterion variable and the predictor variables in each analysis were K-8 teachers' perceived ease of use of the IWB (PEOUIWB), the moderator variable, and the product of ease of use and the moderator variable. Again, the researcher conducted a total of eight multiple regression analyses that were used to explore the question as to whether the relationship between K-8 teachers' perceived ease of use of the IWB and K-8 teacher reported student-centered instructional usage was moderated by teacher or organizational variables.

Table 12. Effect of teacher and organizational variables on the relationship between predictor variable perceived ease of use of the IWB and the criterion variable teacher-centered instructional usage of the IWB (Powers, 2014)

Moderator Term	Beta	*t*	*df*	*p*
PEOUIWB * K-8 teacher reported computer experience	-.122	-1.369	139	.173
PEOUIWB * K-8 teacher reported IWB experience	.117	.803	131	.424
PEOUIWB * K-8 teacher reported quantity of technology professional development	-.072	-.612	139	.541
PEOUIWB * K-8 teacher reported TPACK of the IWB	.609	3.513	133	.001
PEOUIWB * K-8 teacher reported IWB professional development opportunities	-.094	-.829	134	.409
PEOUIWB * K-8 teacher reported IWB technical support at their school	.175	1.481	136	.141
PEOUIWB * IWB K-8 teachers' reported time to plan for IWB use	.010	.087	136	.931
PEOUIWB * administrator reported emphasis on technology	.122	.306	115	.760

Table 13. Effect of teacher and organizational variables on the relationship between predictor variable perceived ease of use of the IWB and the criterion variable student-centered instructional usage of the IWB (Powers, 2014)

Moderator Term	Beta	tx	*df*	*p*
PEOUIWB * K-8 teacher reported computer experience	-.149	-1.487	131	.140
PEOUIWB * K-8 teacher reported IWB experience	.178	1.037	124	.302
PEOUIWB * K-8 teacher reported quantity of technology professional development	.014	.096	131	.924
PEOUIWB * K-8 teacher reported TPACK of the IWB	.471	2.343	127	.021
PEOUIWB * K-8 teacher reported IWB professional development opportunities	-.123	-1.245	127	.216
PEOUIWB * K-8 teacher reported IWB technical support at their school	-0.34	-.337	128	.736
PEOUIWB * IWB K-8 teacher reported time to plan for IWB use	-.166	-1.581	139	.116
PEOUIWB * administrator reported emphasis on technology	-4.17	-1.202	107	.232

In the Series 2 regressions, the VIF for each of the moderators examined, with the exception of administrator's emphasis on technology, was less than 10. A significant finding was also observed in one of the moderator analyses. The Beta associated with the product term K-8 teachers' perceived ease of use of the IWB * reported TPACK of the IWB was.471 and significant (p =.021). Therefore, K-8 teacher reported technological pedagogical content knowledge of the IWB moderated the relationship between teacher's perceived ease of use of the IWB and teachers' reported student-centered instructional usage of the IWB. Also, the effects of multicollinearity appear to have been controlled for because collinearity diagnostics yielded a VIF less than 10 (5.891). Lastly, it should be noted the Beta is positive, and therefore the correlation between K-8 teacher reported TPACK of the IWB and teachers' reported student-centered instructional usage becomes more positive as perceived ease of use of the IWB increases. The results of the Series 2 moderator analyses are presented in Table 13.

Research Question 3

A series of moderator analyses were also carried out to address research question 3, "Is the relationship between K-8 teachers' perceived usefulness of the IWB and their reported instructional IWB usage moderated by teacher and organizational variables?" In each moderator analysis, the question as to whether a particular teacher or organizational variable changed the relationship between instructional usage of the IWB and K-8 teachers' perceived usefulness of the IWB was examined. Moderator terms were calculated following the same procedures described for research question 2, with the only difference being all teacher and organizational variables were multiplied by K-8 teachers' perceived usefulness of the IWB.

In each Series 1 regression for research question 3, teacher-centered instructional usage served as the criterion variable and the predictor variables entered simultaneously into each analysis were K-8 teachers' perceived usefulness of the IWB, the moderator variable, and the product of ease of use and the moderator variable. A total of eight multiple regression analyses were conducted to explore the ques-

Table 14. Effect of teacher and organizational variables on the relationship between predictor variable perceived usefulness of the IWB and the criterion variable teacher-centered instructional usage of the IWB (Powers, 2014)

Moderator Term	Beta	tx	df	p
PUIWB * K-8 teacher reported computer experience	-.026	-.331	139	.741
PUIWB * K-8 teacher reported IWB experience	.147	1.181	131	.240
PUIWB * K-8 teacher reported quantity of technology professional development	-.169	-1.507	139	.134
PUIWB * K-8 teacher reported TPACK of the IWB	.506	3.156	133	.002
PUIWB * K-8 teacher reported IWB professional development opportunities	-.068	-.761	134	.448
PUIWB * K-8 teacher reported IWB technical support at their school	-.076	-.848	136	.398
PUIWB * IWB K-8 teacher reported time to plan for IWB use	-.060	-.660	136	.511
PUIWB * administrator reported emphasis on technology	.202	.645	107	.520

Table 15. Effect of teacher and organizational variables on the relationship between predictor variable perceived usefulness of the IWB and the criterion variable student-centered instructional usage of the IWB (Powers, 2014)

Moderator Term	Beta	tx	df	p
PUIWB * K-8 teacher reported computer experience	-.079	-.910	131	.365
PUIWB * K-8 teacher reported IWB experience	.170	1.148	124	.253
PUIWB * K-8 teacher reported quantity of technology professional development	-.028	-.212	131	.832
PUIWB * K-8 teacher reported TPACK of the IWB	.286	1.582	127	.115
PUIWB * K-8 teacher reported IWB professional development opportunities	-.069	-.680	127	.498
PUIWB * K-8 teacher reported IWB technical support at their school	.063	.603	129	.547
PUIWB * IWB K-8 teacher reported time to plan for IWB use	.089	.876	129	.383
PUIWB * administrator reported emphasis on technology	-.237	-.863	115	.390

tion as to whether the relationship between K-8 teachers' perceived usefulness of the IWB and reported teacher-centered instructional usage was changed by teacher or organizational variables.

The VIF for each of the moderators examined was less than 10, with the exception of administrator's emphasis on technology. A significant finding was observed in one of the moderator analyses. The Beta associated with the product term K-8 teachers' perceived usefulness of the IWB * reported TPACK of the IWB was.506 and significant (p =.002). Therefore, K-8 teacher reported TPACK of the IWB moderated the relationship between perceived usefulness of the IWB and teacher-centered instructional usage of the IWB. The effects of multicollinearity appear to have been controlled for because collinearity diagnostics yielded a VIF less than 10 (5.198). The Beta is positive, and therefore the correlation between K-8 teacher reported TPACK of the IWB and teacher-centered instructional usage becomes more positive as teachers' perceived usefulness of the IWB (PUIWB) increases. The results of the Series 1 moderator analyses are presented in Table 14.

In each Series 2 regressions for research question 3, K-8 teacher reported student-centered instructional usage served as the criterion variable and the predictor variables entered simultaneously into each analysis were K-8 teachers' perceived usefulness of the IWB, the moderator variable, and the product of ease of use and the moderator variable. Again, eight multiple regression analyses were conducted to explore the question as to whether the relationship between perceived usefulness of the IWB and K-8 teacher reported student-centered instructional usage was changed by teacher or organizational variables. No significant findings were observed, indicating that none of the teacher or organizational variables changed the relationship between K-8 teachers' perceived usefulness of the IWB and K-8 teacher reported student-centered instructional usage. The findings are presented in Table 15 below.

DISCUSSION

This chapter examined research that utilized the Technology Acceptance Model (TAM) to investigate factors associated with K-8 teacher reported instructional usage of the IWB. Through a mixed electronic and paper format survey of 155 teachers and 40 administrators the researcher used multiple regression and moderator analyses to examine whether the TAM model helped explain K-8 teachers' instructional IWB usage. A discussion of the implications of the findings of the study is presented in this section of the chapter.

To What Degree Do Teachers' Perceived Ease of Use of the IWB and Perceived Usefulness of the IWB Predict Instructional IWB Usage?

Research question 1 of this study asked: To what degree do K-8 teachers' perceived ease of use of the IWB and perceived usefulness of the IWB predict their reported instructional IWB usage? Multiple regression analysis indicated that both K-8 teachers' perceived ease of use of the IWB and perceived usefulness of the IWB contributed to the prediction of teacher-centered instructional usage of the IWB. The model summary showed that the squared multiple correlation was 0.374, indicating that K-8 teachers' perceived ease of use of the IWB and perceived usefulness of the IWB explained 37.4% of the variance in teacher-centered instructional usage of the IWB. However, just one of the variables, K-8 teachers' perceived usefulness of the IWB, contributed to prediction of teacher reported student-centered instructional usage of the IWB. The model summary showed that the squared multiple correlation was 0.237, indicating that 23.7% of the variance in the criterion variable was explained by the model.

While these results did not establish a cause-and-effect relationship between either of the aforementioned predictor variables and teacher-centered or student-centered instructional usage of the IWB, they may help demonstrate the utility of the TAM model in predicting instructional IWB usage. As noted earlier in this chapter, Davis (1989) theorized that perceived usefulness (PU), which he defined as "the degree to which a person believes that using a particular system would enhance his or her job performance," and perceived ease of use (PEOU), or "the degree to which a person believes that using a particular system would be free of effort," helped to predict actual usage of a given system (Davis, 1989, p. 320). These results supported Davis' (1989) theory that PU and PEOU contribute to the prediction of the actual usage of a given technology system, but PEOU was only a factor when the teacher was the one manipulating the IWB. These findings suggest that teachers' perceptions of the IWBs usefulness for instruction plays a role in its frequency of use for both types of instruction. However, the lack of a significant finding for PEOU when students were manipulating the IWB suggests that teachers' perceptions about ease of use may not matter when the students are interacting with the tool.

Is the Relationship Between Teachers' Perceived Ease of Use of the IWB and Instructional IWB Usage Moderated by Teacher and Organizational Variables?

Research question 2 of this study asked: Is the relationship between K-8 teachers' perceived ease of use of the IWB and their reported instructional IWB usage moderated by teacher and organizational variables? A total of 16 moderator analyses were conducted to address this research question. The moderator analyses yielded two significant findings. These findings indicated that one teacher variable and no organizational variables served as moderators.

First, K-8 teachers reported TPACK of the IWB was found to moderate the relationship between teachers' perceived ease of use of the IWB and reported teacher-centered instructional usage of the IWB (Beta = 0.609, p =.001). The Beta was positive, indicating that teachers' TPACK of the IWB strengthened the relationship between teachers' perceived ease of use of the IWB and teachers reported teacher-centered instructional usage of the IWB. Secondly, the moderator analyses indicated that K-8 teachers reported TPACK of the IWB moderated the relationship between teachers' perceived ease of use of the IWB and teacher reported student-centered instructional usage of the IWB (Beta = 0.471, p =.021). The Beta was positive, indicating that teachers' technological pedagogical content knowledge of the IWB strengthened the relationship between teachers' perceived ease of use of the IWB and teachers reported student-centered instructional usage of the IWB.

These findings suggested that teachers' TPACK of the IWB, described by Mishra and Koehler (2006) as knowledge of content, technology knowledge, and pedagogy, was a moderator of the relationship between perceived ease of use of the IWB and both forms of instructional usage examined in this study. In other words, the easier teachers believed it was to use the IWB for instruction, the more frequently they may be expected to use the tool for both forms of instruction, and this relationship may be expected to be even stronger for teachers with greater levels of TPACK of the IWB. These findings are consistent with the results of Hernandez-Ramos (2005) which suggested that exposure to technology and knowledge of software applications were positively associated with more frequent use of technology by teachers, both for themselves and with their students.

Is the Relationship Between Teachers' Perceived Usefulness of the IWB and Instructional IWB Usage Moderated by Teacher and Organizational Variables?

Research question 3 of this study asked: Is the relationship between K-8 teachers' perceived usefulness of the IWB and their reported instructional IWB usage moderated by teacher and organizational variables? Once again, a total of 16 moderator analyses were conducted to address the research question. The moderator analyses yelled one significant findings, indicating that one teacher variable and no organizational variables served as moderators.

Specifically, the moderator analyses indicated that K-8 teachers reported TPACK of the IWB moderated the relationship between teachers' perceived usefulness of the IWB and teacher-centered instructional usage of the IWB (Beta = 0.506, p =.002). The Beta was positive, indicating that teachers' TPACK of the IWB strengthened the relationship between teachers' perceived usefulness of the IWB and teacher-centered instructional usage of the IWB. These findings were consistent with those of Hughes (2005), who demonstrated how teachers' development of TPACK depends upon a teacher's perceived value of technology as an instructional tool. In the series of moderator analyses in which student-centered instructional usage served as the depended variable no significant moderators were found.

CONCLUSION

This chapter discussed a study that utilized the Technology Acceptance Model (TAM) to examine K-8 teacher reported instructional usage of the IWB. Research suggests that investing in instructional technology does not necessarily lead to teachers' adoption of available technologies into their instructional practice (Dorsen et al., 2004; Fletcher, 2006; Mathews & Guarino, 2000). Scholars have suggested that examining the factors that explain classroom technology use might provide answers to why some teachers embrace new technology while other do not (Hermans et al., 2008). This study helped to shed light on these factors by identifying variables that were significantly related to K-8 teachers' instructional usage of the IWB.

The results of the study indicated that the two variables adapted from Davis' (1989) Technology Acceptance Model, teachers' perceived ease of use of the IWB and perceived usefulness of the IWB, contributed to the prediction of teacher-centered instructional usage of the IWB. Another finding was that the variable teachers' perceived usefulness of the IWB contributed to the prediction of student-centered instructional usage of the IWB. The analysis also indicated that teachers' TPACK of the IWB, a variable adapted from Mishra and Koehler's (2006) TPACK, moderated the relationships between three sets of variables: (a) teachers' perceived ease of use of the IWB and teacher-centered instructional usage of the IWB, (b) teachers' perceived ease of use of the IWB and reported student-centered instructional usage of the IWB, and (c) teachers' perceived usefulness of the IWB and reported teacher-centered instructional usage of the IWB.

These findings suggest that school technology leaders may better facilitate the implementation of IWBs into their schools if they are able to convey the value of the technology to their teaching staff. Although this study did not find any significant relationships for variables relating to professional development, exploring ways to increase teachers' TPACK of the IWB may foster instructional IWB usage in schools. However, it is recommended that further investigation into what constitutes effective instructional IWB usage is conducted in order to determine specific faculty development objectives.

REFERENCES

Alshare, K. A., & Alkhateeb, F. B. (2008). Predicting students' usage of Internet emerging economies using an extended technology acceptance model (TAM). *Academy of Educational Leadership Journal, 12*(2), 109–128.

Bennett, S., & Lockyer, L. (2008). A study of teachers integration of interactive whiteboards into four Australian primary school classrooms. *Learning, Media and Technology, 33*(4), 289–300. doi:10.1080/17439880802497008

Bogazzi, R. P. (2007). The legacy of the technology acceptance model and a proposal for a paradigm shift. *Journal of the Association for Information Systems, 8*(4), 244–254.

Burton-Jones, A., & Hubona, G. S. (2006). The mediation of external variables in the technology acceptance model. *Information & Management, 43*(6), 706–717. doi:10.1016/j.im.2006.03.007

Cochran, W. (2012). *2011-2012 school year Lutheran school statistics.* Retrieved from http://mns.lcms.org/LinkClick.aspx?fileticket=_yiscK2ypjs%3D&tabid=211&mid=813

Davis, F. (1989). Perceived usefulness, perceived ease of use, and user acceptance of information technology. *Management Information Systems Quarterly, 13*(3), 319–340. doi:10.2307/249008

Davis, F., Bogazzi, R., & Warshaw, P. (1989). User acceptance of computer technology: A comparison of two theoretical models. *Management Science, 35*(8), 982–1003. doi:10.1287/mnsc.35.8.982

Davis, F., & Venkatesh, V. (1996). A critical assessment of potential measurement biases in the technology acceptance model: Three experiments. *International Journal of Human-Computer Studies, 45*(1), 19–45. doi:10.1006/ijhc.1996.0040

Dawson, C., & Rakes, C. (2003). The influence of principals technology training on the integration of technology into schools. *Journal of Research on Technology in Education, 36*(1), 29–49. doi:10.1080/15391523.2003.10782401

de Koster, S., Volman, M., & Kuiper, E. (2013). Interactivity with the interactive whiteboard in traditional and innovative primary schools: An exploratory study. *Australasian Journal of Educational Technology, 29*(4). doi:10.14742/ajet.291

Dorsen, A., Gibbs, M., Guerrero, R., & McDevitt, P. (2004). Technology in nonsectarian and religious private schools. *Journal of Research on Christian Education, 13*(2), 289–314. doi:10.1080/10656210409484973

Fletcher, D. (2006). Technology integration: Do they or don't they? A self-report survey from PreK through 5th grade professional educators. *AACE Journal, 14*(3), 207–219.

Fraenkel, J., Wallen, N., & Hyun, H. (2012). *How to design and evaluate research in education* (8th ed.). New York, NY: McGraw Hill.

Franklin, C. (2007). Factors that influence elementary teachers' use of computers. *Journal of Technology and Teacher Education, 15*(2), 267–293.

Gong, M., Xu, Y., & Yu, Y. (2004). An enhanced technology acceptance model for web-based learning. *Journal of Information Systems Education*, *15*(4), 365–374.

Hall, G. E., & Hord, S. M. (2001). *Implementing change: Patterns, principles, and potholes* (2nd ed.). Boston, MA: Pearson.

Harris, J., Mishra, P., & Koehler, M. (2009). Teachers technological pedagogical content knowledge and learning activity types: Curriculum-based technology integration reframed. *Journal of Research on Technology in Education*, *41*(4), 393–416. doi:10.1080/15391523.2009.10782536

Hermans, R., Tondeur, J., Van Braak, J., & Valcke, M. (2008). The impact of primary school teachers educational beliefs on classroom use of computer. *Computers & Education*, *51*(4), 1499–1509. doi:10.1016/j.compedu.2008.02.001

Hernandez-Ramos, P. (2005). If not here, where? Understanding teachers use of technology in Silicon Valley schools. *Journal of Research on Technology in Education*, *38*(1), 39–64. doi:10.1080/1539152 3.2005.10782449

Hughes, J. E. (2005). The role of teacher knowledge and learning experiences in forming technology-integrated pedagogy. *Journal of Technology and Teacher Education*, *13*(2), 377–402.

Kennewell, S. (2006, November). *Reflections on the interactive whiteboard phenomenon: A synthesis of research from the UK*. Paper presented at the AARE 2006 International Education Research Conference. Retrieved from http:www.aare.edu.au/06pap/ken06138.pdf

King, W. R., & He, J. (2006). A meta-analysis of the technology acceptance model. *Information & Management*, *43*(6), 740–755. doi:10.1016/j.im.2006.05.003

Lee, M. (2010). Interactive whiteboards and schooling: The context. *Technology, Pedagogy and Education*, *19*(2), 133–141. doi:10.1080/1475939X.2010.491215

Lee, M., & Winzenried, A. (2006). Interactive whiteboards: Achieving total teacher usage. *Australian Educational Leader*, *28*(3), 22–25.

Mathews, J., & Guarino, A. (2000). Predicting teacher computer use: A path analysis. *International Journal of Instructional Media*, *27*(4), 385–392.

Means, B. (2008). Technology's role in curriculum and instruction. In F. M. Connelly, M. F. He, & J. Phillion (Eds.), *The Sage handbook of curriculum and instruction* (pp. 123–144). Los Angeles, CA: Sage Publications. doi:10.4135/9781412976572.n7

Mishra, P., & Koehler, M. (2006). Technological pedagogical content knowledge: A framework for teacher knowledge. *Teachers College Record*, *108*(6), 1017–1054. doi:10.1111/j.1467-9620.2006.00684.x

Mueller, J., Wood, E., Willoughby, T., Ross, C., & Specht, J. (2008). Identifying discriminating variables between teachers who fully integrate computers and teachers with limited integration. *Computers & Education*, *51*(4), 1523–1537. doi:10.1016/j.compedu.2008.02.003

National Center for Education Statistics. (2011). *Digest of education statistics, 2010*. Retrieved from http://nces.ed.gov/pubsearch/pubsinfo.asp?pubid=2011015

Norris, C., Sullivan, T., Poirot, J., & Soloway, E. (2003). No access, no use, no impact: Snapshot surveys of educational technology in K-12. *Journal of Research on Technology in Education, 36*(1), 15–27. do i:10.1080/15391523.2003.10782400

O'Dwyer, L., Russell, M., & Bebell, D. (2004). Identifying teacher, school and district characteristics associated with elementary teachers' use of technology: A multilevel perspective. *Education Policy Analysis Archives, 12*(48). Retrieved from http://epaa.asu.edu/epaa/v12n48

Pekari, J. (2011). *Reshaping Lutheran education: A systems perspective* (Doctoral dissertation). Available from ProQuest Dissertations and Theses database. (UMI No. 3459161)

Powers, J. R. (2014). *Lutheran school teachers' instructional usages of the interactive whiteboard* (Doctoral dissertation). Florida Atlantic University, Boca Raton, FL.

Reedy, G. B. (2008). PowerPoint, interactive whiteboards, and the visual culture of technology in schools. *Technology, Pedagogy and Education, 17*(2), 143–162. doi:10.1080/14759390802098623

Sandholtz, J. H., Ringstaff, C., & Dwyer, D. C. (1997). *Teaching with technology: Creating student-centered classrooms.* New York, NY: Teachers College Press.

Schmidt, D., Baran, E., Thompson, A., Mishra, P., Koehler, M., & Shin, T. (2009). Technological pedagogical content knowledge (TPACK): The development and validation of an assessment instrument for preservice teachers. *Journal of Research on Technology in Education, 42*(2), 123–149. doi:10.1080/15 391523.2009.10782544

Shulman, L. S. (1986). Those who understand: Knowledge growth in teaching. *Educational Researcher, 15*(2), 4–14. doi:10.3102/0013189X015002004

Spillane, J. P. (2004). *Standards deviation: How schools misunderstand education policy.* Cambridge, MA: Harvard University Press.

Van Braak, J., Tondeur, J., & Valcke, M. (2004). Explaining different types of computer use among primary school teachers. *European Journal of Psychology of Education, 19*(4), 407–422. doi:10.1007/ BF03173218

Vannatta, R. A., & Fordham, N. (2004). Teacher dispositions as predictors of classroom technology use. *Journal of Research on Technology in Education, 36*(3), 253–271. doi:10.1080/15391523.2004.10782415

Watson, D. (2006). Understanding the relationship between ICT and education means exploring innovation and change. *Education and Information Technologies, 11*(3-4), 199–216. doi:10.1007/s10639-006-9016-2

Wells, J. G. (2007). Key design factors in durable instructional technology professional development. *Journal of Technology and Teacher Education, 15*(1), 101–122.

Winzenried, A., Dalgarno, B., & Tinkler, J. (2010). The interactive whiteboard: A transitional technology supporting diverse teaching practices. *Australasian Journal of Educational Technology, 26*(4), 534–552. doi:10.14742/ajet.1071

Wozney, L., Venkatesh, V., & Abrami, P. C. (2006). Implementing computer technologies: Teachers' perceptions and practices. *Journal of Technology and Teacher Education, 14*(1), 173–207.

KEY TERMS AND DEFINITIONS

Behavior Intention (BI): A component of Davis' (1989) original TAM model defined as an individual's intention to perform the behavior (Davis et al., 1989).

Interactive Whiteboard (IWB): For the purposes of this study, an interactive whiteboard is defined as a touch-sensitive presentation system which links together a whiteboard, computer, and multimedia projector.

Instructional IWB Usage (IU): Refers to the ways in which a teacher uses the IWB for classroom instruction.

Perceived Ease of Use (PEOU): A component of Davis' (1989) original TAM model measured through seven self-report questionnaire items defined as "the degree to which a person believes that using a particular system would be free of effort" (p. 320).

Perceived Usefulness (PU): A component of Davis' (1989) original TAM model measured through seven self-report questionnaire items defined as "the degree to which a person believes that using a particular system would enhance his or her job performance" (p. 320).

Rostered Lutheran School Teacher: Refers to a Lutheran school teacher who has been synodically trained by an LCMS through undergraduate work or a colloquy process.

Student-Centered Instructional IWB Usage (SCIU): Refers to instruction during which students are provided with opportunities to interact with the IWB.

Teacher-Centered Instructional IWB Usage (TCIU): Defined as instruction during which the teacher controls the IWB.

Chapter 7
Self–Efficacy and Persistence in a Digital Writing Classroom:
A Case Study of Fifth–Grade Boys

Jessica S. Mitchell
University of North Alabama, USA

ABSTRACT

Utilizing a New Literacies perspective, the purpose of this qualitative case study was to explore the digital writing experiences of one classroom of fifth-grade boys. Research questions for this study included the following: (1) What features of the digital writing environment impact student expressions of confidence in their abilities as writers? (2) How do expressions of confidence align with performance for students who are the least persistent in digital writing tasks? (3) How do expressions of confidence align with performance for students who are the most persistent in digital writing tasks? Through an embedded analysis, eight confidence features were identified. Compared against a holistic analysis of individual focal student experiences, this chapter provides two student vignettes to illustrate the differences between high-persisting and low-persisting students in a digital writing classroom.

In order to succeed, people need a sense of self-efficacy, to struggle together with resilience to meet the inevitable obstacles and inequities of life. Albert Bandura

INTRODUCTION

Many students today spend large portions of their days in digital spaces. From new advances in virtual reality devices to the ever-present barrage of social media notifications, students can easily and affordably connect with anyone, anywhere at any time. While some researchers have argued the accessibility of technology has brought new opportunities for addressing concerns related to a "digital gap" between high performing and low performing students (Morrisett, 2001), researchers over the last decade have reported that the problem of the digital divide is no longer *only* about how to give students greater ac-

DOI: 10.4018/978-1-5225-2838-8.ch007

cess to technology, but *also* how to teach students to use technology to both read and construct meaning within these digital contexts (Leu, Kinzer, Coiro, & Cammack, 2004; Warschauer, Zheng, Niiya, Cotten, & Farkas, 2014). New skills needed for these digital contexts have further extended the definition of the "digital divide" to include a "skills divide" (Mossberger, Tolbert, & Stansbury, 2003). Such a gap in skills from participatory digital culture requires special considerations for educational decisions, as Jenkins, Clinton, Purushotma, Robison, and Weigel (2006) have contended,

The school system's inability to close this participation gap has negative consequences for everyone involved. On the one hand, those youth who are most advanced in media literacies are often stripped of their technologies and robbed of their best techniques for learning in an effort to ensure a uniform experience for all in the classroom. On the other hand, many youth who have had no exposure to these kinds of participatory cultures outside school find themselves struggling to keep up with their peers. (p. 13)

One way to explore the digital skills gap is to explore writing self-efficacy within a digital learning environment. According to Bandura (1977), self-efficacy is the belief in one's ability (confidence) to achieve a specified target and provides a powerful predictor for future performance. The current study explores the nature of boys' self-efficacy when participating in digital writing experiences from perspectives informed by New Literacies Theory (NLT), the body of research seeking to explore the literacy practices created by emerging digital technologies such as blogs, message systems, virtual gaming communities, social networking sites, and a host of continually evolving technologies (Lankshear & Knobel, 2006; Leu, O'Byrne, Zawilinski, McVerry, & Everett-Cocapardo, 2009). Specifically important to the educational context, new literacies embody a nuanced skill set for interpreting information from the Internet and other communication technologies (Kiili, Laurinen, & Marttunen, 2008). Moreover, new literacies extend the definition of traditional literacies as online reading is seen as an increasingly collaborative, social practice (Zawilinski, 2009). Echoing previous sociocultural frameworks for interpreting the social nature of learning and the meaning-making process (Vygotsky, 1986; Wertsch, 1991), such understandings of digital writing experiences are linked to social practices within individual contexts.

Background

Digital writing has gained attention in recent years within the field of writing research, reflecting the growing use of digital writing both inside and outside of the classroom (Anderson, Goode, Mitchell, & Thompson, 2013; Wollscheid, 2016). Research in digital composition in school contexts originally focused on email exchanges among students and cultural writing exchanges during school experiences, highlighting the importance of the role of audience in digital writing experiences (Fabos & Young, 1999; Riel & Levin, 1990). Other studies have since reviewed the role of word processing (Wolfe, Bolton, Feltovich, & Niday, 1996) and assistive technologies for writing achievement in school (MacArthur, 1998; MacArthur, Graham, Haynes, & DeLaPaz, 1996). These studies focused on the effectiveness of technology for improving students' writing achievement, but often found technology was only one component in a larger contextual environment. For example, in Rogers and Graham's (2008) meta-analysis of word processing tools used for revision, they argued that the use of word processing tools alone did not support higher revisions as "the effects are largely dependent on the context in which word processing is used" (p. 251). According to a review of more recent research on early writing development comparing pen and paper with digital tools, new research methodologies are needed to meet the complex context of an "interdisciplinary research topic in rapid development" (Wollscheid, Sjaastad, & Tomte, 2016). Such context dependent features highlight the need to further explore digital writing in the classroom and the potential for digital technologies to create more authentic learning experiences for students.

Digital Writing Integration in Classroom Environments

As technology has become more available for teachers who teach writing, more studies have been conducted on how teachers are implementing digital literacies into the classroom (Hutchison & Reinking, 2011; Purcell, Heaps, Buchanan, & Friedrich, 2013a; Dudeney & Hockly, 2016). Studies demonstrating how secondary and post-secondary teachers have implemented free online collaborative writing tools such *Google Docs* or *SkyDrive*, for example, have been documented (Wood, 2011; Zheng, Lawrence, Warschauer, & Lin, 2015). Although it appears more secondary and post-secondary teachers are implementing digital tools for collaborative writing into the classroom, one study, however, found that the teachers who implemented such tools into the classroom experience did not fully integrate the collaborative potential for peer feedback as only 29% allowed or required students to edit or provide feedback to their peers work (Purcell, Heaps, Buchanan, & Friedrich, 2013b).

Additionally, while the seminal work of researchers have explored collaborative writing with young students, more recent studies are beginning to explore how collaborative digital writing is occurring for younger students (Bogard & McMackin, 2012) with a variety of emerging devices such as iPads (Falloon, 2015). Other studies have demonstrated how teachers have been implementing more "motivating" digital writing practices from outside of the classroom which focus on larger audiences for students' writing (Alvermann, 2008; Guzzeti & Gamboa, 2005; Witte, 2009). Although these studies have concluded that there is a potential for student engagement through the authentic audience established through such experiences, some researchers contend that there is also a danger in "trespassing" into more private student spaces that could potentially present problems for students and teachers alike (Witte, 2009, p. 24).

Even when digital culture has been assimilated into the classroom, some researchers have found that the same level of student engagement and participation was not necessarily transferred from out-of-school experiences to in-school experiences (Alvermann & Hagood, 2000). Researchers such as Gee (2007) point to the ethics of addressing this subject, both cautioning the way teachers attempt to incorporate student culture into the classroom and calling for a greater understanding of how students navigate between digital spaces both inside and outside of the classroom. Especially relevant to the current study researchers such as Aarsand (2010) have called for more research to explore how digital games and social relationships among peers in digital spaces impact their participation in the pedagogical decisions of teachers.

Boys, Writing Self-Efficacy, and Digital Writing

Although it has been heavily critiqued for its lack of attention to dynamic issues across gender such as intersectionality, a literacy gap between boys and girls has been demonstrated in the literature (Coley, 2001; Rutter et al., 2004; Sokal & Katz, 2008) including a gap in writing achievement between boys and girls (Mead, 2006; Kim, Otaiba, Wanzek, & Gatlin, 2015). According to Pajares (2003), studies exploring the relationship of boys' self-efficacy, motivation, and engagement has also been well documented in relationship to writing. More recently, Villalón, Mateos, & Cuevas (2015) directly observed a relationship between male/female performance and beliefs about performance by correlating perceptions of self-efficacy and gender roles to writing performance. High school females in the study were found to have more nuanced writing conceptions and higher levels of writing performance than their male counterparts.

Such concerns for the self-efficacy and writing performance of boys have generated discussion regarding the potential for digital composition to engage boy writers and point to the need to explore the impact of digital technologies with boys and writing achievement. More specific to the current study, new advances in technology hold the potential to expand the existing field of self-efficacy research for boys. According to Bruning & Kaufman, 2015, "Technology-based writing environments afford multi-modalities such as images, videos, and other graphic displays that can affect writing self-efficacy by varying the way a writer connects to audience, incorporates resources, and participates in modes of feedback" (p. 168). By studying how these features impact beliefs about writing, the current study aimed to explore this potential. As Alloway and Gilbert (1997) have argued, the importance of such nuanced approaches to literacy research represents larger issues for consideration:

We remind ourselves and others, as teachers and teacher educators, that concerns for boys, but more importantly, the concerns for boys and girls, need to be understood with a more sophisticated and more nuanced appreciation of what it means to teach in literacy classrooms. (p. 49)

In sum, this study sought to highlight the complexities of a single environment to elucidate understandings of how the boys in the context situated themselves as writers in their digital writing experiences and how, in turn, their perceptions about themselves as writers influenced their digital writing performance.

DIGITAL WRITING IN ONE CLASSRROOM OF FIFTH-GRADE BOYS

The purpose of this qualitative case study was to explore the digital writing experiences of one classroom of fifth-grade boys (ages 10-12) from a context in which traditional access to technology had been previously established for each student on a 1:1 basis (one student per computing device) for over 12 years. Ultimately, by exploring the experiences of students with established access to technology, this qualitative case study (Yin, 2009) answered the call for more studies concerning how digital writing experiences impact self-efficacy within a community of learners (Bruning & Kauffman, 2015). Research questions for this study included the following: (1) What features of the digital writing environment impact student expressions of confidence in their abilities as writers? (2) How do expressions of confidence align with performance for students who are the least persistent in digital writing tasks? (3) How do expressions of confidence align with performance for students who are the most persistent in digital writing tasks?

Selection of Context and Sampling Techniques

This study employed purposeful sampling techniques (Crotty, 1998) to invite the participation of students from one teacher's classroom within a specified school context. To meet the characteristics of the study, the context was required to meet the following criteria: (1) a school site with an established commitment to the development of digital skills across multiple grade levels from early elementary to intermediate students through its general mission statement or action plans, and (2) a classroom site with multiple opportunities for digital integration of writing tasks such as the classroom use of wikis, blogs, microblogs, zines, or digital document sharing through Web 2.0 tools such as Microsoft's SkyDrive or Google's Google Drive.

Consideration of such a school context had been ongoing through the recommendation of researchers specializing in literacy and technology integration in K-12 settings using snowballing (Crotty, 1998) sampling techniques. As the researcher had previously studied and published in this field of research (Anderson, et al., 2013; Anderson, et al., 2014), collaborative writing efforts had been established which allowed the researcher to solicit recommendations from other professionals. Additionally, these partnerships allowed the researcher to meet other educators and school leaders who were committed to technology integration. Ultimately, the cooperating teacher in the study was one such educator whom the researcher had previously met in this work.

Research Context

Although the researcher had an established relationship with one of the teachers from the school site, the selected school context was identified as one of seven school sites in the Mid-South region of the United States that espoused a focus on digital skills development as well as considered specialized approaches to the education of boys. Consideration for how this school context met the criteria above the other identified school contexts was made. First, the school's focus on digital skills development was evidenced through the tenets of its mission statement including a focus on preparation for a "global community" in the "21st century" by incorporating technology for creative thinking, creative application, and collaboration.

Not only did the school site articulate its mission to develop digital skills, but it also demonstrated this commitment in the programs it offered for its students and the training it provided for its teachers. For example, as a 1:1 laptop school for over 12 years, the school site afforded the opportunity to observe students who had been exposed to hands-on approaches to technology throughout their educational experiences. Additionally, teachers from the school had been trained and awarded nationally for their innovative uses of technology into their school curriculum. Furthermore, online courses in various disciplines were offered to students, parents, and teachers, establishing participation in digital environments through communicating within various modes of writing. Thus, the criteria for the selection of the school site were met through identifying these categories.

Data Collection

The study incorporated a variety of data collection methods including classroom artifacts of digital writing tasks and products of one classroom of fifth-grade boys. Additionally, six of the students were randomly selected for interview sessions for understanding their perceptions of themselves as writers after participating in these digital writing tasks. More specifically, the following research data was collected over the 15 weeks of the study: 1) eighteen 20-30 minute semi-structured interviews from six randomly selected focal students (see Appendix 1), 2) student writing products from the six focal students (see Appendix 2), and 3) two weekly classroom observations ranging from one-two hours each (see Appendix 3). While the researcher worked independently for data collection purposes, researcher memos were shared with institutionally approved individuals such as the focal students, the corresponding teacher, and the researcher's colleagues to address issues of reflexivity and transparency in the research process.

Analysis

For this qualitative case study, both an embedded and holistic strategy were employed in the analysis process to explore the complexities of the research problem (Yin, 2009). The embedded strategy was first utilized to account for multiple aspects of analysis from all data sources including whole-class observations, student interviews, and writing artifacts and was analyzed through categorical aggregation (Creswell, 2012). This was accomplished by first utilizing axial or line-by-line coding procedures (Ezzy, 2002) across all data sources. Initial categories included technology facilitation, writing processes, and digital composition. These categories divided the codes from the data into three units of analysis. As codes from the data were sometimes interconnected, careful consideration for the relationship of technology to writing was the first major step of the analysis process. Ultimately, the role of technology in the digital classroom was categorized as a facilitation tool when it did not otherwise overlap with the writing experiences in the classroom. Also, codes associated with writing were categorized as writing processes when they aligned with traditional writing approaches that could occur outside of the realm of technology. Finally, digital composition represented codes that encompassed both technology facilitation and writing processes, creating a category of analysis unique to the digital writing environment. Subcategories explicitly linked to digital composition included the categories of skills, attitudes, and dispositions. As these patterns were developed from a variety of data sources, categories were refined by continually returning to the data set for confirmation that proceeded into naturalistic generalizations.

Next, a holistic strategy was then employed to individual focal students' written products, oral transcripts from interview sessions, and captured observations of focal student experiences in both digital and physical classroom spaces. The patterns from the embedded data analysis were compared against the individual, holistic analysis of the experience of each focal student. As a result, twelve themes emerged from this analysis and included four themes from each of the categories of digital composition from the embedded analysis. Themes for skills included the following: 1) ability to process multiple steps in instructions and procedures, 2) ability to implement writing knowledge, 3) ability to integrate technology as a writing tool, and 4) ability to meet school and classroom behavior expectations. Themes for attitudes included: 1) students' expressions of relationship to others, 2) students' expressions of confidence in participating in tasks, 3) students' expressions of affinity for the task, and 4) students' connections of tasks to future plans or goals. Themes for dispositions included: 1) behaviors of social interactions, 2) emotional responses of students, 3) reactions to restrictions of student participation, and 4) engagement features of students. Thus, combining an embedded and holistic strategy allowed for a more fluid analysis between the students' individual experiences to the larger classroom context. As with the data collection process, the emerging categories were continually informed by focal participant review as well as the classroom teacher and the researcher's colleagues. Inter-rater reliability for this study was established by generalized percent agreement among pairs of raters including the researcher and the focal participants, the researcher and the corresponding teacher, and the researcher and each of the two researcher's colleagues interested in this topic of study.

FINDINGS

As a result of the analysis process, eight confidence features emerged. An overview of the student confidence features is provided in Figure 1. This graphic illustrates a continuum of student responses

Figure 1. Student confidence features compared against expressions of confidence and inadequacy

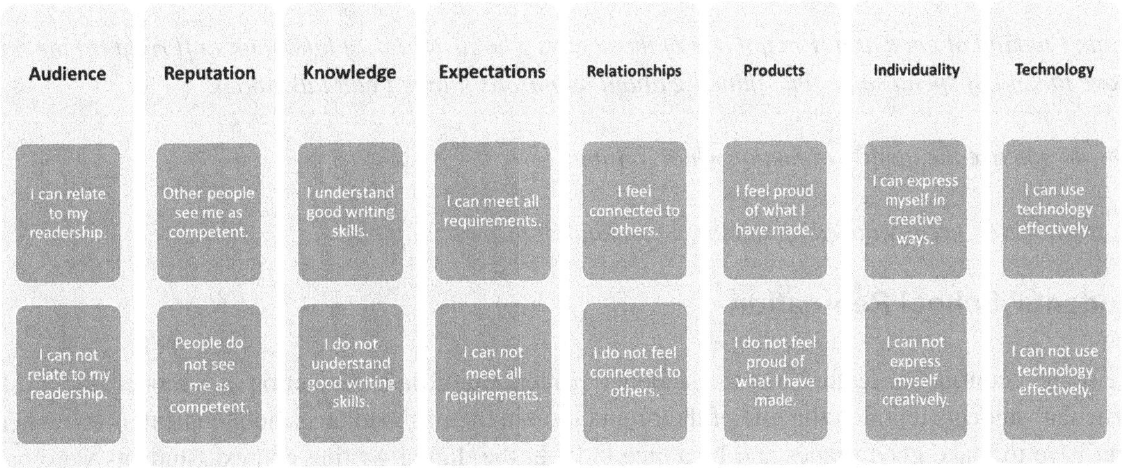

Audience	Reputation	Knowledge	Expectations	Relationships	Products	Individuality	Technology
I can relate to my readership.	Other people see me as competent.	I understand good writing skills.	I can meet all requirements.	I feel connected to others.	I feel proud of what I have made.	I can express myself in creative ways.	I can use technology effectively.
I can not relate to my readership.	People do not see me as competent.	I do not understand good writing skills.	I can not meet all requirements.	I do not feel connected to others.	I do not feel proud of what I have made.	I can not express myself creatively.	I can not use technology effectively.

in regards to their confidence in participating in the digital writing tasks of the classroom. As these categories were developed across the data, an additional section is provided at the end of this section to illustrate two different focal students' experiences throughout the duration of the study.

Ability to Connect to the Audience

The first confidence feature related to the students' sense of audience. When talking about their digital writing experiences, some students reported a greater sense of connection to their audience than others. For example, some students explicitly mentioned their own perception of their writing ability in connection to being able to relate to their audience, while others did not. As one example of students connecting to their audience, some students reported that they were able to "grab the attention" of their peers. Other examples of connecting to the audience included students who reported that they felt that they were good at using "humor" and "making people laugh." The following example illustrates how one student connected his writing identity to his ability to relate to his audience through humorous entertainment.

Brandon, Interview Two

To entertain...I think I'm kind of good at it.

What's a writer?

Somebody that comes up with stories or articles and he writes them down for people to persuade, inform, or entertain.

What qualities of a writer do you think you have?

Probably to entertain.

So is that something you like to do?

I think I'm kind of good at it. I'm not one of those guys who just think of hilarious stuff right off the bat. I have to kind of spend some time thinking about humorous things I can talk about.

How do you use the quality of humor while writing?

My stories aren't really based on humor; I just kind of throw it in there.

Students' School Reputation

The second confidence feature was the students' perception of their reputation as a model student. In particular, students reported the role of their reputation in their immediate school context as one where "you have to make good grades and be a nice kid." In the digital writing context, students were particularly cognizant when their "mistakes" or writing errors were pointed out to them when receiving feedback from peers and their teacher. Students reported that it was "embarrassing" to make mistakes online. The following illustration from one student further demonstrates how the students' perceptions of their reputation impacted their confidence in their abilities as writers.

Franklin, Interview One: "Some people actually look up to me..."

What are your least favorite things with writing?

I don't have a lot of least favorite parts. But some of them are misspelling a word and not realizing it until the end. Or making a mark on my work, I don't really like that.

Ok, what do you mean by making a mark? Your teacher or your friends?

My friends. I mean, that's sort of embarrassing. I'm not bragging, but some people actually look up to me, and they like my work, but that's kind of embarrassing.

Knowledge of Writing Skills

The third confidence feature connected to the students' perceptions of their own knowledge about how to write. For example, students reported there were explicit writing skills in which they perceived that they "knew how to do" or which they were not as confident in implementing. Moreover, some students mentioned spelling specific words and elaborated on their ideas as specific skills in which they experienced difficulty. Some skills which students reported possessing were related to sentence structure, such as using a variety of sentence patterns and punctuating them correctly. In the following example, a student attributes his knowledge of being a writer to the skills that he developed through reading.

Franklin, Interview Two: "I've extended my memory on bigger words..."

What qualities of a writer do you think you have?

I have the ability to extend sentences and be able to use a semicolon correctly. I can find words with context clues easier than some people can. I can see a word I don't know and look at the sentence before and the words around it and see what it looks like, and I'll catch on to the meaning.

How have you used those qualities while writing?

I think I've been writing with bigger words than I did last year or this summer. I've extended my memory on bigger words because I'm reading seventh-grade level books.

Expectations for Responsible Behavior

The fourth confidence feature was associated with students' perceptions of expectations from the teachers and leaders in their school. Students in the study mentioned the importance of "being responsible" since they were now in the "fifth grade" and one of the "oldest" members of the school. Students discussed having their own computer to take home and a personal email account as one in which was a "privilege" given to them from their school. In addition to expectations on behavior regarding their use of the technology given to them, students also expressed that they perceived that they were expected to develop their academic skills through technology. In the following example, a student discusses his perceptions of school expectations for language use when writing with technology.

Ethan, Interview One: "They expect you to use bigger words than you know…"

What are your least favorite things about writing with technology?

I don't like that they expect you to use bigger words than you know because you have a dictionary and thesaurus on your computer so you can look up words a lot. We just wanna use words that we know.

So your teachers want you to use the bigger words? They like the bigger words?

Yes.

Relationships Inside and Outside the Classroom

The fifth confidence feature connected to student reports of their relationships with other individuals. Students expressed a connection to relationships both inside and outside of the classroom when talking about their performance on digital writing tasks. In particular, students related the comments from their relationships with others as an influence for evaluating their own perceptions of their writing abilities. In the following illustration, a student directly reported what his father said about his writing. Later in the same interview, the student responded that he believed that he possessed the same quality of a writer that his father had mentioned.

Dylan, Interview Two

He thought it was really creative.

Have you had a chance to share your story with anyone else outside your classmates?

My dad

What did he think about it?

He liked it. He thought it was really creative.

(...)

So what qualities of a writer do you think you have?

I still think the creativity...

Completion of the Product

The sixth confidence feature of the study was students' perception of their own writing products, particularly in regards to the completion of the product. Students reported concerns regarding how they felt about their writing products. Some students reported feeling "proud" of their final product, stating, "… it makes you feel like you can do anything." Other students reported feeling "frustrated" that they were unable to finish the product. In the following student illustration, a student commented about how he felt after he completed his product.

Ethan, Interview Three

It made me feel better actually about my writing.

So now that you've finished writing, can you give me a brief summary of what your story was about?

It was about these naiads, which are these water mythological creatures, and they are trying to find someone to lead their group because they were lost and had nothing. They went through a whole bunch of places—the Himalayas, the desert. Those were two of the places they went.

So how did that make you feel writing that story?

It made me feel better actually about my writing when I finished.

Ability to Individualize Writing

The seventh confidence feature related to the students' ability to personalize their writing to reflect their personal interests and style. Students reported the preference of being able to express themselves "creatively" with "uniqueness and spice" in their writing. Students also stressed their preference for writing what they wanted to write versus what somebody else wanted them to write. The following illustration demonstrates a student's perception of a writer's ability to choose.

Dylan, Interview Two

Just have fun with it and be you...

What do you think it means to be a writer?

I think it means to have fun with your writing and write about what you want to write about and not what another person says you have to write about. And, you know, just have fun with it and be you because maybe someone will like it, and maybe someone won't. That's basically it.

Technology Competence

The final confidence feature of the study was the students' perception of their competence with technology. Students reported a variety of skills necessary for writing with technology. Some students perceived that they possessed the skills for typing including multi-tasking while typing, while others expressed concerns for not being able to type "fast" enough or not being able to both type and "think" at the same time. Some students also expressed confidence in embedding links for multi-modal components, such as pictures, videos, and sound files. Other students reported that they had trouble remembering passwords, managing files, and following instructions for online navigation across multiple steps. The following illustration demonstrates one student's lack of confidence with technology when he experienced difficulty in the classroom with navigating online across multiple steps for one of his assignments.

Brandon, Interview One

I thought I was good with them until this happened

What kind of skills do you think are necessary to use digital writing?

Definitely be good with computers. You have to know a lot about them and know where to go. If the teacher says you have to pull up something on your toolbar or something, then you have to know where to go after that.

Have you used computers a lot? How do you feel about using computers?

I thought I was good with them until this happened, and it wasn't as easy as I expected.

In the previous sections, the eight confidence features that emerged from the study were presented with an example from the data to illustrate each feature. In the following section, two student vignettes illustrate the variety of student confidence features from a low-persisting student experience to a high-persisting student experience.

Two Student Vignettes of Confidence Features in Sustained Digital Writing Experiences

After the initial analysis, individual differences in confidence features were observed across the sustained digital writing tasks in the classroom. Sustained digital writing experiences consisted of both assigned and voluntary writing tasks as explicitly directed by the teacher and required students to work toward the completion of the task over multiple (3 or more) steps. Of note, two focal students were allowed the opportunity to participate in sustained digital writing experience with other students and reported higher levels of confidence than the four focal students who participated in the same digital writing experience independently. To illustrate these differences, a student who participated in a sustained digital writing experience with peers as well as a student who did not participate with peers in a sustained digital writing experience is presented. In the following student vignette, Andrew represents a student who worked independently on a sustained writing task and was the least persistent in completing the task.

Individual Sustained Writing Experience: Andrew

From the first interview session, Andrew was explicit in expressing his enjoyment of writing. He connected his enjoyment in writing to his interest in comic books, and his interest of extending the possibilities of reality by stating, "I like that, you know, the limit is not the sky. It's way higher." He further expressed that this type of writing was something in which he participated "at home" versus the classroom.

Andrew, Interview One

I like that, you know, the limit is not the sky. It's way higher.

You mentioned that you enjoyed writing about your experiences in your writing reflection from class. What were your favorite parts about writing the reflection assignment?

Everything. I love writing.

What about writing do you like?

I like that, you know, the limit is not the sky. It's way higher. So you can do whatever you want in your story. Put whatever you want in it. I love creating characters. Like writing little comic books sometimes.

So do you do that at home?

Sometimes I do at home. I don't know about sixth grade or later in the year fifth grade, but so far we haven't written any comic books.

As illustrated in the above interview session, Andrew described his interest in writing and his favorite parts of the writing process. Although he later described himself as "creative," he does not explicitly mention why he believes that he is creative in the first interview session. Additionally, he does not credit his own sense of "creativity" to feedback from others, nor does he mention how being creative relates to a respective audience in a piece of writing. In the next interview session, Andrew continued to explain his interest in writing as he further connected it to his perceptions of his own ability as a writer.

Andrew, Interview Two

It's more of just like when you feel like doing it.

What do you think it means to be a writer?

I think it means a good way to do your best at creativity and be creative. And if you're feeling bad about something, you can just write a little story to make you feel better. Or, you can write the story about what you did.

What qualities of a writer do you think you have?

Biggest would be creativity. Things that would never happen in the real world if I am writing a fiction story.

Have you had a chance to use that quality in the classroom yet? To imagine?

Yes, with freelance.

How many times have you gotten to use freelance do you think?

A little bit. It's something she would put up for homework like now just to make sure you have a paragraph or something done by Christmas. It's more of just like when you feel like doing it.

As noted in the second interview, Andrew continued to express his interest in writing fiction. He added that the "biggest" quality of a writer that he possessed was his "creativity" because of his ability to write about "things that would never happen in the real word." Similar to the first interview session, Andrew did not explicitly mention why he perceived himself to be creative, nor did he make other connections concerning how his audience impacted his own writing identity. He further noted that although he was able to participate in the sustained writing experience of "freelance writing," he only did so "a little bit." He also added that it was "more of just like when you feel like doing it." Although the student had previously expressed his interest in writing, the infrequency of his participation in the writing task indicated a gap between his interest in writing and his actual participation in the task. In the final interview, Andrew further explained his experience in the sustained writing task in which he participated on an individual level as well his other experiences participating in periodic writing tasks with his peers.

Andrew, Interview Three

I just got to a point where I wasn't really interested in this anymore.

Have you done any freelance writing yet?

I haven't really started into it, but I got one going. I wasn't really interested in how the story was going, but I thought of a way to change the story to keep it going. I just got to a point where I wasn't really interested in this anymore. I'd much rather be interested in something like a book—maybe like writing about just something I'm more interested in.

What was not interesting in that piece?

I think that I had seen a bunch of movies about that topic, and every time I tried to write something those movies came into my head. I was like, 'If I'm supposed to write when these movies come into my head, how am I supposed to come up with something creative?'

So trying to come up with something creative.

The topic was 'kids in charge.'

So did you ever come up with a topic?

No. I didn't take the time to look at any of the big topics, but nothing really caught my mind.

So what about the other writing you've done this semester in class? Have you done anything else besides the travel journal?

There's one in reading where we had to come up with a figurative language. And an essay. My essay was about Alabama. It was a great weekend place.

What about that writing was interesting?

Probably just all the experiences I've had. I've gone to Alabama all the time and have a lot of family. I get to use my experience in my writing with a bunch of adjectives.

What part did you not like writing?

I can't think of one. I love it. Well, I kind of like it, but it was my least favorite. (When we were) checking each other's in a group of two and we would check each other's. I didn't get a lot of feedback.

How did you feel when you didn't get a lot of feedback?

It kind of worried me a little bit when I didn't get any. I got one or two things, but they were like 'great essay.' It kind of worried me.

What do you mean by worried?

Suspenseful. I was hoping for more feedback. I didn't get what I expected to get.

The final interview with Andrew not only revealed how he had abandoned his sustained writing project, but it also revealed a previously unmentioned "worry" concerning his writing ability. During the first interview, Andrew expressed his interest in writing, and in the second interview, he expressed his perception of his ability as a writer in connection to his own creative ability. In the final interview, however, Andrew reported that he had "lost interest" in his sustained writing project because he "wasn't really interested in writing anymore." Furthermore, when speaking about periodic writing assignments in the classroom, Andrew expressed that his least favorite part of the writing activity was that he did not receive much feedback. He further expressed that this was his least favorite activity because he was a little "nervous" about not receiving enough feedback in his writing. Thus, the lack of social support in the classroom, particularly in relationship to his experiences with the degree of peer interaction, not only impacted his completion of his product, but also his confidence of his ability as a writer. In the following student vignette, Dylan offers a contrast to this experience as a student who participated in the sustained digital writing task with peer support and expressed higher levels of confidence.

Individual Sustained Digital Writing Experience: Dylan

As mentioned in the previous section, Dylan represented one of the two focal students who participated in the sustained digital writing task from start to finish with his peers. In the first interview illustration, the student's perceptions concerning what it means to be a writer is presented.

Dylan, Interview One

I really don't know...I think my desire is not to be a writer when I grow up.

What do you think it means to be a writer?

A writer is someone who writes books. Not any types of books, but books that bring you in and make you want to read the book. And the title of the book is amazing, so you're like 'ooh I wanna read that'! Then you start reading and you're like 'whoa'. It's like you're watching a movie but you can hold the movie. You can imagine what they see. You can imagine how horrible they were. You can imagine how ugly they were. You can imagine how happy he was. You can imagine everything in the book.

What qualities of a writer do you think you have?

I really don't know. I don't want to be bragging and stuff. I think my desire is not to be a writer when I grow up. (Our teacher) has been teaching me some good stuff on prepositions. I just took a test.

How have you used some of these qualities to write in your classroom? Or how do you think you will use what you're learning? How do you think you will use these skills in your own writing?

She's been teaching us prepositions like 'and', no 'and' isn't a preposition. 'After' is a preposition! 'Before' is a preposition. Instead of saying 'Bob...', no you can't have a sentence without a preposition. Like, 'like' is a preposition. "I was behind the cash register." That tells you where you were. We are going to use that in our daily writing, in our college, and in everything that has to do with writing and in our speaking.

In the first interview session, Dylan did not explicitly answer the question concerning his perception of his abilities as a writer. Instead, he addressed the question by explaining that his "desire" was not "to be a writer" in the future. He then proceeded to talk about the writing skills that he was learning from his teacher in his classroom, but he never explicitly mentioned these qualities as characteristics of his own writing identity. At this point in the study, the student had not begun the sustained digital writing task. During the following interview, Dylan continued to talk about his perceptions of himself as a writer while participating in the sustained digital writing task with his peers.

Dylan, Interview Two

I don't want to be a writer when I grow up, but I like writing.

What do you think it means to be a writer?

To be creative in your writing. You just jot your ideas down, and if it's bad, you just delete it and figure out how to make it better. It's a lot of failure, but sooner or later you'll get it. Let me give you an example. In Angry Birds, they took a while to become popular, but now they're over the top popular.

So what do you mean by popular?

It's in the top ten. Each book has its own thing. One book could be horrible, but at least one person will think it's great. More or less if it's horrible, only one person out of a billion will like it. Unless it's a book that you have to read, then you read it and you see what the writer means, and on the back it tells how they became a writer. And sometimes it's like they thought and thought and then finally came up with a good idea, and they think to themselves, "I could be a writer," and then they become one.

So what qualities of a writer do you think you have?

I don't want to be a writer when I grow up, but I like writing. It's pretty fun. If I don't like a book, I won't like reading, but if I like a book, I will like reading. I like fiction and magic and some terrifying stuff and some humor. I like humor a lot.

Have you used any of these qualities or things you like in your writing this semester?

I probably have, but I don't know. The haunted house has some scary stuff like a headless man on a headless horse. And there's a huge black widow and a clown. Clowns scare me.

In the previous interview, Dylan once again did not explicitly address which qualities of a writer he possessed. Instead, he continued to express that he did not wish "to be a writer when he grows up," and added, "but I like writing." This interview represented a shift in the student's outlook from the first interview when he had yet to participate in the sustained writing task with peers as he differentiated the career of a writer from the interest or task of writing itself. Also different from the first interview, the student connected the ultimate success of writing to connecting to an audience. He demonstrated this connection by supplying the example of the makers of *Angry Birds* when he said, "They took a while to be popular, but now they're over the top popular." He further extended this conversation by commenting to his own reading interests by adding, "If I don't like a book, I won't like reading, but if I like a book, I will like reading." The student concluded this connection to reading what he liked by ultimately reporting that he also wrote about what he liked including "some terrifying stuff" in his digital writing. In the final interview, the student further developed the connection between his perceptions of writing and writing in connection to the interest of a readership.

Dylan, Interview Three

I think it means to be creative and make people want to read more.

Has anything changed over the past semester with what you used to do with your writing?

I was in enrichment last time, and this time, I'm not so this time, I'm doing that thing where we had to describe the pictures in a sentence using sentence patterns and stuff.

Did you enjoy writing your story?

Yes, I loved making stories because I can use my own ideas.

So now that you have written your own story, what do you think it means to be a writer?

I think it means to be creative and make people want to read more. Because I'm not really a reader and I don't do it a lot, but I need to start more. And it helps people feel that they can make whatever they want.

What qualities do you have or do you think you have learned this semester?

I think I'm better at sentence structure and things like that now.

As illustrated in the last student interview, Dylan shifted in his response over time to his perceptions of what it means to be a writer and what qualities of a writer that he thought that he possessed. In each interview, Dylan mentioned that being "creative" was an important quality of a writer, but in the last interview, Dylan extended his perception to include the ability to "make people want to read more." This elaboration illustrates the student's developing understanding of writing in connection to audience. Finally, the last interview represented a shift in Dylan's response to the writing qualities which he possessed. During the first two interviews, Dylan did not explicitly comment about his skill level of writing. Instead, he only mentioned the skills that were being taught in the classroom. In the final interview, however, he stated, "I think I'm better at sentence structure and things like that now." Ultimately, Dylan expressed differing perceptions of his understanding of what it meant to be a writer and the qualities which he possessed as the semester progressed. This shift provides evidence of how his experience working with peers in a sustained digital writing project impacted his identity as a writer.

Self-Efficacy and Persistence in Sustained Digital Writing Experiences

The student vignettes in the previous section represented two students who participated in the same digital writing task over a sustained, or prolonged, period. One student participated in this task independently with the opportunity to participate virtually with other students, while the other student participated in this task in a face-to-face group setting with the same virtual access to each other's work. Across the three interview sessions, Andrew discussed working individually on the sustained digital writing project. Although the student reported previous experiences where he had received comments from his peers and family concerning his creative ability, the student reported that he felt "worried" when he did not receive virtual feedback on his work. Additionally, even though the student reported interest in the assignment and his enjoyment of writing, he eventually reported that he "lost interest" in his project and abandoned his topic. In contrast, Dylan worked with other students in a face-to-face group on the same sustained digital writing project. Although initially this student reported that he did not want to be a writer, he persevered through the writing assignment, presented his story to the class, and discussed his ideas for future writing. Thus, the student vignettes illustrated the relationship between the students who participated in sustained digital writing tasks with a higher degree of face-to-face peer interaction than students who participated in the same sustained digital writing tasks without opportunity for face-to-face peer interaction.

DISCUSSION AND RECOMMENDATIONS

Social Writing and Multi-Modalities

A growing body of research demonstrates the new ways in which students are participating in literacies outside of the classroom including gaming (Gee, 2007), fan fiction (Black, 2009), and blogging (Guzzetti & Gamboa, 2005). These activities are embedded social practices that occur over sustained periods of time and engage students in dynamic forms of multimodal production, often involving novel and creative representations for sharing. However, as Burnett and Merchant (2011) contend, the types of digital writing in the classroom often reflect views of technology as a presentation of risk to be monitored which ultimately hinders further integration of students' outside experiences into the classroom. Such disconnects between students' in-school and out-of-school digital literacy practices were most evident in this study when students discussed the ways that they communicated inside and outside of the classroom with technology. Although students reported participating in dynamic forms of communication outside of the classroom through video gaming systems or digital conferencing tools, their digital writing experiences in the classroom did not encompass the breadth of modalities of which they reported participating in contexts outside of school. For example, students in the study reported using *Snapchat* at home for communicating with text, video, and graphics; however, when discussing communication at school, students reported that such use of "chatting" with teachers or students was not considered appropriate communication for school. Thus, students reported a division of tasks that were "approved" for school versus tasks that were not, including communication across modalities. As student engagement continues to be connected to the increasingly social, multimodal environments, concerns for the role of such integration will likely continue to play a role in the educational decisions in the future (Clarke & Besnoy, 2010; Hutchison, Beschorner, & Schmidt-Crawford, 2012).

Peer Interaction and Digital Writing Tasks

Although research in engagement with digital technology (Jenkins, et al., 2006) has been an ongoing area for discussion, the role of peer interaction in student engagement has been an emerging topic of research (Alvermann & Hagood, 2000; Davies, 2012; Gee, 2011). The findings in the current study were particularly significant in that they suggested that engagement in digital tasks extended beyond the inclusion of "engaging" technology tools to include peer interaction as a significant factor for participation. Ultimately, this research added to previous conversations by considering how expressions of interests in the digital writing tasks alone did not necessarily mean a student would complete the task. For some students, the missing engagement factor appeared to be the social component, particularly noted in the lack of peer interaction.

Closely connected, this study related to previous research regarding the reader-writer relationship (Gere, 1987; Moss, Nicholas, & Highberg, 2004). In most of these studies, students favored their own needs as writers without considering the needs of their readers. Thus, helping students to connect to their audience (Gere, 1987) had been found to help students improve their writing skills. The current study illustrates ways in which students who worked together in sustained digital writing tasks were more successful than students who worked on the same tasks independently. These students were observed building connections with each other through participating in the digital writing experience together. Their comments to one another helped them to not only generate ideas, but also to make improvements to their product. These findings are consistent with traditional research on findings from peer interactions in writer's groups (Gere, 1987).

Degree of Peer Interaction and Interaction Spaces

As previously eluded, writing groups, peer response groups, and writer's workshops (Gere, 1987; Moss, et al., 2004) are all bodies of research that have examined the role of peer interaction in traditional writing environments. In particular, these studies have discussed both benefits and challenges of student collaboration in writing environments. Although peer collaboration has been shown to encourage student participation, challenges associated with peer collaboration have often been associated with the students' inability or lack of skills for constructing appropriate feedback (Keh, 1990) for their peers beyond either generic response or superficial suggestions for improvement. In the digital writing environment, however, research has supported modest gains of extended feedback from peers through digital tools (Ellis, 2011; Honeycutt, 2001). In fact, a study by the Pew Foundation has also contributed to this discussion by stating that although digital technologies "encourage greater collaboration among students," teachers still report that students lack the necessary skills for successful peer revision (Purcell et al., 2013a, p. 2). In the current study, the students who participated in sustained digital writing tasks in both physical and digital proximity of peers received more peer comments and made more revisions to their digital writing products than students who worked individually on the same task. Although the students who worked individually could have "shared" their work with a peer in the digital space for peer revision and feedback, the students did not choose this option and expressed frustrations with the development of their ideas and digital writing products. This finding relates to previous studies concerning the nature of peer culture in physical negotiations of digital spaces (Aarsand, 2010). Thus, the nature of physical proximity and verbal feedback in digital writing environments, especially in the consideration for instructional design components, continue to be relevant topics of discussion.

CONCLUSION

This chapter details the experiences of one classroom of fifth-grade boys who encountered digital writing on a daily basis. Eight confidence features were presented with an example of a low-persisting and high-persisting student experience. These findings were similar to the scholarly context of social learning theories and New Literacies studies as it emphasized the social nature of digital writing.

Although the findings are not generalizable as they represent a specific school context, they present significance through providing a detailed picture of one classroom of students who had traditional access to digital tools for writing inside and outside of the classroom. While this study provides unique insights for teachers and students with emerging digital writing experiences, recommendations for future research include continued exploration of the social nature of digital writing from a diverse range of student experiences. In particular, more studies exploring issues of intersectionality among various subgroups of boys are needed to explore how writing self-efficacy is impacted through a variety of student perspectives and experiences.

In sum, the boys in this study with greater peer access in physical spaces of the classroom expressed higher levels of self-efficacy and persisted to make more frequent changes to their products than boys with only access to digital spaces to their peers. While more research is needed to confirm gender differences in the specific social needs of boys and girls in digital classrooms, this study documents a need for teachers to employ strategic scaffolding for students—potentially even more so for boys—in connecting with their peers in both digital and physical spaces. Perhaps with time, more teachers and researchers alike will more closely examine how to best approach the digital writing needs of all students in blended learning environments.

REFERENCES

Aarsand, P. (2010). Young boys playing digital games. *Nordic Journal of Digital Literacy*, *1*(5), 39–54.

Alloway, N., & Gilbert, P. (1997). Boys and literacy: Lessons from Australia. *Gender and Education*, *9*(1), 49–60. doi:10.1080/09540259721448

Alvermann, D. (2008). Why bother theorizing adolescents online literacies for classroom practice and research? *Journal of Adolescent & Adult Literacy*, *52*(1), 8–19. doi:10.1598/JAAL.52.1.2

Alvermann, D., & Hagood, M. (2000). Fandom and critical media literacy. *Journal of Adolescent & Adult Literacy*, *43*(5), 436–446.

Anderson, R. S., Goode, G. G., Mitchell, J. S., & Thompson, R. (2013). Using digital tools to teach writing in K-12 classrooms. In J. Whittingham, S. Huffman, W. Rickman, & C. Wiedmaier (Eds.), *Technological tools for the literacy classroom* (pp. 10–26). Hershey, PA: IGI Global. doi:10.4018/978-1-4666-3974-4.ch002

Anderson, R. S., Mitchell, J. S., Thompson, R., & Trefz, K. (2014). Supporting young writers through the writing process in a paperless classroom. In R. S. Anderson & C. Mims (Eds.), *Handbook of research on digital tools for writing instruction in K-12 settings* (pp. 337–362). Hershey, PA: IGI Global. doi:10.4018/978-1-4666-5982-7.ch017

Bandura, A. (1977). Self-efficacy: Toward a unifying theory of behavioral change. *Psychological Review*, *84*(2), 191–215. doi:10.1037/0033-295X.84.2.191 PMID:847061

Black, R. W. (2009). Online fan fiction and critical media literacy. *Journal of Computing in Teacher Education*, *26*(2), 75.

Bogard, J. M., & McMackin, M. C. (2012). Combining traditional and new literacies in a 21st-century writing workshop. *The Reading Teacher*, *65*(5), 313–323. doi:10.1002/TRTR.01048

Bruning, R. H., & Kauffman, D. F. (2015). Self-efficacy beliefs and motivation in writing development. In C. MacArthur, S. Graham, & J. Fitzgerald (Eds.), *Handbook of writing research* (pp. 160–173). New York, NY: Guilford Press.

Burnett, C., & Merchant, G. (2011). Is there a space for critical literacy in the context of social media? *English Teaching*, *10*(1).

Clark, C., & Dugdale, G. (2009). *Young people's writing: Attitudes, behaviour and the role of technology*. National Literacy Trust. Retrieved from http://www.literacytrust.org.uk/assets/0000/0226/Writing_survey_2009.pdf

Clarke, L. W., & Besnoy, K. (2010). Connecting the old to the new: What technology-crazed adolescents tell us about teaching content area literacy. *The Journal of Media Literacy Education*, *2*(1), 47–56.

Coley, R. J. (2001). *Differences in the Gender Gap: Comparisons across Racial/Ethnic Groups in Education and Work*. Princeton, NJ: Policy Information Center.

Connell, R. W. (1995). *Masculinities*. Cambridge, UK: Polity Press.

Creswell, J. W. (2012). *Qualitative inquiry and research design: Choosing among five approaches*. Thousand Oaks, CA: Sage Publications.

Crotty, M. (1998). *The foundations of social research*. Thousand Oaks, CA: Sage Publications.

Davies, J. (2012). Facework on facebook as a new literacy practice. *Computers & Education*, *59*(1), 19–29. doi:10.1016/j.compedu.2011.11.007

Dudeney, G., & Hockly, N. (2016). Literacies, technology and language teaching. The Routledge Handbook of Language Learning and Technology, 115.

Ellis, J. (2011). Peer feedback on writing: Is on-line actually better than on-paper. *Journal of Academic Language and Learning*, *5*(1), 88–99.

Ezzy, D. (2002). *Qualitative analysis: Practice and innovation*. Crows Nest, Australia: Allen & Unwin.

Fabos, B., & Young, M. D. (1999). Telecommunication in the classroom: Rhetoric versus reality. *Review of Educational Research*, *69*(3), 217–259. doi:10.3102/00346543069003217

Fabry, D. L., & Higgs, J. R. (1997). Barriers to the effective use of technology in education: Current status. *Journal of Educational Computing Research*, *17*(4), 385–395. doi:10.2190/C770-AWA1-CMQR-YTYV

Falloon, G. (2015). Whats the difference? Learning collaboratively using iPads in conventional classrooms. *Computers & Education*, *84*, 62–77. doi:10.1016/j.compedu.2015.01.010

Frater, G. (1998). Boys and literacy. In K. Bleach (Ed.), *Raising boys' achievement in schools*. Stoke-on-Trent, UK: Trentham Books.

Frater, G. (2000). *Securing boys' literacy*. London, UK: The Basic Skills Agency.

Gee, J. P. (2007). *What video games have to teach us about learning and literacy*. New York, NY: Palgrave Macmillan.

Gee, J. P. (2011). The new literacy studies. In *Social linguistics and literacies: Ideology in discourses* (pp. 63–86). London, UK: Routledge.

Gere, A. R. (1987). *Writing groups: History, theory, and implications*. Carbondale, IL: Southern Illinois University Press.

Guzzetti, B., & Gamboa, M. (2005). Online journaling: The informal writings of two adolescent girls. *Research in the Teaching of English*, *40*(2), 168–206.

Hare, S., Howard, E., & Pope, M. (2002). Technology integration: Closing the gap between what preservice teachers are taught to do and what they can do. *Journal of Technology and Teacher Education*, *10*(2), 191–203.

Honeycutt, L. (2001). Comparing e-mail and synchronous conferencing in online peer response. *Written Communication*, *18*(1), 26–60. doi:10.1177/0741088301018001002

Hutchison, A., Beschorner, B., & Schmidt-Crawford, D. (2012). Exploring the use of the Ipad for literacy learning. *The Reading Teacher*, *66*(1), 15–23. doi:10.1002/TRTR.01090

Hutchison, A. C., & Reinking, D. (2011). Teachers' perceptions of integrating information and communication technologies into literacy instruction: A national survey in the U. S. *Reading Research Quarterly*, *46*(4), 312–333.

Jenkins, H., Clinton, K., Purushotma, R., Robinson, A., & Weigel, M. (2006). *Confronting the challenges of participatory culture: Media education for the 21st century*. White Paper. MacArthur Foundation.

Keh, C. L. (1990). Feedback in the writing process: A model and methods for implementation. *ELT Journal*, *44*(4), 294–304. doi:10.1093/elt/44.4.294

Kelly, G. J., & Green, J. (1998). The social nature of knowing: Toward a sociocultural perspective on conceptual change and knowledge construction. In B. J. Guzzetti & C. R. Hynd (Eds.), *Perspectives on conceptual change: Multiple ways to understand knowing and learning in a complex world* (pp. 145–181). New York: Routledge.

Kiili, C., Laurinen, L., & Marttunen, M. (2008). Students evaluating Internet sources: From versatile evaluators to uncritical readers. *Journal of Educational Computing Research*, *39*(1), 75–95. doi:10.2190/EC.39.1.e

Kim, Y. S., Al Otaiba, S., Wanzek, J., & Gatlin, B. (2015). Toward an understanding of dimensions, predictors, and the gender gap in written composition. *Journal of Educational Psychology*, *107*(1), 79–95. doi:10.1037/a0037210 PMID:25937667

Lankshear, C., & Knobel, M. (2003). New technologies in early childhood literacy research: A review of research. *Journal of Early Childhood Literacy, 3*(1), 59–82. doi:10.1177/14687984030031003

Lankshear, C., & Knobel, M. (2006). *New literacies: Everyday practices and cla ssroom learning* (2nd ed.). New York, NY: Open University Press.

Lankshear, C., Knobel, M., & Curran, C. (2012). Conceptualizing and researching "new literacies". The Encyclopedia of Applied Linguistics. doi:10.1002/9781405198431

Leu, D. J. Jr, Kinzer, C. K., Coiro, J., & Cammack, D. (2004). Toward a theory of new literacies emerging from the Internet and other information and communication technologies. In R. B. Ruddell & N. Unrau (Eds.), *Theoretical models and processes of reading* (5th ed.; pp. 1568–1611). Newark, DE: International Reading Association.

Leu, D. J., OByrne, W. I., Zawilinski, L., McVerry, J. G., & Everett-Cocapardo, H. (2009). Expanding the new literacies conversation. *Educational Researcher, 38*(4), 264–269. doi:10.3102/0013189X09336676

Mac an Ghaill, M. (1994). *The making of men.* Buckingham, UK: Oxford University Press.

MacArthur, C. A. (1998). Word processing with speech synthesis and word prediction: Effects on the dialogue journal writing of students with learning disabilities. *Learning Disability Quarterly, 21*(2), 151–166. doi:10.2307/1511342

MacArthur, C. A., Graham, S., Haynes, J. B., & DeLaPaz, S. (1996). Spelling checkers and students with learning disabilities: Performance comparisons and impact on spelling. *The Journal of Special Education, 30*(1), 35–57. doi:10.1177/002246699603000103

Maynard, T. (2002). *Boys and literacy: Exploring the issues.* Routledge.

Mead, S. (2006). *The truth about boys and girls.* Washington, DC: Education Sector.

Millard, E. (1997). Differently literate: Gender identity and the construction of the developing reader. *Gender and Education, 9*(1), 31–48. doi:10.1080/09540259721439

Morrisett, L. (2001). Foreword. In B. M. Compaine (Ed.), *The digital divide: Facing a crisis or creating a myth?* (pp. ix–x). Cambridge, MA: MIT Press.

Moss, B. J., Nicolas, M., & Highberg, N. P. (2004). *Writing groups inside and outside the classroom.* Mahwah, NJ: Lawrence Erlbaum Associates.

Mossberger, K., Tolbert, C., & Stansbury, M. (2003). *Virtual inequality: Beyond the digital divide.* Washington, DC: Georgetown University Press.

Noble, C., & Bradford, W. (2000). *Getting it right for boys...and girls.* London, UK: Routledge.

Pajares, F. (2003). Self-efficacy beliefs, motivation, and achievement in writing: A review of the literature. *Reading & Writing Quarterly, 19*(2), 139–158. doi:10.1080/10573560308222

Penny, V. (1998). Raising boys' achievement in English. In K. Bleach (Ed.), *Raising boys' achievement in schools.* Stoke-on-Trent, UK: Trentham Books.

Pickering, J. (1997). *Raising boys' achievement.* Stafford, UK: Network Education Press Ltd.

Purcell, K., Heaps, A., Buchanan, J., & Friedrich, L. (2013a). How teachers are using technology at home and in their classrooms. Washington, DC: Pew Research Center's Internet & American Life Project; Retrieved from http://www.pewinternet.org

Purcell, K., Heaps, A., Buchanan, J., & Friedrich, L. (2013b). The impact of digital tools on student writing and how writing is taught in schools. Washington, DC: Pew Research Center's Internet & American Life Project. Retrieved from http://www.pewinternet.org

Riel, M. M., & Levin, J. A. (1990). Building electronic communities: Success and failure in computer networking. *Instructional Science*, *19*(2), 145–169. doi:10.1007/BF00120700

Rogers, L. A., & Graham, S. (2008). A meta-analysis of single subject design writing intervention research. *Journal of Educational Psychology*, *100*(4), 879–906. doi:10.1037/0022-0663.100.4.879

Rutter, M., Caspi, A., Fergusson, D. M., Horwood, L. J., Goodman, R., Maughan, B., & Carroll, J. (2004). Gender differences in reading difficulties: Findings from four epidemiology studies. *Journal of the American Medical Association*, *291*, 2007–2012. doi:10.1001/jama.291.16.2007 PMID:15113820

Smith, A. (1996). *Accelerated learning in the classroom*. Stafford, UK: Network Education Press Ltd.

Snider, S., & Foster, J. M. (2000). Stepping stones for linking, learning, and moving toward electronic literacy: Integrating emerging technology in an author study project. *Computers in the Schools*, *16*(2), 91–108. doi:10.1300/J025v16n02_09

Sokal, L., & Katz, H. (2008). Effects of technology and male teachers on boys reading. *Australian Journal of Education*, *52*(1), 81–94. doi:10.1177/000494410805200106

Tweddle, S. (1997). A retrospective: Fifteen years of computers in English. *English Education*, *31*(2), 5–13. doi:10.1111/j.1754-8845.1997.tb00120.x

Villalón, R., Mateos, M., & Cuevas, I. (2015). High school boys and girls writing conceptions and writing self-efficacy beliefs: What is their role in writing performance? *Educational Psychology*, *35*(6), 653–674. doi:10.1080/01443410.2013.836157

Vygotsky, L. (1986). *Thought and language*. Cambridge, MA: MIT Press.

Warschauer, M., Zheng, B., Niiya, M., Cotten, S., & Farkas, G. (2014). Balancing the one-to-one equation: Equity and access in three laptop programs. *Equity & Excellence in Education*, *47*(1), 46–62. doi:10.1080/10665684.2014.866871

Wertsch, J. V. (1991). *Voices of the mind: A sociocultural approach to mediated action*. Cambridge, MA: Harvard University Press.

Witte, S. (2009). "Twitterdee, twitterdumb": Teaching in the time of technology, tweets, and trespassing. *California English*, *15*(1), 23–25.

Wolfe, E. W., Bolton, S., Feltovich, B., & Niday, D. M. (1996). The influence of student experience with word processors on the quality of essays written for a direct writing assessment. *Assessing Writing*, *3*(2), 123–147. doi:10.1016/S1075-2935(96)90010-0

Wollscheid, S., Sjaastad, J., & Tømte, C. (2016). The impact of digital devices vs. Pen (cil) and paper on primary school students writing skills–A research review. *Computers & Education*, *95*, 19–35. doi:10.1016/j.compedu.2015.12.001

Wood, M. (2011). Collaborative lab reports with Google Docs. *The Physics Teacher*, *49*(3), 158–159. doi:10.1119/1.3555501

Yin, R. (2009). *Case study research: Design and methods* (5th ed.). Thousand Oaks, CA: Sage Publications.

Zawilinski, L. (2009). HOT blogging: A framework for blogging to promote higher order thinking. *The Reading Teacher*, *62*(8), 650–661. doi:10.1598/RT.62.8.3

Zheng, B., Lawrence, J., Warschauer, M., & Lin, C. H. (2015). Middle school students writing and feedback in a cloud-based classroom environment. *Technology. Knowledge and Learning*, *20*(2), 201–229. doi:10.1007/s10758-014-9239-z

KEY TERMS AND DEFINITIONS

21ˢᵗ Century Learning: A pedagogical approach to preparing students for college and career contexts beyond the immediate school context by utilizing a core set of skills such as collaboration, critical thinking, and digital literacy.

Digital Divide: A term used to define the differences between individuals with greater access to information and communication tools of the Internet. These discrepancies can be found across geographic locations such as urban or rural areas or across socio-economic status.

Digital Skills Divide: A term to further extend the definition of the digital divide to include the specific skills and knowledge bases required to be proficient with the use of technology.

New Literacies Theory: A body of research involving the multiple ways in which social beings interact through digital technologies. New Literacies continually broaden the definition of literacy to include ways of communicating meaning beyond text.

Self-Efficacy: The belief in one's ability to persevere through a desired or designated task; more commonly referred to as confidence.

Sociocultural Learning Theory: Theories of learning which emphasize the social nature of learning in the meaning-making process.

APPENDIX 1

Student Interview Questions

1a. What experiences do elementary boys bring with them into the classroom concerning the use of digital tools?
    i.   How have you used technology at home or other places besides How have you used technology at school?
    ii. What are your favorite experiences with digital writing tools? What are your least favorite experiences?

1b. How do students individually interact with digital tools throughout digital writing tasks in the classroom?
    iii. If you had a friend outside of your classroom, what would you tell him or her about what you have been learning or doing when you are writing online?
    iv. What did you do when you first got online for this particular project?
    v. Can you walk me through exactly what you did online for this assignment? What were your favorite parts about this assignment? What were your least favorite parts about this assignment?

1c. How do students interact with teachers, classmates, and others throughout digital writing tasks in the classroom?
    vi. Tell me a little bit about what you and your classmates do together online. How do you work together with your classmates when writing online?
    vii. Tell me a little bit about what your teacher does while you are working online. How do you communicate or work with your teacher when you are writing online?
    viii. Tell me a little bit more about how you interact with parents or other people online. How do you communicate or work with people other than your classmates or your teacher online?

2a. What are the characteristics of these writing products?
    i.   Here I have an example of something you have written in class. Can you describe this piece of writing for me?
    ii. What are your favorite parts about this piece of writing?
    iii. What are your least favorite parts about this piece of writing?

2b. How do digital writing tools shape these writing products?
    iv. Can you tell me about the particular digital tools that were used to create this piece of writing?
    v. How did you use those tools to create this piece of writing?
    vi. If someone did not know how to use these digital tools, what would you tell them about how you can use them to create this piece of writing?

2c. How do these digital writing products differ from traditional pen and paper products?
    vii. How do you think this piece of writing would look different if it were on pen and paper?
    viii. What do you think is different about using these digital tools to create this piece of writing than using paper and pencil to write?
    ix. What do you like to do better: writing with pen and paper or writing online? Can you tell me why?

3a. What perceptions does the student express concerning his abilities as a writer?
    i.   What do you think it means to be a writer?

ii.   What qualities of a writer do you have?

iii. How have you used these qualities this semester to write in your classroom?

3b. What perceptions does the student express concerning their abilities as digital composers?

iv.   What skills do you think are necessary to use digital writing tools?

v.   What qualities for using digital writing tools do you have?

vi.   How have you used these qualities this semester to write using digital tools in your classroom?

3c. What perceptions does the student express concerning the relevance for himself of using digital tools for writing?

vii. Why do you think people use technology to write?

viii. What do you think writing would be like if you didn't have these digital tools?

ix.   How do you think you will you use the knowledge that you have learned about writing with these digital tools in your future?

APPENDIX 2

An example of Student Artifact Collection is shown in Figure 2.

Figure 2. A Focal Student's draft of a writing sample from Google Docs

> **Key:**
> Focal Student "Dylan"
> Freelance Writing Draft Version
>
> **The genre from which I am writing is:** Fiction
>
> **The contest in which I am participating is:** Adventure Writers
>
> **The link to the writing contest is:** http://adventurewrite.com/kids/contest.html
>
> **The skill(s) from my unit test in which I still need practice is:**
>
> **Brainstorm** ideas here (the box will get larger if you need more space): Setting: Frightening night. Characters: Me, man with no head, vampire, clown, shark with legs and arms, ogre, black widow. Title: The Frightening Night in Scaryville.
>
> **Draft** your ideas here:
>
> <u>The Frightening Night in Scaryville</u>
>
> So there I was, reading my great uncle's diary in my bed. This is what I read, "One Halloween night I was in the neighborhood of Scaryville. I was about to enter the sc-"
>
> "Honey," my mom said, "time for breakfast."
>
> "I'm coming Mom," I said to her. I was in the middle of reading my great uncle's diary that he gave to me before he died. I was reading about what my great uncle was telling me when I visited him in the hospital. On my way downstairs, I was thinking about what I read this morning. Where was he going, I thought to myself. After I had my breakfast burrito, I went to school. All that day, I was thinking about his diary. Maybe, he was about to enter the Scaddadle Taco House, or maybe it wasn't a taco house, maybe it was a Chinese restaurant, but I wasn't going to stop reading till I find out.
>
> After school, I immediately did my homework, and when I finished it, I went to my bed and read the part where I left off. I read, "I was about to enter the scariest house in the neighborhood. It was all decorated for Halloween. When I walked inside the house, there were live monsters. (...)

APPENDIX 3

Example of Researcher's Expanded Field Observation Memo

(1:05-2:05)

As I walked into the classroom, the "C schedule" is flipped beside the door. I notice there are students in varying apparel from hooded sweatshirts and jackets to short sleeves and shorts. Some of the boys are wearing [polo] style shirts with colors with varying logos including a [Polo] horse, whale, and [Nike] swoosh. I also notice at the back of the room some of the boys are gathered by a table with what appears to be 7-8 bags of candy. As I am observing the students enter the room, one boy welcomes me back. Another boy tells me that he forgot to study for his test today.

On the board, I read the following:

Command, Shift 4

1.   Study for test
2.   Word Voyage
3.   15 sequencing/1 chronological order (hw)
4.   Work on spelling 5 (work ahead)

At this point, the teacher enters the room wearing a [blue] long-sleeved shirt. She is wearing a [knee-length] skirt with a [blue] [checked] pattern and open-toed shoes with [black] straps and a [wooden] platform. She tells the students to open "Haiku" (The learning management platform where the teacher uses the calendar feature in particular to embed links for the students to follow each day). She expresses to the students that she has a feeling that they were not prepared for the test due to the weekend.

As the students are starting their computers and opening their browsers, the teacher tells me hello as she also sits and works at her computer. Here students continuing to start their computers, and a few students ask questions like: "What if you don't finish in sixty minutes?" The teacher replies to this question, "You will." At this point, the teacher connects the projector screen and instructs students to focus their attention to the front of the room and says, "Shh" to the group. Before the teacher was able to begin her instructions, a man with what appears to be a fifth-grade boy gives a piece of chocolate to the teacher (Here the man appears to be the father or caregiver of the child, and I wonder if this is the same family that returned from Ireland of which the class had Skyped the following week.) Teacher says, "Is that for me?" and takes the chocolate and says a [few] more words before returning to the screen. (…)

Chapter 8
Healthcare Education:
Integrating Simulation Technologies

Eva M. Frank
Northern Illinois University, USA

ABSTRACT

The integration of technology into the education and continuous professional education of allied health professionals is evolving. Integrating simulation as an authentic instructional modality has changed how clinicians learn and practice the clinical knowledge, skills, and abilities they are required to be competent in to ensure patient safety. A lot of advances have been made in the utilization of simulation in various domains. Continuing medical education is such a domain, and this chapter will briefly describe the history of simulation, present simulation as an authentic instructional activity, examine education trends of using simulation-based learning, highlight two applicable theoretical frameworks, and present a case study that effectively utilized simulation as an authentic instructional strategy and assessment during a continuing medical education course for athletic trainers.

INTRODUCTION

The integration of technology into the education and continuous medical education of healthcare personnel is evolving. Integrating simulation as an instructional modality has changed how clinicians learn and practice the clinical knowledge, skills, and abilities they are required to be competent in to ensure patient safety. The safety of patients and the ability to integrate a learning tool into education to decrease medical errors has larger healthcare implications. When embedded appropriately, simulation immerses the learner into a real-world environment that provides them with opportunities to practice and refine skills; thereby, decreasing medical errors or their likelihood to harm a patient due to the lack of exposure to specific clinical skills. The ability for the learner to deliberately practice clinical skills, techniques, and behaviors, is imperative to foster and ensure the safety of all patients (Gaba, 2007). Simulation is an ideal instructional strategy that is effective when utilized in teaching clinically relevant knowledge and skills to a multitude of health care providers (Birdane et al., 2012; Fraser et al., 2011; Hatala, Issenberg, Kassen, Cole, Bacchus, & Scalese, 2008; Issenberg & Scalese, 2008; Lavranos, Koliaki, Briasoulis,

DOI: 10.4018/978-1-5225-2838-8.ch008

Nikolaou, & Stefanadis, 2013; McKinney, Cook, Wood, & Hatala, 2013). Simulated educational activities have revolutionized the process of educating health care professionals at all levels (Gaba, 2007). The utilization of simulation is diverse and spans across various domains. Continuing medical education is such a domain, and this chapter will (1) provide a brief history if simulation, (2) present simulation as an authentic instructional activity to enhance learning, (3) review the various types of simulators that are available, (4) examine educational trends of utilizing simulation as an instructional modality, (5) highlight two theoretical frameworks that simulation-based instruction can be grounded in, and lastly, (6) present a case study that effectively utilized high-fidelity and low-fidelity simulation as an authentic instructional strategy and assessment during a continuing medical education course for athletic trainers.

SECTION 1: A BRIEF HISTORY OF SIMULATION

Simulation dates back to the 1940s, when it was successfully incorporated into training professionals on flight simulators who worked in high-risk environments. Since then, simulation and its application broadened into the military, civic aviators, and the National Aeronautics and Space Administration (NASA), who all have utilized simulators to train their pilots and astronauts for hypothetically catastrophic in-flight situations (Rosen, 2008). When utilizing simulation to train professionals, they are provided with the ability to practice their behavior in a high-risk, potentially life-threatening, situation. More importantly, pilots and astronauts learn how to effectively behave and manage such situations without risking an actual injury to themselves or others. With this being said, there is a direct connection with utilizing simulation in the healthcare domain to advance the delivery of healthcare and improve the safety of the patients (Byrne, 2013).

The history of medical simulators and its use in training medical professionals has primitive origins. In the ninth century, simple models aided in explaining the process of childbirth and in the 1600s, the process of childbirth was taught to midwives via manikins referred to as 'phantoms' (Gardner & Raemer, 2008). Over the years, the basic models gradually advanced into more sophisticated simulators that have realistic features and functions. The advancement of the medical simulators largely relied on advances in science and technology. Now a day, simulators are largely used to train healthcare professionals for a variety of clinical situations, especially those that require practice, are high-risk and infrequently experienced. Simulation is an ideal modality to teach students and professionals the behaviors, knowledge and clinical skills necessary to function in clinical environments. Furthermore, the public exposure of the use of simulation in medical training developed an expectation amongst patients who expected professionals to train on simulators before applying their skills on the patients (Barrott, Sunderland, Nicklin, & Smith, 2013). Training on simulators became the new standard for practicing clinical and non-clinical skills. This challenged the educator to develop relevant learning activities to effectively integrate simulators.

SECTION 2: SIMULATION AS AN AUTHENIC ACTIVITY

Healthcare providers in training, and those actively involved in clinical practice, must cultivate their clinical & non-clinical knowledge, skills, and abilities by engaging in relevant learning activities that permit them to acquire and stay abreast on medical information. Relevant activities should be administered in an authentic way; simulation is an example of an authentic activity (Jeffries, 2012). A primary benefit of utilizing simulation as an authentic instructional activity is to eliminate any fears of harming a patient. Authentic activities are based on problems and tasks that replicate, or at minimum, are applicable to situations that clinicians are faced on a regular or not so regular basis (Archbald & Newman, 1988; Wiggins, 1989). The authenticity of an activity or of an assessment can be measured based on the similarity and applicability to real world situations that the student or professional may encounter (Newmann, Brandt, & Wiggins, 1998). A variety of simulators can be used, in isolation or combination, to create an authentic environment; but the most important aspect to consider is the simulator's fidelity configuration. The fidelity configuration is the most distinguishable difference between the simulators and plays a critical role in developing authentic activities or assessments.

The fidelity of a simulator correlates to how effectively and realistically the simulator and the simulated environment mimic life-like situations. To replicate such an environment, the first decision that needs to be made is the degree of realism the simulation requires. To mimic such a situation, attention must be paid to the differences between the physical, functional (Barrott et al., 2013) and environmental fidelity of a simulator and simulation (Ker & Bradley, 2014). The physical fidelity describes the realism of the equipment, such as the way a simulator was engineered to look life-like. The functional fidelity describes the degree to which the physiological functions of a simulator respond to the user manipulations while performing a skill (Barrott et al., 2013). The environmental fidelity includes the degree to which the surroundings replicate real clinical environments (Ker & Bradley, 2014). The physical, functional, and environmental fidelity must imitate and resemble the professional practice environment the learner will encounter (Pointdexter, Hagler, & Lindell, 2015; Smith, Gray, Raymond, Catling-Paull, & Homer, 2012). All, physical, functional, and environmental, fidelity configurations are further divided in two categories: high-fidelity and low-fidelity. The higher the fidelity of a simulator or the simulated environment, the more authentic and life-like the scenario can become (Grady, Kehrer, Trusty, Entin, Entin, & Brunye, 2008; Reznick & MacRae, 2006).

Using a simulator as an authentic activity as part of professional and continuing medical education provides the learner with realistic opportunities to apply and practice the specific knowledge, skills, and attitudes they will require in their medical practice (Gulikers et al., 2004; Pointdexter et al., 2015). Therefore, educators must consider not only creating authentic activities for learners, but also creating authentic assessments to challenge the learner to perform and apply knowledge and/or clinical skill as if he/she would do in real life. An authentic assessment has an educational purpose beyond that of traditional examinations where single and simple responses are required (Hensel & Stanley, 2014; Wiggins, 1998). Authentic assessments and authentic educational experiences need to be meaningful; and with the varying aspects of fidelity, the developer of the simulation-based learning experience is capable of creating a wide range of objective driven occurrences for the learner.

The amount of effort that is put forth by a learner during each of the occurrences has been linked to the learners perceived authenticity of an activity or assessment; the more an environment is perceived to be authentic and the information is transferable to real professional practice, the more engaged the learner is in developing their knowledge, skills, and abilities (Brown, Collins, & Duguid, 1989; Gulikers, Kester, Kirschner, & Bastiaens, 2008). The engaged learner will develop metacognitive practices because the authentic activity requires them to think, act, and reflect on the environment as it resembles the real clinical environment they may encounter (Pointdexter et al., 2015). This in turn uniquely prepares the learner for future circumstances. These circumstances may require the learner to perform frequently practiced skills or on the contrary, infrequently practiced emergency skills in a controlled and low-risk environment, most importantly sparing real patients from potential risks (Issenberg & Scalese, 2008).

It is necessary to develop the authentic learning experiences and assessments in such a way that they align with the professional requirements and engage the learner actively. When the learner is actively engaged, and synthesizes the already existing knowledge, skills, and abilities, the authentic educational activity or assessment becomes even more closely associated with the real world (Pointdexter et al., 2015). Whichever simulator is chosen for a simulation, all of them have diversified how simulation is applied in the healthcare domain (Gaba, 2007); and the more authentic a simulated learning experience or assessments becomes, the more of the necessary knowledge, skills, and abilities will transfer over into the professional career and daily practice of the learner (Frey et al., 2012).

SECTION 3: TYPES OF SIMULATORS

Simulation technologies are multifaceted and therefore an explanation of what types of simulators are currently utilized is necessary. Since the 1950s, the expansion of medical simulation equipment has further developed; primarily, due to scientific and technological advances (Rosen, 2008). The main classifications of simulators that are utilized today can be divided into the following main categories: part-task trainers, computer-enhanced mannequin (CEM) or screen simulators, virtual reality (VR) simulators (Reznek, 2004, as cited in Issenberg & Scalese, 2008; Rosen 2008), real people as simulators, fully immersive and hybrid simulated environments (Byrne, 2013). When utilizing any of the aforementioned simulators on their own or in combination it is necessary to identify specific learning objectives to ensure that the simulation-based instruction is designed to meet those objectives (Grady et al., 2008). Once the specific learning objectives are clearly defined, the authenticity and fidelity configuration should be determined so that the right simulator or combination of simulators can be chosen (Issenberg & Scalese, 2008). As already noted, the fidelity configuration is the most distinguishable difference between the simulators. The simulators and their specific fidelity configuration, whether high-fidelity or low-fidelity, provide a variety of options in creating authentic learning environments and/or assessments.

Part-Task Trainers

Part-task trainers were developed in the 1950s as the development of moldable plastic advanced and the medical community realized the need for timely, targeted training in response to potential medical emergencies (Bryne, 2013). An example of a response to a potential medical emergency would be treating a person in cardiac arrest by providing Cardiopulmonary Resuscitation (CPR). To train medical personnel in CPR, one of the earliest part-task trainers, 'Rescusci Annie', was developed and served as a simple bench top model to practice mouth-to-mouth breathing and chest compressions (Issenberg & Scalese, 2008). A part-task trainer is generally a small model of a body part or a body region that can, but does not have to, mimic realistic anatomical structures or simple physiological functions. With a part-task trainer, the learner can focus on the specific isolated skill while distractions are easily eliminated; therefore, this equipment is most appropriate for novice practitioners that are beginning to acquire and develop clinical skills (Barrott et al., 2013). Part-task trainers are generally low in fidelity, less authentic, and ideal to practice clinical skills that may require the learner to really focus on one specific task (Issenberg & Scalese, 2008; Bryne, 2013), such as accurately performing CPR or mouth-to-mouth breathing.

Some part-task trainers are mobile due to their size; therefore, they can be used in various environments and since they help focus in on one specific skill, they are used when the broader environment (e.g. the whole person) does not play a critical role in the learning of the clinical skill. Another example of a part-task trainer is a breast exam trainer; such a part-task trainer permits the repetitive examination and diagnosis of breast pathologies (Issenberg & Scalese, 2008). Less anatomically specific part-task trainers are oranges and watermelons. Oranges can be utilized to learn and practice how to navigate the needle when using it to inject a solution. Or, watermelons can be used to practice the application of an epidural. Whether a part-task trainer is high in fidelity or not, it provides an excellent resource for novice practitioners to deliberately practice clinical skills to develop competence at no expense to a real patient.

The interactions with a part-task trainer is mostly passive and not likely authentic; however, it still provides the learner deliberate practice opportunities of an isolated skill (Byrne, 2013). Part-task trainers are generally lower in fidelity, less expensive when compared to some other simulators, and composed of either no, or less sophisticated technology (Issenberg & Scalese, 2008; Michael et al., 2014; Rosen, 2008). The cost of a part-task trainer can range from low to moderate with some trainers starting at less than $100 (Gardner & Reamer, 2008).

The cost of a part-task trainer is associated, in part, with the technology that is incorporated. A breast exam part-task trainer does not include any technology. The first version of *Harvey,* a more sophisticated and expensive part-task trainer developed in the late 1960, was attached to a large box that housed electronic equipment to get the part-task trainer to replicate some physiological functions (pulse, heart rate, heart sounds, etc.). This equipment provided less flexibility in moving the part-task trainer to different locations; but, due to the added technology, the learner was able to practice clinical skills associated with the cardiovascular system as many times as they cared to practice. Finding real patients with abnormalities in the cardiovascular system may not be that difficult, but obtaining permission from them to repetitively practice clinical skills is more likely to be difficult. The part-task trainers not only protected real patients from being subject to repetitive evaluations but they also helped certify the learner's clinical competence with a much timelier method (Michael, 1974 as cited in Byrne, 2013) whether it be learning to evaluate breathing pathologies or abnormal heart sounds. This was the beginning of continuous advancements not only in the simulator's physical fidelity but also in it psychological fidelity and capability. With time and progress in science and technologies, more sophisticated simulators emerged as life-sized computer-enhanced mannequins and 2D screen simulators.

Computer-Enhanced Simulators

The progressions from part-task trainers were 2D screen simulators and full body simulators that become known as computer-enhanced mannequins (CEM). Both, screen simulators and full body CEM are more advanced in their technology and may therefore have higher physical and psychological fidelity due to their ability to replicate more than simple anatomical structures and fundamental functions. The computer-enhanced full body patient simulators were not heavily used when they were initially development in the late 1960s. It took pioneers to establish simulated environments first, and then conduct research with selected participants to provide the value of utilizing simulation as a teaching modality; at the time, back in the late 1960s, a full body simulator was an expensive technology that was too complex for routine use (Byrne, 2013).

Screen Simulators

While decisions about the use of full body simulators were made, the 2D screen simulator advanced. These simulators provide less physical fidelity but therefore enough psychological fidelity for learners to acquire and refine clinical skills. These computer based systems provide important feedback to the learner while they progressed through the computer program at their own pace (Ker & Bradley, 2014). Various modules are available to integrate into medical curricula. The case study at the end of this chapter utilized a low-fidelity 2D screen simulator curriculum composed of web sites to provide deliberate practice opportunities for the learner to listen to normal versus abnormal heart sounds. After acquiring and practicing the skills on the low-fidelity 2D screen simulator, the learner was assessed on his or her ability to apply the skills on a high-fidelity simulator, a mannequin. This transfer of skill was explored in this case study because of the growing desire of healthcare professionals to engage in convenient online continuing education courses. For example, allied health professionals are required to stay current with their cardiopulmonary resuscitation (CPR) certification. Currently, various courses are available for professionals to annual obtain re-certification in order to stay certified as clinicians. Computer screen simulation fostered knowledge and skill gains specific to the transfer of knowledge and skill of CPR from the computer to the high-fidelity mannequin (Bonnetain, Boucheix, Hamet, & Freysz, 2010). Are online computer based-simulators valuable strategies to implement into continuing medical education courses due to the busy nature of professionals who seek convenience continuing medical education courses? Online education or computer screen simulators are perhaps more desired for a variety of reasons: a) they require less staff to operate online trainings for a continuing education event; b) the online training with the computer screen simulator is more cost effective; and c) computer screen simulators are more convenient to the learner since the learner can be located anywhere to access the program (Bonnetain et al., 2010).

Computer-Enhanced Mannequins (CEM)

When compared to part-task trainers, one advanced function of CEMs is their ability to simulate and respond to normal and abnormal physiological functions (Issenberg & Scalese, 2008). Physiological functions include but are not limited to multiple peripheral arterial pulses, blood pressure, heart sounds, muscle twitching, heart rate and breathing rate (Issenberg & Scalese, 2008; Rosen, 2008). A computer is what accesses and controls the mannequin's conditions in real time, therefore providing a very realistic environment for the learner to practice situations they may encounter (Laschinger et al., 2008) and simultaneously doing this with increased environmental fidelity (Ker & Bradley, 2014). The CEM is able to respond, by changing the physiological functions, to what the specific scenario entails (Issenberg & Scalese, 2008; Michael et al., 2014; Rosen, 2008). For example, a scenario may entail the learner to inject epinephrine in an attempt to decrease the labored breathing associated with an allergic reaction. Once the evaluator of the simulation identified that the learner injected epinephrine correctly, the simulators labored breathing would subside. On the contrary, if the learner failed to correctly inject the simulator with epinephrine, the evaluator of the simulation can make the mannequins labored breathing worse. These capabilities are what can make the CEM a very high-fidelity simulator and a more authentic environment.

The screen based simulators and high-fidelity computer-enhanced mannequins are amazing tools that can provide training to a variety of healthcare professionals in multiple disciplines because of their high-tech components. Additionally, the mannequin is available in a number of sizes (adult, child, and infant) and therefore adaptable to various scenarios, whether at the entry-level of professional education or at the maintenance stage of clinical knowledge and psychomotor skills (Issenberg & Scalese, 2008; Michael et al., 2014; Rosen, 2008). One of the primary concerns with the computer-enhanced simulators is their associated cost; they range moderate to high because of their computerized ability to provide the user with feedback (Gardner & Reamer, 2008). A simulator or a simulation center/facility has costs related to purchasing simulators, keeping up with the advancement and support of the sophisticated technology. Additionally, the faculty who plans to implement simulation will need to invest a lot of time learning about how to effectively utilize simulation to complement the didactic and laboratory learning environments. Further concerns include the storage of the simulator and the personnel required to upkeep one or multiple simulators. Since these mannequins are computers they are not cheaply attained but the costs may be outweighed when considering the benefits to patient safety and better prepared health care professionals (Barrott et al., 2013; Ker & Bradley, 2014).

Virtual Reality Simulators

Virtual reality simulators are confined to a computer screen and the user interacts in a 3D virtual, simulated world. The immersive nature of a virtual reality simulator can be through the use of an avatar or special goggles and gloves that are composed of special sensors and displays. The display of a virtual reality simulator mimics the physical world and permits real-time human interaction with the capability of receiving visual, auditory, or sensory feedback (Issenberg & Scalese, 2008; Michael et al., 2014; Rosen, 2008). Challenges with a virtual reality simulator can be manifested when the user and the reaction of the computer do not sync in real time; thereby, not contributing to effective learning. The technology has to be extremely advanced and operate at a suitable rate to refresh the graphics and 3D images in real time (Byrne, 2013).

With a virtual environment, the scope of learning is also board. When the technology is compatible, the virtual reality simulator can react to the operator's manipulations and provide haptic feedback while simultaneously altering the environment as determined by the operator's manipulations (Byrne, 2013). The environment becomes truly immersive and authentic, which comes with a very high price tag that can be well over $100,000 (Gardner & Reamer, 2008). Furthermore, another benefit to the virtual environment can be inter-professional distance learning. For example, various clinicians or students can meet in a virtual world and engage in a realistic clinical environment interacting with each other while applying and practicing skills (Issenberg & Scalese, 2008; Rosen, 2008). The virtual reality simulators are applied not only to practice clinical skills such as delivering a baby, but also to practice non-clinical collaborative skills or communication skill, as these are part of the skills required to interact and succeed with patients. A virtual reality simulator would be ideal if the goal of the simulation was to practice how to remove the appendix and due to circumstances of the situation the practitioner had to make decision about the patient's health and effectively communicate those to the assisting staff in the operating room.

Summary

The various types of simulators offer a variety of applications to educate students and healthcare professionals on the relevant knowledge, clinical and non-clinical skills necessary to be competent practitioners. Simulation can be applied across the curriculum because it permits the learner to acquire information through experience (Tiffen, Corbridge, Shen, & Robinson, 2011). It is important that a thorough analysis of the curriculum take place prior to purchasing and adding simulation into every course; faculty must identify where simulation can best be incorporated (Barrott et al., 2013). When utilizing any of the aforementioned simulators, it is imperative to identify the learning objectives for the simulation first and then decide which simulators isolated or in combination, can aid in accomplishing the learning objectives. Besides access to simulators, the simulators fidelity configuration, specific to physical, functional, and environmental, will play the biggest part in identifying which simulator should be used and how it should be incorporated to replicate the most authentic learning environment (Issenberg & Scalese, 2008). Replicating the learning environment uniquely immerses the learner by providing them practical application of knowledge and skills to potential situations to become competent practitioners. Simulation is ideal for practicing and maintaining technical and non-technical knowledge and skills that transfer to real clinical environments (McKimm & Forrest, 2013; Wayne et al., 2006). A paradigm shift to competency-based education is transforming the way that professionals and trainees are educated; teaching and learning in healthcare education is changing to certify the learner demonstrates competence in required clinical knowledge, skills, and abilities (Cannon-Diehl, Rugari, & Jones, 2012; Issenberg & Scalese, 2008).

SECTION 4: EDUCATIONAL TRENDS OF UTILIZING SIMULATION

The healthcare domain is broad and with the existing variety of allied health professions there is a need to prepare the healthcare provider most effectively to ensure competence of clinical knowledge, skills, and abilities. Historically, prior to simulation, the apprenticeship model was commonly utilized in healthcare education (Gaba, 2007; Issenberg & Scalese, 2008). The apprenticeship model required the apprentice, the learner, to follow around and be taught by an expert practitioner (Ericsson, 2008; Gaba, 2007). This traditional approach only utilized real patients and the learner would only have the ability to practice their clinical skills if they encountered an ill or injured patient; or if the expert provided them with the opportunity to react and treat the patient independently, thereby developing the confidence and ability to reason through a clinical case.

Relying on real patients to practice important clinical skills decreased the student-patient interactions. Furthermore, the limited availability of real patients with specific conditions, and the overexertion of the patient serving as the subject for repetitive evaluations decreased the amount of time the students spent learning and practicing skills (Issenberg & Scalese, 2008). Besides, practicing and refining undeveloped clinical skills on patients is unethical (Tang, Tun, Kneebone, & Bello, 2013). Simulation was integrated into the medical domain to protect the patients, provide ample ability for the learner to practice relevant clinical skills, and because the advances in technology and sciences made simulators more authentic. When integrating a simulator into the learning environment the student is provided with a richer learning experience in a low-risk setting that is more flexible and interactive (Fox, 2012). With a simulator, the learner can potentially practice clinical skills more frequently because the variety of simulators are capable of replicating various illnesses and conditions, offer anatomically and physiologically accurate models, and expose the learner to the potential consequences of their decision (Bullock & de Jong, 2014).

Simulation has become an instructional design technique that is capable of replicating the real medical world, fully immerse the learner in an interactive way, and providing immediate feedback and guidance to ensure clinical competence (Gaba, 2007). Never should simulation replace the learners' interactions with real patients in true clinical environments, such as with the apprentice model (McKimm & Forrest, 2013); however, simulation is ideal to replicate the real clinical environment that the learner eventually may encounter. A fully immersive simulation facilitates active learning and involves the learner (Hope, Garside, & Prescott, 2011) in real decision-making, recognition, and management of situations that occur in actual clinical settings (Laschinger et al., 2008).

Caution must be taken when embedding simulation into the curriculum. The faculty who is untrained, not only in the use of a CEM or the required software, but also in the theoretical underpinnings of using simulation as a teaching modality, should not implement simulation into their course (Barrott et al., 2013). Training for faculty that implement simulation is not standardized and certification programs are in the process of being identified and evaluated (McGaghie, Issenberg, Retrusa, & Scalese, 2010). Proficiencies specific to simulation-based learning that educators should possess are: (a) familiarity with the various technologies and application techniques of different simulators; (b) consideration for maintaining a learning environment that is safe as it relates to the physical and psychological properties of learning; (c) the ability to design simulation-based instructional activities that have thoroughly been integrated into the broader curriculum, are objective driven, and are measured and evaluated based on the outcomes; (d) facilitation skills to enhance the students learning in an immersive simulated environment; (e) abilities to provide actual feedback to the learner especially through the process of debriefing; and (f) knowledge in using video recording equipment to aid in debriefing of the learner and reviewing the process as the simulation was implemented (Baxendale, Coffey, & Buttery, 2013).

The nursing and the medical domains have investigated the effectiveness of simulation as students and professionals were taught about CPR (Ackerman, 2009; Bonnetain et al., 2010), cardiac (Botezatu, Hult, Tessma, & Fors, 2010; McKinney et al., 2013; Spatz, LeFrancois, & Ostfeld, 2011; Tiffen et al., 2011), cardiorespiratory (Fraser et al., 2009), pulmonary (Tiffen et al., 2011), and surgical (Gaba, 2007) clinical knowledge and assessment skills. Positive influences on knowledge and skill acquisition after engaging in a simulation-based instruction have been identified when compared to more traditional teaching methods such as didactic lecture methods (Ackerman, 2009; Bonnetain et al., 2010; Fraser et al., 2009; McGaghie et al., 2010; Shinnick, Woo, & Evangelista, 2012). Teaching students and professionals through a combination of didactic and simulation methods significantly influences skills and knowledge acquisition (Spatz et al., 2011) and therefore increases satisfaction of the learner, who have encouraged simulation as part of their learning experience (Tiffen et al. 2011).

The experience and hands-on approach is what facilities learning, leading the knowledge and the clinical skills to be more quickly attained (Butter, McGaghie, Cohen, Kaye, & Wayne, 2010; Kolb, 1984; Tiffen et al., 2011). Simulation can provide the learner the opportunity to acquire and then refine existing knowledge and skill, especially the knowledge and skills already introduced in the didactic lecture. Furthermore, simulation is an optimal strategy for learners to acquire knowledge, critical thinking abilities, confidence in performing clinical skills, and repetitive exposure in a flexible clinical environment (Fox, 2012; Grady et al., 2008) all before the learner would interact with real patients. The apprenticeship model provided the learner with practice opportunities on real patients; however, due to the patient availability the quantity of practice was less. The interaction with a real patient should not be the first time the learner has the opportunity to practice their skills. The ability to identify the deficit in knowledge or skill at the same time the learner is practicing with a simulator is a unique characteristic of simulation; furthermore, identifying a deficit in the learner's knowledge and skill before interacting with real patients is critical.

Simulation-based instructional strategies have been identified as positive influences in the amount of knowledge and skill acquisition of learners in various healthcare fields (Ackermann, 2009; Alinier, Hunt, & Gordon, 2004; Bonnetain et al., 2010; Botezatu et al., 2010; Fraser et al., 2009; McGaghie et al., 2010; Shinnick et al., 2012). Therefore, the future of simulation research will revolve around comparing simulated environments and identifying the different instructional design features and how those influence the clinical and non-clinical knowledge and skill acquisition and retention of healthcare professionals (McGaghie, 1999; McKinney et al., 2013). A case study will be presented at the conclusion of this chapter that compared simulated environments and aimed at identifying instructional design features that need to be considered when incorporating simulation into a continuing education course for athletic trainers.

SECTION 5: TWO PROPOSED THEORETICAL FRAMEWORKS

From an educational perspective, simulation, when used as an activity or assessment, can be grounded in various theoretical frameworks. To prevent the reader for becoming overwhelmed with the volume of theories and for the reader to better understand the later presented case study, only two theoretical frameworks were chosen for the purpose of this chapter. These two frameworks are: Kolb's Experiential Learning Theory and Ericsson's Theory of Deliberate Practice. When using a simulator to create an environment that is either low or high in fidelity, the learner is provided with an opportunity to actively engage in their learning and thereby learn through experience (Hope et al., 2011). By doing so, a safe and effective bridge between theory and practice can be attained through deliberate practice (Ker & Bradley, 2014).

Kolb's Experiential Learning Theory

David Kolb (1984) is credited with the development of the Experiential Learning Theory. Kolb's Experiential Learning Theory is based on John Dewey's (1938) work on the influence of experience on learning, Kurt Lewin's (1951) work on linking theory to practice, and Jean Piaget's (1952) work on how experience influences cognitive development (Kolb, 1984). Kolb's theory has been noted as a theoretical framework for learning and teaching in medical education (Kaufman & Mann, 2014) and conducting simulation-based learning instruction (Clapper, 2010; Poore, Cullen, & Schaar, 2014).

David Kolb (1984) defines learning as "the process whereby knowledge is created through the transformation of experience. Knowledge results from the combination of grasping experience and transforming it" (p. 41). Kolb (1984) proposed that learning occurs in a four-phase cycle. The phases in the learning cycle include (a) concrete experience, (b) reflective observation, (c) abstract conceptualization, and (d) active experimentation. Simulation-based learning experiences are concrete experiences that require the learner to reflect on the hands-on experience, conceptualize for themselves how the experience was significant or how the outcomes could have been altered, and then apply the newly acquired reflected conceptualization to future clinical practice (Poore et al., 2014).

The experiences that are gained during a simulation are transformed into knowledge that the learner internalizes through careful consideration and conceptualization with the hope that the newly acquired knowledge applies to future experiences. Kolb's experiential learning theory provides "the missing link between theory and practice, between the abstract generalization and the concrete instance, between the affective and cognitive domains" (Bennis, 1984, as cited in Kolb, 1984, p. ix). Bridging the gap between theory and practice is a critical component of professional or continuous professional medical education, especially of knowledge and psychomotor skills that are not frequently practiced. It directly translates to better patient care and clinical outcomes (Oermann et al., 2011).

Simulation is well suited to address this missing link between theory and practice. By learning through simulation, learners have the opportunity to directly participate and assume responsibility for their learning; apply previously obtained knowledge, philosophies, experiences, and emotional characteristics to a newly arranged set of capacities, beliefs, and principles; and transfer the wisdom into a practical situation (Kaufman & Mann, 2014). This learning continues from one set of experiences to another, becoming more complex and more deeply embedded within the learner with each additional experience (Poore et al., 2014). This idea stems from Kolb's learning cycle, which is a recurring cycle that allows the continuation of learning through experiences by: (a) apprehending the information; (b) comprehending the information; (c) intension, or reflecting on the information; and (d) extension, or utilizing the information (Ker & Bradley, 2014). This cycle continues for the entire process of learning. Learning is a process, as already noted by Kolb (1984), and learning occurs over time with constant refinement of already existing knowledge and psychomotor skills.

Simulations are perfect for revolving learners around the learning cycle proposed by David Kolb. First, an educator aims to teach the learner a specific skill through a lecture. Second, the learner understands more deeply how the skill can be applied by actually applying the skill on a part-task trainer or more technologically advanced simulator in a simple or an authentic environment. Third, the learner is provided with feedback and multiple opportunities to practice to reflect and refine their skill. Lastly, the newly acquired and purposefully refined knowledge and skills should be deliberately practiced to ensure transferal of the knowledge and skill into the real clinical environment. If the learner still lacks components of the skill, the opportunities for more practice should be available. It is not only through experience, but also through deliberately practicing and refining knowledge and skill that information and capability reaches long-term memory (Hauber, Cormier, & White, 2010). There are tremendous benefits of safely practicing and learning through experience by carefully incorporating any of the aforementioned types of simulators in the curriculum.

Deliberate Practice

Since the 1950s, various factors contributed to the growth of simulation as a teaching technology in healthcare education. Healthcare educators have made changes in the way students acquire clinical knowledge and psychomotor skills because of a declining in-patient hospital population, a concern for the safety of patients, a lack of finding the "right" patient, and a change in learning theory (Laschinger et al., 2008; Perlini et al., 2014). Simulation as a teaching technology addresses the aforementioned challenges with its flexibility to teach by re-creating rare clinical situations thereby increasing opportunities for students to acquire and practice psychomotor skills. When grounding simulated activities and assessments in Ericsson's theory of providing deliberate practice opportunities the development of expert performance and mastery learning is more thoroughly attained.

During stimulation-based activities, the learner is engaging in effective learning environments that are controlled, provide timely feedback, and allow for repetitive practice (Issenberg, McGaghie, Petrusa, Gordon, & Scalese, 2005). According to Ericsson (2004), expert performance is only acquired through deliberate practice of skills and it is only maintained with continuous, deliberate practice of that knowledge and skill. The importance of grounding simulation-based instructional strategies in deliberate practice is for clinicians to practice their clinical skills to be able to perform them "rapidly and intuitively" (Ericsson, 2008, p. 988). Deliberate practice is not just learning through experience. Deliberate practice is a set of conditions that improve performance when the learner is (a) given specific learning objectives, (b) motivated to learn, (c) provided with feedback, and (d) given the opportunity to repeatedly practice their skills (Ericsson, 2008). Mastery learning is achieved by the combination of these conditions and by looping around these conditions to develop and practice behaviors to gradually refine both knowledge and psychomotor skills to achieve more efficient and accurate clinical results (Aebersold & Titler, 2014). Greater patient care quality is attained by deliberately practicing skills, which then leads to mastery learning that has been recognized to increase the transfer of knowledge and skill from the simulated environment to the bedside environment (Ericsson, 2004).

Mastery learning is defined by a set of strict, predetermined, and uniform standards or objectives that have been established through competency-based research (Wayne & McGaghie, 2013). Medical education is competence-based education because a minimum educational standard is necessary to ensure program quality. The professional preparation and continuous education of healthcare professionals must be based on the most up-to-date knowledge, skills, and abilities to ensure competence of clinicians in content areas across all domains specific to each profession (Commission on Accreditation of Athletic Training Education, n.d.). Pre-determined standards guide the certification or re-certification of healthcare professionals, and therefore the aim of continuous professional education courses should be for clinicians to achieve mastery learning.

To achieve mastery learning, Ericsson's (2004) framework is built on developing skills through deliberate practice while under the supervision of clinical experts that provide immediate feedback. Expert performance is only achieved through the combination of experience and practice; experience alone is not automatically going to make someone an expert. Simulation-based instructional strategies need to emphasize the opportunity for learners to engage in deliberate practice at the appropriate level of skill development for the motor skills to permanently become embedded and later transferred to clinical practice (Oermann et al., 2011). During the simulation scenario, the instructor needs to provide opportunities for the learner to execute the skill repetitively, monitor the performance of the skill, provide feedback through debriefing, and collaborate with the learner to analyze the performance in order to refine skills and knowledge and achieve expertise (Ericsson, 2008).

Engaging in simulation and repetitive practice of specific learning outcomes has been shown to increase knowledge and skill acquisition (Ericsson, 2008; McKinney et al., 2013; Spatz et al., 2011; Tiffen et al., 2011). Simulation has been identified as an ideal teaching strategy because it provides the learner an environment that is flexible to the apprentice's learning needs and ideal to practice important clinical skills without causing any harm to patients (Butter et al., 2010; Issenberg et al., 2002; Spatz et al., 2011). Deliberately practicing learning outcomes with simulation is more effective and safer than bedside teaching, which was the traditional method of educating healthcare professionals.

SECTION 6: PRESENTATION OF A CASE STUDY

Implementing simulation-based instructional strategies into continuing medical education for allied health professionals is a realistic method to teach clinical skills and knowledge. This presented case study utilized two types of simulators, screen simulator and computer-enhanced mannequin (CEM), to teach certified athletic trainers how to conduct a comprehensive cardiovascular screening. Specifically, simulation was implemented as part of the pre-test, the intervention, and a post-test. The pre-test and post-test simulation serves as the authentic assessment utilizing a CEM. The intervention, which provided the leaners with deliberate practice opportunities, served as the authentic activity.

The administrators of the continuing education course utilized a pre-test and post-test to measure how simulation fostered the acquisition of knowledge and skill. As part of the pre-test and post-test, a multiple choice knowledge exam and a 4-station objective, structure, clinical exam (OSCE) were utilized to measure if there were any differences in the amount of knowledge and skill attained for each of the professionals that participated the day of the continuing education course. An objective, structured, clinical exam (OSCE) has been identified as an effective authentic activity and assessment (Pointdexter et al., 2015). This continuing education course was of unique design because simulation was used as an authentic activity during the course and as an authentic assessment during the pre-test and post-test.

Procedures

The first part of the continuing education course consisted of a four station OSCE. The OSCE was developed to evaluate the psychomotor skill before and after the lecture and deliberate practice time. The first station assessed the learners' ability to take a thorough personal and family history. The second station assessed the learners' ability to perform the necessary physical examinations required when assessing cardiovascular health. The third station assessed the learners' ability to conduct cardiac auscultation patterns on a high-fidelity computer-enhanced mannequin. The fourth station assessed the learners' ability to identify abnormal versus normal heart sounds that could be heard when performing cardiac auscultations.

The second part of the pre-test and post-test consisted of a 31-item multiple choice exam that members of the course completed in a computer laboratory. This multiple choice exam assessed the learners' knowledge specific to cardiovascular health. The exam was created based on specific objectives that were focused around the anatomy and physiology of the heart and the cardiovascular system.

Once all of the members of the course completed the two pre-exams (skill and knowledge), the lecture began. The lecture was designed to provide the participants with the knowledge and skills necessary to conduct a comprehensive cardiovascular screening. Traditional lecture PowerPoint's were utilized to present the information and intermitted practical application was integrated for participants to practice the skills on each other. All components of the lecture and practical application were instructor led and guided. Participants worked in groups to briefly practice the information as they acquired the knowledge and skill. All members of the course were provided with multiple opportunities to ask the instructor any questions to clarify their own understanding.

As already mentioned, the ability to deliberately practice clinical skills is an essential component to learning. Since simulation-based instructional strategies are not frequently utilized in continuing education the administrators of the CEU course wanted to utilize different simulators based on their fidelity and types of simulations to determine effectiveness of either simulator. The fidelity type of both intervention groups played a role in the perceived authenticity of the experience; thereby, the intervention served as the authentic instruction that directly related to the knowledge and skills that the participants were evaluated on with the authentic assessment before and after the course. The combined consideration of merging authentic instruction with authentic assessments can foster authentic learning, which can be directly transferred into professional clinical practice (Gulikers et al., 2004).

Once the lecture was complete, the participants were divided into two groups. One group was assigned to the low-fidelity 2D screen-based simulation. The other group was assigned to the high-fidelity simulation with the computer-enhanced mannequin and an instructor to readily be available to answer questions.

The computer laboratory was a series of websites that the learners were asked to follow to independently practice the clinical skills in a 2D environment and refine their previously acquired knowledge and skills. The independent nature of this low-fidelity simulation required members of the course to listen with headphones to the directions provided via the websites. All websites were specifically chosen to provide the learner with an opportunity to improve and deliberately practice the various normal and abnormal heart sounds through their auditory system and checking their knowledge and skill through input from a mouse click or the keyboard.

The other group of learners was assigned to the simulation laboratory and utilized the computer-enhance mannequin to deliberately practice and refine their knowledge and skills. The instructor that led the lecture was assigned to stay with this high-fidelity simulation group. The instructor provided queues and ensured that all participants got the opportunity to engage and practice with the mannequin. The various heart sounds, normal and abnormal, were heard through the computer-enhanced mannequin; discussions among participants and facilitator took place as everyone was deliberately practicing, applying, and refining their skills.

Once the allotted time of one hour was over, all participants were asked to re-group in a central location and the official lecture and practice components of the continuing education event was over. To collect post-test data to measure learning gains, all participants were required to complete the OSCE and multiple choice exam one more time. Each member of the course re-visited each of the four stations as part of the objective, structured, clinical exam to evaluate skill, and everyone was required to complete the 31-item multiple choice exam in the computer laboratory to evaluate knowledge. The continuing education course was over once all participants completed the post-tests.

Results

Simulation was utilized as part of this course as an authentic assessment and authentic activity. The data that was collected was analyzed to determine whether high-fidelity simulation fostered more knowledge and/or skill or whether low-fidelity simulation fostered more knowledge and/or skill. Upon arrival, the learners were required to complete an objective, structure, clinical exam; which served the purpose of identifying their clinical competence in conducting a comprehensive cardiovascular screening. The analysis of the exam scores (pre-test and post-test) revealed that as a group, the participating athletic trainers only had 34% clinical diagnostic accuracy. This means that the member of the course really only were 34% competent in performing a comprehensive cardiovascular screening. A comprehensive cardiovascular screening is a skill that athletic trainers are required to know. It is also a skill that is not frequently practiced by athletic trainers; however, due to the nature of their profession, it is very important to be competent in this skill. The authentic pre-assessment identified the deficit in skill of clinically practicing athletic trainers. This identified that the skill itself is worth teaching.

Additionally, further analysis revealed that there was no significant difference between the amount of knowledge gained when the high-fidelity and the low-fidelity simulation groups were compared to each other. Both simulation groups gained significant amounts of knowledge, additionally indicating that if knowledge is not consistently utilized, it is lost. Furthermore, the results specific to skill acquisition revealed that both groups (high-fidelity and low-fidelity) gained significant amounts of skill. It was also identified that the high-fidelity group, when compared to the low-fidelity group, gained significantly more skill. Both methods fostered skill acquisition, but if someone has to choose which method to implement to attain more skill, then a high-fidelity computer-enhanced mannequin would be the recommended simulator. Nevertheless, the pre-exam scores were so low for knowledge and skill of every member of the course, that no matter which method is utilized as part of a continuing education course, there is a great need to re-teach athletic trainers, and probably other allied health professionals, the necessary knowledge and skill to be competent when conducting a comprehensive cardiovascular screening.

RECOMMENDATIONS

First, this case study recommends that considerations should be given to utilizing high-fidelity simulation as an objective driven authentic pre-assessment. Implementing simulation as such could effectively identify the clinicians' professional proficiency deficit. An OSCE is recommended to guide the objective driven pre-assessment. Second, this case study recommends that the lecture portion of the course should be grounded in objective driven authentic instruction to provide the leaner with multiple opportunities to interact with the simulator, obtain feedback from an instructor, and then deliberately practice their skills, specifically those that were identified as deficient. Third, this case study recommends that the pre-test be given as the post-test at the conclusion of the course to identify if the proficiency deficit in skills was narrowed. Utilizing simulation as part of continuing education courses will allow the knowledge and skills that occur less frequently to be practiced, and periodically refreshed, and maintained. This supports the need for high-fidelity simulation to be part of curricula and continuing education (Cannon-Diehl et al., 2012).

Simulation as part of a CPE course is an innovative learning experience (Barr et al., 2014; Cannon-Diehl et al., 2012; Hoadley, 2009; Hope et al., 2011), especially on topics that may have been forgotten, and thus may shift the attitude that professionals have towards continuing education. Authentic assessment strategies have been found to influence the effort put forth by the learner because an environment that is more realistic motivates the learner to study and develop their clinical skills (Gulikers et al., 2008). Simulation, as an objective driven authentic assessment and instructional intervention, can develop the skills by letting the learner experience and discover in an environment that they may actually encounter.

REFERENCES

Ackermann, A. D. (2009). Investigation of learning outcomes for the acquisition and retention of CPR knowledge and skills learned with the use of high-fidelity simulation. *Clinical Simulation in Nursing*, 5(6), e213–e222. doi:10.1016/j.ecns.2009.05.002

Aebersold, M., & Titler, M. G. (2014). A simulation model for improving learner and health outcomes. *The Nursing Clinics of North America*, 49(3), 431–439. doi:10.1016/j.cnur.2014.05.011 PMID:25155540

Alinier, G., Hunt, W. B., & Gordon, R. (2004). Determining the value of simulation in nurse education: Study design and initial results. *Nurse Education in Practice*, 4(3), 200–207. doi:10.1016/S1471-5953(03)00066-0 PMID:19038158

Archbald, D. A., & Newmann, F. M. (1988). *Beyond standardized testing: Assessing authentic academic achievement in the secondary school*. Reston, VA: National Association of Secondary School Principals.

Barr, N., Readman, K., & Dunn, P. (2014). Simulation-based clinical assessment: Redesigning a signature assessment into a teaching strategy. *Australasian Journal of Paramedicine*, *11*(6), 1–9.

Barrott, J., Sunderland, A. B., Nicklin, J. P., & Smith, M. M. (2013). Designing effective simulation activities. In K. Forrest, J. McKimm, & S. Edgar (Eds.), *Essential simulation in clinical education* (pp. 168–195). Chichester, UK: John Wiley & Sons, Ltd. doi:10.1002/9781118748039.ch10

Baxendale, B., Coffey, F., & Buttery, A. (2013). The roles of faculty and simulated patients in simulation. In K. Forrest, J. McKimm, & S. Edgar (Eds.), *Essential simulation in clinical education* (pp. 87–110). Chichester, UK: John Wiley & Sons, Ltd. doi:10.1002/9781118748039.ch6

Birdane, A., Yazici, H. U., Aydar, Y., Mert, K. U., Masifov, M., Cavusoglu, Y., & Timuralp, B. et al. (2012). Effectiveness of cardiac simulator on the acquirement of cardiac auscultatory skills of medical students. *Advances in Clinical and Experimental Medicine*, *21*(6), 791–798. PMID:23457137

Bonnetain, E., Boucheix, J. M., Hamet, M., & Freysz, M. (2010). Benefits of computer screen-based simulation in learning cardiac arrest procedures. *Medical Education*, *44*(7), 716–722. doi:10.1111/j.1365-2923.2010.03708.x PMID:20636591

Botezatu, M., Hult, H., Tessma, M. K., & Fors, U. (2010). Virtual patient simulation: Knowledge gain or knowledge loss? *Medical Teacher*, *32*(7), 562–568. doi:10.3109/01421590903514630 PMID:20653378

Brown, J. S., Collins, A., & Duguid, P. (1989). Situated cognition and the culture of learning. *Educational Researcher*, *18*(1), 32–42. doi:10.3102/0013189X018001032

Bullock, A., & de Jong, P. G. (2014). Technology-enhanced learning. In T. Swanwick (Ed.), *Understanding medical education: Evidence, theory, and practice* (2nd ed.; pp. 149–160). Chichester, UK: John Wiley & Sons, Ltd.

Butter, J., McGaghie, W. C., Cohen, E. R., Kaye, M. E., & Wayne, D. B. (2010). Simulation-based mastery learning improves cardiac auscultation skills in medical students. *Journal of General Internal Medicine*, *25*(8), 780–785. doi:10.1007/s11606-010-1309-x PMID:20339952

Byrne, A. (2013). Medical simulation: The journey so far. In K. Forrest, J. McKimm, & S. Edgar (Eds.), *Essential simulation in clinical education* (pp. 11–25). Chichester, UK: John Wiley & Sons, Ltd. doi:10.1002/9781118748039.ch2

Cannon-Diehl, M. R., Rugari, S. M., & Jones, T. S. (2012). High-fidelity simulation for continuing education in nurse anesthesia. *American Association of Nurse Anesthetists Journal*, *80*(3), 191–196. PMID:22848980

Clapper, T. C. (2010). Beyond Knowles: What those conducting simulation need to know about adult learning theory. *Clinical Simulation in Nursing*, *6*(1), e7–e14. doi:10.1016/j.ecns.2009.07.003

Commission on Accreditation of Athletic Training Education. (n.d.). *Professional programs.* Retrieved from http://caate.net/professional-programs/

Dewey, J. (1938). *Education and Experience*. New York, NY: Simon and Schuster.

Ericsson, K. A. (2004). Deliberate practice and the acquisition and maintenance of expert performance in medicine and related domains. *Academic Medicine, 79*(10Suppl), S70–S81. doi:10.1097/00001888-200410001-00022 PMID:15383395

Ericsson, K. A. (2008). Deliberate practice and the acquisition and maintenance of expert performance: A general overview. *Academic Emergency Medicine, 15*(11), 988–994. doi:10.1111/j.1553-2712.2008.00227.x PMID:18778378

Fox, K. F. (2012). Simulation-based learning in cardiovascular medicine: Benefits for the trainee, the trained and the patient. *Heart (British Cardiac Society), 98*(7), 527–528. doi:10.1136/heartjnl-2011-301314 PMID:22337950

Fraser, K., Peets, A., Walker, I., Tworek, J., Paget, M., Wright, B., & Mclaughlin, K. (2009). The effect of simulator training on clinical skills acquisition, retention and transfer. *Medical Education, 43*(8), 784–789. doi:10.1111/j.1365-2923.2009.03412.x PMID:19659492

Frey, B. B., Schmitt, V. L., & Allen, J. P. (2012). Defining authentic classroom assessment. *Practical Assessment, Research & Evaluation, 17*(2), 1–18.

Gaba, D. M. (2007). The future vision of simulation in healthcare. *Simulation in Healthcare: Journal of the Society for Simulation in Healthcare, 2*(2), 126–135. doi:10.1097/01.SIH.0000258411.38212.32 PMID:19088617

Gardner, R., & Reamer, D. B. (2008). Simulation in obstetrics and gynecology. *Obstetrics and Gynecology Clinics of North America, 35*(1), 97–127. doi:10.1016/j.ogc.2007.12.008 PMID:18319131

Grady, J. L., Kehrer, R. G., Trusty, C. E., Entin, E. B., Entin, E. E., & Brunye, T. T. (2008). Learning nursing procedures: The influence of simulator fidelity and student gender on teaching effectiveness. *The Journal of Nursing Education, 47*(9), 403–408. doi:10.3928/01484834-20080901-09 PMID:18792707

Gulikers, J. M., Bastiaens, T. J., & Kirschner, P. A. (2004). A five dimensional framework for authentic assessment. *Educational Technology Research and Development, 52*(3), 67–86. doi:10.1007/BF02504676

Gulikers, J. T., Kester, L., Kirschner, P. A., & Bastiaens, T. J. (2008). The effect of practical experience on perceptions of assessment authenticity, study approach, and learning outcomes. *Learning and Instruction, 18*(2), 172–186. doi:10.1016/j.learninstruc.2007.02.012

Hatala, R., Issenberg, S. B., Kassen, B., Cole, G., Bacchus, C. M., & Scalese, R. J. (2008). Assessing cardiac physical examination skills using simulation technology and real patients: A comparison study. *Medical Education, 42*(6), 628–636. doi:10.1111/j.1365-2923.2007.02953.x PMID:18221269

Hauber, R. P., Cormier, E., & White, J. (2010). An exploration of the relationship between knowledge and performance-related variables in high-fidelity simulation: Designing instruction that promotes expertise in practice. *Nursing Education Perspectives, 31*(4), 242–246. PMID:20882866

Hensel, D., & Stanley, L. (2014). Group simulation for authentic assessment in a maternal-child lecture course. *Journal of the Scholarship of Teaching and Learning, 14*(2), 61–70. doi:10.14434/josotl.v14i2.4081

Hoadley, T. (2009). Learning advanced life support: A comparison study of the effects of low- and high-fidelity simulation. *Nursing Education Perspectives, 30*(2), 91–95. PMID:19476072

Hope, A., Garside, J., & Prescott, S. (2011). Rethinking theory and practice: Pre-registration student nurses experiences of simulation teaching and learning in the acquisition of clinical skills in preparation for practice. *Nurse Education Today, 31*(7), 711–715. doi:10.1016/j.nedt.2010.12.011 PMID:21237536

Issenberg, S. B., McGaghie, W. C., Gordon, D. L., Symes, S., Petrusa, E. R., Hart, I. R., & Harden, R. M. (2002). Effectiveness of a cardiology review course for internal medicine residents using simulation technology and deliberate practice. *Teaching and Learning in Medicine, 14*(4), 223–228. doi:10.1207/S15328015TLM1404_4 PMID:12395483

Issenberg, S. B., McGaghie, W. C., Petrusa, E. R., Gordon, D. L., & Scalese, R. J. (2005). Features and uses of high-fidelity medical simulations that lead to effective learning: A BEME systematic review. *Medical Teacher, 27*(1), 10–28. doi:10.1080/01421590500046924 PMID:16147767

Issenberg, S. B., & Scalese, R. J. (2008). Simulation in health care education. *Perspectives in Biology and Medicine, 51*(1), 31–46. doi:10.1353/pbm.2008.0004 PMID:18192764

Jeffries, P. R. (Ed.). (2012). *Simulation in nursing education: From conceptualization to evaluation.* New York, NY: National League for Nursing.

Kaufman, D. M., & Mann, K. V. (2014). Teaching and learning in medical education: How theory can inform practice. In T. Swanwick (Ed.), *Understanding medical education: Evidence, theory, and practice* (2nd ed.; pp. 7–29). Chichester, UK: John Wiley & Sons, Ltd.

Ker, J., & Bradley, P. (2014). Simulation in medical education. In T. Swanwick (Ed.), *Understanding medical education: Evidence, theory, and practice* (2nd ed.; pp. 175–192). Chichester, UK: John Wiley & Sons, Ltd.

Kolb, D. A. (1984). *Experiential learning: Experience as the source of learning and development.* Englewood Cliffs, NJ: Prentice-Hall, Inc.

Laschinger, S., Medves, J., Pulling, C., McGraw, D. R., Waytuck, B., Harrison, M. B., & Gambeta, K. (2008). Effectiveness of simulation on health profession students' knowledge, skills, confidence and satisfaction. *International Journal of Evidence-Based Healthcare, 6*(3), 278–302. PMID:21631826

Lavranos, G., Koliaki, C., Briasoulis, A., Nikolaou, A., & Stefanadis, C. (2013). Effectiveness of current teaching methods in cardiology: The SKILLS (medical students knowledge integration of lower level clinical skills) study. *Hippokratia Medical Journal, 17*(1), 34–37. PMID:23935341

Lewin, K. (1951). *Field Theory in Social Sciences.* New York, NY: Harper & Row.

McGaghie, W. C. (1999). Simulation in professional competence assessment: Basic considerations. In A. Tekian, C. H., McGuire, & W. C. McGaghie (Eds.), Innovative simulations for assessing professional competence (pp. 28-50). Chicago, IL: Department of Medical Education, University of Illinois at Chicago.

McGaghie, W. C., Issenberg, S. B., Retrusa, E. R., & Scalese, R. J. (2010). A critical review of simulation-based medical education research: 20032009. *Medical Education, 44*(1), 50–63. doi:10.1111/j.1365-2923.2009.03547.x PMID:20078756

McKimm, J., & Forrest, K. (2013). Essential simulation in clinical education. In S. Edgar, K. Forrest, & J. McKimm (Eds.), *Essential simulation in clinical education* (pp. 1–10). Chichester, UK: Wiley-Blackwell. doi:10.1002/9781118748039.ch1

McKinney, J., Cook, D. A., Wood, D., & Hatala, R. (2013). Simulation-based training for cardiac auscultation skills: Systematic review and meta-analysis. *Journal of General Internal Medicine*, *28*(2), 283–291. doi:10.1007/s11606-012-2198-y PMID:22968795

Michael, M., Abboudi, H., Ker, J., Khan, M., Dasgupta, P., & Ahmed, K. (2014). Performance of technology-driven simulators for medical students–a systematic review. *The Journal of Surgical Research*, *192*(2), 531–543. doi:10.1016/j.jss.2014.06.043 PMID:25234749

Newmann, F., Brandt, R., & Wiggins, G. (1998). An exchange of views on semantics, psychometrics, and assessment reform: A close look at 'authentic' assessments. *Educational Researcher*, *27*(6), 19–22.

Oermann, M., Kardong-Edgren, S., Odom-Maryon, T., Hallmark, B. F., Hurd, D., Rogers, N., & Smart, D. A. et al. (2011). Deliberate practice of motor skills in nursing education: CPR as exemplar. *Nursing Education Perspectives*, *32*(5), 311–315. doi:10.5480/1536-5026-32.5.311 PMID:22029243

Perlini, S., Salinaro, F., Santalucia, P., & Musca, F. (2014). Simulation-guided cardiac auscultation improves medical students clinical skills: The Pavia pilot experience. *Internal and Emergency Medicine*, *9*(2), 165–172. doi:10.1007/s11739-012-0811-z PMID:22767224

Piaget, J. (1952). *The Origins of Intelligence in Children*. New York, NY: International University Press. doi:10.1037/11494-000

Pointdexter, K., Hagler, D., & Lindell, D. (2015). Designing authentic assessment. *Strategies for Nurse Educators*, *40*(1), 36–40. doi:10.1097/NNE.0000000000000091 PMID:25358115

Poore, J. A., Cullen, D. L., & Schaar, G. L. (2014). Simulation-based interprofessional education guided by Kolbs experiential learning theory. *Clinical Simulation in Nursing*, *10*(5), e241–e247. doi:10.1016/j.ecns.2014.01.004

Reznick, R. K., & MacRae, H. (2006). Teaching surgical skills-changes in the wind. *The New England Journal of Medicine*, *355*(25), 2664–2669. doi:10.1056/NEJMra054785 PMID:17182991

Rosen, K. R. (2008). The history of medical simulation. *Journal of Critical Care*, *23*(2), 157–166. doi:10.1016/j.jcrc.2007.12.004 PMID:18538206

Shinnick, M. A., Woo, M., & Evangelista, L. S. (2012). Predictors of knowledge gains using simulation in the education of prelicensure nursing students. *Journal of Professional Nursing*, *28*(1), 41–47. doi:10.1016/j.profnurs.2011.06.006 PMID:22261604

Smith, R., Gray, J., Raymond, J., Catling-Paull, C., & Homer, C. (2012). Simulated learning activities: Improving midwifery students understanding of reflective practice. *Clinical Simulation in Nursing*, *8*(9), e451–e457. doi:10.1016/j.ecns.2011.04.007

Spatz, E. S., LeFrancois, D., & Ostfeld, R. J. (2011). Developing cardiac auscultation skills among physician trainees. *International Journal of Cardiology*, *152*(3), 391–392. doi:10.1016/j.ijcard.2011.08.027 PMID:21917333

Tang, J. J., Tun, J. K., Kneebone, R. L., & Bello, F. (2013). Distributed simulation. In K. Forrest, J. McKimm, & S. Edgar (Eds.), *Essential simulation in clinical education* (pp. 196–212). Chichester, UK: John Wiley & Sons, Ltd. doi:10.1002/9781118748039.ch11

Tiffen, J., Corbridge, S., Shen, B. C., & Robinson, P. (2011). Patient simulator for teaching heart and lung assessment skills to advanced practice nursing students. *Clinical Simulation in Nursing*, 7(3), e91–e97. doi:10.1016/j.ecns.2009.10.003

Wayne, D. B., Butter, J., Siddall, V. J., Fudala, M. J., Wade, L. D., Feinglass, J., & McGaghie, W. C. (2006). Mastery learning of advanced cardiac life support skills by internal medicine residents using simulation technology and deliberate practice. *Journal of General Internal Medicine*, 21(3), 251–256. doi:10.1111/j.1525-1497.2006.00341.x PMID:16637824

Wayne, D. B., & McGaghie, W. C. (2013). Skill retention after simulation-based education. *Journal of Graduate Medical Education*, 5(1), 165. doi:10.4300/1949-8357-5.1.165 PMID:24404250

Wiggins, G. (1989). Teaching to the (authentic) test. *Educational Leadership*, 46(7), 41–47.

Wiggins, G. (1998). *Educative assessment: Designing assessments to inform and improve student performance*. San Francisco, CA: Jossey-Bass.

KEY TERMS AND DEFINITIONS

Allied Health Professional: Medically trained professionals including but not limited to, Athletic Trainers, Nurses, Medical Doctors, and Physical Therapists. These professionals are trained in and apply their knowledge and skill to restore and maintain optimal human health.

Athletic Trainer: An allied health professional that works in collaboration with a physician and is specialized in the prevention, diagnosis, therapeutic intervention, and rehabilitation of orthopedic injuries, and management of emergencies and medical conditions.

Authentic Assessment: An examination that determines the learners' ability and readiness to apply the knowledge, skills, and abilities necessary to be a competent practitioner before encountering situations in real professional life.

Cardiac Auscultation: A skill that healthcare professionals utilize to identify cardiovascular disease with a stethoscope.

Competence: The ability to do something well and according to professional standards.

Continuous Professional Education: A method to promote the development of knowledge, skills, and abilities required to stay current on the changing demands of professional practice.

Fidelity: The designated level of how life-like and realistic the simulator is.

Simulation-Based Learning: A learning environment that provides the learner with hands-on experiences to practice the application of clinically relevant technical or non-technical skills.

Section 2
Diverse Populations

Chapter 9
Technology Shaping Education in Rural Communities

Jillian R. Powers
Florida Atlantic University, USA

Ann T. Musgrove
Florida Atlantic University, USA

Jessica A. Lowe
Florida Atlantic University, USA

ABSTRACT

This chapter examines how technology has shaped the teaching and learning process for individuals residing in rural areas. Research on the history and unique needs of rural communities and the impact of technology in these areas is discussed. Educational experiences of students across all grade levels, from early childhood though post-secondary education, is examined. Examples of innovative and creative uses educational technologies in distance and face-to-face settings are described from the perspective of rural teachers and students.

INTRODUCTION

For decades, rural education advocates have argued that rural students represent a forgotten minority marginalized by poverty and geographic isolation (Azano & Stewart, 2015). According to the 2010 U.S. Census 59,492,276 people, or 19.3 percent of the U.S. population, lived in rural areas (U.S. Census Bureau, 2015). The purpose of this chapter is to examine how technology has shaped the teaching and learning process for individuals residing in rural areas. This chapter presents research and practical examples of technology in rural education across all grade levels, from early childhood through post-secondary education.

The chapter begins by presenting the state of technology use in early childhood rural educational settings. The chapter continues by exploring current technology trends in rural K-12 classrooms. Lastly, the authors examine the history and current application of distance education in rural settings including

DOI: 10.4018/978-1-5225-2838-8.ch009

K-12 and higher education. Each section begin with a vignette of a rural student and paints of picture of how technology shaped their educational experience.

TECHNOLOGY IN RURAL EARLY CHILDHOOD EDUCATIONAL SETTINGS

Meet Maria a Rural Preschooler

Four-year-old Maria hears a car driving up the dirt road to her home in a rural agricultural community. She peeks through the curtain on the window and sees that it is Miss Sarah in the car. She enthusiastically asks her mother if she can open the door before Miss Sarah has a chance to knock. Maria opens the door and asks Miss Sarah, who is just getting out of her car, "What are we going to do on the iPad today?"

"We are going to read a story about a garden and then do so fun activities to learn about different types of plants," Miss Sarah replies.

A few moments later, Maria sits down at the kitchen table with Miss Sarah and touches the iPad in exactly the right places to start the story. She is able to touch words that appear on the screen to hear them read aloud to her as she chooses. She touches a picture of a tomato and then an icon that looks like a tiny speaker that plays recorded information about the tomato plant. "A tomato is really a fruit not a vegetable?" she asks Miss Sarah. After exploring all of pages of the story Maria asks her mother to come and read it with her again, but this time in Spanish, which is accomplished simply by touching another icon on the screen. Her mother has never owned a computer and is not quite sure how to use one, but smiles proudly when she sits down at the table to use the iPad with Maria, who help her to navigate the device effortlessly.

Today's young children are part of a generation of digital natives (Prensky, 2001). They were born and are growing up in a world filled with digital technologies, and are hence native to the digital world (Black, 2010; Prensky, 2001). They are exposed to digital technology by the adults in their lives at school, home, or even on the go. However, statistics indicate that young children residing in rural communities have less access to technology than their urban and suburban peers (Perrin & Duggan, 2015; Smith, 2013). This section of the chapter explores how technology has shaped the types of learning opportunities available to young children from rural communities. Literature on technology use and early learners is reviewed, statistics on the prevalence of technology in young children's lives are presented, and examples of innovative literacy programs for rural preschoolers like 4-year-old Maria are described.

The Impact of Technology on Young Children's' Development

Early education has increasingly focused on language development and emergent literacy skills to prepare children to become strong readers by the third grade. Now professionals are beginning to assess what role exists for digital tools and apps (Guernsey & Levine, 2014, p. 104).

The question as to whether technology helps or hinders early learners has been debated for more than a decade. For example, Healy (1999) examined both sides of this argument in the book *Failure to Connect: How Computers Affect our Children's Minds--for Better and Worse*. Conversely, Armstrong and Casement (2000) pointed out the problems associated with young children and technology use in the book *The Child and the Machine: How Computers Put Our Children's Education at Risk*. A recent study conducted by Hsin, Li, and Tsai (2014) took an empirical approach to examining technology and young learners. The researchers systematically reviewed literature on how technology influences young children's learning. They examined 87 articles published between 2003 and 2013 and used content analysis to identify trends in the research literature and found that the majority of the studies "revealed that the technologies had positive effect on children's performance across developmental domains" (Hsin, Li, & Tsai, 2014, p. 85). However, despite these positive findings, the authors noted that there is still some controversy over whether technology helps or hinders child development.

A study conducted by researchers at The Joan Ganz Cooney Center in partnership with the Sara Lee Schupf Family Center for Play, Science, and Technology Learning examined differences in the ways parents and their preschool-age children interacted when reading print books, basic e-books, and enhanced e-books together (Chiong, Ree, Takeuchi, and Erickson, 2012). In doing so, they recruited 32 parent-child pairs who were patrons of a New York museum to participate in the study. The results of the study indicated that enhanced e-books offered very different co-reading experiences than print and basic e-books. Specifically, the researchers found that reading experiences varied among story formats in the following ways:

- The enhanced e-book was less effective than the print and basic e-book in supporting the benefits of co-reading because it prompted more non-content related interactions. (Chiong, Ree, Takeuchi, and Erickson, 2012, p. 1)
- Features of the enhanced e-book may have affected children's story recall because both parents and children focused their attention on non-content, more than story-related, issues. (Chiong, Ree, Takeuchi, and Erickson, 2012, p. 2)
- The print books were more advantageous for literacy building co-reading, whereas the e-books, particularly the enhanced e-book, were more advantageous for engaging children and prompting physical interaction. (Chiong, Ree, Takeuchi, and Erickson, 2012, p. 2)

These findings support both arguments that technology may help or hinder young children's learning. The interactive nature of the e-books, especially the enhanced e-books, may have made them more engaging yet traditional print books were more effective at building literacy. The researchers concluded that, "Parents and preschool teachers should choose print or basic e-books to read with children if they want to prioritize literacy-building experiences" and that designers should be cautious "when adding features to enhanced e-books, especially when those features do not directly relate to the story" (Chiong, Ree, Takeuchi, and Erickson, 2012, p. 1).

Technology in Young Children's Homes

Statistics indicate that residents of rural communities have less access to digital technologies than those residing in urban and suburban areas, but this gap has closed markedly in the past decade. According to a report published by the Pew Research Center, 56 percent of suburban residents, 53 percent of urban residents, and 42 percent of rural residents were internet users in the year 2000 (Perrin & Duggan, 2015). Today those figures stands at 85 percent, 85 percent, and 78 percent respectively (Perrin & Duggan, 2015). Given this greater access to technology in the home, young children living in rural communities may have greater opportunity to use digital devices than ever before.

Contemporary young children also have more exposure and access to smartphones and tablets due to the increased popularity of these digital devices (McManis & Gunnewig, 2012; Neumann, 2014). According to a study conducted by the Pew Research Center 59 percent of urban and suburban household owned a smartphone in 2013 compared with only 40 percent of rural households. (Smith, 2013). The touch screen nature of these devices marks a major shift from the reliance on using a mouse to control a computer. The tactile nature of these newer touch screen devices enable children with limited fine motor skills to operate them with their fingers (Neumann, 2014). This combination of increased prevalence of smartphones and tablets coupled with increased accessibility of their touch screens for small fingers makes digital technology more accessible to young children than ever before.

Technology in Early Childhood Centers

Another place that young children may have the opportunity to access digital technology is in the classroom at an early childhood center. Blackwell, Wartella, Lauricella, and Robb (2015) conducted a survey of early childhood educators' who were members of the National Association for the Education of Young Children (NAEYC). The researchers collected 945 surveys from early childhood educators serving children from birth through age eight in a member center in 2014. A total of 21 percent of the survey participants reported working in rural communities, compared with 44 percent in suburban and 36 percent in urban areas. Although the study did not break statistics on available technologies down by community type, it did reveal that classrooms contained a variety of technologies including interactive whiteboards (26 percent), computers (82 percent), tablet computers (55 percent), televisions with DVD players (71 percent), digital cameras (88 percent), and e-readers (20 percent) (Blackwell, Wartella, Lauricella & Robb, 2015).

Comienza en Casa: Bringing Technology into the Homes of Rural Children

It is clear that some young children in rural communities have access to technology in either their homes or school, but then there are those who do not. In order to address this problem, some innovative early learning programs have opted to bring technology directly into the homes of rural preschoolers. In an article titled *Pioneering Literacy in the Digital Age,* Guernsey and Levine (2014) described several examples of digital literacy programs, including one called *Comienza en Casa* (It Starts at Home) that serves children in Latino migrant families who settled in rural Maine. The program offered by an organization named Mano en Mano (Hand in Hand) brings iPads directly to rural children's homes (Guernsey & Levine, 2014). The *Comienza en Casa* curriculum was designed to develop early literacy, science, and math skills and promote school readiness (Guernsey & Levine, 2014). Guernsey and Levine (2014) vividly described a *Comienza en Casa Life Science* unit as follows:

It uses the e-book app Red Fox at Hickory Lane, an Interactive app based on a Smithsonian picture book with an audio recording feature. Families can select and listen to the Spanish narration provided to participate together in the story experience and discussions about the fox. They might select an educational game, such as ABC Farm, (available in English and Spanish), or the highly visual and interactive Seed Cycle app. They may decide to help their child tell a story using a creativity app such as Sago Mini Doublecast or Puppet Pals Director's Pals, or they could use Book Creator to make a book about discoveries made while exploring living and nonliving things (p. 105).

This passage paints a picture as to how tablet computing can foster multiple literacies and school readiness for rural migrant children with their families in their own homes. According to interviews conducted by Guernsey and Levine (2014), parents were highly receptive to the program, and parents cited reasons for this approval such as the curriculum promoted teaching and learning, communication, and spending time with their children.

Bringing Technology to Preschoolers in Rural Utah

Another program bringing technology to rural preschoolers is the UPSTART program in the state of Utah. Established in 2009 by the state's legislature, the program delivers a digital school readiness curriculum directly to preschoolers throughout the state of Utah. The software is comprised of adaptive lessons, digital books, songs and interactive activities, and families are encouraged to use the program with their children for 15 minutes a day, 5 days a week (Utah Office of Education, 2016). The program also provides state funding for home computers and Internet access for families of preschool children who cannot afford them (Miner, 2014).

In late 2013, UPSTART was awarded an i3 Validation grant from the federal government which made it possible to expand their presence in the state's 18 most rural school districts (Miner, 2014). With the implementation of the grant, participation in rural districts increased from 100 families with preschool children in 2013 to more than 920 in 2014 (Miner, 2014). The smallest rural district, Tintic, enrolled approximately 10 preschoolers in the program, and Duchesne, the largest district, had approximately 470 (Miner, 2014). In 2015, the program enrolled 5,091 children and increased its presence in both rural and urban districts (Utah Office of Education, 2016).

The Utah State Office of Education reports key statistical outcomes of the UPSTART program annually. Children enrolled in the 2014-2015 UPSTART cohort produced large effect sizes compared to control children not enrolled in the program in the areas of phonological awareness, decoding skills, letter knowledge, vocabulary and syntax, and pre-literacy discrimination (Utah Office of Education, 2016).

Summary

This section of the current chapter examined research and examples of how technology has shaped the educational experiences of young children in rural areas. These children have traditionally lagged behind their urban and suburban counterparts in technology access, but that gap is gradually decreasing. Greater access for children in rural areas is important because it enables them to connect with educational materials from a distance. Although the literature on technology use and early learners reveals that technology may help early learners in some ways but not in others, this access is still important. The potential benefits of developmentally appropriate technologies can reach more young children in rural areas as early childhood centers and mobile device sharing programs such as Comienza en Casa and UPSTART provide them with greater access.

TECHNOLOGY IN RURAL K-12 SETTINGS

Meet Kammie a 2nd Grader in a Small Rural School

Kammie is a 2nd grader in an elementary school located in a small, rural community in the Southeastern United States. She sits down excitedly to begin the project her teacher has assigned her. Today, they are researching animals and creating a project to share with the kindergarten students at her school. She loves animals! Kammie wants to become a zookeeper one day and enjoys observing animals, but has never visited a zoo. Her parents work long hours and the zoo is too far away from where she lives. She quickly forgets her disappointment as she opens her laptop to her classroom website and clicks the first link her teacher has provided. Her teacher is always sending them links to places they have never been since they do not get to take field trips. Kammie is instantly engaged with the live webcam on her screen. She can see penguins in a zoo habitat. Real penguins! There are so many penguins of all different kinds! Her excitement increases. She opens another tab on her browser to view the observation document shared with the other three students on her team. She can see that Wyatt in the 2nd grade classroom next door is working on the same page and they begin to discuss their observations through a live chat as they complete the document together. As she works, Kammie imagines being a zookeeper at the zoo and sharing observations with her coworkers about penguin behaviors. She begins to wonder about the other animals at the zoo. She decides to ask her teacher for more live webcam sites to explore later. Kammie cannot wait until then.

Although Kammie is a fictional student, her experiences are an example of what a 2nd grader in a rural school district might encounter when using a laptop in class. Students in rural school districts often do not have the opportunities to go on field trips due to funding, distance, high numbers of students, and lack of transportation. Using technology in the classroom connects these students to an outside world they may have not known or understood otherwise. According to Behrendt and Franklin (2014), "Field trips have become less common due to limited funding and limited available time due to each school systems' focus on standardized testing" (p. 242). Virtual field trips can be used to enhance student learning by "expanding their social worlds well beyond the confines of the classroom, community, or even a moment in time" (Kirchen, 2011).

Virtual field trips are just one example of how technology is of particular importance to K-12 students residing in rural communities.

History of Technology in K-12 Rural Settings

Technology use is quickly changing and advancing the face of education. Computers and technology have been utilized in education for over 50 years. Thomas Edison was one of the first to produce films for classroom use. Early technology in education included things such as lantern slides, film technology, recorded and broadcast sound, videotapes and broadcast video, and telecourses. In the 1950s, educational technology incorporated computers, and in the 1970s, community colleges developed telecourses. Piaget influenced educational computer software design using interactive learning environments and discovery education in contrast to drill and practice exercises (Berg, 2008).

Historically, rural school districts have lagged behind suburban areas with technological advances in the classroom. In a 1995 study, the National Center for Education Statistics found rural areas had approximately 1,195,000 computers used for instructional purposes with an average number of 54 per school (U.S. Department of Education, 2010). This figure was low compared to approximately 1,536,000 computers used for instructional purposes with an average number of 83 per school in suburban areas. In 2008 that gap had increased to approximately 3,974,000 with an average of 147 per school in rural communities compared to approximately 5,787,000 with an average of 221 per school in suburban communities.

In the 1997 book *Computers and Classrooms: The Status of Technology in U.S. Schools*, Coley, Cradler, and Engel stated, "Students attending poor and high-minority schools have less access to most types of technology than students attending other schools" (p. 5). Technology integration in poor, rural schools can increase options to successfully solve problems such as lack of curriculum and fewer or out of date resources (Hall & Barker, 1995). Some research has shown that technology can help to enhance the learning capabilities of students in isolated areas where resources are not always immediately available (Stern, 1994). The National Center for Education Statistics with the Department of Education, reported that "74% of Pre-K to 12th grade teachers said that technology has helped them reinforce and expand content and has also motivated students to learn" (2009). Although these studies imply that integration of technology could be a positive change for rural education, many rural school districts have had difficulties implementing technology successfully.

In the past, lack of affordability has been a main concern for most districts, even more so in rural districts. Broadband and connectivity issues effect the successful use of technology in classrooms. According to a survey done by the Consortium for School Networking, approximately 46% of schools had access to only one internet provider that delivers internet service to school districts and in rural areas, 54% of school systems had access to only one internet provider (Schaffhauser, 2015). This lack of providers leaves few, or in some cases no options, to decrease the price that these school systems must pay in order to acquire internet capabilities.

The current availability of technology grants for rural schools has had a positive effect on the increase of technology in rural districts. Increasing numbers of companies have made grants available for schools working to increase technology use, science, math, agriculture, and engineering activities in the classroom. Federal and state grants have been implemented in order to support schools struggling with supplying technology resources to teachers and students due to funding (Cullen, 2006). Project Lead the Way (PLTW) is an example of an organization that contributes to rural education by providing curriculum for STEM (Science, Technology, Engineering, and Mathematics), professional development, and more (Smith, 2015). Centurylink, a phone and internet service company, provides teachers with an opportunity to win grants up to $5,000 to increase technology use in classrooms within their service areas. With these opportunities for financial support to increase technology use, rural schools can provide the tools and resources needed to support teachers and students in using technology for teaching and learning.

Current State of Technology in K-12 Rural Education

According to Murphy, DaPasquale, and McNamara (2003), "There is no question that technology has become a common element in most children's lives" (p. 1). Technology use in classrooms has become commonplace. Classrooms without technology are thought to be "lacking."

In recent years, available technology has included teacher desktops or laptops, student computer centers in the classroom, computer labs, document cameras, and interactive whiteboards. Teachers work to use technology in order to engage students in meaningful learning, with little to no professional development or training in the technology they use. Many teachers have gone through short training workshops provided by their school or district in order to learn the newest technology provided to them, or have self-taught themselves the skills needed to successfully implement technology into their lessons.

Rural districts may not have the professional development opportunities that larger suburban and urban districts have access to. Many times, teachers turn to instruction they find online such as instructional YouTube videos, webinars, and other professional development websites in order to receive the extra training or information needed to use the technology to the extent it was intended. For example, a teacher may search for a YouTube video on how to create an interactive slideshow to share with students, or how to upload lessons into the Schoology Learning Management System (LMS). Some teachers have the skills to search for these types of videos to support their technology use, but many teachers do not. Teachers may not know what technologies are available to them using the hardware provided, and therefore, do not know where to start or how to begin searching for resources. If a teacher has never heard of a Learning Management System (LMS), he/she will not be able to search for advice and training on using one.

"Technology is a tool, and as such it should be selected because it is the best tool for the job" (Murphy et. al., 2003). Teachers must be equipped to make judgments on when the technology is the appropriate tool to use and how to use it. As more training becomes available to teachers, more integrated use of technology at the students' hands becomes the norm in the classroom.

Teachers who have more experience with technology have a better idea of what will work the best for certain types of content. If a teacher is not experienced with technology, this becomes a barrier for choosing the appropriate tool for the job. For example, if a teacher with previous technology training is given an electronic whiteboard, he/she may already know that this is a tool that can be used for student engagement and interaction with content material. This teacher may create digital games or slide shows for students to interact with, and give the students the control of the board while teaching. If a teacher without previous technology experience is given this same tool, it may be used just as he/she would have used a dry erase board, just in digital format. Students may still sit in front of the board, taking notes, or raising hands to respond to questions as the teacher writes on the board. This same teacher, if given a class set of laptops, may still teach from the whiteboard and only use the laptops for student drill and practice games. A teacher with more technology experience knows these computers can be used to interact with content and make the current lesson on the board more engaging and differentiated while meeting the needs of all students in the room. This difference in experience and understanding of technology affects how the technology is used throughout lessons with students and how much students are learning.

Students in rural communities are now given more opportunities to use technology through the creative ways their teachers have selected to stretch their available technological resources to meet the needs of both the whole class and individual students. According to Cullen, Frey, Hinshaw, and Warren (2004), "Teacher attitudes toward technology influence the level of technology integration in schools" (p.136). As teachers become more comfortable with the technology, they provide their students with more opportunities to use the technology in order to learn.

Examples of technology use in current classrooms range from Science, Technology, Engineering, and Mathematics (STEM) labs using robotics, to Skype meetings with professionals on a certain subject or content area, or long-distance communication with students in different geographical places and virtual field trips to museums, national parks, and zoos. STEM labs encourage students to take ownership of their learning with challenging and rigorous lessons using technology tools that provide a base for future careers in an increasingly technology-based labor force. These labs, can contain computers for students' use in developing their own games using coding abilities, or robotics kits where students build and create fully operational robots. By using these technologies, students in rural school districts gain more control of their own learning and are able to reach information and experiences they may not have had due to their geographical location or isolation from metropolitan areas.

Research on Technology in Rural K-12 Schools and Policy Implications

Usinger, Ewing-Taylor, and Thornton (2016) examined educational technology projects across a rural western state. A total of twelve school districts and one e-learning consortium that received technology implementation grants by the Commission on Educational Technology were evaluated. Each grant was awarded for unique purposes that addressed one or more of the following problems:

1. Common Core State Standards (CCSS);
2. Smarter Balance Assessment Consortium (SBAC);
3. Growth model;
4. 1:1 Student Computing;
5. Alternative Priority: Innovations in science, technology, engineering, and math (STEM) education (Usinger, Ewing-Taylor, & Thornton, 2016, p. 1155).

Nine of the awardees in the study were rural, and five were classified as frontier districts, with fewer than seven residents per square mile. Sources of data for the evaluation included document analysis, results of teacher and educational technology director surveys, observations, and interviews with key stakeholders. The evaluation revealed that key issues the districts faced included: (a) replacing aging technology, (b) ongoing demands for access to new technology, (c) a need for professional development, and (d) the demand for more computers and related devices (Usinger, Ewing-Taylor, & Thornton, 2016).

Other research suggests that rural school districts face unique administrative challenges that may be alleviated by the use of technology. For example, Yettick, Baker, Wickersham, and Hupfeld (2014) explored whether rural Colorado school districts faced disadvantages in their attempt to follow the Elementary and Secondary Education Act. The researchers analyzed data from a statewide survey of educational administrators (148 respondents) and 11 interviews with educational administrators. The findings suggested that updated technological infrastructure helps rural districts to overcome administrative challenges in different ways. For example, time saving technology may help small rural districts to manage federal funds since such districts generally cannot afford to hire someone who is dedicated to the task. Further, updated technology may make it easier for rural educators to access high quality professional development through either blended or online environments (Yettick, Baker, Wickersham, & Hupfeld, 2014). This research not only highlights the notion that rural districts may benefit from increased technological infrastructure, but may need it even more than their non-rural counterparts in order to meet unique administrative challenges caused by size and geographic isolation.

Azano and Stewart (2015) examined a teacher education program with a rural context. The program sought "to provide pre-service teachers with an introduction to the rural context, strategies for place-based pedagogy, and a field experience in rural schools" (p. 1). Researchers examined how the program's efforts, along with student characteristics related to pre-service teachers' perceived preparedness to teach in a rural school. According to Azano and Stewart (2015), study participants reported several perceived challenges of teaching in rural schools, which included not being able to assign homework, lack of parental support, and lack of access to technology. They also noted a few rural specific challenges such as students missing school during hunting and harvesting seasons.

It is already a challenge for rural districts to recruit teachers and provide them with technology professional development, but once these teachers are in place it can also be more difficult to retain them in rural schools. Miller (2012) explored some of the other unique challenges rural schools face in complying with universal education policies by analyzing differences between rural and non-rural community teacher recruitment and retention efforts. The findings suggested that the rural teacher labor market faced some challenges, but also enjoyed some advantages. In particular, rural schools were challenged by a heavier reliance on beginning teachers. Furthermore, rural teachers were least likely to have graduated from competitive colleges or to have a graduate degree. The study also found that retention rates for the first five years of the teaching career were also lower in rural than in suburban schools, and when teachers transferred between schools it was more likely to be from a rural to a suburban school. As a result, the rural schools examined in this study operated with a less experienced teaching staff than non-rural schools. At the same time, some of the advantages of working in rural schools included lowers class sizes, lower student poverty rates, and higher performing students than in urban schools. Moreover, teachers recruited to work in rural districts had higher SAT scores and were less likely to have failed a teacher certification exam. Finally, teacher salaries in rural school districts were higher than those of other college educated workers in the same communities (Miller, 2012).

The Use of Technology in K-12 Settings: A Rural Florida School District

Okeechobee County School District is the only district within Okeechobee County, Florida. It includes five public elementary schools, two public middle schools, one public alternative school, one public freshman campus, and one public high school. There are multiple private schools within the district. Indian River State College also has a campus in Okeechobee County.

Okeechobee is a rural community depending mostly on agriculture and tourism. The average family income is approximately $34,000 annually. With many families living 20 to 30 minutes away from the city, lack of cellular service, internet service, and transportation causes communication issues between parents and schools. Due to a high population of agricultural workers and of low socio-economic status, students are more mobile within the district, with some changing schools multiple times in one year. Within the school district, approximately 1,200 students qualify for and receive, exceptional student education (ESE) services.

The businesses in Okeechobee County are large supporters of the education system, offering annual mini-grants that teachers may apply for in order to pay for materials or activities for their classrooms. Many of the local restaurants work cooperatively with the schools in order to help raise extra money for funding of different school activities or needs.

In 2015, a team comprised of information technology (IT) personnel, teachers, and administrators identified five long-term goals for integrating technology in the Okeechobee County School District. The *Digital Classroom Plan* set goals as follows:

1. To implement Florida Standards-based instruction and integrate technology into the curriculum in every classroom.
2. Provide ongoing staff development for implementation and use of technology.
3. Increase access to technology for all students.
4. Implement 1:1 computers across the district.

5.   Establish an ongoing process as a means to evaluate the effective implementation of the technology plan (Technology - Okeechobee county school district, 2016).

Prior to the implementation of the *Digital Classroom Plan's* goals, most classrooms in Okeechobee County schools were fortunate if they had 4 to 5 computers in their rooms or access to a computer lab. The bandwidth and internet usage were unreliable and computers were not current models causing any work on the computer to become slow and frustrating for students.

As of the 2015 – 2016 school year, both middle schools have achieved the 1:1 computer initiative. These 1:1 programs make it possible for each student in a classroom to have access to some sort of technology at the same time instead of sharing 4 to 5 computers between 18 to 25 students. Classrooms may be equipped with 1:1 computers, laptops, Chromebooks, iPads, or other types of tablets. Many of the elementary schools have begun using 1:1 in several classrooms. The district piloted a 1:1 program with several elementary classrooms, including kindergarten through 5th grade. Some teachers wrote grants in order to acquire 1:1 computers for their students, and principals began allocating funds to start giving more teachers 1:1 computers.

The district created C@mp IT, a technology camp dedicated to professional development and the training needed to implement technology in the classroom. This two to three day camp started in 2011 and has continued annually each summer. The district provides keynote speakers, representatives from many of the technology companies used in the classrooms, such as Pearson, ExploreLearning, Discovery Education, Apple, and many more. The majority of the professional development sessions are teacher-led by teachers using technology successfully within the district. This peer teaching method has been successful in showing how the technology is being used in a classroom setting by real classroom teachers. Many teachers have given positive feedback to this type of training and several sessions have been made available at separate schools throughout the school year at the requests of the teachers wanting more training and information about using the technology in their classrooms.

The IT department for Okeechobee County has also encouraged technology use by awarding a *Golden Mouse Award* every quarter to a teacher at one of the district's schools. Potential awardees are teachers that exhibit exemplary use of technology in the classrooms and are nominated by their administrators. Next, an IT representative observes each of the nominated teachers using technology in the classroom and selects one to receive the award each quarter.

Impact on Learning Experiences

Teaching and learning have changed with the implementation of technology in rural schools. Classrooms no longer have rows of desks with a teacher at the front of the room leading the discussion. Students are experiencing more individualized and student-led lessons using the teacher as a facilitator. Classroom settings are centered around collaboration of students during instruction and learning. These types of classrooms are consistent with constructivist learning theory with students questioning, summarizing, clarifying, and predicting while working and discussing their thoughts with group members. This encourages teamwork, collaboration, and provides opportunities for feedback. Focus shifts to the students and uses inquiry methods to strengthen problem solving skills and incite an excitement for learning (Jennings, Surgenor, & McMahon, 2013).

According to an action research project completed by Godzicki, Godzicki, Krofel, and Michaels (2013), data showed about one third of students felt that technology was not integrated into lessons in a manner to motivate and engage students in learning. During this study, lesson plans were created implementing technology such as "computers, laptops, iPads, interactive whiteboards, student response systems, overhead projectors, document cameras, video and audio recording devices, computer software," and more (Godzicki et. al., 2013). After completion of the project, students felt more engaged and invested in the activities using technology and were more motivated to learn (Godzicki, et. al., 2013). The results of this study highlight how student's use of technology such as gaming, social media, and apps in the classroom had a positive impact on student motivation and engagement.

Outcomes of Technology Implementation

Technology has made it possible to create more individualized lessons according to student ability. These individualized lessons help to close the achievement gap between low performing students and on-level students by providing remediation and progressing at the student's speed. Individualized lessons help to challenge and enrich high performing students with projects that include research, engineering, and other critical thinking skills.

Research has been both positive and negative in regards to the effects of technology use by students and their learning. According to Doty, Popplewell, and Byers (2001) the comprehension level of a student who read an electronic document as compared to one who read a printed material showed no difference. In contrast, a study by Matthew (1995) showed that there was an increase in comprehension for students using electronic resources. Although these findings contradict each other, students and teachers seem to agree that technology in the classroom increases student motivation to learn, engagement in their learning, and is a critical component of what they will need to be able to use and understand in a future filled with technological advances.

Summary

This section of the current chapter examined research and examples of how technology use is changing education for K-12 students and teachers in rural school districts. The use of technology has increased the ability for rural schools to offer more exposure to the world outside of their small towns and increase their engagement in learning. Technology continues to evolve and change in society and these changes can be seen throughout classrooms even in remote areas. The following section of this chapter will discuss some of these changes and their impact on higher education in rural settings.

TECHNOLOGY SHAPING DISTANCE EDUCATION AND ONLINE LEARNING

Meet Angela a Rural School Teacher

Angela was a nontraditional student. She loves her job teaching at the same local small town in which she grew up. Angela started a family at the same time she was completing her undergraduate studies which delayed her studies but utilizing distance education courses she finished in 6 years. Her roles as a parent and a teacher reinforced her love of children's literature and the technology tools that are so prevalent at home and in the classroom. Now that she's been teaching for a few years she's decided to set her sights on becoming the school librarian. Luckily for Angela her school district was awarded an

Institute for Museum and Library Services (IMLS) grant. Her district set up a program modeled after an IMLS funded grant at Oklahoma State University (Kymes & Ray, 2012). Angela and other students selected for the program received a free laptop computer, with an integrated web cam and specialized software, video camera, and e-reader devices. All books, tuition, fees, professional development opportunities and workshops were paid by the IMLS grant. The program set up by rural educators for rural educators used a combination of distance education and monthly meetings at local hub schools. This combination is a perfect fit for adult learners. The internet and technology resources available at the hub schools provided an opportunity to meet and interact with students and instructors both near and far. This fostered a rich community of practice to support students like Angela to earn a Master's degree in library science. Between the monthly class meetings, learning continued at a distance in a learning management system. Angela reached her new goal with the help of a network of rural educators who understood the needs of rural students and the necessity of flexible and affordable learning.

Angela's story highlights the importance of distance education for nontraditional students, especially those living in rural areas that are geographically isolated from institutions of higher education. Radwin, Wine, Siegel, & Bryan (2013) defined nontraditional students as meeting one of seven characteristics: delayed enrollment into postsecondary education; attends college part-time; works full time; is financially independent for financial aid purposes; has dependents other than a spouse; is a single parent; or does not have a high school diploma. Those criteria fit a wide swath of today's college students.

A Brief History of Distance Education

Distance education started with correspondence courses in the 1800's. An advertisement in a Swedish newspaper in 1833 touted the opportunity to study "Composition through the medium of the post" (Simonson, Smaldino, & Zvacek, 2015, p. 36). Forty years later in 1873, correspondence courses started in the United States when Anna Eliot Ticknor founded the Society to Encourage Studies at Home, a network of women teaching women by mail (Bergmann, 2001). The original target student population then and often now remains the same, adults with occupational, social, and family commitments that interfere with the time constraints of the face-to-face classroom. In recent years distance education has also become a staple in K-12 and professional and continuing education.

In 1992 as distance learning started to become a real option for students, the Alfred P. Sloan Foundation Consortium (Sloan C) began the *Anytime, Anyplace Learning Program,* the purpose of which was to explore educational alternatives for people who wanted to pursue an education via Internet technology. This program included a series of surveys by the Babson College Survey Research Group to examine online learning in Higher Education (Picciano, Seaman, Shea, & Swan, 2012) and American K-12 education (Picciano & Seaman, 2007). These studies were conducted based on national surveys of school district and high school administrators. The focus of these studies was twofold: first, to examine the extent and nature of online learning in K-12 school districts; and second, to examine the role of online learning in high school reform initiatives. The surveys started with the simple question "How many students are learning online?" This year's higher education survey will be the last because the National Center for Education Statistics' Integrated Postsecondary Education Data System (IPEDS) is now tracking distance education. This marks a coming of age for online and distance education now included as a category added to IPEDS.

Table 1. Definitions of higher education distance learning based on percentage of online delivery (Allen, I.E., Seaman, J., 2016, p. 7)

Proportion of Content Delivered Online	Type of Course	Typical Description
0%	Traditional	Course where no online technology used – content is delivered in writing or orally.
1 to 29%	Web Facilitated	Course that uses web-based technology to facilitate what is essentially a face-to-face course. May use a learning management system (LMS) or web pages to post the syllabus and assignments.
30 to 79%	Blended/Hybrid	Course that blends online and face-to-face delivery. Substantial proportion of the content is delivered online, typically uses online discussions, and typically has a reduced number of face-to-face meetings.
80 to 100%	Online	A course where most or all of the content is delivered online. Typically have no face-to-face meetings.

The Current State of Distance Education

Today, traditional and distance education course delivery formats are determined by the percentage of the course that is delivered online. Table 1 shows the widely accepted definitions for distance education in higher education. Percentages of online and face-to-face instruction are used to delineate courses into four categories: (1) traditional, (2) web-facilitated, (3) blended/hybrid and (4) online.

As more and more educational institutions adopt web-based learning and assessment tools the notion of the "traditional" course with no online technology may have to be re-conceptualized. Increasingly paper and pencil educational practices are being replaced with more efficient electronic methods, and there is no telling at what point online methods will be considered the new tradition. The more distinguishing factor to consider may be the percentage of time a course meets face-to-face and online.

A summary of some of the key points from the most recent Babson higher education poll of the Chief Academic Officers (CAO's) in higher education shows the number of students enrolled in distance education continue to grow even in the face of declining overall higher education enrollments (Picciano, et al 2012). It is generally accepted that higher education enrollments decline in times of economic growth and increase in times of challenging economic environments.

Distance Education and Rural Communities

Higher education students in distance education courses are mostly located close to the institution where they are taking the course. A slight majority of students taking all their courses online reside in the same state as the institution offering the course. Forty one percent reside in the United States but not it the same state as the institution. Very few international students are taking distance learning courses in the United States. The majority of distance education students are taking courses at the undergraduate level.

How many distance education students are attending from a rural setting? Most distance education courses are created with a focus on serving the current student base but that does not mean there is not a desire to grow enrollments beyond current students. When the Babson poll asked CAO's about the intended geographic reach of their online courses they reported that 58.2% were targeted for students outside normal service areas. The most recent figures, which are from 2014, show that 72% of higher education distance education students are attending public institutions (Picciano, et al. 2012). Private non-profit institutions of higher education represent 20% of distance enrollment with Private for-Profit institutions coming in with only 8% of students (Picciano, et al.2012).

Distance Education Effectiveness

The effectiveness of distance education has been proven to be equal to other forms of instruction. Clark (1983) stated that:

The best current evidence is that media are mere vehicles that deliver instruction but do not influence student achievement any more that the truck that delivers our groceries causes change in nutrition. Only the content of the vehicle can influence achievement. (p. 445)

Just as Clark (1983) found distance education in higher education has been proven to be equal to other forms of instruction a meta-analysis by Cavanaugh, Gillan, Kromrey, Hess & Blomeyer (2004) also found that distance education was as effective as traditional face-to-face learning for K-12 learners. Further solidifying distance education as an effective alternative to the face-to-face classroom Means, Toyama, Murphy, Bakia, & Jones, (2009) published a meta-analysis and review of online learning studies and concluded that online learning students achieved better than traditional students because they generally allotted more time to studying.

In the Babson polls, over the past 13 years CAO's were asked if online learning outcomes are comparable to face-to-face instruction. These percentages have gone up and down but are mostly level over the last few years with 71.4% of CAO's considering online education as the same or superior to those in face-to-face instruction (Picciano, et al. 2012). The perception of CAO's remained consistent on their view that faculty acceptance of the value and legitimacy of distance education continues to be a matter of debate among faculty members (Picciano, et al. 2012).

K-12 Distance Education

Another way that technology is shaping the educational landscape of students in K-12 rural schools is the expansion of distance education. Distance education is particularly important to rural K-12 school districts. It can be difficult to hire and keep teachers. Shortages are more common in general but especially so in high demand secondary areas of instruction. The highest shortages of teachers are in mathematics, science and special education in both poorer rural and inner city school districts (Ingersoll & Perda, 2006).

The unavailability of teachers with proper certification is not limited to high demand curriculum areas but also in basic classes. As an example, it has been estimated that high school students in rural areas are less likely (6.8% versus 26.5%) to take advanced placement science courses than students in central cities and in suburban fringe areas because of a lack of teachers and resources (U.S. Dept. of Education, 2005). On top of these challenges rural districts have to do more with less with the smallest per pupil funding based on property tax bases.

A major assumption regarding K-12 online learning is that it is widely used for Advanced Placement and the more capable students. While it is true that the vast majority of students enrolled in distance education are in secondary courses the data reported for this survey indicates that online learning is being used to meet the needs of a wide spectrum of students (Picciano & Seaman, 2009). Students who need only a class or two to graduate or even students in correctional settings are also using distance education to finish their high school diploma.

The U.S. Department of Education issued the first comprehensive examination of distance education in K-12 schools, entitled Distance *Education Courses for Public Elementary and Secondary School Students* (Setzer & Lewis, 2005). Key findings included:

- A greater proportion of districts located in rural areas as opposed to suburban and urban areas indicated that they had students enrolled in distance education courses, 46% compared with 28% and 23%, respectively (p 4).
- The proportion of all distance education enrollments that are in Advance Placement (AP) or college level distance education courses is greater in small districts compared to medium or large districts, 24% compared with 10% and 7%, respectively (p.8).

Picciano and Seaman (2007) added to the literature on K-12 Online learning with a survey funded by The Sloan Consortium (since rebranded as the Online Learning Consortium). This is one of the first studies to investigate fully online and blended learning in K-12 schools. The research methodology was based on a survey patterned after the higher education surveys of CAO's now sent to administrators of K-12 school districts. Rural school districts responses to the 2007 survey included 28.4% classified rural outside the Core-Based Statistical Area (CBSA) and 16.7% that were rural inside the CBSA for a total of 45.1% of survey respondents. K-12 online education was growing at such an accelerated pace that this 2007 study was updated in 2009.

Picciano and Seaman (2009) note that how K-12 online learning has evolved much differently from the way it was in higher education. Research indicates that K-12 institutions approached this change with caution, while at the same time a majority of the respondents anticipated growth. Sixty six point three percent of districts expect growth in their fully online course enrollments and 61.2% expect growth in their blended enrollment. The 2007 study found the number of K-12 students enrolled in online courses was estimated to be 700,000. In the 2009 study it was estimated at 1,030,000, a 47 percent increase in two years. This is quite a substantial increase. The 2009 study also consisted of a large rural population with 27.8% of respondents as rural outside the CBSA and 16.3% as rural inside their CBSA, for a total of 44.1% of participants. Statements from school districts participating in the 2009 survey concerning the needs of rural and small district populations summarize the ways in which online learning can help rural districts meet some of their unique challenges. The statements are presented in Table 2 below.

These quotations illustrate how online learning may help alleviate challenges rural districts face, from securing sufficient numbers of certified teachers to connecting students with curriculum to which they may otherwise not have access. Overall, it is clear that the district leaders viewed online education as a solution that helped them better meet the needs of their students.

CONCLUSION

In this chapter, we examined research on technology and education in rural communities. The research highlights both how technology has shaped educational experiences of learners residing in rural areas from preschool through the postsecondary educational levels. However, educational systems in rural

Table 2. Statements from school districts participating in the survey concerning the needs of rural and small district populations (Picciano and Seaman, 2009, p. 24)

"Being a small district with limited revenue sources we are looking at ways to increase our course offerings for students without the expense of hiring costly personnel. Affordable online classes would help us offer more opportunities for our students."
"Community Schools is a small rural district. We would not be able to provide our students with a quality education without online learning. Students have a wide assortment of classes to choose from."
"Online or blended courses would provide the district with more options if we face teacher shortages as a rural district with lower teacher salaries as compared to large urban districts."
"This will become more of an option for students in rural areas as the secondary teacher shortage increases."
"We are in a small rural district and want to be able to offer our students all the opportunities that larger communities can offer. On line courses may fill that need."
"On-line schools serve a vital role in allowing students more flexibility in their schedule at a small school. It also, allows them a large array of courses to choose from."
"[Online learning] provides great opportunities for rural school systems."
"Without this choice [online learning], there may have been 40 fewer high school graduates in our small county last year."
"Online courses have been very beneficial because we are very small and students need credit recovery or they need to take/retake a course we are not offering that semester."
"It has great potential for our district since we are located in a small rural isolated area …."
"Online courses provide needed options for our students in a high poverty area with limited resources. These services expand learning opportunities for our students and enable them [to enroll in] courses they may not be able to take in our school and to accelerate/enhance learning through AP courses."
"I can't speak for urban communities - online courses in rural areas are important. Our teachers have multiple preps, offering electives with only a handful of students is not feasible. As well, some instructors in areas such as foreign language are hard to come by. Another great attribute of distance ed/online courses is availability of dual credit or college credit. Students can graduate high school with a semester of college courses completed."
"I believe that with the decreasing number of certified teachers available and the economically disadvantaged rural area that I live in; this type of teaching and learning will definitely bridge the gap. My district is …in dire need of certified teachers...It will also allow our students the opportunity to be more competitive in education because they will be able to have more Honor, AP and College Preparatory courses."
"We are a rural school. Online courses have been important to making college courses available to our students…"

areas face numerous challenges relating to access, funding, and the implementation of technology in education at all levels.

Rural preschool children have less access to technology in their homes than children in their urban and suburban counterparts. This disadvantage may be mitigated by bringing technology directly into their homes through programs such as the Comienza en Casa in rural Maine and the UPSTART program that extends across the state of Utah.

Rural schools at the K-12 level have traditionally lagged behind urban and suburban districts in the number of classroom computers, but recent research shows they are catching up. In the rural school district of Okeechobee, Florida an innovative *Digital Classroom Plan* is close to reaching its goal of furnishing all K-12 students with laptops. Programs such as this enable children who have never had a computer in their home to have access to one. This has also enabled students in the district to engage in online learning experiences outside of the classroom.

Distance education has become a staple in both K-12 and higher education. It is of perhaps its greatest value to rural students and teachers who have no face-to-face alternative. Distance education began with adults and has trickled down to K-12 and preschool populations. Online higher education provides access to a large population of adults ranging from those pursuing degrees or continuing their education in a variety of ways. Teachers in rural areas use the online classroom to form formal and informal learning communities for professional development.

REFERENCES

Allen, I. E., & Seaman, J. (2016). *Online Report Card Tracking Online Education in the United States.* Babson Survey Research Group and Quahog Research Group, LLC.

Armstrong, A., & Casement, C. (2000). *The child and the machine: How computers put our children's education at risk.* Beltsville, MD: Robins Lane Press.

Aydemir, Z., Öztürk, E., & Horzum, M. B. (2013). The effect of reading from screen on the 5th grade elementary students' level of reading comprehension on informative and narrative type of texts. *Educational Sciences: Theory and Practice, 13*(4), 2272–2276. Retrieved from http://eric.ed.gov/?id=EJ1027653

Azano, A., & Stewart, T. (2015). Exploring place and practicing justice: Preparing pre-service teachers for success in rural schools. *Journal of Research in Rural Education (Online), 30*(9), 1–12.

Behrendt, M., & Franklin, T. (2014). A review of research on school field trips and their value in education. *International Journal of Environmental and Science Education, 9*(3), 235–245.

Berg, G. A. (2008). Educational Technology and Learning Theory. In P. L. Rogers, G. A. Berg, J. V. Boettcher, C. Howerd, L. Justice, & K. D. Schenk (Eds.), *Encyclopedia of Distance Learning* (2nd ed.; pp. 759–763). Hershey, PA: Information Science Reference.

Bergmann, H. (2001). "The Silent University": The Society to Encourage Studies at Home, 1873-1897. *The New England Quarterly, 74*(3), 447-477. Retrieved from http://www.jstor.org/stable/3185427

Black, A. (2010). Gen Y: Who they are and how they learn. *Educational Horizons, 88*(2), 92–101.

Blackwell, C. K., Wartella, E., Lauricella, A. R., & Robb, M. (2015). *Technology in the lives of educators and early childhood programs: Trends in access, use, and professional development from 2012 to 2014.* Center on Media and Human Development at Northwestern University, Evanston, IL. Retrieved from http://www.fredrogerscenter.org/wp-content/uploads/2015/07/Blackwell-Wartella-Lauricella-Robb-Tech-in-the-Lives-of-Educators-and-Early-Childhood-Programs.pdf

Bergmann, H. (2001). The Silent University. *The New England Quarterly, 74*(3).

Cavanaugh, C., Gillan, K. J., Kromrey, J., Hess, M., & Blomeyer, R. (2004). *The effects of distance education on K-12 student outcomes: A meta-analysis.* Naperville, IL: North Central Regional Educational Laboratory.

Chiong, C., Ree, J., Takeuchi, L., & Erickson, I. (2012). *Print books vs. e-books: Comparing parent-child co-reading on print, basic, and enhanced e-book platforms.* Retrieved from http://www.joanganzcooneycenter.org/wp-content/uploads/2012/07/jgcc_ebooks_quickreport.pdf

Clark, R. E. (1983). Reconsidering research on learning from media. *Review of Educational Research, 53*(4), 445–459. doi:10.3102/00346543053004445

Coley, R., Cradler, J., & Engel, P. K. (1997). *Computers and classrooms: The status of technology in U.S. schools.* Policy Information Report. Retrieved from http://eric.ed.gov/?id=ED412893

Cullen, T., Frey, T., Hinshaw, R., & Warren, S. (2004, October). *Technology grants and rural schools: The power to transform.* Chicago: Association for Educational Communications and Technology. Retrieved from http://files.eric.ed.gov/fulltext/ED485134.pdf

Cullen, T. A., Brush, T. A., Frey, T. J., Hinshaw, R. S., & Warren, S. J. (2006). NCLB technology and a rural school: A case study. *Rural Educator, 28*(1).

Doty, D. E., Popplewell, S. R., & Byers, G. O. (2001). Interactive CD-ROM storybooks and young readers reading comprehension. *Journal of Research on Computing in Education, 33*(4), 374–384. doi :10.1080/08886504.2001.10782322

Godzicki, L., Godzicki, N., Krofel, M., & Michaels, R. (2013). *Increasing motivation and engagement in elementary and middle cchool students through technology-supported learning environments.* Retrieved from http://eric.ed.gov/?id=ED541343

Guernsey, L., & Levine, M. (2014). Pioneering literacy in the digital age. In Technology and digital media in the early years: Tools for teaching and learning (pp. 104-114). New York, NY: Routledge.

Hall, R. F., & Barker, B. O. (1995). Case studies in the current use of technology in education. *Rural Research Report, 6*(10). Retrieved from http://files.eric.ed.gov/fulltext/ED391619.pdf

Healy, J. M. (1999). *Failure to connect: How computers affect our children's minds--for better and worse.* New York, NY: Simon and Schuster.

Hsin, C.-T., Li, M.-C., & Tsai, C.-C. (2014). The Influence of Young Children's Use of Technology on Their Learning: A Review. *Journal of Educational Technology & Society, 17*(4), 85–99.

Hunt-Barron, S., Tracy, K. N., Howell, E., & Kaminski, R. (2015). Obstacles to enhancing professional development with digital tools in rural landscapes. *Journal of Research in Rural Education (Online), 30*(2), 1–14.

Ingersoll, R. A., & Perda, D. (2006). *What the data tell us about shortages of mathematics and science teachers.* Paper presented at the NCTAF Symposium on the Scope and Consequences of K12 Science and Mathematics Teacher Turnover. Retrieved from: http://www.ucdoer.ie/index.php/Education_Theory/Constructivism_and_Social_Constructivism_in_the_Classroom

Jennings, D., Surgenor, P., & McMahon, T. (2013). *Education theory/constructivism and social constructivism in the classroom.* Open Educational Resources of University College Dublin Teaching and Learning.

Khattri, N., Riley, K. W., & Kane, M. B. (1997). *Students at risk in poor, rural areas: A review of the research.* Retrieved from http://eric.ed.gov/?id=ED461442

Kirchen, D. J. (2011). *Making and taking virtual field trips in pre-K and the primary grades*. Retrieved from http://www.naeyc.org/yc/files/yc/file/201111/Kirchen_Virtual_Field_Trips_Online 1111.pdf

Kymes, A., & Ray, B. (2012). Preparing school librarians in rural areas through distance education and communities of practice. *School Libraries Worldwide, 18*(2), 35–40.

Matthew, K. I. (1995). *A comparison of the influence of CD- ROM interactive storybooks and traditional print storybooks on reading comprehension and attitude* (Doctoral dissertation). Available from ProOuest Dissertations and Theses database. (UMI No. 9542610)

McManis, L. D., & Gunnewig, S. B. (2012). Finding the education in educational technology with early learners. *Young Children, 67*, 14–24.

Means, B., Toyama, Y., Murphy, R., Bakia, M., & Jones, K. (2009). *Evaluation of evidence-based practices in online learning: A meta-analysis and review of online learning studies*. US Department of Education.

Miller, L. C. (2012). Situating the rural teacher labor market in the broader context: A descriptive analysis of the market dynamics in New York State. *Journal of Research in Rural Education (Online), 27*(13), 1–31.

Miner, C. (2014). Preparing children on the range. *Language Magazine, 14*(4), 20–22.

Okeechobee County School District. (2016). *Technology: District classroom plan, mission, & vision*. Retrieved July 6, 2016, from http://www.okee.k12.fl.us/technology

Picciano, A. G., & Seaman, J. (2007). K-12 online learning: A survey of U.S. school district administrators. *Journal of Asynchronous Learning Networks, 11*(3), 11.

Picciano, A. G., Seaman, J., Shea, P., & Swan, K.Sloan Foundation. (2012). Examining the extent and nature of online learning in American K-12 education: The research initiatives of the Alfred P. Sloan foundation. *The Internet and Higher Education, 15*(2), 127–135. doi:10.1016/j.iheduc.2011.07.004

Picciano, A. G., & Seaman, J.Sloan Consortium. (2009). *K-12 online learning: A 2008 follow-up of the survey of U.S. school district administrators*. Sloan Consortium.

Prensky, M. (2001). Digital natives, digital immigrants. *On the Horizon, 9*(5), 1–6. doi:10.1108/10748120110424816

Prensky, M. (2010). *Reaching digital natives: Partnering for real learning*. Thousand Oaks, CA: Corwin.

Radwin, D., Wine, J., Siegel, P., & Bryan, M. (2013). *2011-12 National Postsecondary Student Aid Study (NPSAS: 12): Student Financial Aid Estimates for 2011-12. First Look. NCES 2013-165*. National Center for Education Statistics.

Setzer, J. C., & Lewis, L. (2005). *Distance Education Courses for Public Elementary and Secondary School Students. 2002-Tab. NCES 2005-010*. US Department of Education.

Simonson, M. R., Smaldino, S., & Zvacek, S. (2015). *Teaching and learning at a distance: Foundations of distance education*. Charlotte, NC: Information Age Publishing.

Smith, A. (2013). *Smartphone ownership 2013*. Retrieved from http://www.pewinternet.org/2013/06/05/smartphone-ownership-2013/

Smith, A. (2015). *How rural schools can support successful STEM programs.* Retrieved from https://www.noodle.com/articles/heres-how-these-rural-schools-offer-top-notch-stem-courses151

Stern, J. (1994). *The condition of education in rural schools.* U.S. Department of Education: Office of Educational Research and Improvement. Retrieved from http://eric.ed.gov/?id=ED371935

U.S. Census Bureau. (2015). *2010 Census urban and rural classification and urban Area criteria.* Retrieved from https://www.census.gov/geo/reference/ua/urban-rural-2010.html

Usinger, J., Ewing-Taylor, J., & Thornton, B. (2016, March). Technology Integration in Rural Districts: A Study in Differences. In *Society for Information Technology & Teacher Education International Conference* (Vol. 2016, No. 1, pp. 1155-1158). Academic Press.

Utah Office of Education. (2016). *UPSTART program evaluation: Year 6 program results.* Retrieved from http://www.schools.utah.gov/CURR/preschoolkindergarten/UPSTART/2016Summary.aspx

Yettick, H., Baker, R., Wickersham, M., & Hupfeld, K. (2014). Rural districts left behind? Rural districts and the challenges of administering the Elementary and Secondary Education Act. *Journal of Research in Rural Education (Online)*, 29(13), 1–15.

KEY TERMS AND DEFINITIONS

1:1 Computing: A model of educational computing that makes it possible for each student to be equipped with a computing device. Students may be equipped with a computer, laptop, Chromebook, iPad, or other types of tablet.

Blended/Hybrid: A course that blends online and face-to-face delivery. Substantial proportion of the content is delivered online, typically uses online discussions, and typically has a reduced number of face-to-face meetings.

Core-Based Statistical Areas: A definition of a United States geographical areas based on their size and distance to metropolitan and micropolitan populations.

Learning Management System: A software application for the administration and delivery of online courses or training programs.

Online: A course where most or all of the content is delivered online. Typically have no face-to-face meetings.

Rural: A community that is not considered to be part an urban or metropolitan area.

Science, Technology, Engineering, and Mathematics Education: is a curriculum based on the idea of educating students in four specific subjects, science, technology, engineering and mathematics, in an interdisciplinary and applied approach.

Traditional: A course where no online technology used – content is delivered in writing or orally.

Web Facilitated: A course that uses web-based technology to facilitate what is essentially a face-to-face course. May use a learning management system (LMS) or web pages to post the syllabus and assignments.

Chapter 10

The Aging and Technological Society:
Learning Our Way Through the Decades

David B. Ross
Nova Southeastern University, USA

Maricris Eleno-Orama
Tacoma Community College, USA & Western Oklahoma State College, USA

Elizabeth Vultaggio Salah
Palm Beach County School District, USA

ABSTRACT

This chapter provides information and support for researchers, family, and medical providers concerning how technology can improve the quality of life for older adults while remain independent as they age in place at home or a community. In examining the available research, the researchers did find continuous developments in Gerontechnology to be beneficial as the aging population is rapidly increasing worldwide. There is increased recognition of the advancement in technology to help the aging in areas of autonomy, socialization, and mental and physical wellbeing. This chapter covered areas of change, independence with a better quality of life, technological devices/adoptions, generational differences and learning with technologies, and university-based retirement communities. This chapter concludes with suggestions for future development in accessibility of technology-based educational programs and the Internet, how to infuse technology to advance the older adults' independence and quality of life, and how older adults are adapting to living in life span communities.

INTRODUCTION

Younger generations such *as iGen, Gen Z*, or *Centennials/Millennials* who grew up with technology, integrate many components of technology into every aspect of our lives. *Baby Boomers/Traditionalists* or the *Silent Generation* did not grow up with the pervasive technology that surrounds us today.

DOI: 10.4018/978-1-5225-2838-8.ch010

Individuals who embraced change when they were younger have the ability to make the transition to newer technologies much more readily and easily than those who resisted change. We have become so accustomed to and dependent on it, that having to put in the time and effort to use new technology generally does not pose any issues.

In addition, using new technology may also take minimal time for younger generations to adapt to, compared to older generations. However, although older generations grew up without the constant use of technology this does not mean that they are incapable of learning or using new technology, but learning and using technology for older generations may require more time and effort than younger generations who are more accustomed to it. "Older adults have special learning needs that differ from younger adults when it comes to technology. Younger adults have not lived life without technology whereas older adults were introduced to it and are challenged to learn it" (Heaggans, 2012, p. 1).

This chapter provides information and support for researchers, family, friends, and medical practitioners as it pertains to how technology can improve the quality of life for older adults. The chapter describes tools that help aging adults remain independent, or as they age in a variety of settings. This chapter also explores how people handle change, remain independent with a better quality of life, technological devices and adoptions, generational differences in technology, learning and technologies, and university-based retirement communities.

BACKGROUND

Heaggans (2012) opined that the baby boomer generation as well as generations prior discover challenges to stay current with the advancement of technology. The older adults find it intimidating to use technology compared to the younger generations as they need to have the readiness to learn and to develop a knowledge base in experiential learning. There is a need to have some sort of assimilation to deal with change, especially with technology. Woods and Clare (2008) mentioned that as people age, they have several challenges (i.e., biological, psychological, and social) that pose anxiety to their "construction of self and personal continuity" (p. 20). Heaggans added that if older adults are taught not to be fearful of the unknown in technology, it would assist them socially, physically, and mentally. In addition, to conform to changes in technology, individuals strategically and actively attempt to change their behavior to deal with the rapid change and need to work with technology. These strategies can assist the aging adult use higher-level functioning skills, especially based on a tech-enabled environment.

Change is part of everyone's life, it takes time and understanding and a long-term commitment by any person or group, or organization to adapt to change. What affects people so dramatically is not the change per se, but the rapid rate of change. Technology is definitely a process that has changed radically over the past few decades. As the rate of change increases, people will have to increase their willingness and ability to adapt and at the art of anticipating the need for productive change. For example, it is imperative that the aging adult keep both body and mind active and healthy moving forward (e.g., exercise their brains, keep active, and engage in social situations).

Older adults will have a better understanding of technology and how it can influence their daily lives; however, they must be willing to embrace it (Heaggans, 2012). This will also help them develop new and stronger social networks and build a better quality of life for health communication with others. Exercising the body facilitates a healthy brain, and a healthy brain facilitates a healthy body. Physical activity has been shown to inhibit the onset of dementia and relative diseases (Lautenschlager, Cox, & Cyarto,

2012). "Physical inactivity is an independent factor contributing to mortality and disability with estimates of 5–10% deaths worldwide being due to inactivity" (Lautenschlager, Cox, & Cyarto, 2012, p. 475).

Mahmood, Yamamoto, Lee, and Steggell (2008) commented that motivation and familiarity has a use in technology and can have a key role in an older person's reasoning to accept technology. To change or adapt, individuals need motivation in some instances as well as the familiarity of devices and/or the operations of the technology.

In the area of technology, if the need is so strong, there needs to be a change process. If having poor health and other deficiencies, this can stimulate the need for change to improve independence and their quality of life. If an older person chooses to age in place by living alone or in a retirement environment, they need to learn to adapt to the change in lifestyle. When an older person is deciding to accept new technology to assist them with their health or personal care, they "must establish whether or not he/she feels a need or has an actual physical or cognitive need that could benefit from using the technology" (Mahmood et al., 2008, p. 109). Fletcher-Watson, Crompton, Hutchison, and Lu (2016) revealed that if older adults increase their engagement with digital literacy skills, the individuals may improve their cognitive aging.

Familiarity is the other factor that Mahmood et al. considered to be beneficial for older adults to adopt technology. Consider simple technological devices such as a remote control or a standard computer, older adults are not so fearful of the functionality compared to new advancements in technology. When older adults are familiar with the technology and have been given knowledge and understanding with the devices, they can apply it to their daily activities and not feel so reluctant in their abilities. Once fear and unfamiliarity are removed, the technology is more readily acceptable by older adults and the results have a positive viewpoint on *Gerontechnology* (Mahmood et al., 2008; Umemuro, 2004).

Change is situational and external compared to the transition, which is internal. Transition is the process that people go through to come to terms with the new situation. For an example with aging adults and technology, these individuals have to learn how to cope with the various technological devices. Change will not work unless transition occurs as the individuals must represent and respect the new situation. Change is either positive or negative. When it is positive and successful, everyone feels good. However, when change is negative, people tend to find liability and barriers for the change or the insiders for resisting the change. Since change is constantly around us, it is essential to learn how to survive and thrive on it.

Melenhorst, Rogers, and Caylor (2001) explored the benefits of technologies by older people. Older adults can expand their social networks with the use of advanced technology to include having a positive outlook to learning more about advanced technologies. Mahmood et al. (2008) additionally mentioned that there are two influencing factors for older adults to adopt technology, which is *attainability* and *desirability*. Conversely, there are negative points to change with technology in older adults. Although the results of technology could allow an individual to adapt more readily, sometimes they can be unwilling to adapt to the changes in technology due to fear, unfamiliarity, lack of skill and training, and isolation of advanced technologies (Melenhorst et al., 2001).

As human beings, we all resist some sort of change. We put up our protective barriers and turn down ideas that we are not comfortable with or the uncertainty of things. In today's technological world, since change happens rapidly, we need time to adapt through the change process. Since people are different and work through change differently, we have to pay more attention to why and how people deal with change. Time constraints, priorities, unfamiliarity, and deadlines have made people resistant to change.

During a change process, in situations with aging adults, this specific age group needs to communicate with their advocates (e.g., family, friends, doctors, social services, health care personnel). Older adults need to have assistance and human interaction to put into place the use of technology in their lives; this increases the success rate of implementation of technology use, establishing new social networks and relationships, enhanced awareness of others, and aiming at ideal results (Mahmood et al., 2008; Melenhorst et al., 2001). There needs to be a common ground of communication between older adults and caregivers, to include family and friends (i.e., advocates) from sending the message, receiving the message, but most importantly to have positive and supportive feedback. These advocates need to communicate to the older adults that technology can be beneficial for their welfare (i.e., socially, mentally, and physically).

The role of the advocates for the aging population must learn how to build one person, one relationship at a time showing the aging that they are personally committed to help them through any personal shift in life: finding suitable and safe living environments, improving health and well-being, being active as the person aging, and learning how to use assistive technology. "Maintenance of health, autonomy, and independent functioning are key needs in older adulthood" (van Bronswijk et al., 2009, p. 6).

These points extend to the research, education, and understanding of an individual's (a) living settings of home or an assisted living location, (b) independence, (c) risky behaviors, (d) ability to use technology in an independent setting, and (e) awareness of environmental hazards and proactive approach to prevent accidents. By building trust and respect to be listened to and valued, advocates for the aging can make a difference to help others change and help them see beyond where they are; motivation, inspiration, and encouragement are key elements.

LITERATURE REVIEW

Gerontechnology and Aging in Place

Practitioners as well as aging adults should have a good understanding of the terms *Gerontechnology* and *Aging in Place*. Chen and Chan (2012) and Hsu and Bai (2016) stated that Gerontechnology is a combination of gerontology and technology. Gerontology developed from the Greek origin meaning *old man* (geron) and *the study of* (logia) was coined this phrase in 1903 by Ilya Ilyich Mechnikov. *The Oxford Dictionaries* (2017) define Gerontology as the study of the social, cultural, psychological, cognitive, and biological aspects of aging and older adults. The scientific study of old age, the process of aging, and the particular problems of old people. *The Oxford Dictionaries* (2017) define *technology* as the application of scientific knowledge for practical purposes, especially in industry such as advances in computer technology. There has been and will be the need to study the area of Gerontechnology.

In 1984, at Eindhoven University of Technology, Eindhoven, Netherlands, a senior social worker felt there was a need to solve problems and barriers for which the aging population can or could encounter. It wasn't until 1988 when researchers at Eindhoven University of Technology formed the term *Gerontechnology* (Mollenkopf, 2016). Bouma and Graafmans (1992) commented that once the researchers defined the inception of the concepts of interdisciplinary dialogue (Mollenkopf, 2016), Herman Bouma became the first acting scientific chair in 1991 at the First International Conference in Eindhoven. After this first conference, a need was created for researchers to collaborate in specific sciences (i.e., technological, social, medical). Hsu and Bai (2016) added that at this First International Congress on Gerontechnology, Gerontechnology became an academic field of research and development technological products and services to assist the elderly in living and working conditions, to include healthcare, safety, and quality of life.

According to van Bronswijk et al. (2009), in the 1990s, there was a continuation of two trends from the 20th century to the 21st century regarding Gerontechnology: the relative and absolute increase in the older segment of society, and a man-made technological environment that is changing fast, especially in the communication domain (p. 4). Mollenkopf (2016) defined Gerontechnology to include

...technology that supports basic and applied research into aging processes, for example imaging techniques, or signal processing of brain activity. More formally, Gerontechnology is defined as the study of technology and aging for the benefit of a preferred living and working environment and adapted medical care for elderly. (p. 217)

Mollenkopf (2016) noted that in the early 1990s, there was a movement to develop technical devices (e.g., mobility, communication aids) that were designed for specific age classifications. These developments had occurred in smaller and personal organizations as the targeted population were based on family and friends who needed the technological offerings. However, there was a shift in the demographics to include an "increasing share of the old and very old people and their special needs and interests, was just beginning to receive attention" (Mollenkopf, 2016, p. 217).

In 2001, the official *Journal of the International Society for Gerontechnology* was founded on the foundation that there is a commitment to assisting and researching for the elderly in balancing their age with technology and knowledge-based society. The International Society for Gerontechnology independently publishes this journal. To promote this as a leading journal in this field, several goals have been developed: (a) reinforce the efficiency of the reviewing and publishing process with experienced reviewers, diversity and professional editorial board members, and improvement of a publishing process management system; (b) enhance the international visibility with a website, social media, and partnerships with other leading journals; (c) increase the journals academic prestige by partnering with researchers and other institutions; and (d) promote studies in Gerontechnology throughout the world and within all cultures (Hsu & Bai, 2016, p. 126). One major accomplishment is to publish this journal and promote advanced research in Gerontechnology in many countries and in different languages.

Since the 1990s, there has been other advanced technology programs such as assistive and adaptive technologies and information and communication technologies. Mollenkopf (2016) commented that one of these scientific and funding programs is the European *TIDE*. *TIDE* is the *Telematics for Integration of Disabled and Elderly* people initiative in the European Union that provides older adults as well as the disabled the opportunity for a healthier quality of life, increase independence, improve safety while lessening the burdens of care (Ballabio & Whitehouse, 1998; Brodin & Persson, 2009; CORDIS, 2014a, 2014b; Mollenkopf, 2016).

There are five key principles to TIDE: (a) market orientation, (b) technology adaption and innovation, (c) multi-disciplinary approach, (d) technology verification, and (e) user-focus approach. Furthermore, there are four technical areas such as control technology (i.e., wheelchairs, robotic aids), communication technologies (i.e., personal computers, alarm systems, satellite systems, wireless systems, enhanced hearing aids), integrated systems (i.e., smart house concepts, navigation systems), and manufacturing techniques (i.e., orthoses and prostheses) (CORDIS, 2014a, 2014b).

Ballabio and Whitehouse (1998) commented that by the year 2020, there would be about 100 million older adults in Europe; in addition, there will be a surge in the disabled population. Based upon the increases of the aforementioned demographics, there is a need to explore healthcare and social well-being to include research and development regarding assistive technologies, information and communication technologies, and control technologies (Ballabio & Whitehouse, 1998). In the United States, Ortman, Velkoff, and Hogan (2014) stated that there will be an increase of older adult population between 2012 and 2050. The older adult age group of 65 years and elder will reach approximately 83.7 million, which will double the 2012 estimation of 43.1 million older adult populace; older adults will pass the number of younger people for the first time in history by 2050 (Nagode & Dolnicar, 2010; Taipale, 2014). Woolrych (2016) identified that the older population of Brazil (i.e., sixth largest population of older adults) of 60 years of age and older will increase 29% by 2050. "Demographic projections indicate that by 2050, over 20% of the world population will be 60+ years old, with a tendency to focus on Latin America, Asia and China" (Alves Pedro, 2016, p. 71).

Based upon the population growth of all generations, especially the older adult populace, there is a need for assistive technologies in supporting older adults and understand how these individuals will age in place by living independently either at home or in a community environment (Woolrych, 2016). In addition, there is a need to invest in the infrastructure of social and health care. "There is increased recognition of the potential of assistive technologies to support the everyday lives of older adults including social participation, activities of daily living and lifestyle monitoring" (Woolrych, 2016, p. 66).

As people increase in age, there is a narrative that must develop between the older adults and their advocates (e.g., family, friends, and medical personnel) regarding a major concern on how aging adults want to age-in-place while retaining their independence and social engagement. To improve the quality of life for the older adults, there is a need for advanced technologies that assist with active aging, social cohesion, and intergenerational cooperation (Nagode & Dolnicar, 2010). Older adults have an option to either age-in-place at home or several types of communities.

An important decision for the older adult is to select an environment that best meets their lifestyle to include living among others who might be at different ages/generations. For example, one type of community to age in place are university-based retirement communities, which are built on university campuses. In this type of environment, there are many age groups where relationships could be built around social support. For the elderly who do not want to bother their children with the burden or someone who might live alone with no family could age in place on a university retirement setting. The social support could be other professional people living on campus to share experiences and work experiences to the younger generations.

Nagode and Dolnicar (2010) stated that strong relationships and informal social support between parents and their children are crucial; however, the pattern of exchange changes over the years. "Informal social support or support exchange usually consists of emotional, financial and instrumental support and is the basis and the central issue of intergenerational solidarity in the family" (Nagode & Dolnicar, 2010, p. 1280). As older adults age in place, it can also place a burden on family members and healthcare individuals.

As a result, selecting the retirement community is vital. If an older adult decides to age in place at home, they would need the support and attention by either family, friends, or healthcare individuals mainly because they could be living alone. A global trend is a one-person household, but this does not refer to being lonely, only living alone. As older adults decide to live alone, there is a need for advanced and innovative technologies and service within different communities and societies (Taipale, 2014). However, if they decide to age in place at a life-care community (i.e., retirement community), there is still the need for support based on the various levels and stages of the older adults' lives.

People are at the mercy of the unknown regarding the level of care (i.e, part time, full time) needed as they age. Decisions are based on which type of community (i.e., independent living, assistive living, and skilled-nursing home), financial standing, medical personnel, medication(s), and stage of health.

The following are the three levels of life-care communities: First, there is independent living by having full autonomy and the choice to live in a one to three bedroom apartment-style environment with many amenities (e.g., dining, library, social activities, meals, resident nurse, nutritionist/licensed dietician, medical director). Secondly, assistive living is an environment of 40 to 60 private rooms with a kitchen, private bathroom, and bedroom. This level is somewhat like the independent living by having a dining room with meal service, socialization, as well as skilled nurses and licensed aides. These communities are designed to keep the residents safe and support a better quality of life. The final level of a life-care community is a skilled nursing home, which represents the hospital-style and sterile environment designed to accommodate the very aging adult to be comfortable during their final stage in life. This environment is also state regulated and receives a rating by each state.

Researchers stated that as people age, they need these levels of aging in place in supporting competencies and quality of life (Mahmood et al., 2008). Wahl (as cited in Mahmood, 2008) opined that *Lawton's Ecological Theory of Aging-Competency-Environment Model* regarding aging and environment was important, especially if an older adult's competencies weaken because the environmental structure "becomes increasingly imposing, resulting in a high potential for negative adaptive outcomes" (p.107).

Independence and Quality of Life

Late-life depression refers to major depressive disorder typically in adults 60 years of age or older and is often associated with coexisting medical illness or cognitive impairment (Taylor, 2014). While depression is not a normal part of the aging process, more than two million of the 34 million American age 65 and older suffer from some form of depression (Mental Health America of Illinois, n.d.; National Alliance for Research on Schizophrenia and Depression, n.d.). Depression is one of the most common conditions in the elderly and is a serious public health problem that needs to be identified and treated. Because many elderly adults battle a number of illnesses, as well as, social and economic difficulties that are accompanied with depression, health care providers may inaccurately diagnose depression in their patients as a normal consequence of these problems. Additionally, there is awareness that depression often times can exhibit for myriad of reasons and is triggered without warning.

Some signs of depression can be restless, avoidance of people, and irritability. Depression affects the whole body and mind, and can be quite debilitating and even life threatening if not treated. Individuals must be aware of the warning signs that manifest in the elderly, such as a change in eating habits, lack of social interaction, being withdrawn, and feeling of helpless, guilt, worthless, or hopeless. Depression can be easily treated with medication as well as without medication. Ruling out medical causes of depression is the first step in treating the individual. Lifestyle changes can bring powerful relief to individuals and can be as effective as medication without the side effects, such as the use of technology.

According to Royal College of Psychiatry (2017), one in five older adults age-in-place in the community as well as two in five age-in-place in retirement homes are affected with depression. There are many issues for older people who feel depressed such as physical symptoms, long-term illness, confusion and memory problems, and loneliness. Most of these issues are medical in nature where they can receive help from healthcare providers. However, in the case of loneliness, technology involving social media can increase quality of life in older people when communicating with family and friends.

Social media is a remarkable tool for staying connected with others, and especially for older people who have limited access to loved ones. Social media can be easily accessible using any device, such as, laptops, desktops, tablets, and smartphones. With the rise in technology use in today's world, access to social media is becoming more popular for both the young and the old. Clearly, grandparents' *Brag Photo Album* has been replaced with social platforms because of technology tools such as *Facebook, Twitter, Instagram*, and Snapchat. Two-thirds of online adults use these social media platforms daily to stay in touch with friends and family members (Smith, 2011). Posting pictures and video clips on these platforms has made *Brag Photo Albums* a thing of the past. Evidently, this has alienated nonusers who are not as tech savvy as everyday users. Connection with family members and friends is paramount for older people, and undoubtedly a major factor across a range of social media users (Smith, 2011).

Zhang and Kaufman (2016) proclaimed that cognitive decline could have a serious effect on the elderly's independence and quality of life. No matter where older adults are aging-in-place, having independence can increase one's quality of life (Edelman & Ficorelli, 2012). Karol (2016) stated that independence for the older adult

... can be translated into feeling normal, respected and able to readily connect with services and people within the community desired. ... In the home itself it means being able to manage daily living require-ments safely whilst retaining a sense of self and personal identity. (p. 227)

Results from a study in Australia, determined that independence was defined as "... being able to continue throughout life to be engaged in the activities and relationships that are important to the in-dividual" (Karol, 2016, p. 227). Use of social media improves cognitive capacity, increases a sense of self-competence and has an overall beneficial impact on mental health and physical well-being (Masedu, Mazza, Di Giovanni, Calvarese, Tiberti, Sconci, & Valenti, 2014; University of Exeter, 2014).

Wellman (2010) opined that the influence of nutrition as it related to independence has been over-looked and that nutrition programs for the aging adults needs more research to link nutrition to gaining at home and independence. Interventions, such as cognitive training, physical activity, social participation, and nutrition, and volunteering, can potentially reduce cognitive decline in aging adults (Chew-Graham, Gask, Shiers, & Kaiser, 2014; Williams & Kemper, 2010). According to Chew-Graham, Gask, Shiers, and Kaiser (2014), psychological interventions and antidepressants have also been used to treat depres-sion in older people. While depression tends to decline with age, the older population seemingly goes untreated (Lill, 2015).

Online social network can support the needs of older people by providing an avenue for building and maintaining social capital as they age. Research on the elderly and the impact of *Facebook* on social capital reported that social media facilitates connections to loved ones and may indirectly facilitate bonding social capital (Erikson, 2011; University of Exeter, 2014). Due to the advances of the *World Wide Web*, there is a more interactive approach in connecting with others compared to the old one-way communication style platform (Nef, Ganea, Muri, & Mosimann, 2013). *Social Network Services (SNSs)* also known as social media (e.g., *MySpace, Flickr, YouTube, Twitter, LinkedIn, Facebook*) can be used for both professional and personal purposes and have been known to help gratify social-emotional needs. *SNSs* serve as a platform for interactive information sharing, social interaction, and collaboration among individuals where users create public profiles, interact with friends, and connect with other users (Masedu et al., 2014; Nef et al., 2013).

SNS platforms are designed where each member has an individual virtual wall where messages and photos are shared with selected "friends." *SNS* encourages its users to engage in dialogues, which in turn, helps reduce social isolation, loneliness, and promote elderly adults to stay connected to their family life (Erickson, 2011). Social networking helps engage groups of people with common interests while fostering relationships with a click of a mouse. Users can use authorized *chat rooms* to share emotional experiences online encourages others users to do the same. Using emotional status, such as "like," is a way to give positive feedback or to connect with things you care about and/or admire on *Facebook*. Users can "like" content posted on *Facebook* as well as posts feedback to their friends' timeline.

Pew Research Center conducted a survey on the American public about their interaction on social media and it was reported that 44% of *Facebook* users reported "like" content posted on their friends' wall at least once day, with 29% posting several times per day (Smith, 2011). SNSs can potentially help elderly adults keep up with existing friends, stay connected with loved ones, reconnect with friends and family, as well as, share experiences via social network platforms. Elderly, who are immobile, can benefit from social network platforms. Coleman (1998) highlighted social network relationships are beneficial to group members as it can foster a sense of confidence, independence, and belonging in individuals. Researchers reported that people who are involved in "social networking sites expect to gratify social-emotional needs rather than information needs, and they are connected in a person-to-person manner, which is more direct and interpersonal" (Rau, Gao, & Ding, 2008, p. 2757).

When asked 'what does social media have to offer older adults', it is clear that this mode of communication can have the greatest benefits for those who are isolated and immobile. Along with these barriers, a person's age, work status, lack of confidence in computer skills, and lack of resources might be barriers for some. Social media can offer individuals who are isolated and immobile a means of communication without leaving the comforts of their home or dwelling. Social media is used by individuals of all ages and has quickly become integrated over the last years into many aspects of daily lives.

Websites such as *Facebook* and *Twitter* helps keep individuals stay in touch with family and friends. Joining online conversations and having access to these social media networks have brought people closer to their loved ones and friends and has improved quality of life (Masedu, Mazza, Di Giovanni, Calvarese, Tiberti, Sconci, & Valenti, 2014). Social media can be an invaluable tool for elderly. Empowering elderly an opportunity to receive and send updates on social media has helped individuals stay connected with the outside world, enhanced feelings of control and self-efficacy, and has become a healthy emotional outlet. In a study conducted by Masedu, Mazza, Di Giovanni, Calvarese, Tiberti, Sconci, and Valenti, (2014), it was reported that

…social network use has a positive impact on mental health and quality of life outcomes in years following a disaster. The use of social networks may be an important tool for coping with the mental health outcomes of disruptive natural disasters, helping to maintain, if not improve QOL [quality of life] in terms of social relationships and psychological distress. (p. 1)

Morrison (as cited in Finn, 2015) revealed that social media gives people, especially the older adults an avenue to connect with others, rather than being isolated from family and friends. The older adults can restore a sense of self by using their social voice from where they are aging in place. By staying in contact with others, it strengthens the relationship among one another as well as provide emotional and moral support (Finn, 2015; Nef et al., 2013).

Gerontechnology Devices, Adoptions, and Security

Gerontechnology relates to technologies that assist in the care of chronic conditions and improve not only the living conditions but also the quality of life and autonomy for the older adult as well as those that require more or less assistance. In addition, it assists the older adults who are aging in place in the areas of housing, communication, health, mobility, leisure, and work (Bouma & Graafmans, 1992; Mollenkopf, 2016). There are numerous areas, which include both high-tech and low-tech options such as, devices and equipment that promote independence and safety for vulnerable individuals as they can both detect and report health hazards. *Smart technology* such as sensors, voice activation, GPS, Bluetooth, cellular connectivity via mobile phones, smart phones, wearable technologies, monitoring apps, and sophisticated computers are making aging in place a viable option for an increasing number of people (Abrams, 2014; Center for Technology and Aging, 2009; Mears, 2015).

Many of these high-tech options do not come into play with older adults who are in an institutional environment, because they have the human interaction, compared to aging in place at home or the community. However, the high-tech options for communicating with family, friends, and others is vitally important (e.g., text, email, web conferencing, continuing education).

Some of these areas are communication/cognitive fitness technologies to include games that exercise the brain, much like physical fitness. These activities help prevent the onset and/or delay various dementias and generally providing a better quality of life. *Social Networking* technologies provide for the creation of building communities of family, friends, and professionals. *Telemonitoring technologies* are designed to manage and monitor an array of health conditions and can support a fully integrated health data collection, analysis, and reporting system that connects to multiple branches of the health system and along with alerts to appropriate responders when either emergencies arise (i.e., fire, police, physicians) or health conditions decline.

Telehealth technologies such as *Medication Optimization*, which "refers to a wide-variety of technologies designed to help manage medication information, dispensing, adherence, and tracking or disease management, which is a patient-centric, coordinated care process for patients with specific health conditions" (Center for Technology and Aging, 2009, p. 5). These programs can include data mining to identify high-risk patients, use medical practice guidelines to support and treat individuals, and a coordinated, data-informed system of patient outreach, feedback, and response. Additionally, *Remote Training and/or Supervision* technologies can be used to train and supervise health and long-term care workers, and offer the potential for continuing education and quality assurance via the Internet, interactive videoconferencing, and satellite (Center for Technology and Aging, 2009).

Technological Devices and Adoption/Apps

"Technologies range from complex, fully integrated devices that use information and communication technologies to the simpler, standalone devices with more limited functionality" (Center for Technology and Aging, 2009, p. 5). Non-computer-based or low-tech assistive technologies include items such as wheelchairs, walkers, grab bars, canes, reading glasses, Braille keyboards, and daily or weekly medication containers. Examples of computer-based or high-tech technologies include those that most people are aware of whether they understand the terms or not such as *smart homes, smart appliances, the internet* and *cloud based technologies, mobile data* and *video conferencing*. Also included in this category are *voice recognition software* and *monitoring and alert systems* that detect and report personal crises.

Fitness trackers, health monitoring, medication distribution, medical alert systems, GPS tracking systems, estate and financial planning programs, interactive real time socialization and transportation, also help the person who needs assistance. These devices allow for the connectivity while the *Apps* provide the solution. It should be noted that many of these high-tech devices provide a physical component, such as insulin pumps that are surgically implanted, can be remotely adjusted and monitor various aspects of the individual's condition. Other technologies that should be addressed are the variety and availability of ultra-high tech medical equipment such as robotics; laser and artificial surgical equipment and procedures, breath controlled wheelchairs, robotic limbs whose technology taps directly into brain and/or neurological activity and the list goes on.

Devices such as smart phones, tablets, e-readers, and smart TVs, allow seniors access to email, news, weather and social media. Seniors can use apps to track their blood pressure, deliver and continue communication with family, friends and/or medical providers. Smart watches, fitness trackers, GPS, and GPS Insoles can provide an alarm button or medication reminder, and track fitness. Optional activity sensors are available for the home with wireless connectivity for use in or away from home to detect falls, and to provide directions home with voice-activated system or find someone who is unresponsive via GPS technology (Mears, 2015).

Individuals of all ages utilize apps such as *Facetime, Instagram, Skype, Uber Conference, What's App*, etc., to continue relationships and to communicate in real time, which keeps them connected with not only family or friends but also the world at large. These devices can now make contact with extended family or lost friends in other parts of the world and keep up with what is happening in their lives, social settings, and surroundings, as well.

External engagement through communication and social skills is particularly vital to the individual who is aging in home and experiencing mobility challenges whether it be physical or emotional. Having contact with other beings is vital to one's mental well-being and quality of life. Being able to be part of the community at large can prevent the feeling of loss, loneliness and/or isolation leading to depression and/or hastening dementia and related conditions. Long distance phone calls are no longer the only option available for communications. Other apps such as *Telekin* and *TelyHD* go further by specifically allowing the older population to continue to communicate both visually and audibly with family members from multiple generations, friends, team mates and so on through real time social media and online games that stimulate both physical and mental activity (Orlov, n.d.).Many, if not all of these applications, utilize smart phones, tablets, e-readers, and/or smart TVs, which are cross platform and provide worldwide connectivity at no additional cost other than the cost of Internet service and is particularly important to fixed income individuals.

Fitness trackers and programs, either monitor physical activity, sleep, and exercise regiments, or provide the regiment directly. Fitbits are an example of this technology Peleton interactive cycling is another. Apps such as *Walkjoy* and *Respondwell* are adaptive technologies that employ non-invasive sensors to stimulate the brains nervous system or develop a physical routine based on the individual's physical abilities, or lack thereof (Center for Technology and Aging, 2009; Mears, 2015; The Online Mom, 2017; Orlov, n.d.). Interactive exercise options such as the many options of *Wii* and *Dance Dance Revolution*, which address multiple areas of training and/or rehabilitative activities including aerobics, balance training, strength training and yoga. All of which promote a healthy body and mind (Heyward, n.d.). Medication monitors and medical alert systems either alert users when it's time to take medications, repeat the alert if the medication is not taken within a certain time and/or contact a caregiver such as *TabSafe* is one such option. Apps like *MedMinder* and *Reminder Rosie* either automatically disburse medication or remind an individual to take meds (and other scheduled activities) and will contact a caregiver alerting them of the person's failure to do so (Abrams, 2014; Mears, 2015; Orlov, n.d.).

Personal Emergency Response System (*PERS*) systems contact the individual first and if unresponsive contact the appropriate responder such as the assigned fire department, which locate the individual via *GPS* tracking. *Great Call, 5 Star, Mobile Help* and *Lifeline apps* are more simple systems, usually a one-touch system whereas *BeClose* is an aging in-place remote wireless technology that helps seniors, families and caregivers stay in touch using wireless sensors placed in the home that tracks daily routine. Caregivers monitor them via a secure web page, are alerted by phone, e-mail or text message. Another *PERS, GrandCare System* provides similar service along with socialization, entertainment and communication elements. Family can send pictures, messages, e-mails, reminders, calendar appointments, voice messages, family videos, music, etc. *Independa* is another app providing similar service and most if not all utilize touch screen options removing physical and dexterity challenges (Orlov, n.d.).

Remote Patient Monitoring include technologies that have been designed to manage and monitor an array of health conditions. Point-of-care (e.g., home) monitoring devices, such as weight scales, glucometers, and blood pressure monitors, may stand alone to collect and report health data, or they may become part of a fully integrated health data collection, analysis, and reporting system that communicates to multiple branches of the health system and can provide alerts when health conditions decline.

These medical uplinks, sometimes referred to as telehealth, are the communications between the individual and either their specific caregiver, physician, pharmacy or hospital or all of them combined. For example, pacemaker recipients have a home health care provider run diagnostics or blood checking/ blood levels and heart rate, and oxygen. This information is then uploaded to their medical record via technology to their doctor, which links their entire medical history and allows for the cycle of medical diagnosis and care to progress uninterrupted while aging in home (Mears, 2015).

Another example of telemedicine would be the testing of a pacemaker function using a smart phone to run an electronic diagnostic of the equipment by transmitting the data to the manufacturers technical support team and the individuals physician.

On a more basic note, the Internet makes it possible for the individual to access more information from finding and researching doctors, hospitals, and other healthcare options to identifying potential treatments for any crises that may arise. Using a smart phone or tablet, medical personnel can now access virtually every resource available whether it be case studies, research, clinical trials, textbooks, journals, or patient history to effectively diagnose and treat an individual. Additionally, they can contact caregivers, specialists, and labs in real time while treating through the same technologies.

Online estate planning, financial trackers and stock trades are another area where the senior population are assisted with technology. Many financial institutions and trading houses have sites similar to *Everplans*. Some sites will provide a digital archive that includes wills, trusts, passwords, advance directives, etc., while others will track your finances, investments and stock trades with information-sharing options (Mears, 2015).

Online legal service can be tremendously beneficial, but may require that the individual obtain notary and/or witness signatures requiring them to leave their home. Programs such as *Lifelock* is a type of service that provides personal financial security by hindering personal identity breaches relative to finances, credit, banking, etc. For the individual who is new to the online service aspect of banking and finances, or has trust issues with technology and sharing information, or simply prefers the brick-and-mortar environment, they no longer have to avoid the high tech options as there are so many that are available, safe, secure and easy to interact with particularly with the aforementioned type of services which monitor online activity for you.

Smart home technologies can be controlled by the individual and accessed by family members/ authorized contacts allowing them to control security systems, lights, thermostats, cameras, even their refrigerator to insure their comfort and well-being. Various online apps such as *PeaPod, Boxed, Instacart,* and *Shipt,* are online grocery pick and delivery services that also provide household sundries (e.g., toilet paper, cleaning supplies, etc.) or meals such as *Fresh, Seattle Sutton,* and others that provide for the standard or medically directed diets.

With the advent of smart home and appliance technology the whole population benefits, but it is of particular importance to the elder adult with a clear mind, but ailing body. For example, if your parent were homebound and not able to utilize online services directly you could look in their refrigerator, see what they need, order it online and have it delivered. This not only serves the individual well, but all parties involved. Many grocery stores and/or businesses provide similar services via low-tech options such as using the phone and placing the order; however, fewer and fewer businesses engage in this option, as it is time consuming.

Home security (alarm systems, cameras, doorbell cameras, door locks), personal security (*First Alert,* etc.) both connect directly via GPS to appropriate responder whether it be the police, fire department or assigned hospital. An individual with mobility issues can utilize the doorbell camera to see who is at their door; if they choose to let that person in, say "a home health care" provider, they can open the door by unlocking it via a wireless connection. Much as the personal emergency response systems or smart home systems can be monitored and controlled by the individual and/or authorized individual whether it be a caregiver, family member or friend. This type of technology provides not only real security but also emotional security for all involved.

Transportation or ride share apps like *Uber/Lyft,* etc. provide transport mobility to medical appointments, social engagements, etc. One service "*Lift Hero* is positioning itself as a ride-sharing service for the elderly, hiring medical professionals and students and training them to meet the needs of older passengers" (Mears, 2015, para. 17).

Educational or brain stimulating games provide the older adult with cognitive or mental exercise, examples are *Tetris* which works spatial recognition, *Trivial Pursuit* which enhances memory, or *Mahjong* honing memory and matching skills. Like many of these technologies, these works in both the institutional and aging in home setting. They are a fun and entertaining way to encourage people of all ages, and particularly the elder population, to work on their own and then can engage with others. Additional online brain stimulating games that foster social interaction are *Words with Friends* and *Scrabble*. Many of these games are based on games that have been played throughout their lives and provide a familiarity not only to the game but also to reminders of previous social engagements such as game night with family (*Home Instead,* 2017).

In short, the technologies that benefit the population at large can and has improved the lives of the older population. The term Gerontechnology address these technologies and those that are specifically designed to assist the older population whether it be the ability to hear or see better through audio and visual enhancing devices or communicate with family and friends through social networking or ensuring a better quality of life through health and safety monitoring and assistance. These technologies also serve to enhance the lives of their family and friends and facilitate the services of their caregivers and physicians to name a few. While there may be upfront individual costs for devices and connecting to either mobile service providers and/or cloud based or Internet services, many if not most of the apps are free of cost. This provides a benefit to the older aging in home individual and potentially reducing the financial drain on healthcare systems and social programs such as *Medicare, Medicaid*, and *Social Security* (Davies, 2016). Technological advancements have accounted for much of this literature regarding a number of areas of existing technology. There are other innovations under way as the present rideshare apps and self-parking car; there are self-driving cars on the horizon.

The impact of the world's aging population will have on health and social systems within this country and around the world, is a growing concern. It is anticipated that over the next decade, the over-60 age group is anticipated to grow 56% faster than the global population. It is projected that in Europe, the 70-79 age group will increase by 50%. This population growth has and continues to place increasing pressure on both the healthcare and social systems prompting an effort to find ways to efficiently provide quality care with ever shrinking resources. These gerontechnologies provide not only a better quality of life for the individual and can make the difference between aging in home and being independent or simply existing in an institutional setting, but also have the potential to streamline healthcare systems, provide a better quality of care, and provide a more cost effective use of declining healthcare resources.

Generational Differences In Technology

Traditional And Technology Generations

Individuals of similar birth year and whose values, behaviors, and general outlook have presumed to be influenced and defined by their shared experiences during fundamental phases within their lifetime are described as generational cohorts (DeVaney, 2015; Huyler & Ciocca, 2016; Sherman, 2006). Currently, literature refers to four generational cohorts (Parry & Urwin, 2011; Sherman, 2006).

- Individuals born between 1925 and 1942-1945 as Traditionalists, Veterans, or the Silent Generation (Fietkiewicz, Lins, Baran, & Stock, 2016; Parry & Urwin, 2011; Sherman, 2006).
- Individuals born between 1943-1945 and 1955-1964 are known as Baby Boomers or the Boomer Generation (Beckett, 2011; DeVaney, 2015; Parry & Urwin, 2011).
- Individuals born between 1961-1963 and 1980-1981 are known as the Baby Busters and as Generation X or the Lost Generation (Parry & Urwin, 2011; Sherman, 2006).
- Individuals born after 1980-1981 are known as Generation Y or the Millenials (Parry & Urwin, 2011).

As noted above, labels, definitions, and birth year ranges within each generational cohort are disputed within current literature. However, the presumed profiles of individuals within each of these generational cohorts help with the understanding of personal values, attributes, and work ethic (Sherman, 2006).

According to Sackmann and Winkler (2013), the access and use of new and basic technologies, in addition to social and cultural environments, have also formed technology generations. Technology generations is a concept that presumes individuals born within birth cohorts may have shared experiences with evolving technology; similar perceptions and usages; and similar technical competence (Gallistl, 2016; Sackmann & Winkler, 2013). Previous research delineated the four main technology generations; Sackmann and Winkler described the formation of a fifth technology generation. These five technology generations include the

- *Mechanical Generation*, for individuals born before 1939;
- *Generation of Household Revolution*, for persons born between 1939 and 1948;
- *Generation of Technology Spread*, consisting of individuals born from 1949 to 1963;
- *Computer Generation*, involving persons born between 1964 and 1978; and
- *Internet Generation*, formed by individuals born after 1978.

Generational Differences In Technology

Not every individual may fit within their traditional or technology generational stereotypes. Lai and Hong (2015) have noted that empirical support for stereotyped characteristics based on access and use of technology for generational cohorts is lacking and that factors, including gender and culture, have been determined to have a greater influence on generational technology-based behaviors and practices. Yet, recognizing that there are some observed generational differences could help further the understanding of support, learning, and technology-related needs for aging and older generations.

Individuals born within the Boomer Generation developed their perceptions and values of life prior to the digital age, despite the fact that the digital age was created and developed primarily by Boomers (Huyler & Ciocca, 2016). According to Huyler and Ciocca (2016), Boomers learned technology much later in life and thus, their outlook and values of daily life were formed without the dependence of technology. Yet, Boomers use technology to adapt to their desired lifestyle, but have a greatly different perception, experience, and relationship with technology. This is in contrast to younger generations that grew up during the digital age: A time when technology was more available and affordable. This early exposure and acceptance of technology for younger generations helped shape their lifestyles, perceptions, and values of daily life to revolve around technology (Huyler & Ciocca, 2016). Additionally, generational differences with regard to social interaction have been observed between individuals within the Boomer Generation and individuals in younger generations. The Boomer Generation developed relationships and social circles without the reliance of technology and appreciate personal and face-to-face interaction (Huyler & Ciocca, 2016; Vroman, Arthanat, & Lysack, 2014). In contrast, younger generations developed relationships and formed social circles during the digital age, digital networking and the use of technology to make connections are a valued method of interaction among individuals within younger generations (Huyler & Ciocca, 2016).

Digital Divide

As Sackmann and Winkler (2013) asserted, the rapid evolution of technology within the last several decades has created an uneven dispersion across generation cohorts in terms of access, possession, and application of technology. This unequal distribution of digital technology and resources has created a digital divide for older generations and other underprivileged populations (Friemel, 2014; Sackmann & Winkler, 2013). With regard to existing technology gaps between generations, current literature distinguishes between the digital divide regarding access and adoption, known as first-level-divide, and the digital divide regarding technology use and skills, known as second-level-divide (Courtois & Verdegem, 2014; Friemel, 2014; Sackmann & Winkler, 2013). Presently, there are distinct differences between generation cohorts with regard to the first-level and second-level digital divides (Friemel, 2014; Sackmann & Winkler, 2013). Sackmann and Winkler stated that younger generations are more likely to use social media and other interactive technologies and will also have faster adaptation rates for new technology, creating greater generational differences in terms of access, adaptation, and use that becomes more evident over time.

Some studies mentioned that the digital divide between generation cohorts will minimize or fade over time since younger generations currently have a higher level of technology appreciation and immersion and will be more likely to continue using technology into retirement (Friemel, 2014; Peels et al., 2013). However, Yu, Ellison, McCammon, and Langa (2016) reported that further research is needed to address the significant digital divide for current older generations. Recent literature has begun to focus on the level of Internet use within older generations, while there is still a need to understand the actual level of Internet access, as well as extent of social networking site usage, for these individuals (Yu et al., 2016). Also, age-related physical limitations and dexterity concerns may present challenges for older generations to use technology (Friemel, 2014; Yu et al., 2016). Lastly, even within the generation cohort, differences with technology adaptation, access, and use may differ between age groups and especially, later in life (Yu et al., 2016). Friemel (2014) mentioned these major differences within older generations, particularly for older adults age 65 and over, deemed the *grey divide*, as remaining prominent with particular needs to focus on older seniors to address unique age-related challenges affecting their technology use and needs.

Learning and New Technologies

Benefits To Learning/Using New Technologies

Boulton-Lewis (2010) stated that continuing education for older adults is vital for our civilization. Older adults have a repertoire of experience and knowledge and a lifetime of learning that can provide wisdom and insight for future generations. Although older generations experience some cognitive and physical decline in their abilities due to the natural aging process, continuing education into the later years of life still presents an advantage over younger generations, as learning helps older adults maintain or enhance the quality of their lives (Boulton-Lewis, 2010; Tam, 2015).

Learning, accepting, and using technology, which includes having access to computers and the Internet, is a challenge aging populations must face in today's modern world (Ordonez, Yssuda, & Cachioni, 2010). Another challenge is providing appropriate and personalized technology-based training for older adults in order to convey how technology can be helpful in supporting an actively aging lifestyle, which includes being mentally and physically active (Arthanat, Vroman, & Lysack, 2016; Boulton-Lewis, 2010). As Fletcher-Watson, Crompton, Hutchison, and Lu (2016) stated,

Educational initiatives for older people should help to convey knowledge and skills that have lapsed in the elderly person's life; make active use of the elderly person's free time; encourage the acquisition of new roles for a new age that are different from those of the preceding life phases; encourage participation in the social life of the community (pp. 162-163).

Additionally, technology-based educational programs should highlight the effective use of technologies to help address or alleviate concerns related to health support, the means to remain independent, keeping socially engaged, and staying safe (Huber & Watson, 2014; Luijkx, Peek, & Wouters, 2015). Current research has revealed that many older adults use information and communication technologies (ICT), but the knowledge, acceptance, and implementation of new and assistive technologies could be greater among older generations (Luijkx, Peek, & Wouters, 2015). Providing relevant technology-based training is one method of providing this information to older adults (Gonzalez, Ramirez, & Viadel, 2012; Wolfson, Cavanagh, & Kraiger, 2014).

Huber and Watson (2014) reported that age was negatively correlated with the level of computer knowledge and interest in new technologies. The researchers also reported that age was positively correlated with computer and technology related anxiety (Huber & Watson, 2014). As noted by Van Volkom, Stapley, and Amaturo (2014), older adults are much less dependent on ICT and have reported lower comfort levels with different technologies than younger generations. Older adults may use devices, such as mobile phones and tablets, as often as younger generations, but have been found to be less likely to have separation anxiety from their mobile phones and do not feel the need to be connected or available at all hours (Huber & Watson, 2014; Van Volkom, Stapley, & Amaturo, 2014). Misgivings have also been reported among older generations about using ICT for social interactions, as personal and physical contact is preferred in building long-term relationships (Huyler & Ciocca, 2016; Vroman, Arthanat, & Lysack, 2014). Without a better understanding of how technology can benefit older adults in actively aging, perceptions and attitudes about learning new technologies will remain low (Vroman, Arthanat, & Lysack, 2014).

Many older adults reported taking advantage of technologies, including ICT, but did so only when they found these technologies to be applicable to their lifestyle, were comfortable with their technology skills, and appreciated the connectedness ICT offers (Arthanat, Vroman, & Lysack, 2016; Huber & Watson, 2014). Several studies indicated the benefits of personal instruction and guidance on how to use new technologies, particularly ICT. These benefits included becoming less intimidated to obtain and use new devices, an increased level of satisfaction and comfort with ICT, a positive overall outlook and acceptance of new technologies, and further confidence in their overall ability to learn (Arthanat, Vroman, & Lysack, 2016; Gonzalez, Ramirez, & Viadel, 2012; Huber & Watson, 2014). ICT can be very helpful for older adults with regard to social connectedness, access to information and resources, and communicate with individuals who provide support (i.e., family, neighbors, help, etcetera) (Arthanat, Vroman, & Lysack, 2016). Arthanat, Vroman, and Lysack (2016) found that the level of ICT activity use in areas of family and social connections and leisure and health management was associated with the level of significance older adults placed on those areas. These researchers also determined that ICT use related to family connections were most regularly performed (Arthanat, Vroman, & Lysack, 2016).

Influence Of Family To Learn And Use New Technologies

Family connectedness is an area that ICT can prove to be very valuable for older populations, particularly if individuals are dealing with health issues or limited by mobility or geographic barriers (Liyanagunawardena & Williams, 2016; Luijkx, Peek, & Wouters, 2015). Luijkx, Peek, and Wouters (2015) highlighted that family members can take on a significant role in encouraging their aging elders in accepting and applying new technologies, as older adults purchase and implement technology as it is influenced by family: spouses, children, and grandchildren. Influence by spouses were found to be natural and unintentional, as spouses provide advice, support, and persuade one another in using certain technologies. Children's influence on their aging parents to implement technologies were found to be natural, but had more intentions of concern. Although parents try to balance help and advice from their children while remaining independent, older adults will be more likely to use technology when children are certain of its positive effects. Furthermore, grandchildren also naturally influence their grandparents to use technology through their enthusiasm to use new technologies and can provide technological assistance, support, and guidance. Older adults are also more likely to be more accepting of technologies that their grandchildren enjoy, which may prove to be truer of ICT than assistive technology (Luijkx, Peek, & Wouters, 2015).

Abilities for Older Adults to Learn

Cognitive And Physical Abilities For Older Adults

Aging does not stop many adults from having the desire to learn and many believe that knowledge and wisdom increases with age (Huber & Watson, 2014; Zaval, Li, Johnson, & Weber, 2015). In fact, continuous intellectual stimulation may improve an older adult's overall well-being and longevity (Morgenroth & Hanley, 2015). Still, due to the natural aging process, many older adults have more trouble adapting to, learning, purchasing and troubleshooting their devices (Huber & Watson, 2014; Van Volkom, Stapley, & Amaturo, 2014; Vermeylen & McClean, 2014). Older adults may have the willingness and desire to learn, as well as continue using new and advancing technologies, but their ability to do so becomes limited by personal factors, including cognitive abilities, and challenges presented by changing life situations experienced later in life (Huber & Watson, 2014; McDonough, 2016; Tam, 2015).

Two types of general intelligence, fluid and crystallized, were recognized by Cattell (1971). *Fluid intelligence* is an individual's innate inductive and deductive reasoning ability; the capability to identify patterns, relationships, and solve problems; and the means to generate and alter acquired information (Becker, Volk, & Ward, 2015; Huber & Watson, 2014; Zaval et al., 2015). Fluid intelligence is known to peak in early adulthood and varying cognitive abilities related to fluid intelligence have been found to gradually decline throughout one's life span, becoming more evident when older adults must perform complex tasks (Huber & Watson, 2014; Zaval et al., 2015). These cognitive abilities include working memory, problem solving, reasoning, and processing speed (Zaval et al., 2015).

In contrast, *crystallized intelligence* consists of skills that are gained through acculturation, learning, and experience and continues to increase in late adulthood. Crystallized intelligence also includes efficient storage of these skills, as well as the efficient application of gained knowledge to new situations and events, including the ability to compromise, recognize one's own limitations, and understand multiple perspectives to one problem (Huber & Watson, 2014; Zaval et al., 2015). Also, crystallized cognitive abilities are generally quantified as our comprehensive knowledge and may be referred to as wisdom (Becker, Volk, & Ward, 2015; Zaval et al., 2015).

As *fluid cognitive functioning* declines in older adults, this type of intelligence becomes less available when learning new technological skills. However, older adults may be able to use their prior experience and general acquired knowledge to develop new technological skills (Huber & Watson, 2014; Zaval et al., 2015).

Current studies have provided sufficient evidence indicating that specific cognitive abilities, such as memory, attention, and creativity, can be improved for healthy older adults through computerized training programs (Kueider, Parisi, Gross, & Robok, 2012; Ordonez, Yassuda, & Cachioni, 2010). Ordonez, Yassuda, and Cachioni (2010) found that an online learning workshop directed to older adults improved certain cognitive abilities, particularly memory, language, and visuospatial skills. The online workshop consisted of fundamental computing instruction and using basic browsing software. The researchers determined that certain cognitive abilities may be enriched by learning new technology skills (Ordonez, Yassuda, & Cachioni, 2010).

Kueider, Parisi, Gross, and Robok (2012) also highlighted the three types of cognitive training programs that enhance cognitive domains the most: classic training tasks, neuropsychological software, and video games. In summary, cognitive domains found to be more responsive to classic cognitive training tasks were working memory, processing speed, and executive functions, including cognitive flexibility, administrative, and abstract thinking abilities.

Neuropsychological software was found to be more influential within memory and visual spatial cognitive domains and the cognitive domains found to be more amenable to video games were processing speed and reaction time (Kueider et al., 2012). Furthermore, Lampit, Hallock, and Valenzula (2014) determined that the effectiveness of computerized cognitive training varies with the program's delivery method, program content, frequency, and domain-specific. The researchers reported that effective computerized cognitive training programs are generally group-based with a trainer or training director; focus more on attention training or use video games; and provide training sessions no more than three times a week (Lampit, Hallock, & Valenzula, 2014).

Barriers To Learning For Older Adults

Other personal factors that influence an older adult's willingness to learn and their perceptions on new technologies, which include education, perceived usefulness, socioeconomic status, previous experience with technology, and current technical knowledge, has been highlighted in current literature (Friemel, 2014; Huber & Watson, 2014). Additionally, older adults may experience challenges and barriers unique to their situation and experiences that influence learning in later life that are associated with the natural aging process. Phipps, Preito, and Ndinguri (2013), as well as Tam (2015), reported that older adults may be met with dispositional, situational, and institutional barriers that may prevent or hamper older adults from learning.

Dispositional barriers are associated with the attitudinal self-perceptions, beliefs, and values that may hinder participation and interest or confidence in learning for older adults. *Situational barriers* arise from circumstances in life, which include time, financial, and transportation limitations, as well as life crises and health problems. Lastly, *institutional barriers* are challenges posed by the practices and procedures of learning institutions that exclude, prevent, or discourage older adults from participating. Institutional barriers may include scheduling conflicts, disinterest in courses being offered, or location (Phipps, Prieto, & Ndinguri, 2013; Tam, 2015).

Education and Older Adults

Online Learning and Education

Learning characteristics have been observed between older adults and their younger peers. Whether these differences are the result of years of maturation and growth that older adults have had the opportunity to develop, or explained through generation cohort characteristics, the circumstances associated with the process of aging, as well as the physical and cognitive changes that occur with aging, make older adults a unique group with particular continuing education needs (Tam, 2015; Vermeylen & McClean, 2014). Older adults have been found to be more purposive, engaged, and varied in approach in comparison to younger learners with regard to learning and education (Tam, 2015; Vermeylen & McClean, 2014). Motivation for older adults to learn was also found to be more varied and include the desire to learn more about specific topics; acquire knowledge on self-improvement, actively aging, and overcoming age-related limitations; positively contributing to their family, community, and society; and making a positive impact on the environment (Liyanagunawardena & Williams, 2016; Phipps, Prieto, & Ndinguri, 2013; Tam, 2015).

Additionally, according to Tam (2015), as older adults obtain more time during retirement to study, explore, and acquire new hobbies and interests, many will consider their time to be very valuable and will want to spend their time on meaningful activities. Older adults do not want to feel as though their time is being wasted. Therefore, when older adults want to learn, they will focus on topics that interest them personally and will initiate learning in order to ensure their learning experience is meaningful. These topics may include retirement issues and adjustment; financial planning and budgeting; exercise, nutrition, and overall health; personal and workplace education; and enhancing physical and mental abilities (Tam, 2015).

Massive Open Online Courses (MOOCS)

Massive open online courses (MOOCs) are free web-based courses offered through higher educational institutions that have partnered with commercial or non-commercial platforms that provide opportunities for anyone to learn (Liyanagunawardena & Williams, 2016; Sanchez-Gordon & Lujan-Mora, 2016). Generally, MOOCs are offered in a very wide variety of topics and provide older adults the chance to learn more about subjects that may interest them, including personal growth, health, workplace learning, and social change (Liyanagunawardena & Williams, 2016; Tan, 2015). According to Sanchez-Gordon and Lujan-Mora (2016), MOOCs have changed the way education is being offered in that there are no limits to who can learn and as the researchers have noted, participants of all ages throughout the world partake in MOOCs. However, accessibility issues, including those of older learners, must be met in order to encourage full participation from diverse learners (Huber & Watson, 2014; Liyanagunawardena & Williams, 2016; Sanchez-Gordon & Lujan-Mora, 2016). For instance, Sanchez-Gordon and Lujan-Mora mentioned several disabilities that may affect older learners, to include visual, hearing, motor, speech, cognitive, and psychosocial disabilities, as well as temporary and progressive combined disabilities that may occur as a result of aging.

Liyanagunawardena and Williams (2016) reported that a considerable number of older adults already partake in MOOCs. These researchers examined the enrollment percentage of older learners for 10 MOOCs offered by the University of Reading on the *FutureLearn* platform and found that the courses consisted of a varied range of participation of older learners. Liyanagunawardena and Williams indicated that the MOOC enrollment for the group of individuals aged 56 years old and over ranged from 3% to almost 40%. Additionally, enrollment for adults over 66 years old and over ranged from approximately 1% to over 16%. Certain classes, particularly those that focused on climate change and heart health, were found to have the higher percentages of older learners (Liyanagunawardena & Williams, 2016). Additionally, Shrader, Wu, Owens, and Santa Ana (2016) found that engagement activity in MOOCs increased with age. These researchers determined that enrolled students aged 30 years old and over were twice as likely, and enrolled older adults, aged 60 years old, were four times as likely to be considered a *high activity* participant in course activities as students between the ages of 18 and 24 years old. Although there were no penalties for not participating or not completing after enrolling in an MOOC, Shrader et al. determined that older adults were also more likely to persevere in MOOCs than younger participants, indicating that older adults may treat MOOCs as they would traditional educational course settings.

University-Based Retirement Communities

University-based retirement communities (UBRCs) were established to help support older adults who choose to remain independent, while continuing a connection to a specific university or college (Herzog, Wilson, & Rideout, 2010; Morgenroth & Hanley, 2015). According to Herzog, Wilson, and Rideout (2010), there are currently two general forms of UBRCs. The first is similar to a continuing care retirement community, in which retired individuals have access to onsite health services and facilities, as well as have the option of a life-care contract. The second is similar to a small community, in which professional staff assists in providing residents services that support independent living. Services provided may include health care, housekeeping, and opportunities to volunteer and socialize (Herzog, Wilson, & Rideout, 2010).

Additionally, as noted by Herzog, Wilson, and Rideout (2010), what makes UBRCs unique is that they are located within a close proximity to a specific university or college; provide independent care to assisted living support to its residents; and have a recorded financial relationship between the two institutions; and have an established program to connect and incorporate the UBRC and higher educational institution. UBRCs support older adults who chose to actively age and maintain a level of independence.

In her dissertation report, Meraz Lewis (2011) noted that the motivation for older adults to choose UBRCs stems from linked interests, life experiences, ideology, and values of further education. Residents of UBRC have the desire to be surrounded by like-minded individuals who have similar educational and career trajectories and would like to stay active, involved, and educated (Meraz Lewis, 2011; Morgenroth & Hanley, 2015). UBRCs also provide older adults opportunities to remain involved and engaged in their community, in which their community, environment, and culture are incorporated into authentic, meaningful experiences. The proximity of university or college campuses also encourages older adults to feel and be socially connected, in contrast to other living arrangements which may present social and spatial isolation concerns (Morgenroth & Hanley, 2015).

The association between universities or colleges and an UBRC also presents advantages from the interaction of students enrolled at the institution and older adults. Sanchez and Kaplan (2014) emphasized the benefit of knowledge, skill, experience, and resource exchange, as well as the added benefit of socialization and discussion, that accompanies intergenerational learning. The information sharing within the classroom encourages students and older adults with more experience to grasp a deeper understanding of subjects and topics learned within the classroom, and provide a broader perspective on information, entertainment, and lifestyle (Morgenroth & Hanley, 2015; Pstross et al., 2016). Additionally, all students within an intergenerational learning environment can learn from others of diverse ages, family backgrounds, socioeconomic statuses, genders, races/ethnicities, and work and life experiences, as long as all students are willing to discuss and share their own knowledge and experiences (Sanchez & Kaplan, 2014). Although opportunities should be created to urge social engagement between students and older adults, Sanchez and Kaplan (2014) caution that planned intergenerational interaction may not lead to positive, beneficial, or healthy outcomes.

Lifelong Learning Programs on College Campuses

Intergenerational learning environments present a unique opportunity to change traditional classroom characteristics and practices (Sanchez & Kaplan, 2014). Current lifelong learning programs that are offered on many university campuses are also another means to engage the older learner. In these situations, creative curriculum programs and services offer enriching educational experiences to adults of all ages including non-credit courses by experts in anthropology, art, concerts, creative writing, current events, dance, environmental awareness, foreign affairs, healthy living, history, law, literature, marine life, medical science, music, philosophy, physics, political science, psychology, religion, science, stress reduction, technology, and entertainment, and a host of other subjects. The lifelong learning programs often include travel opportunities to international locations for those that are able to travel.

Technology is often used to keep the would-be learners informed of activities of interest through their websites and tailored internet and mail system. Seniors are frequently queried to determine what type of programs and services need to be offered to meet their needs.

CONCLUSION AND RECOMMENDATIONS FOR FUTURE RESEARCH

There is a plethora of new research emerging from other countries as well as the United States regarding Gerontechnology. Spanning the decades from 1991 to 2016, The International Society of Gerontechnology has hosted 10 World Conferences of Gerontechnology. These worldwide conferences have represented many countries from the first conference held in Eindhoven, the Netherlands in 1991, to include Finland, Germany, Japan, Italy, Canada, Taiwan, and France. The United States is also part of the representative countries, which had hosted the 2002 conference in Miami, Florida; it will host the 2018 conference in St. Petersburg, Florida.

In previous studies, researchers had examined older adult's perceptions and experiences toward technology to include (a) attitudes, (b) environmental barriers, (c) the need for digital literacy training, (d) negative and positive impacts of social network sites as it pertains to mental health, (e) early discovery and controlling of debilitating chronic conditions and technological advances to promote aging in place, (f) enhancing opportunities for health and security to improve one's quality of life as they age, (g) communication processes with older adults as they interact with technology, (h) inclusion and autonomy with technology, (i) differentiation in technology, and (j) digital inclusion of the elderly. The previously mentioned studies demonstrated concerns for the implementation of the technology with older adults; since the early 1990s, there has been great progress in the study of Gerontechnology.

Since there is the propensity that people are living longer based on advancements in science and technology, researchers and other stakeholders must be cognizant of helping the aging adults with nutrition, medication, physical mobility, and cognition. In addition, there is the need to enable the aging adults to function at the optimal level in their residence (e.g., home, life span community). This type of assistance, with the implementation of technology, can help improve a healthy lifestyle and quality of life of aging adults for the benefit of a preferred living and working environment and adapted medical care. The many advanced technological-based products and services have and will continue to assist all phases of the full human life span.

Regarding suggestions for future exploration, researchers might consider looking at the actual level of Internet access among older adults; as well as the intention to use Internet applications versus their actual use; influence of others, particularly family, in accepting and implementing assistive technologies; and increasing accessibility of technology-based educational programs, as well as MOOCs for older adults. In addition, based on many technological breakthroughs in health care and medical care, there is the need to look at how this can help the older adults with chronic conditions such as dementia, Alzheimer's disease, mild cognitive development, depression, and other physical, mental, emotional, and social needs. A strength of this chapter is the fact that the literature provides a rich description of the Gerontechnology. The recommendation for future studies would also be to conduct a qualitative study regarding the factors and experiences that are affecting how older adults are adapting to living in a life span community located within university environments. Another recommendation would be to involve their families into the sample size. A longitudinal study would be valuable since it would help researchers and family members to follow through and possibly understand the experiences over time. The experiences of family and healthcare providers and caregivers would be beneficial to the overall care and to contribute to Gerontechnology.

Comparing the research from the other countries to include the United States, it is clear that there are many similarities of how to infuse technology to improve the older adults' independence and quality of life. The concerns and similarities appear to be not just limited to one country or one demographic, but is a growing worldwide point at issue. There is a need for more research to determine how these concerns can be addressed and how different countries and different groups can collaborate and research to make the necessary adjustments to increase the use of technology among the older adults as they age in place.

REFERENCES

Abrams, S. (2014). *New technology could allow you or your parents to age at home.* Retrieved from http://www.aarp.org/home-family/personal-technology/info-2014/is-this-the-end-of-the-nursing-home.html

Alves Pedro, W. J. (2016). Aging process assets and social dimensions of science and technology. *1st Brazilian Congress of Gerontechnology, 15*(2), 71-72. doi:10.4017/gt.2016.15.2.006.00

Arthanat, S., Vroman, K. G., & Lysack, C. (2016). A home-based individualized information communication technology training program for older adults: A demonstration of effectiveness and value. *Disability and Rehabilitation. Assistive Technology, 11*(4), 316–324. PMID:25512061

Ballabio, E., & Whitehouse, D. (1999). Ageing and disability in the information society: A European perspective on research and technological development. *Technology and Disability, 10*, 3–10.

Becker, W. J., Volk, S., & Ward, M. K. (2015). Leveraging neuroscience for smarter approaches to workplace intelligence. *Human Resource Management Review, 25*(1), 56–67. doi:10.1016/j.hrmr.2014.09.008

Beckett, F. (2010). *What did the Baby Boomers ever do for us?* London: Biteback.

Boulton-Lewis, G. M. (2010). Education and learning for the elderly: Why, how, what. *Educational Gerontology, 36*(3), 213–228. doi:10.1080/03601270903182877

Bouma, H., & Graafmans, J. A. M. (1992). *Gerontechnology.* Amsterdam, Netherlands: IOS Press.

Brodin, H., & Persson, J. (2009). Cost-utility analysis of assistive technologies in the European Commissions Tide Program. *International Journal of Technology Assessment in Health Care, 11*(2), 276–283. doi:10.1017/S0266462300006899 PMID:7790171

Cattell, R. B. (1971). *Abilities: Their structure, growth, and action.* Boston, MA: Houghton-Mifflin.

Center for Technology and Aging. (2009). *Technologies to help older adults maintain independence: Advancing technology adoption.* Retrieved from http://www.techandaging.org/briefingpaper.pdf

Chen, K., & Chan, A. H. (2012). Use or non-use of Gerontechnology: A qualitative study. *International Journal of Environmental Research and Public Health*, *10*(10), 4645–4666. doi:10.3390/ijerph10104645 PMID:24084674

Chew-Graham, C., Gask, L., Shiers, D., & Kaiser, P. (2014). *Management of depression in older people: Why this is important in primary care*. Retrieved from http://www.rcgp.org.uk/-/media/Files/CIRC/ Mental-Health-2014/5-Older-People-and-depression-Primary-care-guidance-2014.ashx?la=en

Colemen, J. S. (1998). Social capital in the creation of human capital. *American Journal of Sociology*, *94*, S95–S120. doi:10.1086/228943

CORDIS. (2014a). *HS-TIDE 0 - Technology initiative for disabled and elderly people - TIDE pilot action, 1991-1993*. Retrieved from http://cordis.europa.eu/programme/rcn/275 _en.html

CORDIS. (2014b). *HS-TIDE 1 - Technology initiative (EEC) for disabled and elderly people (TIDE), 1993-1994*. Retrieved from http://cordis.europa.eu/programme/rcn/337_en.html

Courtois, C., & Verdegem, P. (2014). With a little help from my friends: An analysis of the role of social support in digital inequalities. *New Media & Society*, *18*(8), 1508–1527. doi:10.1177/1461444814562162

Davies, J. (2016). *Three ways technology is revolutionising elderly care*. Retrieved from https://internetofbusiness.com/technology-revolutionising-elderly-care/

DeVaney, S. (2015). Understanding the millennial generation. *Journal of Financial Service Professionals*, *69*(6), 11–14.

Edelman, M., & Ficorelli, C. T. (2012). Keeping older adults safe at home. *Nursing*, *42*(1), 65–66. doi:10.1097/01.NURSE.0000408481.20951.e8 PMID:22157840

Erickson, L. B. (2011, August). Social media, social capital, and seniors: The impact of Facebook on bonding and bridging social capital of individuals over 65. In *AMCIS*. Retrieved from http://aisel.aisnet. org/cgi/viewcontent.cgi?article=1084&context=amcis2011_sub

Fietkiewica, K. J., Lins, E., Baran, K. S., & Stock, W. G. (2016). Inter-generational comparison of social media use: Investigating the online behavior of different generational cohorts. *IEEE Computer Society*, *16*, 1530–1605.

Finn, K. (2015). *Social media use by older adults*. Retrieved from http://wiserusability.com/wpfs /wp-content/uploads/2015/07/Social-Media-Use-by-Older-Adults.pdf

Fletcher-Watson, B., Crompton, C. J., Hutchison, M., & Lu, H. (2016). Strategies for enhancing success in digital tablet use by older adults: A pilot study. *Gerontechnology (Valkenswaard)*, *15*(3), 162–170. doi:10.4017/gt.2016.15.3.005.00

Friemel, T. N. (2014). The digital divide has grown old: Determinant of a digital divide among seniors. *New Media & Society*, *18*(2), 313–331. doi:10.1177/1461444814538648

Gallistl, V. (2016). The digital divide and technology generations – European Implications from the Austrian Perspective. In *Third ISA Forum of Sociology*. ISACONF.

Gerontology. (2017). In *OxfordDictionaries.com*. Retrieved from http://www.oxforddictionaries.com/definition/english/gerontology

Gonzalez, A., Ramirez, M. P., & Viadel, V. (2012). Attitudes of the elderly toward information and communications technologies. *Educational Gerontology*, *38*(9), 585–594. doi:10.1080/03601277.2011.595314

Heaggans, R. C. (2012). The 60's are the new 20's: Teaching older adults technology. *SRATE Journal*, *21*(2), 1-8. Retrieved from http://files.eric.ed.gov/fulltext/EJ990630.pdf

Herzog, B., Wilson, G., & Rideout, N. (2010). Ageing independently: A Chapel Hill perspective. *North Carolina Medical Journal*, *71*(2), 173–176. Retrieved from http://classic.ncmedicaljournal.com/wp-content/uploads/NCMJ/Mar-Apr-10/Herzog.pdf PMID:20552774

Heyward, V. (n.d.). *Using technology to promote physical activity*. Retrieved from http://www.humankinetics.com/excerpts/excerpts/using-technology-to-promote-physical-activity

Home Instead. (2017). *5 benefits of technology to share with seniors and their caregivers*. Retrieved from http://www.caregiverstress.com/geriatric-professional-resources/5-benefits-of-technology-to-share-with-seniors-and-their-caregivers/

Hsu, Y.-L., & Bai, D. L. (2016). The future of Gerontechnology: Proposals from the new editor-in-chief. *Gerontechnology (Valkenswaard)*, *15*(3), 125–129. doi:10.4017/gt.2016.15.3.001.00

Huber, L., & Watson, C. (2014). Technology: Education and training needs of older adults. *Educational Gerontology*, *40*(1), 16–25. doi:10.1080/03601277.2013.768064

Huyler, D., & Ciocca, D. (2016). Baby Boomers: The use of technology to support learning. *Proceedings from the 15th Annual South Florida Education Research Conference*. Miami, FL: Florida International University.

Karol, E. (2016). Tangible and intangible elements of design for well-being in the home. *Gerontechnology (Valkenswaard)*, *15*(4), 227–232. doi:10.4017/gt.2016.15.4.007.00

Kueider, A. M., Parisi, J. M., Gross, A. L., & Robok, G. W. (2012). Computerized cognitive training with older adults: A systematic review. *PLoS ONE*, *7*(7), e40588. doi:10.1371/journal.pone.0040588 PMID:22792378

Lai, K., & Hong, K. (2015). Technology use and learning characteristics of students in higher education: Do generational differences exist? *British Journal of Educational Technology*, *46*(4), 725–739. doi:10.1111/bjet.12161

Lampit, A., Hallock, H., & Valenzuela, M. (2014). Computerized cognitive training in cognitively healthy older adults: A systematic review and meta-analysis of effect modifiers. *PLoS ONE*, *11*(11), e1001756. PMID:25405755

Lautenschlager, N. T., Cox, K., & Cyarto, E. V. (2012). The influence of exercise on brain aging and dementia. *Biochimica et Biophysica Acta*, *1822*(3), 474–481. doi:10.1016/j.bbadis.2011.07.010 PMID:21810472

Lill, S. (2015). Depression in older adults in primary care: An integrative approach to care. *Journal of Holistic Nursing, 33*(3), 260–268. doi:10.1177/0898010115569350 PMID:25673577

Liyanagunawardena, T. R., & Williams, S. A. (2016). Elderly learners and massive open online courses: A review. *Interactive Journal of Medical Research, 5*(1), e1. doi:10.2196/ijmr.4937 PMID:26742809

Luijkx, K., Peek, S., & Wouters, E. (2015). Grandma, you should do it – its cool Older adults and the role of family members in their acceptance of technology. *International Journal of Environmental Research and Public Health, 12*(12), 15470–15485. doi:10.3390/ijerph121214999 PMID:26690188

Mahmood, A., Yamamoto, T., Lee, M., & Steggell, C. (2008). Perceptions and use of Gerontechnology: Implications for aging in place. *Journal of Housing for the Elderly, 22*(1-2), 104–126. doi:10.1080/02763890802097144

Masedu, F., Mazza, M., Di Giovanni, C., Calvarese, A., Tiberti, S., Sconci, V., & Valenti, M. (2014). Facebook, quality of life, and mental outcomes in post-disaster urban environments: The L'Auila Earthquake experience. *Front Public Health, 22*(286), 1–6. PMID:25566527

McDonough, C. C. (2016). The effect of ageism on the digital divide among older adults. *Journal of Gerontology & Geriatric Medicine, 2*(008), 1–7.

Mears, T. (2015). *10 essential tech tools for older adults.* Retrieved from http://money.usnews.com/money/retirement/articles/2015/11/16/10-essential-tech-tools-for-older-adults

Melenhorst, A.-S., Rogers, W. A., & Caylor, E. C. (2001). The use of communication technologies by older adults: Exploring the benefits from the user's perspective. *Proceedings from the Human Factors and Ergonomics Society 45th Annual Meeting*, 221-225.

Mental Health America of Illinois. (n.d.). *Depression in later life.* Retrieved from www.mhai.org/Depression_Lter_in_Life.pdf

Meraz-Lewis, R. B. (2011). *The lived worlds and life experiences of residents in university linked retirement communities: A qualitative approach* (Doctoral Dissertation). Retrieved from the Eastern Michigan University DigitalCommons. Retrieved from http://commons.emich.edu/cgi/viewcontent.cgi?article=1790&context=theses

Mollenkopf, H. (2016). Societal aspects and individual preconditions of technological development. *Gerontechnology (Valkenswaard), 15*(4), 216–226. doi:10.4017/gt.2016.15.4.011.00

Morgenroth, L., & Hanley, M. (2015). On campus and in the community: How higher education can inform seniors housing models. *Seniors Housing & Care Journal, 23*(1), 70–75.

Morrison, D. (2010). Social media opens social world to elderly, disable. *Wilmington Star News*. Retrieved from http://www.starnewonline.com/article/20100126/articles/10012956>

Nagode, M., & Dolnicar, V. (2010). Assistive technology for older people and its potential for intergenerational cooperation. *Teorija in Praksa, 47*(6), 1278–1294.

National Alliance for Research on Schizophrenia and Depression. (n.d.). *Late life depression.* Retrieved from https://bbrfoundation.org/userFiles/facts.latelifedep.pdf

Nef, T., Ganea, R. L., Muri, R. M., & Mosimann, U. P. (2013). Social networking sites and older users: A systematic review. *International Psychogeriatrics, 25*(7), 1041–1053. doi:10.1017/S1041610213000355 PMID:23552297

Ordonez, T. N., Yassuda, M. S., & Cachioni, M. (2010). Elderly online: Effects of a digital inclusion program in cognitive performance. *Archives of Gerontology and Geriatrics, 53*(2), 216–219. doi:10.1016/j.archger.2010.11.007 PMID:21131070

Orlov, L. M. (n.d.). *An elder care industry veteran offers her picks for must-have aging-in-place technology.* Retrieved from http://www.homecaremag.com/top-10-technology-devices-seniors

Ortman, J. M., Velkoff, V. A., & Hogan, H. (2014). *An aging nation: The older population in the United States: Population estimates and projections.* Washington, DC: United States Department of Commerce.

Parry, E., & Urwin, P. (2011). Generational differences in work values: A review of theory and evidence. *International Journal of Management Reviews, 13*(1), 79–96. doi:10.1111/j.1468-2370.2010.00285.x

Peels, D. A., de Vries, H., Bolman, C., Golsteign, R. H. J., van Stralen, M. M., Mudde, A. N., & Lechner, L. (2013). Differences in the use and appreciate of a web-based or printed computer-tailored physical activity intervention for people aged over 50 years. *Health Education Research, 28*(4), 715–731. doi:10.1093/her/cyt065 PMID:23784076

Phipps, S. T. A., Prieto, L. C., & Ndinguri, E. N. (2013). Teaching an old dog new tricks: Investigating how age, ability, and self-efficacy influence intentions to learn and learning among participants in adult education. *Academy of Educational Leadership, 17*(1), 13–25.

Pstross, M., Corrigan, T., Knopf, R. C., Sung, H., Talmage, C. A., Conroy, C., & Fowley, C. (2016). The benefits of intergenerational learning in higher education: Lessons learned from two age friendly university programs. *Innovation Higher Education,* 1-15.

Rau, P., Gao, Q., & Ding, Y. (2008). Relationship between the level of intimacy and lurking in online social network services. *Computers in Human Behavior, 24*(6), 2757–2770. doi:10.1016/j.chb.2008.04.001

Royal College of Psychiatry. (2017). *Depression in older adults.* Retrieved from http://www.rcpsych.ac.uk/healthadvice/problemsdisorders/depressioninolderadults.aspx

Sackmann, R., & Winkler, I. (2013). Technology generations revisited: The Internet generation. *Geronotechnology, 11*(4), 493–503.

Sanchez, M., & Kaplan, M. (2014). Intergenerational learning in higher education: Making the case for multigenerational classrooms. *Educational Gerontology, 40*(7), 473–485. doi:10.1080/03601277.2013.844039

Sanchez-Gordon, S., & Lujan-Mora, S. (2016). How could MOOCs become accessible? The case of edX and the future of online learning. *Journal of Universal Computer Science, 22*(1), 55–81.

Sherman, R. O. (2016). Leading a multigenerational nursing workforce: Issues, challenges, and strategies. *Online Journal of Issues in Nursing, 11*(2), 3–7. Retrieved from http://www.medscape.com/viewarticle/536480_2 PMID:17201577

Shrader, S., Wu, M., Owens, D., & Santa Ana, K. (2016). Massive open online courses (MOOCs): Participant activity, demographics, and satisfaction. *Online Learning, 20*(2), 171–188. doi:10.24059/olj.v20i2.596

Smith, A. (2011). Why Americans use social media. *PewResearchCenter Internet, Science & Tech.* Retrieved from http://www.pewinternet.org/2011/11/15/why-americans-use-social-media/

Taipale, V. T. (2014). Global trends, policies and Gerontechnology. *Gerontechnology (Valkenswaard), 12*(4), 187–193. doi:10.4017/gt.2014.12.4.001.00

Tam, M. (2014, November 02). A distinctive theory of teaching and learning for older learners: Why and why not? *International Journal of Lifelong Education, 33*(6), 811–820. doi:10.1080/02601370.2014.972998

Taylor, W. D. (2014). Depression in the elderly. *The New England Journal of Medicine, 371,* 1222–1236. PMID:25251617

Technology. (2017). In *OxfordDictionaries.com.* Retrieved from http://www.oxforddictionaries.com/definition/english/technology

The Online Mom. (2017). *7 technologies that can help keep the elderly safe.* Retrieved from http://www.theonlinemom.com/7-technologies-that-can-help-keep-the-elderly-safe/

Umemuro, H. (2004). Computer attitudes, cognitive abilities, and technology usage among older Japanese adults. *Gerontechnology Journal, 3*(2), 64-76. Retrieved from http://journal.gerontechnology.org/archives/340-342-1-PB.pdf

University of Exeter. (2014). Training elderly in social media improves well-being, combats isolation. *ScienceDaily.* Retrieved from www.sciencedaily.com/releases/2014/12/141212111649.htm

van Bronswijk, J. E. M. A., Bouma, H., Fozard, J. L., Kearns, W. D., Davison, G. C., & Tuan, P.-C. (2009). Defining Gerontechnology for R & D purposes. *Gerontechnology (Valkenswaard), 8*(1), 3–10.

Van Volkom, M., Stapley, J. C., & Amaturo, V. (2014). Revisiting the digital divide: Generational differences in technology use in everyday life. *North American Journal of Psychology, 16*(3), 557–574.

Vermeylen, L., & McLean, S. (2014). Does age matter? Informal learning practices of younger and older adults. *The Canadian Journal for the Study of Adult Education, 26*(1), 19–34.

Vroman, K. G., Arthanat, S., & Lysack, C. (2014). Who over 65 is online? Older adults dispositions towards information communication technology. *Computers in Human Behavior, 43,* 156–166. doi:10.1016/j.chb.2014.10.018

Wellman, N. S. (2010). Aging at home: More research on nutrition and independence, please. *The American Journal of Clinical Nutrition, 91*(5), 1151–1152. doi:10.3945/ajcn.2010.29527 PMID:20335549

William, K., & Kemper, S. (2010). Exploring intervention to reduce cognitive decline in aging. *Journal of Psychosocial Nursing and Mental Health Services, 48*(5), 42–551. doi:10.3928/02793695-20100331-03 PMID:20415290

Wolfson, N. E., Cavanagh, T. M., & Kraiger, K. (2014). Older adults and technology-based instruction: Optimizing learning outcomes and transfer. *Academy of Management Learning & Education*, *13*(1), 25–44. doi:10.5465/amle.2012.0056

Woods, B., & Clare, L. (2008). *Handbook of the psychology of ageing* (2nd ed.). Hoboken, NJ: John Wiley and Sons.

Woolrych, R. (2016). Ageing and technology: Creating environments to support an ageing society. *1st Brazilian Congress of Gerontechnology, 15*(2), 66-70. doi:10.4017/gt.2016.15.2.005.00

Yu, R. P., Ellison, N. B., McCammon, R. J., & Langa, K. M. (2016). Mapping the two levels of digital divide: Internet access and social network site adoption among older adults in the USA. *Information Communication and Society*, *19*(1), 1445–1464. doi:10.1080/1369118X.2015.1109695

Zaval, L., Ye, L., Johnson, E. J., & Webber, E. U. (2015). Complementary contributions of fluid and crystallized intelligence to decision making across the life span. *Aging and Decision Making: Empirical and Applied Perspectives*, 149-168.

Zhang, F., & Kaufman, D. (2016). Cognitive benefits of older adults digital gameplay: A critical review. *Gerontechnology (Valkenswaard)*, *15*(1), 3–16. doi:10.4017/gt.2016.15.1.002.00

KEY TERMS AND DEFINITIONS

Aging in Place: The ability for an individual to choose to live in their home or a community as long as possible, while remaining independent, comfortable, healthy, and safe with human connection through the use of technology.

Baby Boomers: This generation made up of 78 million people from 1946 to 1964 grew up during the Civil Rights Movement, the Cold War and the Vietnam War, Race to Space, assassinations, and impeachment. This generation comprised of idealistic and competitive values, yet were free spirited and believed in individualism; in the workplace, they understood they workplace to be about teamwork and building strong relationships to be successful. This was also the first technological generation with computers developing on the horizon.

Centennials (GenZ/iGen): This generation of Centennials are true digital natives; they are considered as the generation best equipped for understanding and using advanced innovations. This generation from 1996 to present are also known as GenZ/iGen. They are a fast-emerging generation in the workplace and marketplace who like instant gratification and are highly connected to the use of communications, yet due to social media, lack a community-oriented nature.

Generation X: From 1965 to 1976, the Generation X, also known as Gen X are defined as slackers, yet are known as the first generation to develop ease and comfort with technology. While independent, they are entrepreneurial, reject rules, mistrust institutions, but are multitaskers and known as the latchkey kids.

Gerontechnology: Gerontechnology, which is derived from gerontology and technology, is defined as implementing successful aging and assisting older adults in meeting the domains of housing, communication, health, safety, comfort, mobility, and leisure and work.

Independence: Allowing older adults to retain a better cognitive function through staying healthier physically, mentally, socially, and emotionally while living independently longer.

Life-Care Retirement Communities: This type of senior living replaces the typical Continuing Care Retirement Community perception and moves toward a new perspective that fosters growth and new experiences for older adults that are aligned with their lifestyles and attitudes. The types of communities are life plan communities on university campuses or retirement corporations that have three levels consisting of independent living, assistive living, or skilled nursing facilities.

Millennials: The fastest-growing generation of customers in the marketplace are the Millennials (1977 to 1995). They challenge various conventional strategies and approaches regarding attitudes toward the workplace, and grew up during the financial crisis. This group also emerged along with the Centennials in the core of the digital age and had technology and social networks that were prevalent in their lives; they seek freedom are innovative, and question authority.

Quality of Life: A psychological theory represented by life satisfaction as well as a clinical and geriatric outcomes symbolized by the core dimensions of health status, physical health, family, finances, religious beliefs, and personal growth.

Silent Generation: The Silent Generation are also known as the Traditionalists who were born prior to 1946 and grew up during the Depression and World War II. This group of 50 million people consist of the largest group of retirees who have the following characteristics: (a) traditional family values; (b) demand quality; (c) patient, respectful, and loyal towards others; (d) possess excellent interpersonal skills; and (e) have a strong work ethic. This generation grew up without modern technology.

Chapter 11
The Impact of Technology on the Teaching and Learning Process

Lisa A. Finnegan
Florida Atlantic University, USA

ABSTRACT

The teaching and learning process of traditionally run classrooms will need to change to meet up with the requirements under the reauthorization of the Elementary and Secondary Education Act as the Every Student Succeeds Act (ESSA). Under the ESSA, the infusion of the Universal Design for Learning (UDL) framework into the teaching and learning environment sets the stage so that instruction and assessment support all levels of learners. Along with UDL, ESSA supports the inclusion of technology-rich learning environments to prepare students for 21st century problem-solving and critical thinking skills. Critical to preparing students comes an understanding of who the 21st century learners are. The current teaching and learning process involving the use of technology continues to hold students back as passive observers of content. Merging technology and the UDL framework in the classroom will be an avenue to meeting the learning needs and wants of 21st century students.

INTRODUCTION

Teachers, now more than ever, have their work cut out for them! What other field or profession has been so scrutinized by politicians, outside professionals, and the general community? The teaching-learning process (TLP) of past decades will no longer work in the current time period or the future. Effective teaching is identified as being an art and a science (Marzano, 2007); but where does that leave learning. An effective TLP means that not only is there an art and science to the teaching; but ultimately, there should be an art and science to the learning as well. If an artful and scientific approach to teaching and learning is the direction to be taken, what then, does teaching and learning look like in the 21st century and beyond? As of the present moment, two decades have passed from the start of the 21st century and within these past two decades technology advancements and applications have continued to evolve daily.

DOI: 10.4018/978-1-5225-2838-8.ch011

The TLP of the 21ˢᵗ century requires teachers to not only teach the state adopted standards; but also support the social, emotional, and intellectual development of the culturally, linguistically, racially, and socio-economically diverse students within their classroom walls. Teachers are no longer preparing their students under college and career ready standards to become highly functional and productive citizens of the nation; but rather to become citizens of the world that are diversely skilled, problem-solving, tech-savvy, innovative and creative.

Wiggins and McTighe (2007) state that a teacher's

role, behavior, and strategies must stem deliberately from an established mission and goals, the curriculum, and agreed-upon learning principles. In other words, the particular approaches, methods, and resources employed are not primarily subjective "choices" or mere matters of style. They logically derive from the desired student accomplishments and our profession's understanding of the learning process. We teach to cause a result. Teaching is successful only if we cause learning related to purpose. (p. 129)

Identifying the purpose of learning for the 21st century learner is the place that the TLP should begin. The TLP in the 21st century must be rejuvenated to cause a result that aligns with a purpose of meeting desired student accomplishments. That result and purpose mean achieving the accomplishments that the students themselves aspire to and the understanding that the profession's learning process must align with that aspiration. The rejuvenated TLP takes into account student learning outcome desires and finds a path to deliver them. Teachers, in the rejuvenated TLP, are the monitors of the path rather than the pavers. Teachers inform students through instruction, support their construction of knowledge through questioning and probing activities that facilitate understanding, and coach students in the complex process of deepening their understanding to apply what they have learned (Wiggins & McTighe, 2007). To arrive at this deepening level of understanding, the way teachers instruct, question, and arrange probing activities must provide a fit for a different generation of learners' needs in the 21st century. Of significance to the TLP are changes in education and the educational environment within which learning occurs.

What is seen as the biggest educational change is actually occurring outside classroom walls rather than in them (Prensky, 2010). Students of the 21st century are actively learning through their peers using social media such as Youtube, Twitter, Facebook, Instagram, and Snapchat or many other cellular apps (Prensky, 2010). They are identified as the iGeneration or digital natives. From the moment of their birth, technology has been a part of their life and they want something different than the generations of learners before them. Prensky (2010) states that

today's leaners want to learn differently than in the past and they want ways of learning that are meaningful to them, ways that make them see – immediately – that the time they are spending on their formal education is valuable, and ways that make good use of the technology they know is their birthright. (p. 3)

Furthermore, this digital generation does not want to be lectured to, but they do want to work collaboratively with their peers, make decisions and share control in their learning goals, be respected, allowed to follow personalized learning goals, and create, using tools of their time (Prensky, 2010). The time has come to put a stop to the stand and deliver teaching that is still very much a part of most pre-Kindergarten through post-secondary classrooms of today and provide digital native students of the 21st century the teaching and learning environments that they deserve. Now is the time to regenerate the TLP for the future.

LEARNING FROM PAST TO PRESENT

Student acquisition of knowledge occurs through the TLP, yet not all students learn the basic knowledge or skills taught and needed for higher order thinking and problem solving while others acquire knowledge more easily. How does learning happen? What factors must be present to make learning occur? Various learning theories have existed for many decades. According to Clayton (1965), "learning theories *have* ranged from specific concerns with particular stimuli and responses to the exploration of the total personality of man in society and his resultant behavior systems, both overt and covert" (p. 47), eventually building toward the construct of a general understanding of human behavior (Clayton, 1965; Pavlov, 1927; Skinner, 1968). Understanding behavior or the underlying motivation of behavior, is important, and can make or break an effective learning environment. Behaviorist theories have long played a critical role in the foundation of learning theories and in turn in the foundational preparation of educators. Understanding the basic aspects of a stimulus-response cycle has been essential for teachers in establishing traditional classroom management. Teachers direct their students to comply with directives and provide reinforcement for their efforts through praise and feedback, yet a gap still exists when connecting the learning to intentional and purposeful motivation.

Learning also has a social nature. Learners acquire information when provided opportunities to interact with others in their environment whether through direct experience or through observing. Teachers are often the primary models learners experience in the classroom. Teachers model the social interactions, emotional and behavioral expectations, and academic strategies that they desire students to practice and perform. The social learning environment provides for rich discourse and varying perspectives as students work alongside and with each other. Basically, the learning of one individual relies on the essential component of another individual with more knowledge, who can guide the first individual to greater learning (Cicconi, 2014; Vygotsky, 1997). Vygotsky's premise focuses on students being at and near two different learning levels to understand how learning occurs: the actual developmental level and the zone of proximal development (Jarvis, Holford, & Griffin, 2003; Vygotsky, 1997). To visualize Vygotsky's theory of learning, think of learning occurring at the point in which a teacher can stretch a student's understanding from their developmental level to a place within their zone of proximal development similar to stretching a rubber band without snapping or breaking it. Learners are taking their foundational knowledge and attempting to acquire new knowledge up to the point of experiencing rigor but not reaching a level of frustration.

Furthermore, students evaluate their performance through self-regulation (Bandura, 1977). Self-regulation requires students to determine which strategies to use to be the most effective as a learner. As students self-regulation skills evolve their understanding of their capabilities to learn or self-efficacy also evolves (Bandura, 1997). A large part of that learning requires teaching self-regulation skills and supporting student metacognition. Metacognition refers to an individual's ability to predict how they perform at a task based on their current accurate level of understanding of their knowledge and mastery level (National Research Council, 2000). A "metacognitive" approach to learning is a student-centered approach that enables learners to take control of their own learning by setting learning goals and monitoring the progress toward those goals (National Research Council, 2000). Metacognition can be attained through what is described in education as instructional scaffolding. Instructional scaffolding provides an approach to mastering higher level tasks through a process of controlling lower level tasks at the learners' capability level thereby allowing the lower level tasks to be learned with ease and ultimately building on each task or concept until the higher level task can be met (Schunk, 2004). During the process of instructional scaffolding, learners are aware of their learning and begin to engage in mindful self-talk related to their learning process. This dialogue with themselves is metacognition. Metacognition is basically learning and understanding about one's own learning and understanding of a concept. Metacognition requires learners to use their brains not only to learn but to understand the where, why, and how of their learning.

Connecting Foundations to Brain-Based Learning

Foundational theories facilitate connections for educators to the TLP as it is today and for the duration of the 21st century. Attempting to grasp the TLP of the 21st century has led educators and educational researchers to a desire to understand the workings of human brain and the impact of using brain-based learning knowledge in the learning environment. Understanding the learning process requires recognizing how the contributions of neuroscience and developmental psychology learning theories inform teaching and learning (Jensen, 2000). "From a neuroscience perspective, instruction and learning are very important parts of a child's brain development and psychological development processes" (National Research Council, 2000, p. 115). Think of the human brain! From the moment of birth the brain is taking in stimuli and processing it in some way. Human beings are born ready to learn! According to Sousa (2006), the brain takes in more information from the environment in a day than the largest computer does in a year. The information that the brain receives is processed through the body's senses; with the senses of sight, hearing, and touch contributing the greatest (Sousa 2006). Just watch as an individual, presented with a new object, looks at it for the first time. They look at the object with their eyes and lean in to listen for any sound that may be coming from or within it, and finally depending on what their brain tells them about its' possible safety, they reach out to touch it. This cycle is repeated with every new object. See, hear, and touch! With every new learning experience knowledge is added to an existing knowledge base.

Educators want to know how the brain learns to better support teaching and learning. Advances in technologies for looking inside the brain and seeing the brain in action have moved faster than scientists predicted less than a decade ago (Sousa, 2008). Neuroscientists have come a long way in studying the physical structures and chemical make-up of the brain that drives understanding of how brain activity relates to learning. "Computer driven technologies such as positron emission tomography (PET), functional magnetic resonance imaging (MRI), and quantitative electroencephalography (Qeeg) are revolutionizing the study of learning as it happens in the brain" (Meyer & Rose, 2005, p. 21). These technological advancements have provided researchers with an inside peek of the brain during various problem-solving learning activities, such as, solving a math problem or analyzing material (Sousa, 2006). Researchers have literally been able to see which part of the brain is activated when it is actively working on different tasks. Understanding that different parts of the brain work during different tasks is vital in supporting the need to include the brain and cognitive processing throughout the TLP.

The Brain and the Added Element of Universal Design for Learning

Universal Design for Learning (UDL) as defined in the 2008 reauthorization of the Higher Education Act (HEA), now known as the Higher Education Opportunity Act (HEOA) is

a scientifically valid framework for guiding educational practices that provides flexibility in the ways information is presented, the ways students respond and demonstrate their knowledge & skills, and the ways students engaged in what they are learning; reduces barriers in instruction, provides appropriate accommodations, supports, and maintains high academic expectations for achievement for students with disabilities and English Learners (Sopko, 2008, p. 94).

Under the HEOA, federally funded teacher preparation programs are required to infuse the UDL framework into the teaching learning process to prepare teachers for the pre-Kindergarten to 12 learning environment. Furthermore, the UDL framework's principles and guidelines are founded and based on brain research (Meyer & Rose, 2005). Recognized as a learner-centered approach, UDL was written into the recently reauthorized Elementary and Secondary Education Act (ESEA), known as the Every Student Succeeds Act (ESSA) (2015). The affirmation of the UDL framework in this educational law is a means to an end that removes the barriers that traditional teaching and learning environments have.

The Universal Design for Learning (UDL) framework stems from universal design (UD) origins, an architectural design mindset of planning and creating structures with accessibility for individuals with disabilities in mind (Gargiulo & Metcalf, 2010). UD has seven foundational principles: equitable use, flexibility in use, simple and intuitive use, perceptible information, tolerance for error, low physical effort, and size and space for approach and use (Burgstahler, 2008). These principles moved architectural design from retrofitted scaffolding to a proactive innovative design, placing accessibility to the forefront and blending it naturally into the architectural environment and landscape which in the long run has benefitted all individuals. Proponents for educational curriculum took what UD did for architecture and applied it to curriculum. In doing so, a framework was created to proactively design learning opportunities by changing teaching, learning, assessment, and curriculum to benefit all students, including those with learning differences (Gargiulo & Metcalf, 2010).

Cognitive Networks in Action

Rose, Meyer, Strangman and Rappolt (2002) indicate that through the various brain-imaging techniques explored, researchers have identified three central nervous system networks in the brain that play an intricate role in the learning framework of UDL. The three brain networks identified in the UDL framework are the affective network, the recognition network, and the strategic network (Coyne, Ganley, Hall, Meo, Murray, & Gordon, 2006; Meyer & Rose, 2005; Rose & Gravel, 2009; Rose, Meyer, Strangman, & Rappolt, 2002). When the UDL framework was initially shared the recognition network was identified and described in the literature first, however the revised framework lists the affective network first. It stands to reason that affect impacts interest or engagement and without engagement it may not matter how content is represented; attentiveness and curiosity of the learner is center to what and how learning happens.

The affective network determines the engagement, motivation, interest, and emotional connection to what an individual is learning. It is described as the 'why' of learning and is what grabs hold of an individual's interest, helps them to sustain and persist through challenging content, and guides their development to self-regulate themselves to the level that they achieve the learning outcome (Coyne, et al, 2006; Meyer & Rose, 2005; Rose & Gravel, 2009; Rose, Meyer, Strangman, & Rappolt, 2002). The affective network relies on "multiple means of engagement" to support the diverse needs students have to personally make meaning to the content (Coyne et al., 2009). When the affective network is working an individual's interest and curiosity has been piqued and quite possibly a personal and emotional connection has been made to the content or learning objective.

The affective system of the brain in the UDL framework is located at the core of the brain and associated with the limbic system; and is touted as the most essential component to learning because it is the area of the brain that engages the learner through emotion, a desire to make a connection, and interest in what is to be learned (Rose, Meyer, Strangman, & Rappolt, 2002). Every individual at some time in their lifetime has had the experience of a class or professional development that they attended and that for some reason, as participants, they were disengaged. Recalling the topic of focus of that class or professional development is next to impossible. Active participants in the teaching and learning environment must move beyond the status quo of district or university provided curriculum resources and extend the content to reach the individual needs of every student. The TLP must pique the curiosity of the learner and provide them with an authentic and real connection to their lives. Educators must examine the full diversity of the classroom and provide the lessons and learning activities that connect to the cultural, social, racial, and socio-economic diversity of every student in the classroom. Teachers that know their students set the stage for great learning. The teacher-student relationship is the crux to the existence of a safe and supportive learning environment. Teachers that understand that their leaners are the most important aspect of teaching and demonstrate a presence of respecting and genuinely caring about their students will take students farther than those that believe the curriculum is the most important aspect of teaching.

The recognition network is located at the back of the brain and is the way the brain allows individuals to take in information through sensory processes, such as, a visual, auditory, tactile, or kinesthetic method (Coyne, et al, 2006). Labeled as the "what' of learning, the recognition network identifies and compartmentalizes the symbols that are seen, determining whether they are letters, numbers, or text; helps individuals to see patterns and ideas, draws upon their background knowledge of a concept, and supports the processing and generalization of new information (Coyne, et al., 2006; Meyer & Rose, 2005; Rose & Gravel, 2009; Rose, Meyer, Strangman, & Rappolt, 2002). The recognition network relies on "multiple means of representation" to support the diverse ways students take in information (Coyne et al., 2009). Basically, the recognition network takes in information and helps an individual to identify what it is and make connections to knowledge they already have.

The recognition network of the UDL framework is one in which many teachers may already be implementing within limits, due to resources. For every curriculum standard or learning objective, it is important that a teacher has solid and timely knowledge of each student's ability to grasp the content presented to them. Knowing each student's level of ability, their strengths and their areas of need provides teachers with the opportunity to modify materials, discover alternative formats of materials and resources, and determine different approaches to teaching the content so that all students have an equal opportunity to build on their conceptual understanding. Multiple means of representation means that resources used to learn the content can come in many sizes, shapes, or forms (Meyer & Rose, 2005). Supporting student learning needs can be achieved through adding closed captioning to videos shown in class, recording lessons or lectures for students to listen to at a later time or as they need to, provide visually appealing or distinctive contrasts in materials, create and modify a website for a class or course, present material in multiple formats such as audio-recorded books as well as at multiple levels of readability, encourage the use of text-to-speech programs, or consider implementing other accessible instructional materials such as textbooks and other instructional material provided in accessible formats and designed for individuals with disabilities (National Center on Universal Design for Learning, 2012).

One critical component of the learning sustained within the recognition network is the guidance toward retrieval of previous learning and background knowledge of a concept that helps scaffold toward acquisition of new concepts. As background knowledge is activated the learner can then make connections to the big ideas of the content standards; identify the patterns of information presented; transform the information into knowledge they can use for future learning and generalize that knowledge to other connected content standards. Teachers can use information support tools such as graphic organizers, learning or concept maps, KWL charts, and reading reflection journals to support students in accessing their background knowledge and as they begin associating new content to previously learned content (National Center on Universal Design for Learning, 2012). Many of these information support tools are also available through technology and are likely to be more efficient for students to use as they modify their responses with the click of a mouse rather than erase and rewrite or redraw. Ideally, for every student in the classroom, teachers are reviewing the content and the materials they are planning to use for instruction and inquiry-based learning and they are modifying them so that every student regardless of their level of ability will gain access to the information and gain some level of understanding or mastery. In the current TLP, meeting the recognition network needs of students with the current resources that teachers have, means a continuation of retrofitting the curriculum rather than fitting the curriculum into the landscape from which students could be learning from.

The strategic network, the area of the brain focused on the "how" of learning is located at the front of the brain and supports the process of learning through the activation of an individual's ability to construct and communicate learned knowledge, exercise planning skills, establish goals, and determine a system to evaluate their progress toward those goals (Coyne, et al, 2006). The strategic network relies on "multiple means of action and expression" to support the diverse needs students have to practice with and share what they know about the content (Coyne et al., 2009). The strategic network is how things get done! It is the process of identifying a task, deciding the way it will get finished, following through with the process, and evaluating the job when it is done.

The strategic brain network is the planning, executing, and monitoring system that guides learning (Rose, Meyer, Strangman, & Rappolt, 2002). As a teacher considers the learning objective they must view the way their learners are able to navigate through the learning environment and demonstrate their knowledge. Successful learning requires that, once again, teachers know each individual student and their needs for accommodating themselves into the learning environment, as well as, the content to be taught. Which students are the kinesthetic learners of the classroom? Which students are visual and need to see models and examples? Who are the students that are auditory learners and only need to hear the lesson once? Which students can express themselves in writing and which students demonstrate mastery of concepts orally. Imagine a classroom where the desks raise and lower to meet a learner's physical need to stretch and move as they work. Or simply a classroom where students are allowed to move around the room and access resources they need to gain information without the direction coming from the teacher.

Learning must be separated into segments that allows learners to move and energize their brains. Lessons should involve action and should be differentiated not only for students with special or different needs but for all students. The learning environment and resources should allow for their active involvement and participation. Choice in different methods and approaches to demonstrating knowledge should be a part of assessment rather than the standard curriculum-based summative assessment tool that is far over-used and requires no problem-solving or creative thinking skills whatsoever. Perhaps the best form of assessment is through an optimal medium of the student's choice rather than paper and pencil or multiple choice using a computer. Providing students with various modalities to express their knowledge means that they deserve opportunities to practice with alternative formats throughout each lesson or unit of study to build fluency. Along with alternative formats of demonstrating knowledge comes the support tools such as concept or thinking mapping tools, outlines, story frames, calculators, manipulatives, etc., that allow students to demonstrate their knowledge efficiently skills (National Center on Universal Design for Learning, 2014). In order for students to be efficient in the use of various tools they must be provided opportunities to become fluent through multiple opportunities to practice and use the tools skills. Furthermore, learning tools cannot be allowed during practice and then not provided during assessment, nor should they be provided during assessment that the students have not had opportunities to practice with. Knowing how to input the information into a tool is equally as important as the product itself. Additionally, other adults, such as, peer teachers, community leaders, para-professionals, and school administrators are tangible human resources that take on a role of support educators in the classroom providing scaffolded mentorship when needed not only for students with disabilities but for all students.

Continuous progress monitoring and feedback must be provided to guide students in making connections in their understanding of the content and planning on their next steps for acquisition and mastery. The strategic network requires the use of an individual's executive functioning skills (National Center on Universal Design for Learning, 2014). Executive function skills are the skills used to organize information and act on it (Morin, 2014). Executive function skills provide individuals with the emotional intelligence that enables them to have impulse and emotional control, flexible thinking, working memory, the ability to self-monitor or self-regulate, and plan, prioritize, organize, and initiate tasks (Morin, 2014). The wiring of executive function skills are held in the prefrontal cortex, the last area of the brain to fully develop (Giedd, 2008, Sousa, 2006). Knowing that the brain is still maturing and that students require support to make important decisions about their learning makes it easy to understand that guidance is still needed in the classroom. Checklists and guides, maintaining a planner, developing schedules, providing models and project planning templates, establishing short and long term goals, demonstrating and teaching planning self-talk such as prompts to reflect on goal achievement, and providing and discussing feedback are tools to assist in the development of executive functioning skills making learning using the strategic network of the brain effective and efficient (National Center on Universal Design for Learning, 2014). Adults in the workplace environment continue to use many of these tools, for example, planners and checklists, although they have moved them from a paper and pencil format to a digital format. Until curriculum is embedded with checklists and planners and opportunities to design models can be tested before projects are completed, teachers will continue to retrofit the curriculum to meet the strategic network needs of students.

When teaching using the UDL framework, the affective, recognition, and strategic brain networks are activated through providing options, choices, or "multiple means" of representation, action, and expression, and engagement correspondingly (Meyer & Rose, 2005). How does each brain network in the UDL framework work in the TLP? What role do educators play in implementing the framework in the teaching and learning process? How does UDL impact teaching and learning as it is known today and needed for the future? To answer these questions, more questions must be answered. Who are the learners in today's classrooms? What are their strengths? What gaps do they have in their knowledge? What are their interests? What is their native language? Implementing the UDL framework means that educators must have knowledge of their learners. Each class every year is different from the next. Effective teaching leading to effective learning means that teachers have knowledge of each student under their charge and have a full understanding of their learning needs. Teachers must know their students' interests, goals for learning, goals for life, their background knowledge and experiences, talents, culture, families, abilities, and their disabilities. Like theory, teachers must know where students are coming from in order to know how they can guide them to where they want to go. Connecting teaching to the UDL framework must be a part of the next step in preparing for the TLP.

Readying the Learner

Students need social, behavioral, and academic expectations that are set to a high standard; however those standards need to be explained to both the students and to their families and must have the supports in place in order to achieve them. Supporting student success requires feedback that engages intrinsic student motivation not just external motivation such as a grade or reward. As with the development of executive function skills, the prefrontal cortex also supports the affective brain network in an individual's ability to self-regulate themselves. The brain deals with planning and thinking, problem-solving, monitoring higher order thinking, and regulating the emotional system (Sousa, 2006). Since the prefrontal cortex is thought to still be developing throughout the teen years until the early to middle 20's (Giedd, 2008), the learning environment must promote activities that support self-regulatory skills of every learner. Self-regulation skills include the ability to persist through a challenging task, identify and resist impulsive actions, regulate emotions, and determine intrinsic motivation (National Center on Universal Design for Learning, 2014). Knowing the late maturity of the pre-frontal cortex helps in understanding the high-school drop-out rate as students give up on a learning task or even themselves or become frustrated and perhaps verbal or volatile when met with an academic or emotional event that disrupts their perceived stability. Scaffolding and differentiating curriculum, providing rubrics, identifying learning goals, supporting students in determining both short term and long term personal academic, college, and career goals, and teaching positive, motivating self-talk are a few ways to provide structure in the attainment of self-regulation (National Center on Universal Design for Learning, 2014). Similar to the recognition network, meeting the affective network needs of students in the current TLP means a continuation of retrofitting the curriculum to align student interests into a set curriculum resource rather than explore where the standard can take students.

The three brain networks of the UDL framework focus or describe separate functions; yet when thinking of the TLP in action, all three networks are working alternatively and simultaneously as an individual acquires new knowledge and attempts to connect newly acquired information into their existing knowledge or make this knowledge part of their foundational background knowledge. This powerful framework was originally designed to incorporate technology as a method to take curriculum and fit students with disabilities into it. UDL has evolved to engage technology into every aspect of the brain network principles and guidelines, yet the evolution has not yet equated to fulfillment with curriculum publishing companies. Technology has the ability to level the playing field for individuals with disabilities and make content accessible. School districts are realizing that what is good for students with disabilities and English Learners is also good for all students. Taking the UDL framework into the classroom is good for all learners. Connecting to who the learners are and what they want in the 21st century classroom will determine how the framework is infiltrated into the TLP landscape.

TECHNOLOGY AND THE LEARNER

Understanding Why and How for the 21st Century Learner

Why is technology infused learning so important today? The reauthorization of the Elementary and Secondary Education Act's Every Student Succeeds Act (ESSA) stipulates that States must

increase access to personalized, rigorous learning experiences supported by technology; develop or use strategies that are innovative or evidence-based for the delivery of specialized and rigorous academic courses and curricula through the use of technology; disseminate promising practices related to technology instruction; provide instructional professionals with instructional support to integrate technology; and make instructional content widely available through open educational resources (2015, p. 220).

Technology use is now written into education laws. It is no longer an option or an enhancement; it is a requirement. A technology infused learning environment will be the norm for both teaching and learning. Most recently technology has become part of assessment as states gradually moved their mandated state assessments from a paper and pencil format to a digital format. Changing to a digital format required districts to develop the infrastructure to support the new format and continues to remain a work in progress. The issue at hand then is not if technology practices will be a part of the future TLP, but will the technology practices used in the classroom today remain the same.

Technology allows individuals to rewrite the definition of the learner from one in which the teacher has the role of being more knowledgeable to one in which the students drive their learning through their own instruction using technology under the masterful guidance of the teacher (Cicconi, 2014). Students entering the classroom today and the near future are learners who have grown up with individualized mobile technologies at their fingertips. Described as the iGeneration or digital natives, they are students that from a very early age have played, gamed, messaged, or talked with a cellular device of their own or their parents (Rosen, 2011). Likewise, they have watched videos and listened to music on cell phones, iPads or tablets, have had an opportunity to practice writing code, print using a 3D printer, and spend every waking minute of the day immersed in media and technology (Rosen, 2011). Currently digital natives live in a world where their cellular devices perform as a mini personal computer allowing them to access information immediately. In fact, many of these students at the middle and high school level may switch among multiple devices such as their laptop and cell phone, take a course online, and even play an interactive computer game with someone located across the country (Rosen, 2011). What is the impact of digital natives on the TLP? Will teachers be required to teach all the content in an online format? Are school districts required to provide access to every Web 2.0 tool available on the web? Using technology to enhance education does not mean providing technology for technology's sake (Rosen, 2011). Technology for technology's sake leaves far too many whiteboards, doc cameras, and laptop carts unused in the classroom or students watching numerous educational videos without class discourse and connections made to content. According to Rosen (2011), teachers can convey content more powerfully and efficiently to all students using technology; bringing the lesson material to life through alternative formats of content or audio and video related resources. This method of incorporating technology aligns with the UDL framework by providing multiple means of representation of content, however, for students to gain knowledge from these sources they need to be engaged in searching for information from them not just passively observing or listening to them.

Critical to every learning environment is the teacher-student relationship and classroom environment. Just as in traditional classrooms of the past, digital native students want to be respected. They want to know that they are in a safe and nurturing environment to explore their interests, share their findings, and ask questions. They want an environment where their cultural differences, interests, and personal learning goals matter (Prensky, 2011). Digital technology in the TLP can provide digital natives with a way to personalize their learning. They can learn at an individualized pace in the way they prefer, delving deeper into areas of interest right from the start of class rather than just perform a technology exercise in between lecture (Prensky, 2011).

Digital natives will require an environment that will support their need to develop the research skills necessary to discover answers to their questions and the questions posed by their teacher. This learning environment will develop students' fluency using multiple literacies through a variety of technology resources necessary. Students will need to be taught the critical thinking skills that will guide their decision-making to evaluate information they have discovered and determine which technology resources will work best for their research needs. In today's digital world critical thinking skills need to be infused in the teaching learning environment by the teacher. Critical thinking skills are promoted and practiced by students outside the class through gaming. Digital natives have grown up gaming on both educational and entertainment type games. "Research and development around learning games seeks to increase student interest while promoting deductive reasoning, collaborative problem-solving, digital literacy, and content knowledge" (Owston, 2009). The National Science Foundation is currently funding research in integrating educational games into the learning environment, such as games and simulations that provide students with opportunities to experience working on a project collaboratively without leaving their classroom, using technology that allows them to bridge abstract concepts with virtual tangible models, or exploring images using three dimensional imaging software (U.S. DOE, 2016, p. 16). Skills required for educational gaming are skills that align with national educational standards to problem-solve and synthesize information. Children of the iGeneration are learning to code and create games that demonstrate the knowledge they have learned. They have the ability and the technology, the TLP environment simply needs to find a way to let it happen.

Searching available online resources can feel as though one has fallen into a dark abyss. Every educator at one time or another has spent hours on the internet searching for that one critical resource that will enable their students to make the desired connections to the content, or so they hope. The resources quite possibly number in the billions throughout the worldwide web which is why it is important to be resourceful. Collaboration, as an educator, is the key to being resourceful. Collaborating with like-minded, tech savvy connected educators through global networking (Nussbaum-Beach & Hall, 2012) or identifying a potential knowledge broker (Rosen, 2011) brings collaboration into the 21st century. A knowledge broker according to Rosen (2011) is a student who was taught previously or is older than current students being taught, may be a student at a local community-college student, a paraprofessional, or perhaps, even a parent that can help search for and locate online resources for a specific content area. Current students can act as knowledge brokers when taught and given guidelines to finding quality online resources. In fact, due to the iGeneration or digital natives desire for immediate information or what Sutherland-Smith (2002) describes as a 'snatch and grab philosophy' toward searching for answers, there is a need to teach students the self-regulation skills that will provide them the ability to persevere and persist through a challenging task and go beyond shallow reading. Digital natives need to use critical thinking skills to evaluate quality resources and strive to find scientific and evidence-based information from authentic sources rather than the general public (Bennett, Maton, & Kervin, 2008).

Increasing students' connectivity under the TLP means not only teaching them how to use the technology tools but to also develop sound judgement and decision-making skills. The U.S. Department of Education, Office of Educational Technology's report Future Ready Learning states that because there will be increased connectivity of students there is also an increase in the importance of teaching learners how to become responsible digital citizens (U.S. DOE, 2016). Students will need to learn and follow standards regarding digital citizenship and technology use practices for their safety and the safety of others.

Students need the tools to dissect information discovered in on-line resources. The TLP of classrooms today and the future will need to assist students in their development of the skills and abilities necessary to make knowledgeable choices regarding their technology practices, rather than hasty judgements based on general public view, to truly be college and/or career ready in a global way. This suggests that what is needed is to take the everyday technology practices that students have and foster them to academic tasks so that they develop the necessary skills required during and beyond their educational years. Digital learners or learners of the iGeneration will need to practice using new literacies in order to be relevant in the 21st century.

Developing the partnering pedagogy for digital natives academic-thinking will mean letting students: find and follow their passion; use whatever technology is available and within their reach; research and find information; answer questions and share not only the information discovered but their thoughts and opinions; practice skills through a method they find motivating; and create presentations and products using text and multimedia (Prensky, 2010, p. 13).

This approach to the teaching learning process definitely moves teachers off the center stage and into a role of partnering and guiding learning.

A partnering for teachers, according to Prensky (2010) means giving teachers the responsibility to generate questions that intrigue students and pique their interests; guide students in the learning process; put material in context; explain concepts to individual students when necessary; create rigor; and ensure quality learning is happening (p. 13).

Teaching students the skills required to examine on-line resources more critically aligns with Prensky's (2010) idea of a partnering pedagogy where students take on the responsibility of using technology. A partnering pedagogy using technology has the teacher moving off the center stage and repositioning themselves behind the scenes where they can support their students as a coach and a guide rather than as the deliverer of content. Moving behind the scenes transpires to teachers asking high level open-ended questions, providing authentic application and context, ensuring rigor, and providing quality feedback to students regarding their work (Prensky, 2010). This does not mean that digital native students are off and on their own answering questions in isolation fulfilling only their own knowledge interests. Learning, even in the 21st century, has a social element. A technology infused learning environment will still require a social element of learning through peers. Students are engaged and motivated by their peers to respond to social media. That same element of engagement and motivation should be part of the current and future TLP. The TLP in the 21st century can capture that level of engagement and motivation by creating opportunities for students to become connected learners. Connected learning is learning through relationships (Nussbaum-Beach & Hall, 2012). Connected learners learn from and with each other both formally and informally by collaborating online, using social media with other globally connected learners, and share what they've learned with their class peers (Nussbaum-Beach & Hall, 2012). Connecting students to other students around the world puts them in touch with others who have the same interests as they do. It provides them with an opportunity to listen to students who have differing opinions and knowledge. Technology use should be meaningful, productive, and accountable; and connected learning helps to make that happen.

Digital natives want to connect and work with their peers. They desire opportunities to collaborate, share their opinions, and expand their thinking through hearing other student's perceptions of concepts not only within their own classroom walls but also globally. This ability to work with their peers is ultimately a real-life, real-work skill that if students acquire will prepare them for work beyond their post-secondary years. Ostroff (2016) states that when a person becomes part of something bigger than themselves, they suddenly get the benefit of identifying with other members. Furthermore, "new activities, with their associated knowledge and expectations, are suddenly available to you and other members will help you do things that interest you. You learn without realizing" (Ostroff, 2016, p. 41). Effective collaborative relationships develop over time. Digital natives want to work with students who are active participants, not do the work for them. Team members need to get to know one another first before they venture into working with one another. Working relationships take time to develop as individuals navigate through differing personalities and working styles. Just as classrooms develop norms of expected behaviors, so too do student working groups (Nausbaum-Beach & Hall, 2012).

Cooperative group learning frequently occurs in most elementary classrooms, but as state assessment plays a greater role in the TLP, teachers tend to focus on individualized learning so that their students are prepared for individualized tests. Implementing both team building and class building cooperative group activities promote a positive classroom culture. Cooperative activities promote trust by developing relationships among students who may not know each other and help students to feel as though they belong by building mutual respect. Nausbeam-Beach & Hall (2010) claim that positive classroom environments have both congenial and collegial relationships. Congenial relationships refer to students being polite and friendly with each other (Nausbeam-Beach & Hall, 2010). Congenial relationships help make collegial relationships work more effectively. Collegial relationships occur when there is a shared belief that no one person holds all the knowledge and that all participants are active contributors to a common learning goal (Nausbeam-Beach & Hall, 2010). It is the mindset that everyone works when on a picnic, not just the person manning the grill. How can digital native's need to collaborate using technology be supported? Classroom digital natives can work together to merge their understanding with that of another to create Wikis and websites to display the information they have discovered and share that information globally. Blogs, Podcasts, Twitter, Snapchat, and Facebook are just a few other technology tools that digital natives can use to express their knowledge, thoughts or perceptions, while also establishing an avenue for feedback, whether it is a confirming or even an opposing view. "Collaboration catapults learning" (Ostroff, 2016, p.42). It is an important opportunity to blend various learning styles, interests, and abilities together preparing them for the working environment they will experience in their future.

Students working together bring opportunity for creativity and creation. Digital natives want to be creators. The digital native looks for novelty and innovation and that desire for novelty and innovation naturally leads to creating. Prensky (2010) states that many digital natives are already creating projects ranging from multimedia presentations, machinima, graphic novels, web sites, blogs, games, how-to Youtube videos, and the list could go on and on. The concern in the TLP is that those creations are happening outside the classroom rather than inside. The types of products students are creating inside the classroom are products when completed have the exact same expected outcome – a shoebox diorama, a poster, a PowerPoint with the same five slides. Students today have "more vehicles to express their learning and their creativity" (Prensky, 2010, p.150) at their fingertips than ever before with no end in sight of what technology tool will surface next. One concern expressed and felt by most teachers is that they themselves do not know how to use many of the vehicles available to students or may not even know what the tools are or do. Digital natives have an innate ability to navigate their way through tools they have not previously experienced. Simply because a teacher is not familiar with a technology tool should not be the reason that students cannot use it. Providing students with the criteria for the expected outcome regardless of the tool will guide students to achieve the expected outcome. Prensky (2010) believes that what is important is that the teacher give students the opportunity to create at their highest level possible with whatever tools are within their grasp.

Providing choice is infused throughout the opportunity to create. The majority of school districts provide classroom teachers with resources to teach their students from a variety of educational publishers. Standards-based curriculum resources that districts provide are a place where teaching to the middle level of learners is the goal. Teachers are required to implement interventions to students who struggle in hopes that they will catch up to the middle, while, students who are already successful at the mid-level and eager to learn more; remain stagnant in their knowledge acquisition. Each district's curriculum resources are designed to prepare students for the annual high-stakes state assignments that they are required to take and pass for promotion to the next grade. Teachers are accountable for ensuring that the state standards are the curriculum to be taught. The way in which the standards are introduced, learned, and assessed throughout the year are, somewhat, at their discretion. Teachers can choose to solely use the resources they are provided by their district for their digital native students or they can choose to provide a rich teaching learning environment framed in UDL and technology. Providing students with a rich learning environment doesn't mean students don't have assignments or learning objectives. Digital natives can and should be given assignments; however allowing students options for completing those assignments and providing effective feedback allows students to be inspired and rise to a higher level of performance (Prensky, 2010). Having choice leads to engagement. Engagement leads to motivation. When students are allowed to make choices they will develop the skills to approach problems or stretch their minds to think of things in new ways (Ostroff, 2016), as will be expected of them beyond their academic career.

Curriculum standards established by the state determine what students are expected to know. Students want what they learn to be relevant and authentic; but mostly they want it to be real (Prensky, 2010). Relevant learning means that students are able to relate something being taught to them to the knowledge or experiences they already have (Prensky, 2010). Relevant learning occurs through scaffolding lessons and building on contexts that are familiar, but according to Prensky (2010) it isn't real learning. Authentic learning incorporates isolated topics into real world experiences and situations of students (Gargiulo & Metcalf, 2010). Relevant and authentic learning attempts to connect students to past events through current events. Real learning as described by Prensky (2010) means "that there is a perceived connection by the students, at every moment, between what they are learning and their ability to use that learning to do something useful in the world" (p. 72). Real learning does not mean that students should not be taught historical events and discoveries. Historical events help connect learners to the past events and their impact on current events. Digital natives want the information they acquire to be real and immediately useful (Prensky, 2010) and personally applicable to their lives. Prensky (2010) compels teachers to "make everything come directly from the world of the students and to make learning not just about the students' world, but also about changing and improving their world" (p. 73). Through the use of technology digital natives can take virtual field trips to historical sites not just in their own state but also around the nation and world. They can follow sea turtles in the Galapagos Islands as they adapt to the weather changes and make predictions on the impact of weather on the existence of an animal that fits somewhere into their personal carbon cycle. The world is truly at the fingertips of digital native students through webcams and the connections students develop with other digitally connected learners.

Humans are a curious lot. Think of infants and young children and the ease with which they learn. Young children can be observed picking up the most challenging of tasks on a daily basis with autonomy and little effort (Ostroff, 2016) "Humans come into this world curious, motivated, and ready to learn" (Ostroff, 2016, p. 23). They are eager to respond to novel tasks and information. Infants, toddlers, and young children avidly watch the adults and other humans in their lives. When no longer engaged, infants, toddlers, and young children are observed moving on to the next object that draws their attention, whether it is a toy, person, or food. Are the learning needs of students in the elementary to post-secondary school environment really any different than those of infants, toddlers, and young children?

The majority of students in classrooms whose curiosity is no longer piqued have been trained through classroom management and discipline to go through the motions of learning for the sake of getting a task done, rather than for the intrinsic pleasure of learning. The rubber hits the road when students refuse to do the status quo and balk at learning for the sake of task completion. Digital natives want what infants, toddlers, and young children seek in their quest for knowledge; they seek to be engaged. Digital natives want to know how newly acquired information will impact their lives now and the foreseeable future. Seeking answers to essential questions is key to that type of learning. Good questions can drive students through a WebQuest eagerly searching for answers. It is an opportunity for them to evaluate the information discovered through their search and an opportunity to share that information with their peers when they are engaged in meaningful, engaging work.

Deeper Learning

In order for students to use technology in meaningful, productive, and creative ways they need to have questions that drive their interest to research for the answers. "Questions are the device that frames, guides, and ultimately evaluates all learning" (Prensky, 2010, p. 84). Guiding questions are driven from the curriculum that teachers are required to teach, that is, the standards. Teachers are responsible for ensuring that students understand the guiding questions clearly enough so that they can answer them and meet the content standards from which they will be judged. Teachers need to know that the questions they create will meet the content standards and that their students have the skills needed in order to answer them.

Questions that challenge students' thinking not only at the moment but throughout their education are identified as essential questions (Brown, 2009). Essential questions are the types of questions that continue to resurface and place learners in a lifelong learning path. Students should respond to questions that address both the big ideas and the supporting details of content (Prensky, 2010). Supporting detail questions scaffold the information learned and big idea questions continue the learning path throughout life. Creating essential questions takes time and effort. Like any part of teaching and learning, they also require reflection related to their effectiveness. Good essential questions start with 'why' or 'how' and similar to what the literature says about classroom rules should be limited, between 5-10, for effective connections to take place (Prensky, 2010). Prensky (2010) suggests novices look at chapter names and subheadings and turn them into questions for starters as long as the resource connects to the standards. Good guiding questions have multiple solutions, local and global implications, and have practical results;

while even better questions can be adapted to different student interests, lead students to real actions to change the world, and catch students interest (Prensky, 2010).

Guiding questions can be differentiated to meet students with varying needs and a highly effective teaching learning environment will scaffold questions in such a way that students can build the knowledge themselves. Questions, regardless of their level, that engage students' interests and propel them into actions to change the world push students to a level where they generate their own questions. Student generated questions certainly align with a digital native's need to learn real information.

Ultimately, the level of questions wanted to achieve are those that require students to probe their own thinking. Socratic questions are rarely, if ever, posed to students in the Kindergarten-12th Grade teaching and learning environment. The current teaching learning environment requires students to learn content to prepare for a test rather than prepare for the world, but Socratic questions should be part of the TLP for digital native students. Socratic questions require dialogue and that dialogue can only truly occur in a learning environment where students feel safe enough to speak freely, without judgement from their peers or teachers. The Socratic learning environment is a learning environment that digital natives seek and that a rejuvenated TLP can offer.

MERGING TECHNOLOGY, UDL, AND THE LEARNER

Technology has supported the type of learner that has an insatiable need to be socially connected to their world. These learners are fueled by discovering information that has been shared ten-fold from the originating individual who they may not know personally. They are intrigued and curious and prepared to learn more. Today's learners, are digital natives, whose lives are surrounded by multiple forms of technology that they easily multitask and process information from. They believe learning should be more than authentic and relevant; it should also be real. They want learning to be immediately useful, fun, and prefer to process information through images, sounds, and video before reading a text (Jeffs, 2010).

A push has been made across the nation to close the "digital divide" of the students of poverty and lower scoring schools having less technological resources than their higher scoring suburban counterparts. The average classroom today does contain technology. At a minimum, most classrooms include a mounted whiteboard, projector, and computer (Reinhart, Thomas, & Toriskie, 2011). Some classrooms may also have a document camera connected to the computer system and perhaps a handful of student computers as well. The district provided curriculum may include a virtual exercise or two, an educational gaming link, and small resource guide for strategies to teach students that are English Learners, students with disabilities, or students that are gifted, however; for the most part they are created to teach to the middle with a "one size fits all" packaging. Additionally, the district provided curriculum will provide a method for a summative assessment of the content in order to prepare students for the annual state assessment. The problem that exists in the current TLP is that the technology in many classrooms is still limited and of the resources available, most are still designed to retrofit the curriculum to meet a few learners' needs (Delgado, A. J., Wardlow, L., McKnight, K., & O'Malley, K., 2015; Ruggerio & Mong, 2015; Inan & Lowther, 2010). A rejuvenated TLP is needed to meet the needs of digital native students and prepare them for their place in the world.

Through the 2004 reauthorization of the Individuals with Disability Act (IDEA); the National Instructional Materials Accessibility Standard (NIMAS) initiated requiring school districts to provide instructional materials to students with varying print disabilities beginning in August 2006 (U.S. DOE,

2004). This innovative standard may seem minimal but in the eyes of educators it is huge since the majority of educational resources used in the classroom are textbooks. The NIMAS initiated alternate formats of curriculum resources for students with visual impairments such as texts in braille, large print textbooks, audio recorded texts, and electronic texts (e-text) (Stahl, 2008). Gains in technology have moved embossed braille print from a 500 page text equating to a nearly 3000 page braille text to a temporary print-to-braille of refreshable braille display (RBD) made through a series of moving pins that can be read on a flexible membrane (Stahl, 2008).

Audio recorded books have been in existence since the early 1930's when the American Federation for the Blind (AFB) along with its collaborating partners established what was known as the "Talking Book" (Stahl, 2008). In the past children's tradebooks could be heard using vinyl records or later cassette tapes. Currently CDs are the material used to produce an audio recording that accompanies a children's picture book or from which an individual listens to, to hear classic and contemporary literature while driving in their car or even while exercising. Although designed initially for individuals with visual impairments the use of audio text benefits students with learning disabilities and other disorders who require auditory support for comprehension or may need to hear a story more than once for complete understanding.

Large print text is typically used by older adults when their vision starts to wane due to age. Publishers of textbooks have printed large print textbooks, however they are used minimally (Stahl, 2008). The primary alternate format of text found in classrooms today is the e-text (Stahl, 2008). Students using an e-text can highlight the text, book mark a page or figure, change the font color or size, access websites through an embedded link, create notes on the page, use an interactive glossary, and listen to the text read aloud by synthetic speech on most computers.

The use of accessible versions of print curriculum provides functional resources for learning for those individuals with a visual impairment, but it still has a retrofitted approach of taking the curriculum and attempting to make it fit an individual student rather than the masses of digital natives waiting to learn in the teaching learning environments in today's classrooms. Closed captioning of video has provided individuals with hearing impairments the opportunity to understand the images of a video. The tools are available, they are just not fluid and efficient. The resources available through the internet are expansive and ever-changing. Federal documents can be pulled, books can be downloaded and read on computers or other e-text readers, and images from around the world and sky at are at the fingertips of the students.

Prensky (2010) poses that it is the student's job to use whatever technology is available. In order to use technology that is available students need to search and discover the tools that fit their needs. If fact, Prensky (2010) proposes that it is the student, and only the student, that should be using the technology whether it be the smartboard, PowerPoint, or a computer, during class time. While this may seem an extreme direction and is not likely to be readily accepted by most current educators; it is one direction that may come to fruition in the future when digital native students become the digital native educators. Until that time arrives, educators in today's teaching learning environment should support digital native learners by providing for full use of technology framed within the UDL principles and guidelines while learning.

Under section 41.04 of the ESSA (2015), education state funds shall be used to support local education agencies in providing programs that increase access to personalized, rigorous learning experiences supported by technology and providing technical assistance to local educational agencies to improve their ability to use technology, consistent with the principles of universal design for learning, to support the learning needs of all students (U.S. DOE 2016). The teaching learning environment should no longer be in a situation where there is a digital divide of students who have and students who do not have technology; nor should the digital divide be about those who have technology in the classroom and they are or are not using it. What the teaching and learning environment should be about is how technology can improve learning for all students. The divide occurring in most classrooms today is identified as a digital user divide (U.S. DOE, 2016). The digital user divide is the divide between students who use technology to actively learn, create, and collaborate and those that use technology as a passive consumer of content (U.S. DOE, 2016). In the digital user divide teachers control the technology in the classroom. They use the technology to present information and show a virtual lab but the students are passive observers. Teachers would be wise to have some knowledge of technology and various tools but they do not need to be the all-knowing source, and in fact, are not likely to be an all knowing source as technology tools change daily. Students involved as active researchers and users of digital resources are likely to be life-long learners. The type of learner who constantly seeks access to information.

The NMC Horizon Report 2015 K-12 Edition (Johnson, Becker, Estrada, & Freeman, 2015) examined how emerging technologies would impact the TLP in Kindergarten to 12th Grade classrooms and identified six trends, six challenges, and six technological developments that would impact educational policy, leadership, and practice. The identified trends facing the 21st century learning environment are: an increasing use of blended learning; the rise in the need for STEAM (science, technology, engineering, art, and mathematics) learning; increasing use of collaborative learning approaches, shift from students as consumers, to creators, rethinking how schools work, and shift to deeper learning approaches (Johnson et al., 2015). A few of the trends identified through the report are not new to most teachers today. STEM and STEAM (art enhanced) learning have been a trend in education for the past decade as the realization that a gap for qualified employable people in those areas exists in the nation. Blended learning, also a trend for the past decade or more, is literally a blending of face-to-face learning with on-line learning. Collaborative group learning has long been an effective strategy to build both whole class and small group relationships. Shifting from students as consumers, to creators, rethinking how schools work, and shifting to deeper learning approaches are trends that align with what digital natives want for their learning environment and although they are more complex to see to fruition can be viable with the merging of technology in a UDL framework environment.

Challenges identified impacting the 21st century classroom were creating real, authentic learning opportunities and integrating technology in teacher education, the need to develop personalized learning opportunities for students and rethinking the roles of teachers, as well as, scaling teaching innovations, and teaching complex thinking (Johnson et al., 2015). It is interesting to connect the similarities between these identified challenges from the NMC Horizon Report and what is known about digital natives and their learning environment. Digital natives have identified these challenges as their wants. They want real, authentic learning that is personalized. They want to take ownership for their knowledge quest and not be passive consumers. It is the TLP that will need to redesign teaching innovations so that teachers are inspiring their digital native students to never quench their thirst for knowledge, and for teacher evaluators to see that real learning continues throughout life and does not end at the end of the secondary school. The technologies identified as needing further develop to meet the needs and challenges listed in the report are "bring your own device" (cell phone or laptop), makerspaces, 3D printing, adaptive learning technologies, digital badges, and wearable technology (Johnson et el., 2015). Cellular devices are a controversial piece of technology in most school districts; and since they are not being used for educational purposes their only purpose is social in nature and therefore are often required to be placed in a locker or they will be confiscated. Students have been using Makerspace and 3D printers however costs are always a factor with new technology resources. Digital badges and wearable technology are projected to be available by the end of this decade (Johnson et al., 2015); however the technological tools that are available currently are being underutilized. Most digital natives are walking into their classrooms with the technology in their lockers that they could be using in the classroom to drive their learning to the level they want it to be.

CONCLUSION

If the TLP of today took the UDL framework and merged it with technology infusion imagine what a dynamic environment it would look like! Take a moment and search the internet for "tools for learning". What appears on the screen? Tools for learning, tools for presentations, elementary tools, high school tools, learning tools, free learning tools, tools for teaching and learning, tools for learning xyz, etc. The list goes on and on not only for computer-based tools but also for apps that can be downloaded to cell phones; as the Apple commercial says, "There's an app for that™". The infusion of technology has lent itself to providing students with tools that provide flexibility in accessing and organization information allowing them to learn through multiple avenues and connecting to all brain networks: recognition, strategic, and affective (Coyne, Ganley, Hall, Meo, Murray, & Gordon, 2008). When looking at each of the brain networks working in the UDL framework it is easy to see that there is a high probability that there is a technology tool or app that is applicable to each principle and guideline providing digital native students the teaching-learning environment they desire. Technology tools are being created with the UD guidelines in mind at the forefront enabling the tools to be accessible for all users.

The TLP needs rejuvenation when thinking about the current learners. Is the TLP ready to unleash all the learning into students' hands? Merging technology practices with the UDL framework and keeping digital natives in mind could open a new energetic approach to learning. The teacher is a critical part to making it happen by providing students with an environment that values respect and creativity and provokes students to think critically from questions that cause real learning to occur. Teacher feedback is necessary to engage students in thinking more deeply and creating their own questions. The UDL framework was originally created to provide individuals with disabilities access to content through the use of assistive technology. UDL is now recognized as an approach to the TLP that benefits all learners by providing all students with options of resources and ways to use various assistive and instructional technologies. Digital learners want access to all the technologies within their grasp to gain information about their world. They want to connect to other learners and make what they learn have personal value. Merging UDL and technology with the digital native in mind can place the learner in the driver seat. It is type of the learning that the digital native desires and will seek on their own if it is not part of their daily TLP. A universally designed framework infused with technology with the digital learner at the helm meets the need for a TLP that is rejuvenated and has future learning goals in mind.

REFERENCES

Bandura, A. (1977). *Social learning theory*. Englewood Cliffs, NJ: Prentice Hall.

Bennett, S., Maton, K., & Kervin, L. (2008). The digital natives debate: A critical review of the evidence. *British Journal of Educational Technology*, *39*(5), 775–786. doi:10.1111/j.1467-8535.2007.00793.x

Brown, K. (2009). Questions for the 21ˢᵗ century learner. *Knowledge Quest, 38*(1), 24–27.

Burgstahler, S. E. (2010). Universal design in higher education. In S. E. Burgstahler & R. C. Coy (Eds.), *Universal design in higher education: From principles to practice* (pp. 1–20). Cambridge, MA: Harvard Education Press.

Cicconi, M. (2014). Vygotsky meets technology: A reinvention of collaboration in the early childhood mathematics classroom. *Early Childhood Education Journal, 42*(1), 57–65. doi:10.1007/s10643-013-0582-9

Clayton, T. E. (1965). *Teaching and learning: A psychological perspective.* Englewood Cliffs, NJ: Prentice Hall, Inc.

Coyne, P., Ganley, P., Hall, T., Meo, G., Murray, E., & Gordon, D. (2008). Applying universal design for learning in the classroom. In D. H. Rose & A. Meyer (Eds.), *A practical reader in universal design for learning* (pp. 1–13). Cambridge, MA: Harvard University Press.

Delgado, A. J., Wardlow, L., McKnight, K., & O'Malley, K. (2015). Educational technology: A review of the integration, resources, and effectiveness of technology in K-12 classrooms. *Journal of Information Technology Education: Research, 14*(24), 397–416.

Every, S. S. A. (ESSA) (Reauthorization of the Elementary and Secondary Education Act). Pub. L. No. 114-95, U. S. C. § 1177 (2015). (n.d.). Retrieved from https://www.congress.gov/bill/114th-congress/senate-bill/1177/text

Gargiulo, R. M., & Metcalf, D. (2010). *Teaching in today's inclusive classroom: A universal design for learning approach.* Belmont, CA: Wadsworth.

Giedd, J. N. (2008). The teen brain: Insights from neuroimaging. *The Journal of Adolescent Health, 42*(4), 335–343. doi:10.1016/j.jadohealth.2008.01.007 PMID:18346658

Inan, F. A., & Lowther, D. L. (2010). Factors affecting technology integration in K-12 classrooms: A path model. *Educational Technology Research and Development, 58*(2), 137–154. doi:10.1007/s11423-009-9132-y

Individuals with Disabilities Education Act, 20 U.S.C. § 1400 (2004). (n.d.). Retrieved http://idea.ed.gov/download/statute.html

Jarvis, P., Holford, J., & Griffin, C. (2003). *The theory & practice of learning.* Sterling, VA: Kogan Page Ltd.

Jeffs, T. (2010). Assistive technologies and innovative learning tool. In R. M. Gargiulo & D. Metcalf (Eds.), *Teaching in today's inclusive classroom: A universal design for learning approach* (pp. 153–177). Belmont, CA: Wadsworth.

Jensen, E. (2000). *Brain-based learning.* San Diego, CA: The Brain Store.

Johnson, L., Adams Becker, S., Estrada, V., & Freeman, A. (2015). *NMC Horizon Report: 2015 K-12 Edition.* Austin, TX: The New Media Consortium.

Marzano, R. J. (2007). *The art and science of teaching: A comprehensive framework for effective instruction*. Alexandria, VA: Association for Supervision and Curriculum Development.

Meyer, A., & Rose, D. H. (2005). The future is in the margins: The role of technology and disability in educational reform. In D. H. Rose, A. Meyer, & C. Hitchcock (Eds.), *The universally designed classroom: Accessible curriculum and digital technologies* (pp. 13–35). Cambridge, MA: Harvard Education Press.

Morin, A. (2014). *At a glance: 8 key executive functions*. Retrieved from https://www.understood.org/en/learning-attention-issues/child-learning-disabilities/executive-functioning-issues/key-executive-functioning-skills-explained

National Center on Universal Design for Learning. (2014). Universal Design for Learning Guidelines. *CAST, Inc*. Retrieved from http://www.udlcenter.org/aboutudl/udlguidelines_theorypractice

National Research Council. (2000). *How people learn: Brain, mind, experience, and school*. Washington, DC: National Academy Press.

Nussbaum-Beach, S., & Hall, L. R. (2012). *The connected learner: Learning and leading in a digital age*. Bloomington, IN: Solution Tree Press.

Ostroff, W. L. (2016). *Cultivating curiosity in K-12 classrooms: How to promote and sustain deep learning*. Alexandria, VA: ASCD.

Owston, R. (2009). Digital immersion, teacher learning and games. *Educational Researcher*, *38*(4), 270–273. doi:10.3102/0013189X09336673

Pavlov, I. P. (1927). *Conditioned reflexes: An investigation of the physiological activity of the cerebral cortex*. Oxford University Press. Retrieved from http://search.alexanderstreet.com.ezproxy.fau.edu/view/work/bibliographic_entity%7Cbibliographic_details%7C2300567#page/3/mode/1/chapter/bibliographic_entity%7Cdocument%7C2300571

Prensky, M. (2010). Teaching digital natives: Partnering for real learning. Thousand Oaks, CA: Corwin.

Reinhart, J. M., Thomas, E., & Toriskie, J. M. (2011). K-12 teachers: Technology and the second level digital divide. *Journal of Instructional Psychology*, *38*(3 & 4), 181–193.

Rosen, L. D. (2011). Teaching the iGeneration. *Educational Leadership*, *68*(5), 10–15. Retrieved from http://www.ascd.org/publications/educational-leadership/feb11/vol68/num05/Teaching-the-iGeneration.aspx

Ruggiero, D., & Mong, C. J. (2015). The teacher technology integration experience: Practice and reflection in the classroom. *Journal of Information Technology Education: Research*, *14*(24), 161–178.

Schunk, D. (2004). *Learning theories: An educational perspective* (4th ed.). Upper Saddle River, NJ: Pearson Education, Inc.

Skinner, B. F. (1968). *The technology of teaching*. New York, NY: Meredith Corporation Appleton-Century-Crofts Educational Division.

Sopko, K. M. (2009). Universal design for learning: Policy challenges and recommendations. In D. T. Gordon, J. A. Gravel, & L. A. Schifter (Eds.), *A policy reader in universal design for learning* (pp. 93–107). Cambridge, MA: Harvard Education Press.

Stahl, S. (2008). Transforming the textbook to improve learning. In D. H. Rose & A. Meyer (Eds.), *A practical reader in universal design for learning* (pp. 103–132). Cambridge, MA: Harvard Education Press.

Sutherland-Smith, W. (2002). Weaving the literacy web: Changes in reading from page to screen. *The Reading Teacher, 55*(7), 662–669.

Sutton, B., & Basiel, A. S. (2014) *Teaching and learning online: New models of learning for a connected world* (Vol. 2). New York: NY: Routledge, Taylor & Francis Group. Retrieved from http://site.ebrary.com/lib/floridaatlantic/reader.action?docID=10752675

U.S. Department of Education, Office of Educational Technology. (2016). *Future Ready Learning: Reimagining the Role of Technology in Education.* Retrieved from http://tech.ed.gov/netp/introduction/

U.S. Department of Education (U.S. D.O.E), Office of Special Education Programs. (2004). *National Instructional Materials Accessibility Standards (NIMAS). Individuals with Disabilities Act 2004.* Retrieved from http://idea.ed.gov/explore/view/p/%2Croot%2Cdynamic%2CTopicalBrief%2C12%2C

Vygotsky, L. S., Davidov, V., & Silverman, R. J. (1997). *Educational psychology.* Boca Raton, FL: St. Lucie Press.

Wiggins, G., & McTighe, J. (2007). *School by design: Mission, action, and achievement.* Alexandria, VA: Association for Supervision & Curriculum Development.

KEY TERMS AND DEFINITIONS

Brain-Based Learning: Learning that connects the functions of the brain as an optimal way of learning.

Connected Learner: A student that is digitally collaborating with their peers.

Connected Teacher: A teacher that collaborates with fellow teachers.

Digital Divide: A groups of students that do not have access to technology.

Digital Native: An individual that has been born in the age of technology.

Digital User Divide: A lack of creative use of technology by students such that they become passive learners through observation only.

Engagement: A point at which a student is interested and becomes an active participant in their learning.

iGeneration: Interchangeable with a digital native. A person born within the age of technology.

Learning Theories: Philosophies of how learning happens.

Multiple Literacies: A variety of ways that individuals can access and share information.

Partnering Pedagogy: The philosophy that both the teacher and the student partner together for learning to occur.

Teaching-Learning Process (TLP): The instruction, feedback, and assessment loop that results in learning.

Technology Rich Environments: A learning environment that promotes the use of technology based on the students interests and skills and not based on teacher selection or district provided technology.

Universal Design for Learning: A framework designed to support all learners by providing option in how material is presented, how student share their knowledge, and how students engage in learning.

Web 2.0 Tool: A technology tool available through the internet that provides a way for students to demonstrate their knowledge and collaborate with their peers.

Chapter 12
Systematic Approach for Improving Accessibility and Usability in Online Courses

Devrim Ozdemir
Des Moines University, USA

Vanessa Preast
Des Moines University, USA

Pamela Ann Duffy
Des Moines University, USA

ABSTRACT

The purpose of this chapter is to provide a systematic approach for improving accessibility and usability in online courses. Accessibility and usability are of particular importance to provide equal human development opportunities to those who have various disabilities in the digital age. The authors developed a systematic approach as a result of a comprehensive accessibility and usability review process of an actual online course. The review involved a team-based collaborative approach. The team consisted of an accessibility professional, an instructional design coordinator, and a course instructor who collaborated to perform the thorough examination process. The presented model is of particular importance to improve accessibility and usability of online courses, which in turn enhances the quality of human development for disabled learners.

INTRODUCTION

Online education promises to bring people levels of independence unparalleled in history. In Fall of 2014, around 5.8 million higher education students in the United States took one or more online education courses (Allen, Seaman, Poulin, & Straut, 2016). People no longer need to feel limited by geography or even physical ability to meet their requirements for intellectual development. Online education can have potential opportunities that traditional education systems fail to provide, but people with disabilities can-

DOI: 10.4018/978-1-5225-2838-8.ch012

not benefit when online education is not completely accessible. Disabilities impacting online learning include visual, hearing, motor, and cognitive impairments (Crow, 2008).

Specific guidelines, laws, regulations and recommended best practices for accessibility are abundant. For example, the World Wide Web Consortium (W3C) developed comprehensive standards for making web content accessible to people with disabilities. The current version is the Web Content Accessibility Guidelines 2.0 (WCAG) (W3C, 2008). WCAG 2.0 provides principle-centered guidelines to help web designers verify their sites meet the standard ("WebAIM: Quick Reference - Web Accessibility Principles," n. d.). Even with these resources available, the literature on accessibility in online education paints a grim picture for the future.

Accessibility initiatives often lose momentum and lack systematic design. In many other cases, taking proper measures to improve accessibility in online courses still does not make these courses usable for the students. Iwarsson and Stahl (2003) stated "accessibility is a necessary precondition for usability" but is not sufficient to ensure usability, which is a subjective measure (p. 62). Usable online courses must not only comply with official accessibility technical standards but also they must provide a satisfactory experience for the student interacting with the environment. Online course designers accomplish this by using expert reviews (Lewis, Yoder, Riley, So, & Yusufali, 2007), end-user tests (Fichten, Asuncion, Barile, Ferraro, & Wolforth, 2009), and automated technologies (Schmetzke, 2001).

This chapter demonstrates a systematic approach to improving accessibility and usability in online courses based on the authors' preliminary analysis on a selected online course. The approach proposes a systematic process which will assure that every individual online course is accessible and usable for all students. This approach may guide other stakeholders who directly or indirectly involved in accessibility and usability within online education. Compliance officers, learning management system (LMS) administrators, faculty development personnel, course instructors, multimedia development specialists, instructional designers, and program administrators may benefit from the proposed approach because improving accessibility and usability of online education requires a team effort.

The proposed systematic approach can benefit a broad range of online courses because it is independent of the instructional technologies, the content domain, and the learner characteristics. This chapter provides online education stakeholders a proactive and sustainable process to make online courses accessible and usable for those who have disabilities.

Background

Equal access to online education opportunities is critical for human development. Persons with disabilities require accessible and usable digital experiences to participate fully in our digital society. Unless we provide accessible and usable online environments, we leave significant portions of our population at a disadvantage. The inaccessibility impacts each of us personally because anyone, at any time, can develop disabilities through aging, disease or trauma.

Higher education institutions encounter three major challenges when providing accessible and usable online learning opportunities. First, institutions may not recognize the magnitude of the problem because the documented disabilities under-represent the actual number of students with disabilities in our classes. Many disabled students in higher education prefer not to disclose their disability for various reasons. According to Brault (2012), "approximately 56.7 million (18.7 percent) of the civilian non-institutionalized population had a disability in 2010" (p. 4) in the United States. Sixty percent of the young adults with disabilities continued to postsecondary education within eight years of leaving high school (Newman et al., 2011). Twenty-eight percent of them informed the postsecondary schools about their disability during their postsecondary education (Newman et al., 2011). Because a reactive approach provides special accommodations upon request by students who disclose their disability, it serves a small fraction of the student body who might be at a disadvantage. Undisclosed student disability leaves many stakeholders in higher education unaware of the actual population of disabled students in their institutions. By designing our learning environments to be accessible and usable, we give more students equal opportunity while removing the burden from students to disclose.

Second, higher education lacks a systematic approach to accessibility and fails to take responsibility for accessibility initiatives. Thus, students with disabilities in higher education experience gaps in services or resources. According to Newman et al., (2011), only nineteen percent of the students who informed the postsecondary schools about their disability received accommodations from their school. Perhaps students did not receive accommodations due to institutions' inadequate approaches to accessibility. In 2013, a survey of 225 higher education institutions in the United States and Canada revealed that at least half of the institutions did not have a systematic way to approach accessibility issues in online education and lacked consensus about who was responsible for ensuring accessibility in online education (Poulin, 2013). Institutions assigned responsibility for accessibility to various parties ranging from the course instructor to the college. Many schools directed the responsibility to one authority rather than a team effort, which could be more efficient. Since these numbers were not much different from the 2011 survey results (Poulin, 2013), the situation may not be improving. The haphazard approach to accessibility may contribute to the poor digital accessibility outcomes in higher education. A study in 2007 reviewed 99 instructional websites and found 87% of them were non-compliant with Section 508 standards (Lewis et al., 2007). Another longitudinal study examining higher education websites found that accessibility issues increase as the websites become more complex (Hackett & Parmanto, 2005). In particular, video conferencing tools, online quizzes, and Adobe Flash™ content were inaccessible to blind students using a particular LMS (Fichten et al., 2009).

Third, higher education lacks effective enforcement mechanisms to increase accountability for accessibility. Two national civil rights laws currently put pressure on higher education regarding accessibility in the U.S. The Americans with Disabilities Act (ADA) prohibits discrimination based on disability anywhere within the United States ("2010 ADA regulations," 2016). The Rehabilitation Act of 1973 "prohibits discrimination on the basis of disability in programs run by federal agencies; programs that receive federal financial assistance; in federal employment; and in the employment practices of federal contractors" ("Rehabilitation Act of 1973," 2016). Section 504 of the Rehabilitation Act of 1973 extends this law to higher education institutions receiving federal financial assistance through student loans and federal research grants. Section 508 of the Act provides certain regulations on the development, procurement, maintenance, or use of electronic and information technology for federal agencies in the United States; the United States Access Board is responsible for developing and maintaining the electronic and information technology accessibility standards ("Section 508 Standards - United States Access Board," 2016). Although these laws exist, Wentz, Jaeger, and Lazar (2011) argue that the wording of current laws provide unenforceable gaps inherent in the "undue burden" clauses. These clauses excuse institutions from making proactive accessibility improvements if those approaches create excessive burdens on its regular operations. In undue burden areas, the institution only provides alternative means in reaction to direct requests for accommodation ("Section 508 Standards - United States Access Board," n.d.). Due to inevitable delays between requesting accommodation and receiving alternative means, this reactive approach creates unequal educational opportunities for students with disabilities. (Wentz et al., 2011). If the content were already accessible, the students with disabilities would not need to ask for accommodations and would not experience any delays or interruptions to their learning. Additionally, the institution would not need to scramble to quickly adapt the content upon request if they had thoughtfully designed the online education from the beginning.

In summary, today's higher education institutions face several obstacles related to accessibility initiatives. First, they are working from inaccurate information about disability numbers on their campuses. Second, they lack consensus about who is responsible for developing accessible online education. Moreover, most institutions do not have a systematic approach to enacting and enforcing accessibility in online education. Third, existing laws may not effectively address accessibility within online education. These challenges leave institutions uncertain about their obligations and leave students with gaps in access.

To address these concerns, the authors for this chapter propose a systematic, proactive approach inspired from the "Universal Design for Instruction (UDI)" model, which provides equal opportunities for all students regardless of their individual differences. This approach considers accessibility and usability to be a core standard for high-quality online courses. The authors recommend that each online course undergoes an accessibility and usability review before it is released to any students, whether or not students with disabilities are enrolled. Furthermore, the authors recommend that stakeholders integrate the accessibility and usability reviews into their existing continuous quality improvement procedures. This way, designing for accessibility is a routine, clearly defined process, not an add-on.

Universal design for instruction adapts the universal design principles identified by the Center for Universal Design at North Carolina State University. The Universal Design Principles focus on making physical environments and products maximally usable for all people without the need for accommodation ("The Center for Universal Design - Universal Design Principles," 2016). Burgstahler (2009) coined "universal design for instruction (UDI)" when she applied the universal design principles to instruction. She explained how UDI could "maximize the learning of students with a wide range of characteristics by applying universal design principles to all aspects of instruction" (p. 1). Applied to the online environment, UDI ensures courses are maximally usable for all students without needing to provide alternative content or accommodations. This approach benefits students with undisclosed disabilities because the inclusive design allows more individuals to learn from the same instructional experiences.

Fortunately, online course developers have tools and resources that can support a more proactive approach. Most important among these is the web content standards that W3C provides in WCAG 2.0. W3C base the standards on the principles that all web content should be perceivable, operable, understandable, and robust (W3C, 2008). W3C also organize the recommendations as testable success criteria statements within twelve guidelines, which "provide the basic goals that authors should work toward in order to make content more accessible to users with different disabilities" (W3C, 2008). The success criteria fall into three conformance levels: Level A (lowest), AA, and AAA (highest). Conforming at a particular level means meeting all the success criteria within that level and the lower level(s). Higher conformance levels should make the content accessible to a wider range of people with disabilities, but it is possible for content to conform at the highest level and still not be accessible to every individual with disabilities. WCAG 2.0 is a very comprehensive and highly technical guide which could intimidate those unfamiliar with web design or the accessibility field. To make identifying and interpreting WCAG 2.0 violations easier, the authors recommend higher education institutions utilize automated accessibility checking software and quick reference guides as appropriate. Institutions can also use accessibility-focused academic, non-profit, and private entities, which provide accessibility analysis services and training or participate in the accessibility conversations occurring in listservs, social media, professional organizations, and accessibility conferences.

The organizational learning and performance literature supports the authors' assertion that a proactive, systematic approach based on UDI can sustainably integrate accessibility into online learning. Successful systems include collaboration, feedback loops, stakeholder participation, openness to new perspectives, and ability to recognize system interactions and interdependencies (Argyris & Schon, 1995; Davis, Dent, & Wharff, 2015; Senge, 1994). The University of Central Florida structured their institution-wide accessibility initiative using an effective systematic approach. Their Online Course Accessibility Support Model has three pillars: Universal Design for Learning, Proactive Requests, and Immediate Need (Bastedo, Sugar, Swenson, & Vargas, 2013). The first pillar involves training faculty about UDI, so they incorporate the principles into their course design from the beginning (Bastedo et al., 2013). The second pillar occurs when faculty proactively request an accessibility review to help them improve the course before students request accommodations. The last pillar occurs when a student requests an accommodation and multiple offices within the institution work together to make the course accessible or provide the accommodation. A UDI approach emphasizes the first and second pillars to minimize the need for the third. Without a systematic, proactive approach to accessibility, many institutions today default to the third pillar, which is less efficient and effective than preventing problems in the first place. Based on this model, the preliminary analysis described in this chapter results from a proactive request because the course instructor sought assistance revising an existing course to improve accessibility before students requested accommodations.

For maximum sustainability, the authors recommend integrating accessibility into the institution's continuous quality improvement process. One example might be a Quality Matters (QM) Course Design Review rubric. QM is a well-known non-profit organization in online education ("Quality Matters Program," 2013). The QM rubric includes some accessibility standards which institutions should apply to all online courses before releasing them to the students. QM also published an online course accessibility policy template which describes the various considerations for accessibility initiatives, including budgets, resources, procurement, and stakeholder roles and responsibilities (Frey, Kearns, & King, 2012). Some components, such as procurement, likely occur at an institutional level and may require a top-down approach for implementation, which is outside the scope of this chapter. However, the authors' proposed approach could provide guidance to the stakeholders from a mid-level or bottom-up manner. The advantage of this approach is that the institutions could implement it anywhere as long as the stakeholders are in agreement.

THE PRELIMINARY ACCESSIBILITY AND USABILITY ANALYSIS

The authors developed the proposed proactive and systematic approach based on a preliminary accessibility and usability analysis of an actual online course. The overall purpose was to analyze an actual online course against the WCAG 2.0 AA success criteria. The results answered some questions about improving the accessibility and usability of existing online courses.

Preliminary Analysis Context

The preliminary analysis was conducted within a university setting which the institution values inclusiveness and embraces "a culture of diversity that accepts and respects the unique characteristics of each individual" (Des Moines University, 2016). Because of this institutional value, authors' university developed the *Digital Information and Services Accessibility Policy* to support its commitment to providing an inclusive environment for students, employees, and guests. This policy established WCAG 2.0 AA (W3C, 2008) as the standard for accessible online content. With this policy in place, the institution began to identify and remove barriers to assure consistent access for everyone, including people with disabilities.

The authors' institution took several steps to implement digital accessibility across the institution. They hired an accessibility professional to lead the initiative. They also formed an advisory group consisting of diverse stakeholders including content consumers with disabilities, content producers, human resources, procurement, risk management, and central administration. Implementation began with several preliminary analyses in different areas across the institution. These focused on developing relationships, processes, and guidelines which could inform future accessibility endeavors at the institution. One such preliminary analysis included the online course analysis that is the focus of this chapter.

A team involving an Instructional Design Coordinator (IDC), an Accessibility Professional (AP) and the course instructor (CI) worked together to analyze one online course. The AP led the accessibility analysis and consulted with the CI and the IDC whenever needed. The team and its members had mutually beneficial goals regarding this project. The AP wanted to identify typical accessibility issues for online courses at the University and to establish some processes to help all online instructors make their courses more accessible. The IDC wanted to experience the entire process of revising an online course to meet WCAG 2.0 AA level. In the meantime, the IDC can understand the accessibility-assurance process to assist faculty when they apply the process to their online course design and development. The CI wanted to change the course design and delivery to meet the WCAG accessibility standards and to learn how to apply Universal Design to all her courses. As a departmental curriculum committee member, the CI also wanted to share her knowledge with the department and plan how to implement accessibility throughout the entire curriculum. With individualized assistance from the IDC and the AP, the CI could develop her course and plan training options for departmental faculty and staff. The team members all hoped that the relationships forged in this process would encourage others in the institution to engage in building accessible courses.

The team carefully selected the course that would feature within the preliminary analysis. The IDC recommended the course, *Overview of the U.S. Health Care System*, for several reasons. Based on his experience consulting with instructors for each course in the program curriculum, the IDC was confident about the quality of this course. The instructor had participated in a peer review process using a public domain version of QM rubric. The program offered this course as a required course for all students every semester. For years, the course consistently received positive feedback about the content, delivery, and instruction. Knowing that the course would not undergo revisions to the objectives or design, the team agreed this course was a reliable starting point for the project.

This 12-week course existed entirely within the LMS. The course template design which included most of the course content consisted of a course homepage and content section. When students entered the course, they first saw the course homepage, which contained announcements, calendar, and resources. The students could access their course materials within the content section. The content section contained a side menu with tabs for the Overview, the course preparation module, and each of the twelve weekly modules. The Overview contained a course description and "Course Tour," an instructor-led review video of course components. The Course Preparation module contained activities and material to help the student be successful in the course. Each weekly module contained the instructional materials for the topic that week. Modules 1 through 12 used a consistent organization for content. Each started with a student progress checklist built within the LMS checklist tool. Microsoft (MS) PowerPoint presentations communicate the weekly lecture content. Additional resources, such as external videos, journal articles, or reports, supported the module's topic. All weekly modules contained scheduled synchronous instant message chats with the instructor and asynchronous discussions. Some modules included quizzes and Dropbox assignments.

The CI started the course by posting a welcome message in an announcement widget on the course homepage. The announcement directed students to the Overview in the content section. The students began by completing a checklist within the "Course Preparation" module. They introduced themselves to classmates within the discussion board. They read the course readiness task list and reviewed the course syllabus. After completing the course preparation module, students began the weekly modules. Checklists allowed students to make sure they completed all required tasks, including reading and assignments. Students could participate in the instant message chats to communicate with the instructor and classmates in real time. They could submit their written papers in the dropboxes and complete their online quizzes within the LMS.

Preliminary Analysis Approach

The team identified the course components which were most common for online courses. The AP conducted the analysis in three stages which started with the most wide-reaching content and moved towards the most course-specific content. Within these stages, the AP used the institution's established automated and manual accessibility review procedures to review the content at that level. In this way, the team could begin addressing issues affecting all users as soon as possible, even as the more course-specific analysis was ongoing. Figure 1 demonstrates the stages of the accessibility analysis.

Figure 1. Preliminary analysis stages

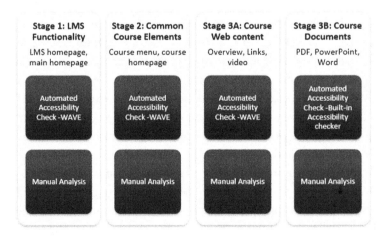

Ultimately, the test for accessibility is whether a person with disabilities can use the system and content. Accessibility testing emulates how individuals with various physical and cognitive disabilities use the content with the aim to identify potential barriers. Accessibility testing frequently combines both automated and manual testing because automated testing alone is insufficient. For web-based content, WebAIM has developed a quick reference on *Testing Web Content for Accessibility* (WebAIM, 2015a), which provides steps for evaluating online course accessibility. This resource informed the institution's accessibility testing procedures with web content. The National Center on Disability and Access to Education created some guides to help people identify common accessibility problems in documents (The National Center on Disability and Access to Education, 2016). These resources informed the institution's accessibility testing procedures for Word, PowerPoint, and PDF files.

The automated approach involves using software to analyze the web page code and stand-alone electronic documents for accessibility. These tools are essential because some code on the website or features within a document may be invisible to sighted visitors, but this code may influence how assistive technology, like screen readers, interprets the content for people with disabilities. For web content, the software can identify issues such as valid HTML, form labels, heading levels, alt text, and color contrast. The AP used the WAVE Chrome browser plugin (WebAIM, 2015b) as the primary automated web content analysis because it provides both accessibility and usability information on any web page currently visible in the browser. To run the analysis, the AP opened the web page in the Chrome browser and activated the WAVE tool. Within a few minutes, the accessibility checker shows a window with the accessibility statistics. For stand-alone electronic documents, software like MS Word, MS PowerPoint, and Adobe Acrobat have built-in accessibility checkers. These accessibility checkers can identify issues such as alt text, heading levels, and table settings. For the automated document analyses, the AP used the built-in accessibility checkers within MS Office and Adobe Acrobat. To run automated analyses on Word or PowerPoint files, AP loaded the file within MS Word 2016 or MS PowerPoint 2016. AP then opened the Accessibility Checker tool. This tool opened a window listing the inspection results categorized as Errors, Warnings or Tips. To run automated analyses on PDF files, AP loaded the file within Adobe Acrobat XI Pro and activated the "Accessibility Full Check" tool. This tool generated an accessibility status report with seven categories (document, page, form, alternative text, tables, lists, and headings).

The manual approach involves a human reviewer inspecting the content to identify problems that the automated approach may have missed. For instance, an automated accessibility checker can identify the presence or absence of alternative text in code for an image, but a human reviewer must decide if the actual message in the alternative text is appropriate for communicating the intended message. For the manual process, the AP first reviewed the results from the automated checker to verify whether the flagged issues are accessibility problems. She then simulated how a user with disabilities might experience the content. The following components are similar for web and document analysis:

- Verify the alternative text is appropriate
- Enlarge the text up to 200% zoom to mimic a low-vision user's experience with scaling content
- Review all multimedia to ensure captions and transcripts are present and accurate for students with auditory disabilities
- Look at all links to make sure the hyperlinked text makes sense even if read out-of-context from the surrounding text
- Make sure colored text has another way to indicate meaning in addition to color, such as bold for emphasized content

- Make sure that students can pause all videos because videos that play immediately upon visiting the page can interfere with students' ability to use the site.
- Navigate the content with only the keyboard to replicate the experience for someone with low mobility.
- Navigate the content with only keyboard and the NonVisual Desktop Access (Teh & Curran, n.d.) screen reader to replicate the experience for someone with blindness.

Since the automated analysis tools within documents do not analyze color contrast, the manual process for documents also included a visual scan to ensure color contrast was sufficient for individuals with low vision.

In Stage 1, the AP analyzed the LMS functionality first because accessibility issues here would affect all users. Additionally, fixing the issues here was more centralized, since only the LMS vendor or the institution's LMS administrators could modify components such as the LMS login page, landing page, and system tools. Thus, identifying and addressing these accessibility issues first was most efficient because the fixes have the broadest impact with least effort. AP used the web content automated and manual analysis methods described above to review the LMS login page, institutional LMS home page, and institutional LMS menu system.

In Stage 2, the AP analyzed common course elements such as the course homepage and course menu format which tends to be similar across courses within a department. Since these were editable by instructors or academic assistants, fixes here involved more people, but the fixes applied to the entire program across multiple courses. Thus, this was the next most efficient way to apply effort. The AP used the web content automated and manual analysis methods described above to review the course home page, course menu, and LMS tools utilized in the course (Discussion boards, DropBox, Checklist, Quiz, Classlist, Chat)

In Stage 3, the AP analyzed the course specific content within the course, including both the web-based content and the documents. Course content varied from instructor to instructor and fixes occurred at an individual course level. Because this course specific content was unique and it made up the largest quantity of material, it was the most challenging part of the online education to make accessible in an efficient way. Each instructor would need to address each piece of content within their courses, which meant we needed to equip each instructor with the skills and resources necessary. The AP analyzed the web-based course content (course overview, embedded videos, and links) using the web-content automated and manual processes described above. The AP analyzed the PowerPoint, Word, and PDF files using the automated and manual processes for documents.

Preliminary Analysis Results

The AP reported the accessibility analysis findings in three categories: web-content issues according to WCAG 2.0, web content usability issues, and accessibility issues in the documents.

Issues Affecting Accessibility According to WCAG 2.0 Level AA

Although the analysis included all guidelines, the authors only reported violations to the applicable standards.

1. **Guideline 1.1 Text Alternatives:** *Provide text alternatives for any non-text content so that it can be changed into other forms people need, such as large print, braille, speech, symbols or simpler language. (W3C, 2008)*
   a. The random image on the login page has the alternative text of "Random Image," which is not meaningful. The alternative text is the information that a screen reader hears when focused on the image, table or graph. This text should concisely describe the image according to its intended meaning. In some cases, it is appropriate to mark the image as purely decorative so the screen reader would skip it entirely.
   b. Form field labels are critical, so individuals using screen readers know what they are supposed to enter into the field. Fortunately, the student view of the landing page was more accessible than the instructor view. The instructor view had several search form fields, which all provided more generic "search" instructions even though each searches a different area of the LMS. This situation could make harder for a screen-reader user to select the desired search box.

2. **Guideline 1.2 Time-based Media:** *Provide alternatives for time-based media. (W3, 2008)*
   a. The video used for the course tour did not have synchronized captions. The video would need captions.

3. **Guideline 1.3 Adaptable:** *Create content that can be presented in different ways (for example simpler layout) without losing information or structure. (W3C, 2008)*
   a. The course appeared to meet this guideline partially. The navigation order was logical. The instructions did not seem to rely on shape, size, auditory cues or visual location alone to complete tasks.
   b. The accessibility checkers did identify form elements without labels and table headings. The vendor should review the markup to ensure the code meets accessibility guidelines.

4. **Guideline 1.4 Distinguishable:** *Make it easier for users to see and hear content including separating foreground from background. (W3C, 2008)*
   a. The color contrast does not meet the minimum contrast ratio of 4.5:1 in many places throughout the LMS. The most problematic issue is that all links throughout the system default to no underline. The links are blue-green (#287993), the body text is dark gray (#353535), the background is white (#FFFFFF). The contrast between the link and background or the body text and background passes. However, there is not enough contrast between the link color and body text color. Links are tough to distinguish from surrounding text. Other color contrast errors include light text over a complex background image on the login page and widgets that use colored text, which does not contrast sufficiently with the background.
   b. In some places, the content author used colored text alone to emphasize the point. Some people may not be able to distinguish between colors and would miss the emphasis. Thus, it is best to add other styling features such as bold or italics in addition to color.
   c. The HTML editor within the LMS allows users to select font sizes, but the editor codes the text with an absolute, not relative, font size. The LMS also allows users to select their default text sizes within the system. When the user changes the personal account settings, the LMS will not alter the size of text coded with absolute sizing. Thus, the user would not benefit from changing the account settings. (Note, the content will scale when using the browser zoom.)
   d. One image within a widget contained an excessive amount of text. Content authors should avoid images of text. The text within the image is not available to a screen reader without

alternative text for the image. Additionally, the image can pixelate and become hard to read when enlarged.

5. **Guideline 2.1 Keyboard Accessible:** *Make all functionality available from a keyboard. (W3C, 2008)*

    a. The course tour video opened in a new window for the third-party streaming video player. The video interface appeared only after allowing mixed content. There was no initial focus indicator to indicate that focus automatically started on the video play button, but pressing enter would launch the video. Video player controls were available to keyboard users after starting the video. The keyboard controls skipped over the help menu item. This situation means that a sighted keyboard user might have challenges accessing the video and the video help.

    b. Keyboard accessibility varied by the browser for certain features. The document viewer was completely keyboard-accessible when using Mozilla Firefox, but Google Chrome and Internet Explorer had some limitations. Navigating the Quiz tool also functioned slightly differently between browsers. In Google Chrome, the tab key jumped between question groups and save buttons and the arrow keys moved within question groups. In Firefox, the tab button would also allow the user cycle through each answer choice.

6. **Guideline 2.4 Navigable:** *Provide ways to help users navigate, find content, and determine where they are. (W3C, 2008)*

    a. The menu on the landing page within the LMS has no visible focus indicator, so it is hard or impossible to know which menu item is active when navigating the site using a keyboard. This situation makes it difficult for someone to choose the desired menu item.

    b. The tab order for some content does not make sense. On the login screen, the focus moves automatically to the username, password form fields, which is convenient. However, other content on the page, including the link to the "System Check" is accessed only after the tabbing cycles back through the browser menu. A screen reader user may not realize there is more content on the screen and may not access "the system check".

    c. The content of at least one widget on the landing page has multiple empty links and some redundant links. This situation can cause confusion for keyboard and screen reader users.

    d. The link text was not as clear as it could be in some places. For example, the hyperlink might be a filename. Avoid ambiguous text that does not make sense out of context because it can cause confusion, especially when screen reader users skip from link to link.

7. **Guideline 3.2 Predictable:** *Make Web pages appear and operate in predictable ways. (W3C, 2008)*

    a. Within the course, the navigation menu met the guideline. The navigation links remained in the same location and retained the same function everywhere on the course site. Instructors are encouraged to adopt a standardized navigation menu for all courses within a program so students can quickly orient themselves when moving between courses.

    b. In some places, a link would open a new window without alerting the user. For example, the instructor-generated content included a link to the course tour, which opened in a new tab. Also, the links to external resources were set to open in a new window. Users who expect content to appear in the same tab could become disoriented when the link opens in a new window.

    c. The LMS may offer a different interface depending on how a user accessed the tool. For example, accessing the Chat tool through the Content did not have an "exit chat" button, but this button is present when accessing Chat through the menu. Additionally, students had more options available, including access to logged chats if they used the menu link rather than the content link. This inconsistency can confuse students and instructors.

8. **Guideline 3.3 Input Assistance**: *Help users avoid and correct mistakes. (W3C, 2008)*
   a. The system partially meets this guideline. Upon submitting a quiz, the tool links to questions that had no responses. How the screen reader read the warning depending on the browser; NVDA read the warning instructions with Firefox but not Chrome. The LMS would also alert the user where there are updates on the course.

9. **Guideline 4.1 Compatible:** *Maximize compatibility with current and future user agents, including assistive technologies. (W3C, 2008)*
   a. The W3C Markup Validation Service (https://validator.w3.org/) identified some errors in the code for the LMS login and a few selected course pages. Assistive technologies are more likely to function well when the code is valid. Software coders are strongly encouraged to ensure their code validates.

Web-Based Usability Issues That Affect Accessibility

The team identified some usability issues which might affect accessibility. WCAG 2.0 guidelines did not address these usability issues. The issues were as follows:

1. The landing page in LMS included very long lists of links to resources. There was also no built-in search. The links to certain tools on the main navigation bar were not functional. For example, the bar included links to Dropbox, Quizzes, and Self Assessments, none of which needed to be active at this level of the system. This situation either produced an error or took users to places within the system that they did not need to access. It could be confusing to include menu items that the user did not need to use.
2. Some of the widgets use underlining as a styling feature. On the web, underlines often signal linked text. It is best to reserve underlines for links and to use other styles, such as bold or italics, to differentiate text. If the underlined text was intended to be a heading, consider adding it to the heading structure at an appropriate level.
3. Some links to non-HTML documents do not alert the user the link opens or downloads a document. Non-HTML files like PDF, Word or PowerPoint documents may require a user to have a separate program installed on their computer or may change the way they access the content. To limit confusion, either the LMS or the content developer needs to alert the viewer about the file type within the link.

File-Based Accessibility Issues

The team identified the following file-based issues which might affect accessibility:

1. Instructors tended to generate the bulk of their course content in the form of standalone document files (Word, PDF, and PowerPoint). Any file uploaded to a website or online course needed to be accessible.

2. The accessibility issues in the Word documents were related to using tables to accomplish a certain aesthetic layout rather than their intended purpose of organizing data in rows and columns. The syllabus was structured almost entirely within tables, sometimes with tables within tables. At times, tabs or carriage returns were used within a table to suggest a new row visually. This design produced a confusing experience for screen readers. The document was also missing headings, which are an important navigational feature.

3. The accessibility issues within the PowerPoint file mostly related to missing alternative text and titles. In some cases, there were additional text boxes added to the basic slide layout. This situation can change the reading order for the content, so the result that a screen reader reads may not be what the instructor intended.

SOLUTIONS AND RECOMMENDATIONS

This section summarizes the authors' solutions to improve the accessibility and usability in the selected online course after the preliminary analysis. The analysis results clearly indicated the need for a systematic approach which authors also recommended in this section.

Institutional Level Solutions

The AP documented the accessibility challenges and provided suggested fixes. She met with several groups according to the issues that they had the ability to fix. First, the team met with a representative from the IT department to discuss the issues relating to the LMS login, landing page, and generic system interface. IT department worked with the vendor and the LMS system administrator resided in this department. In the meeting, the AP demonstrated the accessibility challenges and explained how to fix them. She offered to speak directly to the vendor to discuss issues with the system itself. She also offered to work with the LMS administrator to redesign the landing page and menus to improve accessibility and usability. Fixing these issues would affect everyone because everyone accessed the login page and the landing page in the LMS.

Due to the editing restrictions, several major issues on the login and landing pages required institutional support to resolve. These included suspicious alternative text for an image, insufficient color contrast, menu items without focus indicators, suspicious tab order, and problems with form labels. For the image, the administrator would need to provide meaningful alternative text or code it as null if it was purely decorative. Because links defaulted to having no underline in the LMS, they were tough to distinguish as links. The most straightforward fix was for the vendor or administrator to allow links to have underlined by default. Linked headings and menu items could be exempt. The IT department could fix the menu focus indicators using on the landing page the "navigation bar" design tool. They would merely need to enable the box to outline each menu item when receiving focus. The landing page had several form fields that all say the same thing when activated, so it was hard to distinguish one search box from another. This fix would probably require the software manufacturer to edit their underlying system code to add unique form labels. Fortunately, this issue only appeared in the instructor view, as students did not see the affected widgets. If those widgets were not essential for instructors, the administrators could hide them from the instructor view. It was possible that the tab order on the login page is part of the LMS code, so the vendor might need to make sure the tab sequence would clearly allow the user to cycle through page content right after the fields associated with the login.

The overall page organization and the widget contents on the landing page contributed to a challenging experience for everyone but could be particularly frustrating for individuals with disabilities. The LMS administrator needed to work with an instructional designer and accessibility expert to design a user-friendly, accessible landing page, to identify the most critical components according to user testing data, and to use the data to select menu items and reorganize content. Perhaps the administrator could move the extensive list of resources to a searchable help system and could retain what is necessary on the front page. Therefore, users would quickly learn to ignore it all. The widgets also must be appropriately formatted to avoid color contrast issues, redundant links, broken links and underlines on the non-hyperlinked text.

Some issues, such as the text size scaling has multiple solution options. A system-wide solution was for the vendor to code the HTML editor tool so that the font sizes were relative and that it warned editors when they chose less accessible font types or sizes. In the meantime, the institution would need to advise everyone using the HTML editor to avoid changing font size using the font size tool. Individuals who knew code could use the HTML Source Editor to enter relative text sizing as inline CSS, but most LMS users would not know the code.

The third-party systems that integrate with courses must also be accessible. The current streaming video interface had challenges with keyboard access to all components, color contrast, focus indicators, tab order, and alternative text. IT would need to work with the vendor to fix the accessibility challenges or select a more accessible streaming video interface tool for instructional videos.

Overall, the LMS required more clicks than expected to get to necessary features. Also, the way that students and instructors accessed tools could influence the interface they experience. For example, accessing the chat through the menu offered more choices and different chat interface than the direct link to chat within the content. This situation affected instructors building assessments and students trying to access assessments and interactive tools. IT would need to work with the vendor to encourage them to standardize their interfaces regardless of how the user accesses the tool. That way instructors and students could feel confident they were experiencing the same interface.

Degree Program Level Solutions

Next, the team met with the academic assistants for the program. The academic assistants posted content in the course home pages, so their content affected all courses in a program. The AP created accessible versions of the content from the academic assistants and provided the code for these versions. During the meeting, she demonstrated how the original and the modified versions performed with assistive technologies and simulations. She explained how to accomplish each accessibility feature in the sample. For example, she demonstrated how to use the color contrast checker built into the LMS HTML editor. In this way, the AP tried to educate these employees while also making their work easier. If the academic assistants liked the examples, they could copy and paste the sample code into an accessible template for future content. Presumably, this would decrease barriers to change and increase wiliness to create accessible content in the future.

The accessibility mostly involved readability and text-formatting choices such as insufficient color contrast, underlined text, symbols incorrectly interpreted by screen readers, and absolute font sizes. The content editors could correct these by making different styling choices. When selecting text colors, the content editor could select colors that pass the built-in contrast ratio analyzer within the color selector. The content editor could paste the text into a tool that scores readability; and, then edited the text to simplify the language and use active voice so that the message was as clear as possible. This solution included avoiding ASCII drawings because a screen reader might misinterpret these. For example, screen readers could read hyphens and greater than symbol to form arrows (e.g., -->) as "greater than" which would be confusing. When the content editor linked to the non-HTML document, this person needed to include the file type in the hyperlink text to warn the viewer. For example, the link might be worded as "Syllabus (PDF)" or "Course Overview (PowerPoint file)." Finally, the content editor could avoid pictures of text and make sure that the image has appropriate alternative text.

Individual Course Level Solutions

Finally, the team met to review content peculiar to the course. The AP arranged a series of meetings, each with a different topic, such as Word or PowerPoint. The team met to discuss the accessibility issues in the course that related to those topics. In part, these opportunities were opportunities to train the team members about accessibility. However, they also were opportunities to negotiate best practices and brainstorm ideas for future course design.

When using the HTML editor, instructors had the option to open links in the same frame or new window. If selecting the second choice, instructors were encouraged to include a warning such as "(opens in new window)" at the end of the link title. This message warned the user about the change in context and allowed them to adapt accordingly. The LMS also had a "Create a link" tool, which would add links as external items within the module. When using this tool, instructors needed to leave the "Open as External Resource" option unselected so that the link would open within the LMS. This solution provided a seamless instructional experience and provided better student progress tracking. When choosing the hyperlink title, the instructor could select the text that made sense out of context. For example, "go to the course tour for information about this course" was better than "click here for the course tour for information about this course."

Captioning the videos could be challenging, as there were not yet cost-effective technology options that combined video capture with accurate automatic captioning. Instructors were encouraged to write a script before making the video so that the video transcript was already developed and could be added to a tool like Amara or YouTube to make the captions quickly. Options with existing video might include purchasing captioning services, using speech-to-text tools, or using YouTube auto-caption then correcting the auto-captioning errors.

Instructors could use the accessibility checkers built into Microsoft Office products. These would identify many accessibility issues. Once the Word or PowerPoint document was accessible, the instructor could save as (not print to) a PDF file. This solution increased the likelihood that the resulting file would be accessible.

Using the styles and headings in Word and the layouts in PowerPoint were a good way to make a document accessible and saved time in the long run. The styles and layouts allowed instructors to make changes to the entire document's appearance very quickly. Using headings also permitted automatic table of contents and cross-references. It was important to avoid tables and floating text boxes as styling tools. It was also important to use columns to arrange information side-by-side and simple tables for tabular data.

Instructors might want to consider whether providing an accessible PowerPoint file alone provided the best learning experience. PowerPoint was designed as a live presentation aid and tended to be inadequate for sharing large quantities of information. Thus, instructors might consider making captioned video presentations supplemented with Word or PDF handouts.

A SYSTEMATIC APPROACH FOR ACCESSIBLE AND USABLE ONLINE COURSES

Based on the preliminary analysis, the authors propose the following proactive and systematic approach to accessible and usable online education. The systematic approach involves six-step cycle. After the last step, the first step needs to be revisited. The six steps are:

Step 1: Initiate / Sustain Relationships

The preliminary analysis results demonstrated that improving accessibility and usability requires continuous team effort from those who are directly or indirectly involved in online education. Cultivating relationships with key stakeholders is critical to sustainable success. The accessibility issues for generic LMS tools required the LMS administrator's involvement. The issues that the LMS vendor could resolve required information technology services support. The program assistant became involved when the team identified accessibility and usability issues with the program updates widget. Certain improvements in the course template design required the IDC. The CI needed to maintain the accessibility and usability of course specific content. At the same, the CI needed full support from the AP for developing accessible content templates. The relationships among these stakeholders was symbiotic and critical for success.

The outcomes from the preliminary analysis clearly demonstrated that faculty could not be solely responsible for accessibility in online courses. There are components within the technological tools that may be beyond their knowledge, skills, or access to fix. Accessibility initiatives require collaboration across all levels in the institution. Thus, part of the challenge is to identify all relevant stakeholders. How each stakeholder contributes may not be clear at first, but the team can invite stakeholders to the table as the preliminary analysis makes their roles clearer. Recommended roles for the initial accessibility team is presented in Table 1.

The stakeholders are probably individuals within separate institutional hierarchies or departments. The AP would have less influence using top-down command-and-control approaches because the stakeholders are peers, not subordinates. Thus, the AP may find success leading the team with a "first among equals" approach. The AP can help guide the team with a vision of what is and is not necessary and possible from an accessibility standpoint. However, the AP, and other team members, must listen to and respect each other's experiences. They are likely to devise the best plans together when they take a problem-solving approach which realistically utilizes each person's strengths and addresses each person's legitimate concerns. For example, a faculty member can bring valuable knowledge to the table regarding the classroom experience, student needs, and course content. However, that same faculty member may have little knowledge of accessibility and may fear being overwhelmed by additional activities that can add to workload. The team can honor these strengths and worries by providing time-efficient ways for the faculty member to share her knowledge and by making the accessibility improvement process straightforward and not burdensome to the faculty member. This may mean that the AP and other team members demonstrate willingness to step in, roll up their sleeves, and build accessible course components

Table 1. Relevant stakeholder roles

Role	Responsibility
Instructional Design Coordinator	• Assist course instructors with designing and developing online courses • Support course instructors while implementing online courses • Review online courses for quality assurance
Accessibility Professional	• Lead accessibility initiatives in the entire institution • Develop and disseminate accessibility policies, templates, and best practices • Collaborate with stakeholders regarding accessibility issues • Communicate and resolve accessibility issues with software vendors
Course Instructor	• Design and develop online courses • Teach online courses • Evaluate the online courses they teach • Improve the online courses they teach
LMS Administrator	• Set up the LMS to support accessibility and usability throughout the system • Collaborate with other stakeholders to maintain the accessibility of the LMS
Multimedia Development Specialist	• Provide support for accessible instructional materials

side-by-side with the instructor. Once this instructor gains skills and confidence, she may then be able to be a champion for the initiative and mentor for other faculty.

Step 2: Conduct Preliminary Analysis

The goal for the preliminary analysis is to orient the team to the accessibility and usability issues that they face. Most important is collecting sufficient data to catalog the common tools and features in the online courses and to identify relevant accessibility issues. Even though the preliminary analysis is performed on a handful of courses, the outcomes will reveal problems which could be fixed at the system level to improve all online courses. For example, the outcomes might provide insight about issues with the LMS navigation, or they might show what training and tools faculty need to ensure they use appropriate assessment practices in their courses. Automated accessibility checkers are useful instruments during this stage. It may not be sufficient to conduct the preliminary analysis on only one course when an institution lacks standardized procedures for its online education. Continue performing preliminary analyses on a few courses until the results show recurring patterns. The major overlaps between courses point to the commonalities which will be the focus areas for the next step.

Step 3: Establish Consistent Functionality and Standards

The accessibility team uses the data gathered during the preliminary analysis to establish consistent functionality across all online courses. The team needs to develop policies, standards, and templates to guide the stakeholders how to make online education accessible and usable.

The AP could provide instructors with a document containing instructions on how students can access the LMS using assistive technologies. Instructors can add this document to their course introduction so that students benefit from the accessibility tour. Programs can also include this information as part of a student orientation to the LMS.

Faculty also might benefit from resources that make accessibility changes easy to implement. Some faculty may appreciate one-page guides and checklists to ensure they have considered some of the most common accessibility issues. Some may want attractive and accessible templates for Word and PowerPoint files as a starting point. It is also possible to create some HTML templates that faculty can use when creating a new page. Instructors can use these templates when building course features such as the welcome message and course tour.

Step 4: Train Faculty and Staff to Apply Online Course Development Standards

Instructors need training to help them understand what accessibility means, in an operational sense, within their courses. However, this trainer must carefully scaffold the training activities to help the individuals learn progressively without feeling overwhelmed. Because sequencing is key, workshops may not be the most effective training strategy. In most cases, workshop attendance is voluntary, limited and haphazard. Instead, the AP could work with the department to create a more focused accessibility training series that would occur within regular department meetings. In this way, a captive audience would be present for all the sessions and the content can be tailored to departmental needs.

When designing such instruction, the materials needs to be segmented and sequenced carefully to make each session a meaningful and practical recurring segment. For example, a department might allow ten minutes at each department meeting for a year. At each session, the AP could choose a specific topic, such as heading styles or color contrast or link text, and demonstrate how these appear before and after course redesigns. During these training sessions, it is important to emphasize how to make the changes easily and how accessibility benefits faculty as well as students. Training handouts could be useful so the instructors have a tangible reminder to try the tips when returning to their offices. AP can encourage the faculty to complete specific tasks as "homework" between each session. AP can also have them share their outcomes with peers to generate a faculty learning community and to provide tangible evidence for progress on the accessibility initiative.

Other strategies for faculty training involves identifying what motivates the faculty. Some may enjoy collaborating on teaching and learning research activities with a focus on accessibility. Such scholarly endeavors can teach the faculty about accessibility, support the faculty in promotion and tenure, and increase the institution's visibility in the field. Some faculty may enjoy public recognition of their success. In this step, it is important to find ways to invite the faculty to speak about their accessibility improvement endeavors in front of their peers or acknowledge them in institutional newsletters. Other faculty may find meaning in an ongoing faculty learning community focusing on accessibility. They may enjoy learning and socializing with colleagues. It is critical to listen to their interests and facilitate opportunities to gather together and engage in meaningful learning experiences.

Step 5: Expand Implementation

Once the institution has established policies, consistent functionalities, templates, and ongoing faculty trainings, the stage is set to expand accessibility and usability improvements to all online courses. The relationships established within the community are critical for the success because every instructor needs to apply the best practices into their online courses. The AP or the team works with every academic unit to set accountability standards and a plan to improve accessibility and usability.

Step 6: Evaluate the Accessibility and Usability Outcomes

In an ideal world, the academic culture would embrace accessibility as a normal part of course design. However, most institutions are starting far from the ideal. Accessibility initiatives will inevitably take an incremental approach. This step in the process allows the team to review what did and did not work with the initiative so they can prepare to take the next steps forward. This step also involves ensuring accountability for those involved in online education. Improving accessibility and usability in online education is a continuous systematic process as depicted in Figure 2.

Just as an instructor gives a student a test to ensure that students learned the content, the institution needs measures to ensure stakeholders are applying the institution's accessibility standards. These measurements must be aligned with the institutional goals and stated standards. If an institution considers online course accessibility to be as integral to teaching as responding to students in a timely fashion or creating test questions, the measures must reflect this emphasis to ensure it occurs at the desired level. Teaching effectiveness evaluations must include accessibility. Such evaluations should provide the instructor with valuable feedback about how to improve and allow the institution to document unmet needs for the next phases in the accessibility initiative.

Measuring accessibility as an integral part of teaching effectiveness can be built into existing evaluation methods. The academic unit could include accessibility-related questions on end-of-course student evaluations. Institutions which evaluate teaching within the rank, promotion, and tenure process can include course accessibility as a component in the peer review processes. Faculty curriculum committees which review course syllabi can create and enforce an accessible syllabus template for all courses within an academic unit. Teaching excellence awards can include accessibility attainment as a criterion. Some course quality evaluation models such as QualityMatters™ use faculty peer evaluation and include accessibility as a required item within the quality rubric. An institution can put frameworks in place to support high quality instruction by helping the faculty to run every course on campus through the quality assurance review process (e.g., Ozdemir & Loose, 2014). In the end, it is important to encourage faculty demonstrating accessibility in their courses to become distinguished faculty mentors and champions for the cause.

The evaluation step is also an opportunity to evaluate the implementation progress and report to administrators. The team can use surveys, interviews, focus groups, and course quality data to identify what did and did not work during the last cycle. Identify any new accessibility technologies, laws or resources which might require the institution to modify minimum accessibility standards, training, and budgets. They can use this data to modify their approach as they target the gaps during the next round based. As technologies, standards, faculty, and teaching practices evolve, the institution must revisit all the steps in the approach to maintain minimum accessibility and usability standards in online education. This work is never done; it is a continuous quality improvement process. No course or institution will ever be perfectly accessible, but we can always work towards making more courses accessible to a greater degree while using increasingly efficient approaches (see Figure 2).

FUTURE RESEARCH DIRECTIONS

The future research will involve conducting interviews and observational studies with students who have various disabilities to understand their experiences in the upgraded courses. Even courses which

Figure 2. Systematic approach for improving accessibility and usability in online courses

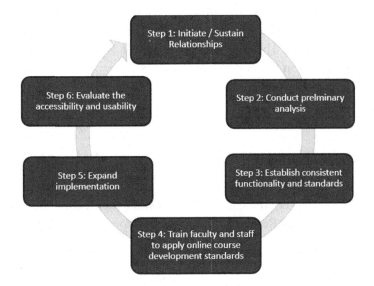

passed the accessibility checker reviews may still be inaccessible to the actual students with disabilities (de Carvalho, da Silva, Fenandes, & Pagliuca, 2014). The data from such an investigation can help the institution further improve the courses. Another research direction involves investigating approaches to larger-scale accessibility improvements in order to develop models and frameworks which can support the institution-wide accessibility initiative. The last research direction includes developing new technologies which will minimize the institution's efforts when improving online course accessibility. An action research approach to improving accessibility benefits an institution because it provides data for the quality improvement efforts while also contributing to the body of knowledge on accessibility and usability.

CONCLUSION

To develop accessible distance learning programs, Burgstahler et al. (2004) explained that distance learning programs need to address policy, guidelines, standards, procedures, dissemination, training, support, enforcement, reward, evaluation, and revision. This preliminary analysis demonstrated that making online courses accessible requires a collective effort. Over the years, the demand for accessible online education has increased, and happily the number of accessibility resources has also increased over time. Online course developers have access to tools, templates, and best practices which can help their efforts. The authors believe that long-term success depends on organizational culture shifting towards embracing accessibility as an institutional value. An institution that utilizes universal design principles takes a proactive approach to accessible online course design and development. Academic units should ensure all courses are designed with accessibility in mind so fewer students need to request accommodation. Every professional development training provided by the institution should have a partial or full emphasis on accessibility concerns. Purchasing decisions should ensure software vendors have adequately addressed accessibility within their products before signing the contract. This organizational culture sets a strong foundation for teamwork to produce excellent educational experiences for all students. The authors believe that every institution must strive towards making online education accessible to students with disabilities. The model proposed within this chapter is based on an organizational structure which resembles many other universities. Thus the authors believe it is likely this model could help many institutions improve accessibility in their own online courses.

REFERENCES

W3C. (2008). *Web Content Accessibility Guidelines (WCAG) 2.0*. Retrieved from http://www.w3.org/TR/WCAG20/

Allen, I. E., Seaman, J., Poulin, R., & Straut, T. T. (2016). *Online report card: Tracking online education in the United States*. Babson Survey Research Group and Quahog Research Group, LLC.

Argyris, C., & Schon, D. A. (1995). Organizational learning II: Theory, method, and practice. Reading, MA: Addison-Wesley.

Bastedo, K., Sugar, A., Swenson, N., & Vargas, J. (2013). Programmatic, systematic, automatic: An online course accessibility support model. *Journal of Asynchronous Learning Networks*, *17*(3), 87–102.

Brault, M. W. (2012). Americans with disabilities: 2010. *Current Population Reports, 7*, 1–131.

Burgstahler, S. (2009). *Universal design of instruction (UDI): Definition, principles, guidelines, and examples*. Retrieved from http://www.washington.edu/doit/universal-design-instruction-udi-definition-principles-guidelines-and-examples

Burgstahler, S., Corrigan, B., & McCarter, J. (2004). Making distance learning courses accessible to students and instructors with disabilities: A case study. *The Internet and Higher Education*, *7*(3), 233–246. doi:10.1016/j.iheduc.2004.06.004

Crow, K. L. (2008). Four types of disabilities: *Their impact on online learning. TechTrends*, *52*(1), 51–55. doi:10.1007/s11528-008-0112-6

Davis, A. P., Dent, E. B., & Wharff, D. M. (2015). A conceptual model of systems thinking leadership in community colleges. *Systemic Practice and Action Research*, *28*(4), 333–353. doi:10.1007/s11213-015-9340-9

de Carvalho, A. T., da Silva, A. S. R., Fenandes, A. F. C., & Pagliuca, L. M. F. (2014). Health education for the blind: Evaluation of accessibility of an inclusive online course. *Creative Education*, *5*(16), 1559–1566. doi:10.4236/ce.2014.516172

Des Moines University. (2016). *Mission, vision and values*. Retrieved January 15, 2016, from https://www.dmu.edu/about/mission-vision-and-values/

Disability Gov. (2016). *Rehabilitation Act of 1973*. Retrieved from https://www.disability.gov/rehabilitation-act-1973/

Fichten, C. S., Asuncion, J. V., Barile, M., Ferraro, V., & Wolforth, J. (2009). Accessibility of e-learning and computer and information technologies for students with visual impairments in postsecondary education. *Journal of Visual Impairment & Blindness*, *103*(9), 543.

Frey, B. A., Kearns, L. R., & King, D. K. (2012). *Quality matters: Template for an accessibility policy for online courses*. Retrieved from http://www.qmprogram.org/template-accessibility-policy-online-courses

Hackett, S., & Parmanto, B. (2005). A longitudinal evaluation of accessibility: Higher education web sites. *Internet Research*, *15*(3), 281–294. doi:10.1108/10662240510602690

Iwarsson, S., & Stahl, A. (2003). Accessibility, usability and universal design: Positioning and definition of concepts describing person-environment relationships. *Disability and Rehabilitation*, *25*(2), 57–66. PMID:12554380

Lewis, K., Yoder, D., Riley, E., So, Y., & Yusufali, S. (2007). Accessibility of instructional Web sites in higher education. *EDUCAUSE Quarterly*, *30*(3), 29.

Newman, L., Wagner, M., Knokey, A.-M., Marder, C., Nagle, K., Shaver, D., & Wei, X. (2011). *The post-high school outcomes of young adults with disabilities up to 8 Years after high school: A Report from the National Longitudinal Transition Study-2 (NLTS2)*. NCSER 2011-3005. National Center for Special Education Research. Retrieved from http://eric.ed.gov/?id=ED524044

Ozdemir, D., & Loose, R. (2014). Implementation of a quality assurance review system for the scalable development of online courses. *Online Journal of Distance Learning Administration*, *17*(1), n1.

Poulin, R. (2013). *Managing online education 2013: Practices in ensuring quality*. WICHE Cooperative for Educational Technologies.

Quality Matters. (2013). *Quality matters program*. Retrieved from https://www.qualitymatters.org/

Schmetzke, A. (2001). Online distance education: "Anytime, anywhere" but not for everyone. Information. *Technology and Disability*, *7*(2), 1–23.

Senge, P. M. (1994). *The fifth discipline: The art & practice of the learning organization* (1st ed.). New York: Doubleday Business.

Teh, J., & Curran, M. (2016). *Nonvisual desktop access*. Retrieved from http://www.nvaccess.org/

The Center for Universal Design. (2016). *Universal design principles*. Retrieved from https://www.ncsu. edu/ncsu/design/cud/about_ud/udprinciplestext.htm

The National Center on Disability and Access to Education. (2016). *Cheatsheets*. Retrieved from http:// ncdae.org/resources/cheatsheets/

United States Access Board. (2016). *Section 508 standards*. Retrieved from https://www.access-board.gov/ guidelines-and-standards/communications-and-it/about-the-section-508-standards/section-508-standards

United States Department of Justice. (2016). *2010 ADA regulations*. Retrieved from https://www.ada. gov/2010_regs.htm

WebAIM. (2015a). *Testing web content for accessibility.* Retrieved from http://webaim.org/resources/evalquickref/

WebAIM. (2015b). *WAVE (Version 1.0.1).* Retrieved from http://wave.webaim.org/

WebAIM. (2016). *Web accessibility principles.* Retrieved January 29, 2016, from http://webaim.org/resources/quickref/

Wentz, B., Jaeger, P. T., & Lazar, J. (2011). Retrofitting accessibility: The legal inequality of after-the-fact online access for persons with disabilities in the United States. *First Monday*, *16*(11). doi:10.5210/fm.v16i11.3666

KEY TERMS AND DEFINITIONS

Accessibility Professional (AP): An individual knowledgeable about best practices, which make products and tools accessible to persons with disabilities.

Course Instructor: An individual whose primary responsibility is to teach the assigned course.

Digital Accessibility: Electronic systems and content, such a website, mobile application or electronic document accessible to all regardless of their disability.

Disability: Any physical and cognitive disability which prevent the individual to access traditional education.

Instructional Design Coordinator: An individual who provides direct support during the design, development, implementation, and evaluation of the course.

Learning Management System: The electronic system which primarily delivers the instruction.

Universal Design of Instruction: A systematic approach which intends to develop learning environments to provide the best opportunities for everybody.

Usability: An attribute of instructional materials which goes beyond accessibility and assures that the materials are easily understandable to the learner.

Chapter 13

Evolution of Covert Coaching as an Evidence–Based Practice in Professional Development and Preparation of Teachers

Kathleen M. Randolph
Florida Atlantic University, USA

Michael P. Brady
Florida Atlantic University, USA

ABSTRACT

There is a tradition of coaching in many fields that prepares and improves performance among professionals. Coaching practices evolved over time, with several technological applications developed to improve the coaching process. An application gaining attention as an evidence-based practice is the use of wireless communication systems in which coaching statements are delivered to individuals while they engage in work. In education this has been called Bug-in-Ear coaching or Covert Audio Coaching, and has demonstrated its efficacy as a coaching intervention with teachers, families, and individuals with developmental disabilities. In this chapter the evolution of coaching across disciplines is summarized and specific applications that hold promise as an evidence-based practice for the professional development and preparation of teachers are described. This chapter summarizes 22 studies which support covert coaching as an evidence-based practice. Covert coaching enables immediate feedback without interrupting the participants, and provides opportunities for immediate error correction.

INTRODUCTION

Technology has greatly affected employment and professional preparation programs. Computers, once relegated to science fiction, are now commonplace tools in academia and most employment settings. Current technologies continue to expand; technology has multiple impacts on the way professionals conduct their work and the way they are prepared for roles in the workplace. Technologies that once relied on

DOI: 10.4018/978-1-5225-2838-8.ch013

computers that were the size of a large room are now portable, and small enough to carry in a pocket. In just two decades, the focus of many technologies has shifted from the hardware to applications and use of portable smart tools. The application of technology to coaching and professional development has the potential to make a greater impact on employees in a variety of employment settings.

BACKGROUND

In many fields, coaching is a common practice used to prepare and improve performance among professionals. Like technology, coaching practices have evolved over time, and several technological applications have been adopted in an effort to improve the process. An application that is gaining attention as an evidence-based practice is the use of wireless communication systems in which coaching statements can be delivered to individuals while they engage in work activity. This coaching practice has been used effectively as an intervention with teachers, families, and individuals with developmental disabilities. In teacher education this practice is referred to as both *Bug-in-Ear* coaching and *Covert Audio Coaching*.

In this chapter the evolution of coaching across several disciplines is outlined. Specific applications that hold promise as an evidence-based practice for professional development and teacher education are described. A review of studies indicate that covert coaching enables immediate feedback without interrupting the participants. Further, this research supports that the combination of covert coaching and immediate feedback provides opportunities for immediate error correction.

RESEARCH ON COACHING AND FEEDBACK

Feedback on employee performance is important for both supervisors and employees. Employment coaching has been used in the private and public employment sectors to provide feedback to employees (e.g., Crowell, Anderson, Abel & Sergio, 1988). Many of the origins of employment coaching can be traced to *organizational behavior management*, a term that has been used to describe an application of behavioral principles including the simultaneous coaching that occurs in various places of employment (Crowell et al., 1988). Feedback and coaching have been used traditionally in employment settings between supervisors and their "subordinate" employees, with feedback delivered after the supervisor has observed the employee or conferred with other management. The purpose of coaching and feedback in the employment sector typically is to develop an employee's skills, provide suggestions to improve or recognize exemplary work, or modify certain workplace practices.

Cunningham and Austin (2007) provide an example of an organizational behavior management practice involving workplace coaching. To reduce injury to hospital staff in an operating room, Cunningham and Austin sought to improve safety practices with direct observation and feedback. Focusing on injuries caused by sharp needles, the researchers set the goal to reduce needle exposure and injury, and to reinforce the "hands-free technique." The study incorporated various coaching practices, and increased safety behavior during inpatient and outpatient procedures in the operating room during treatment, and in outpatient operating rooms during a maintenance condition.

The use of feedback and coaching in employment settings has not been limited to "subordinate" employees. A study by Green, Rollyson, Passante, and Reid (2002) provides an example. Supervisors in a living facility for adults with severe disabilities were coached to improve their supervisory performance by their human service agency administrators. The typical supervision process was enhanced with an alternative management approach that involved direct feedback based on actual observation in the various living facilities. All of the supervisors were trained to use task analysis, reverse fading, prompting, correction, and reinforcement. Compared to traditional management approaches, the use of observation, direct feedback, and coaching was invaluable in developing more effective supervisors.

Kretlow and Bartholomew (2010) summarized the coaching research applied to teachers with a particular focus on its relationship with professional development. In their review of the literature, Kretlow and Bartholomew found teachers reported that coaching in general was a promising practice for promoting high fidelity evidence-based practices. Further they identified that a strength of coaching was to promote the application of skills learned during professional development and in university classes, and to assist in transfer of the skills to real-world classroom settings. The teachers for whom coaching was most successful were provided with individual follow-up, support, and coaching after an initial training period. These teachers noted that the need for collaboration with a coach and time for reflection were imperative to improving their teaching skills. Coaching also helped to prevent isolation for new teachers.

Kretlow and Bartholomew (2010) found two models of coaching were most common in the literature. Supervisory coaching was described as the traditional coaching model, usually accompanied by delayed feedback and recommendations for follow-up. In contrast, side-by-side coaching provided immediate feedback and demonstration in real time alongside the employee. Critical components of both coaching models included highly engaged, instructive group training sessions, and follow-up observation sessions with specific feedback. Feedback sessions often included sharing observational data and self-evaluation. Modeling of specific follow-up actions often followed these observations. The general consensus of the articles reviewed in the Kretlow and Bartholomew report confirmed that coaching should be included as a regular and recurring component of professional development activities for both preservice and inservice teachers.

These and numerous other coaching studies have assisted in improving employment skills in teachers and other professionals. However, much of the early coaching research did not incorporate technology that might reduce the delay between employees' observed performance and the feedback they received from their supervisors. In the studies and other coaching situations, immediate feedback is not always a possibility. The addition of technology to provide immediate feedback has the potential to decrease errors made by participants and provides an opportunity for immediate error correction (Scheeler & Lee, 2002).

Coaching with Technology

Incorporating coaching technology provides an efficient way to deliver feedback to participants, and allows the participant to immediately correct errors. Delayed feedback in traditional coaching situations delays error correction, and promotes the possibility of error practice, which is detrimental to learning. As Scheeler and Lee (2002) noted, "precise, immediate, frequent feedback increases efficacy and efficiency...if feedback is delayed, it allows learners to practice errors, especially in the acquisition phase of learning and when learners are allowed to repeat errors" (p. 232). If immediacy of feedback enhances supervisory practices as Scheeler and Lee described, it is important to examine whether or not using technologies that allow for immediate feedback constitute an Evidence-Based Practice (EBP).

A suggestion that a technology that allowed for coaching with immediate feedback has origins in the 1950s. Employment coaching coupled with a way to provide immediate feedback began with Korner and Brown's use of a "mechanical third ear," a wireless FM listening system made up of two parts—an earpiece receiver and a transmitter (Korner & Brown, 1952). Between 1976 and 1994, the FM listening system was used to train psychometrists, medical students, and marriage and family therapists-in-training during live interviews with clients and patients in different settings. Paired with the traditional one-way mirror, the earpiece provided a way for the supervisor to prompt the student to make immediate corrections or ask additional questions during their sessions with patients and clients (Baum & Lane, 1976; Gallant, Thyer, & Bailey, 1991; Hunt, 1980). The FM listening systems paved the way for what would eventually become known as the *bug-in-ear* (BIE) applications of coaching using a microphone to send a message and an earpiece to receive it.

As BIE technology evolved, other applications were explored in different employment settings. In a study conducted in a Midwestern bank, six tellers were selected and observed on targeted customer service behaviors. Each teller wore a microphone attached to headphones and was able to receive feedback from a supervisor who also had a cassette recorder that recorded teller-customer interactions during 10-second intervals. The researchers saw the importance of BIE technology to track and make improvements in customer service in banking, and found coaching using BIE technology successful with implications for future use (Crowell et al., 1988).

It is unclear whether technology that allows for coaching with immediate feedback has been deemed an EBP in general, and specifically in the professional development and preparation of teachers. In the remainder of this chapter, a review is provided on recent research in which preservice or inservice professional development activities incorporated these coaching technologies. Ways in which the coaching technology was applied is summarized, and evidence is presented that establishes whether coaching that incorporates these technologies is an EBP in teacher education. First, coaching studies in education and other disciplines that used technology that allowed for immediate feedback were eveluted. Next,

Figure 1. Timeline of BIE technology

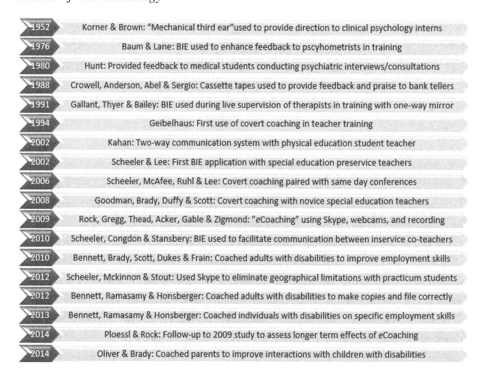

it was determined whether coaching using technology has become an evidence-based practice in the professional development and preparation of teachers. Figure 1 shows the timeline of BIE technology.

What Standards Establish Evidence-Based Practices?

While all professions have customs and traditions that constitute *common practice*, not all common practices have evidence of efficacy that establish them as *evidence-based practices*. For example, reading tea leaves has long been considered a common practice as a way of predicting the future, although the evidence to support this practice does not exist in scientific literature. On the other hand, most scientists accept the evidence of a gradual climate change even though popular arguments exist against this phenomenon. Standards that establish EBP vary dramatically across research methods. They also vary across disciplines. Evidence-based practices are the gold standard which society uses to support, fund, and implement knowledge derived from scientific research. This includes decisions on the validity of practices for the professional development and preparation of teachers.

Much of the research on coaching and in teacher preparation involves experimental research using single subject designs. Grounded in the tradition of behavioral psychology, single subject design research focuses on implementing and evaluating interventions with individual participants. Standards used to support EBP in single subject design research were proposed by Horner et al. (2005) and Kratochwill et al. (2013). A summary of these standards include:

- An experimental, single case design study shows a causal relationship between the independent and dependent variables.
- Within- and between-subject comparisons exist, and controls are provided for major threats to validity, with the ability for systematic replication.
- The participant is the unit of analysis, typically with 3-8 participants per study, and participants serve as their own controls.
- Participants, settings, variables, and selection process are operationally defined.
- Dependent variables are measured repeatedly, selected for social significance, and are constantly assessed over time for change.
- Dependent measures are assessed by at least two observers and the agreement of their observations is reported.
- Independent variables under investigation are actively manipulated, and evaluated for fidelity.
- Baseline condition exists as the comparison condition, where the dependent variable is measured.

By contrast, many coaching studies exist that are grounded in group design research methods. These studies apply traditional research approaches linked to educational and psychological research methods. Standards for establishing evidence-based practices using group research designs vary across disciplines, and several unifying themes are commonly found (Chwalisz, 2003; Flay et al., 2005; & Rycroft-Malone et al., 2004). These standards include evidence that:

- Is generated via a rule-governed methodology.
- Accrues from at least two rigorous trials.
- Describes participants, measurement, and analyses with clear definitions.
- Is based on consistent effects, including at least one example of long-term effects.

- Includes detailed information that supports replication by other researchers.
- Is interpreted in relation to "proof and rationality."
- Is independently observed and verified.
- Is generated via a hierarchical approach that includes (a) random assignment, (b) clinical trials in which some aspects of the most rigorous standards are missing (but not "fatal flaws"), (c) case control studies based on retrospective treatment data, (d) secondary data analysis including meta-analyses, (e) "impressionistic" reviews not based on secondary data analysis, and (f) case studies, and other reports without rigorous methods.

Establishing EBP for Coaching with Technology

To establish whether coaching with technology is indeed an evidence-based practice, consistency of language across the various studies is needed. In some studies that are the focus of this review, the coaching has been referred to as *bug-in-ear* (BIE). Other research has referred to this coaching practice as *covert audio coaching* (CAC). In this review, terminology was adopted that presents *bug-in-ear* as the actual device or technology in use, and *covert audio coaching* as the delivery method of the coaching, whether in-person or via virtual technology (e.g., Skype). As Bennett and colleagues (2013) pointed out, "CAC is a method of delivering ... performance feedback (e.g., supportive or corrective statements) privately through a pair of two-way radios and headsets from a distance" (p. 104). BIE is the equipment that is used to deliver audio messages from one party to another. CAC uses one person (e.g., a coach or co-teacher) to provide guidance or feedback statements, prompts, praise, or corrections – often using various forms of BIE technology.

With this consistency of language, empirical literature was reviewed to determine whether coaching with technology has become an EBP in the professional development and preparation of teachers. The following keywords were used, in combination and alone: *Bug-in-ear, covert audio coaching, immediate feedback, special education, job coaching,* and *employment coaching.* EBSCOhost was the database used for the search, using the education full text database and Boolean/Phrase. Once articles were located, the abstracts were read, and the referenced articles were hand-searched. Studies that did not use covert coaching practices, or those that did not provide a description of the equipment were eliminated. The studies were selected for inclusion if the manuscripts were in peer-reviewed journals, described covert coaching practices using prompts and/or immediate feedback with technology, provided a description of the equipment, and met at least minimum standards established for either single subject or group design research. This review of empirical literature resulted in a pool of 22 studies published between 1952 and 2014 that investigated the use of electronic technologies to provide coaching prompts and/or feedback. Five of these studies targeted employment settings other than education (described previously in the chapter); the remainder of the studies included covert coaching technologies that targeted professional development and preparation of teachers or others who support individuals with disabilities. In the remainder of this chapter, the coaching studies are presented in four categories: (a) preservice applications with general education teachers, (b) preservice applications with special education teachers, (c) inservice applications with general and special education teachers, and (d) applications with others who support individuals with disabilities. Table 1 sunnarizes studies using covert audio coaching with technology.

Table 1. Studies reviewed using covert audio coaching with technology

Author(s), Year, Journal	Participants	Dependent Measure(s)	Results
Baum & Lane (1976) *Counselor Education and Supervision*	Graduate students administering the WISC-R	Delivery of WISC-R during testing	Behaviors corrected during 1st observation were completely developed by 3rd observation
Bennett, Brady, Scott, Dukes, & Frain (2010) *Focus on Autism and Other Developmental Disabilities*	3 adults with disabilities, in supported or competitive employment	**Accuracy**—Percentage and rate of task analysis steps completed correctly (sweeping hallway, washing windows, stacking crates); percentage and rate of trash collected **Durability**—ability to maintain after coaching was removed **Fluency**—rate of performance	**Accuracy**—all 3 increased accuracy to 90% or above **Durability**—2 of 3 maintained skills at 95% or above, and maintained accuracy over baseline **Fluency**—all increased performance rate
Bennett, Ramasamy, & Honsberger (2012) *Journal of Autism and Developmental Disorders*	3 high school students with ASD attending a secondary school only for students with ASD	**Accuracy** in making photocopies	**Accuracy**—all 3 increased accuracy to 90% or above
Bennett, Ramasamy, & Honsberger (2013) *Journal of Behavioral Education*	3 high school students with ASD attending a secondary school only for students with ASD	**Accuracy** and **fluency** using a T-shirt folding board to fold T-shirts, from baseline, intervention, and then maintenance (spm*)	**Accuracy**—All 3 increased accuracy and maintained accuracy during maintenance **Fluency**—All 3 increased fluency
Crowell, Anderson, Abel, & Sergio (1988) *Journal of Applied Behavior Analysis*	Branch manager, operations manager, 6 bank tellers	Customer interactions using 11 "quality points"	Mean scores increased across all participants during all phases of the study (72%; 81.4%; 83%; 88%)
Gallant, Thyer, & Bailey (1991) *Research on Social Work Practice*	4 graduate students enrolled in PhD Marriage and Family Therapy program	Use of supportive statements	Supportive statements (%): Trainee 1-0-18; 18-76 Trainee 2-0-36; 13-56 Trainee 3-0-6; 18-41
Giebelhaus (1994) *Journal of Teacher Education*	22 elementary education student teachers and their cooperating teachers with experimental and control group	14 discrete observable and measurable teacher clarity behaviors	Experimental group increased the average rate of response 88.3% response rate
Goodman, Brady, Duffy, Scott, & Pollard (2008) *Focus on Autism and other Developmental Disabilities*	3 novice special education certified teachers in resource or self-contained classrooms with three or fewer years teaching	Rate and accuracy of learn unit delivery	T1=1-55—93.2% T2-47—94.9% T3-72.8—97.7%
Hunt (1980) *Journal of Medical Education*	34 medical students completing outpatient psychiatric rotations	Suggestions, positive remarks, statements pointing out defense mechanisms, assurances, corrections	3-15 interventions/session (6.2% *M*) Suggestions-36%; Positive-22%; Dynamic statements-21%; Assurances-11%; Corrections-10%
Kahan (2002) *Journal of Teaching in Physical Education*	Student teacher and cooperating teacher in high school physical education	Case study; Duration and rate of communication across lessons and phases	Used two-way radio for 68.8% of communication in softball area; 37.5% in badminton area; duration and rate decreased as student teacher confidence increased
Korner & Brown (1952) *Journal of Consulting Psychology*	Graduate psychotherapy students and interns	Seminal study—provided feedback to graduate psychotherapy students and interns during sessions with patients	Directions ranged from 3-30 per testing hour; Improved interns' clinical sensitivity; Third ear found to improve teaching clinical psychology and supervising student clinical psychologists
Oliver & Brady (2014) *Behavior Analysis in Practice*	3 pairs of mothers and sons with ASD	Percentage of intervals of prompts and praise delivered by mother to child; percentage of steps completed independently by the child on task	Parents increased use of praise and visual prompts, and decreased use of prompts to 0; Children increased task completion **Generalization**-mothers improved interactions and children increased accuracy and independence on task completion

continued on following page

Table 1. Continued

Author(s), Year, Journal	Participants	Dependent Measure(s)	Results
Ploessl & Rock (2014) *Teacher Education and Special Education*	3 co-teaching dyads (general education and special education teacher)	Co-teaching models planned and carried out; student accommodations and modifications; PBIS strategies: redirection, praise, engagement	Co-teaching models: D1: 1-2; D2: 1.25-2.5; D3: 1.75-2.5; Student accomm.: D1: 0-3.75; D2: 2-3; D3: 1-3; Redirection: D1-8.5-1; D2: 1-1 D3: 8.5-11.5; Praise: D1: 25-31.5; D2: 30.5-24.5; D3: 45-56.5; Engagement: D1: 95-97; D2: 98-100; D3: 95-95
Rock, Gregg, Gable, Zigmond, Blanks, Howard, & Bullock (2012) *Journal of Technology and Teacher Education*	13 master's students in a special education hybrid distance education program	Changes in preservice teacher rates of opportunities to respond; changes in classroom climate and student engagement (redirects, reprimands, praise and on-task behavior)	Teacher behavior *M*: Low access-29.08-15.65 High access-29.71-41.29 Redirection-9.85-8.48 Praise-27.15-49.96 Engagement-97.33-97.08
Rock, Gregg, Thead, Acker, Gable, & Zigmond (2009) *Teacher Education and Special Education*	15 teachers enrolled in a federally funded graduate personnel preparation program	Changes in teacher behavior/ instructional practices; Changes in classroom climate; Level of disruption and benefit associate with the advanced online BIE technology and feedback	Hand raising-29.8—11.5 Praise-26.07—54.13 Engagement-73.84—92.79 Disengagement-26.16—7.21
Rock, Schumacker, Gregg, Howard, Gable, & Zigmond (2014) *Teacher Education and Special Education*	14 of the original 15 participants from the 2009 study	Longer term effects of BIE in: Changes in effective teaching behavior; Changes in classroom climate (praise, redirects, reprimands, % students engaged); Participant perception of benefit/ liabilities of eCoaching	Teacher behavior *M*: Low access-34.07-3.98-9.8 High access-11.29-51.01-63.69 Redirection-9.86-5.73-5.44 Praise-27.64-52.35-50.7 Engagement-75-96-99
Scheeler, Bruno, Grubb, & Seavey (2009) *Journal of Behavioral Education*	5 preservice teachers (3 in experiment 1, 2 in experiment 2)	Percentage of completed three-term contingency (TTC) trials by the preservice teacher	Percentage of TTC completed increased Mean completed TTC Baseline, Intervention, Maintenance/ Generalization (%): Experiment 1: T1:1-87.5-66.5; T2: 40-83.7-55; T3: 69.5-94-76.3 Experiment 2: T4: 54.2-74.5-87; T5: 37.6-85.4-93.4
Scheeler, Congdon, & Stansbery (2010) *Teacher Education and Special Education*	3 co-teaching dyads which included one general education teacher and one special education teacher	Completed three-term contingency (TTC) completed by co-teacher; ease and usefulness of receiving feedback through BIE	All 3 dyad pairs increased TTC and maintained when faded TTC *M* (%): D1-T1—21.5-97.4, T2—13.9-96.1; D2-T1—30.5-98.9, T2-7.9-100; D3-T1—29.9-96.5, T2—21.5-98.1
Scheeler & Lee (2002) *Journal of Behavioral Education*	3 preservice special education majors enrolled in a practicum	Percentage of completed three-term contingency (TTC)	Percentage of TTC completed increased Mean completed TTC (%): T1-16-81; T2-52-84; T3-79-87
Scheeler, Macluckie, & Albright (2009) *Remedial and Special Education*	Four female high school seniors	Specific oral presentation self-selected behaviors	Mean frequency of targeted behaviors decreased: S1: 6.8-10.8; S2: 39.6-3.5; S3: 62-62-5.5; S4-33.6-17.4
Scheeler, McAfee, Ruhl & Lee (2006) *Teacher Education and Special Education*	5 preservice teachers in undergraduate special education field experience	Percentage of completed TTC Percent of correct student responses Level of satisfaction provided by feedback with BIE and acclimation to device	Percentage of TTC and correct student responses increased; TTC *M* (%): T1-67.6—94.7; T2-75.6—93.8; T3-61.8—91.6; T4-53.5—86.1; T5-72.5—91.2
Scheeler, McKinnon & Stout (2012) *Teacher Education and Special Education*	5 undergraduate preservice special education majors enrolled in practicum	Percentage of completed three-term contingency (TTC)	Percentage of TTC completed increased TTC *M* (%): T1-45.6—100; T2-36.8—90; T3-63.2—97.6; T4-62—97.6; T5-70—95

Notes: D1, D2, etc. (Dyad 1, Dyad 2); M—Mean ; S1, S2, etc. (Student 1, Student 2); SPM-Shirts per minute ; TTC-Three-Term Contingency; T1, T2, etc. (Teacher 1, Teacher 2)

Table 2. First use of BIE in teacher education

Giebelhaus (1994)

Provided feedback to student teachers using a mechanical third ear. In search of a way to enhance the effectiveness of preservice teacher supervision, Giebelhaus introduced BIE feedback, and changed the field forever.
Study synopsis:
• 22 elementary education student teachers in their final practicum prior to graduating
• Two groups: One received prompting from their cooperating teacher via BIE (experimental group), one did not (control group)
• Experimental group used an observation checklist measuring the frequency and types of prompts delivered, modified to include the following 14 discrete "teacher clarity behaviors":
    1. Give objective
    2. Highlight important points
    3. Repeat something
    4. Use board
    5. Summarize material
    6. Give examples
    7. Demonstrate
    8. Explain unfamiliar things
    9. Repeat, rephrase something
    10. Pause
    11. Ask questions
    12. Provide wait time
    13. Provide practice time to students
    14. Check student work
• Each teacher in the experimental group was required to wear the device seven times
• Cooperating teachers who were comfortable with the equipment tended to be more consistent with the target skills
• 88% of student teachers in the experimental group were able to change their behavior immediately due to the feedback
• The student teachers and cooperating teachers reported the BIE to be an effective discrete communication method
• Student teachers were able to simultaneously teach and receive cuing and feedback to make corrections during their teaching

Preservice Applications with General Education Teachers

The early 90's brought advances in technology and more surreptitious ways to provide feedback. One side-by-side coaching method in particular, *covert audio coaching*, emerged as an efficient way to give unobtrusive immediate feedback in a variety of educational settings via BIE technology. Two studies (Giebelhaus, 1994; Kahan, 2002) were conducted with general education preservice teachers that provided feedback from cooperating teachers to the student teachers. Table 2 shows the background of the first use of BIE in teacher education.

The first documented use of CAC in educational settings was by Giebelhaus in 1994. As is common in supervisory coaching, traditional feedback was given to student teachers after their observations were over, either immediately after the teaching session or later in the day. However, the Giebelhaus study also provided the student teachers with immediate feedback to make corrections *during* the teaching sessions. Fourteen discrete teaching behaviors were targeted, and elementary student teachers were given immediate feedback by their cooperating teachers through BIE during teaching sessions. This enabled Giebelhaus (1994) to incorporate CAC using the BIE technology with cooperating teachers to provide feedback to student teachers in elementary education classrooms. Seeing the delay between the actual observation session and the delivery of feedback, Giebelhaus found that CAC provided immediate feedback compared to the delayed feedback method common to supervisory coaching. Considered a pioneer study with BIE and feedback, this study sparked interest in the possibilities that CAC could bring by providing immediate feedback to student teachers.

The Giebelhaus (1994) research was extended by Kahan (2002) who used CAC to create a two-way communication and interaction system between a physical education student teacher and cooperating teacher pair (using a wired earphone and attached microphone). The goal of the study was to evaluate whether this side-by-side communication enhanced the student teaching experience. The study helped to provide role clarity, role functions, and personal and professional compatibility between the student teacher and cooperating teacher. The participants assured that CAC provided discrete, immediate feedback that helped to prompt and facilitate communication, and communication was less restrictive than vocal proximity.

Preservice Applications with Special Education Teachers

Teachers-in-training typically obtain feedback from their university supervisors during several points in their preparation. Once hired, these teachers receive feedback in post-observation conferences by administrators, coaches, or peer teachers, and this feedback typically is delayed by several hours or days. Delayed feedback for classroom teachers can enable them to practice instructional errors, resulting in days or weeks of ineffective instruction, which affects students in the classroom. Immediate feedback corrects the errors in situ and results in effective instruction while practicing a skill (Goodman, Brady, Duffy, Scott, & Pollard, 2008; Scheeler & Lee, 2002). Seven studies with preservice teachers were included in this review (Rock et al., 2009; Rock et al., 2012; Rock et al., 2014; Scheeler, Bruno, Grubb, & Seavey, 2009; Scheeler & Lee, 2002; Scheeler, McAfee, Ruhl, & Lee, 2006; Scheeler, McKinnon, & Stout, 2012).

A series of studies conducted by Scheeler and colleagues include preservice special education teachers and the use of BIE technology to provide feedback. In the first study to include special education teachers-in-training (Scheeler & Lee, 2002), three preservice teachers received CAC through BIE technology during a field-based practicum. Participants took a course on effective instruction before the study and were prepared for the intervention using short, specific coaching statements delivered through BIE. Teachers-in-training provided direct instruction lessons during 90-minute teaching sessions with students whose Individual Education Programs (IEP) identified specific needs in reading. The teachers received immediate feedback, given within one to three seconds, on their instructional delivery through BIE from a supervisor located in the back of the classroom. Feedback consisted of short statements to prompt students, deliver error corrections, or provide praise. Faster acquisition of effective teaching behaviors, along with greater accuracy in delivery, was found when the coaching feedback was delivered immediately via BIE rather than being delayed.

In a follow-up study by Scheeler and her colleagues (Scheeler et al., 2006), BIE technology was used to deliver coaching feedback during preservice teacher observations. Though conferences were held after the observation, BIE enabled immediate feedback and correction opportunities. Successful completion of three-term contingencies was measured. (An example of a three-term contingency in education is a teacher's question, followed by a student response, with a teacher correction or praise statement.) Using what they had learned in previous BIE studies, supervisors delivered feedback and found that CAC enabled more completed three-term contingencies in less time, because the supervisor was able to focus on the quality of the preservice teacher's delivery of lessons. The researchers also noted that immediate feedback allowed the teachers to correct their less effective teaching practices, and allowed their students to receive more effective instruction. The researchers also found that with the increased completion of three-term contingencies, student responses increased. Scheeler and colleagues conducted additional studies with preservice teachers, as well as peer tutors, that included systematic measures of maintenance, and explored generalization outcomes (Scheeler et al., 2009; Scheeler, Mackluckie, & Albright, 2010b).

In an effort to lessen the possible limiting factors of BIE, Rock and colleagues integrated several wireless mobile technologies into student teacher observations in a series of studies that analyzed student engagement and effective teacher behavior (Rock et al., 2009; Rock et al., 2012; Rock et al., 2014). The participants in these studies were master's degree students in the clinical portion of their program. The researchers incorporated Bluetooth© and Skype© technology, as well as an online recording system, to measure changes in teaching behavior and classroom climate. They also measured the levels of disruption and benefit associated with CAC and feedback. The study enhanced the use of traditional BIE technology by incorporating newer technology and had similar outcomes as previously mentioned BIE studies with immediate feedback using CAC.

The Rock et al. (2009) research helped support the efficacy of immediate feedback, while drawing attention to the importance of a non-interruptive means of providing that feedback. This study, and the follow-ups (Rock et al., 2012; Rock et al., 2014), showed that feedback given immediately and in situ provided little to no interruption to the teachers during their instructional practice. In addition, the Rock et al. studies incorporated a virtual component to the previous coaching technology. That is, the feedback was provided using a wireless internet connection that did not require the researcher to be in the same proximity. The minimal cost and time of the additional technology, as well as the simple integration of Bluetooth© and Skype© (i.e., the virtual component), allowed coaches to observe student teachers and teachers alike, from live and remote locations.

In addition to the Rock studies, Scheeler and colleagues (2012) also investigated virtual coaching applications using Skype© to provide feedback to preservice teachers when faced with geographic challenges. Supervisors provided feedback to student teachers using short phrases during 15-minute observation sessions. Immediate feedback delivered via Skype© was successful in increasing the targeted teaching behaviors in five preservice teachers. Teachers were able to improve the delivery of their lessons -- in the midst of the act of teaching. The intervention proved to be an effective solution to geographically limiting situations (Scheeler et al., 2012).

Because the feedback in these studies was delivered in real time to the teachers-in-training, they were able to make immediate improvements to their instruction while they delivered lessons to students in the classroom. This enabled faster active responding, and strengthened the instructional response, which in turn resulted in more student opportunities for learning. Teachers in all studies deemed the immediate feedback helpful, and did not find the CAC intervention or the BIE equipment distracting. Immediate corrective feedback was considered to be more effective than traditional delayed feedback in improving instruction (Scheeler & Lee, 2002; Scheeler et al., 2006).

Inservice Applications With General and Special Education Teachers

Goodman and colleagues (2008) observed novice special education teachers in resource and self-contained classrooms. The researchers focused on three separate components of teacher-delivered instruction: lesson delivery (e.g., a teacher's question to the class), student response to the lesson, and the teacher follow-up (e.g., praise or a correction). This three-step interaction (similar to the three-term contingency described earlier) is the smallest "unit" of teaching, and is particularly useful when analyzing teacher-directed lessons. When a teaching coach delivered feedback on the completeness and accuracy of their lessons via CAC, the teachers increased the accuracy and rate of the lessons that they delivered. This indicated that the teachers were successful in discriminating between complete and incomplete lessons. These teachers improved the delivery of their lessons within one to two coaching sessions, and maintained these gains when the coaching intervention was removed (Goodman et al., 2008).

Another application of CAC with already-employed teachers involves planning and delivering instruction via co-teaching (Ploessl & Rock, 2014; Scheeler, Congdon & Stansbery, 2010a). Co-teaching typically includes a special education and a general education teacher working together to provide instruction when students with disabilities are included in general education classrooms, and feedback is necessary to make the partnership successful. Immediate feedback can enhance that working relationship and strengthen the teaching skills of the teachers involved.

In one study, co-teaching pairs used BIE technology to give each other feedback during instruction (Scheeler et al., 2010a). Each dyad developed examples of short specific phrases to say to each other when delivering feedback (e.g., "Good praise," and "Give positive feedback"). Coaching elements were infused into the school's professional development program, and training was provided to the participants. It was continuous and non-evaluative by nature. Participants rated the coaching with BIE as an acceptable, nonintrusive, and efficient way to deliver feedback in real time. Teachers reported that the technique was user-friendly; as important, it helped to rapidly change their teaching behavior, maintained after it was faded, and showed potential for generalization to other settings without the co-teaching partners. This differs from the focus by Ploessl and Rock (2014) where coaching was delivered by a third party, rather than as an interaction between the co-teachers. However, like the Scheeler et al. co-teaching study, the Ploessl and Rock outcomes showed positive effects on the co-teachers' targeted behaviors.

Applications With Others Who Support Individuals With Disabilities

As this coaching technology expands for teachers, other applications have emerged that directly target individuals with disabilities, or those who support them, as the recipients of coaching. This includes family members, job coaches, paraprofessionals, and others. When preparing individuals with disabilities for community employment, Wehman (2012) noted that job coaching is a reliable and effective support. Coaching provided prior to employment placement can assist future employees to master job skills, while coaching provided during and after placement can help new employees with disabilities adjust to the workplace and improve their performance.

A series of studies by Bennett and colleagues explored uses of CAC in supported employment settings for young adults with disabilities by delivering performance feedback directly to them via CAC. In the first study (Bennett, Brady, Scott, Dukes, & Frain, 2010), when a job coach provided prompts and feedback, the employees showed rapid and substantial improvements in the accuracy and fluency of various employment tasks (e.g., washing windows, sweeping, preparing trays for food service). In two follow-up studies (Bennett, Ramasamy & Honsberger, 2012; Bennett, Ramasamy & Honsberger, 2013), job coaches used CAC to teach employment-related skills to students with Autism Spectrum Disorders. The researchers used task-specific training and feedback to provide the students with skills needed at community employment sites. In the 2012 study, Bennett et al. taught students to make photocopies and then sort them into the correct bins when they were finished with the task. CAC was used to provide feedback to students, which included support statements, prompts and error correction. Participants not only acquired the skills, but also maintained them after the coaching intervention was removed. In the 2013 study, Bennett et al. incorporated the needs of a community-based instruction site where students were required to fold laundry. CAC was used to provide feedback after the task was completed correctly, immediately after an error occurred, or if a student was non-responsive during a step for 30 seconds. Again, the work tasks were acquired rapidly and maintained when the coaching was withdrawn.

Finally, Oliver and Brady (2014) applied this coaching technology to improve interactions between parents and their children with Autism Spectrum Disorders. Prompts and praise statements were delivered to the parents via CAC to encourage them to provide verbal reinforcement to their children during household routines (e.g., getting dressed; taking a bath), and to prompt their children to complete these routines. Parents were taught to deliver more effective prompts (including more visual prompts and fewer verbal ones), and to praise their children's improvements in their performance of the routines. Each of the parents increased the amount of praise given to their child and their effective prompts; each decreased their ineffective interactions. A second positive outcome involved the children's performance; as the parents' interactions with their children improved, the task performance of the children also improved. Finally, generalization of the skills for both the parents and their children were an additional desired outcome of the study. Parents transferred their improved interaction patterns with their children to other household routines that were not targeted for coaching, and the children also improved their performance of these tasks.

Limitations of Coaching Technology

As the addition of technology as a coaching practice has created numerous advances, several limitations have also been discovered. Many of the limitations noted in the studies and in practice are technological in nature. These limitations include firewall challenges in school districts, unreliable Internet connections, inability to use the Internet in some districts, poor connections between the observer and participant, and occasional equipment malfunctions. As educators have discovered when using any type of technology, flexibility and familiarity is essential for successful implementation. Figure 2 shows the types of technology that have been used as BIE.

The biggest limitation of the coaching research with covert electronic technology so far may be that the limits of CAC have yet to be found. For example, of the 22 studies reviewed for this chapter, few systematically explored CAC as a generalization strategy (Goodman et al., 2008; Oliver & Brady, 2014; Scheeler et al., 2009; Scheeler et al., 2010a). Although a few investigations explored the spread of experimental results to settings that were not part of the intervention, a more accurate presentation of generalization outcomes requires a measure of the intended generalization performance during all conditions. In both research and practice, for a specific focus on the transfer of learning, multiple measures of potential generalization outcomes prior to the coaching should be collected. These measures should also be collected during and after the intervention so that any generalization effects can be established.

SOLUTIONS AND RECOMMENDATIONS

Despite limitations or glitches encountered in research and practice, technology is constantly evolving and improving. The addition of technology to coaching for the professional development and preparation of teachers has demonstrated its' effectiveness across many learning environments. This coaching has also had a positive impact on family members, job coaches, paraprofessionals, and others in classroom settings, community employment work sites, and family homes.

Figure 2. Types of technology used as BIE

Korner & Brown, 1952	•Hearing-aid device with extended wire connected to the chest microphone and amplifier
Baum & Lane, 1976	•AM/FM transistor radio and FM wireless microphone with miniature earphone (Juliette, No. FPR-1255A, Radio Shack, 33-1048; Realistic, No. 33-175)
Hunt, 1980	•Radio transistor, audio mixer, radio receiver, standard cassette tape recorder, extension cord for the earphone, earphone
Crowell, Anderson, Abel, & Sergio, 1988	•Microphone, stereo cassette recorder, headphones
Gallant, Thyer, & Bailey, 1991	•Farrell Instruments bug-in-the-ear device
Kahan, 2002	•Two-way personal radios (Radio Shack, Cat. No. 21-1859), peripheral device (Radio Shack telephone headset adaptor, Cat. No. 21-1832) and ear set connector (Jabra EarBoom™)
Scheeler & Lee, 2002; Scheeler, McAfee, Ruhl & Lee, 2006; Scheeler, Bruno, Grubb, & Seavey, 2009; Scheeler, Macluckie, & Albright, 2009	•Personal FM System (Model 300, Williams Sound) with portable transmitter, receiver, and two AA batteries
Rock, Gregg, Thead, Acker, Gable, & Zigmond,2009	•Webcam, Bluetooth USB adapter, Bluetooth headset, Skype, and Pamela for Skype Business version 3.5 (to record sessions)
Scheeler, Congdon, & Stansbery, 2010	•Webcam, Bluetooth earpiece, Skype
Bennett, Brady, Scott, Dukes, & Frain, 2010; Bennett, Ramasamy, & Honsberger, 2012, 2013	•Two-way radios with headsets (Midland, Model LXT276VP; Midland X-tra Talk Adventure Headsets, Model AVP-H4)
Rock, Gregg, Gable, Zigmond, Blanks, Howard, & Bullock, 2012	•MacBook Pro, internal webcam/ microphone; or Mac desktop, external webcam/microphone (researcher); Skype , Bluetooth earpiece, wide-angle lens (teachers)
Scheeler, McKinnon & Stout, 2012	•Webcam, Bluetooth earpiece, Skype
Oliver & Brady, 2014	•Motorola two-way radios, model T-6500, a single ear bud, and single ear bud/microphone system
Ploessl & Rock, 2014	•Mac computers; webcam/ microphone, Skype , Bluetooth , existing videoconferencing equipment; Call recorder for Mac

Covert audio coaching with BIE and other technologies provides a bridge for the gap between delayed feedback and immediate feedback, and reduces many of the geographic challenges that interfere with the professional development and preparation of teachers. The application of covert technology in coaching increases the usefulness and efficiency of feedback, and has proven to be an effective delivery method. From the inception as a large, conspicuous, equipment-intensive system to the current state of long range transmission via covert sending and listening devices, numerous possibilities exist for future covert coaching uses in the professional development and preparation of teachers. These possibilities require specific guidelines for the successful implementation of covert coaching.

Implementation Guidelines

To implement covert audio coaching with these various electronic technologies, at least five variables must be considered:

1. *Participants* must be willing to receive immediate feedback. Covert audio coaching has been most effective when it focused on performance improvement. This contrasts with traditional supervision models in schools that have an evaluation function. Evaluations of educators frequently create anxiety during live observations. Even immediate feedback might not improve professional performance in anxious or unwilling participants.

2. *Behaviors* targeted for improvement should be agreed-upon prior to implementation. In the studies we reviewed, those that were most successful focused on a few high-value skills rather than a wide range of possible targets. These skills were observable, operationally defined, and easily measurable. The selected target behaviors must be important to the overall intent, relevant to participants, maintain high social validity, and affect student achievement.

3. *Feedback* delivered by the coach must be defined prior to implementation. Coaching feedback serves a variety of purposes and can include initial prompts, corrective feedback, reinforcement, questions, and other comments. Across the studies, feedback has ranged from concise directions to narrative discussion. Consideration should be given to the delivery, purpose, and ability of the participant to act on the feedback.

4. *BIE tools* should be selected based on the intended audience, purpose, and settings. Possible tools include a one- or two-way communication system (e.g., radio, personal FM system), with a Bluetooth, Skype, and Wi-Fi connection, if needed. Prior to purchasing tools, assess the intended location for the presence of firewall limitations. Criteria for selecting tools include that they are user-friendly, portable, applicable across settings, reasonably priced (with possible maintenance agreements), durable, and reliable.

5. *Practice* sessions must be conducted for participants prior to implementation. Participants will need to acclimate to the equipment and to the method of coaching. Participants will need to create contingency plans if limitations are encountered along the way (e.g., hang-ups, lost connections).

Based on the combination of coaching studies from education and other employment settings, coaching with electronic technologies has evolved into an *evidence-based practice*. Covert audio coaching can be incorporated into professional development programs and settings with the appropriate tools and support from coaches. By incorporating aspects from the studies included in the literature review, teachers, supervisors, and researchers alike can infuse coaching with technology into the supervision and professional development process.

FUTURE RESEARCH DIRECTIONS

As applications of coaching with technology continue to evolve, there is an obvious need for research to guide these coaching practices. For example, specific research practices that target the generalization issues described previously will be an important research direction. In addition, there will always be a need to establish the efficacy of different forms, formats, and equipment to deliver feedback during coaching. Several platforms exist that have been supported by the evidence as a *promising practice* including different types of earpieces (standard headphones, Bluetooth, and ear buds) and different types of delivery systems (two-way radios, FM wireless). One future direction includes coaching through Apple iPods (iCoaching) using one of the standard communication applications provided on Apple products (FaceTime).

Figure 3. Future research implications for eliminating professional development shortages in geographically isolated areas

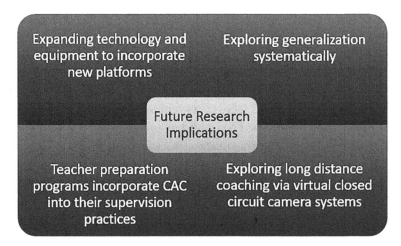

These and other platforms will need to be examined along with technology that allows for wireless internet paired with computer, tablet, or smart phone applications. Also, long-distance virtual communications will most likely join the short list of delivery systems. For example, different forms of multi-media coaching can be extended across states, countries, and even continents using wireless connections. This technology is only beginning to be studied in a systematic fashion. For example, if teacher educators discover that virtual supervision is both effective and cost efficient, then more teacher preparation programs will explore this practice. This has tremendous implications for eliminating professional development shortages in geographically isolated areas. Figure 3 summarizes several future research implications.

CONCLUSION

The BIE and CAC studies reviewed for this chapter met at least the minimum standards for establishing coaching with technology as an evidence-based practice. This conclusion holds for standards proposed for both single-case (Horner et al., 2005 Kratochwill et al., 2013) and group studies (Chwalisz, 2003; Flay et al., 2005; & Rycroft-Malone et al., 2004). It is evident that the use of covert electronic technologies is an evidence-based coaching practice for professional development and preparation of teachers and others. Like other uses of technology in the digital age, this coaching practice will continue to evolve, and future research will continue to support the efficacy of this practice.

REFERENCES

Baum, D. D., & Lane, J. R. (1976). An application of the Bug-in-the-Ear communication system for training psychometrists. *Counselor Education and Supervision*, *15*(4), 309–310. doi:10.1002/j.1556-6978.1976. tb02010.x

Bennett, K., Ramasamy, R., & Honsberger, T. (2012). The effects of covert audio coaching on teaching clerical skills to adolescents with autism spectrum disorder. *Journal of Autism and Developmental Disorders, 43*(3), 585–593. doi:10.1007/s10803-012-1597-6 PMID:22798051

Bennett, K., Ramasamy, R., & Honsberger, T. (2013). Further examination of covert audio coaching on improving employment skills to adolescents with autism spectrum disorder. *Journal of Behavioral Education, 22,* 103–119. doi:10.1007/s10864-013-9168-2

Bennett, K. D., Brady, M. P., Scott, J., Dukes, C., & Frain, M. (2010). The effects of covert audio coaching on the job performance of supported employees. *Focus on Autism and Other Developmental Disabilities, 25*(3), 173–185. doi:10.1177/1088357610371636

Chwalisz, K. (2003). Evidence-based practice: A framework for twenty-first-century scientist-practitioner training. *The Counseling Psychologist, 31*(5), 497–528. doi:10.1177/0011000003256347

Crowell, C., Anderson, D., Abel, D., & Sergio, J. (1988). Task clarification, performance, feedback and social praise: Procedures for improving the customer service of bank tellers. *Journal of Applied Behavior Analysis, 21*(1), 65–71. doi:10.1901/jaba.1988.21-65 PMID:16795713

Cunningham, T., & Austin, J. (2007). Using goal setting, task clarification, and feedback to increase the use of hands-free technique by hospital operating room staff. *Journal of Applied Behavior Analysis, 40*(4), 673–677. doi:10.1901/jaba.2007.673-677 PMID:18189098

Flay, B. R., Biglan, A., Boruch, R. F., Castro, F. G., Gottfredson, D., Kellam, S., & Ji, P. et al. (2005). Standards of evidence: Criteria for efficacy, effectiveness and dissemination. *Prevention Science, 6*(3), 151–175. doi:10.1007/s11121-005-5553-y PMID:16365954

Gallant, J. P., Thyer, B. A., & Bailey, J. S. (1991). Using bug-in-the-ear feedback in clinical supervision: Preliminary evaluations. *Research on Social Work Practice, 1*(2), 175–187. doi:10.1177/104973159100100205

Giebelhaus, C. R. (1994). The mechanical third ear device: A student teaching supervision alternative. *Journal of Teacher Education, 45*(5), 365–373. doi:10.1177/0022487194045005009

Goodman, J., Brady, M. P., Duffy, M. L., Scott, J., & Pollard, N. (2008). The effects of bug-in-ear on special education teachers delivery of learn units. *Focus on Autism and Other Developmental Disabilities, 23*(4), 207–216. doi:10.1177/1088357608324713

Green, C., Rollyson, J., Passante, S., & Reid, D. (2002). Maintaining proficient supervisor performance with direct support personnel: An analysis of two management approaches. *Journal of Applied Behavior Analysis, 35*(2), 205–208. doi:10.1901/jaba.2002.35-205 PMID:12102142

Horner, R. H., Carr, E. G., Halle, J., McGee, G., Odom, S., & Wolery, M. (2005). The use of single subject research to identify evidence-based practice in special education. *Exceptional Children, 71*(2), 165–179. doi:10.1177/001440290507100203

Hunt, D. (1980). 'Bug-in-ear' technique for teaching interview skills. *Journal of Medical Education, 11,* 964–966. PMID:7441683

Kahan, D. (2002). The effects of bug-in-the-ear device on intralesson communication between a student teacher and a cooperating teacher. *Journal of Teaching in Physical Education*, *22*(1), 86–104. doi:10.1123/jtpe.22.1.86

Korner, I. N., & Brown, W. H. (1952). The mechanical third ear. *Journal of Consulting Psychology*, *16*(1), 81–84. doi:10.1037/h0061630 PMID:14907954

Kratochwill, T. R., Hitchcock, J., Horner, R. H., Levin, J. R., Odom, S. L., Rindskopf, D. M., & Shadish, W. R. (2013). Single-case intervention research design standards. *Remedial and Special Education*, *34*(1), 26–38. doi:10.1177/0741932512452794

Kretlow, A., & Bartholomew, C. (2010). Using coaching to improve the fidelity of evidence-based practices: A review of studies. *Teacher Education and Special Education*, *33*(4), 279–299. doi:10.1177/0888406410371643

Oliver, P., & Brady, M. P. (2014). Effects of covert audio coaching on parents interactions with young children with autism. *Behavior Analysis in Practice*, *7*(2), 112–116. doi:10.1007/s40617-014-0015-2 PMID:27547702

Ploessl, D. M., & Rock, M. L. (2014). eCoaching: The effects on co-teachers planning and instruction. *Teacher Education and Special Education*, *37*(3), 191–215. doi:10.1177/0888406414525049

Rock, M., Gregg, M., Gable, R., Zigmond, N., Blanks, B., Howard, P., & Bullock, L. (2012). Time after time online: An extended study of virtual coaching during distant clinical practice. *Journal of Technology and Teacher Education*, *20*(3), 277–304.

Rock, M., Gregg, M., Thead, B., Acker, S., Gable, R., & Zigmond, N. (2009). Can you hear me? Evaluation of an online wireless technology to provide real-time feedback to special education teachers-in-training. *Teacher Education and Special Education*, *32*, 64–82. doi:10.1177/0888406408330872

Rock, M. L., Schumacker, R. E., Gregg, M., Howard, P. W., Gable, R. A., & Zigmond, N. (2014). How are they now? Longer term effects of eCoaching through online bug-in-ear technology. *Teacher Education and Special Education*, *37*(2), 161–181. doi:10.1177/0888406414525048

Rycroft-Malone, J., Seers, K., Titchen, A., Harvey, G., Kitson, A., & McCormack, B. (2004). What counts as evidence in evidence-based practice? *Journal of Advanced Nursing*, *47*(1), 81–90. doi:10.1111/j.1365-2648.2004.03068.x PMID:15186471

Scheeler, M., Congdon, M., & Stansbery, S. (2010a). Providing immediate feedback to co-teachers through bug-in-ear technology: An effective method of peer coaching in inclusion classrooms. *Teacher Education and Special Education*, *33*(1), 83–96. doi:10.1177/0888406409357013

Scheeler, M., & Lee, D. (2002). Using technology to deliver immediate corrective feedback to preservice teachers. *Journal of Behavioral Education*, *11*(4), 231–241. doi:10.1023/A:1021158805714

Scheeler, M., McKinnon, K., & Stout, J. (2012). Effects of immediate feedback delivered via webcam and bug-in-ear technology on preservice teacher performance. *Teacher Education and Special Education*, *35*(1), 77–90. doi:10.1177/0888406411401919

Scheeler, M. C., Bruno, K., Grubb, E., & Seavey, T. L. (2009). Generalizing teaching techniques from university to K-12 classrooms: Teaching preservice teachers to use what they learn. *Journal of Behavioral Education, 18*(3), 189–210. doi:10.1007/s10864-009-9088-3

Scheeler, M. C., Macluckie, M., & Albright, K. (2010b). Effects of immediate feedback delivered by peer tutors on the oral presentation skills of adolescents with learning disabilities. *Remedial and Special Education, 31*(2), 77–86. doi:10.1177/0741932508327458

Scheeler, M. C., McAfee, J. K., Ruhl, K. L., & Lee, D. L. (2006). Effects of corrective feedback delivered via wireless technology on preservice teacher performance and student behavior. *Teacher Education and Special Education, 29*(1), 12–25. doi:10.1177/088840640602900103

Wehman, P. (2012). Supported employment: What is it? *Journal of Vocational Rehabilitation, 37*, 139–142.

KEY TERMS AND DEFINITIONS

Bug-in-Ear (BIE): Device with microphone used to deliver coaching comments delivered by a coach directly to a participant wearing a receiver; the BIE is the equipment used to deliver audio messages.

Covert Audio Coaching (CAC): Method of delivery of unobtrusive coaching comments and feedback from a coach to participant using a BIE device from a distance; uses one person (e.g., a coach) to provide guidance or feedback statements, prompts, praise, or corrections using various forms of BIE technology.

Employment Coaching: Coaching and feedback provided for the purpose of developing an employee's skills; providing suggestions to improve or recognize exemplary work, or modifying certain workplace practices.

iCoaching: The use of Apple© products (such as iPods) connected to an earpiece enabling a participant to receive coaching comments from a researcher/coach who has a direct connection to the participant's earpiece.

Immediate Feedback: Feedback provided to an individual about a targeted behavior during or immediately after the specific act.

Inservice Teachers: Teachers currently employed in a K-12 school setting.

iPod: A small, portable handheld electronic device with a touch screen that can be used to take pictures and video, email, play digital media, and make calls using wireless internet connection to another device on the Apple platform.

FaceTime: An application used to make audio or video calls to other people using both the wireless internet connection and an Apple product (iPod Touch, iPad, Mac, iPhone).

Preservice Teachers: Adult students enrolled in teacher preparations programs, also referred to as student teachers, teachers-in-training, or intern teachers.

Professional Development: Training, coaching, and support provided to inservice teachers.

Chapter 14
Differentiated Animated Social Stories to Enhance Social Skills Acquisition of Children With Autism Spectrum Disorder

Bee Theng Lau
Swinburne University of Technology – Sarawak, Malaysia

Ko Min Win
Swinburne University of Technology – Sarawak, Malaysia

ABSTRACT

This study developed a web-based social skills intervention system accessible via a tablet/laptop computer which combines differentiated instructions, social stories, multimedia, and animations. This creates an interactive learning environment which (1) allows children to learn social skills repeatedly and pervasively; and (2) promotes teacher/caretaker-parent collaborations to boost the ASD children's social skills acquisition as, a simple logon to the portal enables parents/ caretakers and teachers to view the media prepared by others; track and reinforce the skills a child has learnt at home/ in school, and add his/her social stories which others can view. The prototype evaluation and observation of voluntary participants from the special education school who were treated with differentiated animated social stories demonstrates that digital-based differentiated social story interventions have made the learning of social skills more interactive, appealing and effective compared to the traditional social skill tools.

INTRODUCTION

Social communication impairment is pervasive among children diagnosed with Autism Spectrum Disorder (ASD) and participating in the respective community as a full-fledged member requires social communication skills. Ignoring this significant deficit means denying these children access to society. As such, research has been carried out to explore means and methods to help these children learn these skills. One among them is the Social Story™ developed by Carol Grey in 1991 which has acquired its

DOI: 10.4018/978-1-5225-2838-8.ch014

reputation as an effective method. This approach makes use of social stories which describe social situations and appropriate responses to these situations to enable children to learn or acquire social skills. At its inception, social stories were delivered by a teacher to one individual child face-to-face. Though effective, this requires a lot of human intervention, in this case, teachers (and parents) and time to make learning interactive and interesting. In addition, repetition is needed for the children to retain and apply what they have learned. Reinforcement of these social skills for each individual child at school is beyond what teachers can do when they are handling many children at the same time. Accomplishing this at home also requires a proper system of communication and collaboration between teachers and parents.

Given all these requirements and issues that teachers and parents may have, the authors developed a web-based social skills intervention system accessible via a tablet/laptop computer which combines differentiated instruction, social stories, multimedia and animations to create a learning environment for children to learn social skills interactively, repeatedly, and pervasively. This also promotes collaborations between teachers and parents/caretakers to boost the ASD children's social skills acquisition. Logging on to the portal of this web-based application enables both parents and teachers/caretakers to (i) track the skills a child is learning or has learned, (ii) view and use the media prepared by teacher/caretaker/parents to reinforce the social skills at home/school and (iii) add his/her social stories to the portal so that others can view them from school/home.

This chapter presents the evaluation of digital based social story interventions implemented through web-based application prototype developed for this study and observation of behavioral responses of voluntary participants from a special school and an early intervention care center in Kuching, Sarawak, Malaysia. The first section presents background to this study which describes Autism Spectrum Disorder, social skills deficits common to children with ASD, and Social Story™ as one of the effective methods to train children with ASD in social skills and its various delivery methods to improve or increase the effectiveness of Social Story™. Against the backdrop of certain boundaries of Social Story™, the second section of this chapter presents the main focus of this study to figure out method(s) to overcome certain limitations of Social Story™ approach and improve effectiveness of social stories, and technology(s) as a catalyst.

AUTISM AND SOCIAL SKILLS

Autism Spectrum Disorders, as described by National Institute of Mental Health (2014), are a group of complex disorders of brain development which cause deficiencies in social and communication skills which are vital to human lives and to survival in the workplace. They are interactive skills learned through socialization to stimulate positive responses from people whom they interact with. The ASD problem is serious and ASD cases are on the rise. According to the report released by the Centers for Disease Control and Prevention in 2012, 1 in 88 American children have some form of ASD, a 78% increase in the number compared to that of about a decade before (Falco, 2012; Centers for Disease Control and Prevention, 2014). According to the National Autistic Society United Kingdom (2013), 1.1% of its population (2011 population census) had autism. Although no one has so far been able to identify what exactly triggers ASD, there are two factors which seem to be related to ASD: genetic factors and environment factors (National Institutes of Mental Health, 2014; Research Autism, 2015).

According to DSM-V (Diagnostic and Statistical Manual of Mental Disorders 5th edition, American Psychiatric Association, 2013), ASD is diagnosed based on two areas which are:

1. Deficits in social communication which include social-emotional reciprocity (e.g., two ways conversations), nonverbal communicative behaviors for social interaction such as abnormal eye contact and body language, and developing, maintaining and understanding relationships such as making friends and

2. Fixated interests and repetitive behaviors which include stereotyped or repetitive motor movements, use of objects, or speech (e.g., simple motor stereotypes, lining up toys or flipping objects, echolalia, idiosyncratic phrases), insistence on sameness, inflexible adherence to routines, or ritualized patterns of verbal or nonverbal behavior (e.g., extreme distress at small changes), hyper- or hypo-reactivity to sensory input or unusual interest in sensory aspects of the environment (e.g., apparent indifference to pain/temperature)(American Psychiatric Association 2013).

On the other hand, basic social skills essential for children as pointed out by McGrath & Francey (1991); Burke et al. (2006); Eskay & Willis (2008) include imitation, emotional expressions, facial expressions, making eye contact, following instructions, obeying rules and regulations, sharing, taking turns, playing together, accepting failures, empathy and offering support, giving and receiving compliments, disagreeing with other people properly, saying "no" to peers when appropriate, paying attention to peers, asking for help, asking to join the group and respect for other people's opinions. It can clearly be seen that deficits highlighted as symptoms of ASD in ASD diagnosis manual stated above are in fact the basic social skills essential for children.

As the social skills are crucial for daily lives, lack of these social skills prevents these children from becoming independent individuals of the society. Hence, training social skills that they lack becomes the most effective and efficient way to help children with ASD not only to improve their personalities such as self-esteem, motivations and satisfaction, but to enable them to gain better achievements in schools and at work (Loomis 2008; Bohlander et al. 2012). Most importantly, successful social skills acquisition will empower them to contribute their talents fully to the community in which they live.

As pointed out by Wilson (2013), social skills can be improved by using specific teaching methods systematically, and tools and methods for teaching and learning social skills specifically designed for children with ASD have emerged. Some typical effective treatments include behavior modification therapies, computer based therapies, robot-based therapies, visual and audio based therapies and Social Story™. The following section will describe the social story approach which is the focus of this study.

SOCIAL STORY

Social Story™ developed by Carol Grey in 1991 (Gray & Garand 1993) has acquired a good reputation for teaching or improving social skills of children with ASD (Schneider & Goldstein 2009). It is a short story which describes a detailed situation which may bring obstacles or problems in social communication and provides the learners with solid information to face the situation or overcome the obstacles (Scurlock 2008, Gabbert 2010). Helping children with ASD to have the capacity to show concern for other people suggests that the social story endeavors to tackle the social communication impairment of children with ASD.

Three basic steps required for the development of a social story include: (1) identification of a problematic social situation for the targeted child to be used as the focus situation of the social story; (2) establishment of the setting in which such a situation occurs through observation of the targeted child and his/her opinions about that situation, interview with parents, teachers and caretakers (Gray & Garand 1993; Gray 1996) and (3) sharing collected data with the targeted child as well as all other stakeholders such as parents, caretakers and teachers.

It is of paramount significance to write social stories at the level that the targeted children can understand (Gray & Garand 1993, Gray 1996). For instance, if the targeted child has problems in either reading or understanding the story read by someone, as pointed out by Kokina & Kern (2010), there may be little or no effect on social skill acquisition by that child.

The original guideline of social story writing suggests use of four types of sentences: 1) descriptive sentences which describe when and where the situation occurs, who are involved, and what and why they are doing, 2) directive sentences which depict a favorable response(s) to the social situation in a positive tone, 3) perceptive sentences which provide responses, aspects, opinions and emotions of other people involved in the social situation and 4) affirmative sentences which describe common belief(s) in a given situation (Gray & Garand 1993). Gray (2000) later added control sentence and cooperative sentence to the list. Control sentences are more like key sentences for the audience either to recall or apply the information. Cooperative sentences inform the audience who are able to help them in a given situation. Note that not all types of sentences need to be used in composing a story (Washburn 2006). Descriptive and perspective sentences are mandatory in a social story because the purpose of social story is to describe a specific situation and provide solid information about possible expected response to the situation and emotions and opinions of other people.

The formal method of presenting social story is that teachers or caretakers read aloud to the children the story in plain text on paper without any graphic. This method is most effective when one teacher reads stories and takes care of one single pupil at a time (Mandasari 2012). The social story delivered through this formal method was proved to be positively effective to train sportsmanship to a 10-year old participant with Asperger Syndrome according to Scurlock (2008). However, given the use of one single participant, the result of this research could not be generalized. In addition, the advantage of this formal method was outweighed by the fact that it was time-consuming and needed a lot of human intervention.

According to the reviews, however, as highlighted by Sansosti, Powell-Smith and Kincaid (2004), Reynhout and Carter (2006), and Kokina and Kern (2010), the effectiveness of the social story approach was unstable. The formal method of presenting the social story read aloud by someone to an individual at a time is handy to be used in a class of children with ASD whose attentions are scattered (Crozier & Tincani 2007). However, the method has to be customized according to the number of students involved.

In fact, the social story approach was proven to be more effective when the children read the stories themselves instead of teachers, parents and caretakers reading for them (Kokina & Kern 2010). This method can also save time and human resources in the classroom and home setting. However, this method is not feasible if the children involved either have poor reading skill or cannot read at all.

Bearing in mind the limitations of the formal delivery approach and recognizing ASD children as visual learners, different researchers have combined social stories together with other components to achieve better outcomes. As pointed out by Wallin (2009), addition of visual cues such as picture, drawing and real objects to social story could improve the effectiveness of the social story. For example, Reynhout & Carter (2006) suggested use of illustrations together with the written text although Gray and Garand (1993) recommended avoiding illustrations given the possibility that children might portray them in the ways that they were not meant for.

People's quest for a better and more effective approach to presenting social stories has resulted in a shift from the formal delivery to ones which employ different media and emerging information technology. Social stories employing different media have been proven to be effective although in some cases the results may not be generalizable given the small number of participants (Agosta et al. 2004; Scurlock 2008; Schneider & Goldstein 2009).

With emergence of computer and other related electronic gadgets, most ASD children find computers intrinsically motivating (Sansosti & Powell-Smith 2008), and they appear to learn more on computer than from the teacher (Heimann et al. 1995). Hagiwara and Myles's intervention which combined the social story and use of computer as the platform in 1999 showed that the combined intervention was effective and that it was possible to employ advanced technology in presenting social stories. In 2008, Sansosti and Powell-Smith combined video modeling and social stories and presented them to the participants using computers. The intervention was successful, resulting in significant behavioral changes. Social stories presented in PowerPoint slide show on computer were also effective (More 2008).

According to the reviews, the effectiveness of social story was unstable (Sansosti, Powell-Smith, Kincaid 2004; Reynhout & Carter 2006; Kokina & Kern 2010). The formal method of presenting social story read aloud by someone to an individual at a time is handy to be used in a class of children with ASD whose attentions are scattered (Crozier & Tincani 2007). However, the method has to be customized according to the number of students involved.

This seems to suggest the use of illustration instead of the written text for students to read. Although Gray and Garand (1993) suggested avoiding illustration because the children might portray them in the ways which were not meant to, Reynhout & Carter (2006) suggested using illustration together with written text. Mandasari (2012) combined social stories, animation and computer to save both reading time and human resources required in the formal delivery. Using flash technology, she created five 2D animated social stories, and presented the children with ASD using a laptop. These social stories were made available in two languages, English and Bahasa Malaysia, the National Language of Malaysia. The results of her research showed that the animation was able to capture children's attention and improve the effectiveness of the social stories. Laptop also motivated the children with ASD to learn independently.

As technology advances, laptop computers are not the only choice of technology which children with ASD are interested in nowadays. Tablet computers, especially iPad, become very useful and appealing to students not only in general education but also in special education (Shore & Rastelli 2006). According to Shore, use of iPad decreased such symptoms as control and attentions of autism (Shore & Rastelli 2006). According to Brandon (2011), a mother claimed that iPad not only lessened her son's disorder symptoms but also improved his communication skills. Kim et al. (2014) investigated the effect of tablet-assisted social stories on three participants with ASD. Social stories were created using Prezi and presented to the children using a tablet. According to their research data, this tablet-assisted social stories intervention not only decreased disruptive behaviors but also increased academic engagement.

All the research reviewed so far suggests that social stories presented in media (via different gadgets) bring the following advantages to children with ASD who have problems with concentration and attention span:

1. Motivating and capturing their attention;
2. Helping them acquire the necessary social skills
3. Decreasing their disruptive behavior
4. Increasing academic engagement

A point worthy of note is that though improving effectiveness of social stories, those animated social stories were designed and applied generally as interventions to all participants regardless of their backgrounds. As Guskey (2008, p.198) points out, "due to students' individual differences, no single method of instruction works best for all". Kokina & Kern (2010) also explained that effectiveness of social stories may vary depending on the background of individual children – varying level of reading skills, background knowledge, learning preferences and styles etc. These stories were not designed to be dedicated to individual participants' unique needs of social skills. Kokina & Kern (2010) explained that effectiveness of social stories may vary depending on the background of individual children – varying level of reading skills, background knowledge, learning preferences and styles etc. This also calls for the attention of the social story writer that social stories created for one specific group of children might not work well with another group of children (see also Vicker 1998).

In a nut shell, this section has drawn our attention to the fact that the researchers' creative venture of making social stories using application in the compatible gadgets appealing to the children has given rise to an increase in the effectiveness of social stories in social skills training, and consequently, an increase in these children's independence while noting varying degrees of effectiveness given the diverse backgrounds of individual children. This discrepancy in effectiveness has led this study to integrate the animated social story intervention with *differentiated instruction* (refer to the next section) to accommodate distinctive needs of these children and make social stories more effective.

INTEGRATION OF DIFFERENTIATED INSTRUCTION

Differentiated Instruction or differentiation is an effective teaching framework which encourages teachers to differentiate their instructions to meet the needs of every student in the classroom. As suggested by Aldridge (2010), it should be applied in a way that does not change learning outcomes but rather change how the content is delivered. The aim of implementing differentiated instruction is to amplify each student's development based on their culture, strength, characteristics and learning styles instead of changing them to fit with the curriculum (Hall 2002). Tomlinson (2001) recommends that teachers should personalize or customize teaching materials and instructions congruent with varied learning needs of different students based on the need analysis data. According to Tomlinson & Susan (2000), differentiation can be implemented in the *content*, *process* and *product* of the curriculum as can be seen in Figure 1.

Content includes anything the students need to learn and how the students need to achieve them. Different elements and material can be used to support students for easy access to contents (learning materials). An individual can learn best in "zone of proximal development (ZPD)" where moderate levels of context are provided (Vygotsky & Cole, 1978). Each student has different scales of ZPD which can be analyzed through their learning profiles. Sometimes it is hard to adjust content in some extreme cases. For example, some students still practice multiplying by two while other students are able to multiply by seven. In such cases, content differentiation should focus more on concepts rather than very detailed or unlimited facts.

Process or activity is how the student gets the key points or concepts of the targeted subject. Consistent use of dynamic grouping is suggested. Students are expected to cooperate together to accomplish the given task(s). Either small or big groups of students will be formed based on the content, the nature of project and students' skills. Teacher must consider how to organize efficiently and deliver contents effectively.

Figure 1. Differentiated instruction (Hall, 2002)

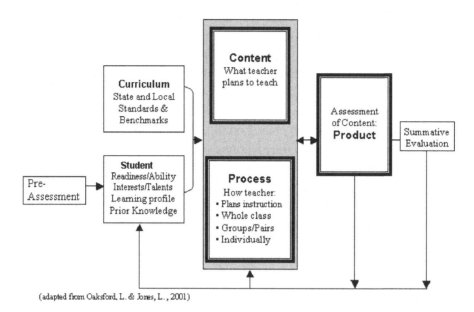

(adapted from Oaksford, L. & Jones, L., 2001)

Products are what students produce at the end of the lessons to exhibit the mastery of the subject.

Preparation for differentiation requires use of assessment/formative data. The success of differentiation depends on purposeful pre-assessment, be it formal or informal. The assessment here refers to both pre-assessment that serves as a pedagogical tool to diagnose or analyze details about the students to understand more about them and on-going assessment to measure instructions (Hall, 2002). The success of differentiation depends on purposeful pre-assessment, be it formal or informal. Combination of pre and on-going assessments can assist teachers to create better approaches, more choices and efficient learning styles for the students. Teachers should create tasks which are fascinating, enthralling, and accessible to key comprehension and skills but challenging for the children. The products may vary depending on the students' understanding and knowledge.

According McAdamis (2001), using differentiated instruction significantly improves test scores of students who previously scored low in the Rockwood School District. Differentiated instruction improves not only student growth but also teachers' self-confidence (Affholder, 2003). Baumgartner et al. (2003)'s research implemented differentiated strategies such as flexible grouping, increasing self-selected reading time and easy access to a wide range of reading materials to improve primary and middle school students' reading skills. According to Baumgartner et al. (2003), its successful implementation resulted in improved reading skills. The effectiveness of differentiation in curriculum was investigated between the students who received differentiated intervention and the students who did not receive (Tieso, 2005). An assessment based on the curriculum was used to test before and after the curriculum for the evaluation purpose. The assessment results showed that students who received the intervention achieved significantly more highly than those who did not. Karadag & Yasar (2010) also investigated the effectiveness of differentiated instruction approach on the attitudes of thirty students in Turkish course and found that the effectiveness of the differentiated instruction was positive and students' academic performances were improved. According to Chamberlin and Power (2010), findings of a similar research reported that implementing differentiated instruction in mathematics (college level) remarkably fulfilled the needs of the students.

The differentiated instruction was formerly used with special children but the idea of differentiated instruction has also been well accepted in inclusive classrooms (Lawrence-Brown 2004). Differentiated instruction has been proven as effective in special education (Daily 2005) based on the study Darrow (2015) who investigated the effectiveness of differentiated instruction on five students with different disabilities in the music classroom. According to the data stated in the research, the effectiveness of differentiated instruction was positive and the learning outcomes of students were better than what had been expected. Affholder (2003) conducted a research which implemented differentiated instruction in an inclusive elementary classroom. One of the findings from the research is that some differentiated contents which were meant for high functioning students were also effective with a wide range of the students. The research investigated effectiveness of differentiated instruction not only on students but also on teachers. Twenty six teachers who received 15 hours of training on differentiated instruction were tested using the Stage of Concern (SOC) to find out their opinions and mastery of differentiated instruction. Only 6 teachers got the lower level of concern for implementing differentiated instruction. The research showed overall positive outcomes. Differentiated instruction has also been proven as effective in special education (Daily 2005). Darrow (2015) investigated the effectiveness of differentiated instruction on five students with different disabilities in the music classroom. According to the data stated in the research, the effectiveness of differentiated instruction was positive and the learning outcomes of students were better than what had been expected.

PROPOSED SOLUTION

This study proposed that the issue of satisfying varying needs of individual students stated above could be addressed by integrating *differentiated instruction* into the social story approach. This has led the researchers to determine which delivery method should be used for integration. Choosing the original delivery of the social story would pose the same issue - too much consumption of time and energy. Mandasari (2012)'s approach on social story is considered a better choice because her approach was proved to save time and human resources, and more significantly, using animation and the IT gadget (laptop) was attested to engaging ASD children well. In addition, using animation solves the issue of readability for ASD children who cannot read at all. As justified in the review of Social Story™, using the latest gadget like the tablet computer (e.g. iPad) does produce positive outcomes. As such, this research study also proposed that the animated social story (employing Mandasari's approach) be delivered via the tablet computer instead of the laptop. This proposed solution called for the development of an application which could assist both the integration of differentiated instruction and the presentation of animated social stories on the tablet computer.

In this study, the framework of differentiated instruction was integrated into the intervention of animated social stories in 4 stages:

1. **Pre-Assessment**: First of all, pre-assessment was conducted to find out the targeted students' background, what these students needed and what they had already known. This prevented us from repeatedly teaching them what they had already known.

2. **Content**: Secondly, contents of animated social stories were then differentiated based on the outcomes of the analysis of pre-assessment data to reach out every targeted student.
3. **Process**: Thirdly, differentiated animated social stories, the products of the second step, were delivered using the latest popular gadget, an electronic tablet in replacement of computer in Mandasari (2012)'s approach, to capture rapt attention from targeted students.
4. **Product**: Fourthly, ongoing assessments were used to track the improvements and the demonstrated actions/responses of children in their daily lives were observed to see whether or not they had acquired the required skills.

The following section will describe how the Social Story App as the intervention tool was developed for this study.

INTERVENTION TOOL

Social Story App (SSA) is a simple web-based application which was developed (1) to assist in differentiation processes and (2) to be able to run on most of modern devices. SSA developed for this study makes the following possible:

1. Create and differentiate (modify) animated social stories
2. Import animated social stories into SSA
3. Assign suitable animated social stories to individual students differently according to their social skill needs reflected in the pre-assessment
4. Create and modify assessments to assist with on-going assessments
5. Take the created assessments and save assessment answers for improvement tracking and the course evaluation

There are two main benefits of choosing the web platform for SSA.

1. SSA can be used on any popular device which has the browser and Internet access. This allows students to use any device they prefer as long as it has a browser and Internet access. As the browser is a pre-installed application on popular devices, no extra software is needed to install. More importantly, web applications are very efficient and they can be run on devices with low specifications.
2. SSA can be accessed from anywhere as long as there is a device with Internet. Using SSA, students can learn at home again what they have learned in school. This repetition reinforces the learning or growth of neural connections in children's brains (Kindermusik 2014). Parents and caretakers can also view what their children are learning just by logging into SSA. Within SSA, parents and caretakers can create or upload animated social stories or modify existing animated socials stories for their children and track their children's improvements via assessment results once they have taken the assessment. This also offers the means to teacher- parents/care-taker collaborations to boost the social skills acquisition by the children with ASD.

In order to investigate the usability of SSA, two teachers and four students with some prior knowledge on using information technology for teaching and learning from two research sites (see the following section) were asked to test SSA on different platforms i.e. windows desktop computer and android tablet computer. Firstly, SSA was reported by teachers to be comprehensive and easy to use with very little explanation. Secondly, as the drawing board of SSA is a basic tool with no effect at all, it was suggested to include some pre-set animation characters so that users could drag and drop instead of drawing, as creating animation requires skills in painting to get a good animation. Thirdly, as SSA only accepts videos with MP4 format to be compatible with browsers from mobile operating systems for upload, this restriction requires the user to convert other video file types to MP4 before uploading pre-made animation videos. This requirement was reported to be difficult for the teachers. Finally, as expected, students were motivated to use the tablet PC while some still needed some more time to get familiar with tablet PCs. Although students were able to use SSA, they still needed help from teachers in some cases such as logging in and taking assessments.

SOCIAL STORY INTERVENTION

The study was carried out in a special school and an early intervention care center located in Kuching, Sarawak, Malaysia. As this study aims to investigate the effectiveness of animated social stories complemented by the differentiated instruction in the social skills training of children with ASD, this study mainly targeted students aged between 5 and 16 who had been diagnosed with any disorders under ASD. 12 students together with their parents/caretakers and class teachers who were invited through school principals agreed to participate in this study.

A field study was conducted to develop content for this study. Using data from the field study and literature reviews, seven animated social stories - "Asking for Help", "Calming Down", "Greeting Friends", "Paying Attention", "Playing and Singing with Friends", "Snack Time" and "Waiting" - were developed for all children with ASD in general.

Common or general animated social stories in this chapter refer to general animated social stories created for children with ASD regardless of their individual differences. *Differentiated animated social stories*, on the other hand, refer to those which are differentiated based on the data from the pre-assessment.

Goal Attainment Scaling (GAS)

As it was very important to observe behavioral responses of the participants to measure the success or failure of interventions, observation rules for each story were defined using GAS developed by Thomas Kiresuk and Robert Sherman (1968). Initially used to evaluate a wide range of mental illnesses, GAS has been used as a standard evaluation tool in normal and special education settings (Oren and Ogletree 2000; Sladeczek et al. 2001; Ruble et al. 2012).

Following GAS steps, five scales (from -2 to + 2) were needed for each goal. Zero is the expected outcome or targeted goal. -2 and -1 are somewhat less expected of the outcomes and +1 and +2 are somewhat more expected. The baseline is usually considered as -2 (Kiresuk et al. 1994). Importance and/ or difficulty of the goal should also be considered in calculating the weight of the goal (Turner-Stokes 2009). The simplified equation of GAS is shown in Figure 2.

In the formula,

Figure 2. Simplified formal for calculating overall goal attainment scores (Turner-Strokes, 2009)

$$50 + \frac{10\Sigma(w_i x_i)}{\left[0.7\Sigma w_i^2 + 0.3(\Sigma w_i)^2\right]^{\frac{1}{2}}}$$

Table 1. GAS of animated social stories

	much less than expected (-2)	less than expected (-1)	expected (0)	more than expected (+1)	much more than expected (+2)
Asking for Help (Importance = 3, Difficulty = 2)	bad moods	do nothing	raise hand (or) call teacher	raise hand and call teacher (or) give signals to teacher (for non-verbal)	raise hand and call teacher and ask for help politely (or) give signals to teacher in proper manner (for non-verbal)
Calming Down (Importance = 3, Difficulty = 3)	bad moods	calm down when teacher/assistant/caretaker interacts with him/her	partially control emotion (take a deep breath (or) count 1 to 10)	control emotion properly (take a deep breath and count 1 to 10)	control emotion properly and explain to teacher/parent/caretaker
Greeting Friends (Importance = 3, Difficulty = 2)	ignore/aggressive when he/she is asked to greet	reluctant to greet even he/she is asked	greet when he/she is asked to do	greet friends without being asked	greet friends with good expressions (smiling or waving hand or both)
Paying Attention (Importance = 3, Difficulty = 3)	totally ignore	need to be reminded frequently to pay attention	pay attention when he/she is asked to do	pay attention on his/her own	pay attention and respond properly
Playing and Singing with Friends (Importance = 3, Difficulty = 2)	ignore/refuse to play with friends even he/she is asked repeatedly	participate when he/she is asked repeatedly	engage with friends easily when he/she is asked	play with friends on his/her own	invite friends to play with him/her
Snack Time (Importance = 3, Difficulty = 2)	ignore/refuse to share snacks	need to be asked more than once to share snacks (or) need to remind him/her to ask the owner before grabbing other people's snacks.	share food when he/she is asked (or) exchange snack	share food on his/her own (or) ask other people properly for food	share food and exchange food in proper manner
Waiting (Importance = 3, Difficulty = 3)	do not wait at all	need to be reminded frequently to wait	need to be reminded once for waiting	wait on his/her own but not with proper manner (noisy while waiting	wait in proper manner

w_i = the weight assigned to the ith goal
x_i = the numerical value achieved (between -2 and +2)

Following the steps of GAS, five scales for each story were defined and these are provided in Table 1. Importance and difficulty of stories were decided based on literature review and observation. All levels were consulted with teachers to avoid disparity in levels and ratings.

Although baseline scores should be -2 according to Kiresuk et al. (1994) and Ruble et al. (2012), the baseline score in this study was set at -1 (less than expected) for two reasons. Firstly, the higher score was set as the baseline score to determine whether or not the intervention made the situations worse. Secondly, very few students scored -2 based on the observation data and consultation with teachers. The common cause of those scores was students' mood (angry, sulking and so on). The normal overall GAS for the expected outcome should be 50 and that the score should be used to determine whether the participant has acquired the skill or not. To merge all scores from all sessions, scores are being averaged and it does affect some variations in the final GAS scores. To compensate for the score variation, the mean score (45) between the normal and baseline values was used for judging. An observation form was created to align with GAS.

Pre-Assessment

Pre-assessment conducted in this study include (1) data collected from parents through the social skill survey and (2) the outcomes of common animated social story intervention conducted with the participant children with ASD. Firstly, parents of participants were requested to fill in the social skill survey to find out the primary languages and social skills situation of participants from the parents' perspective. Data collected from the survey were used to tentatively assign common animated social stories to participants individually. To ensure appropriate social stories were assigned to individual students, this tentative assignment was checked against observation and confirmed with respective teachers. Using data from the survey, observation and confirmation with teachers, appropriate social stories were assigned to individual students in SSA. Table 2 below provides the summary of the participants' profile and social stories assigned to each individual student.

After assigning suitable animated social stories to individual participants, a preliminary intervention using common animated social stories started. The purposes of this intervention were (1) to collect more data for differentiation purpose and (2) to use as the point of departure in comparing the effectiveness between the common and the differentiated versions of the animated social stories. Using SSA on a tablet, a total of 6 sessions of the common animated social story intervention were conducted for each participant. After each session, the participants' behavioral responses were observed and observation scores were given using the GAS as discussed above. Each participant's score in each session and the average for all sessions were calculated using the GAS formula. As discussed in the setup of the study, any participant whose average GAS for any common animated social story was lower than 45 was considered "failed" for that story.

Scores based on the participants' demonstrated behaviors in response to all assigned common animated social stories tabulated. As a sample, Table 3 presents behavioral responses of 7 participants who were assigned to the common animated social story "Asking for Help."

Table 4 below summarizes the results of observation with regard to all common social stories conducted.

Table 2. Animated social stories assigned to individual participants

Participant	Age (Years)	Gender	Fluency of Language (In order)	Asking for Help	Calming Down	Greeting Friends	Paying Attention	Playing and Singing with Friends	Snack Time	Waiting
01	12	Female	Malay, English, Chinese	✓	▪	▪	▪	✓	✓	✓
02	14	Male	Malay, English	✓	▪	✓	▪	▪	▪	✓
03	12	Male	Chinese, Malay, English	✓	✓	▪	✓	▪	✓	▪
04	12	Female	English, Malay, Chinese	✓	✓	✓	✓	▪	▪	▪
05	15	Male	Chinese, English, Malay	✓	✓	✓	▪	✓	▪	▪
06	08	Male	Chinese, English, Malay	✓	✓	✓	▪	▪	▪	▪
07	11	Female	Chinese, English, Malay	▪	✓	▪	✓	▪	▪	✓
08	06	Male	English, Malay	▪	✓	▪	✓	▪	▪	✓
09	05	Male	Chinese, English	▪	✓	✓	✓	▪	✓	▪
10	05	Male	Chinese	✓	▪	▪	✓	▪	✓	✓
11	05	Male	English, Chinese	▪	✓	▪	✓	▪	▪	✓
12	05	Male	Chinese, English	▪	✓	▪	✓	▪	▪	✓

As can be seen, Table 4 provides the summary of the participants' performance in each common animated social story: the highest and lowest GAS and the participants who scored these (participant number in parentheses), the success and failure rates of each common animated social story.

The failure rate of common animated social stories was 28.57% for the story "Asking for Help", 88.89% for the story "Calming Down", 00.00% for the story "Greeting Friends", 75.00% for the story "Paying Attention", 00.00% for the story "Playing and Singing with Friends", 25.00% for "Snack Time" and 85.71% for "Waiting". The failure rates of three common animated social stories, "Calming Down", "Paying Attention" and "Waiting" were significantly higher compared to those of the other four.

Detailed observations and teachers' feedback on those three animated social stories highlighted the following:

Most participants assigned to the story "Calming Down" did not understand both the concept of the story and the gesture for taking a deep breath. The researcher had to demonstrate the action for them

Table 3. Responses of assigned participants for "Asking for Help"

	Session 01						Session 02						Session 03						Session 04						Session 05						Session 06						Avg GAS
	-2	-1	0	1	2	GAS	-2	-1	0	1	2	GAS	-2	-1	0	1	2	GAS	-2	-1	0	1	2	GAS	-2	-1	0	1	2	GAS	-2	-1	0	1	2	GAS	
01		2				40		2				40		2	1			43			3	1		53			3			50		1	3			48	45.56
02		2	1			43		1	2			47			1	1		55			1	1		55				2		60				2		60	53.33
03		2	1			43		1	2			47			2			50			2			50		1	1	1		50			1	1		55	49.17
04		2				40		2	1			43		2	2			45		1	3			48		1	2			47		1	2			47	44.86
05		2	1			43		2	1			43		2	2			45		1	3			48		1	2	1		50		1	2	1		50	46.53
06		2	1			43		2	2			45		1	2			47			2			50			2			50			3			50	47.50
10	1	4				38	1	4				38		5				40		4	1			42		3	2			44		2	2	1		48	41.67

Table 4. Summary of effectiveness of common animated social stories

Common Animated Social Story	Lowest Average GAS (Participant who achieved)	Highest Average GAS (Participant who achieved)	Passed	Failed	Total	Failure Rate
Asking for Help	41.67 (10)	53.33 (02)	5	2	7	28.57%
Calming Down	40.56 (07)	47.78 (03)	1	8	9	88.89%
Greeting Friends	48.00 (04)	52.78 (02)	5	0	5	00.00%
Paying Attention	41.11 (07, 11)	46.11 (03)	2	6	8	75.00%
Playing and Singing with Friends	51.17 (05)	51.25 (01)	2	0	2	00.00%
Snack Time	42.92 (01)	50.83 (03)	3	1	4	25.00%
Waiting	41.11 (12)	45.56 (02)	1	6	7	85.71%

to understand better. Some participants especially participants 04 and 09 lost interest while watching this animation. Besides, as pointed out by the teachers, sentences used in this story were too long for participants to understand.

For the story "Paying Attention", all the participants especially 04, 07, 09 and 10 needed to be reminded frequently when their teachers were giving instructions. Most of the participants did lose their attentions to this animated social story while watching. Their interest declined from time to time. They seemed quite confused with both the gestures of characters and the story line. Even participant 03 with the highest score partially understood this animated social story. He was also confused with gestures of characters from animation. Teachers recommended that the story should focus on the teacher character only instead of two characters, teacher and friend. One of the teachers also advised to include appreciation from the teacher character to the student character.

Most participants assigned to the story "Waiting", especially participants 01 and 10, needed to be reminded frequently to wait because they ran to their busy teachers straight away most of the time when they wanted to show their homework or they wanted to ask for permission to go to the washroom. Some participants, participants 02 and 08 waited once they were asked in the last few sessions though sometimes they needed to be reminded repeatedly. Participants 10 and 12 did not show the same interest in this animation as in other animated social stories they were assigned to. Except for the participant 02, other participants did not understand the gestures of animated characters. The instructions were somewhat complicated for them. Even the participant 02 partially understood this animated social story.

In this study, the tablet PC was used as the medium through which the social story intervention was implemented. This preliminary intervention proves that using tablet motivated the participants well as even participants 04 and 10, who showed less interest in the animated social stories, did not decline any intervention session due to the tablet.

As for the use of animation, the preliminary intervention suggests that the animation worked, but to a certain extent, for some participants especially participant 10 who showed less interest in these animated social stories. Participants such as participant 02 who can read and are willing to read was observed to be reading subtitles/lyrics from educational videos and watching at the same time. It seemed they were more interested to read than to listen to audio from videos.

A point worthy of note is that some participants, participants 10 and 12 who were less interested in the animated social stories they were assigned to were observed to be more attracted towards animal characters (animals acting like human, for example, Tom & Jerry) than human characters. During observation, they showed keen interest in educational videos and animations in which animal characters were featured.

Data generated from the preliminary common animated social story intervention were fed into the development of the differentiated animated social stories as explained below.

Content

Data collected from pre-assessment data were analyzed to pave the way for the differentiation of social stories.

As mentioned earlier, the failure rate of common social stories was set to 50% to get reliable data though the effectiveness could be seen through 30%. Out of seven common animated social stories assigned to participants, the failure rates of three common animated social stories, "Calming Down", "Paying Attention" and "Waiting" were above 50%. The failure rates show clearly that participants did not improve much on social skills linked to those three common animated social stories. They failed to attract most participants' attention, as a decline in their interest in these stories was observed from time to time. Observation data and feedback from teachers also indicated that (1) gestures from those three animated social stories confused most participants and (2) instructions in the stories "Paying Attention" and "Waiting" were unnecessarily long and somewhat complicated. In short, those three animated social stories were not good enough to help the participants acquire associated social skills.

Both the failure rates and observation data suggested that those three animated social stories needed to be differentiated to meet the needs of the participants on the basis of teachers' feedback and observation data. It was also decided that the other four stories would be neither differentiated nor included in the next intervention as the results of these stories clearly indicated that they worked well. Steps taken to differentiate those three animated social stories are as follows:

1. Scripts of those three stories were rewritten at the level all participants could easily understand;
2. Animations were differentiated as a response to teachers' input and observation data. These include:
    a. Gestures which made participants confused were either removed or modified based on feedback, observations data and consultation with some artists.
    b. The main character was switched to the animal character as the participants 10 and 12 were observed to prefer animal characters to human characters.
3. Subtitles were added for participants who can read.

In addition to differentiation made to these stories described above, an on-going assessment was also added to monitor children's progress as this study believes that integration of on-going assessment can help not only parents and teachers to track improvement, as stressed by Croker (1999), but also children to have a better understanding of what they have learned. Multiple choice questions (MCQ) were used as an on-going assessment in this study. The differentiated animated social story intervention which differentiated the process coupled with the on-going assessment was conducted.

Effectiveness of Differentiated Animated Social Stories

As stated earlier, three animated social stories - "Calming Down", "Paying Attention", and "Waiting"- with the highest failure rate in the preliminary intervention were differentiated and MCQ questions were added as an on-going assessment for each story.

The same steps taken in the preliminary intervention were repeated in the differentiated animated social story intervention together with added on-going assessments. 6 sessions of three differentiated animated social story intervention were conducted. As before, these differentiated animated social stories were presented to the participants on SSA using an electronic tablet. Participants were then asked to take on-going assessments (MCQ) related to the differentiated animated social stories to which they were assigned. This was followed by the observation as in the preliminary intervention.

Two more observation rules were added to align with added MCQ. If a participant can answer an MCQ of a differentiated animated social story correctly, 0 was given to the participant for that differentiated animated social story based on the expectation or assumption that providing a correct answer means understanding the story. If he or she got it wrong, -1 was given. Details of the participants' behavioral responses for three differentiated animated social stories are presented in the following sub-sections.

Behavioral Responses to the Differentiated Version of "Calming Down"

A total of 9 participants were assigned to the differentiated version of the social story "Calming Down" and their behavioral responses are tabulated in Table 5.

The scoring rules were the same as those in the first intervention. The highest average GAS score was 52.64 by participant 03 and the lowest 46.94 by participant 12. None of the participants obtained average GAS score below 45. Details of their responses are as follows:

1. Participant 03 tried to calm himself down for a few times in the early session. But he only counted 1 to 10. He was given the score -1 in the first session because he chose a wrong answer to MCQ. He chose correctly in the later sessions.
2. Observation highlighted that participant 04 loved to write. During the first intervention, she was observed to read subtitles. She did choose the wrong MCQ answer till the third session. She counted 1 to 10 when she tried to use the eraser repeatedly.
3. Participant 05 was getting better in controlling his temper from session to session when his rubber bands were taken away by his teacher. He chose the wrong answer only once in the first session.
4. Participants 06, 07 and 09 seemed to understand this differentiated animated social story. Though they could not calm themselves down properly, they were able to do partially.
5. Participant 08 did not cry as easily as he used to and he was able to count 1 to 10 when he was about to cry. But he chose the wrong MCQ answer sometimes.
6. Participants 11 and 12 counted 1 to 2 and learned how to take a deep breath. But they had to be reminded to calm down.
7. The focus of participant 04 was getting better when she read subtitle. The attention of participant 12 seemed to improve.

During the intervention, all participants understood the story line well though some of them did not understand the revised gestures "taking a deep breath" and the researcher had to demonstrate how to

Table 5. Responses of assigned participants for differentiated version of "Calming Down"

	Session 01						Session 02						Session 03						Session 04						Session 05						Session 06						Avg GAS
	-2	-1	0	1	2	GAS	-2	-1	0	1	2	GAS	-2	-1	0	1	2	GAS	-2	-1	0	1	2	GAS	-2	-1	0	1	2	GAS	-2	-1	0	1	2	GAS	
03		1	3			48			2			50			2	1		53			2	2		55			2	2		55			2	2		55	52.64
04		2	2			45		1	2			47		1	3			48			3			50			2	1		53			1	2		57	49.86
05		2	2			45		1	2			47			3			50			3			50			2	1		53			2	1		53	49.72
06		3	2			44		2	3			46		2	3			46		2	3			46			4			50			4			50	47.00
07		2	1			43		2	1			43		1	2			47			2			50			3			50			2			50	47.22
08		2	1			43		1	2			47		1	2			47			2			50		1	2			47			2			50	47.22
09		2	1			43		2	2			45		1	3			48		1	4			48			3			50			3	1		53	47.72
11		2	1			43		1	1			45		1	2			47			2			50			2			50			2			50	47.50
12		2	1			43		1	1			45		1	2			47		1	2			47			2			50			2			50	46.94

Table 6. Responses of assigned participants for differentiated version of "Paying Attention"

	Session 01						Session 02						Session 03						Session 04						Session 05						Session 06						Avg GAS
	-2	-1	0	1	2	GAS	-2	-1	0	1	2	GAS	-2	-1	0	1	2	GAS	-2	-1	0	1	2	GAS	-2	-1	0	1	2	GAS	-2	-1	0	1	2	GAS	
03		1	2			47		1	2			47			3			50			3			50			2	1		53			2	1		53	50.00
04		1	2			47		1	2			47		1	2			47			2			50			2	1		53			2	1		53	49.44
07		2	2			45		1	2			47		1	2			47			3			50			2			50			2			50	48.06
08		2	1			43		1	2			47			2			50			2			50			2			47			2			50	47.78
09		2	2			45		1	2			47			2			50		3	4			46		1	3			48			3			50	47.48
10		3	1			43		4	3			44		3	3			45		3	4			46		1	3			48			3			50	45.83
12		2	1			43		1	2			47		1	2			47			2			50			2			50			2			50	47.78
13		2	1			43		2	1			43		2	2			45		1	1			45			2			50			2			50	46.11

Table 7. Responses of assigned participants for differentiated version of "Waiting"

	Session 01						Session 02						Session 03						Session 04						Session 05						Session 06						Avg GAS
	-2	-1	0	1	2	GAS	-2	-1	0	1	2	GAS	-2	-1	0	1	2	GAS	-2	-1	0	1	2	GAS	-2	-1	0	1	2	GAS	-2	-1	0	1	2	GAS	
01		1	2			47			3			50			3			50			2	1		53			2	1		53			1	2		57	51.67
02		1	2			47			3			50			3			50			2	2		55			1	2		57			1	2		57	52.50
07		1	2			47			2			50			2			50			3			50			2			50			2			50	49.44
08		2	1			43		1	2			47		1	2			47			2			50		1	2			47			2			50	47.22
10		4	1			42		3	3			45		3	4			46		3	4			46		2	3			46			4			50	45.74
11		2	1			42		2	1			45		2	1			46		1	1			46		1	2			46			2			50	45.74
12		2	1			43		1	1			45		2	1			45		2	2			45		1	1			45			2			50	45.28

take a deep breath. Nevertheless, GAS score clearly validates that this differentiated animated social story was able to help participants acquire one of social skills "calming down". MCQ also helped them recall what to do and apply what they had acquired easily when they felt angry.

Behavioral Responses to the Differentiated Version of the Story "Paying Attention"

8 participants were assigned to the differentiated version of the story "Paying Attention" and their behavioral responses are tabulated in Table 6.

The highest average GAS score 50.00 was achieved by participant 03 and the lowest 45.83 by participant 10. As in the first differentiated story, no participant scored lower than 45. Details of their responses are as follows:

1. Participant 03 behaved better during giving instructions from session to session.
2. Participant 04 did not lose her interest in this animated social story any more. Her focus was improved by reading subtitles from the animated social story.
3. Nearly half of the participants especially participants 09 and 10 had to be reminded frequently while giving instructions until the fourth session.
4. Attention of both participants 11 and 12 to this animated social story and their behaviors were improved session by session.
5. All participants except participant 10 did very well in on-going assessment (MCQ). They still chose wrong answers till the fifth session.
6. Some participants such as participants 03, 08, 11 and 12 understood this animated social story while others such as participant 04 and 10 partially understood it.

To sum up, the scores as the outcomes of the observation of participants' behavioral responses highlight that all participants acquired the social skill to pay attention to teacher with the help of the differentiated animated social story "Paying Attention".

Behavioral Responses to the Differentiated Version of the Story "Waiting"

As in the first intervention, 7 participants were assigned to the differentiated version of "Waiting" and their behavioral responses are presented in Table 7.

The highest average GAS score was 52.50 obtained by participant 02 and the lowest 45.28 by participant 12. As in the two previous stories, no single participant scored lower than 45 for the story "Waiting" though average GAS scores of some participants were so close to the marginal score 45. Details of their responses are as follows:

1. Participant 01 was reminded more than once in the first session. Her waiting skill was improved session by session. The same applied to participants 02, and 07. They became better in waiting. Those 4 participants chose correct MCQ answers in every session. Some of their negative scores came from their hyper activeness. They were reminded multiple times because they were simply too active to wait.

2. Participant 10 was reminded multiple times in many sessions. He chose MCQ answers correctly half of the time but sometimes he chose the wrong ones intentionally.
3. Improvement of participants 11 and 12 was quite slow compared to that of other participants in this animated social story. But they chose MCQ answers correctly in most sessions.

Some participants such as participants 01, 02, and 07 understood the concept completely. Participants 11 and 12 understood partially. Although participant 10 was easily distracted, his focus was much better in this intervention than in the previous intervention. Based on GAS scores and observation data, all participants seemed to have acquired "waiting" skill with the help of this differentiated animated social story.

As in the preliminary intervention, the attraction of electronic tablet worked very well. It improved participants' attentions. The revised scripts were good enough for participants to have a better understanding of the animated social story. The revised gestures worked well for most of the participants and not much for some. Subtitles also improved focuses of participants who can read. Participant 04 read subtitles, her focus improved and she understood concepts of the stories better. Integration of MCQ also helped most of the participants to be able to recall what they had learned which in turn enabled them to apply and to behave accordingly. But it did not work for some participants (participants 04 and 10) who chose answers recklessly. It is obvious that all three differentiated animated social stories indeed helped most participants to acquire associated social skills.

DISCUSSION

It is clear from the tables of scores of both versions of stories that all differentiated animated social stories worked very well. To get much clearer results, results of each are compared according to individual social stories in the following.

First, the comparison of the results between the common and differentiated versions of the story "Calm Down" can be seen in Table 8.

There were totally 2 times of scoring -2 in the common version but none in the differentiated version. No more behaviors which were expected much less were observed in the differentiated version. The common version scored 105 times of the score -1 and the differentiated one had 42 times only. The unexpected behavior rate was more than 50% down in the differentiated version. The score of 0 occurred 38 times and 117 times in the common and differentiated versions respectively. The rate of expected behaviors rose up three times much more in the differentiated version than the common version. The common version achieved the score 1 twice and differentiated version 13 times. Both versions had no occurrence of scoring 2 and p value was less than 0.001. Thus, the results clearly show an increase in the frequencies of occurrence of positive behavior and a significant decrease in the frequencies of occurrence of negative behavior in the differentiated intervention.

Second, Table 9 compares two sets of the results of the social story "Paying Attention".

In this story, both versions did not have any occurrence of score -2 and 2. The common version had 109 times of the score -1 and 48 times of 0 respectively. It had no occurrence of score 1. The differentiated version, however, had 45 times of the score -1, 103 times of score 0 and 4 times of score 1. Behaviors which were less than expected went down more than 50% in the result of the differentiated version. More expected behaviors were found in the differentiated version although the figure was not

Table 8. Results comparison of both versions of "Calm Down"

	Calm Down											
	Common Animated Social Stories						Differentiated Animated Social Stories					
	-2	-1	0	1	2	GAS	-2	-1	0	1	2	GAS
Session 01	1	22				39.57		18	14			44.38
Session 02	1	21	3			40.80		11	16			45.93
Session 03		19	8			42.96		8	22	1		47.74
Session 04		19	6			42.40		4	23	2		49.31
Session 05		14	11	1		45.00		1	22	4		51.11
Session 06		10	10	1		45.71			20	6		52.31
Total	2	105	38	2		256.44		42	117	13		290.77
P value						$p < 0.001$						$p < 0.001$

Table 9. Results comparison of both versions of "Paying Attention"

	Paying Attention											
	Common Animated Social Stories						Differentiated Animated Social Stories					
	-2	-1	0	1	2	GAS	-2	-1	0	1	2	GAS
Session 01		23	2			40.80		15	12			44.44
Session 02		22	2			40.83		12	16			45.71
Session 03		19	8			42.96		8	18			46.92
Session 04		16	12			44.29		7	21			47.50
Session 05		16	10			43.85		3	18	2		49.57
Session 06		13	14			45.19			18	2		51.00
Total		109	48			257.91		45	103	4		285.15
						$p < 0.001$						$p < 0.001$

Table 10. Results comparison of both versions of "Waiting"

	Waiting											
	Common Animated Social Stories						Differentiated Animated Social Stories					
	-2	-1	0	1	2	GAS	-2	-1	0	1	2	GAS
Session 01		19				40.00		13	10			44.35
Session 02		17	3			41.50		7	15			46.82
Session 03		16	5			42.38		8	16			46.67
Session 04		15	5			42.50		6	16	3		48.80
Session 05		12	8			44.00		5	13	3		49.05
Session 06		10	9			44.74			14	4		52.22
Total		89	30			255.12		39	84	10		287.90
						$p < 0.001$						$p < 0.001$

clear-cut like "Calming Down". The same goes for better behaviors which mean more than expected. As in the story "Calming Down", p value was less than 0.001.

Third, the results of both versions of the story "Waiting" are juxtaposed in Table 10.

As illustrated in the table, the common version had 89 times of the score -1 and 30 times of the score 0 but none of the score -2, 1 and 2. On the other hand, the differentiated version had 39 occurrences of the score -1, 84 of the score 0 and 10 of the score 1. Undesirable behaviors which were less than expected were reduced more than half in the differentiated version. Expected behaviors were doubled and behaviors which were more than expected were found in the differentiated version. In this story, *p* value is the same as other modified stories - less than 0.001.

As can be seen from the comparison tables presented above, it is obvious that all differentiated versions of animated social stories helped participants acquire associated social skills better than the respective common counterpart of these stories. Intervention using the common animated social stories failed to assist participants in their acquisition of some social skills because the common animated social stories associated with those skills did not meet the needs of the participants. When the needs were not met, participants could not understand the social skills presented in those animated social stories. In addition, their interest in those stories was observed to fall gradually. Some participants lost their interests even in the first session. By this way, the participants were pushed away by those common animated social stories instead of learning from them. This called for social stories that would cater to these participants' needs which in turn necessitated identification of their needs.

With these learning needs in mind, common animated social stories which failed to help participants acquire associated social skills were differentiated. Scripts of less successful animated social stories were rewritten concisely to pitch at participants' comprehensibility. Confusing gestures for participants were revised. The main human character was replaced with the animal character for participants who preferred animal characters. Subtitles were added for visual participants who learned better by reading. Most importantly, MCQ questions were added as on-going assessment for each differentiated social story for parents and teachers to monitor their children's progress in learning and for children to reflect what they have learned and be motivated to learn more. In that way, common animated social stories were differentiated according to the learning styles and needs of participants and became differentiated animated social stories.

Participants who did not understand before came to understand the concepts of the social stories with the help of rewritten scripts. With the aids of revised gestures, some participants understood these animated social stories better. Some participants who were distracted due to the appearance of the human characters came to be interested in the stories as they were attracted to the replaced animal character. Participants who learned better by reading focused better and performed better with differentiated social stories with added subtitles. Participant 04 was exceptional because her desire to read never appeared during observation in the first intervention. Her focus became better and better with reading subtitles.

The electronic tablet attracted participants' attractions and motivated them to learn. Some participants were eager to touch the tablet rather than learning. That might be the downside of using electronic tablet. More time was needed for participants like them to get familiar with the gadget.

Integration of on-going assessments (MCQ) did help most participants to recall the social skills they had learned through these differentiated animated social stories. Some participants showed their interest in SSA and some parents asked about it. They were interested in animation and MCQ features.

Based on data analysis and discussion above, the differentiated animated social stories helped partici-pants acquire associated social skills by attracting the attentions of participants to the stories, improving their interests and creating a better understanding of the stories. Tablet computer was useful to attract and maintained the attentions of participants. MCQ helped participants recall what they had learned. These are the testimonials to the fact that the proposed approach which integrated differentiated instruction into animated social stories worked as expected.

FUTURE WORKS

First future work is to upgrade the animation feature of SSA. According to the users' feedback, animation feature was way too basic. Animation feature can be upgraded to the level whereby teachers can create animation using pre-set characters and motions easily without drawing anything. Although technology exists to upgrade, another essential factor is art skill. The researcher of this study did not have necessary arts skills to draw pre-set characters with pre-set motions and had to use the software to create animation for this study. Collaboration with someone with great art skill is needed for upgrading animation feature of SSA. This will help both teachers and parents/caretakers to create or modify more animated social stories easily to meet the needs of their ASD children.

Implementing automatic video recording during watching animated social stories and taking on-going assessments is part of the future works. Recorded videos can be used as reference to check the learners' detailed facial expressions. Parents and caretakers can check how their children are learning in the schools and vice versa teachers can also check how their children are learning at their homes. This will also help teachers and parents/caretakers to judge whether their children enjoy learning or the animated social stories are working for their children. But this upgrade needs both surveys to find out the rate of approval of this feature by both parents/caretakers and teachers, and technical works to ensure unauthorized access to recorded videos.

This study also recommends that SSA be upgraded to a level in which artificial intelligence (AI) is implemented. The current stage of SSA is completely manual. Pre-assessment can be implemented with AI. Pre-assessment with AI may enable users to explore the background of users. It may be able to assign users to animated social stories which are considered fit based on the background data. But extensive research on background, preferences and learning styles of children with ASD are needed to compile data from research into pre-assessment so that SSA would be able to assign best-fit animation social stories to the participant based on input data.

CONCLUSIONS

To get clear results of integrating differentiated instruction into animated social stories, two interventions were conducted with the aid of prototype (constructed using up-to-date technologies) which can run on popular IT gadget, an electronic tablet. The web-based tool allows usability, accessibility and communication across setting, motivates the targeted children to learn and enables users to tailor animation to individual needs. The preliminary intervention was conducted using common animated social stories to find out which stories did not work out well with most participants. Based on observation data and feedback from teachers, animated social stories which did not work well were differentiated according to the combined teaching method. The actual invention was then conducted using modified/differentiated animated social stories. Then, results of two interventions were compared and evaluated. The results clearly highlight that the combination of differentiated instruction and animated social stories with the aid of SSA worked well.

In conclusion, the findings of this study suggest that differentiated instruction is definitely imperative to meet varying needs of ASD children and maximize their social skills learning potentials through animated social stories. Findings of this study also show that the integration of differentiated instruction into animated social stories on SSA helped participants in their social skills acquisitions by eliminating least unwanted behaviors of participants, trimming participants' behaviors which were less expected down at least half of occurrences and shaping expected behaviors up to mostly double. Although the results are positive, there is a need to improve the integration of differentiated instruction into animated social stories. There may be more problems/issues which could not be revealed by findings of this study. This study is considered preliminary to investigation of the integration of differentiated instruction into animated social stories to emerge as a reliable approach to the social skills acquisition of children with ASD.

REFERENCES

Affholder, L. P. (2003). *Differentiated instruction in inclusive elementary classrooms* (Doctoral dissertation). University of Kansas.

Agosta, E., Graetz, J. E., Mastropieri, M. A., & Scruggs, T. E. (2004). Teacher researcher partnerships to improve social behavior through social stories. *Intervention in School and Clinic, 39*(5), 276–287. doi:10.1177/10534512040390050401

Aldridge, J. (2010). Among the periodicals: Differentiated instruction. *Childhood Education, 86*(3), 193–195. doi:10.1080/00094056.2010.10523147

American Psychiatric Association. (2013). *Diagnostic and statistical manual of mental disorders* (5th ed.). Washington, DC: Author.

Baumgartner, T., Lipowski, M. B., & Rush, C. (2003). *Increasing reading achievement of primary and middle school students through differentiated instruction* (Master's thesis). Chicago: Saint Xavier University.

Bohlander, A. J., Orlich, F., & Varley, C. K. (2012). Social skills training for children with autism. *Pediatric Clinics of North America, 59*(1), 165–174. doi:10.1016/j.pcl.2011.10.001 PMID:22284800

Brandon, J. (2011, March 9). *Is the iPad a 'Miracle Device' for Autism?* Retrieved from http://www.foxnews.com/tech/2011/03/09/can-apple-ipad-cure-autism

Burke, R., Herron, R., & Barnes, B. A. (2006). *Common sense parenting: using your head as well as your heart to raise school-aged children* (3rd ed.). Boys Town Press.

Centers for Disease Control and Prevention. (2014, March 27). *CDC estimates 1 in 68 children has been identified with autism spectrum disorder*. Retrieved from http://www.cdc.gov/media/releases/2014/p0327-autism-spectrum-disorder.html

Chamberlin, M., & Powers, R. (2010). The promise of differentiated instruction for enhancing the mathematical understandings of college students. *Teaching Mathematics and Its Applications, 29*(3), 113–139. doi:10.1093/teamat/hrq006

Croker, R. (1999). Fundamentals of ongoing assessment. *Shiken, 3*(1), 10-15. http://jalt.org/test/cro_1.htm

Crozier, S., & Tincani, M. (2007). Effects of social stories on prosocial behavior of preschool children with autism spectrum disorders. *Journal of Autism and Developmental Disorders, 37*(9), 1803–1814. doi:10.1007/s10803-006-0315-7 PMID:17165149

Daily, M. (2005). *Inclusion of Students with Autism Spectrum Disorders*. Retrieved from http://education.jhu.edu/PD/newhorizons/Exceptional Learners/Autism/Articles/Inclusion of Students with Autism Spectrum Disorders/index.html

Darrow, A. (2015). Differentiated instruction for students with disabilities: Using DI in the music classroom. *General Music Today, 28*(2), 29–32. doi:10.1177/1048371314554279

Eskay, M., & Willis, K. (2008). Implementing social skills for students with autism. *Autism and Developmental Disabilities: Current Practices and Issues, 18*, 45-17. Retrieved from http://www.emeraldinsight.com/doi/abs/10.1016/S0270-4013(08)18003-5

Falco, M. (2012, March 29). *CDC: U.S. kids with autism up 78% in past decade*. Retrieved from http://edition.cnn.com/2012/03/29/health/autism

Gabbert, C. (2012, December 7). *Using Social Stories to Teach Kids with Asperger's Disorder*. Retrieved from http://www.brighthub.com/education/special/articles/29487.aspx

GoAnimate. (2014). *Create Animated Videos for your Business*. Retrieved from https://goanimate.com/

Gray, C. A. (1996). *Social stories and comic strip conversations: unique methods to improve social understandin*g [Videotape]. Arlington, TX: Future Horizons.

Gray, C. A. (2000). *Writing social stories with Carol Gray – workbook for video*. Arlington, TX: Future Horizons.

Gray, C. A., & Garand, J. D. (1993). Social stories: Improving responses of students with autism with accurate social information. *Focus on Autism and Other Developmental Disabilities, 8*(1), 1–10. doi:10.1177/108835769300800101

Guskey, T. (2008). Mastery Learning. In 21st Century Education: A Reference Handbook. Thousand Oaks, CA: Sage Publications. doi:10.4135/9781412964012.n21

Hall, T. (2002). *Differentiated Instruction*. Retrieved from http://www.cast.org/publications/ncac/ncac_diffinstruc.html

Heimann, M., Nelson, K. E., Tjus, T., & Gillberg, C. (1995). Increasing reading and communication skills in children with autism through an interactive multimedia computer program. *Journal of Autism and Developmental Disorders, 25*(5), 459–480. doi:10.1007/BF02178294 PMID:8567593

Karadag, R., & Yasar, S. (2010). Effects of differentiated instruction on students attitudes towards Turkish courses: An action research. *Procedia: Social and Behavioral Sciences*, *9*, 1394–1399. doi:10.1016/j.sbspro.2010.12.340

Kim, M., Blair, K. C., & Lim, K. (2014). Using tablet assisted social stories™ to improve classroom behavior for adolescents with intellectual disabilities. *Research in Developmental Disabilities*, *35*(9), 2241–2251. doi:10.1016/j.ridd.2014.05.011 PMID:24927518

Kindermusik. (2014, November 4). *Repeat After Me: Kids Learn from Repetition.* Retrieved from https://www.kindermusik.com/mindsonmusic/benefits-of-music/repeat-after-me-kids-learn-from-repetition/

Kiresuk, T. J., & Sherman, R. E. (1968). Goal attainment scaling: A general method for evaluating comprehensive community mental health programs. *Community Mental Health Journal*, *4*(6), 443–453. doi:10.1007/BF01530764 PMID:24185570

Kiresuk, T. J., Smith, A., & Cardillo, J. E. (1994). *Goal attainment scaling: Applications, theory and measurement.* Hillsdale, NJ: Lawrence Erlbaum Associates.

Kokina, A., & Kern, L. (2010). Social story™ interventions for students with autism spectrum disorders: A meta-analysis. *Journal of Autism and Developmental Disorders*, *40*(7), 812–826. doi:10.1007/s10803-009-0931-0 PMID:20054628

Lawrence-Brown, D. (2004). Differentiated instruction: Inclusive strategies for standards-based learning that benefit the whole class. *American Secondary Education*, *32*(2), 34.

Loomis, J. W. (2008). *Staying in the game: providing social opportunities for children and adolescents with autism spectrum disorder and other developmental disabilities.* Autism Asperger Publishing Company.

Mandasari, V. (2012). *Learning social skills with 2D animated social stories for children with autism spectrum disorders* (Master's thesis). Kuching, Sarawak: Swinburne University of Technology.

McAdamis, S. (2001). Teachers tailor their instruction to meet a variety of student needs. *Journal of Staff Development*, *22*(2), 1–5.

McGrath, H., & Francey, S. (1991). *Friendly kids, friendly classrooms: teaching social skills and confidence in the classroom* (1st ed.). Melbourne: Pearson Australia.

More, C. (2008). Digital stories targeting social skills for children with disabilities: Multidimensional learning. *Intervention in School and Clinic*, *43*(3), 168–177. doi:10.1177/1053451207312919

National Autistic Society. (2014). *Autism facts and history.* Retrieved from http://www.autism.org.uk/about/what-is/myths-facts-stats.aspx

National Institute of Mental Health. (2014). *Autism Spectrum Disorders.* Retrieved from http://www.nimh.nih.gov/health/topics/autism-spectrum-disorders-pervasive-developmental-disorders/index.shtml?utm_source=rss_readers&utm_medium=rss&utm_campaign=rss_full

Oren, T., & Ogletree, B. T. (2000). Program evaluation in classrooms for students with autism: Student outcomes and program processes. *Focus on Autism and Other Developmental Disabilities*, *15*(3), 170–175. doi:10.1177/108835760001500308

Research Autism. (2015). *Causes of Autism*. Retrieved from http://researchautism.net/autism/causes-of-autism

Reynhout, G., & Carter, M. (2006). Social stories™ for children with disabilities. *Journal of Autism and Developmental Disorders*, *36*(4), 445–469. doi:10.1007/s10803-006-0086-1 PMID:16755384

Ruble, L., McGrew, J. H., & Toland, M. D. (2012). Goal attainment scaling as an outcome measure in randomized controlled trials of psychosocial interventions in autism. *Journal of Autism and Developmental Disorders*, *42*(9), 1974–1983. doi:10.1007/s10803-012-1446-7 PMID:22271197

Sanrattana, U., Maneerat, T., & Srevisate, K. (2014). Social skills deficits of students with autism in inclusive schools. *Procedia: Social and Behavioral Sciences*, *116*, 509–512. doi:10.1016/j.sbspro.2014.01.249

Sansosti, F. J., & Powell-Smith, K. A. (2008). Using computer-presented social stories and video models to increase the social communication skills of children with high-functioning autism spectrum disorders. *Journal of Positive Behavior Interventions*, *10*(3), 162–178. doi:10.1177/1098300708316259

Sansosti, F. J., Powell-Smith, K. A., & Kincaid, D. (2004). A research synthesis of social story interventions for children with autism spectrum disorders. *Focus on Autism and Other Developmental Disabilities*, *19*(4), 194–204. doi:10.1177/10883576040190040101

Schneider, N., & Goldstein, H. (2010). Using social stories and visual schedules to improve socially appropriate behaviors in children with autism. *Journal of Positive Behavior Interventions*, *12*(3), 149–160. doi:10.1177/1098300709334198

Scurlock, M. (2008). *Using social stories with children with Asperger syndrome* (Master's thesis). Athens, OH: Ohio University.

Shore, S., & Rastelli, L. G. (2006). *Understanding Autism for Dummies* (1st ed.). For Dummies.

Sladeczek, I. E., Elliott, S. N., Kratochwill, T. R., Robertson-Mjaanes, S., & Stoiber, K. C. (2001). Application of goal attainment scaling to a conjoint behavioral consultation case. *Journal of Educational & Psychological Consultation*, *12*(1), 45–58. doi:10.1207/S1532768XJEPC1201_03

Tieso, C. (2005). The effects of grouping practices and curricular adjustments on achievement. *Journal for the Education of the Gifted*, *29*(1), 60–89. doi:10.1177/016235320502900104

Tomlinson, C. A. (2001). *How to Differentiate Instruction in Mixed-Ability Classrooms* (2nd ed.). Alexandria, VA: Association for Supervision & Curriculum Development.

Tomlinson, C. A., & Susan, D. A. (2000). *Leadership for differentiating schools & classrooms* (1st ed.). Alexandria, VA: Association for Supervision & Curriculum Development.

Turner-Stokes, L. (2009). Goal attainment scaling (GAS) in rehabilitation: A practical guide. *Clinical Rehabilitation*, *23*(4), 362–370. doi:10.1177/0269215508101742 PMID:19179355

Vicker, B. (1998). Behavioral issues and the use of social stories. *The Reporter*, *3*(2), 13–14.

Vygotsky, L. S., & Cole, M. (1978). *Mind in society: The development of higher psychological processes*. Cambridge, MA: Harvard University Press.

Wallin, J. M. (n.d.). *An introduction to social stories.* Retrieved from http://www.polyxo.com/socialstories/introduction.html

Washburn, K. P. (2006). *The effects of a social story intervention on social skills acquisition in adolescents with Asperger's syndrome* (Doctoral dissertation). University of Florida.

Wilson, K. P. (2013). Incorporating video modeling into a school-based intervention for students with autism spectrum disorders. *Language, Speech, and Hearing Services in Schools, 44*(1), 105–117. doi:10.1044/0161-1461(2012/11-0098) PMID:23087158

KEY TERMS AND DEFINITIONS

Autism Spectrum Disorders: A set of complex brain developmental disorders which cause deficits in social and communication skills.

Baseline: An original state of a certain social skill of a participant before interventions of this study.

Differentiated Instruction: An effective teaching framework which encourages teachers to differentiate instructions to meet the needs of every student in the classroom add in its features.

Differentiated animated social story: An animated social story which is differentiated according to the data from intervention with generalized animated social story to meet the needs of assigned participants to the story to help them acquire associated social skill.

Generalized animated social story: An animated social story which is created to help children with Autism Spectrum Disorders in general (i.e. without targeting any specific group or individual) in acquiring associated social skill.

Intervention: A process of intervening or treatment to help children with ASD in acquiring social skills.

Social skills: Interactive skills which we acquire by socializing with people in the society, use to communicate and significantly build relationship with people in the society.

Social story: A short story used in the Social Story Approach to teach social skills to children diagnosed with ASD; each story presents a certain social situation together with responses from different aspects and gives advice on interactions.

Social Story App (SSA): A web-based software prototype developed in this study to aid in differentiating and delivering processes.

Chapter 15
Applied Behavior Analysis as a Teaching Technology

Amoy Kito Hugh-Pennie
Hong Kong Association for Behavior Analysis, China

Hye-Suk Lee Park
KAVBA ABA Research Center, South Korea

Nicole Luke
Brock University, Canada

Gabrielle T. Lee
Michigan State University, USA

ABSTRACT

Applied behavior analysis is known as an effective way to address the needs of people with autism spectrum disorders. The layperson may also associate behavior analysis with forensic psychology through their experience of crime dramas such as Criminal Minds: Behavior Analysis Unit. However accurate or simplified these portrayals they are a very narrow view of the larger field of behavioral science. Behavior analysis has a host of applications in the real world. Some of these applications include but are certainly not limited to the determination of social policies, advertising, policing, animal training, business practices, diet and exercise regimens and education. In this chapter the authors will focus on how applied behavior analysis can be used as a teaching technology from the behavioral and educational literature that has the potential to help lead the way out of the educational crisis faced in the United States of America and abroad.

INTRODUCTION

Applied behavior analysis (ABA) is a science traditionally tied to solving practical problems based on the discoveries from the basic science of behavior. It is the application of behavioral principles to change socially significant behavior to a meaningful degree through careful observations and systematic experimentation (Baer, Wolf, & Risley, 1968). Webster's Dictionary (n. d.) defines technology as the

DOI: 10.4018/978-1-5225-2838-8.ch015

use of scientific knowledge to solve a practical problem. One of the defining characteristics of ABA as "technological" is that its effects are replicable and available to others via precise descriptions of procedural operations (Baer et al., 1968). Thus, not only any instruments, apparatus, or techniques, but also strategic methodological processes developed within the behavior analytic tradition, are included in the definition of technology (Layng & Twyman, 2013) herein described in this chapter. Simply, ABA is a technology which is used to change behavior.

Lattal (2008) further distinguished technologies developed within the behavior analytic discipline as endogenous technology (e.g., the operant chamber) while those developed outside of this discipline as exogenous technology (e.g., the iPad™). Assimilating or merging exogenous technology with endogenous technology can produce powerful effects on evaluation in our society, particularly when applied to our education system (Escobar & Twyman, 2014).

Endogenous technology can be defined as the applications of discoveries from the laboratory to solve student learning problems in the classroom via systematically sequenced educational outcomes with frequent measures to mastery, learner-centered active responding opportunities, and individualized pacing toward the ultimate goals. Pedagogy has always been an integral part of the research tradition of behavior analysis (Keller, 1968; Lindsley, 1991; Skinner, 1968). Despite the existence of empirically validated pedagogical practices shown effective in facilitating student learning, advances of exogenous technology applied in the classroom seem to remain independent of and ignorant of endogenous technology.

For example, in a review of evidence-based online instructional strategies, it was reported that online instructions involving multi-media did not produce superior effects in student performance (Means, Toyama, Murphy, Bakia, & Jones, 2010). Such results were not surprising, as those studies compared lectures delivered via either in-person or video formats. Both instructional methods were literally identical and consisted of passive learning without active student responding. Advanced exogenous technology alone, without integrating endogenous technology as the foundation, yielded no significant educational outcomes. ABA offers many benefits if implemented in the classroom. These include ways to teach, ways to organize teaching materials and objectives, and ways to think about schooling in general.

Unfortunately, adapting exogenous technology without endogenous technology in the education system is common. In its 2016 National Education Technology Plan, the Office of Educational Technology defines technology as those tools that a classroom has for learning such as: laptops, computers, iPads™, and phones (US Department of Education, 2016). This definition does not fully account for the essential learning process necessary for successful educational outcomes and ignores the role of teachers who serve as scientists to apply scientific knowledge to solve practical learning problems. Such a prevailing notion has contributed to an ongoing culture that dismisses teachers as valued and technological, which has become a barrier when discussing practical solutions to a serious problem. As a result, ABA is not being consistently used in schools and this may pose a problem.

Recent test results still show that children in the United States are performing in school below average when compared to other children in the world (Carnoy & Rothstein, 2013). The need to improve our education system is imperative; even though we have spent money and time to do so, we have yet to be competitive on the world stage. Science and digital technology have given us access to a great number of wonderful tools, but without a science of teaching we cannot effectively use these tools to improve the learning of our children. The process or the way we teach is an area of opportunity for change.

Hundreds of effective pedagogical tactics and strategies have been identified as evidence-based procedures in the behavioral literature (See Greer, 2002, Chapters 5 and 6 for a list of over 200 such tactics). These tactics and strategies constitute a technology of teaching and as such should be included in our consideration of advancements in the digital age. We have seen inclusion of some of these strategies in special education where there has been wide spread adoption of tools like functional behavior assessment and positive behavior supports. Nearly 7,000 schools in over 37 states in the United States have adopted School Wide Positive Behavior Supports (SWPBS) in conjunction with Response to Intervention (RTI) to increase prosocial and academic behaviors while decreasing incidence of conduct referrals, seclusion, restraints, suspensions and juvenile incarceration of school-aged children ("What is School-Wide Positive Behavior Support?" 2009). These tools are endogenous technology but on a whole due to the precision and depth of understanding required to implement such technologies and the system of schooling they will require their own treatment outside the scope of this chapter.

Lastly, academic teaching strategies such as scaffolding instruction, use of Direct Instruction, using scripted curriculum for core subjects of math, reading and social studies, along with progress monitoring of academic interventions, are all based on fundamental principles of behavior. As such a science of teaching benefits learners at all ability levels (e.g., general education, gifted and talented, and students with learning differences) and represents, additionally, an opportunity to offer greater equity (fiscal and human resources) across the board for all, regardless of race, gender or socioeconomic status (SES). In this way we can fulfill the mandate of President Barack Obama of the United States through Exec. Order No. 13707, 3 C.F.R. 56365 (2015) to use behavioral science to improve lives and to improve the access to educational opportunities for all. Our focus in this chapter will be on the use of ABA as a technology for teaching.

BACKGROUND

Why ABA as a Teaching Technology?

ABA has a number of strengths when considered as a technology of teaching. Teachers who are strategic scientists of instruction learn to know immediately when to change what they are doing in the classroom because they are constantly measuring learning and they are providing intensive learning opportunities for their students. With the knowledge of the science of teaching, they understand how to arrange the learning environment in such a way as to optimize the students' learning.

According to Cooper, Heron and Heward (2007), ABA has six important elements that make it what it is: effective, accountable, public, doable, empowering, and optimistic. ABA is effective because it produces practical results for teachers and for the students they are teaching. ABA is accountable because it allows us to learn from our mistakes and we can try something else if it doesn't work. ABA is public because there is no hidden "magic or miraculous event."

This public aspect allows others to replicate what we do. This is an important aspect because we want to support effective teaching across the field of education. ABA is doable because it is simply the things that we already know how to do like: repetition, consistency, reinforcement, and so on. We just use a scientific terminology and a scientific practice to move what we "know" how to do from the common understanding and into a scientific technology. ABA is empowering because it is about practical tools that can be learned by practitioners and gives them confidence in their skills. ABA is optimistic because it is a science that assumes that all people have the ability to change for the better and to make the world a better place.

One of the earliest examples of ABA as a teaching technology is that of Skinner's teaching machines. In 1954, Skinner designed machines that students could use to learn new information. The machines incorporated two important elements of ABA as a teaching technology. Firstly, they allowed for each student to learn individually, at their own pace. Secondly, they provided immediate feedback to the learner, telling the learner whether they had responded correctly or incorrectly (Hill, 1977).

Another example of using ABA in education with a bit more modern twist is that of using Programmed Instruction (an ABA tactic) to teach students how to write a simple Java™ computer program. This computer-based programmed instruction tutoring system was used with lectures and collaborative learning experiences to successfully teach students to write their own computer programs (Emurian, Hu, Wang, & Durham, 2000). This type of learning lends itself particularly well to this teaching strategy and highlights the importance of teachers learning how to match the teaching technology to the teaching task or goal.

Direct and continuous measurement in ABA allows the detection of small improvements that may otherwise be overlooked. The more you use ABA with positive outcomes the more optimistic your outlook on your work and on your effectiveness as a teacher, creating positive supports for people who are often stressed and feeling overwhelmed and overworked. ABA is an evidence-based practice and a field where peer-reviewed literature such as journals and books give many examples of successful practice that has been replicated over decades in many subjects.

Lastly, ABA is not only an effective teaching technology, it also meets all of the requirements of a *Response to Intervention* (RTI) tiered approach to remediating learning and behavioral problems required by the "No Child Left Behind Act of 2001" (VanDerHeyden, Witt, & Gilbertson, 2007). RTI requires screening for learning and behavioral problems (e.g., curriculum based or other academic and functional behavior assessments), ongoing progress monitoring (e.g., ongoing data collection and analysis), data based decision making (e.g., decision analysis protocol of changes to instructional strategies post visual inspection of student data and verbally-mediated behaviors), and a multi-level prevention system (e.g., ongoing implementation of evidence-based procedures, teaching and expanding of student's communities of reinforcers). There are specific characteristics of teaching as applied behavior analysis as shown in Table 1 and which qualify ABA as an approved RTI approach.

Table 1. Characteristics of teaching as applied behavior analysis (adapted from Greer, Keohane, & Healy, 2002, p. 121)

Screening for learning and behavioral problems: Teachers continuously measure teaching and student responses. Teaching is driven by the moment-to-moment responses of each individual student and existing research findings. All instruction is individualized whether the instruction is provided in a one-to-one setting or in groups.
Ongoing progress monitoring: Graphs of the measures of student's performance are used for decisions about which scientifically-tested tactics are best for students at any given instructional decision point.
Data-based decision making: Expertise in the science is used to make moment-to-moment decisions based on the continuous collection of data, its visual summary in graphs, and the precision of the vocabulary of the science used with the data. Indeed, the data language is part of that science. The precision of the vocabulary of the science drives the production of good outcomes. The progress of students is always available for view in the form of up-to-date graphs that summarize all of the students' responses to instruction.
Multi-level prevention system: Logically and empirically tested curricula and curricular sequences are used that are repertoires of behavior. The goals of instruction (antecedents, responses, and consequent contingencies within setting events) are educationally and socially significant repertoires. The principles of the basic science of the behavior of the individual and the 200+ tactics from the research are used to teach educationally and socially significant repertoires. Tactics must be fitted to the individual needs of students. Teachers/practitioners are strategic scientists of pedagogy/therapy and applied behavior analysis because the process of determining what each student needs at any given point requires a strategic scientific analysis.

Educational Technologies Derived from Applied Behavior Analysis

The appendix to this chapter describes the Applied Behavioral Analysis in detail including case studies and practical examples. The theoretical, experimental and applied branches of behavior analysis all converge to establish a multitude of avenues from which new behaviors can be taught, learned behaviors can be maintained, and socially undesirable behaviors can be reduced. Our focus in this chapter is to describe how this convergence of science and education has led to the development of over 200 tactics and strategies that make up a technology of teaching. In the next section and throughout the chapter, we will describe some of these technologies and how some models of schooling are training teachers to be effective users of the technology available to them. The following are some of the methods derived from ABA used to teach these objectives.

Discrete Trial Training

Discrete trial training (DTT) refers to delivery of discrete trials which are instructional units. Each unit is a potential operant targeted to teach. Within DTT, tasks are broken down into smaller parts. There are four main components of DTT: (a) present an antecedent with a child's motivation and attention in place (e.g., the student is looking at the teacher and the teacher points to a map and delivers an instructional command, "What is the capital city of New York State?"), (b) wait up to three seconds for the child's response, (c) the child's response (e.g. The student says, "Albany" or "Manhattan"), and (d) deliver a consequence for the response (e.g. reinforcement for a correct response or a correction for an incorrect response (e.g, The teacher says, "Yes, it is Albany" or in the second instance, "The capital city is Albany.") (Smith, 2001; Sarokoff & Sturmey, 2004).

Another example of DTT is as follows: 1. A teacher gains student attention (e.g., eye contact), 2. A teacher presents an instructional command, "do this" while simultaneously modeling hands clapping, 3. the child imitates the teacher's clapping correctly within three seconds, 4. the teacher provides reinforcement in the form of verbal praise for the correct response. The delivery of a discrete trial ends when the teacher records "+" on the data sheet. In this scenario, a three-term contingency is delivered and thus operant conditioning is conducted through DTT. Skills in academic, social, communication, self-help and play skills can all be taught using DTT.

Direct Instruction

Direct Instruction (DI) (Engelmann & Carnine, 1982) is one of the most well-known and researched forms of scripted programmed instruction. DI has been researched in over 150 studies comparing it to other such teaching methods. Results of Adams & Engelman's (1996) meta-analysis showed that DI is more effective than other methods in 64% of those studies. With DI the teaching procedures include: student responses to instructional objectives, opportunities for teacher guided performance and finally independent demonstration and performance of skills taught.

Direct instruction (DI) refers to an explicit teaching of a skill-set and relies on a systematic curriculum that are delivered through a prescribed behavioral script. DI is teacher-centered and focuses on clear behavioural and cognitive objectives.

The theoretical basis of DI is operant conditioning models developed by Skinner. Engelmann and Carnine (1982) identified three major categories of cognitive knowledge which are presented in order from simple to complex: Basic forms, joining forms, and complex forms. Classifying knowledge forms provides teachers with a basis for designing instructional sequences that can be used repeatedly with similar forms of knowledge.

For example, teachers can arrange an instructional sequence starting by teaching basic discriminations, then related discriminations, teaching rules and then teaching cognitive operations (Kenny, 1980). Core features of DI include using scripts that permit the use of pretested examples and sequences. A response signal is an integral part of the scripts which enable teachers to pace their instruction at a high rate.

DI in a small group with the features mentioned above enable teachers to provide repetitious practice with students acting as models for each other. *Choral responding* in a high rate, immediate corrective feedback, and differential praise are other core features of direct instruction strategies (Binder & Watkins, 1990). DI is used in resource rooms in special education programs as well as the general classroom setting to teach all core subject: math, reading, spelling, social studies, science and English Language Learners. They are not only an effective approach for academic remediation for children at risk, but provide opportunities for movement from one group to another for students who are paced faster through the curriculum (i.e., advanced learners).

Precision Teaching

Precision teaching (PT) is a precise and systematic method of evaluating instructional tactics and curricula. It emphasizes rate of responding and the standardization of visual displays. Counts per minutes are used to evaluate the student's mastery and fluency with tool or component skills of more complex repertoires (Greer, 2002). By focusing on fluency, teachers can adjust the curricula for each learner to maximize the learning based on the learner's personal fluency measurements (Lindsley, 1990; Lindsley, 1991).

PT has been utilized for teaching a variety of behaviors such as handwriting, mathematics, vocational skills and recreational skills with a variety of populations including typically developing individuals and persons with emotional disorders or developmental disorders (Ramey, Lydon, Healy, McCoy, Holloway, & Mulhern, 2016). With Precision Teaching (PT) (Pennypacker, Gutierrez, & Lindsley, 2003; White & Harring, 1976) the skills learned through DI are then practiced. Practice occurs typically in pairs, self-timed, until students can perform within a specified criterion for number and rate of responses (i.e. how many and how fast). Students then plot their own data on Standard Celeration Charts and follow or monitor their own progress until a fluency criterion is achieved for mastered skills. The expectation for learning and demonstrating skills is marked on the graph. The nature of this type of instruction mixes DI, PT as well as Personalized System of Instruction (PSI) discussed in the next section.

Through this process students learn to become sufficient at self-monitoring and self-management. Additionally, they learn to work cooperatively with others (e.g. peer-tutoring) and gain important organizational skills by using fluency methods such as SAFMEDS (Say all fast, minute each day, shuffled) (Eschelman, 2004). Group contingencies are implemented to assign points and provide reinforcement to the group based on individual student academic performance. These types of methods build motivation into the process of learning.

Personalized System of Instruction

Personalized System of Instruction (PSI), developed by Fred S. Keller in 1968, is a behavioral system of instruction. In PSI, each study unit is divided into subunits and objectives and students move through instructional material at their own pace. Students must meet preset criteria for each unit. Information of instruction is transmitted in written form between teachers and students. Proctors or tutors provide individualized instruction when needed. (Greer, 2002; Sherman, Raskin, & Semb, 1982)

Class Wide Peer Tutoring

Class Wide Peer Tutoring (CWPT) is a form of peer-mediated instruction where pairs of students alternately play roles of tutor and tutee. The tutors ask questions, mark whether tutees' responses are correct or incorrect, and provide feedback. Teachers supervise tutoring and reinforce good tutoring. CWPT has been used for learning spelling, math facts, reading, vocabulary, and facts related to a subject area. CWPT benefits both of the tutors and tutees in learning academic and social skill by providing them more opportunities to practice those skills, encouraging them to engage in active learning (Greenwood, Delaquadri, & Hall, 1989; Kamps, Barbetta, Leonard, & Delaquadri, 1994).

Stimulus Equivalence and Relational Frame Theory

Stimulus Equivalence (SE) and Relational Frame Theory (RFT) explain sources of "derived" or "emergent" human verbal behavior which don't have direct reinforcement history within stimulus-response relations for an individual (Barnes-Holmes, Barnes-Holmes, Smeets, Cullinan, & Leader, 2004).

SE is an empirical phenomenon which was first explained by Murray Sidman. SE provides a logical basis for explaining "derived" or "emergent" stimulus-response relations exhibited in human verbal behavior. Sidman (1982) conceptualized SE in terms of the mathematical relations of reflexivity, symmetry, and transitivity. Reflexivity of a stimulus relation can be demonstrated when each stimulus bears the relation to itself ("if A then A"). Symmetry requires reversibility between stimuli A and B ("if A then B", "if B then A"). To determine whether stimulus relation is transitive, it requires a third stimulus, C. Once "if A, then B" and "if B, then C" have been established, transitivity requires "if A, then C" to emerge without differential reinforcement. If an individual learns the relations "if A, then B" and "if A, then C" through differential reinforcement, "if B, then C" relation emerges with direct reinforcement history (Sidman & Tailby, 1982).

RFT provides a basis to explain other derived stimulus relations (e.g., mutual entailment, combinatorial entailment, transformation of stimulus functions) and are more general than the terms in SE (e.g., reflexivity, symmetry, and transitivity). Sidman's (1982) SE explains equivalence relations but this does not work for other relations (e.g., bigger than, before-after, opposite, etc.). In RFT, stimulus functions can be changed based on the derived relations. Research demonstrated that stimulus functions can transfer between members of an equivalence class and these functions will be changed.

Exogenous Technologies Used to Enhance the Practice of Applied Behavior Analysis

Although Applied Behavior Analysis itself has been discussed in this chapter as a scientific "technology" of teaching there are also many other applications of what the mainstream refer to as technology (i.e. exogenous technology) used throughout the greater field of applied behavior analysis. In this section technology that is not a part of the science of teaching (such as evidence-based teaching strategies and resultant curriculum) will be referred to as exogenous technology. The use of exogenous technology is not new to the field of Applied Behavior Analysis. From the advent of the teaching machine by B.F. Skinner (Hill, 1977); that takes students through a learning module frame by frame allowing advancement to the next step only after first mastering the previous step, to the use of Microsoft Excel programs to input and graph data for the purpose of visual analysis (Alberto & Troutman, 2012) this chapter will discuss some of those technologies and how they have been applied in the field. Exogenous technology has allowed for multiple advancements in both the dissemination and application of behavior analytic procedures in education, home, and other institutions around the world. In this section we will focus on the use of exogenous technologies to educational applications as they relate to students of applied behavior analysis, practitioners of applied behavior analysis, and students in educational settings with learning differences.

Examples of Exogenous Technologies Used to Increase Communication Skills

Picture Exchange Communication Systems (PECS) (http://www.pecsusa.com/research.php) is a form of communication training that uses picture icons from single pictures, to strings of pictures to text of words in a sentence strip to allow individuals with no communication skills to develop first instances of non-vocal communication while gradually shaping up vocal communication skills in children with autism spectrum disorder and other communication disorders. The advent of more Hi-tech applications include but are not limited to the use of text to speech functions in different text programs across platforms like Mic vocal output devices such as Sound Buttons, the Dynavox (http://www.dynavoxtech.com/products) to digital applications that can be used on ever smaller devices like an iPad or Smartphone like Proloquo2Go (http://www.assistiveware.com/product/proloquo2go) which uses similar principles of communication training as PECS. In Proloquo2Go the difference is that the picture icons and text are programmed with different choices of vocal output: from male to female and adult to children's voices, allowing for individuals with limited to no vocal capacity for speech to communicate through vocal output sources.

Examples of Exogenous Technologies Used to Increase the Dissemination of Applied Behavior Analysis

Correspondence and distance learning has long been a method for learning new skills and enhancing one's practice. In the 21st Century we have seen universities all over the world develop on-line: certificate, master's, and doctoral level programs, that can all be accessed from a computer without ever having to step foot into a classroom. Additionally, with the advent of Skype's visual conference calling and other communication platforms it has become ever easier to connect practitioners and teachers of Applied Behavior Analysis to people in more remote locations with limited access to trained professionals. On-line educational programs in conjunction with digital conferencing platforms have allowed for trained professionals to provide a level of education, training, and supervision of practitioners to a degree not seen in any previous time in history. These exogenous technologies have allowed for the further development of skills and increased dissemination of ABA around the world. Exogenous technology is not without limitations. One limitation of the growing propensity for distance learning and distance supervision models using such technologies is the limited in-person contact with trained professionals. This may lead to an inability to closely monitor students of applied behavior analysis who participate in distance practicums and receive distance supervision in the same ways that you could in person or when in the same local professional community.

Many on-line instructional practices used have not led to greater student performance (Means, Toyama, Murphy, Bakia, & Jones, 2010). These types of concerns have led the credentialing body for Behavior Analysts, The Behavior Analyst Certification Board (BACB) (http://bacb.com) to create strict regulations around the amount and extent to which distance supervision can occur within the required hours for certification. This was done while establishing quality indicators and requirements for BACB Supervisors to ensure the quality of supervised experiences for practitioners. Finally, restrictions to the number of hours of supervision that can be done remotely was enacted to ensure the majority of training and supervision be hands-on practical experiences.

The positive aspect of this use of exogenous technology has been the greater dissemination of information to parents, teachers, and social service personnel who live and work in remote areas with little to no contact with licensed and/or credentialed professionals. This has led to the increase in awareness of applied behavior analysis as well as the increased development of instructional and training programs around the world in consultation with qualified professionals.

Examples of Exogenous Technologies Used to Enhance the Practice of Applied Behavior Analysis

The practice of applied behavior analysis requires great attention to detail. It requires that often, large amounts of data be collected, graphed and visually analyzed, and used to make timely instructional decisions to increase student attainment of specified goals. More and more educators are using exogenous technologies to engage in these types of practices. For example if you were to input ABA or data collection into Google Play for Android and/or iTunes store for Mac platforms you will now find a multitude of such applications. Practitioners are using such exogenous technologies to assist in the timely tracking of data as well as graphing. Advanced technology companies such as TNAC (Technology North Active Care) are enriching such technologies with the use of behavior analytic consultants to not only allow for data collection and the generation of visual displays of data via graphs but also to incorporate the use of evidence-based data analytic rules as published in the field (Keohane & Greer, 2005) to assist in alerting practitioners to view the data to make more timely decisions about intervention. Additionally, these technologies are also including ways to communicate this information to multiple stakeholders such as parents, school support team members, and anyone else involved in the educational process further allowing for tracking of behavior analytic services and generation of billing for insurance agents and government funding bodies.

A Model of Schooling Incorporating ABA as a Teaching Technology

There are several examples of *applications of behavior analysis* in education. In this section we will name and describe one of these models. The intent of such approaches are to make everyone in the system accountable for outcomes. Additionally, the goal is to effectively use the technology of ABA as a means to increase student outcomes. ABA as a model of schooling has a purpose to change socially significant student behavior to a meaningful degree in such a way that the results can be shown to be a result of the instructional procedures applied. Administrators and supervisors are held accountable for the outcomes of teachers who in turn are accountable for student outcomes. This system of accountability allows the learner (i.e. student) to drive the system. Models of schooling that integrate ABA as a teaching technology share the following core features:

1. Regular and ongoing data collection and data analysis
2. Ongoing core teacher training inclusive of regular supervision with corrective feedback.
3. Implementation of over 200 evidence-based teaching strategies, tactics and curriculum that make-up a technology of teaching including but not limited to: Direct Instruction (DI) (Becker, 1977; Becker & Carnine, 1981; Engelmann & Carnine, 1991), Personalized System of Instruction (PSI) (Keller, 1968; Sherman, Raskin, & Semb, 1982), the consulting behavior analyst model (Greenwood, Delaquadri & Hall, 1984), and the Precision Teaching Model (PT) (Lindsley, 1990; Lindsley, 1991).

The Comprehensive Application of Behavior Analysis to Schooling (CABAS®)

CABAS® (Albers & Greer, 1991; Greer, 1994; Greer, McCorkle & Williams, 1989; Ingham & Greer, 1992; Lamm & Greer, 1991; Selinske, Greer & Lodhi, 1991) is a student driven school-wide systems approach that creates a symbiotic relationship between all elements of the school program. The goals and objectives of the school program are constantly changing and adapting based on regular ongoing analysis of relevant student outcome data (Bushell & Baer, 1994). The first CABAS® school; the Fred S. Keller School, was established in 1986 in New York by Dr. R. Douglas Greer. Currently five schools are fully certified by the CABAS® Board in New York, New Jersey, Louisiana, and England while others are in the certification process in Italy, Spain, and other countries. See Figure 1 for an example of the components of a fully certified CABAS® program.[1]

Additional defining features of the CABAS® model include use of the following: The learn unit (Albers & Greer, 1991; Lamm & Greer, 1991; Ingham & Greer, 1992, Greer & McDonough, 1999; Selinski, Greer & Lodhi, 1991) as the smallest unit of instruction, teacher observations using the Teacher Performance Rate and Accuracy Assessment Scale (TPRA) (Ingham & Greer, 1992; Ross, Singer-Dudek & Greer, 2005), decision-tree protocol for data analysis, Preschool Inventory of Repertoires for Kindergarten Assessment (C-PIRK) (Waddington & Reed, 2009) and other curriculum based measures (CBM), CABAS® Teacher Training Modules/ Ranks (Keohane & Greer, 2005) inclusive of verbal behavior about the science, verbally-mediated, and contingency-shaped behaviors, Skinner's *Verbal Behavior* (Skinner, 1954) and Verbal Behavior Developmental Theory (VBDT) (Greer & Keohane, 2005) used to determine student verbal behavior repertoires identifying their verbal capabilities to individualize instruction, a university connection to allow for ongoing learning and provide teacher internships, and CABAS® curriculum/ protocols based on research on effective teaching strategies.

The purpose of this model is to use ABA as a teaching technology to implement an approach to schooling that is focused on the entire system: students, teachers and parents using scientifically driven effective procedures with ongoing learning built in. ABA has more recently and commonly been associated with children diagnosed with an Autism Spectrum Disorder and other such diagnoses that fall under the purview of special education. However, the CABAS® schools have used ABA as a technology of teaching that is also applied to general education with 7 general education classrooms currently using the Accelerated Independent Learner Model (AIL) developed as a means to increase student outcomes in a general education setting. The components of the AIL classroom in CABAS® are detailed in Table 2.[2]

Figure 1. Description of CABAS® program components (adapted from Greer, Keohane, & Healy, 2002, p. 126)

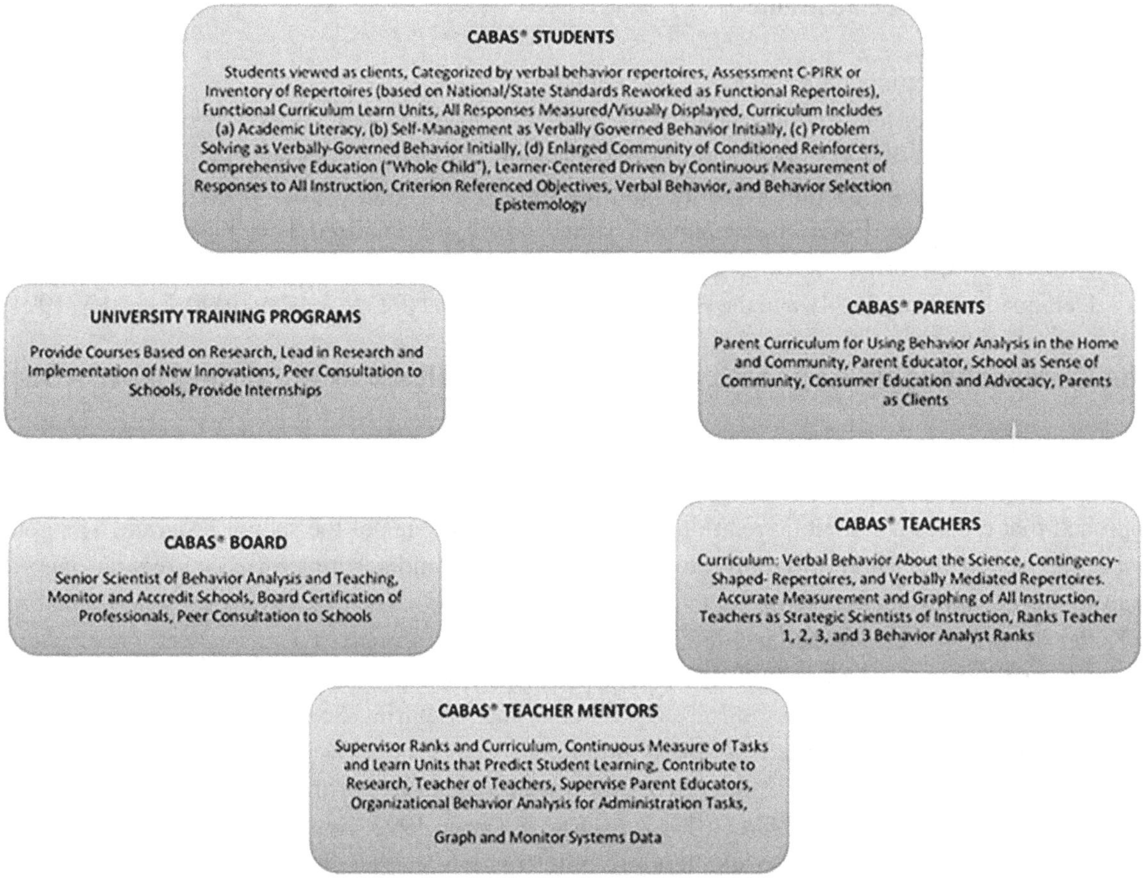

Table 2. Components and instructional procedures of a CABAS® AIL classroom (adapted from Broto & Greer, 2014, p. 9)

a) Learn unit (direct and observed)
b) Model demonstration learn units for more advanced students with observational learning (model of how to do the problem followed by probes and learn units)
c) Rule posting and reinforcement for following rules
d) Point system (individual, small group, and whole classroom) for accuracy and social behavior
e) Class wide peer tutoring
f) Differentiated instruction by small groups across all academic areas
g) Choral responding in small or large groups
h) Response board responding
i) Mastery objectives followed by fluency objectives
j) Personalized System of Instruction (PSI) for advanced students (Keller, 1968; Sherman, Raskin & Semb, 1982)
k) The use of book reports to assess students' reading comprehension skills. (The book reports included a summary of events of a story including the beginning, middle, and end, description of characters, and description of story setting)
l) Public posting of responses to math facts fluency, reading scores, correct completion of book reports, and class-wide learning data
m) CABAS® AIL decision protocol for when interventions are needed and where to locate the source of the learning problem
n) Use of Learning Pictures on a web server (showing mastery of objectives in the curricula and numbers of learn units needed to achieve mastery or fluency)

Every person involved in the school including: top level administrators, teachers, teaching assistants and parents are provided with instruction and training in implementing tactics and strategies of applied behavior analysis through a series of training modules. The training modules are set up in a way that allow each staff member or parent to go through them at their own pace using *Personalized Systems of Instruction* (PSI) (Keller, 1968) based procedures.

Fundamental modules required for a minimum standard of practice within the school system are to be completed within a given time frame while others are left at the discretion of the employee. The completion of training modules leads to professional ranks and incremental merit based pay raises. Professional ranks include, but are not limited to,: Teacher 1, Master Teacher, Senior Behavior Analyst and Research Scientist. These ranks are equated to a specific level of expertise and are awarded upon the completion of modules in conjunction with the demonstration of specific skills within the school, home or other required settings across three major teaching behaviors that collectively make up repertoires of a teacher required to effectively implement ABA as a teaching technology that will be described later in this chapter.

Defining Features of CABAS®

The Learn Unit

The learn unit (Albers & Greer, 1991; Lamm & Greer, 1991; Ingham & Greer, 1992, Greer & McDonough, 1999; Selinski, et al. 1991) is a set of inter-locking three-term contingencies for both the student and the teacher. It is the interaction between teacher delivery and student receipt of instruction (i.e., Instructional Antecedents), student/ teacher responses (i.e., Behavior) and outcomes in the form of reinforcement (e.g., praise) and/or corrections (i.e., Consequences) for which learning can then occur. For an in depth definition and examples of the learn unit (Albers & Greer, 1991; Lamm & Greer, 1991; Ingham & Greer, 1992, Greer & McDonough, 1999; Selinski, et al. 1991) see Greer (2002) chapter 2.

Teacher Training and the Teacher Performance Rate and Accuracy Scale

Teacher training is an essential feature in that you cannot effectively use any technology without proper training and guidance. The CABAS® model provides training of teachers that allow for the development of teaching behaviors that lead to repertoires of teachers as strategic scientists described later in this chapter. For this purpose, the CABAS® teaching modules/ranks require mentor teachers to provide modeling, and in-situ training through the use of the TPRA (Ingham & Greer, 1992; Ross, et al. 2005), which is a measure of both teacher and student behavior in the form of learn units (Albers & Greer, 1991; Lamm & Greer, 1991; Ingham & Greer, 1992, Greer & McDonough, 1999; Selinski, et al. 1991).

The TPRA (Ingham & Greer, 1992; Ross, et al. 2005) provides information on both teacher and student correct/incorrect responses and delivery of instruction as correct and incorrect learn units. Additionally, information is gathered about the learning environment such as direct and indirect behavior management in the form of teacher provided praise and other forms of reinforcement to all students. Further the TPRA (Ingham & Greer, 1992; Ross, et al. 2005) requires the teacher to provide information to the observer (i.e., teacher mentor) about the student, teaching procedures, objectives of instruction and under what conditions student responses are to occur (e.g., schedules of reinforcement and other behavior management strategies), as well as operational definitions of the target skills or social behaviors.

Decision Tree Protocol

The decision tree protocol (Keohane, & Greer, 2005) is used as another tool to train teachers how to analyze visual displays of student data (i.e., graphs) and make decisions based on a visual analysis in combination (when more advanced teaching repertoires are gained) with verbally-mediated strategies to decide when and what interventions to implement. In summary, the protocol states that when visually inspecting a graph of student data one should look at the trends in the data to determine: 1) when an intervention is needed and 2) what intervention strategies should be implemented.

Data trends include the following: ascending (i.e., increasing), descending (i.e., decreasing), no trend (i.e., flat), and variable trend (i.e., changes of direction). Once a trend is identified the teacher will determine if the method of instruction should change or remain the same. Additionally, a teacher as strategic scientist would then ask a series of verbally-mediated questions to identify the problem in the learn unit and make a determination about what tactics or strategies would best remediate those problems. For an in depth description of the decision tree protocol procedures see Keohane, & Greer (2005).

Student Assessment

Students are assessed in pre-school using the C-PIRK (Waddington & Reed, 2009) and those at higher grades are assessed using curriculum based assessments tied to national, state or country standards and translated into functional repertoires.

Verbal Behavior Repertoires

Skinner's (1957) treatment of verbal behavior, the *Verbal Behavior Development Theory* (Ross, et al. 2005) and other research that helped to develop such theories of verbal behavior are used to determine a student's current learning needs based on a functional analysis of their verbal behavior repertoire. Students are classified as pre-listeners, listeners, speakers, speaker as own listeners, and readers. Additionally, at more complex stages of verbal behavior students are classified as readers (with mathematical repertoires), writers, writer as own reader, and problem-solvers. Each of these repertoires is characterized by a set of skills that the student currently emits. *Pre-listeners* are completely dependent on those around them for their survival as they are unable to manipulate their environment through their own behaviors. *Listeners* can follow simple directions and with assistance can direct change within their environment. *Speakers* can manipulate their own environment through the mediation of another person (a listener) who can then make necessary changes to the environment that in turn control a speaker's behavior. *Speaker as own listener* is someone who can make changes to their environment through directing a listener and can self-edit their behavior based on the environmental contingencies. Readers can manipulate their environments without the need for a listener as they also have the skills to wait for or recruit reinforcement through the use of written and other verbal behavior repertoires. For an in depth description of each verbal behavior repertoire see Greer, 2002, chapters 5 and 6.

TEACHERS AS STRATEGIC SCIENTISTS OF INSTRUCTION

What is a teacher as a "strategic scientist of instruction" (Greer, 1991; Greer 2002)? As discussed previously in the chapter teachers in the CABAS® system are trained using training modules across three specific behaviors that make up a teaching repertoire: verbal behavior about the science, verbally-mediated behaviors and contingency-shaped behaviors. Teachers are acting as strategic scientists of instruction when they have mastered these teaching repertoires allowing them to speak a common language, effectively replicate evidence-based teaching procedures, ask high level questions about whether instruction is effective or ineffective and make moment to moment decisions about changes to instructional methods and the instructional environment based on an analysis of student data and the student's history of instruction.

As a strategic scientist of instruction these skills are applied in the setting to remediate learning problems. Teachers become "strategic scientists of behavior" when evidence-based procedures are shown to be ineffective with students in their learning environment. The "strategic scientist of behavior" uses the same skills but additionally creates new procedures and tests their effectiveness through functional or experimental analysis in the classroom setting (Greer, 2002).

In order for teachers to master skills required to develop the necessary repertoires to implement ABA as an effective teaching technology they must be carefully supervised. The supervision of a teacher as a strategic scientist of instruction further requires specific repertoires of a supervisor to be discussed later in the chapter.

Teaching Repertoires of Strategic Scientists of Instruction

The CABAS® training modules are constructed based on one major premise. In order for students to succeed people in their learning environments (inclusive of school and home) must speak a common language, provide consistency and support for their learning so that students maintain and apply what they have learned across time and settings (i.e. generalization) as well as become independent learners. The CABAS® training modules are derived from this premise and focus on training the following repertoires of the teacher as a strategic scientist of instruction (Greer, 1991; Greer 2002): verbal behavior about the science, verbally-mediated teaching repertoires and contingency-shaped teaching repertoires.

Verbal Behavior about the Science

The key to any technology of teaching is the common vocabulary or terminology of a science. In order to provide effective instruction educators must first use precise language to name and describe instructional problems. Further educators must also name and describe the teaching tactics and strategies that will remediate those instructional problems. To this end a common language allows educators to contact educational and behavioral research, understand what is read, and translate that information to others in the student's learning environments resulting in the development and implementation of effective instructional procedures to remediate specific learning problems. Furthermore, teachers and parents can then access the greater community of educators and behavior analysts in a way that allows for ongoing professional development and training opportunities to occur.

Contingency-Shaped Behavior

Speaking a common language through the use of a similar technical vocabulary is not enough. Teachers and parents must also replicate evidence-based teaching procedures in the classroom and home. This repertoire allows the teacher to use the verbal behavior about the science to contact the research literature in education and behavior analysis and systematically follow the procedures given in their own setting. When a teacher has gained these skills they should be able to consistently apply evidence-based procedures in the classroom. However, additional skills will be necessary for those behaviors that are not affected by the mere implementation of such procedures. As we know there are multiple variables that may act as barriers to students accessing the curriculum or changing behavioral patterns. In order for teachers to be effective in addressing behaviors resistant to change they must gain additional skills.

Finally, teachers must learn to, "go with the flow" so to speak. They must evaluate student performance on a regular basis (i.e., daily) to determine whether students are responding favorably to instruction or not. In the case they are, teachers must stay the course. In the case they are not, teachers must quickly and effectively make changes to instruction to engage students in ways for learning to occur or behaviors to come under control of the learning environment. This requires teachers to design instruction based on direct assessment of students, use scripted teaching procedures and be ever present and responsive to students by providing: flawless instructional antecedents, reinforcement for appropriate responses/behaviors, and behavior specific corrective feedback in order to increase correct responding and decrease student errors (Greer, 1991).

Verbally-Mediated Behavior

To speak a common language and to successfully replicate evidence based procedures in the instructional setting are necessary first steps in effectively using ABA as a teaching technology. However, in order to truly provide for ongoing effective use of such a technology one must be able to remediate instructional problems that have been resistant to change or the effects of evidence-based procedures. This is done by asking high level questions about instructional problems in order to identify and remediate them (Keohane & Greer, 2005). Some examples of verbal-mediation include asking the following types of questions: Is this learning problem due to the student's history of instruction (i.e., prerequisite skills? ability to respond to the instruction? environmental arrangements? presentation of the material? opportunities to respond to instruction?) or barriers to contacting instructional antecedents such as attention and/or behavioral issues?

Answering these types of questions allow teachers as strategic scientists of instruction to use the technology of ABA to make informed decisions about the appropriate strategies to remediate learning problems based on their interaction with the student and learning environment. Teachers can then make adjustments to their teaching, student response modalities, classroom environments and/or positive behavioral supports to ensure the removal of instructional barriers and increase the opportunity for learning to occur.

Supervision for Training Teachers as Strategic Scientists

In order for teachers to become strategic scientists of instruction they need to become fluent in the three teaching behaviors discussed throughout this chapter. To this end training requires direct instruction in all three teaching behaviors. To build a repertoire as a strategic scientist the following behaviors must be learned and demonstrated to a mastery and/or a fluency criterion. This is done for verbal behavior about the science by reading and learning definitions of the terminology of the science. Teachers take quizzes and recycle to a mastery criterion until they become fluent in the verbal behavior about the science. They begin with basic terms required for initial stages of ABA as a teaching technology (e.g. basic behavioral principles of reinforcement and punishment) through more complex terms that define and describe teaching strategies and tactics to remediate learning problems (e.g., differential reinforcement of alternative behaviors and behavioral shaping and chaining procedures).

Contingency-shaped behaviors are taught through in-situ modeling and supervision with corrective feedback in the form of a TPRA (Ingham & Greer, 1992; Ross, et al. 2005) completed in the classroom or other learning environment. One demonstration of fluency in this area requires a teacher to deliver intensive and flawless learn units (Albers & Greer, 1991; Lamm & Greer, 1991; Ingham & Greer, 1992, Greer & McDonough, 1999; Selinski, et al. 1991) in the classroom with high rates of student accuracy of responding over a period of time. Additional demonstrations of mastery and fluency in this area require ongoing adaptations to the classroom environment through daily classroom routines and procedures such as delivering reinforcement for student pro-social behaviors and rule-following while ignoring or implementing procedures to change maladaptive behaviors. This also requires the ability to make in the moment changes to instructional procedures as needed.

Verbally-mediated behaviors are taught through an ongoing analysis of visual representations of both student and teacher data using high-level questions to determine instructional problems, name and describe tactics and strategies to remediate them as well as develop proactive solutions for possible learning barriers. Verbally-mediated behaviors are demonstrated through a supervisor's' review of student visual data (i.e., graphs).

Supervisors themselves must have mastered these teaching repertoires in order to train others. They use tools such as the TPRA (Ingham & Greer, 1992; Ross, et al. 2005) to measure learn units (Albers & Greer, 1991; Lamm & Greer, 1991; Ingham & Greer, 1992, Greer & McDonough, 1999; Selinski, et al. 1991) consisting of: teacher delivered instruction in the form of instructional antecedents, student responses to instruction (i.e. student behavior), and teachers correct or incorrect application of student reinforcement for correct responses or student corrective feedback as consequences for incorrect student responses to teacher led instruction. The TPRA (Ingham & Greer, 1992; Ross, et al. 2005) allows an in depth analysis of complete flawless presentations of the *learn unit* (Albers & Greer, 1991; Lamm & Greer, 1991; Ingham & Greer, 1992, Greer & McDonough, 1999; Selinski, et al. 1991). The *learn unit* is considered the smallest unit of instruction and a complete learn unit is a requirement for learning to occur (Albers & Greer, 1991; Lamm & Greer, 1991; Ingham & Greer, 1992, Greer & McDonough, 1999; Selinski, et al. 1991).

In CABAS®, students drive the system through teachers and administrators regular and ongoing analysis of relevant student outcome data (Bushell & Baer, 1994) in the forms of total delivered and correct learn units, learn units to mastery criterion, number of objectives met, increases in prosocial behaviors, decreases in maladaptive behaviors as well as the development of more independent and complex student verbal behavior repertoires. A combination of high rates of correct teacher decisions based on the decision tree protocol, low rates of teacher errors and high rates of correctly implemented learn units (Albers & Greer, 1991; Bahadourian, 2000; Lamm & Greer, 1991; Ingham & Greer, 1992, Greer & McDonough, 1999; Selinski, et al. 1991) as measured by the TPRA (Ingham & Greer, 1992; Ross, et al. 2005), combined with the other CABAS® components show a cumulative effect of higher rates of student learning overall as measured in decreased numbers of learn units to criterion, the increased high rates of correct and low rates of incorrect teacher decisions and student responses to instruction, as well as gains on standardized, and criterion referenced assessments show the system to be an extremely effective one (Greer et al., 2002; Singer-Dudek, Speckman, & Nuzullo, 2010).

The student outcome data is reflexive of the extent of teacher effectiveness and leads to school-wide goal setting both academically and from an operations perspective. This information relayed in the form of schoolwide evaluative data allows administrators to: set schoolwide goals, determine training needs and remediation for specific classrooms, teaching staff, and students as well as make adjustments to tuition fees, teacher salaries, etc. This level of data collection and analysis additionally allows for a cost-benefit analysis through the determination of actual cost per student goal achieved (Greer, 1994a; Greer, 1994b; Greer, Keohane & Healy, 2002). This leads to effective data based decision making that benefits everyone in the system from students to the local taxpayers.

CONCLUSION

In conclusion, there are a number of specific examples that exist as evidence of the ability of ABA to offer an endogenous technology that is essential and critical to support the development of humans as learners when combined with exogenous technology in this digital age. The authors have briefly reviewed several of those examples, both practical examples of teacher skills and real life examples of the successful use of these strategies and tools in classrooms and schools.

One of the major areas of focus that the authors recommend in order to improve the effectiveness of schools and in turn student outcomes is to increase training of teachers in the use of educational technologies afforded us from the behavioral sciences. The President of the United States himself has issued an executive order, Executive Order No. 13707 (2015), supporting the use of behavioral science to improve lives and to improve the access to educational opportunities for all. Training teachers to use ABA as a teaching technology is one way in which we can meet this mandate. The authors feel ABA as a science is important for educators to use in order for them to leverage the advances we have seen in the digital age to contribute to advances in human development and learning which will be necessary if we are to prepare our children to be successful in the modern world.

REFERENCES

Adams, G. L., & Engelmann, S. (1996). *Research on direct instruction: 25 years beyond DISTAR*. Seattle, WA: Educational Achievement System.

Alberto, P. A., & Troutman, A. C. (2012). Applied behavior analysis for teachers (9th ed.). Pearson.

Baer, D. M., Wolf, M. M., & Risley, T. R. (1968). Some current dimensions of applied behavior analysis. *Journal of Applied Behavior Analysis*, *1*(1), 91–97. doi:10.1901/jaba.1968.1-91 PMID:16795165

Baer, D. M., Wolf, M. M., & Risley, T. R. (1987). Some still-current dimensions of applied behavior analysis. *Journal of Applied Behavior Analysis*, *20*(4), 313–327. doi:10.1901/jaba.1987.20-313 PMID:16795703

Barnes-Holmes, D., Barnes-Holmes, B., Smeets, P. M., Cullinan, V., & Leader, G. (2004). Relational frame theory and stimulus equivalence: Conceptual and procedural issues. *International Journal of Psychology & Psychological Therapy*, *4*, 181–214.

Barnes-Holmes, D., Barnes-Holmes, Y., & Cullinan, V. (2000). Relational frame theory and Skinner's Verbal Behavior: A possible synthesis. *The Behavior Analyst*, *23*, 69–84. PMID:22478339

Becker, W. C. (1977). Teaching reading and language to the disadvantaged. *Harvard Educational Review*, *47*(4), 518–543. doi:10.17763/haer.47.4.51431w6022u51015

Becker, W. C., & Carnine, D. W. (1981). Direct Instruction: A behavior therapy model for comprehensive educational intervention with the disadvantaged. In S. W. Bijou & R. Ruiz (Eds.), *Behavior modification: Contributions to education* (pp. 145–207). Hillsdale, NJ: Lawrence Erlbaum.

Binder, C., & Watkins, C. L. (1990). Precision teaching and direct instruction: Superior instructional technology in schools. *Performance Improvement Quarterly*, *3*(4), 74–96. doi:10.1111/j.1937-8327.1990.tb00478.x

Broto, J., & Greer, R. D. (2014). The effects of functional writing contingencies on second graders writing and responding accurately to mathematical algorithms. *Behavioral Development Bulletin*, *19*(1), 7–18. doi:10.1037/h0100568

Bushell, D., & Baer, D. M. (1994). Measurably superior instruction means close, continual contact with the relevant outcome data: Revolutionary. *Behavior analysis in education: Focus on measurably superior instruction*, 3-10.

Carnoy, M., & Rothstein, R. (2013). *What do international tests really show about U.S. student performance?* Economic Policy Institute. Retrieved from http://www.epi.org/publication/us-student-performance-testing/

Cipani, E., & Schock, K. M. (2007). *Functional behavioral assessment, diagnosis, and treatment: A complete system for education and mental health settings.* New York: Springer Publishing Company.

Cooper, J. O., Heron, T. E., & Heward, W. L. (2007). *Applied Behavior Analysis* (2nd ed.). Pearson.

Davis, J., & Kershaw, G. (Producers). (2005). Criminal Minds: Behavior Analysis Unit [Television series]. Los Angeles, CA: The Mark Gordon Company.

DeLeon, I. G., Iwata, B. A., Goh, H., & Worsdell, A. S. (1997). Emergence of reinforcer preference as a function of schedule requirements and stimulus similarity. *Journal of Applied Behavior Analysis*, *30*(3), 439–449. doi:10.1901/jaba.1997.30-439 PMID:9378681

Emurian, H. H., Hu, X., Wang, J., & Durham, A. G. (2000). Learning Java: A programmed instruction approach using Applets. *Computers in Human Behavior*, *16*(4), 395–422. doi:10.1016/S0747-5632(00)00019-4

Engelmann, S., & Carnine, D. (1975). *Distar arithmetic I.* SRA/McGraw-Hill.

Engelmann, S., & Carnine, D. W. (1982). Theory of instruction: Principles and applications. New York: Irvington.

Escobar, R., & Twyman, J. S. (2014). Editorial: Behavior analysis and technology. *The Mexican Journal of Behavior Analysis*, *40*(2), 1–2.

Eshelman, J. W. (2004). *SAFMEDS on the Web: Guidelines and considerations for SAFMEDS*. Retrieved from http://members.aol.com/standardcharter/safmeds.html

Fisher, W., Piazza, C. C., Bowman, L. G., Hagopian, L. P., Owens, J. C., & Slevin, I. (1992). A comparison of two approaches for identifying reinforcers for persons with severe and profound disabilities. *Journal of Applied Behavior Analysis*, *25*(2), 491–498. doi:10.1901/jaba.1992.25-491 PMID:1634435

Greenwood, C. R., Delaquadri, J., & Hall, R. V. (1984). Opportunity to respond and student academic performance. In Behavior analysis in education (pp. 58-88). Columbus, OH: Charles E. Merrill Co.

Greenwood, C. R., Delaquadri, J. C., & Hall, R. V. (1989). Longitudinal effects of classwide peer tutoring. *Journal of Educational Psychology*, *81*(3), 371–383. doi:10.1037/0022-0663.81.3.371

Greer, R. D. (1991). The teacher as strategic scientist: A solution to our educational crisis? *Behavior and Social Issues*, *1*(2), 25–41. doi:10.5210/bsi.v1i2.165

Greer, R. D. (1994a). A systems analysis of the behaviors of schooling. *Journal of Behavioral Education*, *4*(3), 255–264. doi:10.1007/BF01531981

Greer, R. D. (1994b). The measure of a teacher. In R. Gardner III, D. M. Sainata, 1. O. Cooper, T. E. Heron, W. L. Heward, J. Eschelman, & T. A. Grossi, (Eds.), Behavior analysis in education: Focus on measurably superior instruction (pp. 325-335). Pacific Grove, CA: Brooks Cole.

Greer, R. D. (2002). *Designing teaching strategies: An applied behavior analysis systems approach*. San Diego, CA: Academic Press.

Greer, R. D., Keohane, D., & Healy, O. (2002). Quality and comprehensive applications of behavior analysis to schooling. *Behavior Analyst Today*, *3*(2), 120–132. doi:10.1037/h0099977

Greer, R. D., & Keohane, D. D. (2005). The evolutions of verbal behavior in children. *Behavioral Development Bulletin*, *1*(1), 31–47. doi:10.1037/h0100559

Greer, R. D., McCorkle, N. P., & Williams, G. (1989). A sustained analysis of the behaviors of schooling. *Behavioral Residential Treatment*, *4*, 113–141.

Greer, R. D., & McDonough, S. H. (1999). Is the learn unit a fundamental measure of pedagogy? *The Behavior Analyst*, *22*(1), 5–16. PMID:22478317

Hill, W. F. (1977). *Learning: A Survey of Psychological Interpretations*. New York, NY: Thomas Y. Crowell Company.

Ingham, P., & Greer, R. D. (1992). Changes in student and teacher responses in observed and generalized settings as a function of supervisor observations. *Journal of Applied Behavior Analysis*, *25*(1), 153–164. doi:10.1901/jaba.1992.25-153 PMID:1533855

Iwata, B. A., Dorsey, M. F., Slifer, K. J., Bauman, K. E., & Richman, G. S. (1994). Toward a functional analysis of self-injury. *Journal of Applied Behavior Analysis*, *27*(2), 197–209. doi:10.1901/jaba.1994.27-197 PMID:8063622

Iwata, B. A., Pace, G. M., Dorsey, M. F., Zarcone, J. R., Vollmer, T. R., Smith, R. G., & Willis, K. D. et al. (1994). The functions of self-injurious behavior: An experimental-epidemiological analysis. *Journal of Applied Behavior Analysis*, *27*(2), 215–240. doi:10.1901/jaba.1994.27-215 PMID:8063623

Kamps, D. M., Barbetta, P. M., Leonard, B. R., & Delaquadri, J. (1994). Classwide peer tutoring: An integration strategy to improve reading skills and promote peer interactions among students with autism and general education peers. *Journal of Applied Behavior Analysis*, *27*(1), 49–61. doi:10.1901/jaba.1994.27-49 PMID:8188563

Keller, F. S. (1968). Good-bye, teacher.... *Journal of Applied Behavior Analysis*, *1*(1), 79–89. doi:10.1901/jaba.1968.1-79 PMID:16795164

Kenny, D. T. (1980). Direct instruction: An overview of theory and practice. *Journal of the Association of Special Education Teachers*, *15*, 12–17.

Keohane, D. D., & Greer, R. D. (2005). Teachers use of a verbally governed algorithm and student learning. *International Journal of Behavioral and Consultation Therapy*, *1*(3), 252–271. doi:10.1037/h0100749

Lamm, N., & Greer, R. D. (1991). A systematic replication of CABAS. *Journal of Behavioral Education*, *1*, 427–444. doi:10.1007/BF00946776

Lattal, K. A. (2008). JEAB at 50: Coevolution of research and technology. *Journal of the Experimental Analysis of Behavior*, *89*(1), 129–135. doi:10.1901/jeab.2008.89-129 PMID:18338681

Layng, T. V., & Twyman, J. S. (2013). Education + technology + innovation = learning? In M. Murphy, S. Redding, & J. Twyman (Eds.), *Handbook on innovations in learning* (pp. 135–150). Philadelphia, PA: Center on Innovations in Learning, Temple University. Retrieved from http://www.centeril.org

Lindsley, O. R. (1990). Precision teaching: By teachers for children. *Teaching Exceptional Children*, *22*(3), 10–15. doi:10.1177/004005999002200302

Lindsley, O. R. (1991). Precision teachings unique legacy from B. F. Skinner. *Journal of Behavioral Education*, *1*(2), 253–266. doi:10.1007/BF00957007

Malott, R. W., Malott, M. E., & Trojan, B. (1999). *Elementary Principles of Behavior* (4th ed.). Pearson Education.

Means, B., Toyama, Y., Murphy, R., Bakia, M., & Jones, K. (2009). *Evaluation of evidence-based practices in online learning: Meta-analysis and review of online learning studies*. US Department of Education.

Meyer, G. R., Sulzer-Azaroff, B., & Wallace, M. (2011). *Behavior analysis for lasting change*. New York: Sloan Publishing.

Pace, G. M., Ivancic, M. T., Edwards, G. L., Iwata, B. A., & Page, T. J. (1985). Assessment of stimulus preference and reinforcer value with profoundly retarded individuals. *Journal of Applied Behavior Analysis*, *18*(3), 249–255. doi:10.1901/jaba.1985.18-249 PMID:4044458

Pennypacker, H. S., Gutierrez, A., & Lindsley, O. R. (2003). *Handbook of the Standard Celeration Chart (deluxe edition)*. Cambridge, MA: Cambridge Center for Behavioral Studies.

Piazza, C. C., Fisher, W. W., Hagopian, L. P., Bowman, L. G., & Toole, L. (1996). Using a choice assessment to predict reinforcer effectiveness. *Journal of Applied Behavior Analysis*, *29*(1), 1–9. doi:10.1901/jaba.1996.29-1 PMID:8881340

Ramey, D., Lydon, S., Healy, O., McCoy, A., Holloway, J., & Mulhern, T. (2016). A systematic review of the effectiveness of precision teaching for individuals with developmental disabilities. *Journal of Autism and Developmental Disorders*, *3*(3), 179–195. doi:10.1007/s40489-016-0075-z

Robbins, J. K., Layng, T. V. J., & Jackson, P. J. (1995). *Fluent thinking skills*. Seattle, WA: Robbins/Layng & Associates.

Roscoe, E., Iwata, B. A., & Kahng, S. W. (1999). Relative versus absolute reinforcement effects: Implications for preference assessments. *Journal of Applied Behavior Analysis*, *32*(4), 479–493. doi:10.1901/jaba.1999.32-479 PMID:10641302

Ross, D. E., Singer-Dudek, J., & Greer, R. D. (2005). The teacher performance rate and accuracy scale (TPRA): Training as evaluation. *Education and Training in Developmental Disabilities*, 411–423.

Sarokoff, R. A., & Sturmey, P. (2004). The effects of behavioral skills training on staff implementation of discrete-trial teaching. *Journal of Applied Behavior Analysis*, *37*(4), 535–538. doi:10.1901/jaba.2004.37-535 PMID:15669415

Selinske, J., Greer, R. D., & Lodhi, S. (1991). A functional analysis of the Comprehensive Application of Behavior Analysis to Schooling. *Journal of Applied Behavior Analysis*, *13*, 645–654. PMID:1829071

Sherer, M. (2011). Transforming education with technology: A conversation with Karen Cator. *Educational Leadership*, *68*(5), 16–21.

Sherman, J. G., Raskin, R. S., & Semb, G. B. (1982). *The personalized systems of instruction: 48 seminal papers*. Lawrence, KS: TRI.

Shrestha, A., Anderson, A., & Moore, D. W. (2013). Using point-of-view video modeling and forward chaining to teach a functional self-help skill to a child with autism. *Journal of Behavioral Education*, *22*(2), 157–167. doi:10.1007/s10864-012-9165-x

Shukla-Mehta, S., Miller, T., & Callahan, K. J. (2010). Evaluating the effectiveness of video instruction on social and communication skills training for children with autism spectrum disorders: A review of the literature. *Focus on Autism and Other Developmental Disabilities*, *25*(1), 23–26. doi:10.1177/1088357609352901

Sidman, M., & Tailby, W. (1982). Conditional discrimination vs. matching to sample: An expansion of the testing paradigm. *Journal of the Experimental Analysis of Behavior*, *37*(1), 5–22. doi:10.1901/jeab.1982.37-5 PMID:7057129

Simpson, A., Langone, J., & Ayres, K. M. (2004). Embedded video and computer based instruction to improve social skills for students with autism. *Education and Training in Developmental Disabilities*, *39*(3), 240–252.

Singer-Dudek, J., Speckman, J., & Nuzullo, R. (2010). A comparative analysis of the CABAS® model of education at the Fred S. Keller School: A twenty-year review. *Behavior Analyst Today*, *11*(4), 253–265. doi:10.1037/h0100705

Skinner, B. F. (1938). *The Behavior of Organisms: An Experimental Analysis*. Acton, MA: Copley Publishing Group.

Skinner, B. F. (1953). *Science and human behavior*. New York: Pearson Education, Inc.

Skinner, B. F. (1957). *Verbal Behavior*. Prentice Hall. doi:10.1037/11256-000

Skinner, B. F. (1968). *The Technology of Teaching*. New York: Appleton-Century-Crofts.

Smith, T. (2001). Discrete trial training in the treatment of autism. *Focus on Autism and Other Developmental Disabilities, 16*(2), 286–292. doi:10.1177/108835760101600204

Steege, M. W., & Watson, T. S. (2009). *Conducting School-Based functional behavioral assessment: A practitioner's guide*. New York: The Guilford Press.

Technology. (n.d.). In *Merriam-Webster*. Retrieved June 23, 2016, from http://www.merriam-webster.com/dictionary/technology

U. S. Department of Education. (2016). *Future ready learning: Reimagining the role of technology in education*. Office of Educational Technology. Retrieved from http://tech.ed.gov

VanDerHeyden, A. M., Witt, J. C., & Gilbertson, D. (2007). A multi-year evaluation of the effects of a response to intervention (RTI) model on identification of children for special education. *Journal of School Psychology, 45*(2), 225–256. doi:10.1016/j.jsp.2006.11.004

Waddington, E. M., & Reed, P. (2009). The impact of using the Preschool Inventory of Repertoires for Kindergarten (PIRK) on school outcomes for children with Autistic Spectrum Disorders. *Research in Autism Spectrum Disorders, 3*(3), 809–827. doi:10.1016/j.rasd.2009.03.002

What is School-Wide Positive Behavior Support? (2009, March). *School-wide Positive Behavior Support (SWPBS)*. Retrieved from http://swpbs.org/schoolwide/Training/files/Kansas_School-Wide_Positive_Behavior_Support_Newsletter.pdf

White, O. R., & Haring, N. G. (1976). *Exceptional teaching: A multi-media approach*. Columbus, OH: Merrill.

Wilson, K. P. (2013). Teaching social-communication skills to preschoolers with autism: Efficacy of video versus in vivo modeling in the classroom. *Journal of Autism and Developmental Disorders, 43*(8), 1819–1831. doi:10.1007/s10803-012-1731-5 PMID:23224593

KEY TERMS AND DEFINITIONS

Applied Behavior Analysis: The application of evidence-based intervention strategies used to change socially significant behaviors to a meaningful degree such that the interventions applied can be shown through experimental manipulation to be responsible for the change of behavior that occurred.

Exogenous Technology: Hardware, software, and other downloadable applications for use on computers, smartphones, or tablets used for advancing learning and/or assisting in behavior change.

Response to Intervention: A multi-tier approach to identify students who require academic, social and behavioral interventions in general education classrooms and school settings. The effectiveness of such interventions subsequently measured to determine the need to refer the student for additional academic, social and/or behavioral supports via special education services.

Operant Conditioning: A type of learning that occurs through the consistent application of a set of consequences in relation to antecedent stimuli. This is done using the principles of behavior: positive reinforcement, negative reinforcement, positive punishment and negative punishment.

Task Analysis: The observation of a competent individual or group completing a task for the purposes of breaking the skill down into smaller components to teach a novice.

Shaping: Differential reinforcement (i.e. application of behavioral principles of reinforcement and punishment) for successive approximations to a terminal behavior such that some responses are reinforced while others are punished leading to the accurate behavior being emitted by an individual.

Modeling: Providing visual examples of an individual or group performing a skill or set of skills accurately and fluently for the purposes of teaching others through the visual medium.

Behavior Chaining: A chain of complex behaviors broken down into small incremental steps that build upon each other to complete a task at varying levels of difficulty. Each step in the chain builds upon the other serving as both antecedent and consequence to student behaviors. Each step is differentially reinforced resulting in a completed task. (e.g. reciting the alphabet or brushing one's teeth.)

Discrete Trail Training: The delivery of instruction that breaks down each unit of teaching into a three-term contingency such that there is a teacher delivered antecedent followed by student behavior and teacher applied consequence as a means of delivering individualized instruction.

ENDNOTES

[1]   CABAS® is a registered trademark of R. Douglas Greer. The circular pattern represents the symbiotic relationship between all components of the system. Adapted from Greer, R.D., Keohane, D., & Healy, O. (2002). Quality and comprehensive applications of behavior analysis to schooling. *The Behavior Analyst Today, 3*(2), 120.

[2]   Reproduced from Broto, J., & Greer, R.D. (2014). The effects of functional writing contingencies on second graders' writing and responding accurately to mathematical algorithms. *Behavioral Development Bulletin, 19*(1), 7.

APPENDIX

Foundations of ABA

Operant Conditioning

Operant conditioning is a key process of changing behavior. Its theoretical basis is from Skinner's experimental analyses of behavior which were conducted in his research laboratories from the 1930s to the 1950s (Cooper, et al., 2007). Skinner (1938) formulated principles of behavior from his experiments. The behavioral principles (i.e., reinforcement, punishment, stimulus control, etc.) describe relationships between environmental conditions and the behavior of organisms subject to those conditions.

Operant conditioning is a behavioral technology in which behavioral principles of reinforcement and punishment are key elements of the process (Cooper et al., 2007). It describes the selective effects of consequences which follow behavior and influence its future occurrence. However, functional relationships between behavior and the consequences that follow the behavior are also associated with antecedent conditions (events preceding the behavior). Operant conditioning is a term used to describe "learning." Operant conditioning occurs when a three-term contingency of antecedent, behavior, and consequence events repeated together can accurately predict behavior. When an organism comes under the control of this three-term contingency we say that "learning" has occurred. Therefore, learning occurs when antecedent stimuli (a stimulus or condition occurring prior to a predicted behavior) becomes a discriminative stimulus (S^D) for the occurrence of a specified behavior or set of behavioral responses. This behavior and or set of behaviors regularly comes into contact with a specified consequence or consequence event which either reinforces the behavior (i.e. increases the probability of future occurrence), or punishes the behavior (i.e. decreases the probability of future occurrence). The S^D is repeatedly presented until the three-term contingency becomes a discriminated operant to an individual.

Operant conditioning, when used as an educational technology, entails assessment of specific, observable, measurable behaviors, operationalized behavioral intervention to change behaviors, and progress monitoring through ongoing data collection and analysis. In order to target appropriate skills to teach or behaviors to improve it is imperative to assess current student repertoires. In the next section the authors will discuss behavioral assessment and how ABA offers ways of teaching new behaviors, maintaining behaviors, and reducing unwanted behaviors.

Behavioral Assessment

Typical psycho-educational assessments involve norm- and/or criterion-referenced standardized tests. The main purpose of those types of assessments is to find an individual's strengths and weaknesses by comparing his/her skill levels in assessed domains with those of a normed group (Cooper et al., 2007). Skill-based assessments offer a complete picture of an individual's current repertoires, upon which an individualized instruction can be built for more advanced learning to occur. Typical psycho-educational assessments and skill-based, or performance-based, assessments serve to answer specific types of questions about the learner. They can tell us about how the learner performs compared to his/her peers and they can tell us how the learner's skills in one area of learning are compared to their skills in another area of learning.

Behavioral assessments are designed to ask questions about how the learner's behavior relates to operant principles. The purpose of behavioral assessment is to identify behavior targeted for change and, equally importantly, to identify antecedent conditions and consequences which establish and maintain the behavior. Antecedent conditions and consequences are environmental variables that increase or decrease the future probability of a behavior and, further, are important, too, for maintenance and generalization of the induced behavior change. Identification of those variables; especially those for problem behavior, often requires a variety of methods including: interview, checklists, and direct observation.

Through a comprehensive behavioral assessment and an understanding of the contexts where the behavior occurs, reinforcers and competing contingencies for the behavior of interest can be identified. Thus behavioral assessment provides information about the behavior and how to change it (Cooper et al., 2007). Behavioral assessment identifies current operant behaviors and competing contingencies. It also provides information about how to change the operants including alternative contingencies. Behavioral assessment enables us to make scientifically and ethically appropriate decisions whereby a behavior change can be induced successfully and effectively (Mayer, Sulzer-Azaroff, & Wallace, 2012). The followings are brief examples of behavioral assessment:

Classroom Scenario 1

A kindergarten teacher, Sara, wants to know whether Jim, who struggles to make friends, greets his peers when he meets them. First she interviews a teacher's aide who stays with Jim during lunch time and recess. Sara also interviews Jim's mother to gain relevant information within and about his community settings. Through the interviews, Sara learns that Jim raises his hand without smiling or saying anything when he sees his peers. More detailed information is revealed when Sara directly observes the behavior of interest. Jim raises his hand too far away from his peers for them to recognize him. Jim doesn't say hello to his peers when they are near him.

With information gathered through the assessment, Sara identifies problems within the three-term contingency that cause barriers to appropriate socialization with peers. A potential intervention is selected to teach the necessary operant while applying the principles of reinforcement to correct the faulty operant (i.e., learned behavior), and to provide support to people in his social environment. Sara decides to provide prompts to Jim to greet peers when in close proximity. Additionally, she provides prompts to teach an appropriate distance from which to wave hello. When he engages in the behaviors with guidance, prompts are removed (i.e., faded) until the behavior comes under control of the proximity of peers.

Classroom Scenario 2

Ethan is a fourth grader in an integrated classroom of a public school. He has been referred for a functional behavior assessment due to his aggressive and disruptive behaviors in class. Ethan yells, swears at the teachers, and sometimes sweeps things off his desk when he is required to complete tasks in class. Ethan's behavior usually occurs during literacy and history class. His behavior interrupts the learning of himself and his peers. A behavior analyst conducts a comprehensive assessment including: reviewing documents, interviewing relevant adults, practitioners and/or peers, using a checklist and/or behavior rating scale, and direct observation. The assessment reveals that Ethan needs help with tasks where he is required to process auditory input. Results of the assessment suggest that his aggressive behavior is to communicate a need for help or a break when frustrated. "I need help" or "I need a break."

The assessment has provided information about the faulty operant (e.g. antecedent = task demands, behavior = yelling, reinforcement = teacher attention and escape). The assessment further provides information about alternative replacement behaviors (i.e., newly targeted operant behavior), resources within school, key people involved, and supporting personnel. Based on the results of assessment, an effective intervention is implemented. The intervention includes preparing environmental supports such as the use of visual aids and additional time to complete tasks, a system of reinforcement for his completion of tasks, extinction strategies (i.e., withholding reinforcement for previously reinforced behaviors) to make the current operant ineffective, and reinforcing alternative socially acceptable behaviors (e.g. saying, "I need help" and/or "I need a break"). The assessment is also a basis for monitoring and experimentally analyzing the function of the intervention plan and its outcomes.

Teaching New Behavior

When making a decision about what behavior to target for change considerations need to be made about how effectively the behavior change will induce adaptive and habilitative outcomes for an individual (i.e., social significance) (Cooper, et al., 2007). An observable and measurable definition of target behaviors to teach; often referred to as a "behavioral objective," is the first step when teaching a new behavior.

Ongoing progress monitoring through data collection on the target behavior provides a basis for analyzing the effect of a teaching procedure and allows the professional to test for function which is a core feature of a scientific technology. For example, you may want to increase reading fluency. The problem with stating this as a student goal when writing objectives for students with learning differences on an Individualized Education Plan (IEP), Accelerated Learning Plan or Response to Intervention (RTI) is that there is no way to observe and measure this behavior. In education it is vastly important to write student goals and objectives in a way that allows one to determine whether or not the teaching strategies and methods of intervention are effective.

Teaching strategies are considered effective if the student masters the material taught. To increase reading fluency is very vague and difficult to measure. However, when written as a behavioral objective the goal reads: Given a leveled reader (stimulus) and the teacher direction to, "read" (antecedent) the student will read 20% more words per minute read (method of measurement) over initial baseline measures with 90% accuracy (criterion) for pronunciation, additions and omissions (student behavior).

The teacher in the setting will then provide reinforcement for correctly read words and consequences in the form of corrections for any additions, omissions or mispronounced words (consequence). This breakdown of antecedent stimuli, student behavior and teacher consequence constitute the three-term contingency of operant conditioning (i.e. teaching). For "good" teachers this is a naturally occurring condition in the classroom when working with students. The behavioral objective; consisting of the three-term contingency, method of measurement and criterion to meet the objective, of increasing reading fluency can then be measured and teaching strategies therefore found effective or ineffective.

The criterion for improvement can be incrementally increased over the course of the school year such that it begins with 20% and ends with 75% over baseline measures resulting in the student reading at a pace 75% faster or more fluent than when initially tested. As a matter of course these figures are not chosen arbitrarily. A measure of student's word per minutes read will be based on the "norm" for the age/grade level of the student and/or their class peers.

As you can see from the previous example teaching a new behavior involves behavioral pedagogy. A core procedure of behavioral pedagogy is operant conditioning. A targeted and thus potential operant is presented until learning occurs and the potential operant becomes a discriminated operant. The potential operant consisting of the three-term contingency is the main agent for learning to occur.

Through the operant conditioning procedure, the individual establishes a history of reinforcement within the three-term contingency. The identification of reinforcers is a major component of the process of operant conditioning. Through preference assessment and reinforcer assessment, potential reinforcers can be identified (DeLeon, Iwata, Goh, Worsdell, 1997; Fisher, Piazza, Bowman, Hagopian, Owens, & Slevin, 1992; Pace, Ivancic, Edwards, Iwata, & Page, 1985; Piazza, Fisher, Hagopian, Bowman, & Toole, 1996).

Reinforcers for an individual can be primary, secondary or tertiary. Primary reinforcers include food or physical contact, those things that are part of human phylogeny (i.e. built into the system- DNA), and secondary reinforcers (requiring some training after birth) include a variety of environmental stimuli such as toys, activities, and events. Praise, tokens, and even money are generalized reinforcers with which different response classes can be taught. It is important for educators to understand that verbal praise alone does not always act as a reinforcer for students. Many students are shy or dislike public attention therefore student preference and reinforcer assessments are strongly encouraged as the use of verbal praise alone to reinforce student behavior is not always adequate for them to learn new operants.

Another important element of the three-term contingency delivered during operant conditioning is the antecedent condition. When a response-reinforcer relation is associated with an antecedent condition, the three-term contingency becomes a discriminated operant. Thus, identifying whether an additional antecedent stimulus is needed and what type of stimulus that might be is critical in the operant conditioning process. Providing an additional stimulus to a natural antecedent stimulus is technically known as prompting.

For example, a young child may need a hand gesture or vocal signal (i.e. prompt) when he/she is required to discriminate a tiger from a lion initially. A mother might point to a lion asking her child, "Where is a lion?" when they look at an animal book together. A picture of a lion (stimulus) and mom's asking, "Where is a lion?" (antecedent) together are antecedent stimuli and gesturing to the picture is an additional stimulus or prompt. Later, the gesturing can be removed once the child reliably points to the picture of the lion. Eventually, the child will be able to point to the picture of a lion without the additional stimulus (i.e., prompt). This procedure is referred to as prompt fading and transfer of stimulus control. In this case, with the aid of an additional antecedent stimulus the child is exposed to the potential operant easily and learning is induced more efficiently.

These prompts include physical guidance, instructing, modeling, and vocal prompts (Alberto & Troutman, 2013). Using technical terms for this process allows the professional to teach others to engage in the same teaching process with precision and accuracy.

Modeling

Modeling is one of many widely used prompt procedures for establishing a variety of behaviors. A physical movement may function as a model when it evokes an imitative behavior of a child which brings about acquisition of a new skill. In that case, a model is an antecedent stimulus that functions as a prompt. For example, seeing a jungle gym alone won't evoke appropriate play when a child sees it for the first time. The child will learn how to play on the jungle gym after the child observes and imitates others' actions on the jungle gym.

Video modeling emerged in the 1990s as an effective tool to teach new skills (Wilson, 2013). For example, video modeling was used to teach functional living skills, social-communication skills such as toy play or social initiations (Shukla-Mehta, Miller, & Callahan, 2010; Simpson, Langone, Ayres, 2004). Shrestha, Anderson and Moore (2013) taught a 4-year old boy to prepare and serve himself Weetabix. Thirteen steps for setting-up, eating, and cleaning -up were identified and three videos were produced with the boy's mother as the model.

The first video included Steps 1-4 which began with the model saying, "I'm hungry! Let's get some Weetabix without any help!" The second video included Steps 1-10 and the third one included Steps 1-13. The results of using video modeling in teaching the self-help skill indicated that the modeling procedure was effective and the learned skill was maintained. The 13 steps identified are shown in Figure 2.

It should be noted that often, providing prompts is not enough to induce learning of a new skill. For example, it is unrealistic for a young child to draw a triangle with straight lines when they connect two dots with a curvy line. In this case, shaping can be a useful strategy.

Figure 2. Task analysis for the target behavior using a video model (adapted from Shrestha, Anderson, & Moore, 2013)

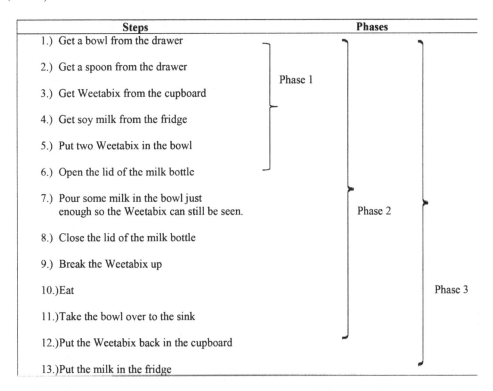

Shaping

Shaping is defined as "the process of systematically and differentially reinforcing successive approximations to a terminal behavior (Cooper, et al., 2007, p. 421). Through differential reinforcement for drawing more straight lines in the triangle, the child draws a triangle with less curvy and straighter lines. The strategy is used until the child produces an acceptable triangle.

Shaping can be used for a child who can't sit even a minute to teach sitting for 15 minutes. A certain length of time sitting is reinforced selectively during each stage of shaping and gradually, the length of his sitting behavior is shaped up to 15 minutes. Again, the professional can more effectively apply this strategy when it is treated as a technology.

Case Example 1

A special education preschool teacher Martha has a 4-year old boy Ethan who has feeding problems in her classroom. Ethan would not accept any food delivered on a spoon. In addition to that, he has no history of swallowing food with texture. The main source of his nutrition was in liquid form such as

Table 4. Three-term contingency to shape feeding behaviors

Step	Antecedent	Behavior	Consequence
1	A spoon with a small amount of oatmeal & teacher gesture to the spoon	Bring the spoon to his lip within 10 seconds	Video for 30 seconds
2	A spoon and tray with oatmeal	Put the spoon in his mouth within 10 seconds	Video for 30 seconds
3	A spoon and tray with oatmeal	Put the oatmeal in his mouth and swallow within 10 seconds	Video for 30 seconds
4	A spoon and tray with a spoonful of oatmeal	Scoop and put the oatmeal in his mouth and swallow within 10 seconds	Video for 30 seconds
5	A spoon and tray with a spoonful of oatmeal	Finish the oatmeal within 1 minute	Video for 30 seconds
6	A spoon and tray with 2 spoonfuls of oatmeal	Finish the oatmeal within 1 minute	Video for 30 seconds
7	A spoon and tray with 3 spoonfuls of oatmeal	Finish the oatmeal within 1 minute	Video for 1 minute
8	A spoon and tray with 5 spoonfuls of oatmeal	Finish the Oatmeal within 5 minutes	Video for 3 minutes
9	A spoon and a tray with 5 spoonfuls of oatmeal with 1/10th slice of bread mixed	Finish the oatmeal within 5 minutes	Video for 3 minutes
10	A spoon and tray with 5 spoonfuls of oatmeal with 3/10ths slice of bread mixed	Finish the oatmeal within 5 minutes	Video for 3 minutes
11	A spoon and tray with 5 spoonfuls of oatmeal and a 1/10th slice of bread separate	Finish the oatmeal and the bread within 5 minutes	Video for 3 minutes
12	A spoon and tray with 5 spoonfuls of oatmeal and a 3/10ths slice of bread separate	Finish the oatmeal and the bread within 5 minutes	Video for 3 minutes

PediaSure®. Martha decided to teach Ethan a critical skill, feeding himself textured food using a spoon. First, she interviewed Ethan's mother to ensure that he didn't have a medical reason causing his inability to swallow food with texture. She then broke down the target skill into small steps (i.e. a task analysis). The steps are shown in Table 4.

Martha established criteria for moving from one step to the next: independent responses with 90% accuracy for three to 12 consecutive sessions depending on the target responses. One session is consisted of 1 to 20 trials depending on the target responses. Once Ethan maintained learned feeding responses for 10 school days, Ethan's mother tried to generalize the responses at home very carefully following Martha's guideline. When teaching feeding skills, data were collected and summarized in a graph. Martha monitored the effectiveness of her teaching procedure by regular visual inspection of the graph and received consultation as needed from a supervisor.

Martha realized that she needed reinforcers of very high value to Ethan. Martha used Ethan's favorite video as a reinforcer for his correct responses during the feeding sessions. For example, she gestured to a tray where she placed a spoonful of Oatmeal and waited for 1 minute. If Ethan ate the food on the tray using the spoon, she marked "+" on her data sheet and provided reinforcement by turning on the video Ethan selected on an iPad™ for 1 minute. If he didn't eat within 1 minute, the tray and the iPad™ were removed for 10 seconds. Ethan had another opportunity after a 10-second pause.

The amount and texture (i.e. solidity) of the food was gradually and carefully increased. Finally, Ethan could feed himself foods with soft textures such as oatmeal and bread. Martha realized that teaching feeding required careful monitoring and persistence. Martha still had a long way to go, but Ethan's mother was very happy with the outcome.

Behavior Chaining

Behavior chaining is another useful technology and is used to teach complicated skills which require a sequence of discrete responses. "Each response in a chain produces a stimulus change that simultaneously serves as a conditioned reinforcer for the response that produced it and as a discriminative stimulus for the next response in the chain" (Cooper et al., 2007, p. 435).

One example of behavior chaining is making a peanut butter sandwich. The first response is to place two slices of bread on a plate, which is a discriminative stimulus for the next response, opening a jar of peanut butter. A series of specific discrete responses lead to a terminal response, having a peanut butter sandwich ready on the plate. In behavior chaining, a task analysis is an important component. "Task analysis involves breaking a complex skill into smaller, teachable units, the product of which is a series of sequentially ordered steps or tasks" (Cooper et al., 2007, p. 437).

For example, a parent can teach his/her child to brush their teeth by using a behavior chaining procedure with a task analysis. The parent breaks down steps for brushing teeth into smaller units and teaches the child to perform each of the behaviors in the chain in a specified order. This contributes to the parent behaving as a technologically savvy teacher--a goal the authors would have for any parent.

Maintaining Behavior

Any behavior changed through operant conditioning is not maintained by itself without a persisting behavioral consequence (Malott, Malott, & Trojan, 1999). When a behavior analyst or teacher as strategic scientist teaches a new skill by delivering potential three-term contingencies to a student, he/she might use a continuous schedule of reinforcement by delivering a reinforcing consequence for every correct response. Once the child begins to emit correct responses, the behavior analyst fades the schedule of reinforcement by using a gradually intermittent schedule until it approximates the "natural" environment.

For example, a third grader, Jake is receiving special education services. He is integrated into a general education classroom for 50% of his school day. Jake receives verbal praise from an adult every time he follows a direction in his special education class. One of his behavioral objectives is following directions with an intermittent schedule of reinforcement. The special education teacher expects that Jake will maintain his direction-following after the teacher systematically reduces her delivery of verbal praise. This schedule fading (i.e., schedule thinning) will help him gain skills needed to spend greater amounts of time in the inclusive setting where he may experience fewer opportunities to be praised by his teacher.

The maintenance of learned behavior is influenced by the amount of and types of reinforcers used during operant conditioning. If Jake, in the above scenario, doesn't follow directions with verbal praise alone, the teacher may need to use other prosthetic reinforcers such as cookies or toys at the initial stage of training. Eventually, this type of reinforcer will need to be faded to a natural reinforcer for following directions such as receiving praise or acknowledgement from teachers or finding reinforcement in completion of the task alone. This fading process is another example of a teaching technology as many learners will need systematic support to transition from one type of learning environment, set of expectations, or type of reinforcement to another.

Based on the same behavior principles, problematic behavior that is maintained by intermittent (i.e. variable) schedules of reinforcement also persist and last longer than behavior with continuous schedules of reinforcement (Cooper, et al., 2007; Malott et al., 1999). This is one of the greatest challenges and poses the most difficulty when there is an inconsistent application of an intervention strategy for either teaching a new skill or reducing a problem behavior.

The student continues to behave in ways that have been reinforced in the past due to what is referred to as an "instructional history". The longer the instructional history (i.e., history of reinforcement that maintains a behavior); be it academic, social, or maladaptive, the longer the behavior will persist in the face of changing intervention strategies.

This may at times lead to teachers feeling as though the intervention strategies are ineffective and they may choose to change direction too soon. On the bright side; when teaching a new skill, intermittent (i.e., variable) schedules of reinforcement increase the probability that the behavior will persist (i.e. be maintained). Over time a new skill becomes the norm or expected behavior. The student is now reinforced by the naturally occurring contingencies such as completing an assignment. This is called *transfer of stimulus function*.

A prosthetic reinforcer is no longer needed to reinforce student behavior. When this occurs there is no need to provide the same levels of reinforcement for the same behavior as used when initially teaching the skill. This form of fading is one of many behavioral strategies used in academic interventions such as scaffolded instruction. As new skills are being taught different levels of guidance, prompting or additional tools are provided to the student. These levels of modeling, guidance and use of tools become part of a student's repertoire which are then maintained as new skills are being acquired and build upon the prior knowledge or skill.

Generalizing Behavior

Generalizing behavior requires that the behavior learned in one environment (e.g., school) also has reinforcement provided by other significant people in the student's life in settings where the behavior should also occur. This is the definition of social significance.

If a behavior is learned in one environment or can only be elicited by one person there is no opportunity for the change in behavior to significantly change the person's access to higher instruction and or access to appropriate social experiences. For example, when you first teach a child to use a graphic organizer to organize their ideas before writing you may model its use, prompt them to place items in different categories and other such procedures while providing verbal praise for using the graphic organizer. Over time you reduce the number of prompts, provide less guidance and verbal praise is no longer necessary for the student to use a graphic organizer in the pre-writing stages. If the same is done at home by parents the student will then generalize those skills to home when doing homework allowing them to become more independent and complete work outside of school independent of tutors or adult prompting.

Reducing Behavior

Problem behaviors are also operants which are learned and maintained by environmental effects produced by the problem behavior. In other words, problem behaviors are maintained due to functions of the behaviors within an individual's environment. Simply speaking, problem behaviors are maintained because they serve some purpose or function. An individual may obtain attention they don't regularly receive or avoid having to complete a difficult task (an aversive condition). These types of consequences can lead to problem behavior.

Reducing problem behavior is another area where a technological approach is just as effective as the technological approach to assessment of behavior and the learning of new behavior. Relevant literature reports that environmental events such as social attention, aversive tasks, tangible items, or sensory stimulation (Iwata, Pace, Dorsey, Zarcone, Vollmer, Smith, et al., 1994) can be related to problem behavior. Prior to determining an intervention, a functional behavior assessment (FBA) to determine the relevant environmental events is required.

The main purpose of an FBA is to identify functions of the behavior; setting events (things occurring prior to any antecedent stimuli not necessarily under control of anyone in the environment (e.g., hunger, illness, restless night), antecedent conditions including antecedent stimulus or stimuli and consequences (i.e., environmental changes which follow the behavior). Once the function of the behavior has been determined practitioners can effectively alter three-term contingencies of the problematic behaviors to socially acceptable behaviors with the same functions (Iwata, Dorsey, & Slifer, 1994).

FBA procedures can be classified into three types: (a) indirect assessment, (b) descriptive assessment, and (c) functional analysis which requires experimental manipulations to identify function(s) of the behavior (Cipani & Schock, 2007). Indirect assessment involves interviews, checklists, rating scales, or questionnaires to obtain information to identify possible functions of the behavior within natural contexts from caregivers or stakeholders. This type of assessment is easy to conduct but is limited in accuracy.

Descriptive assessment involves direct observation of the problem behaviors within natural environments to identify relevant three-term contingencies. Main procedures of this type of FBA are ABC recording and scatterplots. ABC recording enables practitioners to make a hypothesis about three-term contingencies (antecedent-behavior-consequence) relationships of the behavior. Scatterplots provide a temporal pattern for the occurrence of the behaviors. Functional Analysis (FA) involves systematically manipulating antecedent events and consequences of the problem behaviors. One advantage of using FA is more accurate information about three-term contingencies involved. However, it requires personnel with extensive training on FA. All of these types of assessment procedures serve one function: identification of three-term contingencies of problem behaviors (Iwata, Dorsey, et al., 1994).

Section 3
Theoretical and Experiential Perspectives

Chapter 16
Youths and Cyberbullying:
Description, Theories, and Recommendations

Michelle F. Wright
Pennsylvania State University, USA

ABSTRACT

Youths are immersed in a digitally connected world, where blogs, social networking sites, watching videos, and instant messaging tools are a normal part of their lives. Many of these youths cannot remember a time in which electronic technologies were not embedded within their lives. Electronic technologies afford a variety of opportunities for youths, but there are also risks associated with such use, such as cyberbullying. This chapter draws on research from around the world to explain the nature, extent, causes, and consequences of cyberbullying. This chapter concludes with a solutions and recommendation section, emphasizing the need for cyberbullying to be considered a global concern.

INTRODUCTION

Millions of youths use electronic technologies (e.g., cell phones, the Internet) everyday, engaging in a variety of different online behaviors, such as looking up information, watching videos for entertainment, and communicating with people from around the world (Lenhart, 2015). Although there are many benefits associated with youths' electronic technology use, they are also at risk for identity theft, sexual predators, addiction, and being exposed to unwanted, sexually graphic, or gory content via videos and images. Cyberbullying is also a risk factor associated with youths' electronic technology use. Defined as an extension of traditional face-to-face bullying, cyberbullying involves harming others via electronic technologies (e.g., email, instant messaging, social networking websites, text messages through mobile devices; Bauman, Underwood, & Card, 2013; Grigg, 2012). Bullying through electronic technology offers cyberbullies the flexibility to harm their victims at almost any time of day, without having to be concerned with the consequences of their actions, due to the ability to remain anonymous (Wright, 2014b). The ability to remain anonymous through interactions in the cyber context can potentially trigger the online disinhibition effect among youths. This effect can lead some youths to do or say things

DOI: 10.4018/978-1-5225-2838-8.ch016

online to others that they would never do or say in the offline world (Suler, 2004; Wright, 2014a). Electronic technologies also allow bullies to target their victims quicker (e.g., spreading a rumor in the online world can occur in a matter of moments), administer multiple attacks in a short period of time, and the ability to involve various more people or bystanders (e.g., posting a degrading or humiliating video online can receive thousands of watches versus only a handful of students witnessing teasing in the hallway of a middle school).

The aim of this chapter was to review literature on cyberbullying among youths in elementary, middle, and high schools. The literature review draws on research from various disciplines, including psychology, sociology, education, social work, communication studies, gender studies, and computer science. The research involves cross-sectional, longitudinal, qualitative, quantitative, and mixed methods research designs. The chapter also includes research studies conducted by researchers from around the world. The chapter is organized into the following seven sections:

1. Definition and description of cyberbullying
2. Characteristics and risk factors associated with cyberbullying
3. The outcomes or consequences related to youths' involvement in cyberbullying
4. Theoretical underpinnings
5. Solutions and recommendations
6. Future research directions
7. Conclusion

BACKGROUND

Using electronic technologies to hostilely, intentionally, and maliciously harass, embarrass, and intimidate others is known as cyberbullying (Smith, Del Barrio, & Tokunaga, 2013). These online behaviors must be hostile, intentional, and malicious to qualify as cyberbullying. Cyberbullying can also include repetition and an imbalance of power between the bully and the victim, similar to the definition of traditional face-to-face bullying. Although these characteristics of the traditional face-to-face bullying definition can be present in cyberbullying acts, these characteristics are often much more pronounced. For instance, repetition of a cyberbullying act might involve targeting the victim multiple times through the sharing of a humiliating video or a text message with one or multiple people (Bauman, Underwood, & Card, 2013). Sending this video or text message to one person could trigger this person to share the content with multiple other people who could then share the contents with yet more people. This cycle can continue over and over again, perpetuating the cycle of cyberbullying victimization. The ability to remain anonymous while engaging in cyberbullying acts can also widen the imbalance of power between the victim and the bully.

Because cyberbullying acts occur through electronic technology, this characteristic separates it from traditional face-to-face bullying (Curelaru, Iacob, & Abalasei, 2009). Some examples of cyberbullying include sending unkind text messages and emails, theft of identity/personal information, pretending to be someone else, making anonymous phone calls, spreading nasty (and oftentimes false) rumors using social networking websites, threatening to harm someone physically (in the offline world), or uploading or sending a picture or video of the victim with the intention to embarrass the victim (Bauman et al., 2013). Cyberbullying acts can also be similar to those acts in the offline world, such as insults, verbal attacks, teasing, physical threats, social exclusion, humiliation, harassment, and intimidation. Furthermore, cyberbullying behaviors can be carried out via a variety of electronic technology mediums, such as social networking sites, text messages, and online gaming sites, creating websites to defame someone else, and making fake social networking profiles using someone else's identity (Rideout, Roberts, & Foehr, 2005). The most frequently used electronic technologies to perpetrate cyberbullying include gaming consoles, instant messaging tools, and social networking websites (Ybarra, Diener-West, & Leaf, 2007). Other forms of cyberbullying acts include happy slapping and flaming. Happy slapping is defined as a group of people insulting another person at random while filming the incident on a mobile phone (Rideout et al., 2005). These individuals later post the images or videos online for everyone to see. Flaming is defined as posting provocative or offensive messages in a public forum with the intention of eliciting an angry response or arguments from other forum users.

Similar to the earlier investigations of traditional face-to-face bullying, earlier investigations of cyberbullying involved assessing the prevalence rates of youths' involvement in cyberbullying. In one of the earliest studies on this topic, Kowalski and Limber found that 11% of the 3,767 middle school students (aged 11-14) they sampled admitted that they had been cyberbullied, 4% indicated that they had bullied other youths, and 7% were involved as cybervictims and cyberbullies. Similarly, Patchin and Hinduja (2006) found that 29% of the youths in their sample reported that they were cyberbullies, while 47% admitted that they had witnessed cyberbullying at least once. Using a sample of high schools in grades 9th through 12th, Goebert, Else, Matsu, Chung-Do, and Chang (2011) reported that 56.1% of their sample from Hawaii admitted to being victimized by cyberbullying at least once. Inconsistent patterns of prevalence rates have been found in more recent research as well. In particular, Hinduja and Patchin (2012) found that 4.9% of the 6th through 12th grade youths in their sample perpetrated cyberbullying in the past 30 days.

Cyberbullying Across the Globe

The differences in prevalence rates are most likely the result of differences in sampling techniques and measurement techniques employed in the studies on cyberbullying. Despite such a consideration, it is important to understand the frequency rates of cyberbullying as such rates indicate that these behaviors are a concern for youths across the globe. Consequently, some researchers have examined cyberbullying in regions other than the United States. Cappadocia, Craig, and Pepler (2013) reported that 2.1% of the Canadian 10th graders in their study admitted that they were cyberbullies, while 1.9% were cybervictims and 0.6% were cyberbullies and cybervictims. Bonnanno and Hymel (2013) found slightly higher prevalence rates in their sample of Canadian youths in the 8th through 10th grades. In particular, 5.8% reported that they were victims only, 6% admitted that they were cyberbullies only, and 5% indicated that they were cyberbullies and cybervictims.

Outside of North America, increasing evidence indicates that cyberbullying perpetration and victimization occur in Asia, Australia, and Europe as well. Using a sample of 22,544 Swedish youths between the ages of 15 and 18 years old, Laftman, Modin, and Ostberg (2013) found that 5% were cybervictims, 4% were cyberbullies, and 2% were both cyberbullies and cybervictims. Beckman, Hagquist, and Hellstrom (2012) also investigated cyberbullying among Swedish youths. Although they used a younger sample of Swedish youths (grades 7th through 9th), Beckman et al. found that 1.9% were cybervictims, 2.9% were cyberbullies, and 0.6% were cyberbullies and cybervictims. Similar prevalence rates of cyber victimization were found in a study conducted among Irish youths. In this study, Corcoran, Connolly, and O'Moore (2012) found that 6% of the 876 Irish youths, ages 12 through 17 years, they sampled were cybervictims. Higher prevalence rates have been found among Italian youths. Brighi, Guarini, Melotti, Galli, and Genta (2012) reported that 12.5% of their 2,326 sample (*M* age = 13.9 years old) indicated that they had experienced cyber victimization. German youths also report similar levels of involvement in cyberbullying. For instance, Festl, Scharkow, and Quandt (2013) found that 13% of their sample of 13 through 19 year olds (*N* = 278) reported that they were cyberbullies and 11% indicated that they were cybervictims.

Rates of cyberbullying perpetration and victimization are slightly higher in Israel than in some European countries. In particular, Olenik-Shemesh, Heiman, and Pieschl (2010) found that 16.5% of the 242 youths in their sample, ages 13 through 16 years old, were classified as cyberbullies. On the other hand, Lazuras, Barkoukis, Ourda, and Tsorbatzoudis (2013) reported that the rate of cyberbullying victimization or witnessing cyberbullying was 32.4% among their sample (*N* = 355) of youths between the ages of 13 and 17 years old.

Research on the prevalence of cyberbullying rates in Turkey has been increasing. In particular, rates of cyberbullying victimization range from 18% to 32% (e.g., Erdur-Baker, 2010; Yilmaz, 2011), while rates of cyberbullying perpetration range from 6% to 19% (Ayas & Horzum, 2012; Yilmaz, 2011). Higher rates of cyberbullying perpetration were found by Aricak and colleagues (2008). They found that 36% of the 269 Turkish secondary students in their study reported that they were cyberbullies.

Although a bit slower to develop, cyberbullying research has also been conducted in Asian countries as well. Huang and Chou (2010) found that 63.4% of the 545 Taiwanese youths in their sample had witnessed cyberbullying, 34.9% were classified as cybervictims, and 20.4% were classified as cyberbullies. Among a sample of Korean youths (N = 3,238), Jang, Song, and Kim (2014) indicated that 43% of the sample were involved in cyberbullying as either perpetrators or victims. Zhou et al. (2013) found similar prevalence rates among 1,438 Chinese youths in their sample. In particular, 34.8% reported that they were cyberbullies and 56.9% indicated that they were cybervictims. Using a sample of Singaporean youths, Kwan and Skoric (2013) found that 59.4% were exclusively victimized through Facebook and 56.9% reported that they perpetrated cyberbullying through Facebook.

Little attention has been given to cross-cultural differences in youths' cyberbullying involvement. This research has focused on understanding differences among countries with an independent self-construal and those with an interdependent self-construal. An independent self-construal means that the person views himself or herself separate from the social context. On the other hand, someone with an interdependent self-construal views himself or herself within the context of his or her social environment or society. Generally, people from Western countries, like the United States, Canada, and Sweden, are reinforced and primed for behaving in ways that align with an independent self-construal, while people from Eastern countries, like China, Korea, and Japan, are reinforced and primed for displaying an interdependent self-construal. Depending on people's self-construals, they act in different ways.

In the cross-cultural cyberbullying literature, youths with independent self-construals typically report more cyberbullying involvement than youths with interdependent self-construals. In particular, youths from the United States reported higher levels of cyberbullying perpetration and victimization in comparison to youths from Japan (Barlett et al., 2013). Similar patterns have been found for youths from Austria and Japan, with Austrian youths reporting higher levels of cyberbullying involvement than youths from Japan (Strohmeier, Aoyama, Gradinger, & Toda, 2013). Chinese youths reported that they engaged in less cyberbullying perpetration and were victimized less by cyberbullying than Canadian youths (Li, 2006, 2008). Other research has also revealed that East Asian youths from Canada engaged in less cyberbullying than Caucasian youths from Canada (Shapka & Law, 2013). Different patterns emerged in Shapka and Law's research when they delineated cyberbullying perpetration into proactive and reactive forms. They found that when East Asian youths from Canada engaged in cyberbullying they typically did so for proactive reasons (i.e., to obtain a goal), while Canadian youths perpetrated cyberbullying more often for reactive reasons (i.e., response to provocation).

Few studies have focused on cyberbullying involvement among youths in Africa, India, and South America. More research should be focused on cyberbullying perpetration and victimization in these regions. In one of the few studies conducted on cyberbullying in India, Wright and colleagues (2015) found that the highest rates of cyberbullying perpetration and victimization were reported by youths from India in their sample, followed by youths in China and then in Japan. Taken together, the literature reviewed in this section strongly suggests that cyberbullying is a global concern.

Characteristics and Risk Factors

More recent attention on cyberbullying involvement among youths have focused on the characteristics and risk factors associated with their involvement in these behaviors. A commonly investigated risk factor is age. Early adolescents have the highest rates of cyberbullying perpetration and victimization when compared to younger and older youths. In other research, Williams and Guerra (2007) delineated between physical forms (i.e., hacking) and nonphysical forms of cyberbullying. They investigated the prevalence rates of cyberbullying among youths in middle school and high school. The findings revealed that physical forms of cyberbullying peaked in middle and then declined throughout high school, while such patterns were not found for nonphysical forms of cyberbullying. Other research has found that age is not always a consistent predictor of cyberbullying involvement. Wade and Beran (2011) found that 9th graders in their sample were at an elevated risk of cyberbullying involvement when compared to middle school youths.

Another frequently examined characteristic associated with cyberbullying involvement is gender. Some researchers (e.g., Boulton, Lloyd, Down, & Marx, 2012; Li, 2007; Ybarra et al., 2007) found that boys were more often the perpetrators of cyberbullying, while girls were more often victimized by cyberbullying (e.g., Hinduja & Patchin, 2007; Kowalski & Limber 2007). Opposite patterns have been found by other researchers (e.g., Dehue, Bolman, & Vollink, 2008; Pornari & Wood, 2010) who concluded that girls were more likely to perpetrated cyberbullying and that boys were more often victims of cyberbullying (e.g., Huang & Chou, 2010; Sjurso, Fandrem, & Roland, 2016). Yet other researchers (e.g., Stoll & Block, 2015; Wright & Li, 2013b) have found no gender differences in youths' cyberbullying involvement. Similar to age, gender is not a consistent predictor of cyberbullying perpetration or victimization.

Research has also focused on youths' involvement in traditional face-to-face bullying perpetration and victimization as risk factors associated with cyberbullying involvement. Ample research evidence links cyberbullying perpetration with traditional face-to-face bullying perpetration, cyber victimization with traditional face-to-face bullying victimization, cyber victimization with traditional face-to-face bullying perpetration, and cyberbullying perpetration with traditional face-to-face bullying victimization (Barlett & Gentile, 2012; Mitchell, Ybarra, & Finkelhor, 2007; Wright & Li, 2013a; Wright & Li, 2013b). Due to these associations, it is important for researchers interested in youths' involvement in cyberbullying to also consider youths' involvement in face-to-face traditional bullying.

The amount of time that youths use electronic technologies is another risk factor associated with cyberbullying involvement. Positive relationships are found between internet use and cyberbullying perpetration and victimization (Ang, 2016; Aricak et al., 2008). Researchers have also found that cybervictims reported using instant messaging tools, email, blogging sites, and online gaming at higher rates than nonvictims of cyberbullying (Smith et al., 2008). The linkage between electronic technology use and cyberbullying involvement can be explained by cybervictims increased disclosure of personal information (Ybarra et al., 2007). In particular, disclosing more personal information online, such as geographic location, puts youths at a greater risk of cyber victimization.

Externalizing difficulties, such as alcohol use and drug use, and internalizing difficulties, such as depression, loneliness, and anxiety, also have a role in cyberbullying involvement. More specifically, alcohol and drug use are related positively to cyberbullying perpetration (Cappadocia, Craig, & Pepler, 2013; Wright, 2016). These difficulties are hypothesized to reduce cybervictims' coping abilities, making them vulnerable to victimization (Cappadocia et al., 2013; Mitchell et al., 2007).

Researchers have also examined other risk factors associated with cyberbullying involvement among youths. Holding higher levels of normative beliefs concerning traditional face-to-face bullying and cyberbullying were associated positively with cyberbullying perpetration (e.g., Burton, Florell, & Wygant, 2013; Wright, 2014b). Therefore, youths with more favorable attitudes toward bullying are much more likely to perpetrate cyberbullying. Youths with lower levels of provicitm attitudes (i.e., believing that bullying is unacceptable and that defending the victim is valuable), lower peer attachment, less self-control and empathy, and greater levels of moral disengagement were each related to cyberbullying perpetration (e.g., Sevcikova, Machackova, Wright, Dedkova, & Cerna, 2015; Wright, Kamble, Lei, Li, Aoyama, & Shruti, 2015).

Because cyberbullying research is in its infancy, few studies have been conducted utilizing longitudinal research designs. Consequently, it is difficult to understand the longitudinal associates of risk factors to youths' cyberbullying involvement. Using a longitudinal design, Fanti, Demetriou, and Hawa (2012) found that media violence exposure was related positively to cyber victimization, assessed one year later. Furthermore, Wright's (2014a) findings revealed that perceived stress from parents, peers, and academics increased youths' cyberbullying perpetration one year later.

There are a variety of characteristics that increase youths' risk for cyberbullying perpetration and victimization. As the cyberbullying research is advancing, researchers are beginning to look beyond frequency rates and the risk factors associated with individual characteristics, such as age, gender, and normative beliefs. They are beginning to consider contextual predictors of youths' involvement in cyberbullying, such as parents.

Parents

The traditional face-to-face bullying literature is consistent regarding the linkages between this form of bullying, parental monitoring, and parenting styles. Permissive parenting styles are associated with parents who have less knowledge about their children's offline activities (Nikiforou, Georgiou, & Stavrinides, 2013). This lack of awareness places these children at risk for traditional face-to-face bullying victimization. Indifferent-uninvolved parenting styles increase the risk of youths being classified as bully-victims, due to their parents' inconsistent monitoring styles (Totura et al., 2009). Overprotective parents also have children who are at risk for traditional face-to-face bullying (Hokoda, Lu, & Angeles, 2006). Such overprotective families do not allow their children to develop the autonomy, assertive behaviors, or social skills needed for peer interactions. Poor social skills increase youths' risk of being targeted by their peers for bullying. Furthermore, without these skills, children have difficulties navigating their interpersonal relationships, which increases their risk of experiencing poor interpersonal relationships. A strong social network of peers provides children with protection from peer victimization.

Electronic technologies also require parental monitoring. In research on this topic, Mason (2008) found that 30% of the youths in his sample used the internet often, about three hours or more daily. However, about 50% of these youths indicated that their parents monitored their online activities. Parental mediation of youths' electronic technology use can serve a protective function for reducing youths' exposure to online risks. In particular, Wright (2015) found that parental mediation of electronic technology use buffered against the negative psychosocial adjustment difficulties associated with youths' cyber victimization. Findings from the research on parental mediation of electronic technology use is mixed. For example, Aoyama, Utsumi, and Hasegawa (2011) did not find support that parental mediation and parental monitoring reduced youths' cyberbullying perpetration or victimization. To explain these findings, Aoyama et al. proposed that many parents lack the technological skills necessary to effectively monitor and discuss online activities with their children, which might lead them to inconsistently implement internet safety guidelines. Because of this limitation, parents are often unsure of how to intervene when their children experience online risks. Such a proposal is consistent with research suggesting that parents are often unsure of how to discuss online activities with their children (Rosen, 2007). When parents do not discuss appropriate electronic technology use with their children, this can increase the risk of their children perpetrating cyberbullying. Parents need to also update their mediational strategies and technology-related rules as their children become more independent and savvy electronic technology users.

Although many parents are not certain of how to monitor their children's electronic technologies use, 93% of parents in one study indicated that they set limits on their children's online activities (McQuade, Colt, & Meyer, 2009). In contrast, only 37% of their children reported that their parents had set rules concerning online activities. There are a few ways to interpret these discrepancies. Parents might be over reporting how often they monitor their children's online activities or they might monitor children's online activities without their children's awareness. Furthermore, these results might also suggest that parents are ineffective at implementing monitoring strategies and consequently their children do not recognize any utilized strategies. Regardless of the correct interpretation of these findings, more research attention should be given to how parents navigate conversations with their children about online risks and opportunities.

Other family characteristics are related to youths' cyberbullying involvement. In particular, Arslan, Savaser, Hallett, and Balci (2012) found that parental unemployment related to youths' cyberbullying perpetration and victimization. On the other hand, Ybarra and Mitchell (2004) did not find any evidence that family income, parental education, and marital status of caregivers were associated with youths' involvement in cyberbullying. Neglectful parenting is associated with youths' cyberbullying involvement, while youths with authoritarian parents are more likely to be victims of cyberbullying (Dehue, Bolman, Vollink, & Pouwelse, 2012). Furthermore, youths are also at an increased risk of experiencing cyberbullying when their parents do not monitor their online technology use or set rules concerning the use of electronic technology (Hokoda, Lu, and Angeles, 2006; Wright, 2015). To explain these associations, Wright (2015) argues that parents who monitor their children's electronic technology use are more likely to provide opportunities to discuss online risks and opportunities. Such monitoring, she proposes, serves a similar function as social support. In somewhat related research, Hinduja and Patchin (2013) and Wright (2013a) found that youths who believed that their parents would punish them for engaging in negative online behaviors, like cyberbullying, were less likely to engage in cyberbullying. Ultimately, parents have an important role in mitigating their children's exposure to various online risks. Other research has focused on the role of other adults, such as teachers, and peers in youths' involvement in cyberbullying.

Schools

There is great debate regarding the role of schools in monitoring and punishing youths for being involved in cyberbullying. Many cases of cyberbullying are perpetrated off school grounds, making it incredibly difficult for schools to be aware of such cases and how to respond (deLara, 2012; Mason, 2008). The issue is even more complicated because many cyberbullying incidences occur among youths who attend the same school. Because the perpetrator and victim might attend the same school, it is likely that knowledge of the incident might spread across the school. It could also mean that cyberbullies might engage in additional negative behaviors while on school grounds, potentially disrupting the learning process.

Regardless of the potential for cyberbullying incidences to "spill over" onto school grounds, it is unsurprising that some administrators' and teachers' perceptions and awareness of cyberbullying vary (Kochenderfer-Ladd & Pelletier, 2008). In particular, some administrators and teachers do not perceive cyberbullying as a problematic behavior, leading them to not perceive such behavior as serious and harmful as physical forms of bullying (Sahin, 2010). In addition, some administrators and teachers are unaware of the harmful consequences associated with relational bullying and cyberbullying.

Teacher training often does not properly inform teachers on how to deal with and recognize cyberbullying. Cassidy, Brown, and Jackson (2012a) also found that many Canadian teachers were unfamiliar with newer technologies, which are used at increasing rates among their students. Being unfamiliar with these technologies makes it incredibly difficult for teachers to deal with cyberbullying because they might be unsure of how to respond to the incident or how to implement strategies to reduce harm or stop the behavior. Even when teachers are concerned with cyberbullying, many schools lack the policies and programs needed to deal with these behaviors, leading to an inability to implement solutions and strategies (Cassidy, Brown, & Jackson, 2012b).

Research has also indicated that teachers are more likely to encourage prevention programs designed to reduce traditional face-to-face bullying (Tangen & Campbell, 2010). Such a finding suggests that some school officials might not consider cyberbullying or other forms of covert bullying behavior as needing their attention. It is crucial that schools recognize the importance of developing and implementing training and strategies designed to deal with cyberbullying, particularly since these behaviors can impact the learning environment (Shariff & Hoff, 2007).

Youths recognize their schools' inability to respond to cyberbullying. In particular, youths involved in cyberbullying, as victims and perpetrators, perceive their school, teachers, and administrators more negatively when compared to uninvolved youths (Bayar & Ucanok, 2012). When youths believe that their school will not be there for them if they were to experience cyberbullying, they are more likely to fear that a classmate could be a cyberbully (Eden, Heiman, & Olenik-Shemesh, 2013). Such fear reduces their ability to concentrate on learning, resulting in poor academic attainment and performance. Perceptions of negative school climate and having lower school commitment increase youths' perpetration of cyberbullying because they feel less connected to their school (Williams & Guerra, 2007). Furthermore, cyberbullying involvement relates to poor academic functioning among youths, including lower school grades, poorer attendance, and more classroom misbehaviors (Wright, in press).

Teacher training is needed to increase their awareness of cyberbullying. Such training might trigger the development and implementation of policies at the school level to reduce these behaviors. Teachers with more confidence in their ability have greater school commitment and are more likely to learn about cyberbullying (Eden et al., 2013). Furthermore, greater confidence increases the likelihood that teachers will intervene in cyberbullying incidences more often, which reduces youths' risk of cyberbullying involvement (Elledge et al., 2013). The desire to learn about cyberbullying increases teachers' awareness of these behaviors, allowing them to deal effectively with cyberbullying (Eden, Heiman, & Olenik-Shemesh, 2013). Awareness and knowledge of cyberbullying helps to prevent youths' involvement in these behaviors. The motivation to learn about cyberbullying is highest among teachers in elementary school (Ybarra et al., 2007). However, such motivation declines among middle school teachers, which is problematic as cyberbullying involvement is at peak levels in middle school. More attention needs to be devoted to developing educator training programs designed to raise awareness of cyberbullying.

Peer group social norms are learned through interactions with peers. Such norms dictate the acceptable and unacceptable behaviors within the peer group. As a result of such norms, youths will engage in acceptable behaviors, as determined by the peer group, even if such behaviors are negative. This effect also applies to cyberbullying involvement. In one study, the best predictor of cyberbullying involvement was being in classrooms with the highest rates of cyberbullying perpetration and victimization (Festl et al., 2013). The classroom climate of such classrooms encourages cyberbullying behaviors. Furthermore, having friends who engaged in cyberbullying also increased youths' risk of cyberbullying perpetration (Hinduja & Patchin, 2013).

Peer attachment is defined as youths' beliefs about whether their peers will be there for them when they need them. Poor peer attachment relates to negative interactions with peers. Peer attachment also has a role in youths' cyberbullying involvement. In particular, youths with low levels of peer attachment are more likely to be involved in cyberbullying than youths with higher levels of peer attachment (Burton et al., 2013). Other research indicates that peer rejection increases youths' risk of perpetrating and experiencing cyberbullying (Sevcikova et al., 2015; Wright & Li, 2013b). On the other hand, cyberbullying behaviors might be used to promote youths' social standing among their peer group. In this research, Wright (2014c) found that higher levels of perceived popularity, a reputational type of popularity in the peer group, was associated positively with cyberbullying perpetration six months later among adolescents. Because many youths are immersed in electronic technologies, Wright explains that such technologies might be used to promote and maintain youths' social standing. A new line of research indicates that having friends who discuss online risks helps to protect youths from cyber victimization (Wright, 2015). More attention is needed to better understand the role of peers in youths' involvement in cyberbullying.

Negative Adjustment Outcomes

Interest in cyberbullying is the result of the negative psychological, academic, and behavioral consequences associated with this behavior. Cyberbullying disrupts the emotional well-being of youths, whether they perpetrate or are victimized by these behaviors. Cybervictims report lower levels of global happiness, general school happiness, school satisfaction, family satisfaction, and self-satisfaction (Toledano, Werch, & Wiens, 2015). Furthermore, cybervictims are also more likely to report feeling angry, sad, and fearful when compared to uninvolved youths (Dehue et al., 2008; Machackova, Dedkova, Sevcikova, & Cerna, 2013; Patchin & Hinduja, 2006). Cyberbullying also disrupts youths' academic achievement. In particular, cyberbullies and cybervictims are both at an increased risk for academic problems, including having less motivation for school, poor academic performance, lower academic attainment, and more school absences

(Belae & Hall, 2007; Yousef & Bellamy, 2015). Youths who are cyberbullies and cybervictims are more likely to experience lower school functioning when compared to uninvolved youths (Wright, in press).

Cyberbullies and cybervictims are also at risk for internalizing and externalizing difficulties (e.g., Mitchell et al., 2007; Patchin & Hinduja, 2006; Wright, 2014b; Ybarra et al., 2007). They also experience suicidal ideation and attempt suicide more often than uninvolved youths (Bauman et al., 2013). Other research findings indicate that youths involved in cyberbullying are at an increased risk for experiencing mental health problems, including psychiatric and psychosomatic problems (Beckman et al., 2012; Sourander et al., 2010). Much of the previous research on the internalizing and externalizing difficulties associated with cyberbullying involvement do not take into account youths' involvement in traditional face-to-face bullying and victimization. Considering youths' involvement in these behaviors is important because these behaviors are highly correlated with cyberbullying (Williams & Guerra, 2007; Wright & Li, 2013b). Furthermore, both types of bullying and victimization are each associated with depression, anxiety, loneliness, and alcohol and drug use. One study revealed that cyberbullying perpetration and victimization was related to higher levels of depressive symptoms and suicidal ideation, after controlling for face-to-face bullying and victimization (Bonnano & Hymel, 2013).

Due to the strong linkages between cyberbullying and traditional face-to-face bullying involvement, some researchers have focused on the conjoint effects of these experiences on youths psychological and behavioral outcomes. In particular, victims of both traditional face-to-face bullying and cyberbullying reported more internalizing symptoms when compared to youths who only experienced one type of victimization (Gradinger, Strohmeier, & Spiel, 2009; Perren, Dooley, Shaw, & Cross, 2012). Consequently, a combination of various types of victimization might worsen youths' experience of depression, anxiety, and loneliness. Therefore, researchers should consider the importance of examining youths' experiences of both traditional face-to-face bullying and cyberbullying to better understand how to intervene and mitigate the associated negative adjustment difficulties.

THEORETICAL FRAMEWORKS

Theoretical frameworks of cyberbullying have been slow to develop. There have been some attempts to apply existing theories to youths' involvement in cyberbullying. Some of these research investigations have involved the development of new theories. In this section, two theories, namely the social cognitive theory and the online disinhibition effect, will be applied to cyberbullying. The social cognitive theory explains that parents, other adults, and/or friends serve as models of youths' behaviors (Hinduja & Patchin, 2008; Mouttapa, Valente, Gallaher, Rohrbach, & Unger, 2004). Therefore, youths' aggressive behaviors are sometimes modeled by someone who is stronger than the observer (Olweus, 1993). The effects of the model depend on the observer's positive evaluation of the model. If the model is rewarded for aggressive behaviors, this increases the likelihood that the observer will be less inhibited when it comes to engaging in aggression. This model has also been applied to youths' involvement in cyberbullying (Barlett & Gentile, 2012). Youths are often observing incidences of cyberbullying. These incidences might often involve zero to no consequences for cyberbullies, leading youths to develop the belief that such behaviors are acceptable, normative, and tolerable. Because there are often no consequences for engaging in cyberbullying, many youths believe that they can engage in these behaviors and not be caught, especially if they can remain anonymous. Being positively reinforced for cyberbullying behaviors increases youths' positive attitudes toward these behavior (Barlett & Gentile, 2012). Such attitudes relate to subsequent perpetration of cyberbullying (Wright & Li, 2013a; Wright & Li, 2013b).

The online disinhibition effect suggests that people often act or behave in different ways online than they would offline (Suler, 2004). Cyberspace loosens, reduces, or dismisses the typical social restrictions and inhibitions present in face-to-face interactions (Mason, 2008). Research evidence supports the proposal that people behave differently in cyberspace than they do in the offline world. This research also indicates that people are blunter in their communications via electronic technologies (McKenna & Bargh, 2000). Analysis of various computer-mediated communication revealed that there were more misunderstandings, heightened hostility, and increased aggressive and hostile behaviors through these communications when compared to face-to-face communication. Many communications via electronic technologies occur without being able to see the emotional reactions of the people on the other side of the technology, which prevents people from modulating their own behaviors because they are not usually aware of the consequences associated with their actions in the online world (Kowalski & Limber, 2007). Many times cyberbullying behaviors are perpetrated without the cyberbully witnessing the cyber-victim's reactions or the social disapproval, punishment, and other consequences that might occur. After cyberbullying, many cyberbullies might realize that it is easy to engage in negative online behaviors via electronic technologies. This might lead them to become even more disinhibited over time, especially if they receive positive reinforcement for their behaviors, do not recognize, are unaware of, or do not care about the consequences of their behaviors (Hinduja & Patchin, 2010; Wright, 2014a). Deindividuation is also another characteristic associated with the online disinhibition effect (Joinson, 1998). This occurs when people are not held accountable for their actions. The ability to engage in behaviors anonymously via electronic technologies might further reduce people's accountability. Considering that anonymity is easier in the cyber context and that cyberspace can promote the online disinhibition effect, youths might not be able to separate their online actions from their real world identities, making it much easier for them to disengage from others, leading to increases in harmful online behaviors (Wright, 2014a).

SOLUTIONS AND RECOMMENDATIONS

Many individuals in our communities are concerned with cyberbullying. Educational curriculum should be designed to teach children and adolescents about cyberbullying, digital literacy, and citizenship in both the online and offline worlds (Cassidy et al., 2012b). Such curriculum should also focus on the opportunities afforded by electronic technologies, including empathy, self-esteem, and social skills. Schools should also aim to improve school climate by learning students' names, praising good behavior, and staying technologically up-to-date (Hinduja & Patchin, 2012). All schools should develop and adopt a code of conduct that addresses the appropriate use of electronic technologies. Furthermore, administrators and teachers should follow through with advocating and enforcing the policies described in the code of conduct.

Parents should also do their role in helping to address cyberbullying. This might involve parents partnering with schools and increasing their own awareness and knowledge electronic technologies (Cassidy et al., 2012a; Diamanduros & Downs, 2011). By having an increased knowledge of electronic technologies, parents are better able to understand their children's online behaviors and the risks that their children might encounter while using these technologies. Such knowledge is instrumental for parents implementing their own electronic technology monitoring strategies. The implementation of effective strategies might diminish their children's risk of cyberbullying involvement. Children are constantly observing their parents and therefore it is important for parents to model appropriate electronic technology behavior in an effort to serve as good role models for their children. Furthermore, parents and their children should engage in a continuous and open dialogue about the appropriate use of electronic technologies. This dialogue should involve how often children should spend using electronic technologies and a discussion of appropriate online behaviors.

This section began by stating that cyberbullying is a concern for our communities. Communities can also do their part in helping to reduce youths' risk of cyberbullying involvement. In particular, many of us go through our day acting as bystanders within our communities. We might not notice when someone in our community needs help or know how to respond. Instead of being a bystander to someone who needs help, we should help others, instead of expecting others to help. This will help to model appropriate behaviors for the whole community.

On a larger scale, there also needs to be cyberbullying legislation, which is important for helping to address these behaviors. Cassidy and colleagues (2012b) argue that cyberbullying laws should be reformulated so that these laws further societal values. Society needs to recognize that cyberbullying is a threat and understand how it affects everyone. We need to be united to deal with these behaviors. Governmental agencies should also take cyberbullying seriously by developing initiatives to fund research studies devoted to understanding more about prevention. The more that we understand cyberbullying the better we are able to develop solutions designed to prevent these behaviors and promote positive online interactions.

FUTURE RESEARCH DIRECTIONS

There are some noticeable gaps in the cyberbullying literature. Although anonymity is an important component of cyberbullying, little attention has been given to investigations of these variables associations. Future research should consider examining youths' perceptions of anonymous online behaviors, and attempt to understand what factors motivate youths to engage in anonymous forms of cyberbullying. This research should also consider the differences in non-anonymous forms of cyberbullying and anonymous forms of cyberbullying. Such an understanding is important as it could explain youths' motivations for engaging in these behaviors. Furthermore, anonymity allows youths to become more disinhibited in their online interactions, leading to an increased risk of perpetrating negative online behaviors that they would typically not engage in offline. In addition, the anonymity of cyberbullying might also impact adolescents' coping strategies and the associated psychosocial adjustment difficulties. For instance, non-anonymous cyberbullying, perpetrated by a known peer from school, might exacerbate depressive symptoms more so than if the youth experienced cyberbullying from an unknown perpetrator.

Given that cyberbullying research is in its infancy, many of the studies described in this literature use concurrent research designs. Such designs hinder our ability to understand the long-term implications of cyberbullying involvement. In addition, much of the current research focuses on middle-school aged youths, without much consideration of younger or older youths. This is an important consideration because electronic technology use is increasing among all age groups of youths, and youths' use of these technologies increases their risk of cyberbullying involvement (Ybarra et al., 2007). Additional attention to younger age groups makes it possible to understand the developmental trajectory of traditional face-to-face bullying and cyberbullying, and it could potential answer questions about the temporal ordering of these behaviors. This research could also reveal the age in which youths are the most vulnerable to cyberbullying involvement. Consequently, intervention and prevention programs could be developed with consideration to the online risks most prominent at a particular age group.

CONCLUSION

This chapter provides a strong foundation for understanding the literature on youths' involvement in cyberbullying. Furthermore, it is important for researchers to look beyond prevalence rates of cyberbullying and to focus more attention on the predictors of and consequences associated with youths' cyberbullying involvement. Many of the studies involve investigations of individual level predictors of youths' cyberbullying involvement. More attention should be given to the role of parents, schools, peers, and communities in cyberbullying. It is important that cyberbullying is recognized as a global concern that undermines ethical and moral values in our society. Therefore, it is important that we unite and do our part to reduce cyberbullying.

REFERENCES

Ang, R. P. (2016). Cyberbullying: Its prevention and intervention strategies. In D. Sibnath (Ed.), *Child safety, welfare and well-being: Issues and challenges* (pp. 25–38). New, NY: Springer. doi:10.1007/978-81-322-2425-9_3

Aoyama, I., Utsumi, S., & Hasegawa, M. (2011). Cyberbullying in Japan: Cases, government reports, adolescent relational aggression and parental monitoring roles. In Q. Li, D. Cross, & P. K. Smith (Eds.), *Bullying in the global playground: Research from an international perspective*. Oxford, UK: Wiley-Blackwell.

Aricak, T., Siyahhan, S., Uzunhasanoglu, A., Saribeyoglu, S., Ciplak, S., Yilmaz, N., & Memmedov, C. (2008). Cyberbullying among Turkish adolescents. *Cyberpsychology & Behavior*, *11*(3), 253–261. doi:10.1089/cpb.2007.0016 PMID:18537493

Arslan, S., Savaser, S., Hallett, V., & Balci, S. (2012). Cyberbullying among primary school students in Turkey: Self-reported prevalence and associations with home and school life. *Cyberpsychology, Behavior, and Social Networking*, *15*(10), 527–533. doi:10.1089/cyber.2012.0207 PMID:23002988

Ayas, T., & Horzum, M. B. (2010). *Cyberbullg / victim scale development study*. Retrieved from: http://www.akademikbakis.org

Barlett, C. P., & Gentile, D. A. (2012). Long-term psychological predictors of cyber-bullying in late adolescence. *Psychology of Popular Media Culture*, *2*, 123–135. doi:10.1037/a0028113

Barlett, C. P., Gentile, D. A., Anderson, C. A., Suzuki, K., Sakamoto, A., Yamaoka, A., & Katsura, R. (2013). Cross-cultural differences in cyberbullying behavior: A short-term longitudinal study. *Journal of Cross-Cultural Psychology*, *45*(2), 300–313. doi:10.1177/0022022113504622

Bauman, S., Toomey, R. B., & Walker, J. L. (2013). Associations among bullying, cyberbullying, and suicide in high school students. *Journal of Adolescence*, *36*(2), 341–350. doi:10.1016/j.adolescence.2012.12.001 PMID:23332116

Bauman, S., Underwood, M. K., & Card, N. A. (2013). Definitions: Another perspective and a proposal for beginning with cyberaggression. In S. Bauman, D. Cross, & J. Walker (Eds.), *Principles of cyberbullying research: Definitions, measures, methodology* (pp. 26–40). New York, NY: Routledge.

Bayar, Y., & Ucanok, Z. (2012). School social climate and generalized peer perception in traditional and cyberbullying status. *Educational Sciences: Theory and Practice*, *12*, 2352–2358.

Beckman, L., Hagquist, C., & Hellstrom, L. (2012). Does the association with psychosomatic health problems differ between cyberbullying and traditional bullying? *Emotional & Behavioural Difficulties*, *17*(3-4), 421–434. doi:10.1080/13632752.2012.704228

Bonanno, R. A., & Hymel, S. (2013). Cyber bullying and internalizing difficulties: Above and beyond the impact of traditional forms of bullying. *Journal of Youth and Adolescence*, *42*(5), 685–697. doi:10.1007/s10964-013-9937-1 PMID:23512485

Boulton, M., Lloyd, J., Down, J., & Marx, H. (2012). Predicting undergraduates self-reported engagement in traditional and cyberbullying from attitudes. *Cyberpsychology, Behavior, and Social Networking*, *15*(3), 141–147. doi:10.1089/cyber.2011.0369 PMID:22304402

Brighi, A., Guarini, A., Melotti, G., Galli, S., & Genta, M. L. (2012). Predictors of victimisation across direct bullying, indirect bullying and cyberbullying. *Emotional & Behavioural Difficulties*, *17*(3-4), 375–388. doi:10.1080/13632752.2012.704684

Burton, K. A., Florell, D., & Wygant, D. B. (2013). The role of peer attachment and normative beliefs about aggression on traditional bullying and cyberbullying. *Psychology in the Schools*, *50*(2), 103–114. doi:10.1002/pits.21663

Cappadocia, M. C., Craig, W. M., & Pepler, D. (2013). Cyberbullying: Prevalence, stability and risk factors during adolescence. *Canadian Journal of School Psychology*, *28*(2), 171–192. doi:10.1177/0829573513491212

Cassidy, W., Brown, K., & Jackson, M. (2012a). Making kind cool: Parents suggestions for preventing cyber bullying and fostering cyber kindness. *Journal of Educational Computing Research*, *46*(4), 415–436. doi:10.2190/EC.46.4.f

Cassidy, W., Brown, K., & Jackson, M. (2012b). Under the radar: Educators and cyberbullying in schools. *School Psychology International*, *33*(5), 520–532. doi:10.1177/0143034312445245

Corcoran, L., Connolly, I., & OMoore, M. (2012). Cyberbullying in Irish schools: An investigation of personality and self-concept. *The Irish Journal of Psychology*, *33*(4), 153–165. doi:10.1080/0303391 0.2012.677995

Curelaru, M., Iacob, I., & Abalasei, B. (2009). *School bullying: Definition, characteristics, and intervention strategies*. Lumean Publishing House.

Dehue, F., Bolman, C., & Vollink, T. (2008). Cyberbullying: Youngsters experiences and parental perception. *CyberPscyhology & Behavior*, *11*(2), 217–223. doi:10.1089/cpb.2007.0008 PMID:18422417

Dehue, F., Bolman, C., Vollink, T., & Pouwelse, M. (2012). Cyberbullying and traditional bullying in relation to adolescents' perceptions of parenting. *Journal of Cyber Therapy and Rehabilitation*, *5*, 25–34.

deLara, E. W. (2012). Why adolescents dont disclose incidents of bullying and harassment. *Journal of School Violence*, *11*(4), 288–305. doi:10.1080/15388220.2012.705931

Diamanduros, T., & Downs, E. (2011). Creating a safe school environment: How to prevent cyberbullying at your school. *Library Media Connection*, *30*(2), 36–38.

Eden, S., Heiman, T., & Olenik-Shemesh, D. (2013). Teachers perceptions, beliefs and concerns about cyberbullying. *British Journal of Educational Technology*, *44*(6), 1036–1052. doi:10.1111/j.1467-8535.2012.01363.x

Elledge, L. C., Williford, A., Boulton, A. J., DePaolis, K. J., Little, T. D., & Salmivalli, C. (2013). Individual and contextual predictors of cyberbullying: The influence of childrens provictim attitudes and teachers ability to intervene. *Journal of Youth and Adolescence*, *42*(5), 698–710. doi:10.1007/s10964-013-9920-x PMID:23371005

Erdur-Baker, O. (2010). Cyberbullying and its correlation to traditional bullying, gender and frequent and risky usage of internet-mediated communication tools. *New Media & Society*, *12*(1), 109–125. doi:10.1177/1461444809341260

Fanti, K. A., Demetriou, A. G., & Hawa, V. V. (2012). A longitudinal study of cyberbullying: Examining risk and protective factors. *European Journal of Developmental Psychology*, *8*(2), 168–181. doi:10.1080/17405629.2011.643169

Festl, R., Schwarkow, M., & Quandt, T. (2013). Peer influence, internet use and cyberbullying: A comparison of different context effects among German adolescents. *Journal of Children and Media*, *7*(4), 446–462. doi:10.1080/17482798.2013.781514

Genta, M. L., Smith, P. K., Ortega, R., Brighi, A., Giasrini, A., & Thompson, F. et al.. (2012). Comparative aspects of cyberbullying in Italy, England and Spain: Findings from a DAPHNE project. In Q. Li, D. Cross, & P. K. Smith (Eds.), *Bullying goes to the global village: Research on cyberbullying from an international perspective* (pp. 15–31). Chichester, UK: Wiley-Blackwell. doi:10.1002/9781119954484.ch2

Goebert, D., Else, I., Matsu, C., Chung-Do, J., & Chang, J. Y. (2011). The impact of cyberbullying on substance use and mental health in a multiethnic sample. *Maternal and Child Health Journal*, *15*(8), 1282–1286. doi:10.1007/s10995-010-0672-x PMID:20824318

Gradinger, P., Strohmeier, D., & Spiel, C. (2009). Traditional bullying and cyberbullying. *The Journal of Psychology*, *217*, 205–213.

Grigg, D. W. (2012). Definitional constructs of cyberbullying and cyber aggression from a triagnulatory overview: A preliminary study into elements. *Journal of Aggression, Conflict and Peace Research*, *4*(4), 202–215. doi:10.1108/17596591211270699

Hinduja, S., & Patchin, J. W. (2007). Offline consequences of online victimization. *Journal of School Violence, 6*(3), 89–112. doi:10.1300/J202v06n03_06

Hinduja, S., & Patchin, J. W. (2008). Cyberbullying: An exploratory analysis of factors related to offending and victimization. *Deviant Behavior, 29*(2), 129–156. doi:10.1080/01639620701457816

Hinduja, S., & Patchin, J. W. (2010). Bullying, cyberbullying, and suicide. *Archives of Suicide Research, 14*(3), 206–221. doi:10.1080/13811118.2010.494133 PMID:20658375

Hinduja, S., & Patchin, J. W. (2012). Cyberbullying: Neither and epidemic nor a rarity. *European Journal of Developmental Psychology, 9*(5), 539–543. doi:10.1080/17405629.2012.706448

Hinduja, S., & Patchin, J. W. (2013). Social influences on cyberbullying behaviors among middle and high school students. *Journal of Youth and Adolescence, 42*(5), 711–722. doi:10.1007/s10964-012-9902-4 PMID:23296318

Hokoda, A., Lu, H. A., & Angeles, M. (2006). School bullying in Taiwanese adolescents. *Journal of Emotional Abuse, 6*(4), 69–90. doi:10.1300/J135v06n04_04

Huang, Y., & Chou, C. (2010). An analysis of multiple factors of cyberbullying among junior high school students in Taiwan. *Computers in Human Behavior, 26*(6), 1581–1590. doi:10.1016/j.chb.2010.06.005

Jang, H., Song, J., & Kim, R. (2014). Does the offline bully-victimization influence cyberbullying behavior among youths? Application of general strain theory. *Computers in Human Behavior, 31*, 85–93. doi:10.1016/j.chb.2013.10.007

Joinson, A. (1998). Causes and implications of behavior on the Internet. In J. Gackenbach (Ed.), *Psychology and the Internet: Intrapersonal, interpersonal, and transpersonal implications* (pp. 43–60). San Diego, CA: Academic Press.

Kochenderfer-Ladd, B., & Pelletier, M. (2008). Teachers views and beliefs about bullying: Influences on classroom management strategies and students coping with peer victimization. *Journal of School Psychology, 46*(4), 431–453. doi:10.1016/j.jsp.2007.07.005 PMID:19083367

Kowalski, R. M., & Limber, S. P. (2007). Electronic bullying among middle school students. *The Journal of Adolescent Health, 41*(6), 22–30. doi:10.1016/j.jadohealth.2007.08.017 PMID:18047942

Kwan, G. C. E., & Skoric, M. M. (2013). Facebook bullying: An extension of battles in school. *Computers in Human Behavior, 29*(1), 16–25. doi:10.1016/j.chb.2012.07.014

Laftman, S. B., Modin, B., & Ostberg, V. (2013). Cyberbullying and subjective health: A large-scale study of students in Stockholm, Sweden. *Children and Youth Services Review, 35*(1), 112–119. doi:10.1016/j.childyouth.2012.10.020

Lazuras, L., Barkoukis, V., Ourda, D., & Tsorbatzoudis, H. (2013). A process model of cyberbullying in adolescence. *Computers in Human Behavior, 29*(3), 881–887. doi:10.1016/j.chb.2012.12.015

Lenhart, A. (2015). *Teens, social media & technology overview 2015.* Retrieved from: http://www.pewinternet.org/2015/04/09/teens-social-media-technology-2015/

Li, Q. (2007). Bullying in the new playground: Research into cyberbullying and cybervictimization. *Australasian Journal of Educational Technology*, *23*(4), 435–454. doi:10.14742/ajet.1245

Li, Q. (2008). A cross-cultural comparison of adolescents experience related to cyberbullying. *Educational Research*, *50*(3), 223–234. doi:10.1080/00131880802309333

Machackova, H., Dedkova, L., & Mezulanikova, K. (2015). Brief report: The bystander effect in cyberbullying incidents. *Journal of Adolescence*, *43*, 96–99. doi:10.1016/j.adolescence.2015.05.010 PMID:26070168

Machackova, H., Dedkova, L., Sevcikova, A., & Cerna, A. (2013). Bystanders support of cyberbullied schoolmates. *Journal of Community & Applied Social Psychology*, *23*(1), 25–36. doi:10.1002/casp.2135

Mason, K. (2008). Cyberbullying: A preliminary assessment for school personnel. *Psychology in the Schools*, *45*(4), 323–348. doi:10.1002/pits.20301

McKenna, K. Y. A., & Bargh, J. A. (2000). Plan 9 from cyberspace: The implications of the internet for personality and social psychology. *Personality and Social Psychology Review*, *4*(1), 57–75. doi:10.1207/S15327957PSPR0401_6

McQuade, C. S., Colt, P. J., & Meyer, B. N. (2009). *Cyber bullying: Protecting kids and adults from online bullies*. Westport, CT: Praeger.

Mitchell, K. J., Ybarra, M., & Finkelhor, D. (2007). The relative importance of online victimization in understanding depression, delinquency, and substance use. *Child Maltreatment*, *12*(4), 314–324. doi:10.1177/1077559507305996 PMID:17954938

Mouttapa, M., Valente, T., Gallagher, P., Rohrbach, L. A., & Unger, J. B. (2004). Social network predictor of bullying and victimization. *Adolescence*, *39*, 315–335. PMID:15563041

Nikiforou, M., Georgiou, S. N., & Stavrinides, P. (2013). Attachment to parents and peers as predictors of bullying and victimization. *Journal of Criminology*, *2013*, 1–9. doi:10.1155/2013/484871

Olenik Shemesh, D., Heiman, T., & Pieschl, S. (2011). *Adolescents' cyberbullying: Moods, loneliness and social support*. Oral presentation at the 32nd International Conference of the Stress and Anxiety Research Society (STAR), Munster, Germany.

Olweus, D. (1993). *Bullying at school. What we know and what we can do*. Malden, MA: Blackwell Publishing.

Patchin, J. W., & Hinduja, S. (2006). Bullies move beyond the schoolyard: A preliminary look at cyberbullying. *Youth Violence and Juvenile Justice*, *4*(2), 148–169. doi:10.1177/1541204006286288

Perren, S., Dooley, J., Shaw, T., & Cross, D. (2010). Bullying in school and cyberspace: Associations with depressive symptoms in Swiss and Australian adolescents. *Child and Adolescent Psychiatry and Mental Health*, *4*(1), 1–10. doi:10.1186/1753-2000-4-28 PMID:21092266

Pornari, C. D., & Wood, J. (2010). Peer and cyber aggression in secondary school students: The role of moral disengagement, hostile attribution bias, and outcome expectancies. *Aggressive Behavior*, *36*(2), 81–94. doi:10.1002/ab.20336 PMID:20035548

Rideout, V. J., Roberts, D. F., & Foehr, U. G. (2005). *Generation M: Media in the lives of 8-18-year-olds: Executive summary.* Menlo Park, CA: Henry J. Kaiser Family Foundation.

Rosen, L. D. (2007). *Me, Myspace, and I: Parenting the Net Generation.* New York: Palgrave Macmillan.

Sahin, M. (2010). Teachers perceptions of bullying in high schools: A Turkish study. *Social Behavior and Personality*, *38*(1), 127–142. doi:10.2224/sbp.2010.38.1.127

Sevcikova, A., Machackova, H., Wright, M. F., Dedkova, L., & Cerna, A. (2015). Social support seeking in relation to parental attachment and peer relationships among victims of cyberbullying. *Australian Journal of Guidance & Counselling*, *15*, 1–13. doi:10.1017/jgc.2015.1

Shapka, J. D., & Law, D. M. (2013). Does one size fit all? Ethnic differences in parenting behaviors and motivations for adolescent engagement in cyberbullying. *Journal of Youth and Adolescence*, *42*(5), 723–738. doi:10.1007/s10964-013-9928-2 PMID:23479327

Shariff, S., & Hoff, D. L. (2007). Cyber bullying: Clarifying legal boundaries for school supervision in cyberspace. *International Journal of Cyber Criminology*, *1*, 76–118.

Sijtsema, J. J., Ashwin, R. J., Simona, C. S., & Gina, G. (2014). Friendship selection and influence in bullying and defending. *Effects of moral disengagement. Developmental Psychology*, *50*(8), 2093–2104. doi:10.1037/a0037145 PMID:24911569

Sjurso, I. R., Fandream, H., & Roland, E. (2016). Emotional problems in traditional and cyber victimization. *Journal of School Violence*, *15*(1), 114–131. doi:10.1080/15388220.2014.996718

Smith, P. K., Del Barrio, C., & Tokunaga, R. S. (2013). Definitions of bullying and cyberbullying: How useful are the terms? In S. Bauman, D. Cross, & J. Walker (Eds.), *Principles of cyberbullying research: Definitions, measures, methodology* (pp. 26–40). New York, NY: Routledge.

Smith, P. K., Mahdavi, J., Carvalho, M., Fisher, S., Russell, S., & Tippett, N. (2008). Cyberbullying: Its nature and impact in secondary school pupils. *Journal of Child Psychology and Psychiatry, and Allied Disciplines*, *49*(4), 376–385. doi:10.1111/j.1469-7610.2007.01846.x PMID:18363945

Sourander, A., Brunstein, A., Ikonen, M., Lindroos, J., Luntamo, T., Koskelainen, M., & Helenius, H. et al. (2010). Psychosocial risk factors associated with cyberbullying among adolescents: A population-based study. *Archives of General Psychiatry*, *67*(7), 720–728. doi:10.1001/archgenpsychiatry.2010.79 PMID:20603453

Stoll, L. C., & Block, R. Jr. (2015). Intersectionality and cyberbullying: A study of cybervictimization in a Midwestern high school. *Computers in Human Behavior*, *52*, 387–391. doi:10.1016/j.chb.2015.06.010

Strohmeier, D., Aoyama, I., Gradinger, P., & Toda, Y. (2013). Cybervictimization and cyberaggression in Eastern and Western countries: Challenges of constructing a cross-cultural appropriate scale. In S. Bauman, D. Cross, & J. L. Walker (Eds.), *Principles of cyberbullying research: Definitions, measures, and methodology* (pp. 202–221). New York: Routledge.

Suler, J. (2004). The online disinhibition effect. *Cyberpsychology & Behavior*, *7*(3), 321–326. doi:10.1089/1094931041291295 PMID:15257832

Tangen, D., & Campbell, M. (2010). Cyberbullying prevention: One primary schools approach. *Australian Journal of Guidance & Counselling, 20*(02), 225–234. doi:10.1375/ajgc.20.2.225

Toledano, S., Werch, B. L., & Wiens, B. A. (2015). Domain-specific self-concept in relation to traditional and cyber peer aggression. *Journal of School Violence, 14*(4), 405–423. doi:10.1080/15388220.2014.935386

Totura, C. M. W., MacKinnon-Lewis, C., Gesten, E. L., Gadd, R., Divine, K. P., Dunham, S., & Kamboukos, D. (2009). Bullying and victimization among boys and girls in middle school: The influence of perceived family and school contexts. *The Journal of Early Adolescence, 29*(4), 571–609. doi:10.1177/0272431608324190

Wade, A., & Beran, T. (2011). Cyberbullying: The new era of bullying. *Canadian Journal of School Psychology, 26*(1), 44–61. doi:10.1177/0829573510396318

Williams, K. R., & Guerra, N. G. (2007). Prevalence and predictors of internet bullying. *The Journal of Adolescent Health, 41*(6), S14–S21. doi:10.1016/j.jadohealth.2007.08.018 PMID:18047941

Wong, D. S., Chan, H. C. O., & Cheng, C. H. (2014). Cyberbullying perpetration and victimization among adolescents in Hong Kong. *Children and Youth Services Review, 36*, 133–140. doi:10.1016/j.childyouth.2013.11.006

Wright, M. F. (2013). The relationship between young adults beliefs about anonymity and subsequent cyber aggression. *Cyberpsychology, Behavior, and Social Networking, 16*(12), 858–862. doi:10.1089/cyber.2013.0009 PMID:23849002

Wright, M. F. (2014a). Cyber victimization and perceived stress: Linkages to late adolescents' cyber aggression and psychological functioning. *Youth & Society.*

Wright, M. F. (2014b). Predictors of anonymous cyber aggression: The role of adolescents beliefs about anonymity, aggression, and the permanency of digital content. *Cyberpsychology, Behavior, and Social Networking, 17*(7), 431–438. doi:10.1089/cyber.2013.0457 PMID:24724731

Wright, M. F. (2014c). Longitudinal investigation of the associations between adolescents popularity and cyber social behaviors. *Journal of School Violence, 13*(3), 291–314. doi:10.1080/15388220.2013.849201

Wright, M. F. (2015). Cyber victimization and adjustment difficulties: The mediation of Chinese and American adolescents' digital technology usage. *CyberPsychology: Journal of Psychosocial Research in Cyberspace, 1*(1), article 1. Retrieved from: http://cyberpsychology.eu/view.php?cisloclanku=2015051102&article=1

Wright, M. F. (in press). Adolescents' cyber aggression perpetration and cyber victimization: The longitudinal associations with school functioning. *Social Psychology of Education.*

Wright, M. F., Kamble, S., Lei, K., Li, Z., Aoyama, I., & Shruti, S. (2015). Peer attachment and cyberbullying involvement among Chinese, Indian, and Japanese adolescents. *Societies, 5*(2), 339–353. doi:10.3390/soc5020339

Wright, M. F., & Li, Y. (2012). Kicking the digital dog: A longitudinal investigation of young adults victimization and cyber-displaced aggression. *Cyberpsychology, Behavior, and Social Networking*, *15*(9), 448–454. doi:10.1089/cyber.2012.0061 PMID:22974350

Wright, M. F., & Li, Y. (2013a). Normative beliefs about aggression and cyber aggression among young adults: A longitudinal investigation. *Aggressive Behavior*, *39*(3), 161–170. doi:10.1002/ab.21470 PMID:23440595

Wright, M. F., & Li, Y. (2013b). The association between cyber victimization and subsequent cyber aggression: The moderating effect of peer rejection. *Journal of Youth and Adolescence*, *42*(5), 662–674. doi:10.1007/s10964-012-9903-3 PMID:23299177

Ybarra, M. L., Diener-West, M., & Leaf, P. (2007). Examining the overlap in internet harassment and school bullying: Implications for school intervention. *The Journal of Adolescent Health*, *1*(6), 42–50. doi:10.1016/j.jadohealth.2007.09.004 PMID:18047944

Ybarra, M. L., & Mitchell, K. J. (2004). Online aggressor/targets, aggressors, and targets: A comparison of associated youth characteristics. *Journal of Child Psychology and Psychiatry, and Allied Disciplines*, *45*(7), 1308–1316. doi:10.1111/j.1469-7610.2004.00328.x PMID:15335350

Yousef, W. S. M., & Bellamy, A. (2015). The impact of cyberbullying on the self-esteem and academic functioning of Arab American middle and high school students. *Electronic Journal of Research in Educational Psychology*, *23*(3), 463–482.

Zhou, Z., Tang, H., Tian, Y., Wei, H., Zhang, F., & Morrison, C. M. (2013). Cyberbullying and its risk factors among Chinese high school students. *School Psychology International*, *34*(6), 630–647. doi:10.1177/0143034313479692

ADDITIONAL READING

Bauman, S. (2011). *Cyberbullying: What counselors need to know*. Alexandria, VA: American Counseling Association.

Bauman, S., Cross, D., & Walker, J. (2013). *Principles of cyberbullying research: Definitions, measures, and methodology*. New York, NY: Routledge.

Hinduja, S., & Patchin, J. W. (2015). *Bullying beyond the schoolyard: Preventing and responding to cyberbullying*. Thousand Oaks, CA: Sage Publications.

Li, Q., Cross, D., & Smith, P. K. (2012). *Cyberbullying in the global playground*. Malden, MA: Blackwell Publishing. doi:10.1002/9781119954484

Menesini, E., & Spiel, C. (2012). *Cyberbullying: Development, consequences, risk and protective factors*. New York, NY: Psychology Press.

Tokunaga, R. S. (2010). Following you home from school: A critical review and synthesis of research on cyberbullying victimization. *Computers in Human Behavior*, *26*(3), 277–287. doi:10.1016/j.chb.2009.11.014

KEY TERMS AND DEFINITIONS

Anonymity: The quality of being unknown or unacknowledged.

Anxiety: A mental health disorder which includes symptoms of worry, anxiety, and/or fear that are intense enough to disrupt one's daily activities.

Collectivism: A cultural value that stressed the importance of the group over individual goals and cohesion within social groups.

Cyberbullying: Children's and adolescents' usage of electronic technologies to hostilely and intentionally harass, embarrass, and intimidate others.

Empathy: The ability to understand or feel what another person is experiencing or feeling.

Externalizing Difficulties: Includes children's and adolescents' failure to control their behaviors.

Individualism: The belief that each person is more important than the needs of the whole group or society.

Loneliness: An unpleasant emotional response to isolation or lack of companionship.

Normative Belief: Beliefs about the acceptability and tolerability of a behavior.

Parental Mediation and Monitoring: The strategies that parents use to manage the relationship between their children and media.

Parenting Style: The standard strategies that parents use in their child rearing.

Peer attachment: The internalization of the knowledge that their peers will be available and responsive.

Peer Contagion: The transmission or transfer of deviant behavior from one adolescent to another.

Provictim Attitudes: The belief that bullying is unacceptable and that defending victims is valuable.

Social Exclusion: The process involving individuals or groups of people block or deny someone from the group.

Traditional Face-To-Face Bullying: The use of strength or influence to intimidate or physically harm someone.

Chapter 17
Constantly Connected:
Managing Stress in Today's Technological Times

Jennifer Lynne Bird
Florida Atlantic University, USA

ABSTRACT

As society has transitioned from landlines to iPhones, people find themselves connected to their mobile devices 24/7. While the advantages of new technologies have led to constant availability, it has also led to additional stress and disconnection. For example, how many times have you seen a group of people out to dinner but they are all looking at their phones and not at each other? The problem is not the technology; instead, people need better coping strategies to deal with stress and the constant flood of information. This chapter will address the health consequences of stress and provide suggestions for how people can deal with stress in their lives. It will also illustrate the need for connection and the value of people being their authentic selves instead of portraying an image for social media.

INTRODUCTION

It is not yet five in the morning. My alarm goes off, and as I reach over to shut it off, I grab my iPhone from my bedside table. I check the texts I received since I went to sleep, then check my email. I haven't even been awake for two minutes, but already I am typing a reply to a coworker that can certainly wait until I've had breakfast. My mind is racing thinking of my endless to do list before my feet even hit the floor. The tone has been set for the day, and I'm not sure it's a good one.

Technology has made the world a better place by connecting people. My out of state relatives are only a text message away, and we can send each other pictures on our phones to bridge the distance between us. I love research, and when looking up information for this chapter, as much as I love the feeling of books in my hands, it is comforting to know there is a wealth of information that is only a mouse click away when I type key words into a search engine. The flip side of the advantages of technology, however, is that we as a society are constantly connected. This constant connection can bring a feeling of stress.

DOI: 10.4018/978-1-5225-2838-8.ch017

When my parents were my age, they had a landline to call people. Before the invention of answering machines, if someone wasn't home, a call was missed. Even with an answering machine, my parents had to wait until they got home to know who called them. Their dinners at restaurants and trips to the movies were not disturbed by phone calls. Granted, they were difficult to reach if there was ever an emergency, but true emergencies are few and far between. My parents could actually look into each other's eyes at dinner. How many times have my friends and I been at a restaurant and everyone is looking at their cell phones instead of each other? When my parents were my age, if they were gone when a favorite television show was on, they missed it. Thanks to the invention of the VCR, they could record their favorite shows, but only one show at a time. Members of my generation tend to get overwhelmed by the volume of television shows and all the recording options. When my parents were my age, it may be difficult to fathom they lived in a world without social media or email. My mom wrote handwritten letters to her family and friends. My dad left work at the office and the only inbox he ever had to check was the paper one on his desk. Email brings people together while simultaneously making it difficult to disconnect. How many times have I been distracted by the ping of an email? How many times have I been misled by someone's social media post because that person wants to present a constructed persona instead of an authentic self? Recently, I visited a friend's high school classroom. The students asked us how we communicated before social media. My friend and I attempted to explain going to high school football games and meeting friends in the college dining hall and were met with blank stares from the teenagers in her classroom. I found myself thinking of this question: How do you cope when the incredible gift of technology concurrently brings stress?

This chapter represents an ongoing odyssey to navigate the world of technology and the concurrent stress that sometimes accompanies it. Technology itself is not stressful; it's the reaction by people to the technology that often creates stress. This chapter will be presented in the form of a narrative and will explore different dimensions of this topic such as the author's temporary technology fast, observations of stress in college students, and research from the fields of medicine and education that provide the theory behind the practice of stress management.

FIRST PERSON NARRATIVE INQUIRY

In order for you as the reader to comprehend my personal experiences with technology, I present this chapter in the form of a narrative inquiry. Narratives are subjective, as each person views his or her story through the lens of experience. Clandinin and Connelly (2000) argue, "in narrative thinking, interpretations of events can always be otherwise" (p. 31). Asking questions and finding themes in stories involves inquiry. Narrative inquiry is the qualitative interpretive field of research where researchers find narrative threads in stories that reflect themes. Connelly and Clandinin (1988) elaborate, "try to understand a narrative unity as a thread or theme that runs through the narrative of experience and that provides a way to see how the rules, principles, images, and metaphors relate one to the other as they are called out by the practical situations in which we find ourselves" (p. 75). In other words, when a person shares a story, he or she selects what details to share or not to share. For example, to share every detail would make this writing much longer than a chapter, so details that enhance the theme of the chapter appear here and contribute to the narrative thread that runs through each vignette. Clandinin and Connelly (2000) describe the process of converting informal field texts into a formal research text by stating, "we find ourselves frequently engaged in writing a variety of different kinds of interim texts, texts situated in the spaces between field texts and final, published research texts" (p. 133). In other words, the following narrative represents informal research that was never submitted to an institutional research board because it is comprised of my own personal observations about how my life changed when I temporarily cut back from my use of technology.

Nevertheless, the interim texts of my journal entries don't make those texts any less worthy than the formal research projects I designed and implemented. Connelly and Clandinin (1988) argue that education, especially when it comes to narratives, does not have to take place in the classroom and they elaborate, "education, in this view, is a narrative of experience that grows and strengthens a person's capabilities to cope with life" (p. 27). People view their lives through the lenses of narratives of experience, and sharing narratives enables people to own their stories. Brown (2015) discusses the value of owning stories and explains, "I know that it takes more than courage to own your story. We own our stories so we don't spend our lives being defined by them or denying them" (p. 40). When people own their stories and find the strength to share their narratives with others, they find the courage to write new chapters to their stories and change the endings of their narratives.

Furthermore, when presenting narratives, writers can choose which genres best illustrate their ideas. Harrison (2002) explains, "I used narrative to refer to the way we tell our stories. It is the form our stories take when we use our language and our own voice to record or tell the experiences of our lives" (pp. 83-84). Sometimes a story of my experience may present itself best as a journal entry, a letter, or a poem instead of an essay. Romano (2000) describes this format as multigenre writing and discusses narrative as a foundation as he explains, "multigenre papers, however, as I conceive them, demand that writers think narratively. Writers must meld the cognitive with the emotional" (p. 24). Therefore, you will read my personal experiences with technology in the form of a variety of genres, all of which feature the first person pronoun "I" as I own my story.

A Multigenre Narrative

Dear Technology,

I love you, but we need to take a break. I am not a person anyone would describe as mellow, but my stress level has been increasing recently. I am feeling like I have no downtime and feeling that I always have to be on without any breaks. Even now as I write this I am checking my phone for text messages. People know how to find me, so why I am I so concerned that I am going to miss something? This has to stop.

Best wishes until we meet again,

Jen

INFORMAL TECHNOLOGY EXPERIMENTS

I decided to complete informal technology experiments because my life was becoming consumed by email. I would check my email periodically throughout the day, only to stop whatever activity in which I was currently engaged to answer the email. Pipher (2006), advises, "don't let the urgent crowd out the important" (p. 91). Too often, the urgent email eclipsed the important activity that required more of my attention.

As you probably already know, email is a wonderful resource. The reality is that most people do not have the time to pick up a pen and write a handwritten letter, but they do have time to type a few lines from their phone or computer keyboard. Information can be transmitted quickly, and an entire conversation can take place in a matter of minutes if both people are checking their email.

However, email should not be used in place of real conversations. Several of my friends eventually found true love on dating websites, but sitting at a computer sending emails back and forth wasn't going to make a true connection. That could only be done in person. The same applies for work issues. Emails can't convey writing voice or subtle nuances. If your colleagues work down the hall, consider chatting in person occasionally. If your colleagues work across the country, consider picking up the phone and calling them. Email is an incredible technological tool, but not when it takes the place of in person conversation.

Informal Technology Experiment #1: Not Sending Emails to My Phone

I stopped sending my email to my phone for a month. It feels weird. Now whenever I want to check email I have to go to an actual computer. No more grabbing my phone as soon as I open my eyes in the morning. I have to admit it also feels kind of nice. I wake up, feed my two cats, go for a workout, eat breakfast, get ready for work, and then check emails. I'm not missing much. In fact, there isn't anything in my email inbox that couldn't wait while I was sleeping. Sure, I know the information a few hours later, but if someone needed an instant response they have my phone number and can call me. No one called me about a work issue and now that I've eased into my day I can better deal with things. I like this.

One Month Later....

I confess I couldn't keep it up. Despite the peacefulness of easing into my day, I started sending emails to my phone again. I just felt like I was going to miss something. But is reading emails before I do anything else in my day really how I want to live my life? There is a time and a place for everything, and like I learned the past month, emails can be a part of life without consuming it.

Two Months Later....

I have managed to find a balance in my life; just because an email goes to my phone doesn't mean I have to read it as soon as it arrives. If something is important, I will receive a phone call or text. Most email is not urgent and can wait until I have time to read it. I now save designated times during the day to check email.

Informal Technology Experiment #2: Leaving My Phone at Home

I confess I am guilty of needing to know the constant whereabouts of my beloved iPhone. Too often I can be found looking down at my phone when I should be looking up at my surroundings. So for a month I decided not to bring my phone to church with me. Granted, my church is within walking distance of my home and I have a large group of friends who attend my church. If I had car trouble, I could walk home. If I needed help, numerous people would volunteer. I sing in the choir at my church, so I have a limited of amount of things I can carry with me anyway, and why do I need to have my phone with me when I am trying to concentrate on the minister's inspirational message? This worked for about three weeks. One week the choir director asked us all to pull out our cell phones for a special musical number. I ran home to get my phone. I now bring my cell phone to church, although it is turned off during the service.

So what did I learn from my informal technology experiments? With both of them, it became about finding a balance between using helpful technology and not letting that technology consume too much of my time. While email and the apps on my iPhone enhance my life, they are not a substitute for interaction with other people. During a conversation, I need to look other people in the eyes instead of talking to them while looking at my phone. There are also times when it becomes beneficial to put my phone away with the knowledge that time spent with others is more meaningful than any content that might appear on my phone screen.

End Notes of What I Learned

Technology enhances people's lives. Cameron (1998) describes that technology can enhance writing, "because it is instantaneous, email tricks people into evading their censor" (p. 33). While the use of email, like other technology, can enhance people's lives, too often people abuse the technology. Carter (2015) asks the questions, "Do you check your email, texts, voicemails, Facebook, Instagram account, or Twitter feed within an hour of waking up or going to sleep? While you're in line at the store? During dinner with your family? Would you check it at church while waiting for a funeral to start? If so, ya ain't alone" (p. 97). Carter explains that there is a reason for such behavior. She elaborates, "there is something gratifying about constantly checking our email and social-media feeds. The distraction is pleasurable because it gives us what researchers call 'variable ratio reinforcement.' In other words, we are drawn to our smartphones in the way we are drawn to slot machines. We never know when we'll get a satisfying message on Facebook or an email with good news, so we just keep checking" (p. 97). Even though there is research to provide a rationale for this behavior, it doesn't mean it is healthy behavior. Brickman (2015) observes, "so far, I haven't missed any career or life-changing moments by not facing the morning with a first-thing phone fling" (p. 20). He recommends easing into the morning before checking technology so that you control the technology instead of letting the technology control you.

Brown (2012) discusses research on anxiety and elaborates, "when it comes to anxiety, we all struggle. Yes, there are different types of anxiety and certainly different intensities. Some anxiety is hardwired and best addressed with a combination of medication and therapy, and some of it is environmental – we're overextended and overstressed" (p. 143). Brown observed differences between two groups of people and discovered, "participants from both groups often used today's dominating technology as an example of an anxiety-producing source during the interviews" (p. 143). While both groups shared the experiences of anxiety from technology, one group found ways to manage the anxiety while the other changed behaviors that led to anxiety. Brown provided the example that the first group constantly checked emails and made sure they were all answered although sometimes at the expense of sleep, while the second group asked people not to send unnecessary emails and indicated it might take several days for a reply. Brown concluded, "when we asked that group about the process of setting boundaries and limits to lower the anxiety in their lives, they didn't hesitate to connect worthiness with boundaries. We have to believe we are enough in order to say, 'Enough!'" (pp. 144-145). Consequently, while technology can enhance our lives, abuse of it can cause anxiety and it helps to set boundaries for when the technology is used.

Carter (2015) concurs that there is a connection between technology and anxiety with the explanation, "even though our brain tends to seek that variable ratio reinforcement, which suggests pleasure, usually we aren't consciously checking our email for fun or recreation. We check constantly to abate our anxiety that we are missing something" (p. 98). Carter offers suggestions such as disabling push features that provide instant alerts on phones and computers, designating spaces in which technology will be used, and deciding on times when not to use technology. She concludes, "what all this means is that unless we want to feel overwhelmed and exhausted, we need to unplug. A lot" (p. 99). As I found from my informal experiments of taking breaks from technology, this advice is not easy but necessary for a life filled with less stress.

Enayati (2015) discusses the connections between technology and stress and explains, "the effects of stress are compounded by the fact that we are rarely turned off and are always connected. Stress in its various forms has access to us at all times. In the old days people got upset and were able to go for a walk to get away. Now we are never far from all sorts of bad news. The solution: turn it off! Go on technology fasts" (pp. 158-159). Enayati concludes, "we can choose narratives that help us reframe stressors, thereby strengthening our ability to withstand (or avoid) the stress coming our way and to counter it with positive emotions" (p. 159). Once again, we are reminded to own our stories and change the narratives if we are not happy with them.

As previously mentioned, taking this advice is not easy. I admit that while writing these paragraphs, I have paused to check my email several times because of fear of missing something. I have also responded to several texts and admit it took me a short time after each one to regain my train of thought for this chapter. I am reminded I need to get better at setting boundaries with technology and realize that understanding people will wait for a response.

DISCONNECTED

It is the middle of the week, and I am finished with work for the day. My family members have other plans on this weekday evening, and I am too tired from a busy day to call friends and go out for the evening. So I send some emails and text a few friends. Even though I have communicated with them, I feel restless and disconnected. Texting someone is not the same as looking a person in the eyes or sharing a hug. I open the YouTube app on my iPhone and discover that old television shows from my childhood are only a few clicks away. I watch a few clips, but don't feel the same happiness I did when I originally watched the shows years ago in the living room of my childhood home with my family. I talk to my cats, Lucy and Andy, just to be able to hear the sound of my own voice and know someone is listening even if they can't reply with anything other than a meow. I have difficulty sleeping and wake up the next morning tired, completely defeating the purpose of a quiet evening at home.

Stress Relief Strategy #1: Self-Compassion and Connection

Whether caused by technology or another source, stress can feel overwhelming. In this chapter, you will be reading stress management strategies interspersed with my multigenre narrative. Perhaps from the tone of my writing voice in the last passage, you could infer that I wasn't being too kind to myself. It would have helped if I practiced self-compassion and did not mentally beat myself up for what I thought was a wasted evening of my life watching YouTube videos. Neff (2011) describes self-compassion as, "if we can compassionately remind ourselves in moments of falling down that failure is part of the shared human experience, then that moment becomes one of togetherness rather than isolation" (p. 65). I am certainly not the first person to use technology to waste time, and I will certainly not be the last. Therefore, the fact that I am willing to share my story in this chapter will perhaps cause you as the reader to smile, relate to it, and know that you are not alone either. Germer (2009) concurs, "self-compassion is the foundation for kindness toward others. When we're accepting of our own idiosyncrasies, we become more accepting of others" (p. 87). And kindness and connection with others can lead to less stress.

Even though I attempted to connect with friends through text messages, I didn't feel as happy as when I see them in person. I needed more connection than a text could provide. Rankin (2013) discusses the value of community and explains, "chronic social isolation can lead to loneliness, and multiple studies demonstrate that loneliness can trigger stress responses in the body, the same kind of fight-or-flight responses fear of bodily harm can elicit" (p. 93). Being part of a strong community can help reduce loneliness and consequently reduce stress. Used well, technology can bring people together. A text message can remind a person that a loved one is thinking about him or her. Skype enables people across the country and even around the world to see each other. But there is a time for technology and a time to get out of the house and get together with people in person.

Some people find strength in spirituality and their community in churches. Spirituality can provide comfort in times of need. Ortberg (2014) believes, "for much of our lives, we live in the shallows. Then something happens – a crisis, a birth, a death – and we get this glimpse of tremendous depth. My soul becomes shallow when my interests and thoughts go no further than myself. A person should be deep because life itself is deep" (p. 57). This chapter does not serve as an endorsement of any particular religion, since spirituality is unique and personal to each individual reading these words. Furthermore, while some people find their community in a church, a church is not the only place to go for community connection. It is possible to find community in a gym, in a classroom, or around a table in a restaurant. The point is that no one needs to experience social isolation and there are numerous opportunities to reach out and connect with others. Germer (2009) believes, "connecting with others is another form of self-care – to stop isolating" (p. 108). He explains that this is important because "a sense of isolation can turn even ordinary unhappiness into despair or minor anxiety into dread" (p. 108). Technology can bring people together in the form of a community of practice, where a group uses technology as a platform to share their ideas and collaborate on projects.

Whether it is directed toward self or others, compassion becomes essential for increased health and happiness. Neff (2011) shares, "one of the most robust and consistent findings in the research literature is that people who are more self-compassionate tend to be less anxious and depressed" (p. 110). She discovered that self-compassionate people had lower levels of the stress hormone cortisol and concluded, "self-compassion gives us the calm courage needed to face our unwanted emotions head-on" (p. 124). Remaining calm lowers stress while helping people assess a situation and take ownership of their emotions. The next time you make a mistake or feel isolated and lonely, try to be kind to yourself and rely on your community where others will demonstrate kindness toward you.

I Just Had to Check That Text Message

I am at the doctor's office in the middle of an appointment. The doctor has left the room for a moment to check on another patient. My phone is on silent, but I hear it buzz. What is in that text message? I debate for a moment. I am in a doctor's office. I have greater priorities at this moment in time other than the content of that text message, such as making sure I ask my doctor all the medical questions I have written down so I don't forget anything. But what if something has happened to someone in my family? What if there is important information in that text that cannot wait until I leave the doctor's office? I probably have a couple minutes before the doctor returns, so I quietly creep over to my purse and steal a glance at my phone. The pharmacy is informing me that I have a prescription ready. It was nothing that couldn't have waited. Even though no one saw me, I am embarrassed. Why did I think that text message was so important that I had to interrupt something even more important to check it? I am reminded of the billboards I see on the interstate urging drivers that text messages can wait, that nothing in that phone is worth a life. At least I wasn't driving. I make a mental note to be more mindful, to perhaps even turn my phone to off and not silent when I am involved in something serious such as a doctor's appointment, or when I am involved in something fun such as a meal with family or friends where we all put our phones away and take the time to look at each other.

It seemed appropriate that I was in a doctor's office when I received that text message, because it serves as a nice transition to the next section about stress and your health. I preface the following section by stating that while I am a certified health coach who focuses on the emotional side of healing, and while I did complete an internship in a hospital, the words you are about to read in no way take the place of a conversation with your doctor. I do not know what your personal health history is, but the medical professionals in your life do, so if you have any questions related to your personal health needs, please consult with your doctor even if it means putting down this chapter and returning to it later. These words will always be here for you to read, and it is more important for you to be aware of your health and take care of yourself!

Stress Relief Strategy #2: Focus On Your Health

Concerned about something you looked up on an internet search engine or worried about a friend's post on social media? It can influence your health. Tindle (2013) reports, "anxiety, self-doubt, and related thoughts and feelings are associated with increases in blood pressure, heart rate, and stress hormones such as adrenaline and cortisol, all of which pound our organs like waves on the beach" (p. 100). Tindle discusses that a positive outlook can lead to better health, and one way to change outlook is through exercise because "physical activity can temporarily catapult you out of the territories of depression, relapse, and other unsavory outlook addresses long enough to get your bearings and steer yourself in a different direction" (p. 138). For specifics about the right exercise plan for you, consult a physician or physical therapist.

Research has shown that stress can make people sick. Rankin (2015) explains, "when exposed to stress, the body tends to whisper before it yells. Stress often manifests through less immediately life-threatening physical symptoms, such as backache, headache, eye strain, insomnia, fatigue, dizziness, appetite disturbances, and gastrointestinal distress" (p. 35). If you find yourself experiencing any strange health symptoms, check the stress level in your life and call your doctor, since emotional stress can manifest physically in your body. If you are experiencing stress, meditation and letting everything go can help. Schmidt (2014) elaborates, "when we are able to let go of ruminating about the past or worrying about the future, we can see the gifts and opportunities in the present moment. We are better able to recognize our blessings, even in the midst of our challenges and stress" (p. 114). It becomes very easy to focus on what you don't have, but stopping for a moment to think about gratitudes and what you do have is an effective method of relaxing and relieving stress. Beck (2008) provides the reminder, "remember, you can't force this kind of calm; pressuring yourself to feel no anxiety merely creates more anxiety" (p. 101). Beck (2001) advocates facing fears and addressing anything that may be creating stress, and she describes an experience where writing down her anger at a situation helped with her back pain because "as soon as I wrote it down, I felt a tingle along my own spine, and the pain in my back relaxed significantly" (p. 195). As you will read in the next section, writing serves as a valuable resource for stress management; however, before you continue reading take a deep breath and give yourself permission to let go of any stress you may be feeling today.

Writing as Healing Research

In addition to my informal technology experiments, I had the privilege of conducting formal research studying college students and anxiety (Bird and Wanner, 2015). The research project began as a study to find connections between writing and healing. From two separate research studies, my physical therapist colleague and I discovered "college students who used a positive writing voice demonstrated lower anxiety and stronger emotional health, just like physical therapy patients who used a positive writing voice throughout their treatment interventions demonstrated higher recovery gains for objective measures on pre-existing physical therapy surveys. The results illustrate that a strong positive writing voice can help people heal both physically and emotionally" (pp. 279-280).

Our first research study asked physical therapy patients at an outpatient clinic to respond throughout their treatment to short answer questions on a survey designed by the researchers while simultaneously having their body part in pain evaluated by existing physical therapy measures. Our second research study asked college students in a writing classroom to respond to both short answer writing prompts on a survey designed by the researchers and a health survey called the HRQOL (Health Related Quality of Life) survey, a general health survey in the public domain and able to be used by researchers without securing permission or paying copyright fees. While conducted in two different environments, the results of both studies dovetailed together by illustrating the difference a positive writing voice makes in both physical and emotional healing.

Our research added to the existing literature in the field. Pennebaker (1997) completed a research study that showed "people who wrote about their deepest thoughts and feelings surrounding a trauma evidenced an impressive drop in illness visits after the study compared with the other groups" (p. 34). More studies confirmed the results of the original, as Enayati (2015) reports, "study after study bore out Pennebaker's thesis that putting negative experiences into words has positive physical and psychological effects" (p. 73). Brown (2015) adds, "what's important to note about Pennebaker's research is the fact that he advocates limited writing, or short spurts" (p. 87). Short answer responses effectively lead the writer to process emotions and eliminate both physical and emotional stress. Writing also does not have to be about a trauma to be beneficial to the writer. Pennebaker and Smyth (2016) conclude, "writing can be an inexpensive, simple, albeit sometimes painful way to help maintain our health" (p. 80). The pain they refer to is that sometimes people may feel worse short term after writing if they explore an emotional topic, but long term they feel better by releasing their emotions because "writing moves us to a resolution. Even if there is no meaning to an event, it becomes psychologically complete" (p. 152). Writing can also release physical tension in the body when emotional tension is released onto the page.

When writing, it becomes essential to trust initial impressions and not overthink. Goldberg (2000) describes this process as "first thoughts have their own structure, move in their own rhythm, rise full-muscled from the bottom of the mind. They appear and disappear, present themselves and fade away unless we try to smother them, frightened by their power and truth, or smash them into polite second or third thoughts" (pp. 30-31). The first response to a prompt such as "How are you feeling?" is often the truest and most honest response before a person's self-censor can reevaluate and change the perspective. Sharp (2000) suggests, "whatever it takes, don't think, don't second-guess, don't edit. This exercise must come as directly as possible from your head to the page, traveling without censorship" (p. 18). When I teach writing classes to high school and college students, sometimes I provide writing prompts to help students think about a specific topic, but other times I encourage students to write whatever is on their minds. Lamott (1994) advises writers, "you need to start somewhere. Start by getting something – any-thing – down on paper" (p. 25). Brown (2015) agrees, "what you write doesn't have to be a sweeping narrative. It can be a bulleted list on a Post-it note or a simple paragraph in a journal. Just get it down" (p. 86). Determining if the act of completing the writing process would have healing benefits for students regardless of the topic discussed provided the foundation for the writing as healing research.

After completing the research studies, I included writing workshops as a daily part of the curriculum of my college classroom. Stress can be contagious. As Enayati (2015) observes, "we volley emotions back and forth all the time, as part of every interaction – however brief or extended – that we have with each another. We can 'catch' other people's stress, all with amazing speed" (p. 154). One student would walk into the classroom sharing concern about an upcoming exam, and soon most of the students in the classroom were worried. Each class, I attempted to shift the momentum by beginning with a reading/ writing workshop. At the end of the semester, students shared with me that it helped. Students had ten minutes to write in their journals about either a topic of their choice or a quote I wrote on the board. I did not grade the writing in order to encourage students to share their feelings with the pages of their notebooks. If students didn't want to write, they could read a book of their choice. I share the belief of Gruwell and her students, The Freedom Writers (2009), who write, "the greatest lesson the Freedom Writers and I have learned is to validate that everyone has a story" (p. 283). My goal as a teacher, writer, and researcher is for students to share their stories through writing.

Stress Relief Strategy #3: Write Your Story

Stressed? Pick up a pen and put it to paper or let your fingers roam over the keyboard of your computer. Writing, whether handwritten or typed, enables expression because a piece of paper or the computer screen won't criticize the writer, thus allowing for the emergence of writing voice. Romano (2004) be-lieves, "I'm a narrative creature. Through telling stories I experience the power of my voice and come to understand what the stories mean" (p. 29). He continues, "one of the great things about writing is that by doing it, we can construct a persona. We can craft an authentic voice" (p. 218). And that voice can be constructed using multiple outlets. Pipher (2006) discusses the value of blogs because "writing a blog is instant self-publication, which is its own special kind of creativity" (p. 200). While technology allows blogs to be shared with a large audience, writing does not have to be shared if the writer does not wish it to be.

While there can be value in sharing written words, writing can have healing benefits even if no one sees it except the writer. Brickman (2015) believes journaling is a great method of self-exploration be-cause, "it is a wonderful way to explore your life and figure out what's working and what's not. You'll also find reviewing your journal at the end of the year a great way to explore your accomplishments and figure out what you want to do over again" (p. 104). Journaling can also have healing benefits if a person is experiencing medical symptoms. Keeping track of symptoms and pain levels in a journal can help patients remember information to share with their medical providers. Tindle (2013) wanted to know the stories her patients were telling themselves because "if we can briefly slow down our internal dialogue long enough to take a look at it, we gain yet another window into our current outlook in action and catch glimpses of a new outlook" (p. 111). Journal writing helps English teachers determine the stories students tell themselves; consequently, writing can provide the same benefit for professionals in the medical field. Cameron (1998) believes, "when there is something we are not telling ourselves, our writing points that out" (p. 140). Writing helps reveal the stories we are telling ourselves. We can then choose the path our writing can take. Goldberg (1990) states, "think of something now that you sincerely want to tell and go ahead and tell it" (p. 7). We can share our writing with a trusted medical professional who can see patterns to our pain. We can publish our writing in a blog and share it with readers we may not even know. Or we can keep the writing private in a journal, letting the page worry about an issue so we can experience a little less stress and perhaps a little more sleep. Heard (1995) believes, "the task of every writer is to dig beneath the surface and find complexity in each situation" (p. 45). Life can be complex. Stories can be complex. Your story is your story. Sharing it, even with only yourself, can help you heal physically, heal emotionally, and relieve stress.

A Curriculum of Change

I've lost track of the amount of time I have checked my email and text messages while writing these pages. It's ironic that while I am offering stress relief strategies to help you cope with this constantly connected culture that I am experiencing technology induced stress. I witness both sides. On the one hand, one piece of technology, my computer laptop, enables my fingers to fly over the keys and make my ideas reality. On the other hand, another piece of technology, my iPhone, keeps distracting me from this writing. Yet, my beloved iPhone has made my life easier and better with all its apps, from the map app that keeps me safe and keeps me from getting lost, to my photo apps that allow me to preserve my family's memories.

To integrate technology into our lives without letting it overwhelm us, it helps to borrow a page from the playbook of curriculum design and integration. Beyer (1996) explains, "the belief that significant educational and social change is possible has been fueled by a number of forces – both theoretical and practical" (p. 16). Even though twenty years have passed since that statement was written, the sentiment remains the same. Both theoretical and practical forces fuel change. For example, in theory it would be nice to tell people to only use cell phones at certain times of the day if they are going to be a distraction. But in practice, people remain attached to cell phones and depend on them. The compromise, therefore, is to find a balance and that balance will be different for everyone. For example, my family has agreed to put the cell phones away during dinner so we have time for conversation with each other. Other families may have different boundaries for technology. With technology and stress, answering some questions can help. Does using this technology at this moment in time make me happy and enhance my life, or does it bring me additional stress?

Continuing with the theme of curriculum integration, Beane (1997) provides the information, "the ideas that people have about themselves and their world – their perceptions, beliefs, values, and so on – are constructed out of their experiences" (p. 4). Past experiences can provide insight for how to help live in the present moment as well as set goals for the future. For example, my informal technology experiences such as not sending my email to my cell phone made me more present in each moment and overall more relaxed. Remembering that feeling will help me integrate that strategy into my life.

Similarly, my formal research experiences will help me use what I learn to help others. Connelly and Clandinin (1988) believe, "administering the curriculum meant the narrative living out of a personal philosophy of education" (p. 196). When maximizing technology use in your life while simultaneously minimizing stress, design your curriculum of a personal philosophy and live it.

WELLNESS RESOURCES

To help you put the theories in this chapter into practice, here are some additional wellness resources. Sandberg (2013) writes, "we cannot change what we are unaware of, and once we are aware, we cannot help but change" (p. 156). Feel free to take these ideas and incorporate them into your life in whatever ways work best for you.

Heart Maps

When you look at heart pictures, you might think of love, Valentine's Day, and happiness. Or you might think of health or a trip to the doctor. Too often in life we worry about things, which can lead to stress on our bodies. Ever feel your heart race when you are nervous about something? One way to stress less and smile more is to spend time with people and things you love by creating a heart map.

Heart maps originally started as a writing strategy; teachers use them in classrooms when students can't think of a writing topic. What is important to you? Look in your heart map! Writing teachers such as Georgia Heard discuss the value of falling in love with life and the sense of peace it can bring. Heard (1999) instructs her students, "today, I'd like you to make a map of all the important things that are in your heart, all the things that really matter to you. You can put: people and places that you care about; moments and memories that have stayed with you; things you love to do, anything that has stayed in your heart because you care a lot about it" (pp. 108-109). Here's how to create your own heart map:

- Draw a heart on a sheet of paper. The artistic quality doesn't matter. What is important is that you leave enough blank space to write words inside the heart.
- Inside the heart, write down the names of people, places, and things you love. No one has to see this except you. Remember it's not always the big things in life but the small things that can cause you to smile. A walk in the park when it is sunny outside. Spending time with my family. A great book. That's part of my list. What makes you happy?
- Look at your list. How much of your day is spent with the people, places, and things in your heart map? If you are not spending part of your day with people, places, and things you love, how can you arrange your schedule so you can do this?
- No one has to see this heart map except for you, but you may want to use your heart map as a reality check. You may love things that are not healthy for you, and it's also fine to enjoy some things in moderation or occasionally, such as spending a Saturday watching reruns of a favorite television show or eating your favorite dessert. The key is balance.
- Don't have enough hours in the day for things you love? Try to rearrange your schedule to spend more time with the people and things in your heart map.
- Below is an example of a heart map I created.

Figure 1. Heart map designed by the author

An example heart map is presented in Figure 1 below.

525,600 Minutes of What Brings You Energy

In the song *Seasons of Love*, a year is measured in 525,600 minutes. Everyone has an equal amount of time in a year. How do you use it? Teacher Donald Graves discusses four types of activities. Graves (2001) states, "I know that you already have a sense of what takes energy, gives it, and is a waste of time. What you need now are the specifics from your own life in order to chart a different course from the one you know. Awareness that grows out of the specifics of your own situation produces energy" (p. 11). What do you do that gives you energy? What do you do that takes away energy? What do you do that is neutral? What do you do that wastes energy? Time to take a look at how you spend your time.

- Write out your schedule, or choose a computer program or the calendar feature on your phone that will do it for you.
- Hour by hour, list how you spend your time during a day. Be honest with yourself. No one has to see this except for you. Now look at how your energy level feels with each activity.
- Which activities give you energy? For me, I love spending time with loved ones, teaching, and making a difference in the world. List yours.
- Which activities take away energy? For me, I hate waiting in long lines, cleaning, and running boring errands. Some activities, such as a long walk, may take away physical energy but bring you emotional energy.
- Which activities are neutral? I consider driving and eating in this category, although driving may take away energy if I'm driving in a thunderstorm and eating may give energy if I am having a meal with a group of friends.

- Which activities waste energy? I have to play computer solitaire until I win. After ten or eleven games, this wastes both time and energy.
- Now that you have categorized the activities, how many of each do you have in your day? Are you spending too much time doing activities that take away energy and not enough time doing activities that give energy?
- If the answer to the above question is yes, consider pairing activities that take away energy with ones that bring you energy. For example, I might read a magazine (something that gives me energy) while sitting in the waiting room during a car oil change (something that takes away energy).
- Can you eliminate activities that take away energy or waste energy from your schedule? In other words, if you said no to someone or something, how bad would the consequences be? If you can't make the dessert for the party, the odds are someone else will do it. Probably not a big deal.
- You should notice some connections between the activities that bring you energy and the ones in your heart map. More energy = the feeling of more hours in a day.

10-10-10

Suzy Welch designed a strategy called 10-10-10. Welch (2009) explains that to reclaim her life, she needed "to start making my decisions differently – proactively – by deliberately considering their consequences in the immediate present, near term, and distant future. In ten minutes….ten months….and ten years" (p. 9). What will be important to you ten minutes from now, ten months from now, and ten years from now? Answer these questions in your own life. Sometimes what seems like a big deal now may not be a big deal later.

Here's an example of how I used this recently:

- **Issue:** I have numerous emails to answer but also want to meet my family for dinner. I picture how the results of my decision might look in the short term, midterm, and long term future.
- **Life 10 Minutes From Now:** I really need to answer these emails so I can start work tomorrow without having to worry about them, but I also don't want to disappoint my family.
- **Life 10 Months From Now:** I won't remember the content of those emails, but I will remember dinner with my family and smile when I look at the pictures of that event.
- **Life 10 Years From Now:** I love my job, but I love my family more. I don't want to be a person who was so distracted by work at the expense of family relationships. So I'm going to put aside the emails and focus on being in the moment with people I love.
- **So if an Issue is Bothering You**: How will you feel about it in the immediate, distant, and really distant future?

Important/Urgent

Stephen Covey designed a matrix of urgent vs. important. Covey, Merrill, and Merrill (1994) explain, "clearly, we deal with both factors – urgency and importance – in our lives. But in our day-to-day decision making, one of these factors tends to dominate. The problem comes when we operate primarily from a paradigm of urgency rather than a paradigm of importance" (p. 39). If something is both urgent and important (the bills need to be paid), people usually do it. If something is not urgent and not important (reading junk mail), people rarely do it. The middle categories can get confusing. Some things that seem urgent aren't that important. For example, the phone rings during a family dinner, you grab it, and it is a telemarketer. Don't take time away from family dinner (not urgent but important) to deal with the telemarketer (urgent but not important).

Here's an example of how I used this recently.

I'm working on lesson plans for class (urgent, important). Emails appear in my inbox (urgent, not important). I also want to have dinner with my family (not urgent, important). I wonder if I will have time to watch my favorite television show (not urgent, not important). I make my decisions based on my values and priorities of what is important. I finish the lesson plans and remind myself they do not have to be perfect, enjoy dinner with my family, save the emails for later, and will watch the television show if I have time.

Don't let urgent demands eclipse what is truly important in life.

Revising a Technological Life

Since writing the first draft of this chapter, I left my college classroom for a high school English one. My new high school has integrated technology into the curriculum and every student has a laptop. As I reflect on potential obstacles and opportunities, I am reminded that students look to me to set the tone of the classroom. Clandinin and Connelly (2000) remind me that "the teacher is part of the curriculum and therefore part of the establishment of the goals in the first place and part of the ensuing achievement" (p. 29). My classroom, like my life, will have both goals and boundaries for technology, which I will continue to reflect on and revise. Much like writers revise their compositions, people can revise the lives they compose. Welch (1997) states, "we become, as we write and revise, exposed to competing ideas of ourselves and to competing social forces that would shape our voices and beliefs" (p. 50). I know now to reconcile the competing forces of my love for technology and the stress I sometimes feel when overwhelmed by it.

Narrative inquiries such as this one often conclude in the middle of a story. As I write these words I have only been teaching English at my current high school for a month. I hope to continue to find a balance for technology in my own life and encourage students there is a time and place for technology so they may decrease stress and anxiety. The events that happen will be a story to share for another time. While technology may make us as a society feel like we are constantly connected, the connections we need to be making are with each other.

REFERENCES

Beane, J. A. (1997). *Curriculum integration.* New York, NY: Teachers College Press.

Beck, M. (2001). *Finding your own North Star.* New York, NY: Three Rivers Press.

Beck, M. (2008). *Steering by starlight.* New York, NY: Rodale.

Beyer, L. E. (1996). Introduction: the meanings of critical teacher preparation. In L. E. Beyer (Ed.), *Creating democratic classrooms* (pp. 1–26). New York: Teachers College Press. doi:10.1515/9783110889666.xi

Bird, J. L., & Wanner, E. T. (2015). Research as curriculum inquiry: helping college students with anxiety. In V. C. X. Wang (Ed.), *Handbook of research on scholarly publishing and research methods* (pp. 273–295). Hershey, PA: Information Science Reference. doi:10.4018/978-1-4666-7409-7.ch014

Brickman, J. (2015). *Soothe*. New York, NY: Rodale.

Brown, B. (2012). *Daring greatly*. New York, NY: Gotham Books.

Brown, B. (2015). *Rising strong*. New York, NY: Spiegel & Grau.

Cameron, J. (1998). *The right to write*. New York: Tarcher/Putnam.

Carter, C. (2015). *The sweet spot*. New York, NY: Ballantine.

Centers for Disease Control and Prevention. (2011). *Health Related Quality of Life*. Health Related Quality of Life Surveillance Program. Retrieved from http://www.cdc.gov/hrqol/hrqol14_measure.htm

Clandinin, D. J., & Connelly, F. M. (2000). *Narrative inquiry*. San Francisco, CA: Jossey-Bass.

Connelly, F. M., & Clandinin, D. J. (1988). *Teachers as curriculum planners*. New York, NY: Teachers College.

Covey, S. R., Merrill, A. R., & Merrill, R. R. (1994). *First things first*. New York, NY: Free Press.

Enayati, A. (2015). *Seeking serenity*. New York, NY: New American Library.

Germer, C. K. (2009). *The Mindful path to self-compassion*. New York, NY: The Guilford Press.

Goldberg, N. (1990). *Wild mind*. New York, NY: Bantam.

Goldberg, N. (2000). *Thunder and lightning*. New York, NY: Bantam.

Graves, D. H. (2001). *The energy to teach*. Portsmouth, NH: Heinemann.

Gruwell, E., & the The Freedom Writers. (2009). The Freedom Writers diary (2nd Ed.). New York, NY: Broadway.

Harrison, M. D. (2002). *Narrative based evaluation*. New York, NY: Peter Lang Publishing.

Heard, G. (1995). *Writing toward home*. Portsmouth, NH: Heinemann.

Heard, G. (1999). *Awakening the heart*. Portsmouth, NH: Heinemann.

Lamott, A. (1994). *Bird by bird*. New York: Anchor Books.

Larson, J. (2005). Seasons of love [Recorded by the cast of Rent]. On Rent: Original motion picture soundtrack [CD]. Burbank, CA: Warner Brothers Records.

Neff, K. (2011). *Self compassion: The proven power of being kind to yourself*. New York, NY: HarperCollins.

Ortberg, J. (2014). *Soul keeping*. Grand Rapids, MI: Zondervan.

Pennebaker, J. W. (1997). *Opening up: the healing power of expressing emotions*. New York, NY: The Guilford Press.

Pennebaker, J. W., & Smyth, J. M. (2016). *Opening up by writing it down*. New York, NY: The Guilford Press.

Pipher, M. (2006). *Writing to change the world*. New York, NY: Riverhead.

Rankin, L. (2013). *Mind over medicine*. Carlsbad, CA: Hay House.

Rankin, L. (2015). *The fear cure*. Carlsbad, CA: Hay House.

Romano, T. (2000). *Blending genre, altering style*. Portsmouth, NH: Heinemann.

Romano, T. (2004). *Crafting authentic voice*. Portsmouth, NH: Heinemann.

Sandberg, S. (2013). *Lean in*. New York, NY: Alfred A. Knopf.

Schmidt, B. (2014). *The practice*. Deerfield Beach, FL: Health Communications, Inc.

Sharp, C. (2000). *A writer's workshop*. New York: St. Martin's Press.

Tindle, H. (2013). *Up: How positive outlook can transform our health and aging*. New York, NY: Hudson Street Press.

Welch, N. (1997). *Getting restless*. Portsmouth, NH: Heinemann.

Welch, S. (2009). *10-10-10*. New York, NY: Scribner.

KEY TERMS AND DEFINITIONS

Anxiety: Different clinicians have different definitions of anxiety, and a person who lives with anxiety will describe it from a different point of view than a clinical definition in a textbook, but the general consensus is that anxiety is chronic fear or stress that can result in panic attacks and a person feeling an inability to cope with life's stressors.

Heart Maps: Writing teacher Georgia Heard believes in the value of heart maps, which ask writers to draw a heart and inside the heart write things that the writer loves.

Journal Writing: The process of a person responding to prompts and writing about his or her thoughts and feelings. While journal writing is typically associated with writing classrooms, writing teachers including Julia Cameron and Natalie Goldberg advocate that journal writing can be done by anyone, anywhere.

Medical Professionals: People in the medical profession such as primary care doctors, specialists, physical therapists, and emotional therapists provide support and consultation to patients about health issues. Medical doctors Hilary Tindle and Lissa Rankin discuss in their research that patients experience improved health when they have a positive outlook and a willingness to share their stories with their doctors.

Multigenre Writing: Introduced to the field of education by Tom Romano, multigenre writing consists of creative writing in multiple genres and the writer's analysis of the genres.

Narrative Inquiry: Described in depth by F. Michael Connelly and D. Jean Clandinin, narrative inquiry is a qualitative interpretative form of research that focuses on the telling, retelling, and sharing of stories.

Story Sharing: By sharing a story with a supportive audience, either in conversation or in writing, it frees the storyteller of unneeded physical and emotional stress caused by holding the story inside and worrying about it. Brene Brown explains that it helps people to share stories instead of numbing pain with unhealthy choices.

Urgent vs. Important: Mary Pipher, Don Graves, and Stephen Covey all discuss the type of choices people make of how they spend their time and the resulting increased or decreased energy experienced.

Writing as Healing: James Pennebaker is a leader in the field which explores the health benefits of writing. Numerous studies have been conducted by researchers investigating the influence of writing on physical and emotional health.

Writing Voice: Voice in writing describes how a writer uses word choice and tone to reflect the unique personality of the writer. Just like each person has a unique speaking voice, each writer has a unique writing voice.

Chapter 18
Digital Technologies and 4D Customized Design:
Challenging Conventions With Responsive Design

James I. Novak
Griffith University, Australia

Jennifer Loy
University of Technology Sydney, Australia

ABSTRACT

Digital design tools are rapidly changing and blurring the boundaries between design disciplines. By extension, the relationship between humans and products is also changing, to the point where opportunities are emerging for products that can co-evolve with their human users over time. This chapter highlights how these '4D products' respond to the vision laid out three decades ago for ubiquitous computing, and have the potential to enhance human experiences by creating more seamless human-centered relationships with technology. These developments are examined in context with broader shifts in sociocultural and environmental concerns, as well as similar developments being researched in Responsive Architecture, 4D printing and systems designed to empower individuals during the design process through interactive, parametric model platforms. Technology is fundamentally changing the way designers create physical products, and new understandings are needed to positively guide these changes.

INTRODUCTION

Human-centered product design, where the end users of a product remain at the forefront of all design decisions, is evolving rapidly as the opportunities of the digital age become better understood. The boundaries between design disciplines are blurring as digital technologies break down traditional practices, creating products that challenge design conventions. This chapter discusses the significance of changes to product design and design systems enabled by digital technologies in relation to human

DOI: 10.4018/978-1-5225-2838-8.ch018

development. In particular it considers how the relationship between people and products could change with a shift in thinking from static, resolved outcomes to digitally enabled products, in particular ones that are capable of changing over time—4D products—and the implications of that change. This affects the designer-product relationship, and the customer-product relationship as well as the systems within which they operate.

Examples of practice-led design research in the latter part of this chapter introduce different approaches to the development of 4D products. These provide starting points for a practical and theoretical framework for design research and education in the changing digital design environment from user experience, through interaction, to a digitally enabled product service system. Designs based on ubiquitous computing allow for the development of products that change the relationships and experiences in human-centered product design. Based on additive manufacturing processes, 4D printing allows for products that morph under certain conditions, as do examples from the field of responsive architecture (Meagher, 2014). These approaches challenge designers to think less about static, final outcomes, and more about the opportunities for objects to evolve into different states through their lifespan. As such, designers are called on to develop systems and parameters for product permutations, rather than fixed product outcomes, and rethink their role and relationship to products and users, and the impact of their designs in a digitally connected world. This aligns with current theory on the relationship between human evolution and digital technologies.

HUMAN EVOLUTION IN A DIGITAL ERA

There is an argument that the biological mechanisms that have governed human evolution for 3.5 million years have been disrupted by the development of human cognition and cultural behaviors, overwhelming natural systems, and resulting in what is termed "Human Evolutionary Stasis" (Powell, 2012). The suggestion is that humans have the ability to collectively circumvent the challenges they may otherwise face as individuals, and that this is impacting the biological evolution of the species as a whole.

The human organism is a paradigmatic case of ontogenetic adaptation: thanks to an enormously flexible cognitive and behavioral repertoire, including the ability to acquire and transmit cumulative (intergenerational) cultural adaptations, humans can survive and reproduce across a wide range of otherwise hostile developmental conditions. (Powell, 2012, p. 150)

Yet the impact of technological development on early learning and ontogenetic adaptation could be argued to be challenging the idea of a stalled evolution of the species. If human evolution is seen as referring to its adaptation to the complex systems in which humans operate, then human development in a technological age is evidenced by the ability of each successive generation to adapt more quickly to evolving digital systems:

Gen Y have grown up in a world of rapid technological advances affecting the way they learn, their approach to knowledge acquisition and the forms of interaction between themselves... as a result of their techno-dependency and the fact they are accustomed to using computers and Internet to perform any given task, Gen Y has formed unique characteristics and competences... (Petrova, 2014, p. 525)

As the pace of technological innovation increases, there is a tendency to assume that humans will continue to adapt cognitively to keep pace, yet, as suggested by Al Gore, humans will soon be in a situation where their cognitive abilities are surpassed by their own inventions:

The emergence of a planet-wide electronic communications grid connecting the thoughts and feelings of billions of people and linking them to rapidly expanding volumes of data, to a fast growing world of sensors being embedded ubiquitously throughout the world, and to increasingly intelligent devices, robots, and thinking machines, the smartest of which already exceed the capabilities of humans....and may soon surpass us in manifestations of intelligence we have always assumed would remain the unique province of our species. (Gore, 2013, xiv)

For designers operating in a world where technological innovation could assume an intelligence that drives change itself—beyond human cognition—it is tempting to focus on the potential of technology to create new object mitigated interactions and complex support systems without taking into account the implications for humanity. This is a pitfall into which the commercial world has already fallen: "Could the people who began the Industrial Revolution foresee the ecological effects and loss of life caused by the rise of factory systems, chemical manufacturing, machine tools, coal burning, and mining?" (St Clair, 2016, p. 42) The publication of *Wealth of Nations* through to the development of the moving assembly line by Ford (Sparke, 1987) and the establishment of the Ford Motor Co in 1903 could hardly have been expected to lead to the economic problems for Detroit in the 1950s. Understanding economic and social implications in a period of significant change are consistently problematic. Understanding the implications for the development of the human psyche, already linked to cognitive behavior changes, brought on by technological immersion at an early age of subsequent generations in a rapidly evolving digital age, are nigh on impossible. Who could have predicted the overwhelming initial response to the launch of the augmented reality Nintendo game of Pokémon Go (*Pokemon Go*, 2016) in 2016 and the unexpected consequences of players, such as being injured through inattention to their surroundings and collaborating with strangers, all in the pursuit of Pokémon?

The challenge for all people, from designers creating new products to the end users openly embracing them, is that "we are morphing so fast that our ability to invent new things outpaces the rate we can civilize them. These days it takes us a decade after a technology appears to develop a social consensus on what it means" (Kelly, 2010, p.3). Similarly Gore argues that there have never before been "so many revolutionary changes unfolding simultaneously and converging with one another" and that there is a "clear consensus that the future now emerging will be extremely different from anything we have ever known in the past. It is a difference not of degree but of kind" (2013, xv). His reasoning is that global digital connectivity, the expansion of information collection and data mining techniques are fostering the emergence of a collective "global mind" that requires a re-imagining of human interaction and organization (Gore, 2013).

One of the inevitabilities widely assumed over the last 30 years has been cultural homogenization through globalization. A consequence of the digital connectivity described by Gore is that country borders become porous, and after an unprecedented era of relative stability across the globe allowing for increased trade and co-operation, the predictions have been for a linear pattern of growth in the amalgamation of individual countries into larger trade groups, such as in the European Union. Yet the signs in 2016 are that globalization is facing a crisis. The fallout from the Brexit vote, the crisis in France under the onslaught of ISIS, and the concerns in Germany over their open borders policy during the Syrian refugee crisis provide contrary indications that suggest the possibility of a trend reversal.

Within product design, there is evidence of a corresponding drive for diversity over homogenization, with cultural difference and individuality paradoxically supported by the very digital technology predicted to alienate people from production. While Aldersey-Williams' (2011) predictions of a return to a pre-industrial era of individual craftsmanship may have sounded farfetched in 2011, the exponential growth of the digitally enabled maker society highlighted by Anderson (2012) suggests there could be a change in paradigm, where people become significantly more engaged in the design and development of the products around them.

This shift in thinking is already resulting in a new breed of digitally enabled product designer, who uses generative modeling techniques as part of their process, only possible because new Computer-Aided Design (CAD) software and 3D printing (additive manufacturing) allows for individual objects to be built without tooling. Designers such as Lionel Dean (Dean, 2016) and Fung Kwok Pan ("Fung Kwok Pan: Fluid Vase," 2010) evidence this trend where the designer and consumer both contribute to decision making on the form of the product, communicating through digital platforms. Also in both these cases, the designers are exploring the interaction itself and the power of digital communication facilitated by additive manufacturing. Recognizing the human-centered aspects to the development of products in a digital age remains at the core of the role of the designer. Yet the nature of that human-centered focus is changing as the digital age matures, and designers will have to renegotiate their role and responsibilities alongside it, while also keeping pace with broader design theory including the sustainability imperative and systems thinking.

PEOPLE, PRODUCTS AND SYSTEMS

Over the last 20 years, design theory has moved the focus of design from discrete products to the design of systems (Hawken, Lovins & Lovins, 2000). This strategy began as a response to economic drivers with practices such as "Lean Manufacturing" and "Just in Time" extending out to the re-evaluation of the supply chain to a value chain approach, but it gained momentum with the sustainability imperative introduced to design and manufacturing in response to the Brundtland commission report in 1987. Technology and the digital age in which humans now live is allowing for a more holistic understanding of the lifecycle of designs not previously possible, with quantifiable measurement and standardization at all stages making designers increasingly accountable for their decisions. It is only in the current era that this complex connectivity is becoming overt, changing the relationship between designers, products and consumers. However, these rapid changes in information gathering and technical possibility need to take into account the corresponding changes to the collective human psyche mentioned in the previous section, as well as the specific experiences of individuals. The scope, pace and scale of change currently being experienced have not previously been part of human evolutionary history. Therefore the impact of current thinking in technology as it informs the design of products and its subsequent impact on humans requires sufficient attention, and the responsibilities designers face for affecting ontogenetic adaptation need to be addressed.

It is essential for humans at this time in our evolution to begin to identify what is being lost through our utter dependence on technology and to determine how it may affect humanity long term. Furthermore, we must not think only of the long-term effects: we must also ask ourselves about the intentions of our actions. (St Clair, 2016, p. 43)

The impact on human development and the realities of the human response to the covert introduction of technology into everyday living is not linear and predictable. There are unexpected consequences, just as there were with the impact of manufacturing on the health of the planet, and the human response can be equally unexpected, even perverse, and often emotional—as illustrated by the recent resurgence in "low-tech" vinyl record sales, for example, despite the proliferation of high quality digital music. One of the issues is the technology promise tends to focus on ideas of simplifying the human experience, and reducing choice, rather than focusing on user experience and the individual needs of people to be unique and valued for their differences. The growing move to cloud-based services and intangible goods can clash with a human need to be connected to the tangible world. Focusing on the direct marketing aspects in transactions with online travel companies, clothing shops and bookshops, ignores the very human need for the hunt—for meeting the curiosity cognitive driver identified in the updated Maslow's hierarchy (McLeod, 2016).

The problem of information technology (IT) driven change is that the user-centered experiences are rarely understood or catered for, let alone central to the product discourse. Digitally enabled user-experience products have typically evolved from user-interface, screen-based product design. IT professionals are not traditionally trained to focus on the user experience beyond the boundaries of the screen in the way that product designers are, but, equally, product design disciplines do not usually contain the technical understanding of electronics and coding needed to maximize the possibilities for digitally enabled design. Yet, that human understanding and focus are vital for design—both in a business sense and in a broader, social and human development point of view.

As technology evolves, designers and IT specialists alike have the opportunity to integrate more functionality, data capture, information sorting and communication into everyday products, but the challenge is how to keep a level head to maximize integrated digital technologies for actual benefit to the users. Evgeny Morozov describes this modern dilemma as "solutionism": when a designer "presumes rather than investigates the problems that [the product] is trying to solve" (2013, p. 6) and too readily adopts new technologies without thoroughly understanding the human-centered problem—if there is even a problem at all. With the rapid pace of technological adoption, the opportunity to slow down to understand all facets of a problem as suggested by Morozov can be a challenge. If one of the fundamental characteristics predicted for the post digital revolution era is that technology will evolve at an ever more rapid pace, then creating products that center the human experience within that change become even more important. Helping individuals to define and support their identities should be a driver for design in an era of homogenization. Equally, supporting the confidence of the individual to navigate in a technological era should be vital for designers, rather than losing all decision making power to machines, as emphasized by St Clair (2016).

Developing users who are effective lifelong learners matters in a time of technological development, as does designing products that are fully expected to evolve as situations and needs change. Developing lifelong learners depends on empowering the individual to take control of their own learning going forward. In her work on student learning in higher education, Weimer (2002) discusses the importance of shifting the balance of power in the learning experience from the lecturer to the student. She argues that this enables the student to build resilience in learning terms to facing new challenges that are initially difficult. If this approach is applied to design, then for designers to create products that allow for an evolution of use or interaction, they must fundamentally empower the user during use, rather than disempowering the individual in service of the organizational system. This making of the individual experience subservient to support the efficiencies in management practices is short sighted and could well lead to a very human rejection of technologically based products.

Collaboration between disciplines in developing technology-driven products is becoming essential in the current sociocultural and environmental sustainability context (Loy, Canning, & Haskell, 2016). The goal is arguably to reinforce identity and sense of self, supporting diversity in a global community, by using technology to collaborate to enhance the human experience and sense of engagement and responsibility, rather than to make interaction more efficient, or organizationally more effective.

DESIGNING IN CONTEXT

For the last 20 years, designers have been striving to design more "lightly"; that is, to design to reduce the impact of the manufacture, use, and disposal of their products on the environment. This has extended to include the social impact of their products for their full lifecycle right from the impact on communities of sourcing raw materials (e.g. foreign-owned mono-culture plantations on local communities dependent on natural, diverse forestation, or the mining of bauxite for aluminum smelting on aboriginal communities and farming communities). In *Design Activism: Beautiful Strangeness in a Sustainable World*, Fuad-Luke (2009) looked at the discourses and context informing design strategies at a point in time. Hindsight highlights the unexpected consequences of design decisions, suggesting that the information available at a point in time is context specific, and that there could be layers of impact initially unknown that could eventually become clear. The impact on human development is one of those layers. So, just as sustainable design theory has shifted the focus of product design from a "cradle to grave" approach to a "cradle to cradle" approach (Braungart & McDonough, 2002), then correspondingly an approach to design taking into account human development needs to be considered equally "lightly". "In considering 'value' during product definition, then, we should expand this usual definition to include intangibles such as personal aspirations and model codes of behavior" (Rowland, Goodman, Charlier, Light, & Lui, 2015, p. 187).

This moral imperative suggests designers need to consider their work even more holistically, as part of a complex team that includes sociologists and psychologists. However, with the bourgeoning digital technology environment, IT specialists need to be integrated into that team more effectively than in current practice. Where user-interface design is morphing into user-experience design, the body of knowledge in product design is lost or diluted. A new approach is needed, perhaps one whereby designers are able to adopt new technologies to take greater control of—or at least have a greater understanding of—the design solution in its entirety. Without a vantage point to see both the problem and solution in entirety, it is difficult for a designer to appreciate the impact of their designs on the users, and on stakeholders indirectly affected during the product's lifecycle.

Designer-maker John Makepeace (1995) described good design as being informed by the knowledge and understandings available at a particular point in time. He also argued that good design embodies the aspirations for society of the period, expressing its values and ideals. Rowland et al. suggest that ideas of value and aspirations are linked to what people care about: "If your business model involves helping people feel closer to specific dreams, it's worth taking time to clearly articulate what those dreams are" (Rowland et al., 2015, p.187). Whether individuals currently care sufficiently about the impact of the digital age on human development in order for it to be overtly mandated as a design imperative is open to debate, but for the design discipline, leading the development of products post the digital revolution, these issues need to be articulated and discussed. Designers working to Makepeace's ideal should not ignore the potential of their work to influence human development and, equally, should recognize that where humans are concerned, the impacts are impossible to predict and they should tread lightly.

The main learning from the pace of technological development is that change is perpetual, and the current rate of change should be a key consideration for the development of products. Aligned with the recognition that agile and evolving products are part of a product service systems approach is the planned "graceful degradation" of products (products that decline to obsolescence with as little harm as possible) and the "cradle to cradle" product lifecycle ideal that addresses the sustainability imperative (economic, environmental and sociological). Extending the essential criteria of this approach to a new era of data generation, collection and analysis, and technologically enhanced functionality, designers need to focus on the fundamentals of really designing for people and for change, not impose values and behaviors on users for the sake of efficiencies and technical enhancements. Just as sustainability theory has been extended to include socio-cultural sustainability in the face of challenges to cultural diversity brought about by digital connectivity and globalization (Loy et al., 2016), so design theory needs to respond to current thinking around supporting the development of the human psyche, and human learning after the digital revolution. The following sections of this chapter describe ideas on the development of responsive products as the role and responsibilities of the designer change again.

THE CHANGING ROLE OF DESIGNERS

A key theme of this chapter is that technological development is becoming symbiotic with humanity. Indeed, Kelly, cofounder of *Wired* magazine, argues that technology can be viewed as a living force:

The technium [the broader interconnected system of technologies] is now as great a force in our world as nature, and our response to the technium should be similar to our response to nature. We can't demand that technology obey us any more than we can demand that life obey us. Sometimes we should surrender to its lead and bask in its abundance, and sometimes we should try to bend its natural course to meet our own. (Kelly, 2010, p. 17)

In Kelly's view, if technology is considered as a living force then the next logical step forward is for "living products" or products that act independently, directed by technologies referred to as ubiquitous computing. The term ubiquitous computing can be used interchangeably with the terms pervasive computing and physical computing (Greenfield, 2006, p. 1), and is credited to the seminal paper by Mark Weiser in 1991 titled "The Computer for the 21st Century." In this paper Weiser describes the most profound technologies as "...those that disappear. They weave themselves into the fabric of everyday life until they are indistinguishable from it" (1991, p.1). These go beyond conspicuous computers, such as smart phones and tablets, to more rudimentary products that have sensors and computing power in them, as seamlessly gathering and processing data, and reacting to this information.

The Internet of Things (IoT) is an extension of ubiquitous computing, with the key difference described by Adrian McEwen and Hakim Cassimally as the element of "the Internet" (2013, p. 10). Assa Ashuach's AI light (*Assa Ashuach Studio*, 2016) is an example of ubiquitous computing because it responds to movement in a room autonomously, without needing to be connected to the Internet for control. In contrast, home LED lighting solutions that can be controlled via mobile phone applications, such as the Philips Hue (*Philips Hue*, 2016) are examples of Internet of Things solutions where the product relies on being able to connect to other devices via the Internet in order to function.

While it is clear that many elements of theorist Weiser's ubiquitous computing vision from the early 1990s have come to pass, in particular the concepts of "tabs [mobile phones], pads [tablet computing] and boards [interactive displays]" (Weiser, 1991, p. 9), the examples of research-led design described in the following section take this vision further. The concepts explore the creation of products embedded with computing technology to add value to users' experiences while remaining relatively inconspicuous during daily life. As with many digital technologies, ubiquitous computing has been a research focus for IT and computer science disciplines, with innovation largely a response to the opportunities provided by new technologies and reduced size of processors and sensors in line with Moore's Law. User-driven design has taken a back seat. However, Adam Greenfield (2006, p. 3) and Peter Nowak (2015, p. 7) argue that the majority of technical hurdles to ubiquitous computing in products have now been overcome, suggesting it is time for designers to determine how ubiquitous computing can enhance the experiences of consumers. As Greenfield asserts, "All the necessary pieces of the puzzle are sitting there on the tabletop, waiting for us to pick them up and put them together" (2006, p. 92).

One of the challenges for designers in creating ubiquitous computing products is the quantity and variation of skills involved in working in this field. In addition to the traditional understanding of form, function, materials and sustainability familiar to industrial designers, there is an added necessity to work with electrical hardware, computer programs, interfaces and Internet protocols. Splitting the product into separate components and responsibilities, as is historically the case in product development where industrial designers, engineers, IT, graphic designers, manufacturers and numerous other parties work on aspects of the same product in relative isolation, is unlikely to result in the high value output described by visions of ubiquitous computing. The results can be feature creep or solutionism, rather than the genuine engagement with improving user experience needed for a paradigm shift. This is because, by definition, a product designed to seamlessly integrate into the complex daily lives of humans is made up of numerous elements, systems and sub-systems that must operate as a unified whole, or else expose themselves through glitches and errors that break the illusion of being at one with the surrounding environment. The fractured growth of the field has yet to provide a unified, informed approach sufficient to meet the challenges involved.

Bruce Sterling describes current offerings of ubiquitous computing products as low-level gizmos—products that "have enough functionality to actively nag people. Their deployment demands extensive, sustained interaction: upgrades, grooming, plug-ins, plug-outs, unsought messages, security threats and so forth" (Sterling, 2005, p. 11). An example would be the mobile phone, a so-called "smart" device that demands attention with ring tones, flashing lights, vibrations and messages. While alerts may relate to a human-centered social contact, the phone itself may send alerts to demand an update to an app, its system, or security settings. Most smart objects and humans are still essentially discrete entities, and while Kevin Kelly describes humans as "coevolving with our technology" (2010, p. 37), the technology is not yet a reflection of humanity. Sterling describes this when he says:

It's mentally easier to divide humans and objects than to understand them as a comprehensive and interdependent system: people are alive, objects are inert, people can think, objects just lie there. But this taxonomical division blinds us to the ways and means by which objects do change, and it obscures the areas of intervention where design can reshape things. (Sterling, 2005, pp. 8-9)

Perhaps the struggle for designers in developing innovative ubiquitous computing products lies in historical baggage, including the term "industrial" design. In Stuart Walker's book *Sustainable by Design: Explorations in Theory and Practice*, this concept is explored from a sustainability perspective, but applies equally to the struggles in adopting new digital technologies. Walker argues:

The very term 'industrial design' brings with it a great deal of baggage. It defines an approach, carrying with it a set of expectations, and it represents a particular set of knowledge and skills. Industrial design is closely linked, as a term and as a discipline, with the development of mass production and consumer goods in the early years of the 20th century. It is generally understood as the design of products for large-scale distribution and it is commonly described as a service profession to the manufacturing industry. (2006, p. 35)

However, design is no longer just industrial in nature, nor is it necessarily focused on mass production or even the creation of physical objects. The digital revolution provides a paradigm shift away from focusing on the atoms of products to the bits of technology. Gore cites an example of this shift in his book *The Future*, through the company Narrative Science, which uses computer algorithms to write entirely new newspaper and magazine articles on topics ranging from sports to finance. Gore observes, "The few human writers who work for the company have become 'meta-journalists' who design the templates, frames, and angles into which the algorithm inserts data" (2013, p. 8). The meta-journalists, or rather, their algorithms, can now write millions of stories at a time rather than just one, with huge implications for the future employment opportunities for journalists. Should this trend to rethink entire operational approaches to conventional disciplines spread as is predicted by Gore, all industries, including industrial design, must adapt or risk becoming obsolete to computers.

Adapting is made all the more challenging because of the rapid progress of technologies. No sooner has the latest software upgrade to a smart phone been delivered than a new model is created with yet more features and power. This is also the case with software. The digital tools used by industrial designers, including optimized software to keep pace with technological developments such as 3D printing (additive manufacturing), 3D scanning, virtual reality, and the Internet of Things challenge designers in staying current and relevant in their practice. An example to illustrate how industrial design is changing as a profession is found in the evolution of bicycle design. Bicycles are industrial products, with their materials, construction, and form a result of the machine age. While new materials have been applied to bicycle frames over the decades, and there are multiple configurations of tube cross-sections and frame size, bicycle design has remained relatively unchanged over the last hundred years. Under the mass production paradigm, bicycle manufacturers need to sell a large number of the same bicycle to offset the expense of tooling its individual components. To reduce costs, models are produced in a limited range of sizes. Customers choose the closest-fitting size for their anthropometry, but frames are rarely perfect for the rider because of different body shapes, so adjustments are made through components such as the saddle and handlebars, to create as close to fit as possible. This longstanding model of practice is poised for significant change—in part because of the opportunities provided by additive manufacturing (3D printing) technology, and in part because of the advances in 3D CAD tools. For example, topological optimization software utilizes mathematics and computer simulation to calculate "the 'logical place' for material—normally using iterative steps and finite element analysis" (Renishaw, 2014). The design of a product—from both a functional and an aesthetic point of view—can theoretically be calculated by computer, and because of the opportunities to use additive manufacturing to bring complexity into the real world, a topologically optimized seat post by Renishaw can be designed 44% lighter than before (Renishaw, 2014). From the digital design perspective, if software using topology optimization is creating complex lightweight forms for the bicycle frame previously impossible to manufacture, then consider the following:

1. If the computer can automatically design a better product from an engineering perspective than a human being, does this reduce the need for designers?
2. If additive manufacturing allows for every design to be different, will designers be left to micromanage every variation of a design rather than creating a single static product and moving on to something else?

This shift could be viewed as confrontational for the design discipline. However, depending on the response of the industrial design discipline, it is possible that the designer's role could evolve positively alongside emerging digital tools. To research this, the customization of products through data manipulation has been investigated, looking at projects such as "Fab Form" (Shugrina, Shamir, & Matusik, 2015), "Project Shapeshifter" (AutoDesk, 2016), and "Parametric Parts" (*Parametric Parts*, 2016). These projects use parametric relationships as constraints while limiting objects to a range of values known to produce manufacturable results. This means a novice user can, within limits, customize the CAD data for a pre-defined product within a simplified user interface. A shift in the industrial designer's role is required because these systems mean the designer is no longer creating a single 3D model of a final product, but is responsible for creating the system whereby a product concept can be manipulated into forms not necessarily envisaged by the designer. This is referred to as "Meta-Design" (Bezirtzis, Lewis, & Christeson, 2007; Fischer & Scharff, 2000). A second shift is that the customer is a participant in the design process, as discussed by Tseng, Jiao and Wang (2010, p. 177) and Jack Hu (2013, p. 6)—no longer being limited in what they must purchase by designers, but actively involved in creating it themselves. This shift from consumer to "prosumer" (Abel, Evers, Klaassen, & Troxler, 2011; Ahluwalia & Miller, 2014) radically transforms the relationship between people buying products and those creating products to sell. It is also part of a response to the imperative to create proactive users, who are invested in the products they use, with potential positive ramifications for the sustainability imperative.

However, the changes confronting modern designers go deeper: "Over the last two decades designers have mastered algorithms alongside visual thinking, and today we can witness the first generation of computational designers mature. The coming generation of designers sees code as a kind of material just as a potter sees clay" (Klanten, Ehmann, & Hanschke, 2011, p. 5). Algorithms and coding have developed in order to create software or control complex electronics. Intuitive visual programming, while not new, is only now becoming readily accessible, with programs such as Scratch (MIT Media Lab, 2016) and App Inventor (MIT, 2015) providing a visual method of coding where blocks of code can be graphically linked together in-tune with designers' visual understanding of the world. Furthermore, Rhino, popular CAD program amongst industrial designers and architects, has a range of plug-in packages including Grasshopper and Firefly, allowing the form of a product to be developed alongside its electronics or mobile application, within the same piece of software. These capabilities are also being newly embedded within PTC's Creo 3D design software through their addition of the "Designworx" Internet of Things platform. In both cases, Arduino and other electronic devices can be directly prototyped and controlled in the real world utilizing plug-ins, allowing the designer to manage additional aspects of the design relating to digital technologies, and rapidly iterate this integrated approach during design development more efficiently than previously. These examples signal a breaking down of barriers between formerly distinct roles, such as Electrical Engineer, Software Developer, User Interface Designer and Industrial Designer, with a single creator able to design, prototype, test and even manufacture complex ubiquitous computing based products. A new breed of industrial designer, the "Digital Technologist" (Loy, Canning, & Little, 2015), is emerging as education responds to these changes.

While designers might have access to a rapidly transforming range of new tools and technologies, it is crucial that human-centered design remains the focus of all design endeavors. How would humans react if simple tasks such as running a bath or making a phone call became part of autonomous systems, and what would be the level of frustration when those autonomous systems break down or misinterpret the sensor data designed to predict a person's needs? No doubt most people with a smart phone have experimented with the voice-recognition features, whether it is Siri on the Apple system, Google Now on Android, or Kortana from Microsoft, and experienced the frustrations of having to repeat the query or speak in an unnatural way in order for the system to "hear" what was being said. These systems highlight how challenging a ubiquitous system could be if it struggled to interpret user needs. Adam Greenfield calls this a needless application of technology complexification, and warns "whatever marginal 'improvement' is enacted by overlaying daily life with digital mediation has to be balanced against the risk of screwing up something that already works, however gracelessly or inelegantly" (2006, p. 125). The design of ubiquitous systems is a delicate balancing act that designers are still working to understand and implement with the kind of finesse imagined by Mark Weiser.

Emerging digital design tools, such as those in Rhino or Creo, will give designers the ability to take a holistic control of product development combined with sensors and data collection tools. However, designers will face a seemingly contradictory challenge—to design "invisible" products that enhance user experiences from the background, while being obvious in function so that they can be understood. As products move towards being truly ubiquitous, consumers will be faced with the challenge of not necessarily knowing if a product they encounter is "smart" or not, or to what degree it might be capable of responding to their needs. Greenfield explains "we should get used to the idea that there will henceforth be little correlation between the appearance of an artifact and its capabilities—no obvious indications as to how to invoke basic functionality nor that the artifact is capable of doing anything at all" (2006, p. 134). Traditionally designers include indicators of how a product functions with a visual language intended to transcend written language and culture. An example would be a handle that indicates where a product should be held, a few raised edges on a plastic enclosure to show how it can be opened, a variation in color or material to suggest where a lid can be removed. These cues replace an instruction manual, as the intention is that the user can unconsciously recognize them through their life experiences. However, how does a designer integrate visual cues describing to someone that in order to have a custom multi-vitamin 3D printed each day, as is under development by researchers at the Nestle Institute of Health Sciences (Boyle, 2014)? They may need to use a variety of inter-connected devices, such as a toilet that can analyze urine, a physical activity tracker, a fridge monitoring the foods consumed, and a pill that will only print in response to a retinal eye scan. Such complex, networked systems are as yet more science fiction than reality, but the individual technologies are possible, and demonstrate the sort of complex interactions that designers will need to consider if ubiquitous computing is embraced by mainstream consumers.

INTRODUCING 4D PRODUCT DESIGN

The authors propose an emerging type of product to fulfill the vision of Mark Weiser's ubiquitous computing—the 4D product. A 4D product may be described as one having "four dimensions, typically the three dimensions of space (length, breadth, and depth) plus time" ("four-dimensional," 2010), with time being the critical factor in this category. Time is not related to the longevity of the product, nor the time to produce it, but the ability for the product to physically evolve over time to suit changes in user needs. The emergence of 4D products is strengthened by the growing interest in 4D printing by digital revolution authors such as Eujin Pei (2014) and Dan Headrick (2015). It also relates to the field of responsive architecture at the "intersection of architecture and computer science... and implies the capacity of the building to respond dynamically to changing stimuli" (Meagher, 2014, p. 95). With relevant literature emerging relatively recently, the relationship between time and products specifically is yet to find a clear voice. With their capacity to seamlessly integrate into existing human experiences, 4D products not only meet the goals of ubiquitous computing, but they are only made possible by the concurrent developments in digital tools for designers.

The origins of 4D products are found in nature: there are numerous living examples of creatures capable of transforming or adapting to their environment in real time, such as color-changing chameleons and the blue-ringed octopus. There is also the example of the Mutable Rain Frog, only discovered in 2006, capable of transforming its skin texture from soft and smooth to sharp and spiny. Even humans are capable of a similar, if smaller, change, as cold, stress, or even euphoria can cause small bumps, known as goosebumps (or goose pimples), to be raised on the skin. This is thought to be left-over reflex from when sapiens were covered in thick hair, and when confronted by a potential predator, their goosebumps would cause the hair to stand out, making the person look more intimidating. This reaction can still be seen in animals such as porcupines and cats. If technology is a natural evolutionary force, and humans have spent millennia surrounded by living organisms capable of rapid and ongoing change, then 4D products could be considered a form of biomimicry inevitable because of technological evolution. To illustrate what a 4D product does and why it represents a shift in product design thinking, the following section provides product examples considered in the context of developments such as responsive architecture, 4D printing, and robotics.

4D DESIGN EXAMPLES

The MIT Media Lab has developed "bioLogic" (Yao et al., 2015), a form of nano-actuator powered by bacteria cells. When exposed to moisture, the cells expand to move thin biofilm materials, working like a hinge to open small vents in clothing. The product operates autonomously without the user needing to control the vents. The effect is similar to the reflexive goosebumps mentioned earlier. Although in the early stages of development, critically this work embodies the concept of being 4D in terms of its human-object relationship changing form continuously over time without specific instructions from the user or even an interface to interact with. Another company experimenting with moving forms is BMW, with both their GINA and more recent Vision Next 100 concept cars. While both cars employ a range of technologies in response to the future of driving and automation, most relevant is their capacity to change their exterior shape for functional purposes. In the case of GINA, the frame is hydraulically controlled to reveal things such as headlights or the engine, or change the shape of the rear of the car to increase traction at high speeds. As with MIT's bioLogic, these form changes are automatically controlled by the car's onboard sensors to improve the driving experience and safety on the road. The Vision Next 100 car adopts the same capabilities of "physically altering the car itself on the go and anticipating and even improving the driver's performance" (Szondy, 2016), with the addition of moving fender skirts to expand the car body as the wheels turn, reducing the drag coefficient to reportedly 0.18 C_d. This feature also improves visibility on the road, revealing a glowing red sub-structure to alert oncoming drivers the car is turning. While such a dynamic car body is yet to be seen on the mainstream market, elements of this transformation can be seen in Formula 1 racing cars. These vehicles have movable rear wing flaps to modify drag for overtaking in certain sections of a race (known as the Drag Reduction System or DRS). Consumer-level cars, such as the Audi TT, are also capable of automatically increasing the rear spoiler angle at high speeds to increase traction and safety. This suggests these life-like movements are slowly finding their way into the mainstream.

Inspired by these conceptual visions of the future, "Dynaero" by James Novak is a research project focusing on the development of a bicycle helmet capable of autonomously adjusting its aerodynamic and thermal regulation properties. The intention is to enhance the performance of the wearer through the use of integrated electronics, sensors and actuators. Research shows that "an aerodynamically efficient helmet can reduce the riders drag by up to 8% of the total aerodynamic drag that a cyclist usually generates" (Alam et al., 2010). During time trial events, cyclists typically wear aerodynamic race helmets with no ventilation, sacrificing thermal regulation for speed over short distances; however over long distances this becomes dangerous for the rider's health so they must sacrifice aerodynamics for helmets with large vents to maintain their body temperature. New helmets from Bell (Star Pro) and KASK (Infinity) have recently emerged allowing riders to manually adjust ventilation with sliders while riding. However, Dynaero draws on recent computing developments in cycling, where sensors relay data on the bodily responses of the cyclist and their bicycle during performance to the support team. Dynaero uses this data to create a responsive helmet that automatically adjusts its vents based on the riders' data, and independent of that rider or even the support team within a predetermined system. This ensures accuracy in using the data patterns to adjust the vents, rather than relying on rider awareness in the heat of competition (Figure 1).

The current working prototype of Dynaero (Figure 2) operates from a custom-designed mobile application and uses the built-in mobile phone sensors to calculate the rider's movements, sending a signal to the helmet via Bluetooth technology to control the opening angle of the large vents. The full design of this system, including both hardware and software, has been created by Novak through the use of graphical tools such as MIT App Inventor and Rhino with Grasshopper discussed previously, exemplifying the way in which designers are becoming empowered to control a greater breadth of the design process through new digital tools. While the prototype is linked to a mobile phone, the final product would be driven by its own sensors and expanded to engage with a variety of common sensors already used by cyclists and transmitting and recording using wireless signals, such as Bluetooth. As such, this project is an example of a product that upholds the ubiquitous computing vision—the helmet responds autonomously to changes in the riders' needs, with its own sensors, and those already installed on a bicycle, communicating simultaneously with the helmet to determine the second-by-second optimum position of the openings. In this way, just like the previous examples from MIT and BMW, the athlete can be immersed in the experience of riding without distraction, yet their performance and safety is improved. Such an "awareable" (i.e., a wearable technology that is itself aware of its surroundings or use) device aims to reduce the attentive demands of the user by raising the "awareness" of the products.

Figure 1. James Novak, Key stages of elite cycling races with relevant speed and power information indicating specific combinations that can be used to control air vents

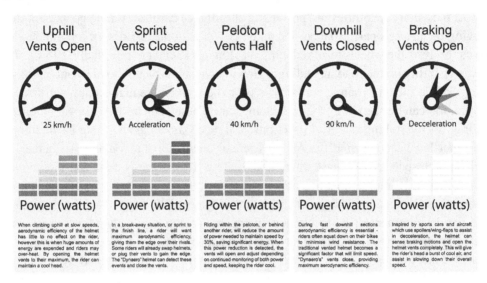

There are key criteria for the design of 4D products (as defined in this chapter). Fundamentally, a 4D product must be human-centered in this digitally enabled era. It must physically adapt over time—this emerging field is not concerned with software responses alone, such as notifications or other methods of alerting a user as currently utilized by gizmos such as smart phones. The product must autonomously analyze its situation based on the information from sensors, and reflexively respond through actuators. As such, 4D products are inherently tangible and tactile, and act symbiotically with the human user. Adam Greenfield suggests that the word "user" is inadequate to describe these new relationships with the ubiquitous computing objects; "the whole point of designing ubiquitous systems was that they would be ambient, peripheral, and not focally attended to in the way that something actively "used" must be" (Greenfield, 2006, p. 70). In their most basic sense, 4D products are driven by functional and emotional requirements, to enhance the human experience in some way that relates to performance, safety, comfort,

Figure 2. James Novak, Dynaero 2.0 with prototype mobile application 2016, polyamide 3D printed

ergonomics etc. While ideally these will be engaging aesthetic transformations, the examples discussed here are all driven from a need to improve the functional characteristics of the object with measurable results. However, this is the starting point for the development of 4D products rather than their conclusion.

THE 4D LANDSCAPE

Products that are 4D relate to the field of responsive architecture that emerged in environmentally responsive building practices (Meagher, 2014). In Jean Nouvel's Institut du Monde Arabe, the building's facade includes hundreds of mechanical diaphragms that open and close in response to the changing climate to regulate building temperature and lighting. The Al Bahar Towers in Abu Dhabi, designed by Aedas Architects, features a similar mechanically responsive climate control façade. Designed to suit the harsh desert weather, the façade elements open and close as the sun tracks around them, shutting the building off from direct sun to keep them cool, and then opening as the sun passes to let in natural light without the heat. It is estimated that such a system could reduce solar gain by up to 50% (Cilento, 2012). Both examples use sensors and weather simulation to control the facades, operating as ubiquitous systems with no need for human control. They are also designed to improve the experience of users inside through temperature control and exposure to natural light.

The development of 4D products can also be related to the emerging field of 4D printing, a term coined by the head of Massachusetts Institute of Technology (MIT)'s Self-Assembly Lab, Skylar Tibbits. In his own words:

4D printing... entails multi-material prints with the capability to transform over time, or a customized material system that can change from one shape to another, directly off the print bed. This technique offers a streamlined path from idea to reality with performance-driven functionality built directly into the materials. The fourth dimension is described here as the transformation over time, emphasising that printed structures are no longer simply static, dead objects; rather, they are programmably active and can transform independently. (Tibbits, 2014, p. 119)

4D printing uses 3D printing technology to create structures capable of transforming shape over time under certain stimuli, including liquids or electrical current. This means the object created by the printer will not initially look like the object 15 minutes later, or a week later, or a year later. The object is "programmed" to morph into various states under specific conditions, with much in common to the bioLogic garment discussed earlier. In fact, it is possible to imagine bioLogic as a 4D print as it too uses multiple materials in order to create the opening effect of the panels. However, it currently uses screen-printing techniques to layer materials rather than a 3D printer. The development and application of 4D printing can be considered as related to the broader development of 4D products, and has potential to be a valid method of manufacturing a 4D product similar to the bioLogic garment. Tibbits acknowledges this idea, suggesting that it is the broader ideas around 4D printing that are of significance. The opportunities—and challenges—of programming materials and what this might mean for designers and consumers (Headrick, 2015, p. 8) add to the body of knowledge for the design discipline in the evolving design landscape.

Figure 3. James Novak, MyPen customized by four test subjects 2015, ABS 3D Prints

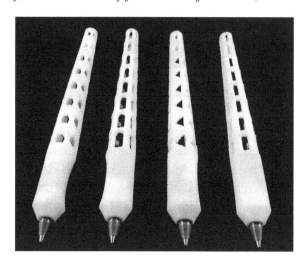

An example of a 4D printed product is the "Minimal Shoe" by Christophe Guberan and Carlo Clopath from MIT's Self-Assembly Lab. The shoe starts out as a shallow 3D print created with Fused Deposition Modeling (FDM) printed over a stretched textile. When removed from the printer, the material automatically folds itself into a three-dimensional shoe, and will further morph to suit the wearer's foot over time. This can be combined with other materials for the shoe sole for durability as a hybrid manufacturing approach, allowing for greater customization. This type of product has movements free of electronics, whereas 4D products, such as the Dynaero helmet or BMW concept cars, rely on actuators, power and programming and change the relationship between users and products. For example, although fountain pens were often valued objects, disposable pens have generally superseded these invested objects. However, if a person's relationship to the use of a pen were regarded as a system, then advances in digital technology create a different approach to design. "MyPen", published in the proceedings for the 2015 Drawing International Brisbane conference (Novak, 2015), embeds sensors in a pen that detect the user's grip and how the pen moves through space. This information can be used to 3D print a customized pen that can be embedded with sensors that monitor the evolution of a person's grip over time—short term, for different uses or from childhood to adulthood. Each evolution of the print refines the grip, responding to changes of writing style or weaknesses or strengths in the hand. Further, this system allows for change in consultation with a clinician if the user experienced difficulties, for example, following a medical incident, such as a stroke. This is arguably a form of evolutionary robotics, or alternatively part of what A. E. Eiben terms the Evolution of Things (Eiben, 2014), and figure 3 shows four different pens customized to the grip and aesthetic preference of four different test subjects in Novak's study.

Just as MyPen builds a body of knowledge on the evolving requirements of an individual, product designer Tom Dixon used digital technology to build up a body of cultural knowledge. He embedded the cultural history in a product, designed to evolve over time when he relaunched second-hand Artek stools on the market with the story of where they had previously been used contained in an RFID chip and accessed by smart phone (Loy, 2008). In *Sustainable by Design* (2006), Walker discusses building such opportunities for emotional connections between people and objects to invest objects with additional meaning to keep the product in use for longer, spreading the embodied energy invested in its manufacture. Digitally enabled 4D products designed for socio-cultural sustainability embed more than technology; they embed cultural information, such as storytelling, images, sounds and other sensory information specific to an individual or a group. This approach builds shared memory into product systems that supports the evolution of the group, and retains and enhances community. Based on this approach, conventional ideas of digital customization through 3D printing and parametric modeling have to change, with products customized through engagement, building value through use because of the embedded cultural connections. A 4D product may therefore itself change over time, or may spawn a new iteration of itself when it senses it is no longer performing optimally, or it may change as information tagged to that product or provided as data to a system is updated. This begins to describe what Bruce Sterling calls SPIMES, objects that:

...begin and end as data. They are designed on screens, fabricated by digital means, and precisely tracked through space and time throughout their earthly sojourn. SPIMES are sustainable, enhance-able, uniquely identifiable, and made of substances that can and will be folded back into the production stream of future SPIMES. (Sterling, 2005, p. 11)

With the digital revolution, and complex sustainability imperatives, including socio-cultural sustainability as well as environmental, and the aspirations for a society that responds to inclusion and diversity there is a shift towards the fourth dimension that will impact the man-made world, from the macro to the micro. This challenges what it means to be a designer and raises the question as to what degree this will affect human development in an increasingly digital age. Responsive architecture, 4D products, and 4D printing together suggest how designers are embracing new technologies with an understanding of the flux attached to rapid technological development, choosing to embed their designs with the capability to change and adapt to a changing world.

EMPOWERING PRODUCTS

It has been shown how the relationship between designers and products inherently changes as the designer's role moves from creating single products for mass production, to more of a systems approach where products change over time. The relationships between consumers and 4D products are likely to be different to those already in existence and need to be studied. This is suggested by the emotional responses noted in "The Never Hungry Caterpillar" project. At a functional level, this is an extension cable for the home designed by Matthias Laschke, Marc Hassenzahl, and Sarah Diefenbach (2011). However rather than blending into the background, this device will squirm, twist and turn as if in pain when it detects devices wasting power in standby mode, using "the metaphor of a caterpillar [to] touch upon (at least some) people's tendency to help and take care of living things" (Laschke et al., 2011). Trial users in the study could not help but unplug devices in standby mode to stop the perceived "pain" of the device. Of course "technically, the Caterpillar could just detect connected devices in stand-by and simply switch them off automatically. This would be practical, it would save energy, but it would not engage in any argument or dialogue" (Laschke et al., 2011).

This type of product is 4D in nature, having the capacity to autonomously transform in order to affect the habits of the user. What is particularly important to consider in 4D products, especially those that may be as life-like as The Never Hungry Caterpillar, is the psychological and emotional connection between users and such products, who may begin to see them as living entities to be cared for like a pet, rather than an inanimate object with little value as would be the case of a standard extension cord. This is highlighted in the work of Moyle et al. (2013) on the use of robots in the care of Alzheimer patients, where the emotional relationship between the robot and the user was explored through studies on robotic animals and toys. What happens when these "living" products stop working? Will users be more likely to try and repair these products than throw them away, much like a beloved family pet, and could this be a response to more sustainable design? With 4D products only newly emerging through research it is difficult to say, however it is conceivable based on research in robotics that this will be the likely scenario. Matthias Scheutz explores these unidirectional relationships, explaining that robots:

... affect humans in very much the same way that animals (e.g., pets) or even other people affect humans. In particular, the rule-governed mobility of social robots allows for, and ultimately prompts, humans to ascribe intentions to social robots in order to be able to make sense of their behaviors (e.g., the robot did not clean in the corner because it thought it could not get there). The claim is that the autonomy of social robots is among the critical properties that cause people to view robots differently from other artefacts such as computers or cars. (Scheutz, 2011, p. 207)

Scheutz uses numerous examples to evidence this trend, from soldiers becoming attached to robots used to detect and detonate improvised explosive devices in Iraq, to the popular robotic Roomba vacuum cleaner and the personality's people ascribe to them. As such, new scenarios and systems become important long-term considerations for 4D products, including the necessity to provide better means for product repair and maintenance, ethical regulation to prevent products influencing humans to do things inappropriate or outside their normal behavior, psychological and counseling services to help people move on after a product 'dies', control over product memory so that traits or sensitive data can be removed when a product is sold second hand. As technology moves closer to nature, these considerations will transform the relationship between consumers and products, and the industries built around them.

In responding to the ideas expressed in this chapter about human empowerment in an increasingly technological age, it might be assumed that ambient intelligence would be at odds with ideas of enhancing the human experience based on empowerment. However, this would be an oversimplification. Ubiquitous computing might be a utopian ideal, alongside modernist ideas of houses as "machines for living", but the development of ambient intelligence just needs to be developed with an underlying recognition of the importance of empowerment in the same way environments must focus on human emotion, social interaction and behavior rather than being completely machine-like. Light bulbs that wirelessly transmit their status and trigger a replacement order, as shown at the 2013 *The Future Is Here* exhibition in the London Design Museum walk a fine line between enhancing the human experience through the development of freedom from day to day minutia, and alienating people from their environment. Complete freedom from responsibility can equate to feelings of a loss of control. This is not aligned with current aspirations for society, and alternative strategies, such as delegation, should be considered in the development of the product service system.

There's a tendency in connected products and service design to assume that having machines take over human work is a good in itself....however, there are good reasons to treat automation as a choice, not a default. Instead of talking about automation, philosophers of technology often talk about 'delegation'—that is, the distribution of responsibility and effort among different kinds of humans and machines. (Rowland et al., 2015, p. 211)

However, there is an opposing argument that computing provides humans with the opportunity to extend their faculties and connection to the real world, becoming more sensitive to the nuances of their surroundings and better informed about the systems that operate within it. For example, MIT have embedded sensors into marshland (Tidmarsh, Plymouth, Massachusetts) and even their Media Lab building. This allows users to virtually explore the landscape, honing in on details such as pockets of noise, or temperature change that would otherwise be impossible for individuals to be aware of. This has the potential to create people with a very different sense of the world, in the same way that television and the Internet has changed collective understandings of the world by different populations (depending on the way it is presented). That shift in perception, triggered by an increase in information, causing a transformational change in understanding is illustrated by, for example, the reported impact of the first image of the earth taken as the Apollo rounded the moon in 1968.

Although the signs have been there with augmented reality products such as Google Glass and QR codes, Pokémon Go has heralded in a democratization of augmented reality technology that has the potential to change the human perception of the world and interactions with their environment and each other. Kuniavsky makes the comment that to have computing embedded in a forest would make no sense "…in an office it is not surprising to have wires running under the floor, but forest trees with embedded electronics seem wrong" (Kuniavsky, 2010, p. 286), yet if that technology allowed the individual to walk through the forest with the option of technologically heightened senses, they could zoom in on the movement of insects in the forest floor, hear chicks hatch high above their heads, feel the direction and strength of the wind at the top of the trees. Biohackers such as Stelarc and Neil Harbisson suggest that information sent to the brain in any form can be learned and interpreted by the brain to increase the information received through traditional senses. Augmented experience and ambient intelligence could have the potential to support the human development in a digital age if the focus is on the human experience.

Even so, the inevitability of unexpected consequences could have an equally negative impact on development. Will real life become less real? As the opportunities provided by ubiquitous computing create temptations for designers to strive for all encompassing systems, the ability to opt out at any point must be provided. The most amazing technology in the world "…will mean little if we don't, as individuals, have genuine power to evaluate its merits on our own terms, and make decisions accordingly…a paradise without choice is no paradise at all" (Greenfield, 2006, p. 247).

CONCLUSION

While there is a cautionary note in working with the power of digital technology in human-centered products, the ontogenetic adaptation capabilities of humans should allow for the evolution of the collective to rise to the opportunities—and challenges—digital technology provides. The essential criteria, though, involve designing in context, and not get swept along with what is technologically possible, but rather what responds to design theory, aspirations and values for now, for positive human development. That is, for designs to align with current thinking about sustainability, connectivity, experience-centered design, design for change, and to support inclusion and diversity.

As defined here, 4D products are about responding to the drivers behind design now, and working with time as an essential ingredient of that design approach. Going beyond the design of customizable, parametric models for individual 3D printing, and beyond the design of products embedded with sensors that send information to a management system, and going beyond augmented reality, 4D products are capable of changing over time. Ideas evolve, people's needs and desires change. Sustainability drivers support the idea of designing for that change. Digitally enabled 4D products are an emerging class of products that work towards these ideals, in sync with the natural flux of human behaviors, needs and learning.

This shift from static, resolved 3D products that make up today's retail market to 4D products is only beginning to emerge. It has the potential to encompass the next state beyond cradle to cradle, with an iterative development lifecycle, rather than a rehabilitated but still linear lifeline. The proposal is that they can work with the reality of human behaviors and interactions. The assumption will be that they require repair and are therefore designed for that inevitability, and be flexible enough to have their functionality revised and updated over time. They will be responsive, agile, and embedded with information on how to use, how to repair, and how to alter for new needs—data is their life-blood.

What does that mean for designers? What does it mean in terms of the use of technology in products? What does it mean in relation to the psychology of those products? If an essential driver for selling products is for economic growth, then there will be significant changes in how economic growth is sustained. In the past, products made for manufacturing utilized as many common components as possible, and costs of tooling constrained ideas of iterative change. Digitally enabled design has the potential to alter understandings of systems of products and production, not only for practical reasons, but also in response to the normal, human desire for change. The need now is to expand this approach to a more fluid, flexible, empowering approach. Design can become more iterative, allowing for bespoke development and evolution of products. This ability for customization in a technological era responds to the need for designers to keep referring back to the human-centered core in their design work, highlighted by Greenfield (2006, p.13): "It would be wise for us all to remember that, while our information technology may be digital in nature, the human beings interacting with it will always be infuriatingly and delightfully analogue".

The difficulty of designing in this way is that even basic designs are creating complex problems for teams across disciplines. If designers are to respond effectively, creating positive product experiences that respond to the aspirations for society at this time, they need to be basing their work on updated understandings of the human psyche and ecological interconnection as well as the technological opportunities and potential pitfalls. A new approach to the education and development of designers and teams working in this space needs to be devised, and, fundamentally, a paradigm shift in thinking and research is needed to keep pace with designing for the human experience in a digital age.

REFERENCES

Abel, B. V., Evers, L., Klaassen, R., & Troxler, P. (2011). *Open design now: Why design cannot remain exclusive*. Amsterdam, Netherlands: BIS.

Ahluwalia, P., & Miller, T. (2014). The prosumer. *Social Identities*, *20*(4-5), 259–261. doi:10.1080/13 504630.2015.1004830

Alam, F., Chowdhury, H., Elmir, Z., Sayogo, A., Love, J., & Subic, A. (2010). An experimental study of thermal comfort and aerodynamic efficiency of recreational and racing bicycle helmets. *Procedia Engineering*, *2*(2), 2413–2418. doi:10.1016/j.proeng.2010.04.008

Aldersey-Williams, H. (2011). *The new tin ear: Manufacturing, materials and the rise of the user-maker.* London: RSA Design Projects.

Anderson, C. (2014). *Makers: The new industrial revolution.* New York, NY: Crown Business.

Assa Ashuach Studio. (2016). Retrieved from http://assaashuach.com/#!/portfolio/assa-studio-micro-3d-design/0

AutoDesk. (2016). *Project Shapeshifter.* Retrieved from www.shapeshifter.io

Bezirtzis, B. G., Lewis, M., & Christeson, C. (2007). Interactive evolution for industrial design. In *Proceedings of the 6th ACM SIGCHI conference on Creativity & Cognition* (pp. 183-192). New York, NY: ACM. doi:10.1145/1254960.1254986

Boyle, M. (2014, June 23). *Nestle aiming to develop a Nespresso of nutrients.* Retrieved from http://www.bloomberg.com/news/articles/2014-06-22/nestle-aiming-to-develop-a-nespresso-of-nutrients?_ga=1.134810162.210344514.1402054238

Braungart, M., & McDonough, W. (2002). *Cradle to cradle: Remaking the way we make things.* New York, NY: North Point Press.

Cilento, K. (2012, September 5). Al Bahar Towers responsive facade / Aedas. *Archdaily.* Retrieved from http://www.archdaily.com/270592/al-bahar-towers-responsive-facade-aedas

Dean, L. T. (2016). *Future factories.* Retrieved from www.futurefactories.com

Eiben, A. E. (2014). *In vivo veritas: Towards the evolution of things.* Paper presented at the 13th International Conference on Parallel Problem Solving from Nature, Ljubljana, Slovenia. doi:10.1007/978-3-319-10762-2_3

Fischer, G., & Scharff, E. (2000). Meta-design: design for designers. *Proceedings of the 3rd conference on Designing interactive systems: Processes, practices, methods, and techniques* (pp. 396-405). New York, NY: ACM.

Four-dimensional. (2010). *Oxford Dictionary of English* (3rd ed.). Oxford University Press.

Fuad-Luke, A. (2009). *Design activism: Beautiful strangeness for a sustainable world.* London: Earthscan.

Fung Kwok Pan. Fluid vase. (2010). *Design Boom Newsletter 440071.* Retrieved from http://www.designboom.com/technology/fung-kwok-pan-fluid-vase/

Gore, A. (2013). *The future.* New York, NY: Random House.

Greenfield, A. (2006). *Everyware: The dawning age of ubiquitous computing.* Berkeley, CA: New Riders.

Hawken, P., Lovins, A., & Lovins, L. H. (2000). *Natural capitalism: The next industrial revolution.* London: Earthscan.

Headrick, D. (2015). 4D printing transforms product design. *Research-Technology Management, 58*(2), 7–8.

Hu, S. J. (2013). Evolving paradigms of manufacturing: From mass production to mass customization and personalization. *Procedia CIRP*, *7*, 3–8. doi:10.1016/j.procir.2013.05.002

Kelly, K. (2010). *What technology wants*. New York, NY: Penguin Group.

Klanten, R., Ehmann, S., & Hanschke, V. (2011). *A touch of code: Interactive installations and experiences*. Berlin, Germany: Gestalten.

Kuniavsky, M. (2010). *Smart things: Ubiquitous computing user experience design*. Burlington, MA: Morgan Haufmann.

Laschke, M., Hassenzahl, M., & Diefenbach, S. (2011). *Things with attitude: Transformational products*. Presented at the Create 11 Conference, Shoreditch House, London, UK. Retrieved from http://static1. squarespace.com/static/52722face4b02a66778dc9d0/t/53318711e4b09837d5a328f8/1395754769468/ Laschke%2C+Hassenzahl%2C+Diefenbach+-+Things+with+attitude+Transformational+Produc ts+-+2011.pdf

Loy, J. (2008). Strategies for teaching sustainable design practice with product design students. *Proceedings of E&PDE 2008, the 10th International Engineering and Product Design Education Conference* (pp. 491-496). Design Society.

Loy, J., Canning, S., & Haskell, N. (2016). 3D printing sociocultural sustainability. In S. S. Muthu & M. M. Savalani (Eds.), *Handbook of sustainability in additive manufacturing, environmental footprints and eco-design of products and processes* (pp. 145–168). New York, NY: Springer. doi:10.1007/978-981-10-0549-7_7

Loy, J., Canning, S., & Little, C. (2015, June-July). *Digital industrial design*. Paper presented at the International Design Technology Conference, DesTech2015, Geelong, Australia.

Makepeace, J. (1995). *Makepeace: Spirit of adventure in craft and design*. London: Octopus.

Massachusetts Institute of Technology. (2015). *MIT App Inventor*. Retrieved from http://appinventor. mit.edu/explore/

McEwen, A., & Cassimally, H. (2013). *Designing the Internet of Things*. Oxford, UK: John Wiley & Sons.

McLeod, S. A. (2016). *Maslow's hierarchy of needs*. Retrieved from www.simplypsychology.org/maslow. html

Meagher, M. (2014). Responsive architecture and the problem of obsolescence. *International Journal of Architectural Research*, *8*(3), 95–104.

MIT Media Lab. (2016). *Scratch*. Retrieved from https://scratch.mit.edu/

Moyle, W., Beattie, E., Jones, C., Klein, B., Cook, G., & Gray, C. (2013). Exploring the effect of companion robots on emotional expression. *Journal of Gerontological Nursing*, *39*(5), 46–53. doi:10.3928/00989134-20130313-03 PMID:23506125

Novak, J. (2015). *Drawing the pen: From physical to digital and back again.* Presented at the Drawing International Brisbane Conference, Brisbane, Australia. Retrieved from http://static1.squarespace.com/static/55779bbce4b004acf1e1479d/t/56aef970b6aa60cdf1c253d6/1454307702608/JAMES+XXXX_DRAWING+THE+PEN_DIB2015.pdf

Nowak, P. (2015). *Humans 3.0: the upgrading of the species.* London: Harper Collins.

Parametric Parts. (2016). Retrieved from http://www.parametricparts.com/

Pei, E. (2014). 4D printing: Revolution or fad? *Assembly Automation, 34*(2), 123–127. doi:10.1108/AA-02-2014-014

Petrova, M. (2014). Educating designers from Generation Y: Challenges and alternatives. In *DS 78: Proceedings of the 16th International conference on Engineering and Product Design Education (E&PDE14), Design Education and Human Technology Relations* (pp. 524-529). New York, NY: ACM.

Philips Hue. (n.d.). Retrieved from http://www2.meethue.com/en-au/

Pokémon Go. (n.d.). Retrieved from http://www.pokemongo.com/

Powell, R. (2012). The future of human evolution. *The British Journal for the Philosophy of Science, 63*(1), 145–175. doi:10.1093/bjps/axr027

Renishaw. (2014, February 2). *First metal 3D printed bicycle frame manufactured by Renishaw for Empire Cycles.* Retrieved from http://www.renishaw.com/en/first-metal-3d-printed-bicycle-frame-manufactured-by-renishaw-for-empire-cycles--24154

Rowland, C., Goodman, E., Charlier, M., Light, A., & Lui, A. (2015). *Designing connected products: UX for the consumer internet of things.* Sebastopol, CA: O'Reilly.

Scheutz, M. (2011). *The inherent dangers of unidirectional emotional bonds between humans and social robots. In Robot ethics: The ethical and social implications of robotics* (pp. 205–221). Cambridge, MA: The MIT Press.

Shugrina, M., Shamir, A., & Matusik, W. (2015). *Fab forms: Customizable objects for fabrication with validity and geometry caching.* Paper presented at the ACM Siggraph 2015, Los Angeles, CA. Retrieved from http://cfg.mit.edu/content/fab-forms-customizable-objects-fabrication-validity-and-geometry-caching

Sparke, P. (1987). *Design in context.* London: Quarto Books.

St Clair, A. (2016). Critical thinking, wisdom and paying homage to the human experience. *Voices, 42*(1/2), 41-43.

Sterling, B. (2005). *Shaping things.* Cambridge, MA: MIT Press.

Szondy, D. (2016, March 9). BMW looks to the future with shape-shifting. *Vision Next 100 Concept.* Retrieved from http://www.gizmag.com/bmw-group-vision--next-100-concept/42194/

Tibbits, S. (2014). 4D printing: Multi-material shape change. *Architectural Design, 84*(1), 116–121. doi:10.1002/ad.1710

Tseng, M. M., Jiao, R. J., & Wang, C. (2010). Design for mass personalization. *CIRP Annals: Manufacturing Technology*, *59*(1), 175–178. doi:10.1016/j.cirp.2010.03.097

Walker, S. (2006). *Sustainable by design: Explorations in theory and practice*. London: Earthscan.

Weimer, M. (2002). *Learner-centered teaching: Five key changes to practice*. San Francisco, CA: Jossey Bass.

Weiser, M. (1991). The computer for the 21st century. *Scientific American*, *265*(3), 94–110. doi:10.1038/scientificamerican0991-94 PMID:1675486

Yao, L., Ou, J., Cheng, C.-Y., Steiner, H., Wang, W., Wang, G., & Ishii, H. (2015). bioLogic: Natto cells as nanoactuators for shape changing interfaces. In *Proceedings of the 33rd Annual ACM Conference on Human Factors in Computing Systems* (pp. 1-10). New York, NY: ACM. doi:10.1145/2702123.2702611

KEY TERMS AND DEFINITIONS

Additive Manufacturing (3D Printing): A process of producing three-dimensional forms directly from 3D computer data by depositing material layer by layer. This is in contrast to subtractive manufacturing, whereby material is removed from a solid piece of material to reveal the final object.

Generation Y (Gen Y): People born between approximately 1980 and 1995.

Human-Centred Design: An approach to design where the user remains at the forefront of all design decisions, resulting in solutions that are more in tune with user needs.

Industrial Design: A profession responsible for developing the form and function of physical products, traditionally for the intention of mass production.

Internet of Things (IoT): Extends the concept of ubiquitous computing by adding the element of the Internet, allowing objects to communicate with each other or the cloud.

Ontogenetic: The entire sequence of events influencing the development of an organism.

Stasis: A state in which there is no action or progress.

Ubiquitous Computing: The concept of embedding computing capabilities into any ordinary object, in any location. May also be known as "pervasive computing".

Chapter 19
Distributed Work Environments:
The Impact of Technology in the Workplace

Edwiygh Franck
The Greatest You Yet!, USA

ABSTRACT

Technology is making the traditional workplace obsolete. Companies are taking advantage of the myriads of digital resources available to make their processes leaner, cut costs and have a larger presence in the global market through the concept of distributed work environment. In this chapter, the author provides an overview of the distributed work environment, as well as the impact it has on the human condition in the workplace. Although this technology driven work concept can be beneficial, companies have to ensure that it is the right business model for them and their employees. The author looks at different factors that companies need to consider in deciding to adopt a distributed work environment model. Several companies, over 125 of them, have successfully implemented the concept and the author shares some examples on how they were able to achieve success and employee satisfaction.

INTRODUCTION

Technology has had a significant impact on how humans live their lives from entertainment, medicine, education, to family life, dating, and social media. Technology has taking center stage in our lives and have allowed us to achieve things that we would not think possible a decade ago. We are sharing and consuming information at lighting speeding due to the availability and capabilities of technology. Technology has allowed for the development of robotic surgery to enhance the preciseness and accuracy of surgery as well as recovery time for patients. The popularity of online learning has increased tremendously as technology has become readily available for students to learn anywhere and at any time. We have self-driving cars on our roads and we can conduct videos chat sessions with anyone around the world by simply using our cellular devices. In other words, we live in a digital and technologically advanced age and almost everything around us is connected by technology, including organizations and their employees.

As Roper and Kim (2007) stated:

DOI: 10.4018/978-1-5225-2838-8.ch019

A clear revolution is underway in when, where and how work is accomplished. The workplace of the future will be more physically distributed due to a variety of reasons, such as the high cost of land and buildings in urban areas, air pollution resulting from mass commuting, and changes in the nature of work (p. 103).

In the past two decades the landscape of our workforce has changed dramatically from traditional brick and mortar buildings to distributed work environments because of the advancement of technology. From having all employees in a physical building to having employees spread all over the world in an array of physical locations. By definition, a distributed work environment is an organization structure where "... the vast majority of employees work from wherever they are comfortable and productive. Perhaps most importantly, communication and culture are moved outside the boundaries of a physical location so that everyone is able to be included wherever they live" (Robins, 2014, p. 3). A more technical definition explains the distributed work environment as "... an environment in which a plurality of mobile workers using portable computing devices can gain access to a network via network access stations installed within the work environment" (Cole et al., 2002, p. 1). Both definitions reiterate the idea that traditional company headquarters are gradually changing from one main location to wherever an employee wants it to be.

As we begin to understand the concept of what a distributed work environment is, it is important to also understand what it is not. According to Jeff Robbins (2014), from Lullabot, a strategy, design and development company that has embraced and implemented a distributed work environment for his company, a distributed work environment is not:

- *... One with a prominent central office where the majority of people work most of the time* (Robins, 2014, p. 4)
- *A corporation with multiple locations* (Robins, 2014, p. 4)
- *A company where people are often allowed to work from home* (Robins, 2014, p. 4)
- *A company that takes advantage of outsourcing, freelancers, or subcontractors* (Robins, 2014, p. 4)
- *A co-working space where people freelance on similar projects* (Robins, 2014, p. 4)
- *A single freelancer* (Robins, 2014, p. 4)
- *A department within a large company where most people work from home (for instance, the customer service branch of an airline) – though this may qualify as a distributed team* (Robins, 2014, p. 4)

Robbins (2014) goes on to say that it is also important to understand the difference between a distributed work environment and remote employees. In his words:

...the truth is that in-person communication and activities will always trump virtual/tele/digital communications. After all, humans have been communicating in-person since the beginning of time. It is our default setting. So a company with remote employees begins with the deck stacked against them. It's not an even playing field. It's really going to be a challenge to make remote employees feel like they're part of the team. Resentment and imbalance can build up between those who "get to stay at home" and those who "get to have lunch with the boss every day"(p. 4).

Differentiating between remote employees and a distributed work environment is important, because by confusing them or making them synonymous, the above sentiments begin to be shared by several other companies that are thinking about implementing a distributed work environment. The fear that employees will be disengaged if they are removed from the physical office is real, and it preventing organizations to take the leap forward and try this new concept. However, Robbins (2014) describes what a true distributed work environment is below by saying:

A distributed company doesn't have these problems. Most of its communications happen online and are available for everyone in the company to participate. Whether these are phone conferences, email threads, or message-board and issue-queue posts, it's very easy to be inclusive despite geographical separation (p. 4).

Today's technological advancements are making the traditional brick and mortar headquarters slowly obsolete. Employers are realizing that they have the ability to have a larger top talent pool by having opportunities and presence around the world instead of the country. Josh Kramer (2011), CEO of Full-Stack, a software development company, describes the traditional work environment as a handicap where companies are "Geographically Challenged:"

Your company has probably been operating under a handicap for its whole existence. It's a handicap that has been so common that the vast majority don't even see it as such. The handicap is this: most companies are limited in their ability to find and hire the right people by a fixed geographic radius set up around their central office. We will call these type of companies "Geographically Challenged". Your geographically challenged company may have attempted to overcome this handicap by opening branch offices in multiple cities or paying for a new employee's relocation or maybe even introducing flextime into the mix. Though these steps help the situation, you are only slightly mitigating the root problem (p. 1).

We live a society where we are constantly connected and the cost of staying connected is decreasing everyday due to emerging competitors in the industry. Technology has made it possible for employers and employees to connect with their colleagues across the world in real time to collaborate on projects and expand their business. Employers are catching on to the idea that in order for their employees to perform at their high potential, they need to provide a technological experience in the workplace equivalent to the technological experience that employees have at home. One could further argue that employees have better technology at home than they have in the office, so distributed work environments make sense because employers can take advantage of these advanced technologies by paying for them and decreasing their overhead costs. This sounds like a win-win situation: employees can work wherever they want and be more productive then they would be at the office; and employers are reducing overhead costs and making profits due to the increased level of productivity of the employees and the reduced operating costs. Of course, there are no perfect systems, so this chapter will explore some of the benefits and downfalls of this logic later in the chapter.

THE CONCEPT OF DISTRIBUTED WORK ENVIRONMENT

An Overview

The economy is changing, so it only makes sense that organizations would be looking at strategies to improve and streamline their processes and services to reduce their operating costs and maintain or gain competitive edge. This change is mainly because of the rise and refinement of technology where information is being shared at an unprecedented speed and industries that were once human driven, are now technology driven. Once example of that is the newspaper industry. Long gone are the days of having a paper boy (or girl) ride on a bicycle to deliver newspapers; news is readily available the minute we open our eyes in the morning, on our cellphones, tablets and computers. Due to this technology boom, the nature of running a business has to change in order to keep up with all of these changes. One option many organizations are looking into or implementing is the concept of distributed work environment. Such a work environment is attractive to companies because it yields many benefits such as the rapid growth of affordable telecommunication technology, a decrease in overhead costs, as well as linkage to improved employee retention, more efficient use of office space, improve productivity and greater staffing flexibility (Holman, 2003).

As companies look to examine the landscape of the workforce, more and more they are looking closely at the distributed work environment concept as a way to preserve their existence and sustainability through the use of technology. In a book titled, *The Distributed Workplace: Sustainable Work Environments* (Harrison, Wheeler, & Whitehead, 2004), the authors expressed the concern that most companies have had on their minds in the past decade:

The relationship between sustainability and the build environment has always been a tortuous one: close but not warm. They're an uneasy pair Sustainability with its sometimes conflicting imperatives: ethical, practical, physical, economical. The built environment—a work of will masquerading as a force of nature. Perhaps as clash of fact and value. But at least, in certain key aspects, fixed. No longer (p. 1).

The above phenomenon is faced by companies around the globe and they have to strategically think about how they will tackle this issue as a competitive edge is harder and harder to get due to the changing market and workforce. Harrison et al. (2004) continue on the matter of sustainability by adding:

...Sustainability, once a simple matter for better resource use—difficult but achievable—now claims its rightful place at the shifting centre of all the issues raised by globalization. And the built environment—particularly the work environment- loses its monolithic status to stand revealed as a mercurial participant in the new economy. It is evident that the workplace is evolving in a distributed form to deal with these changed circumstances. It is equally evident that the fluidity of the distributed workplace will set society some urgent problems—not least in the field of sustainability (p. 1).

The authors described the issue that is in most CEO and executive teams' minds and narrows it down to sustainability. Staying relevant in this ever changing economy means that companies have to understand the true meaning of sustainability as it pertains to the barriers that have been broken down by the advancement of technology. Companies have to actively seek out strategies and solutions that will work for their organizations and employees while being financially responsible. As the authors of *The Distributed Workplace: Sustainable Work Environments* (2004) explain:

Sustainability needs to be seen as a dynamic process, not a fixed and attainable state. It is rather like the mathematical concept of a limit—an end point that does not exist as such, and cannot be reached, but represents the hypothetical end point of a tendency (p. 3).

Companies are constantly looking for ways to improve their practices on all aspect of the business: human and operational. Trying to stay ahead of the curve to maintain their competitive edge is a difficult task. As technological advancements continue to happen, and employee needs continue to evolve companies need to respond accordingly or it will cost them in the long run. Many organizations are either taking steps or making provisions to enter the distributed work environment community, or they are thinking about it as a strategic move for them to meet the needs of their talent pool and to ensure their survival. They understand that they are operating in a digital and knowledge age, and the "business as usual" concepts are no longer valid. Organizations need to keep up with the changing work patterns, which can be difficult, and at times, almost impossible to do. In a research paper titled *Successful Distributed Work Arrangements: a Developmental Approach* (2007), the authors explained that, given these economical and workforce circumstances, implementing a distributed work framework can look attractive to organizations, especially large organizations, because of the potential financial benefits; however they need to be sure that it is the right move for their organizations (Roper & Kim, 2007). As executive teams are turning toward distributed work environments, experts suggest that there are four factors surrounding this concepts that companies need to examine to make an informed decision: the organization, the employee, the work, and the support system that is needed to sustain such an environment (Roper & Kim, 2007).

First off, companies have to align their goals, objectives and culture as a whole to determine if a distributed work environment would work for them. They need to ensure that all three of these components are in sync and will not create any disadvantages for all or some of their employees, as well as the organization. In addition, they have to look at their current financial structure to ensure that they have the funds or can strategically locate funds to finance this major change in infrastructure. Further, they have to spend time determining if this change will positively or negatively impact their processes and productivity (Roper & Kim, 2007). Next, they have to examine the work that their companies perform to determine how conducive such an environment would be for that work. Distributed work environments work best with work that requires minimal interaction, such as programming, graphic design copy-writing, etc. (Roper & Kim, 2007). These types of work require only periodic interaction with team members and clients, as opposed to positions that need frequent interactions with others to complete their work: managers, and customer service representatives, as examples. Having a clear understanding of the work that is produced in the organization will guide an educated decision. Lastly, they have to examine how the work is completed. Roper and Kim (2007) referred to the concept of sequential and mutual work processes. Sequential work processes refer to "…process that reflect a one-way work flow and do not need frequent information exchange among workers to accomplish tasks" (Roper & Kim, 2007, p. 106). Mutual work processes refer to a "…work process that has a complex work flow and needs frequent and fast information exchange, frequent coordination and team-work" (Roper & Kim, 2007, p. 106). Understanding these type of processes support the decision making process as organizations can determine whether they can fully, partially or not venture out in the distributed work environment depending on if it makes sound business sense to them. Although technology advances allow for both processes to occur virtually, being comfortable that it will give the organization a competitive advantage is key.

Organizations need to also review the types of employees who are part of their organizations. Although technology can connect us in ways that we could not imagine, employees who need constant interactions with others whether because of the nature of their work, or need assistance in completing their work may not be the best candidates for distributed work environments. If the majority of the organization's employees fit in that category, then this concept may be detrimental to the company instead of helpful. Organizations with self-directed, self-motivated and disciplined employees who hold positions that do not require a high level of interaction would be ideal for the distributed work environment as they would be able to self-manage and thrive. Organizations have to be comfortable with the fact that not all employees are cut out for a distributed work environment. As Roper and Kim (2007) explain that organizations need to look for two attributes when analyzing if their employee base would be a good fit for a distributed work environment.

The two attributes to consider, according to Roper & Kim (2007), are the employees' work setting preferences and their ability to work in a distributed work style. Some employees would welcome the idea of work schedule flexibility, which in turn would allow them to take care of family obligations; on the other hand, there are workers who prefer the consistency of coming to and leaving work at a specific time and working in a specific office location (Roper & Kim, 2007). Organizations also need to look if the employees can effectively handle the level of flexibility and self-directedness that comes with a distributed work environment. Roper and Kim (2007) explained that:

Some workers need a high degree of face-to-face interaction and direct communication to effectively undertake their work, whereas other professional and knowledge workers usually a high degree of choices available to when, where, and how their work is undertaken. The former type of worker might need a permanent work location and the latter type of worker would be better for DWA [distributed work arrangements] (Roper & Kim, 2007, p. 107).

Further, organizations need to assess the level of employee engagement and motivation to determine if a distributed work environment would be beneficial to the employees and the company. Because of the rise of the distributed workplace, companies have had to deal with a concept called cyberslacking (O'Neil, Hambley & Chatellier, 2014). Cyberslacking refers to "...a phenomenon in which employees are distracted by non-work Internet browsing when they should be accomplishing work tasks" (O'Neill, Hambley, & Bercovich, 2014). This is an issue that has been present in the office environment and has transferred over to a larger scale into the distributed work environment due to the flexibility and autonomy provided to employees. This can be caused by the idea that the employees feel less engaged by virtue of being removed from a physical office location (O'Neill, Hambley, Greidanus, MacDonnell, & Kline, 2009). O'Neil et al. (2014) went on to explain that:

...we treat both cyberslacking and engagement as indicators of distributed work effectiveness, given that these are top-of-mind issues for employees and their managers in distributed contexts. Moreover, this suggests that advancing knowledge of the antecedents of distributed work effectiveness could be valuable for theory building and practical application (2014, p. 152).

As a result, employers need to assess employee personalities to determine if they would thrive or fail in a distributed work environment. The trait activation theory (Tett & Burnett 2003) suggests that employee effectiveness and performance level are high when there is a strong fit between the employee and the job duties that he needs to complete. O'Neil et al. (2014) furthers this concept by stating "specifically, person-job fit theory posits that employee attributes need to match the job environment to create high effectiveness levels, and distributed work may contain unique conditions that affect personality-job fit levels." This suggest that employers need to pay close attention to these traits to either conduct organizational restructuring to place employees in the right fit before moving them into a distributed work environment, or be selective about who participates in a distributed work environment versus who stays in a physical office. The most extreme case, if an employer wants to go 100% in the distributed work space, would be to let go of the employees who are not a great fit and hire new employees to fill the gaps.

Finally, organizations have to ensure that they have the necessary technology and other resources that will support the distributed work environment infrastructure. They have to make sure that workers can easily gain access to equipment and resources to be able to complete their work. The access to important data requires resources such as laptops, internet connectivity, wireless phones, satellite, cable, etc. which are all directly connected to technology (Roper & Kim, 2007). Without the necessary equipment and resources, distributed employees will not be able to perform their work which may be construed as them not doing what they are supposed to be doing, instead of the fact they cannot actually do their work because they do not have the needed tools. Organizations have to take a serious look at their technological infrastructure and assess their capabilities to determine if, in fact, they have the necessary platform to support a distributed work environment.

DISTRIBUTED WORK ENVIRONMENT IMPACT ON THE HUMAN CONDITION

Influencing Factors on the Human Condition

Employment in general has positive and negative impacts on the human condition. On the positive side, it allows employees to earn a living, care for their families, and save for retirement. In contrast, there are instances where employment has interfered with family life, caused undue stress and sickness, and fostered unhealthy environments filled with conflict and lack of trust. Distributed work environments comes with positive and negative impacts as well, some similar to the above listed, but manifested in different ways.

Distributed work environments provide employees with many potential benefits such as: "more flexible working hours, more time for home and family, reduced commuting, greater job autonomy, less disturbance whilst working, and the chance to remain in work despite moving home, becoming ill or taking family care roles" (Holman, 2003). As well, this type of work environment also brings societal benefit which include increases entrepreneurial activities, less pollution, increased community stability, and more efficient use of energy resources (Cascio, 2000).

In contrast, there are some negatives impacts that may emerge in a distributed work environment such as fewer chances for development and promotion, increased conflict between work and home; and social isolation (Holman, 2003.) However, to truly understand the impact of a distributed work environment on the human condition, there are social and individual factors that need consideration. Social factors that may determine the feasibility, success or failure of employees in this type of work environment include:

the socialization of distributed workers, communication between distributed workers and traditional office workers, decision making and communication within virtual teams (Holman, 2003). In regards to individual factors, some determinants of feasibility, success or failure of employees include the connection between personality, competencies and the distributed work environment, employee motivation and the psychological contract in which they enter, the connection of job characteristics and the well-being of employees, and the home and work interface (Holman, 2003).

Social Factor 1: Socialization of Distributed Workers

Employees need to be able to socialize with their colleagues and managers in order to build rapport and trust, which in turn fosters highly effective and cohesive teams and a healthy work environment. Distributed workers need this socialization even though they are not physically present in a physical traditional office. These employees do not have the natural opportunities to interact with other employees as they would if they were in the office on a regular basis, which then affects their immersion in the organizational culture. Of course if the organization starts off on a distributed work environment platform, this problem is lessened as no organizational culture has been created with the walls of an officer, but they still need to address this issue. This socialization issue may impact distributed workers differently depending on their level of intra-organizational contact within the organizations. Employees with high intra-organizational contact will have an easier time socializing virtually with other virtual employees or their office counterparts, and employees with low intra-organizational contact will have a harder time dealing with this issue. As Holman (2003) expresses:

...teleworkers with high intra-organizational contact, or who regularly use real-time communication media (e.g. telephone, [instant messaging]) are more likely to be socialized through natural processes. In contrast teleworkers with low intra-organizational contact and that use non-real time telecommunications (e.g. E-mail), are less likely to be socialized through natural means (2003, p. 205).

Therefore, especially for the workers with low intra-organizational contact, organizations who engage in distributed work environments must intervene and ensure that they are putting in place socialization mechanisms, using technology, of which distributed workers can take advantage to stay connected and feel part of the organization. Interventions such as regular virtual weekly meetings, minimum office presence requirements, social programs participation and off-site social events are all good strategies to use and tackle this issue (Holman, 2003) are all good strategies to use to tackle this issue. Such interventions prevent employees, especially the ones with low intra-organizational contact, from feeling isolated from the rest of the organization and begin to be disengaged and de-motivated, which then will lead to larger issues.

Social Factor 2: Communication Between Distributed Workers and Traditional Office Workers

Effective formal and informal communication is key to the success of an organization. It is often difficult to ensure that all lines of communication in an organization are being utilized effectively, and it can be even harder within a distributed work environment where workers are spread across the country and around the globe. The types of communication that occur between employees and managers within one physical office naturally are going to be different from the types of communication that occur with distributed workers. As well, group communication will be higher in the office than in the distributed work environment.

However, organizations have to mimic the office type communications as much as possible for the distributed workers in order to keep them informed and engaged in a timely manner. Using technology, they need to recreate the office communication experience for the distributed workers so that the lines of communication stay open and the distributed employees feel part of the team no matter how far away they are. Technologies such as instant messaging, voice-over IP phones, online meeting platforms, are just a few ways to mitigate this issue. Obtaining these technologies is the first step, but organizations have to ensure that the implementation and communication on the use of these technologies are thorough so that employees understand what, why and how to use them. Such communication integration will help both the employees with high and low intra-organizational contact within the company. Another aspect of communication integration, if these all of these technologies are not accessible, is to be comfortable with a lower level of communication among office workers and distributed workers, and most importantly ensure that employees being assigned to distributed work are comfortable with that level of communication and that it will not hinder their job satisfaction, productivity and quality of work. Holman (2003) summarizes this idea by saying:

Whilst teleworkers with lower intra-organizational communication requirements to perform their work tasks may experience fewer problems with task-related communication ... communication can have an important function beyond direct facilitation of work. Therefore, it is important to be sure that managers and co-workers are happy with low levels of intra-organizational communication, a separate "cyberspace" subculture based on mutual support and information sharing may be beneficial to teleworkers (2003, p. 206).

Communication can have a large impact, positive or negative, on distributed workers' engagement and motivation; therefore, it behooves organizations to invest time and technological resources into ensuring that communication is not a barrier for their employees.

Social Factor 3: Decision Making and Communication within Virtual Teams

Decision making is a normal part of the work environment and team members often need to communicate in order to ensure that everyone is on the same page to make decisions on how to approach and complete projects. Although distributed workers are virtually located, they are not exempt from team decision making. In fact, is it crucial that these employees stay in communication with their team members and are included in the decision making process so that they can effectively make their contributions to the projects. Often distributed workers report that the quality of the information that received, related to performance feedback, organizational politics and organizational strategy is reduced (Holman, 2003). This is often due to the subpar quality of the technology infrastructure of the organizations. They are not taking into account the impact of technology, or the lack thereof, can have on the productivity and motivation of employees when it begins to interfere with their work.

As a result, organizations are encouraged to create channels where the virtual employees can participate in the decision making process. Research has shown that opportunities to take part in decisions have decreased for distributed workers due to the remote access of their job, unless they are in high "extra-organizational" positions where they are in constant contact with their office counterparts and/or clients (Holman, 2003). Therefore, companies have to find viable solutions to include these workers in making decisions. Some examples of channels could be attending meetings at the office, online meeting tools with video capabilities, etc. However the organizations choose to address this issue to up to them; but the bottom line is to continue to foster a psychologically healthy work environments, employees need to feel vested in the organization through the decision making process.

Individual Factor 1: Connection between Personality, Competencies and Distributed Work Environment

Not all employees are suited to be distributed workers. Some employees thrive in the traditional office environment, but may not thrive as much in a distributed work environment. The same goes for some people whose performance will increase if they have an opportunity to participate in a distributed work environment, assuming that they have the proper technological resources to effectively completer their work and communicate with their virtual colleagues. One way to determine if an employee would be best suited for the office or a distributed work environment is to analyze employee personalities through the five basic dimensions, also referred to as the "Big Five" (Holman, 2003). These dimensions include extraversion, emotional stability, agreeableness, conscientiousness, and openness to experience (Holman, 2003). Evaluating employees using these dimensions can shed light and give a fairly accurate indication on whether or not they will do well in a distributed environment. If some employees score low on these dimensions, it may be an indication that they would do better in an office environment because they will have the needed interactions to help them develop these dimensions over time. On the other hand, employees who score high on these dimensions may be well-suited, and probably would even perform at a higher level because of their self-directedness and motivation level.

According to Holman (2003), personality plays a big role in making the determination of who would be best suited for distributed work especially in the case of manager feedback. In the distributed work environment manager feedback is either minimal or non-existent. Therefore, if employees require regular feedback to validate their performance, then it is best that they remain in an office environment because they will have direct contact with the manager. Holman (2003) goes further to make the point that:

… the characteristics associated with conscientiousness, such as persistence, care, capacity for hard work, and being responsible have been shown to influence the accomplishment of tasks. We would also expect that people who work with high levels of intra and/or extra-organizational communication are likely to be successful if they are higher on extraversion, agreeableness, and openness to experience (2003, p. 207).

In addition, personality plays a role in the way employees acquire knowledge. In terms of the employees' preferred learning medium, personality can be an indicator of potential success or failure in a distributed work environment. Some employees are not comfortable with using technology to complete their work or to learn new concepts. These employees who are more comfortable and learn better in a classroom environment and would be better suited for the office environment where they can attend training sessions being offered through the organization's training department or attend other outside face-to-face trainings. Their learning preference does not necessarily fit into a distributed work environment platform, as, due to the various locations, distributed workers usually attend online training and courses to further their knowledge. They require minimal supervision and are self-directed to complete the course or training at their own pace, and they are comfortable with using technology as an avenue through which their learning opportunities are administered. Consequently, having high levels of extraversion, openness to experience and conscientiousness would be important to have because they relate to how well people perform in training programs (Holman2003). Research has indicated that intelligence is directly and positively related to work performance, which furthers the idea of learning preferences and also be an indicator of how well employees will perform as distributed workers in terms of success in training programs, knowledge retention and application (Holman 2003).

Finally, personality also affects how individuals interact in teams. Employees in distributed work environments still need to have and practice the traditional teamwork skills such as collaboration, effective communication, performance orientation and goal clarity (Holman, 2003). However, they have to find new ways to perform these skills since they no longer have the office environment where a meeting can be called at any given time and all team members gather in a room to discuss a project. Given this fact, researchers have established the below list of personality competencies that employees should possess in order to be effective distributed team members. The competencies have been grouped into four major categories (Holman, 2003, p. 208):

1. Personal competencies, such as self-discipline, self-direction, self-motivation, capacity for self –assessment, tough-mindedness, tenacity, personal integrity and self-confidence
2. Inter-personal competencies, such as strong verbal and written communication skills, negotiation skills, trusting others and assertiveness
3. Generic task competencies, such as organization skills, practical orientation, basing decisions on facts, flexibility, ability to take independent decision, time management skills, and possessing consistent, productive and organized work habits
4. Technical competencies, such as information and communications technology literacy, and good subject-matter knowledge

Although further research needs to be conducted on the connection of personality, competencies as they relate to a distributed work environment, employers and employees can use the above practices as means to determine fit. Interacting in a distributed work environment is an extensive undertaking; therefore, using all available avenues to make the right decisions is imperative as the impact is great both on the organization and employees in terms of business success, employee engagement and job satisfaction.

Individual Factor 2: Employee Motivation and the Psychological Contract

The landscape of human resources in organization has evolved over the years and has shifted from offering employees stability and predictability in their work to asking employees to be intrinsically motivated and take control of their role in the workplace. Holman (2003) expresses it as such:

...there has been a movement away from the traditional psychological contract where employers have offered career and employment stability. Instead, the emerging psychological contract emphasizes flexibility, mobility, where employees should expect to be flexible in their work practices, be prepared to take responsibility for their own training and career development, and be prepared to move jobs regularly (2003, p. 208).

Due to this shifting philosophy, employee motivation and commitment are affected because they no longer have the guarantee that as long as they perform their job tasks satisfactorily, they will remain stable in their jobs. Such uncertainty pushes employees to always be looking for the next job as they do not know if they will be able to fulfill the future demands of their current jobs. In terms of distributed workers, this can cause problems due to the isolation factor that exists with working virtually. Components such as an office network, counseling services and unions are not readily accessible to them, so they may see it as psychological contract violation on the part of the organization (Holman, 2003). Therefore, to attempt to remedy this issue and promote successful distributed work environments, organizations need to present "…clear career paths and training opportunities [which] may encourage employee retention and motivation without necessarily affecting the establishment of a mutually beneficial flexible psychological contract" (Holman, 2003, p. 208).

Individual Factor 3: Connection of Job Characteristics and Employee Well-being

Just as traditional work environments can be psychologically healthy or toxic and harmful, distributed work environments are no exception. Researchers have explored this topic and have identified that psychologically healthy jobs generally include …"greater skills use, greater variety of work, greater opportunities for control through task discretion or participation in decisions, balanced demands from work, performance feedback and job security, high clarity concerning tasks, better physical working conditions, higher wages, greater social value accorded to the nature of the work and more support and contact with others" (Holman, 2003). Depending on the type of job within the distributed work environments, it is likely that task discretion, variety in work and skill usage may decrease. For example, this can be in jobs that have low knowledge intensity due to established output control and monitoring mechanisms given the routine nature of the work. In that case task discretion variety and skill usage are decreased, taking away from the psychological health of the job. One way to resolve this issue by allowing distributed workers, whether in low or high knowledge intensity positions, to have the autonomy over their work schedule and task completion. Technology plays a big role in accomplishing this because it has the capabilities to provide the employees with a sense of autonomy and support their success if organizations invest in the right technological resources for these employees. This will give them a sense of ownership and responsibility to the work that they do.

To enhance employee well-being, organizations have to take steps to ensure their distributed workers have psychologically healthy jobs. Researchers have suggested several ways in which employers can accomplish this task. One strategy, is to ensure that the employees have access to all of the technology needed to successfully complete their work, as they would have access in a traditional office. Another strategy is to establish clear goals and objectives for the workers and help them identify the important role that they play (Holman, 2003). Another strategy is to ensure that employees have readily access to information and channels of communication to discuss and clarify the information if needed. This practice can also help in the reduction of the social isolation that distributed workers too often experience due to the non-existent office experience (Holman, 2003). To reduce the risk of poor physical working conditions that may occur in low knowledge intensity jobs due to low wages and the routine nature of the work, companies need to ensure that they are providing the necessary resources to those employees, in addition to sharing information. These employees are more likely to experience isolation and burn out due lack of resources, where they have to perform additional steps to complete tasks that can be streamlined with the proper resources and equipment. Finally, offering appropriate training opportunities to not only training on job function, but on maintaining a healthy distributed work environment. Knowing steps they can take to improve their work conditions promotes autonomy and higher levels of job satisfaction and fulfillment.

Individual Factor 4: Home and Work Interface

Working from home comes with its set of benefits and challenges. As previously mentioned in this chapter, employees enjoy work flexibility and autonomy, as well as more time to spend completing family obligations. However, distributed workers who work from home face certain issues whether or not they have families. For employees without families, they struggle with creating an environment that is conducive to productive work by restricting distraction from neighbors, community activities, friends, and other social activities. For workers with families, they struggle with setting boundaries of work and home especially if there are family members present during their self-set work hours. The idea of separating work from family for a period of time as in a traditional office environment is non-existent for remote workers as their office is also home. The idea of work and family conflict arises and creates a certain level of stress on both the worker and family members (Holman, 2003).

These issues are sure to have an impact on work performance and job satisfaction if not handled appropriately. As organizations work with distributed workers to help them create a healthy and productive work environment, considering and being emotionally intelligent to the family and home demands placed on these workers can help. Training managers to be sensitive to these demands and structuring their work using a project based format with milestones and deadlines may be a positive alternative that supports flexibility and autonomy. In turn, employees' stress level will decrease, and they will be better positioned to deliver quality work and have high levels of job satisfaction and vested interest in the organization.

MANAGEMENT AND DISTRIBUTED WORK ENVIRONMENTS

Distributed workers require a different kind of manager than traditional office employees. To begin with, based on the earlier explanations of social and individual factors associated with distributed work environment, selecting of remote employees and their managers need to be a systematic process that goes beyond just matching job duties to personal candidate characteristics (Omari & Standen, 2000).

Given the nature of distributed work, management style matters in that specific, sometimes non-traditional and unconventional, strategies have to be employed to support the needs of the remote worker. Managing based on outputs may not be the best approach. As stated by Holman (2003) based on the work of Sparrow and Omeeren (2000) "Consequently, the usual adage of managing teleworkers by outputs—in of and by itself—may prove inappropriate for teleworkers, possibly leading to problems such as reduces well-being, reduced trust and low quality work." Holman (2003) suggests that managers need to play close attention to the social aspect of remote work due to the removal of the traditional office, they need to make a conscious effort is developing social networks, support systems, open channels of communication and establish trust in order to create environment where organizational learning can take place (Tregaski & Daniels, 2000). Further, human resources has an important role in identifying the organizational culture that currently exists and ensure that proper matching of managers and employees, as well as providing appropriate trainings occur to promote culture integration in the distributed work environment. As summarized by Holman (2003):

...human resource managers should be aware of the cultures and contexts in each area of their organization and should endeavor to ensure that telework schemes, workers and managers suit those cultures and contexts (since changing the cultures and contexts to suit teleworking is a longer-term strategy) (2003, p. 212).

One final important aspect of management involvement in distributed work environment is the training of distributed workers. Training and development of remote workers is just as important, if not more important than traditional office workers due to the added circumstance of distance. Holman (2003) suggests that there are several areas where training can be beneficial to remote workers, such as communication, self-management, corporate values, time management, off-site health and safety requirements, company cyber security policy, legal and tax requirements related to working from home, computer operation and maintenance, and job-specific trainings. Managers need to work with distributed workers to facilitate access to these trainings and create a communication system that will allow them to monitor the application of knowledge gained from these trainings. As well, they need use different methods of training delivery such as face-to-face, online learning, webinars, online instructional manuals, etc. to ensure that the employees have all the resources and training they need to perform at their highest potential. In addition, managers of distributed workers also need to attend trainings to prepare them for the different aspects of distributed work compared to the traditional office environment, as well as company policies and procedures of distributed work, communication and socialization needs, and support systems (Tregaskis & Daniels, 2000).

Properly selecting and preparing managers to support distributed workers is a crucial function, as they can determine the success or failure of the remote work process. If understanding, empathy and mutual trust and respect do not exist between managers and employees, then the odds of a positive, productive and long term working relationship are slim to none.

EXAMPLES OF IMPLEMENTING DISTRIBUTED WORK ENVIRONMENTS USING TECHNOLOGY

In researching the popularity of distributed work environments, over 125 companies have adopted this method of doing business, some of them are in their first or second year in the adoption, and others have been employing this method for over 14 years, and from the looks of it seems to be working for them. A company named FlexJobs, which provides services to candidates seeking flexible schedules, telecommuting, freelance and part-time jobs and as well as a distributed work environment company itself, keeps track of other companies that have fully or partially adopted the distributed work environment (Shin, 2016). The list of companies that they provide has grown 26 companies in 2014 to 76 companies in 2015, and in 2016 the list grew to 125 companies (Shin, 2016). These companies range for HR/recruiting and education to IT/computer. Based on these increases, Flexjobs is estimating that by the year 2020, 50% of employees will work remotely (Shin, 2016). Included in that list are:

Articulate which is a company that develops web, mobile, and desktop applications for online learning space that are rapidly growing, and for which it has won awards. Articulate has been a distributed work environment company for over 14 years, and the management team has found the method successful for both their employees and the business. According to their founder and CEO, Adam Schwartz, all 150 employees work 100 percent of the time from home and their productivity level and quality of work is exemplary. Schwartz (Reynolds, 2015) added "We've always been fully distributed, so it's in our DNA. Because working remotely requires a lot of trust, you have to put people front and center. Ours are smart, kind, fun, and results-oriented, which makes Articulate a pretty magical place to work." Schwartz further expressed ""Being able to choose where and when we work empowers us to be more productive, more engaged, and more balanced in every aspect of our lives. After 14 years as a fully remote company, we're convinced a distributed environment isn't just good for our employees. It's also one of the key reasons we've been so successful as a company" (Shin, 2016).

Mozilla, a not-for-profit organization and the developer of Firefox, also support a distributed work environment, as well as remote workers around the world. They accommodate employees who want to work from home or in one of their remote offices in 30 countries around the world. The company explains "We have 13 global offices and people working in more than 30 countries. If you work best from home, that's not a problem. We can support you anywhere" (Reynolds, 2015).

Equation Research, is a strategic research company working with clients on brand equity and strategy, concept testing, advertising testing and tracking, and community panels (Reynolds, 2015). Its business model is quite impressive and the way they deliver services to their clients is quite unconventional. The CEO, Mike Travis commented and said "When we launched back in 2000, we set out to build and grow a company that NEVER HAD AN OFFICE. It was not a fear of the old food in the back of the refrigerator that drove us—it was the inspiration of building a different kind of experience for the people that shared in this adventure. It was part of the innovation we craved" (Reynolds, 2015).

Varsity Tutors, a private tutoring company that provides virtual and in home tutoring services, or where ever it is convenient for their clients. They provide one-on-one tutoring, they have over 20,000 instructors and a 24/7 online learning platform. The company prides itself in the "no commuting time" concepts as their instructors do most of their work using the online learning platform (Reynolds, 2015).

The list of these companies continues to grow and from the initial response to this movement, it is highly unlikely to see a decrease in this growth anytime soon.

In looking at the list of over 125 companies implementing the distributed work environment model, it begs the question: how do they do it? What strategies have they use to ensure that their employee and business needs are being met? In looking at companies that have been leading the way in distributed work environments, three main strategies have helped them be successful with this method and have grown their companies substantially over the years. These three main strategies are open communication, adequate resources and equipment, and promoting work/life balance.

Open Communication

In researching these companies, open communication, as a key to their success, was a recurring theme. Without having a strong communication system, these companies would most likely crumble as most or all of their employees are located across the country and the globe and not in central locations. Being a remote employee who feels that he/she is missing out on important information and discussions because the avenues of communication are not as robust as they need to be can be a very scary and demotivating position to be in. As a result, these companies employ several communication methods to keep their employees informed, engaged and productive. Let's take Automattic, for example. Automattic is the company that created WordPress.com and several other services for WordPress.com customers. They have over 400 employees spread across 40 countries to help to power companies' websites and their website needs (CloudPeeps, 2015). In their business model, to promote open communication, they have chosen to not use email. Instead they have worked on streamlining their communication channels to ensure that it is open and engaging. To replace the use of email, Automattic employees use an instant messaging chat system and an internal blog system, called P2, which comes with its own Google alert system so that employees are notified whenever new content has been posted on the blog (CloudPeeps, 2015). Automattic is also using an unconventional way of communicating with potential employees. Instead conducting traditional or virtual initial interviews, their process includes the following (Cloud-Peeps, 2015, p. 2):

1.   The CEO screens all resumes
2.   The hiring lead sends quality candidates a note
3.   The hiring lead then pings them on Skype – and has a Q&A via Skype chat
4.   The candidate completes a paid trial project on their own time
5.   The CEO has a final review chat on Skype with the candidate

Even more unconventional is that there have been times when new hires have been brought on board without ever having a single voice interview (CloudPeeps, 2015). This method seems to be working for Automattic because it has seen 100% employee retention in its design and growth department (Cloud-Peeps, 2015). The CEO supported this process by saying "This has been amazing for the company in that we can attract and retain the best talent without them having to be in New York or San Francisco or one of the traditional tech centers" (CloudPeeps, 2015).

Another example is with Zapier, the company that creates software that connects applications (apps) that are used for the automation of tasks and leveraging more out of exciting data. Zapier takes communication very seriously with its remote teams, and it uses a series of communication apps across the company that are specific to each department and its functions. For example, when a new hire comes on board in their marketing team, he/she is provided with a list of communication apps, such as the one shown below to get them acquainted and equipped to engage in the open communication platform (CloudPeeps, 2015, p. 5):

1.   Slack for ongoing chatter in their designated channels
2.   Trello Editorial Calendar board for discussion around individual blog posts
3.   Google Docs for Weekly Marketing Meeting notes
4.   Google Calendar for keeping up with each other's schedules, including out of office
5.   Async (their internal blog modeled after Automattic's P2 mentioned above) for Friday Updates and Monthly Marketing Updates
6.   The team@zapier.com email for Daily Recaps (automated), hiring decisions, hiring announcements, time-sensitive news or questions

The above tools and several others have kept the employees engaged and productive, which in turn has made the company successful.

Another method of open communication being using is called "daily standup meetings. A company named Groove, known for its exemplary story telling approach to present website content for their customers, values communication and understands its importance to keep a remote team productive and engaged. Groove also supports the idea of employees working during the times they are most productive; in other words, they do not have the expectations for employees to be at their desk at home or wherever at all times. This provides great flexibility for the employees and allow them to produce their best work every time. However, Groove also understands that, with this type of flexibility, having a good grip on what everyone is working on is crucial to keep projects moving and delivered; therefore, they instituted "daily stand up meetings" where everyone comes on and shares with the rest of the team what they are working on for the day, have weekly team calls, share their quarterly and annual goals, as well as ask or answer any questions, as well as have weekly meetings calls to discuss projects and any other issues that may have arisen throughout the week (CloudPeeps, 2015). Groove is able to provide such flexibility to its employees because of the strong culture of trust, principle and habits that they have engraved in their company. They are selective in their hiring practices; they look for candidates that will fit in their culture and move their mission forward. As they are screening potential employees, they look for specific qualities in the candidates such as (CloudPeeps, 2015, p. 6):

1.   Have they worked remotely before or ran their own small business
2.   Are they mature decision maker, meaning they can make the best decisions for customers and manage their energy on their own
3.   Are they extraordinary communicators

A combination of these attributes is hard to find, but when it is found, Groove is confident that the employee will be a valuable asset to company and contribute to its success.

Companies like Automattic, Zapier and Groove, along with many others, have found that one key component of having a successful distributed work environment is open and streamlined communication. Keeping up with employees across the globe and not at a specific central location can be a difficult task; however, they seem to have figured a system that works for them, that just may work for other companies who are thinking about moving in the distributed work environment direction.

Adequate Resources and Equipment

Another strategy that companies in the distributed work environment have employed is ensuring that their remote employees have adequate resources and equipment to do their work. These companies realize that without the appropriate resources, employees will get frustrated and not perform to their highest potential. In addition, having remote employees means low overhead costs as these companies do not usually have headquarters or central locations. Therefore, they are able to invest in top of the line equipment and resources needed. On example of this strategy comes from Automattic. They ensure that they provide everything that the employees need to be comfortable and do their best work. Some examples of the resources that Automattic provides to its employees are (CloudPeeps, 2015, p. 2):

1.   The best equipment for doing their jobs
2.   A stipend for improving their home offices
3.   Allowing any team to meet wherever they want for a "hack week"
4.   Once a year, the entire company gets together for a "grand meetup" in a beautiful location
5.   Employees make their own schedules

Another example comes from a company called Buffer, which provides services to clients to help them drive traffic to their website, increase fan engagement and save time through social media. They too understand that they need to provide the best resources and equipment to their employees. Being present around the globe means that their employees have to be available to clients at different time zones. Therefore, employee satisfaction is key as these employees interact directly with the clients and need to provide impeccable customer service. As a result, Buffer ensures that its employees have Kindles, laptops, software such as Timezone.co, used to know when and where team members and clients are; Speak.io, used to provide fast video conferencing; and Hipchat, for regular chat communication among team members (CloudPeeps, 2015). Buffer, like Automattic, also puts on gatherings in a nice location for all of its employees to meet face-to-face, networking and engage in team building activities (CloudPeeps, 2015).

Providing these resources motivate employees to do their best because they see that the companies invested in them and understands the value they bring to the team. So many times, employees do not have the adequate resources to do their work; they have to get creative and make do with what they have. After a while, they get frustrated and demotivated and end up leaving the company. This is an issue for companies as these employees who leave, take with them vast amount of knowledge that was not transferred and companies basically have to scramble to get the work done. So it behooves all companies, remote or headquartered to be sure and invest in providing the necessary resources to their employees as the companies mentioned above have, to ensure productivity, job satisfaction and success.

Promoting Work/Life Balance

Another aspect of distributed work environment is the work/life balance concept. Chances are that being remote employees most likely means that they work from home where their families live. Therefore, it is important to ensure that a balanced work/life environment exists where there is a precise amount of time set aside for work and a precise amount of time set for family. This way employees can enjoy their work and their family lives and not feel that they have to choose one over the other. Companies who are part of the distributed work environment community understand the importance of this concept and take steps to support their employees in maintaining that crucial balance.

One example involves a company called Baremetrics that provides data mining services to companies. They strongly believe in the work/life balance concept and have created an environment where employees are able to achieve the balance while performing at their highest potential and spending quality time with their families. One thing that they recognize as a priority is self-care, and they encourage employees to practice self-care by providing them with these tips (CloudPeeps, 2015, p. 7):

1. Have set work hours and stick to them
2. Exercise every single day
3. Alternate between sitting and standing
4. Eat well
5. Take frequent breaks

They feel that by following these tips, employees are less likely to burn out and their job satisfaction level will continue to increase.

A second example comes from a company called Help Scout, that leads the help desk software support industry. At Help Scout, they understand the anxiety that new employees face especially of they are remote employees. As a result, they have developed a buddy system that is solely there to support the new employees when they first get on board, and ease the stress and anxiety that comes with starting a new job. One of their marketing team members had this to say about the buddy system:

We figure being new at work isn't so far removed from being the new kid at school. Wouldn't it be nice to make a friend on the first day? For every new Help Scout teammate, someone who's been on board for a while steps up and becomes their go-to guy/gal who shows them the ropes. Work friends matter, and although they naturally form over time, feeling settled in shouldn't wait... A new buddy is especially important for remote work because you're not meeting a ton of people face-to-face your first few weeks. With so much to take in, now is not the time to let things get quiet (CloudPeeps, 2015, p. 10).

When new employees come onboard, team members have a list of activities that they can engage in with their buddy. Some of these activities include (CloudPeeps, 2015, p. 10):

1. Check-in every couple of days to see how things are going
2. Share a story from the team retreats, or what it's like to hang out in Boston
3. Share "unwritten rules," like the subtle difference between the #general and #offtopic channels in Slack
4. Have a video chat over Appear.in or Skype
5. Give them the run-down on who to ask for what

Such a system allows the new employees to get engrained in the Help Scout culture and be part of the family. Alleviating the stress of a new job in this way allows the new employees get on boarded at a much faster pace, which reduces the backlash that stress can have on their own families. Employees from this company and others mentioned above have written and expressed gratitude for the care they have been afforded through these companies which has allowed them to live happier and more fulfilled lives due to the unconventional way they work.

CONCLUSION

As presented in this chapter, the landscape of the work environment is changing due to the advancement of technology and more companies are considering or implementing distributed work environments. This type of work environment can be beneficial to organizations and employees if implemented correctly, using the right technology with the right employees and managers. In contrast, they can come at the detriment of organizations and employees if proper human and technological systems are not put in place. Over 125 companies in 2016 have fully or partially implemented the concept of a distributed work environment. They all have had their lessons learned, but they are pushing forward with the concept and are seeing positive results for their companies and employees.

As we examined the concept of a distributed work environment, we focused on the reasons why companies are entering this realm. The main reasons are for sustainability and having a competitive edge. In addition, companies have to respond to the needs of a new generation of employees who are looking for flexibility and autonomy in how, when and where they complete their work.

In implementing a distributed work environment, organizations have to consider several things, such as aligning their goals, objectives and culture as a whole so that they can clearly see if a system as a distributed work environment would work for their business and employees. They have to ensure that they have a robust technology infrastructure to support such an environment. They also have to look at the types of work and services that they provide to ensure that the same level of service and productivity or higher can be accomplished through a distributed work environment. In addition, companies have to examine the types of employees they have to determine if they would be a good fit for such a work environment. They need to figure out, based on what they know and have observed about employees, if they would thrive in a remote work environment. Looking for behaviors like self-directedness, self-motivation, time management, to name a few, are key to a successful distribute work environment employee integration. Further, employers need to make sure that they have the necessary resources, equipment and systems to support the distributed work environment infrastructure to promote business and employee success.

As with any system, distributed work environment have a definite impact on the human condition. As a result, careful considerations must be made to ensure that a distributed work approach is the best course of action for their employees. To make this determination, companies and employees need to pay attention to social and individual factors that surround the distributed work environment concept. The social factors include socialization, communication between remote and office workers, and decision making and communication with virtual teams. Individual factors include the connection that exists between personality, competencies and distributed work environments; employee motivation and psychological contract; the connection that exists between job characteristics and employee well-being; and the home and work interface. Failure to examine all of these factors to determine the best course of action on deciding on distributed work environments, will put organizations at a disadvantage because they will not have a clear picture of how their employees measure up against these factors in order for them to make sound decisions.

We also looked at the management of distributed work employees and how it differs from managing traditional office employees. Managing remote workers is not an easy task; therefore, human resources professionals have to ensure that they match the right employees and managers together for such a work environment as the communication, socialization and resource needs for these employees are different from the needs, for the most part, of traditional office employees. In addition, human resources and managers have to ensure that adequate training opportunities are available for both managers and employees to become familiar with the components of distributed work environments.

Finally, we looked at some examples of companies that have implemented a distributed work environment and how they have managed to make it successful. In reviewing these companies, there were three main practices they had in common that seem to be integral parts of their success: open communication, adequate resources and equipment, and promoting work/life balance. These three components seem to resonate with employees at these companies, and have allowed them to become stronger teams.

In the end, although distributed work environments need to be further researched both on the organizational and human aspects, the concept seems promising to companies as long as it makes sense for them. Given the continued rise of the digital age, distributed work environments may become the norm in the near future; therefore, it behooves organizations to be proactive and take the necessary steps to prepare their employees and organizational infrastructure for a possible change in that direction.

REFERENCES

Behling, O. (1998). Employee Selection: Will intelligence and conscientiousness do the job? *The Academy of Management Executive, 12*, 77–86.

Cascio, W. F. (2000). Managing a virtual workplace. *The Academy of Management Executive, 14*, 81–90.

CloudPeeps Team. (2015). Top 10 companies winning at remote work culture and their secrets. *CloudPeeps*. Retrieved from http://blog.cloudpeeps.com/top-10-companies-winning-at-remote- work- culture/

Cole, S. M., Achanhals, J. A., & Vallilww, G. W., IV. (2002). System and method for supporting a worker in a distributed work environment. *IFI Claims Patent Services*. Retrieved from https://www.google.com/patents/US6359711

Harrison, A., Wheeler, P., & Whitehead, C. (2004). *The distributed workplace: Sustainable work environment*. New York, NY: Spoon Press.

Holman, D. (2003). *The new workplace: A guide to the human impact of modern working practices*. Hoboken, NJ: Wiley.

Kramer, J. (2011). Why distributed teams are making your traditional office obsolete. *Fullstack*. Retrieved from http://gofullstack.com/why-distributed-teams-are-making-your-traditional-office- obsolete

Omari, M., & Standen, P. (2000). Selection for telework. In K. Daniels, D. Lamnf, & P. Standen (Eds.), Managing Telework: Perspectives from Human Resource Management and Work Psychology. London: Thomson Learning.

ONeill, T. A., Hambley, L. A., & Chatellier, G. S. (2014). Cyberslacking, engagement, and personality in distributed environments. *Computers in Human Behavior, 40*, 152–160. doi:10.1016/j.chb.2014.08.005

ONeill, T. A., Hambley, L. A., Greidanus, N. S., MacDonnell, R., & Kline, T. J. B. (2009). Predicting teleworker success: An exploration of personality, motivational, situational, and job characteristics. *New Technology, Work and Employment, 24*(2), 144–162. doi:10.1111/j.1468-005X.2009.00225.x

ONeill, T. A. A., Hambley, L. H., & Bercovich, A. (2014). Prediction of cyberslacking when employees are working away. *Computers in Human Behavior, 34*, 291–298. doi:10.1016/j.chb.2014.02.015

Reynolds, B. W. (2015). 76 virtual companies and distributed teams. *FLexjobs*. Retrieved from https://www.flexjobs.com/blog/post/76-virtual- companies-and-distributed-teams/

Robins, J. (2014). *What is a Distributed Company?* Lullabot. Retrieved from https://www.lullabot.com/articles/what-is-a-distributed-company.

Roper, K. A., & Kim, J. H. (2007). Successful distributed work arrangements: A developmental approach. *Journal of Facilities Management, 5*(2), 103–114. doi:10.1108/14725960710751852

Shin, L. (2016). At these 125 companies, all or most employees work remotely. *Forbes*. Retrieved from http://www.forbes.com/sites/laurashin/2016/03/31/at-these-125-companies- all-or-most- employees-work-remotely/#7ebf93554d94

Sparrow, P., & Omereen, V. (2000). Teleworking and psychological contract: a new division of labour. In K. Daniels, D. Lamnf, & P. Standen (Eds.), Managing Telework: Perspectives from Human Resource Management and Work Psychology. London: Thomson Learning.

Tett, R. P., & Burnett, D. D. (2003). A personality trait-based interactionist model of job performance. *The Journal of Applied Psychology*, 88(3), 500–517. doi:10.1037/0021-9010.88.3.500 PMID:12814298

Tregaskis, O., & Daniels, K. (2000). Organizational Learning. In K. Daniels, D. Lamnf, & P. Standen (Eds.), Managing Telework: Perspectives from Human Resource Management and Work Psychology. London: Thomson Learning.

KEY TERMS AND DEFINITIONS

Self-Motivation: Initiative to undertake or continue a task or activity without another's prodding or supervision.

Teleworker: Employees who work from home or satellite locations for an organization.

Socialization: A continuing process whereby an individual acquires a personal identity and learns the norms, values, behavior, and social skills appropriate to his or her social position.

Intra-Organizational: The level to which an employees has built strong relationships with their colleagues within an organization.

Self-Directed: The ability to guide, manage or regulate oneself without supervision.

Communication: The process of imparting or interchange of thoughts, opinions, or information by speech, writing, or signs.

Virtual Teams: A team of employees working together from different remote locations. The majority of their collaboration occurs online.

Personality: The sum total of the physical, mental, emotional, and social characteristics of an individual. The organized pattern of behavioral characteristics of the individual.

Chapter 20
Cognitive Investment Into the Interaction Society

Linda Marie Ellington
Southern New Hampshire University, USA

ABSTRACT

There is a cascade of interest in the topic of interactive time and space. and it might may be useful to align our cognitive investment that contributes to the operational goals of our thinking, our beliefs, and reactions to the phase of co-evolution of the human with the interaction society. If we want to build a rich understanding of how our mental assets influence involvement into this unique society, we need to be able to make a case for the crucial role of framing how the digital intergalactic transforms individuals and society. The mode of interactions may not be instruments of cognitive evolution, but the how of weaving together different perspectives of human development and engagement with cutting-edge interaction technology may be a significant player in the new cyborg society order.

"If every tool, when ordered, or even of its own accord, could do the work that befits it ... then there would be no need of either of apprentices for the master or of slaves for the lords. -Aristotle

INTRODUCTION

Even though fiction, let us begin with Syne Mitchell's book, *Technogenesis* (2002) that introduced her readers to an interaction society where almost everyone on earth is connected to a worldwide net, and in which the main character discovered the existence of an intelligence called Gestalt-a-self-aware entity generated by the collected consciousness of eight billion networked people. One might ask before we begin this chapter, is her book really fiction? So, let us get underway with this chapter that hopefully peaks the reader's inquisitive mind to seek to affirm their curiosity for experimentation with, and expansion of, the scope of cognitive embodiment within the digital space. Rather than providing exuberant accounts, this chapter illustrates and tries to make sense of the important changes occurring in relational life.

The digital space raises a variety of issues as we try to understand them, their place in our lives, and their consequences for our personhood and relationships with others in society (Baym, 2015). Churchill,

DOI: 10.4018/978-1-5225-2838-8.ch020

Snowden & Munroe (2012) defined space in this interaction society landscape as a terrain that can be inhabited or populated by individuals, encouraging a sense of shared place. They expanded on this by sharing an example of two avatars, or embodiments, who are currently inhabiting the virtual space – an angel and a round, floating face. Both embodiments can navigate through the space; they can see each other and can both see the landscape clearly. They can interact through audio connections and can orient their bodies to each other, which in some ways can approximate real-life interactions. When the interaction interfaces are new, they affect how we see the world, our communities, our relationships, and ourselves. They lead to social and cultural reorganization and reflection. While people in ancient times fretted about writing and Victorians fretted about electricity, today we are in a state of anxiety about our immersion into technology that demands a cognitive investment (Baym, 2015).

This chapter is grouped into three different areas: (a) how immersion into the digital space may impact cognitive experiences; (b) how to understand the impact interaction technologies have on centrality of beliefs; and (c) gain a heightened understanding of the impact this phenomenon has on individuals (self) in a society. Even though briefly, each of these three parts are presented with a short preface of the scope and perspective taken from a literature review.

There is a high priority for society to engage in this study of intellectual inquiry – not only the engineering of cognitive abilities, but an understanding of how our brains work and how it generates the mind when engaging in the interaction society (Poggio, 2016). The uniqueness of this chapter is that it provides a perspective of a technological view point with an individual and social aspect of users who invest cognitive time and space into an interaction society. Hopefully, the simplistic approach in writing this chapter will be interesting to both the academic environment as well as the human development field.

Informational Society Versus Interaction Society

Let's first ask if there is a difference in the typical characteristics of informational society and interaction society; and if so, how do the differences impact cognitive experiences moving into the future where cutting edge interaction is in the making? Not only the human development field of study as it understands, explains, or even predicts the impact of interactions within the digital domain, but whether individual or societal interactions expand or limit cognitive capacity. Indeed, there is a shift occurring from the information society with its focus on information processing and transactions, to the interaction society with related issues including ongoing and fluid networks of connections, interaction management and attention management (Wiberg, 2005).

The field of cognitive investment in the digital space has become multidisciplinary, borrowing from engineering, mathematics, computer science, psychology and more recently, neuroscience (Oberst & Sanders, 2016). The transferring process of cognitive abilities is defined as the application of knowledge learned in one situation to another situation that leads to improve cognition (Davis, 1989). This improvement forms the basis of collective intelligence, which includes similar images or impressions each user creates and then links to previous experiences (Ren, Chen, Yuan, & Zheng, 2016). Does this collective acumen then allow for new perceptions or experiences that challenge existing schemas, a process of reorganization and adaption that possibly occurs, leading to new schemas, thus affecting more diverse and independent thoughts during immersion into the digital interfaces?

In recent years, neuroscientists have gained insights into the cognitive connections that influence cognitive ability when interacting with digital interfaces, and according to studies, immersion in a digital environment can enhance cognition in at least three ways: 1) enabling multiple perspectives; 2) situated learning; and, 3) transfer. First, the ability to change one's perspective or frame of reference is a powerful means of understanding a complex phenomenon (Dede, 2009). Secondly, through the changes in perspective a user of digital technology enables her or his actional immersion, as well as symbolic insights gained from distancing oneself from the context (Dede, 2009). The potential advantage of cognitive immersion in digital interfaces means taking advantage of higher cognitive skills; thus, the third way is to be able to demonstrate near-transfer of knowledge for future preparation in real world settings (Greenfield, 2009).

We can expect to see the expansion, and even next generation of digital absorption of information, in the building of cognitive abilities that were once thought of in a traditional sense, but rather now the ability to navigate rapid change valuable to human development. If digital interaction is substituted for personal interactive experience, the approach to what will tailor the cognitive abilities is not only possible but desirable for world technological interactions with users of that technology. However, not surprisingly researchers and practitioners alike are concerned with the issue of how users of that information understand and manage the information (Agarwal & Karahanna, 2000). An additional concern is that information technology is a double edge sword, which has the power to exploit for malicious purposes and there may be a propensity for this to transfer into interaction technology (Liang, & Xue, 2009). In response to those concerns, there are several theoretical models that we could examine, such as *innovation diffusion theory* (Brancheau & Wetherbe, 1990; Rogers, 1995), the theory of reasoned action (Ajzen & Fishbein, 1980; Fishbein & Ajzen, 1975), and possibly the theory of planned behavior (Ajzen, 1985, 1988; Ajzen& Madden, 1986), but to do so would be outside the scope of this chapter.

Whereas, the emphasis of this chapter places its attention on the vast, ever-changing world of digital technology; knowing it can be difficult to pin-point, the best approach that sheds light on relevant information for human development, whether history, theory, philosophies of development, processes, implementation or evaluation as humans interact within the digital age. And yet, hopefully the value of such attention is to assist those who study the phenomena; becoming symbiotic with digital interfaces and growing into interconnected societies (Sparrow, Liu & Wegner, 2011). One might ask are we exploiting these digital interfaces to keep up with computer power or is there a demand for richer input and output possibilities through the experiences within the interaction society?

Given the limitlessness of this field of study, the author of this chapter decided simplicity was the best approach. Rather than invoking an in-depth conceptual framework based on a specific theory or theories, the intent is to extend the curiosity of those studying human development and the impact interaction interfaces have on cognition investment into a cyborg society. Cyborg meaning the borders between human and machine collapse, which another way to state this is by Haraway's (as cited in Baym, 2015) *cyborg manifesto* where self and body are thrown into flux; a time when some people feel that their real self is expressed best through digital; e.g., virtual. And yet, the other side of that manifesto, is exciting elements that the new interaction interfaces allow us to communicate personally within what used to be prohibitively large groups.

Interaction Impacting Cognitive Investment

Interaction is the subjective impression that one is participating in a comprehensive, realistic experience. The more a virtual immersive experience is based on design strategies that combine actional, symbolic, and a perception of ease of use and usefulness, the greater the participant's suspension of disbelief that she or he is "inside" a digitally enhanced setting (Dede, 2009). His study has shown that immersion in a digital environment can enhance cognition in at least three ways: 1) allowing multiple perspectives;

2) situated learning; and, 3) transfer of that learning. However, there is research that warns against an artefactual approach to any interactional technology, insisting that we must learn to understand the technology as a system of social practice, and thus widen the perspective and regard digital interfaces as tools, rather than an intelligent addiction or even mindlessness, and a host of other dismissive and pathologizing perspectives (de Castell & Jensen, 2007).

Of utmost importance is that the cognitive behavior in the interaction society can behave in ways that our physical counterparts cannot: the rules of "real world" physics do not apply here. Scholarly work is ongoing considering future models for human development between virtual and reality that may create ways in which we may not have thought of before when examining cognitive consequences in such virtual world physics (Churchill, Snowden & Munroe, 2012).

Actional Interaction

Actional engagement empowers the participant in an experience to initiate actions impossible in the real world that have novel, intriguing consequences. Modern mass societies are made up of a bewildering variety of social worlds. Each is an organized outlook, built up by people in their interaction with one another; hence, each communication channel gives rise to a separate world (Blumer, as cited in Herman & Reynolds, 1994). Probably the greatest sense of solidarity is to be found in the various communal structures, such as when individuals are engaged in virtual reality and have the opportunity to make new discoveries such as by becoming a bird and flying around; the degree of cognitive concentration this activity creates is intense and 'real' to the participant immersed in this action (Dede, 2009).

Another relevant illustration is in the gaming society of the *World of Warcraft*, in which individuals are heroes that come in all shapes and sizes, and the epic challenge is to become one of Azeroth's legends. Thus, the actional experience in building epic knowledge and produce epic wins for problem solving knowingly comes with intriguing consequences for those who immerse themselves in this virtual reality game. There is empirical data that illustrates the importance of mutual understanding of locations (space) to successfully perform collaborative tasks. For example, in the game *World of Warcraft*, the participants are not sufficient in the performance of just their own tasks; it is rather the mutual understanding of being in proximity, or other visual virtual clues, which are of importance to epic winning (Wiberg, 2005).

An important implication of the fact that the human being makes indications to himself in his actional immersion during the gaming activity, such as *World of Warcraft*, is that his action is constructed or built up instead of being a mere release. Whatever his action in this gaming scenario is, the human individual proceeds by pointing out to himself that divergent things have to be taken into account in the course of his actions. There are various conditions which may be instrumental to his actions and those which may obstruct his actions. In the actional experience in the interaction society, such as the *World of Warwick*, the human being has to take into account the demands, the expectations, the prohibitions, and the threats that may arise in the situation in which he is acting (Blumer, as cited in Herman & Reynolds, 1994).

Symbolic Interaction

The term *symbolic interaction* refers to the peculiar and distinctive character of interaction as it takes place between human beings. The peculiarity consists in the fact that human beings interpret or define each other's actions instead of merely reacting to each other's actions (Blumer, as cited in Herman & Reynolds, 1994). A human's response is not made directly to the actions of one another, but instead is based on the meaning which she or he attach to such actions. Thus, human interaction is mediated by the use of symbols, by interpretation, or by ascertaining the meaning of one another's actions.

The human individual is born into a society characterized by symbolic immersion. The use of these symbols by those around the individuals enable them to pass from the conversation of gestures – which involves direct, unmeaningful responses to the overt acts of others (Herman & Reynolds, 1994). Thus, a basic proposition of symbolic immersion is that humans live in a world of meanings and respond to objects and events based on the subjective meanings that these things have for them. This interaction involves triggering powerful semantic, psychological associations by means of the content of an experience. As an illustration, digitally fighting a horrible virtual monster can build a mounting sense of fear, even though one's physical context is unchanging and rationally safe. Invoking digital versions of situations from one's familiarities deepens the immersive experience by drawing on the participant's beliefs, emotions, and values about the real world (Venkatesh, Morris, Davis et al., 2003).

This immersion, as a distinctive perspective in social psychology, focuses on the nature of human social interaction. Humans are portrayed as acting as opposed to being acted upon; as such, interactionists present an active image of beings, and they reject any view of humans as passive, robot-like entities (Herman & Reynolds,1994). From their vantage point Herman and Reynolds used scholars such as Blumer, 1969; Manis & Meltzer, 1978; Rose, 1962, to enumerate basic assumptions about symbolic immersion:

1. Humans live in a symbolic world of learned meanings.
2. Symbols arise in the social process and are shared.
3. Symbols have motivational significance; meanings and symbols allow individuals to carry out distinctively human action and interaction.
4. The mind is a functional, volitional, teleological entity serving the interests of the individual. Humans, unlike the lower animals, are endowed with the capacity for thought; the capacity for thoughts is shaped by social interaction.
5. The self is a social construct; just as individuals are born mindless, so too, are they born selfless; our selves arise in social interaction with others.
6. Society is a linguistic or symbolic construct arising out of the social process; it consists of individuals interacting.
7. Sympathetic introspection is a mandatory mode of inquiry.

These assumptions are conceived as social products arising through the defining acts of individuals as they engage in social interaction – social products that may, in turn, exert influences up them. One might agree that socially-created and socially-shared meanings are motivational significances in the interactions with emerging haptic technologies; for example, 3D glasses. However, 3D was once the essence of reality, and now the degree of physical involvement is the measure of immersion and its relationship to haptic technologies (Hansen, 2006).

According to Blumer (as cited in Herman & Reynolds, 1994) there are essential features that form the basis of symbolic interaction and they presuppose that human society is made up of individuals who have selves (that is, make indications to themselves); that individual action is a construction and not a release being built up by the individual through noting and interpreting features of the situations in which he acts; that group of collective action consists of the aligning of individual actions, brought about by the individuals' interpreting or taking into account each other's actions. Blumer argues that all three premises apply to the human group; e.g., interaction society. Symbolic meanings can be altered through the creative capabilities of humans, and individuals may influence the many meanings that form their society, as well as being influenced by these meanings themselves (Herman & Reynolds, 1994).

Impact on Centrality of Beliefs

Beliefs represent the cognitive structures that an individual develops after collecting, processing, and synthesizing information about information technology and incorporating various outcomes associated with technology use. Hence, the belief formation process is clearly worthy of further investigation, such as this section highlights. Although there are studies that have chosen to focus on many factors unique to beliefs in informational technologies, the primary purpose here is to illustrate that beliefs exhibit significant interactions toward usefulness and ease of use; thus, the acceptance of, and not avoidance of, the practical implications of the characteristic of technology from the vantage point of their own internal cognitive processes.

A variety of theoretical models have attempted to develop explanation of the criticality of beliefs in the use of information technologies with each garnering varying levels of theoretical and empirical support (Lewis, Agarwal & Sambamurthy, 2003). Within these various studies, a central construct and recurrent theme are the notion of an individual's cognition outcomes are associated with the use of targeted technology; referred to in the literature as beliefs. Uniqueness of beliefs about information technology has been shown to have a profound impact on subsequent perception toward technology. In their study, Lewis, Agarwal & Sambamurthy, (2003) argued that individuals form beliefs about their use of technologies within a broad milieu of influences emanating from the individual, institutional, and social contexts in which they interact with the technology. Their findings suggested that the three sets of influences on beliefs about information technology use are influenced by: 1) internal psychological processes; 2) the individual factors of self; and, 3) social influences.

Individuals perceive technology from the vantage point of their own internal cognitive processes and develop beliefs about them. Lewis, Agarwal & Sambamurthy (2003) suggested that the influence of all other variables on technology, acceptance outcomes have a significant impact of perceived ease of use and perceived usefulness. When individuals perceive the technology to be relatively free of cognitive effort, they will view it as releasing important cognitive resources that may be productively applied to other activities.

One might then ask if the technology is too hard to use and that the performance benefits of usage are outweighed by the effort of using the application; is the perception of usefulness influenced by the perception of ease of use? Perceived usefulness is defined as the degree to which a person believes that using a particular technology would enhance his or her life. This follows from the definition of the word useful: "capable of being used advantageously" (Davis, 1989, p.320.) Perceived ease of use, in contrast, refers to the degree to which a person believes that using a particular technology would be free of effort. This follows from the definition of "ease", "freedom from difficulty or great effort" (Davis, 1989, p. 320). The importance of perceived ease of use is supported by Bandura's (1982) research on self-efficacy, defined as "judgments of how well one can execute actions required to deal with in prospective situations" (p. 122, and cited in Davis, 1989, p. 321). Focusing for a moment on this notion of self-efficacy, Richards (2004) conjectures there may be unintended consequences for cognitive functioning which may involve concealing outward reality in perceptions when one is a new participant to the interaction society.

This then may be a good time and space in the chapter to ask what causes individuals to construct beliefs about a specific digital technology? Lewis, Agarwal & Sambamurthy (2003) would answer that by stating individual characteristics and influences emanating from the social milieu within which the individual is situated. In the traditional sense, some researchers surmise that social influences affect usage intentions in a manner like attitude. However, there is an argument that in addition to its effects on intentions, social influences have an important relationship with beliefs about the usefulness of a technology and others have suggested that this effect is manifested via the psychological pathways of internalization and identification.

The individual incorporates the opinion of an important referent as part of her own belief structure; the referent's beliefs become one's own. Via identification, the individual seeks to believe and act in a manner like those possessing referent power. Therefore, compelling messages received from important others are likely to influence one's cognition about the expected outcomes of technology use. At the heart of the centrality of beliefs is confusion about what is virtual – that which seems real but is ultimately a mere simulation – and what is real (Baym, 2015). Interaction society therefore calls into question the very authenticity of our identities, relationships, and practices and yet some critics noted that these disruptions are part of a movement from modern to postmodern times in which time and space are compressed, speed is accelerated, people are ever more mobile, communication is person-to-person, rather than place-to-place, identities are multiple, and communication media are ubiquitous (Baym, 2015).

Impact on Individuals (Self) Within Interaction Society

Nothing profound in this statement, *human being has a self*, but this idea should not be cast aside as esoteric or glossed over as something that is obvious and hence not worthy of attention (Blumer, as cited in Herman & Reynolds, 1994). The individual, e.g., self, is an outgrowth of social interaction; is developed and defined during interaction with others. Individuals are constantly changing because of social interactions with technology and we recognize this as no mystical conjuration. And yet, with the speed of digital changes impacting the interaction society, history often is still relevant in today's study of self and in 1902 Cooley stated:

Self takes the form of a somewhat definite imagination of how one's self that is, any idea he appropriates appears in a particular mind, and the kind of self-feeling one has is determined by the attitude toward this attributed to the other mind. A social self of this sort might be called the reflected or looking-glass self. (pp. 151-152, as cited in Herman & Reynolds, 1994)

Just as Cooley stated in 1902, scholars still agree that just as the mind is conceived of as a social product and develops within the social process, self undergoes continual development and modification throughout the lifespan of the individual. Herman & Reynolds posit:

The distinctive aspect of the self is its duality; that is, it has the capacity to be both subject and object unto itself. As that which can be an object to itself, the self is basically a social structure, arising in the social context. In this sense, the self can be said to exist in the act of viewing oneself in a reflexive manner. Such activity is made possible through the use of language, a group of symbols which allows one to employ the standpoints of others in order to view oneself as an object – to see oneself as others do. (1994)

Is it possible to separate cognitive self from society when initiated into digital technologies? To converse about possible retorts to the question, there is literature that identifies three implications of selfhood in human development, and that implores to offer the inquiry as to do these implications transfer into the digital space? The implications are summarized by a statement that the individual (self) and the mind (mental activity) are twin emergent in the social process. Those implications are:

1. The possession of a self makes the individual a society in miniature. That is, he may engage in interaction with himself, just as two or more different individuals might. In the course of this interaction, he can come to view himself in a new way, thereby bringing about changes in himself.
2. The ability to act toward oneself makes possible an inner experience which need not reach overt expression. That is, the individual by virtue of having a self, is thereby endowed with the possibility of having a mental life. He can make indications to himself-which constitutes mind.
3. The individual with a self thereby enables to direct and control his cognitive investment and he is then, not a mere passive agent in an interaction society. (Herman & Reynolds 1994)

The core concept of self, like society, is in an evolution toward a global and digital society, in which the dialogical self is described as a spatial and temporal process of positioning. Technological developments and their relationship to cognitive interconnectedness provide new opportunities for innovation of the self as multivoiced and dialogical (Hermans, 2004).

Perspectives of The Interaction Society

In his introduction to his book, *Constructivist Learning Environments*, Wilson (1996) pointed out that the idea of cognitive investment, e.g., learning, evokes the notions of place and space, room to move and explore and generous access. He suggested that among the many ways we think of knowledge, the notion of cognitive collaboration with technology resonates best with a vision of knowledge as meaning constructed by interaction with that technology.

Even prior to Wilson's era, Dewey (1859-1952) emphasized, society exists in and through communication; common perspective – emerge through participation in common communication channels. It is through social participation that perspectives shared in a group of internalized (Blumer as cited in Herman & Reynolds,1994). A digital layer on top of traditional society has emerged to the extent that modern information technology is used almost everywhere in today's society to support various kinds of technology-enabled human activities not possible to perform without the technology. An example is the cinema which has the capacity to present the world from a nonhuman perspective, linking virtual reality technologies with natural perception (Hansen, 2006). In its fantasy form, though certainly not in reality, virtual reality works – or rather would work – like an externalization of neuroscientist Antonio Damasio's analogy for consciousness: if consciousness can be likened to a *movie-in-the-brain* with no external spectator, then virtual reality would comprise something like a *movie-outside-the-brain*, again, importantly with no external spectator (2006).

In de Castell and Jensen's (2007) work they highlighted Michael Tomasello's insight into the development of human cognition which states that the immersion into digital interfaces may be fun, and that could be the primary motivation for immersion into them. Are we hardwired to explore for the simple pleasure of exercising our faculties and exploring the world in non-survival ways? This may serve the purpose of expanding a wider range of cognitive patterns to apply to differing points of view, thus alternate perspectives in understanding this phenomena. Human experience in virtual environments are made of the same elements that all other experiences consist of, and can be defined as an ensemble made up of sensations, thoughts, feelings, actions, and meaning-making in a setting (de Castell & Jensen, 2007). Thus, an emergence in a unique interaction process between self as individual of the technology and the technology itself.

For a moment, let us travel to Moroco, where one of the unique interactions is called Virtual *Hrig*, a technology-mediated interaction and cybercafe' culture appropriated by individuals and groups. This digital communication mediates the construction of cybernetic identities and promotes the rehearsal of invented social relations (Wiberg, 2005). The term 'virtual hrig' is an inventive accommodation of the Internet made possible through the discursive forum of chatrooms and e-mail discussion groups that can act as a backtalk to dominant patriarchal and conservative power structures; e.g., *hrig* means leaving one space for another, such as from reality into virtual. While Wyberg (2005) postulated it is too early to draw conclusions on the extent of the impact of digital interfaces on individual and group identities, the point he made is that cyber interaction is contributing to the expansion of the public sphere.

Staying with the café concept, the patterning of the interaction society in markets, bureaucracies, solidarity groups, and others is that their respective core values are considered. Thus, a core value of communication plays a key mode of interaction, to reveal monologic and dialogic conceptions of communication. Richard Varney, as cited in Wiberg, 2005, wrote around the theme of interactive communication and appreciation in a society constituted by an interaction that requires presence, not absent. However, Baym (2005) raised important questions for scholars and lay people alike: How can we be present yet also absent? What is a self if it is not in a body? How can we have so much control yet lose so much freedom? What does personal communication mean when it is transmitted through a mass medium, such as twitter? What is a mass medium if it is used for personal communication? What do 'private' and 'public' mean anymore? What does it even mean to *be* real?

CONCLUSION

While the technology of yesterday was occupied with basically crunching numbers, today and tomorrow's technology will be occupied with maintaining our social needs with one another and with technology itself. The interaction interfaces are already being labeled as social belonging technologies, awareness technologies, and community support interaction interfaces (Wiberg, 2005). On top of the interaction technologies and the societies in which they sit, new use patterns and human behaviors are emerging around this digital space. In sum, we are still standing on shifting ground in our efforts to make sense of the benefits of the digital interfaces and their cognitive consequences.

New interfaces are constantly developing, new populations are taking up these tools, and new users are emerging. However, who is excluded from interaction society is neither random nor inconsequential. The same tools may take on very different meaning for different populations in different contexts or different times. It is too soon to tell what the final consequences will be, but it seems unlikely that they will never be universal or stable (Baym, 2015). And yet, the excitement is considering how much more we have to learn, as we continue to invest our cognitive abilities as a player in an interaction society.

Future analysis of cognitive investments in interaction societies is an intriguing opportunity as in mass societies, such as those in the gaming world, virtual reality world, and so forth, the key may be to ascertain how a person defines the situation, which perspectives he uses in arriving at such a definition, and who constitutes the audience whose responses provide the necessary confirmation and support for his position (Blumer as cited in Herman & Reynolds, 1994). One might ask are cognitive abilities and investment changing or maybe re-arranging through differing perspectives as a human development study? To extend this question for future exploration is it important for those who work in the field of human development to analyze operations for the description of the manner in which each cognitive investment is oriented toward a successful immersion into mass society, e.g., interaction society? Since perception is selective and perspectives differ, different items are noticed and a progressively diverse set of images arise, even among those engaged in the same interface technology. Would this then be the impetus to develop a tool for comprehending the diversity and dynamic investment of the kind needed in an interaction society, such as we are in today?

Human cognitive functions achieve close collaboration with brain inspired digital technology, comprising of certain capabilities the brain trumps over technologies, including adaptability, robustness, flexibility and learning ability (Zhang, Shi, & Song, 2016). Thus, can we declare that immersive virtual environments can break the deep, everyday connection between where our senses tell us we are and where we are actually located and whom we are with? The concept of presence refers to the phenomenon of behaving and feeling as if we are in the virtual world created by interactive technologies (Sanchez-Vive & Slater, 2005). Does this then provide the argument that cognitive investment and cognitive presence is worthy of future studies which might aid in a deeper understanding of consciousness as it enters the realm of the interaction society?

REFERENCES

Agarwal, R., & Karahanna, E. (2000). Time flies when youre having fun: Cognitive absorption and beliefs about information technology usage. *Management Information Systems Quarterly, 24*(4), 665–694. doi:10.2307/3250951

Baym, N. (2015). Personal connections in the digital age. Cambridge, UK: Polity Press.

Churchill, E. F., Snowdon, D. N., & Muro, A. J. (2012). *Collaborative Virtual Environments: Digital places and spaces for interaction.* New York, NY: Springer Science and Business Media.

Davis, R. D. (1989). Perceived Usefulness, perceived ease of use, and user acceptance of information technology. *Management Information Systems Quarterly, 13*(3), 319–340. doi:10.2307/249008

de Castell, S., & Jensen, J. (2007). *Words in play: International perspectives on digital games research.* New York, NY: Peter Lang Publishing.

Dede, C. (2009). Immersive interfaces for engagement and learning. *Science, 323*(5910), 66–69. doi:10.1126/science.1167311 PMID:19119219

Dede, C. (2009). Introduction to virtual reality in education. *Themes in Science and Technology Education, 2*(1-2).

Greenfield, P. M. (2009). Technology and information education: What is taught, what is learned. *Science, 323*(5910), 69–71. doi:10.1126/science.1167190 PMID:19119220

Hansen, M. B. N. (2006). *Bodies in Code: Interfaces with Digital Media.* New York, NY: Routledge Taylor and Francis Group.

Herman, N. J., & Reynolds, L. T. (Eds.). (1994). *Symbolic Interaction: An Introduction to Social Psychology*. Dix Hills, NY: General Hall, Inc.

Hermans, H. (2004). Introduction: The Dialogical self in a global and digital age. *An International Journal of Theory and Research*, *4*(4), 297–320.

Lewis, W., Agarwal, R., & Sambamurthy, V. (2003). Sources of influence on beliefs about information technology use: An Empirical study of knowledge workers. *Management Information Systems Quarterly*, *27*(4), 657–678.

Liang, H., & Xue, Y. (2009, March). Avoidance of information technology threats: A theoretical perspective. *Management Information Systems Quarterly*, *33*(1), 71–90.

Mitchell, S. (2002). *Technogenesis*. New York, NY: Penguin Publishing.

Oberst, J., & Sanders, S. (2016). Realizing Intelligent Robotics. In Brain-Inspired intelligent robotics: The Intersection of robotics and neuroscience. Beijing, China: Chinese Academy of Sciences.

Poggio, T. (2016). *Deep learning: Mathematics and neuroscience. In Brain-Inspired intelligent robotics: The Intersection of robotics and Neuroscience* (pp. 9–12). Beijing, China: Chinese Academy of Sciences.

Ren, P., Chen, B., Yuan, Z., & Zheng, N. (2016). Toward robust visual cognition through brain-inspired computing. In Brain-Inspired intelligent robotics: The Intersection of robotics and neuroscience. Beijing, China: Chinese Academy of Sciences.

Richards, J. M. (2004, August). The cognitive consequences of concealing feelings. *Psychological Science*, *13*(4), 131–134.

Sanchez-Vives, M., & Slater, M. (2005, April). From presence to consciousness through virtual reality. *Nature Reviews. Neuroscience*, *6*(4), 332–339. doi:10.1038/nrn1651 PMID:15803164

Sparrow, B., Liu, J., & Wegner, D. M. (2011). Google effects on memory: Cognitive consequences of having information at our fingertips. *Science*, *333*(6043), 776–778. doi:10.1126/science.1207745 PMID:21764755

Venkatesh, V., Morris, M., Davis, G., & Davis, F. (2003). User acceptance of information technology: Toward a unified view. *Management Information Systems Quarterly*, *27*(3), 425–478.

Wiberg, M. (2005). *The Interaction society: Practice, theories and supportive technologies*. Hershey, PA: Information Science Publishing. doi:10.4018/978-1-59140-530-6

Wilson, B. (1996). *Constructivist learning environments*. Englewood Cliffs, NJ: Educational Technologies Publication.

Zhang, B., Shi, L., & Song, S. (2016). Creating more intelligent robots through brain-inspired computer. In Brain-Inspired intelligent robotics: The Intersection of robotics and neuroscience. Beijing, China: Chinese Academy of Sciences.

KEY TERMS AND DEFINITIONS

Actional Immersion: Empowers the participant in an experience to initiate actions impossible in the real world that have novel, intriguing consequences.

Brain Inspired Digital Technology: Human cognitive functions achieve close collaboration with brain inspired digital technology comprising of certain capabilities the brain trumps over technologies, including adaptability, robustness, flexibility and learning ability,

Centrality of Belief: At the heart of the centrality of beliefs is confusion about what is virtual – that which seems real but is ultimately a mere simulation – and what is real.

Concept of Self: The core concept of self, like society, is in an evolution toward a global and digital society, in which the dialogical self is described as a spatial and temporal process of positioning. Technological developments and their relationships to cognitive interconnectedness provided new opportunities for innovation of the self as multivoiced and dialogical.

Digital Space: The digital space raises a variety of issues as we try to understand them, their place in our lives, and their consequences for our personhood and relationships with others in society. A space is a societal landscape such as a terrain that can be inhabited or populated by individuals, encouraging a sense of shared space.

Symbolic Immersion: Refers to the peculiar and distinctive character of interaction as it takes place between human beings. The peculiarity consists in the fact that human beings interpret or define each other's actions instead of merely reacting to each other's actions.

Technogenesis: Syne Mitchell's book, Technogenesis (2002) introduced her readers to an interaction society where almost everyone on earth is connected to a worldwide net, and in which the main character discovered the existence of an intelligence called Gestalt-a-self-aware entity generated by the collected consciousness of eight billion networked people.

Virtual Hrig: Is an inventive accommodation of the internet made possible through the discursive forum of chatrooms and e-mail discussion groups that can act as a backtalk to dominant patriarchal and conservative power structures; e.g., meaning leaving one space for another space, such as from reality to virtual.

Compilation of References

Aarsand, P. (2010). Young boys playing digital games. *Nordic Journal of Digital Literacy*, *1*(5), 39–54.

Abel, B. V., Evers, L., Klaassen, R., & Troxler, P. (2011). *Open design now: Why design cannot remain exclusive*. Amsterdam, Netherlands: BIS.

Abrams, S. (2014). *New technology could allow you or your parents to age at home*. Retrieved from http://www.aarp.org/home-family/personal-technology/info-2014/is-this-the-end-of-the-nursing-home.html

Ackermann, A. D. (2009). Investigation of learning outcomes for the acquisition and retention of CPR knowledge and skills learned with the use of high-fidelity simulation. *Clinical Simulation in Nursing*, *5*(6), e213–e222. doi:10.1016/j.ecns.2009.05.002

Adams, G. L., & Engelmann, S. (1996). *Research on direct instruction: 25 years beyond DISTAR*. Seattle, WA: Educational Achievement System.

Aebersold, M., & Titler, M. G. (2014). A simulation model for improving learner and health outcomes. *The Nursing Clinics of North America*, *49*(3), 431–439. doi:10.1016/j.cnur.2014.05.011 PMID:25155540

Affholder, L. P. (2003). *Differentiated instruction in inclusive elementary classrooms* (Doctoral dissertation). University of Kansas.

Agarwal, R., & Karahanna, E. (2000). Time flies when youre having fun: Cognitive absorption and beliefs about information technology usage. *Management Information Systems Quarterly*, *24*(4), 665–694. doi:10.2307/3250951

Agosta, E., Graetz, J. E., Mastropieri, M. A., & Scruggs, T. E. (2004). Teacher researcher partnerships to improve social behavior through social stories. *Intervention in School and Clinic*, *39*(5), 276–287. doi:10.1177/10534512040390050401

Ahluwalia, P., & Miller, T. (2014). The prosumer. *Social Identities*, *20*(4-5), 259–261. doi:10.1080/13504630.2015.1004830

Alam, F., Chowdhury, H., Elmir, Z., Sayogo, A., Love, J., & Subic, A. (2010). An experimental study of thermal comfort and aerodynamic efficiency of recreational and racing bicycle helmets. *Procedia Engineering*, *2*(2), 2413–2418. doi:10.1016/j.proeng.2010.04.008

Alberto, P. A., & Troutman, A. C. (2012). Applied behavior analysis for teachers (9th ed.). Pearson.

Aldersey-Williams, H. (2011). *The new tin ear: Manufacturing, materials and the rise of the user-maker*. London: RSA Design Projects.

Aldridge, J. (2010). Among the periodicals: Differentiated instruction. *Childhood Education*, *86*(3), 193–195. doi:10.1080/00094056.2010.10523147

Alexander, B., & Levine, A. (2008, November 1). Web 2.0 Storytelling: Emergence of a New Genre. *EDUCAUSE Review, 43*, 6.

Aliaga, M., & Gunderson, B. (2000). *Interactive statistics*. Saddle River, NJ: Prentice Hall.

Alinier, G., Hunt, W. B., & Gordon, R. (2004). Determining the value of simulation in nurse education: Study design and initial results. *Nurse Education in Practice, 4*(3), 200–207. doi:10.1016/S1471-5953(03)00066-0 PMID:19038158

Allen, I. E., & Seaman, J. (2016). *Online Report Card Tracking Online Education in the United States*. Babson Survey Research Group and Quahog Research Group, LLC.

Allen, I. E., Seaman, J., Poulin, R., & Straut, T. T. (2016). *Online report card: Tracking online education in the United States*. Babson Survey Research Group and Quahog Research Group, LLC.

Alloway, N., & Gilbert, P. (1997). Boys and literacy: Lessons from Australia. *Gender and Education, 9*(1), 49–60. doi:10.1080/09540259721448

Alshare, K. A., & Alkhateeb, F. B. (2008). Predicting students' usage of Internet emerging economies using an extended technology acceptance model (TAM). *Academy of Educational Leadership Journal, 12*(2), 109–128.

Alvermann, D. (2008). Why bother theorizing adolescents online literacies for classroom practice and research? *Journal of Adolescent & Adult Literacy, 52*(1), 8–19. doi:10.1598/JAAL.52.1.2

Alvermann, D., & Hagood, M. (2000). Fandom and critical media literacy. *Journal of Adolescent & Adult Literacy, 43*(5), 436–446.

Alves Pedro, W. J. (2016). Aging process assets and social dimensions of science and technology. *1st Brazilian Congress of Gerontechnology, 15*(2), 71-72. doi:10.4017/gt.2016.15.2.006.00

American Psychiatric Association. (2013). *Diagnostic and statistical manual of mental disorders* (5th ed.). Washington, DC: Author.

Anderson, J., & Rainie, L. (2014). The Internet of things will thrive by 2025. *Pew Research Internet Project, 14*. Retrieved from http://www.pewinternet.org/2014/05/14/internet-of-things/

Anderson, M. (2015, October 29). Technology device ownership: 2015. *Pew Research Center: Internet, Science, and Technology*. Retrieved from http://www.pewinternet.org/2015/10/29/technology-device-ownership-2015/

Anderson, C. (2014). *Makers: The new industrial revolution*. New York, NY: Crown Business.

Anderson, R. S., Goode, G. G., Mitchell, J. S., & Thompson, R. (2013). Using digital tools to teach writing in K-12 classrooms. In J. Whittingham, S. Huffman, W. Rickman, & C. Wiedmaier (Eds.), *Technological tools for the literacy classroom* (pp. 10–26). Hershey, PA: IGI Global. doi:10.4018/978-1-4666-3974-4.ch002

Anderson, R. S., Mitchell, J. S., Thompson, R., & Trefz, K. (2014). Supporting young writers through the writing process in a paperless classroom. In R. S. Anderson & C. Mims (Eds.), *Handbook of research on digital tools for writing instruction in K-12 settings* (pp. 337–362). Hershey, PA: IGI Global. doi:10.4018/978-1-4666-5982-7.ch017

Ang, R. P. (2016). Cyberbullying: Its prevention and intervention strategies. In D. Sibnath (Ed.), *Child safety, welfare and well-being: Issues and challenges* (pp. 25–38). New, NY: Springer. doi:10.1007/978-81-322-2425-9_3

Aoyama, I., Utsumi, S., & Hasegawa, M. (2011). Cyberbullying in Japan: Cases, government reports, adolescent relational aggression and parental monitoring roles. In Q. Li, D. Cross, & P. K. Smith (Eds.), *Bullying in the global playground: Research from an international perspective*. Oxford, UK: Wiley-Blackwell.

Archambault, L. M., & Crippen, K. (2009). Examining TPACK among K-12 online distance educators in the United States. *Contemporary Issues in Technology & Teacher Education*, 9(1), 71–88.

Archbald, D. A., & Newmann, F. M. (1988). *Beyond standardized testing: Assessing authentic academic achievement in the secondary school*. Reston, VA: National Association of Secondary School Principals.

Argyris, C., & Schon, D. A. (1995). Organizational learning II: Theory, method, and practice. Reading, MA: Addison-Wesley.

Aricak, T., Siyahhan, S., Uzunhasanoglu, A., Saribeyoglu, S., Ciplak, S., Yilmaz, N., & Memmedov, C. (2008). Cyberbullying among Turkish adolescents. *Cyberpsychology & Behavior*, 11(3), 253–261. doi:10.1089/cpb.2007.0016 PMID:18537493

Armstrong, A., & Casement, C. (2000). *The child and the machine: How computers put our children's education at risk*. Beltsville, MD: Robins Lane Press.

Arslan, S., Savaser, S., Hallett, V., & Balci, S. (2012). Cyberbullying among primary school students in Turkey: Self-reported prevalence and associations with home and school life. *Cyberpsychology, Behavior, and Social Networking*, 15(10), 527–533. doi:10.1089/cyber.2012.0207 PMID:23002988

Arthanat, S., Vroman, K. G., & Lysack, C. (2016). A home-based individualized information communication technology training program for older adults: A demonstration of effectiveness and value. *Disability and Rehabilitation. Assistive Technology*, 11(4), 316–324. PMID:25512061

Assa Ashuach Studio. (2016). Retrieved from http://assaashuach.com/#!/portfolio/assa-studio-micro-3d-design/0

Association for Talent Development. (2015). *Bridging the skills gap: Workforce development is everyone's business*. Alexandria, VA: ATD Public Policy.

Association for Talent Development. (2017a). *Together we create a world that works better*. Retrieved from https://www.td.org/About

Association for Talent Development. (2017b). *Why ATD 2017?* Retrieved from http://www.atdconference.org/?_ga=1.36520672.1906492158.1488225871

Association for Talent Development. (2017c). *Communities of practice*. Retrieved from https://www.td.org/Communities-of-Practice

AutoDesk. (2016). *Project Shapeshifter*. Retrieved from www.shapeshifter.io

Ayas, T., & Horzum, M. B. (2010). *Cyberbullg / victim scale development study*. Retrieved from: http://www.akademik-bakis.org

Aydemir, Z., Öztürk, E., & Horzum, M. B. (2013). The effect of reading from screen on the 5th grade elementary students' level of reading comprehension on informative and narrative type of texts. *Educational Sciences: Theory and Practice*, 13(4), 2272–2276. Retrieved from http://eric.ed.gov/?id=EJ1027653

Azano, A., & Stewart, T. (2015). Exploring place and practicing justice: Preparing pre-service teachers for success in rural schools. *Journal of Research in Rural Education (Online)*, 30(9), 1–12.

Baer, D. M., Wolf, M. M., & Risley, T. R. (1968). Some current dimensions of applied behavior analysis. *Journal of Applied Behavior Analysis*, 1(1), 91–97. doi:10.1901/jaba.1968.1-91 PMID:16795165

Baer, D. M., Wolf, M. M., & Risley, T. R. (1987). Some still-current dimensions of applied behavior analysis. *Journal of Applied Behavior Analysis*, 20(4), 313–327. doi:10.1901/jaba.1987.20-313 PMID:16795703

Ballabio, E., & Whitehouse, D. (1999). Ageing and disability in the information society: A European perspective on research and technological development. *Technology and Disability*, *10*, 3–10.

Bandura, A. (1977). Self-efficacy: Toward a unifying theory of behavioral change. *Psychological Review*, *84*(2), 191–215. doi:10.1037/0033-295X.84.2.191 PMID:847061

Bandura, A. (1977). *Social learning theory*. Englewood Cliffs, NJ: Prentice Hall.

Baran, E., Correia, A., & Thompson, A. (2013). Tracing successful online teaching in higher education: Voices of Exemplary Online Teachers. *Teachers College Record*, *115*(3), 1–41.

Barlett, C. P., & Gentile, D. A. (2012). Long-term psychological predictors of cyber-bullying in late adolescence. *Psychology of Popular Media Culture*, *2*, 123–135. doi:10.1037/a0028113

Barlett, C. P., Gentile, D. A., Anderson, C. A., Suzuki, K., Sakamoto, A., Yamaoka, A., & Katsura, R. (2013). Cross-cultural differences in cyberbullying behavior: A short-term longitudinal study. *Journal of Cross-Cultural Psychology*, *45*(2), 300–313. doi:10.1177/0022022113504622

Barnes-Holmes, D., Barnes-Holmes, B., Smeets, P. M., Cullinan, V., & Leader, G. (2004). Relational frame theory and stimulus equivalence: Conceptual and procedural issues. *International Journal of Psychology & Psychological Therapy*, *4*, 181–214.

Barnes-Holmes, D., Barnes-Holmes, Y., & Cullinan, V. (2000). Relational frame theory and Skinner's Verbal Behavior: A possible synthesis. *The Behavior Analyst*, *23*, 69–84. PMID:22478339

Barr, N., Readman, K., & Dunn, P. (2014). Simulation-based clinical assessment: Redesigning a signature assessment into a teaching strategy. *Australasian Journal of Paramedicine*, *11*(6), 1–9.

Barrott, J., Sunderland, A. B., Nicklin, J. P., & Smith, M. M. (2013). Designing effective simulation activities. In K. Forrest, J. McKimm, & S. Edgar (Eds.), *Essential simulation in clinical education* (pp. 168–195). Chichester, UK: John Wiley & Sons, Ltd. doi:10.1002/9781118748039.ch10

Basso, K. H. (1996). *Wisdom sits in places: Landscape and language among the Western Apache*. Albuquerque, NM: University of New Mexico Press.

Bastedo, K., Sugar, A., Swenson, N., & Vargas, J. (2013). Programmatic, systematic, automatic: An online course accessibility support model. *Journal of Asynchronous Learning Networks*, *17*(3), 87–102.

Bauman, S., Toomey, R. B., & Walker, J. L. (2013). Associations among bullying, cyberbullying, and suicide in high school students. *Journal of Adolescence*, *36*(2), 341–350. doi:10.1016/j.adolescence.2012.12.001 PMID:23332116

Bauman, S., Underwood, M. K., & Card, N. A. (2013). Definitions: Another perspective and a proposal for beginning with cyberaggression. In S. Bauman, D. Cross, & J. Walker (Eds.), *Principles of cyberbullying research: Definitions, measures, methodology* (pp. 26–40). New York, NY: Routledge.

Baum, D. D., & Lane, J. R. (1976). An application of the Bug-in-the-Ear communication system for training psychometrists. *Counselor Education and Supervision*, *15*(4), 309–310. doi:10.1002/j.1556-6978.1976.tb02010.x

Baumgartner, T., Lipowski, M. B., & Rush, C. (2003). *Increasing reading achievement of primary and middle school students through differentiated instruction* (Master's thesis). Chicago: Saint Xavier University.

Baxendale, B., Coffey, F., & Buttery, A. (2013). The roles of faculty and simulated patients in simulation. In K. Forrest, J. McKimm, & S. Edgar (Eds.), *Essential simulation in clinical education* (pp. 87–110). Chichester, UK: John Wiley & Sons, Ltd. doi:10.1002/9781118748039.ch6

Bayar, Y., & Ucanok, Z. (2012). School social climate and generalized peer perception in traditional and cyberbullying status. *Educational Sciences: Theory and Practice*, *12*, 2352–2358.

Baym, N. (2015). Personal connections in the digital age. Cambridge, UK: Polity Press.

Beane, J. A. (1997). *Curriculum integration*. New York, NY: Teachers College Press.

Becker, W. C. (1977). Teaching reading and language to the disadvantaged. *Harvard Educational Review*, *47*(4), 518–543. doi:10.17763/haer.47.4.51431w6022u51015

Becker, W. C., & Carnine, D. W. (1981). Direct Instruction: A behavior therapy model for comprehensive educational intervention with the disadvantaged. In S. W. Bijou & R. Ruiz (Eds.), *Behavior modification: Contributions to education* (pp. 145–207). Hillsdale, NJ: Lawrence Erlbaum.

Becker, W. J., Volk, S., & Ward, M. K. (2015). Leveraging neuroscience for smarter approaches to workplace intelligence. *Human Resource Management Review*, *25*(1), 56–67. doi:10.1016/j.hrmr.2014.09.008

Beckett, F. (2010). *What did the Baby Boomers ever do for us?* London: Biteback.

Beck, M. (2001). *Finding your own North Star*. New York, NY: Three Rivers Press.

Beck, M. (2008). *Steering by starlight*. New York, NY: Rodale.

Beckman, L., Hagquist, C., & Hellstrom, L. (2012). Does the association with psychosomatic health problems differ between cyberbullying and traditional bullying? *Emotional & Behavioural Difficulties*, *17*(3-4), 421–434. doi:10.1080/13632752.2012.704228

Behling, O. (1998). Employee Selection: Will intelligence and conscientiousness do the job? *The Academy of Management Executive*, *12*, 77–86.

Behrendt, M., & Franklin, T. (2014). A review of research on school field trips and their value in education. *International Journal of Environmental and Science Education*, *9*(3), 235–245.

Bennett, K. D., Brady, M. P., Scott, J., Dukes, C., & Frain, M. (2010). The effects of covert audio coaching on the job performance of supported employees. *Focus on Autism and Other Developmental Disabilities*, *25*(3), 173–185. doi:10.1177/1088357610371636

Bennett, K., Ramasamy, R., & Honsberger, T. (2012). The effects of covert audio coaching on teaching clerical skills to adolescents with autism spectrum disorder. *Journal of Autism and Developmental Disorders*, *43*(3), 585–593. doi:10.1007/s10803-012-1597-6 PMID:22798051

Bennett, K., Ramasamy, R., & Honsberger, T. (2013). Further examination of covert audio coaching on improving employment skills to adolescents with autism spectrum disorder. *Journal of Behavioral Education*, *22*, 103–119. doi:10.1007/s10864-013-9168-2

Bennett, S., & Lockyer, L. (2008). A study of teachers integration of interactive whiteboards into four Australian primary school classrooms. *Learning, Media and Technology*, *33*(4), 289–300. doi:10.1080/17439880802497008

Bennett, S., Maton, K., & Kervin, L. (2008). The digital natives debate: A critical review of the evidence. *British Journal of Educational Technology*, *39*(5), 775–786. doi:10.1111/j.1467-8535.2007.00793.x

Berg, G. A. (2008). Educational Technology and Learning Theory. In P. L. Rogers, G. A. Berg, J. V. Boettcher, C. Howerd, L. Justice, & K. D. Schenk (Eds.), *Encyclopedia of Distance Learning* (2nd ed.; pp. 759–763). Hershey, PA: Information Science Reference.

Bergmann, H. (2001). "The Silent University": The Society to Encourage Studies at Home, 1873-1897. *The New England Quarterly, 74*(3), 447-477. Retrieved from http://www.jstor.org/stable/3185427

Bergmann, H. (2001). The Silent University. *The New England Quarterly, 74*(3).

Beyer, L. E. (1996). Introduction: the meanings of critical teacher preparation. In L. E. Beyer (Ed.), *Creating democratic classrooms* (pp. 1–26). New York: Teachers College Press. doi:10.1515/9783110889666.xi

Bezirtzis, B. G., Lewis, M., & Christeson, C. (2007). Interactive evolution for industrial design. In *Proceedings of the 6th ACM SIGCHI conference on Creativity & Cognition* (pp. 183-192). New York, NY: ACM. doi:10.1145/1254960.1254986

Binder, C., & Watkins, C. L. (1990). Precision teaching and direct instruction: Superior instructional technology in schools. *Performance Improvement Quarterly, 3*(4), 74–96. doi:10.1111/j.1937-8327.1990.tb00478.x

Birdane, A., Yazici, H. U., Aydar, Y., Mert, K. U., Masifov, M., Cavusoglu, Y., & Timuralp, B. et al. (2012). Effectiveness of cardiac simulator on the acquirement of cardiac auscultatory skills of medical students. *Advances in Clinical and Experimental Medicine, 21*(6), 791–798. PMID:23457137

Bird, J. L., & Wanner, E. T. (2015). Research as curriculum inquiry: helping college students with anxiety. In V. C. X. Wang (Ed.), *Handbook of research on scholarly publishing and research methods* (pp. 273–295). Hershey, PA: Information Science Reference. doi:10.4018/978-1-4666-7409-7.ch014

Black, A. (2010). Gen Y: Who they are and how they learn. *Educational Horizons, 88*(2), 92–101.

Black, E., DiPietro, M., Ferdig, R., & Polling, N. (2009). Developing a survey to measure best practices of K-12 online instructors. *Online Journal of Distance Learning Administration, 12*(1).

Black, R. W. (2009). Online fan fiction and critical media literacy. *Journal of Computing in Teacher Education, 26*(2), 75.

Blackwell, C. K., Wartella, E., Lauricella, A. R., & Robb, M. (2015). *Technology in the lives of educators and early childhood programs: Trends in access, use, and professional development from 2012 to 2014.* Center on Media and Human Development at Northwestern University, Evanston, IL. Retrieved from http://www.fredrogerscenter.org/wp-content/uploads/2015/07/Blackwell-Wartella-Lauricella-Robb-Tech-in-the-Lives-of-Educators-and-Early-Childhood-Programs.pdf

Bogard, J. M., & McMackin, M. C. (2012). Combining traditional and new literacies in a 21st-century writing workshop. *The Reading Teacher, 65*(5), 313–323. doi:10.1002/TRTR.01048

Bogazzi, R. P. (2007). The legacy of the technology acceptance model and a proposal for a paradigm shift. *Journal of the Association for Information Systems, 8*(4), 244–254.

Bohlander, A. J., Orlich, F., & Varley, C. K. (2012). Social skills training for children with autism. *Pediatric Clinics of North America, 59*(1), 165–174. doi:10.1016/j.pcl.2011.10.001 PMID:22284800

Bonanno, R. A., & Hymel, S. (2013). Cyber bullying and internalizing difficulties: Above and beyond the impact of traditional forms of bullying. *Journal of Youth and Adolescence, 42*(5), 685–697. doi:10.1007/s10964-013-9937-1 PMID:23512485

Bonnetain, E., Boucheix, J. M., Hamet, M., & Freysz, M. (2010). Benefits of computer screen-based simulation in learning cardiac arrest procedures. *Medical Education, 44*(7), 716–722. doi:10.1111/j.1365-2923.2010.03708.x PMID:20636591

Borja, R. R. (2005). Evaluating online teachers is largely a virtual task. *Education Week, 24*(44), 8.

Botezatu, M., Hult, H., Tessma, M. K., & Fors, U. (2010). Virtual patient simulation: Knowledge gain or knowledge loss? *Medical Teacher, 32*(7), 562–568. doi:10.3109/01421590903514630 PMID:20653378

Boulton-Lewis, G. M. (2010). Education and learning for the elderly: Why, how, what. *Educational Gerontology, 36*(3), 213–228. doi:10.1080/03601270903182877

Boulton, M., Lloyd, J., Down, J., & Marx, H. (2012). Predicting undergraduates self-reported engagement in traditional and cyberbullying from attitudes. *Cyberpsychology, Behavior, and Social Networking, 15*(3), 141–147. doi:10.1089/cyber.2011.0369 PMID:22304402

Bouma, H., & Graafmans, J. A. M. (1992). *Gerontechnology.* Amsterdam, Netherlands: IOS Press.

Boyle, M. (2014, June 23). *Nestle aiming to develop a Nespresso of nutrients.* Retrieved from http://www.bloomberg.com/news/articles/2014-06-22/nestle-aiming-to-develop-a-nespresso-of-nutrients?_ga=1.134810162.210344514.1402054238

Brandon, J. (2011, March 9). *Is the iPad a 'Miracle Device' for Autism?* Retrieved from http://www.foxnews.com/tech/2011/03/09/can-apple-ipad-cure-autism

Brault, M. W. (2012). Americans with disabilities: 2010. *Current Population Reports, 7,* 1–131.

Braungart, M., & McDonough, W. (2002). *Cradle to cradle: Remaking the way we make things.* New York, NY: North Point Press.

Brickman, J. (2015). *Soothe.* New York, NY: Rodale.

Brighi, A., Guarini, A., Melotti, G., Galli, S., & Genta, M. L. (2012). Predictors of victimisation across direct bullying, indirect bullying and cyberbullying. *Emotional & Behavioural Difficulties, 17*(3-4), 375–388. doi:10.1080/13632752.2012.704684

Brodin, H., & Persson, J. (2009). Cost-utility analysis of assistive technologies in the European Commissions Tide Program. *International Journal of Technology Assessment in Health Care, 11*(2), 276–283. doi:10.1017/S0266462300006899 PMID:7790171

Broto, J., & Greer, R. D. (2014). The effects of functional writing contingencies on second graders writing and responding accurately to mathematical algorithms. *Behavioral Development Bulletin, 19*(1), 7–18. doi:10.1037/h0100568

Brown, B. (2012). *Daring greatly.* New York, NY: Gotham Books.

Brown, B. (2015). *Rising strong.* New York, NY: Spiegel & Grau.

Brown, J. S., Collins, A., & Duguid, P. (1989). Situated cognition and the culture of learning. *Educational Researcher, 18*(1), 32–42. doi:10.3102/0013189X018001032

Brown, K. (2009). Questions for the 21st century learner. *Knowledge Quest, 38*(1), 24–27.

Bruner, J. (1990). *Acts of meaning.* Cambridge, MA: Harvard University Press.

Bruning, R. H., & Kauffman, D. F. (2015). Self-efficacy beliefs and motivation in writing development. In C. MacArthur, S. Graham, & J. Fitzgerald (Eds.), *Handbook of writing research* (pp. 160–173). New York, NY: Guilford Press.

Bullock, A., & de Jong, P. G. (2014). Technology-enhanced learning. In T. Swanwick (Ed.), *Understanding medical education: Evidence, theory, and practice* (2nd ed.; pp. 149–160). Chichester, UK: John Wiley & Sons, Ltd.

Burgstahler, S. (2009). *Universal design of instruction (UDI): Definition, principles, guidelines, and examples.* Retrieved from http://www.washington.edu/doit/universal-design-instruction-udi-definition-principles-guidelines-and-examples

Burgstahler, S. E. (2010). Universal design in higher education. In S. E. Burgstahler & R. C. Coy (Eds.), *Universal design in higher education: From principles to practice* (pp. 1–20). Cambridge, MA: Harvard Education Press.

Burgstahler, S., Corrigan, B., & McCarter, J. (2004). Making distance learning courses accessible to students and instructors with disabilities: A case study. *The Internet and Higher Education, 7*(3), 233–246. doi:10.1016/j.iheduc.2004.06.004

Burke, R., Herron, R., & Barnes, B. A. (2006). *Common sense parenting: using your head as well as your heart to raise school-aged children* (3rd ed.). Boys Town Press.

Burnett, C., & Merchant, G. (2011). Is there a space for critical literacy in the context of social media? *English Teaching, 10*(1).

Burton-Jones, A., & Hubona, G. S. (2006). The mediation of external variables in the technology acceptance model. *Information & Management, 43*(6), 706–717. doi:10.1016/j.im.2006.03.007

Burton, K. A., Florell, D., & Wygant, D. B. (2013). The role of peer attachment and normative beliefs about aggression on traditional bullying and cyberbullying. *Psychology in the Schools, 50*(2), 103–114. doi:10.1002/pits.21663

Bushell, D., & Baer, D. M. (1994). Measurably superior instruction means close, continual contact with the relevant outcome data: Revolutionary. *Behavior analysis in education: Focus on measurably superior instruction*, 3-10.

Butter, J., McGaghie, W. C., Cohen, E. R., Kaye, M. E., & Wayne, D. B. (2010). Simulation-based mastery learning improves cardiac auscultation skills in medical students. *Journal of General Internal Medicine, 25*(8), 780–785. doi:10.1007/s11606-010-1309-x PMID:20339952

Byrne, A. (2013). Medical simulation: The journey so far. In K. Forrest, J. McKimm, & S. Edgar (Eds.), *Essential simulation in clinical education* (pp. 11–25). Chichester, UK: John Wiley & Sons, Ltd. doi:10.1002/9781118748039.ch2

Cameron, J. (1998). *The right to write*. New York: Tarcher/Putnam.

Cannon-Diehl, M. R., Rugari, S. M., & Jones, T. S. (2012). High-fidelity simulation for continuing education in nurse anesthesia. *American Association of Nurse Anesthetists Journal, 80*(3), 191–196. PMID:22848980

Cappadocia, M. C., Craig, W. M., & Pepler, D. (2013). Cyberbullying: Prevalence, stability and risk factors during adolescence. *Canadian Journal of School Psychology, 28*(2), 171–192. doi:10.1177/0829573513491212

Carnoy, M., & Rothstein, R. (2013). *What do international tests really show about U.S. student performance?* Economic Policy Institute. Retrieved from http://www.epi.org/publication/us-student-performance-testing/

Carter, C. (2015). *The sweet spot*. New York, NY: Ballantine.

Cascio, W. F. (2000). Managing a virtual workplace. *The Academy of Management Executive, 14*, 81–90.

Cassidy, W., Brown, K., & Jackson, M. (2012a). Making kind cool: Parents suggestions for preventing cyber bullying and fostering cyber kindness. *Journal of Educational Computing Research, 46*(4), 415–436. doi:10.2190/EC.46.4.f

Cassidy, W., Brown, K., & Jackson, M. (2012b). Under the radar: Educators and cyberbullying in schools. *School Psychology International, 33*(5), 520–532. doi:10.1177/0143034312445245

Cattell, R. B. (1971). *Abilities: Their structure, growth, and action*. Boston, MA: Houghton-Mifflin.

Cavanaugh, C., Gillan, K. J., Kromrey, J., Hess, M., & Blomeyer, R. (2004). *The effects of distance education on K-12 student outcomes: A meta-analysis*. Naperville, IL: Learning Point Associates/North Central Regional Educational Laboratory. Retrieved from ERIC database. (ED489533)

Cavanaugh, C., Gillan, K. J., Kromrey, J., Hess, M., & Blomeyer, R. (2004). *The effects of distance education on K-12 student outcomes: A meta-analysis*. Naperville, IL: North Central Regional Educational Laboratory.

Center for Technology and Aging. (2009). *Technologies to help older adults maintain independence: Advancing technology adoption.* Retrieved from http://www.techandaging .org/briefingpaper.pdf

Centers for Disease Control and Prevention. (2011). *Health Related Quality of Life.* Health Related Quality of Life Surveillance Program. Retrieved from http://www.cdc.gov/hrqol/hrqol14_measure.htm

Centers for Disease Control and Prevention. (2014, March 27). *CDC estimates 1 in 68 children has been identified with autism spectrum disorder.* Retrieved from http://www.cdc.gov/media/releases/2014/p0327-autism-spectrum-disorder.html

Chaille, C., & Britain, L. (1991). *The young child as a scientist: A constructivist approach to early childhood science education.* New York: HarperCollins.

Chamberlin, M., & Powers, R. (2010). The promise of differentiated instruction for enhancing the mathematical understandings of college students. *Teaching Mathematics and Its Applications, 29*(3), 113–139. doi:10.1093/teamat/hrq006

Chen, B., Seilhamer, R., Bennett, L., & Bauer, S. (2015, June 22). Students' mobile learning practices in higher education: A multi-year study. *EDUCAUSE Review.* Retrieved from http://er.educause.edu/articles/2015/6/students-mobile-learning-practices-in-higher-education-a-multiyear-study

Chen, K., & Chan, A. H. (2012). Use or non-use of Gerontechnology: A qualitative study. *International Journal of Environmental Research and Public Health, 10*(10), 4645–4666. doi:10.3390/ijerph10104645 PMID:24084674

Chew-Graham, C., Gask, L., Shiers, D., & Kaiser, P. (2014). *Management of depression in older people: Why this is important in primary care.* Retrieved from http://www.rcgp.org.uk/-/media/Files/CIRC/Mental-Health-2014/5-Older-People-and-depression-Primary-care-guidance-2014.ashx?la=en

Chiong, C., Ree, J., Takeuchi, L., & Erickson, I. (2012). *Print books vs. e-books: Comparing parent-child co-reading on print, basic, and enhanced e-book platforms.* Retrieved from http://www.joanganzcooneycenter.org/wp-content/uploads/2012/07/jgcc_ebooks_quickreport.pdf

Churchill, E. F., Snowdon, D. N., & Muro, A. J. (2012). *Collaborative Virtual Environments: Digital places and spaces for interaction.* New York, NY: Springer Science and Business Media.

Chwalisz, K. (2003). Evidence-based practice: A framework for twenty-first-century scientist-practitioner training. *The Counseling Psychologist, 31*(5), 497–528. doi:10.1177/0011000003256347

Ciccone, A. A. (2009). Foreward. In R. Gurung, N. Chick, & A. Haynie (Eds.), *Exploring signature pedagogies: Approaches to teaching disciplinary habits of mind* (pp. xi–xvi). Sterling, VA: StylusPublishing.

Cicconi, M. (2014). Vygotsky meets technology: A reinvention of collaboration in the early childhood mathematics classroom. *Early Childhood Education Journal, 42*(1), 57–65. doi:10.1007/s10643-013-0582-9

Cilento, K. (2012, September 5). Al Bahar Towers responsive facade / Aedas. *Archdaily.* Retrieved from http://www.archdaily.com/270592/al-bahar-towers-responsive-facade-aedas

Cipani, E., & Schock, K. M. (2007). *Functional behavioral assessment, diagnosis, and treatment: A complete system for education and mental health settings.* New York: Springer Publishing Company.

Clandinin, D. J., & Connelly, F. M. (2000). *Narrative inquiry.* San Francisco, CA: Jossey-Bass.

Clapper, T. C. (2010). Beyond Knowles: What those conducting simulation need to know about adult learning theory. *Clinical Simulation in Nursing, 6*(1), e7–e14. doi:10.1016/j.ecns.2009.07.003

Clark, C., & Dugdale, G. (2009). *Young people's writing: Attitudes, behaviour and the role of technology.* National Literacy Trust. Retrieved from http://www.literacytrust.org.uk/assets/0000/0226/Writing_survey_2009.pdf

Clarke, L. W., & Besnoy, K. (2010). Connecting the old to the new: What technology-crazed adolescents tell us about teaching content area literacy. *The Journal of Media Literacy Education, 2*(1), 47–56.

Clark, R. E. (1983). Reconsidering research on learning from media. *Review of Educational Research, 53*(4), 445–459. doi:10.3102/00346543053004445

Clayton, T. E. (1965). *Teaching and learning: A psychological perspective.* Englewood Cliffs, NJ: Prentice Hall, Inc.

CloudPeeps Team. (2015). Top 10 companies winning at remote work culture and their secrets. *CloudPeeps.* Retrieved from http://blog.cloudpeeps.com/top-10-companies-winning-at-remote- work- culture/

Cochran, W. (2012). *2011-2012 school year Lutheran school statistics.* Retrieved from http://mns.lcms.org/LinkClick. aspx?fileticket=_yiscK2ypjs%3D&tabid=211&mid=813

Cohen, D. K., Moffitt, S. L., & Goldin, S. (2007). Chapter four. In S. Fuhrman, D. Cohen, & F. Mosher (Eds.), *The state of education policy research* (pp. 63–83). Mahwah, NJ: Academic Press.

Cole, S. M., Achanhals, J. A., & Vallilww, G. W., IV. (2002). System and method for supporting a worker in a distributed work environment. *IFI Claims Patent Services.* Retrieved from https://www.google.com/patents/US6359711

Colemen, J. S. (1998). Social capital in the creation of human capital. *American Journal of Sociology, 94*, S95–S120. doi:10.1086/228943

Coley, R., Cradler, J., & Engel, P. K. (1997). *Computers and classrooms: The status of technology in U.S. schools.* Policy Information Report. Retrieved from http://eric.ed.gov/?id=ED412893

Coley, R. J. (2001). *Differences in the Gender Gap: Comparisons across Racial/Ethnic Groups in Education and Work.* Princeton, NJ: Policy Information Center.

Commission on Accreditation of Athletic Training Education. (n.d.). *Professional programs.* Retrieved from http://caate. net/professional-programs/

Connell, R. W. (1995). *Masculinities.* Cambridge, UK: Polity Press.

Connelly, F. M., & Clandinin, D. J. (1988). *Teachers as curriculum planners.* New York, NY: Teachers College.

Conrad, D. (2008). From community to community of practice: Exploring the connection of online learners to informal learning in the workplace. *American Journal of Distance Education, 22*(1), 3–23. doi:10.1080/08923640701713414

Cooper, J. O., Heron, T. E., & Heward, W. L. (2007). *Applied Behavior Analysis* (2nd ed.). Pearson.

Corcoran, L., Connolly, I., & OMoore, M. (2012). Cyberbullying in Irish schools: An investigation of personality and self-concept. *The Irish Journal of Psychology, 33*(4), 153–165. doi:10.1080/03033910.2012.677995

CORDIS. (2014a). *HS-TIDE 0 - Technology initiative for disabled and elderly people - TIDE pilot action, 1991-1993.* Retrieved from http://cordis.europa.eu/programme/rcn/275 _en.html

CORDIS. (2014b). *HS-TIDE 1 - Technology initiative (EEC) for disabled and elderly people (TIDE), 1993-1994.* Retrieved from http://cordis.europa.eu/programme/rcn/337_en.html

Cotreras, M. (2014). *Digital story from vivir Mexico study abroad.* Retrieved from YouTube: https://www.youtube.com/ watch?v=mdQeEwahcxo

Courtois, C., & Verdegem, P. (2014). With a little help from my friends: An analysis of the role of social support in digital inequalities. *New Media & Society, 18*(8), 1508–1527. doi:10.1177/1461444814562162

Covey, S. R., Merrill, A. R., & Merrill, R. R. (1994). *First things first*. New York, NY: Free Press.

Coyne, P., Ganley, P., Hall, T., Meo, G., Murray, E., & Gordon, D. (2008). Applying universal design for learning in the classroom. In D. H. Rose & A. Meyer (Eds.), *A practical reader in universal design for learning* (pp. 1–13). Cambridge, MA: Harvard University Press.

Crawford-Ferre, H. G., & Wiest, L. R. (2012). Effective online instruction in higher education. *Quarterly Review of Distance Education, 13*(1), 11.

Creswell, J. W. (1998). *Qualitative inquiry and research design: Choosing among five traditions*. Thousand Oaks, CA: Sage Publications.

Creswell, J. W. (2012). *Qualitative inquiry and research design: Choosing among five approaches*. Thousand Oaks, CA: Sage Publications.

Croker, R. (1999). Fundamentals of ongoing assessment. *Shiken, 3*(1), 10-15. http://jalt.org/test/cro_1.htm

Crompton, H. (2013). Mobile learning: New approach, new theory. In Z. L. Berge & L. Y. Muilenburg (Eds.), *Handbook of Mobile Learning*. New York: Routledge.

Crotty, M. (1998). *The foundations of social research*. Thousand Oaks, CA: Sage Publications.

Crowell, C., Anderson, D., Abel, D., & Sergio, J. (1988). Task clarification, performance, feedback and social praise: Procedures for improving the customer service of bank tellers. *Journal of Applied Behavior Analysis, 21*(1), 65–71. doi:10.1901/jaba.1988.21-65 PMID:16795713

Crow, K. L. (2008). Four types of disabilities: *Their impact on online learning. TechTrends, 52*(1), 51–55. doi:10.1007/s11528-008-0112-6

Crozier, S., & Tincani, M. (2007). Effects of social stories on prosocial behavior of preschool children with autism spectrum disorders. *Journal of Autism and Developmental Disorders, 37*(9), 1803–1814. doi:10.1007/s10803-006-0315-7 PMID:17165149

Cullen, T., Frey, T., Hinshaw, R., & Warren, S. (2004, October). *Technology grants and rural schools: The power to transform*. Chicago: Association for Educational Communications and Technology. Retrieved from http://files.eric.ed.gov/fulltext/ED485134.pdf

Cullen, T. A., Brush, T. A., Frey, T. J., Hinshaw, R. S., & Warren, S. J. (2006). NCLB technology and a rural school: A case study. *Rural Educator, 28*(1).

Cunningham, T., & Austin, J. (2007). Using goal setting, task clarification, and feedback to increase the use of hands-free technique by hospital operating room staff. *Journal of Applied Behavior Analysis, 40*(4), 673–677. doi:10.1901/jaba.2007.673-677 PMID:18189098

Curelaru, M., Iacob, I., & Abalasei, B. (2009). *School bullying: Definition, characteristics, and intervention strategies*. Lumean Publishing House.

Daily, M. (2005). *Inclusion of Students with Autism Spectrum Disorders*. Retrieved from http://education.jhu.edu/PD/newhorizons/Exceptional Learners/Autism/Articles/Inclusion of Students with Autism Spectrum Disorders/index.html

Danaher, P., Gururajan, R., & Hafeez-Baig, A. (2009). Transforming the practice of mobile learning: Promoting pedagogical innovation through educational principles and strategies that work. In *Innovative Mobile Learning: Techniques and Strategies*. Hershey, PA: IGA Global. doi:10.4018/978-1-60566-062-2.ch002

Danielson, C. (2007). *Enhancing professional practice: A framework for teaching.* Alexandria, VA: Association for Supervision and Curriculum Development.

Darling-Hammond, L. (2010). *Evaluating teacher effectiveness: How teacher performance assessments can measure and improve teaching.* Retrieved from https://edpolicy.stanford.edu/sites/default/files/publications/evaluating-teacher-effectiveness_0.pdf

Darling-Hammond, L. (2006). *Powerful teacher education: Lessons from exemplary programs.* San Francisco, CA: Jossey-Bass.

Darling-Hammond, L. (2014). One piece of the whole: Teacher evaluation as part of a comprehensive system for teaching and learning. *American Educator, 38*(1), 4–13.

Darrow, A. (2015). Differentiated instruction for students with disabilities: Using DI in the music classroom. *General Music Today, 28*(2), 29–32. doi:10.1177/1048371314554279

Daudelin, M. W. (1996). Learning from experience through reflection. *Organizational Dynamics, 24*(3), 36–49. doi:10.1016/S0090-2616(96)90004-2

Davies, J. (2016). *Three ways technology is revolutionising elderly care.* Retrieved from https://internetofbusiness.com/technology-revolutionising-elderly-care/

Davies, J. (2012). Facework on facebook as a new literacy practice. *Computers & Education, 59*(1), 19–29. doi:10.1016/j.compedu.2011.11.007

Davis, J., & Kershaw, G. (Producers). (2005). Criminal Minds: Behavior Analysis Unit [Television series]. Los Angeles, CA: The Mark Gordon Company.

Davis, A. P., Dent, E. B., & Wharff, D. M. (2015). A conceptual model of systems thinking leadership in community colleges. *Systemic Practice and Action Research, 28*(4), 333–353. doi:10.1007/s11213-015-9340-9

Davis, F. (1989). Perceived usefulness, perceived ease of use, and user acceptance of information technology. *Management Information Systems Quarterly, 13*(3), 319–340. doi:10.2307/249008

Davis, F., Bogazzi, R., & Warshaw, P. (1989). User acceptance of computer technology: A comparison of two theoretical models. *Management Science, 35*(8), 982–1003. doi:10.1287/mnsc.35.8.982

Davis, F., & Venkatesh, V. (1996). A critical assessment of potential measurement biases in the technology acceptance model: Three experiments. *International Journal of Human-Computer Studies, 45*(1), 19–45. doi:10.1006/ijhc.1996.0040

Dawson, C., & Rakes, C. (2003). The influence of principals technology training on the integration of technology into schools. *Journal of Research on Technology in Education, 36*(1), 29–49. doi:10.1080/15391523.2003.10782401

de Carvalho, A. T., da Silva, A. S. R., Fenandes, A. F. C., & Pagliuca, L. M. F. (2014). Health education for the blind: Evaluation of accessibility of an inclusive online course. *Creative Education, 5*(16), 1559–1566. doi:10.4236/ce.2014.516172

de Castell, S., & Jensen, J. (2007). *Words in play: International perspectives on digital games research.* New York, NY: Peter Lang Publishing.

de Koster, S., Volman, M., & Kuiper, E. (2013). Interactivity with the interactive whiteboard in traditional and innovative primary schools: An exploratory study. *Australasian Journal of Educational Technology, 29*(4). doi:10.14742/ajet.291

Dean, L. T. (2016). *Future factories.* Retrieved from www.futurefactories.com

Deaton, C. M., Deaton, B., Ivankovic, D., & Norris, F. A. (2013). Creating stop-motion videos with iPads to support students understanding of cell processes: "Because you have to know what youre talking about to be able to do it. *Journal of Digital Learning in Teacher Education, 30*(2), 25–31. doi:10.1080/21532974.2013.10784729

Dede, C. (2009). Introduction to virtual reality in education. *Themes in Science and Technology Education, 2*(1-2).

Dede, C. (2009). Immersive interfaces for engagement and learning. *Science, 323*(5910), 66–69. doi:10.1126/science.1167311 PMID:19119219

Dehue, F., Bolman, C., & Vollink, T. (2008). Cyberbullying: Youngsters experiences and parental perception. *CyberPscyhology & Behavior, 11*(2), 217–223. doi:10.1089/cpb.2007.0008 PMID:18422417

Dehue, F., Bolman, C., Vollink, T., & Pouwelse, M. (2012). Cyberbullying and traditional bullying in relation to adolescents' perceptions of parenting. *Journal of Cyber Therapy and Rehabilitation, 5*, 25–34.

deLara, E. W. (2012). Why adolescents dont disclose incidents of bullying and harassment. *Journal of School Violence, 11*(4), 288–305. doi:10.1080/15388220.2012.705931

DeLeon, I. G., Iwata, B. A., Goh, H., & Worsdell, A. S. (1997). Emergence of reinforcer preference as a function of schedule requirements and stimulus similarity. *Journal of Applied Behavior Analysis, 30*(3), 439–449. doi:10.1901/jaba.1997.30-439 PMID:9378681

Delgado, A. J., Wardlow, L., McKnight, K., & O'Malley, K. (2015). Educational technology: A review of the integration, resources, and effectiveness of technology in K-12 classrooms. *Journal of Information Technology Education: Research, 14*(24), 397–416.

Dennen, V. P., & Hao, S. (2014). Intentionally mobile pedagogy: The M-COPE framework for mobile learning in higher education. *Technology, Pedagogy and Education, 23*(3), 397–419. doi:10.1080/1475939X.2014.943278

Des Moines University. (2016). *Mission, vision and values.* Retrieved January 15, 2016, from https://www.dmu.edu/about/mission-vision-and-values/

DeVaney, S. (2015). Understanding the millennial generation. *Journal of Financial Service Professionals, 69*(6), 11–14.

Dewey, J. (1938). *Education and Experience.* New York, NY: Simon and Schuster.

Dewey, J. (1938). *Experience and education.* New York: Macmillan.

Diamanduros, T., & Downs, E. (2011). Creating a safe school environment: How to prevent cyberbullying at your school. *Library Media Connection, 30*(2), 36–38.

Diekelmann, N. L. (2003). *Teaching the practitioners of care: New pedagogies for the health professions.* Madison, WI: University of Wisconsin Press.

DiPietro, M. (2010). Virtual school pedagogy: The instructional practices of K-12 virtual school teachers. *Journal of Educational Computing Research, 42*(3), 327–354. doi:10.2190/EC.42.3.e

DiPietro, M., Ferdig, R. E., Black, E. W., & Preston, M. (2008). Best practices in teaching K-12 online: Lessons learned from Michigan virtual school teachers. *Journal of Interactive Online Learning, 9*(3), 10–35.

Disability Gov. (2016). *Rehabilitation Act of 1973.* Retrieved from https://www.disability.gov/rehabilitation-act-1973/

Dorsen, A., Gibbs, M., Guerrero, R., & McDevitt, P. (2004). Technology in nonsectarian and religious private schools. *Journal of Research on Christian Education, 13*(2), 289–314. doi:10.1080/10656210409484973

Doty, D. E., Popplewell, S. R., & Byers, G. O. (2001). Interactive CD-ROM storybooks and young readers reading comprehension. *Journal of Research on Computing in Education, 33*(4), 374–384. doi:10.1080/08886504.2001.10782322

Dudeney, G., & Hockly, N. (2016). Literacies, technology and language teaching. The Routledge Handbook of Language Learning and Technology, 115.

Duffy, T. M., & Jonassen, D. H. (Eds.). (1992). *Constructivism and the technology of instruction: A conversation.* Lawrence Erlbaum Associates.

Dyson, L. E., Andrews, T., Smyth, R., & Wallace, R. (2013). Toward a holistic framework for ethical mobile learning. In Z. L. Berge & L. Y. Muilenburg (Eds.), *Handbook of Mobile Learning.* New York: Routledge.

Edelman, M., & Ficorelli, C. T. (2012). Keeping older adults safe at home. *Nursing, 42*(1), 65–66. doi:10.1097/01. NURSE.0000408481.20951.e8 PMID:22157840

Eden, S., Heiman, T., & Olenik-Shemesh, D. (2013). Teachers perceptions, beliefs and concerns about cyberbullying. *British Journal of Educational Technology, 44*(6), 1036–1052. doi:10.1111/j.1467-8535.2012.01363.x

Edwards, M., Perry, B., & Janzen, K. (2011). The making of an exemplary online educator. *Distance Education, 32*(1), 101–118. doi:10.1080/01587919.2011.565499

Eiben, A. E. (2014). *In vivo veritas: Towards the evolution of things.* Paper presented at the 13th International Conference on Parallel Problem Solving from Nature, Ljubljana, Slovenia. doi:10.1007/978-3-319-10762-2_3

Elledge, L. C., Williford, A., Boulton, A. J., DePaolis, K. J., Little, T. D., & Salmivalli, C. (2013). Individual and contextual predictors of cyberbullying: The influence of childrens provictim attitudes and teachers ability to intervene. *Journal of Youth and Adolescence, 42*(5), 698–710. doi:10.1007/s10964-013-9920-x PMID:23371005

Ellis, J. (2011). Peer feedback on writing: Is on-line actually better than on-paper. *Journal of Academic Language and Learning, 5*(1), 88–99.

Emurian, H. H., Hu, X., Wang, J., & Durham, A. G. (2000). Learning Java: A programmed instruction approach using Applets. *Computers in Human Behavior, 16*(4), 395–422. doi:10.1016/S0747-5632(00)00019-4

Enayati, A. (2015). *Seeking serenity.* New York, NY: New American Library.

Engelmann, S., & Carnine, D. (1975). *Distar arithmetic I.* SRA/McGraw-Hill.

Engelmann, S., & Carnine, D. W. (1982). Theory of instruction: Principles and applications. New York: Irvington.

Entwistle, N. (2001, July 1). Styles of learning and approaches to studying in higher education. *Kybernetes, 30*(5/6), 593–603. doi:10.1108/03684920110391823

Erdur-Baker, O. (2010). Cyberbullying and its correlation to traditional bullying, gender and frequent and risky usage of internet-mediated communication tools. *New Media & Society, 12*(1), 109–125. doi:10.1177/1461444809341260

Erickson, L. B. (2011, August). Social media, social capital, and seniors: The impact of Facebook on bonding and bridging social capital of individuals over 65. In *AMCIS.* Retrieved from http://aisel.aisnet.org/cgi/viewcontent.cgi?article=1084&context=amcis2011_sub

Ericsson, K. A. (2004). Deliberate practice and the acquisition and maintenance of expert performance in medicine and related domains. *Academic Medicine, 79*(10Suppl), S70–S81. doi:10.1097/00001888-200410001-00022 PMID:15383395

Ericsson, K. A. (2008). Deliberate practice and the acquisition and maintenance of expert performance: A general overview. *Academic Emergency Medicine, 15*(11), 988–994. doi:10.1111/j.1553-2712.2008.00227.x PMID:18778378

Escobar, R., & Twyman, J. S. (2014). Editorial: Behavior analysis and technology. *The Mexican Journal of Behavior Analysis, 40*(2), 1–2.

Eshelman, J. W. (2004). *SAFMEDS on the Web: Guidelines and considerations for SAFMEDS*. Retrieved from http://members.aol.com/standardcharter/safmeds.html

Eskay, M., & Willis, K. (2008). Implementing social skills for students with autism. *Autism and Developmental Disabilities: Current Practices and Issues, 18*, 45-17. Retrieved from http://www.emeraldinsight.com/doi/abs/10.1016/S0270-4013(08)18003-5

Evans, B. (2016, March 29). *Mobile is eating the world*. Retrieved from http://ben-evans.com/benedictevans/2016/3/29/presentation-mobile-ate-the-world

Every, S. S. A. (ESSA) (Reauthorization of the Elementary and Secondary Education Act). Pub. L. No. 114-95, U. S. C. § 1177 (2015). (n.d.). Retrieved from https://www.congress.gov/bill/114th-congress/senate-bill/1177/text

Ezzy, D. (2002). *Qualitative analysis: Practice and innovation*. Crows Nest, Australia: Allen & Unwin.

Fabos, B., & Young, M. D. (1999). Telecommunication in the classroom: Rhetoric versus reality. *Review of Educational Research, 69*(3), 217–259. doi:10.3102/00346543069003217

Fabry, D. L., & Higgs, J. R. (1997). Barriers to the effective use of technology in education: Current status. *Journal of Educational Computing Research, 17*(4), 385–395. doi:10.2190/C770-AWA1-CMQR-YTYV

Falco, M. (2012, March 29). *CDC: U.S. kids with autism up 78% in past decade*. Retrieved from http://edition.cnn.com/2012/03/29/health/autism

Falk, J. H., & Dierking, L. D. (2002). *Lessons without limit: How free-choice learning is transforming education*. Walnut Creek, CA: AltaMira Press.

Falloon, G. (2015). Whats the difference? Learning collaboratively using iPads in conventional classrooms. *Computers & Education, 84*, 62–77. doi:10.1016/j.compedu.2015.01.010

Fanti, K. A., Demetriou, A. G., & Hawa, V. V. (2012). A longitudinal study of cyberbullying: Examining risk and protective factors. *European Journal of Developmental Psychology, 8*(2), 168–181. doi:10.1080/17405629.2011.643169

Farkas, M. (2012). Participatory technologies, pedagogy 2.0 and information literacy. *Library Hi Tech, 30*(1), 82–94.

Fenwick, T., Edwards, R., & Sawchuk, P. (2012). *Emerging approaches to educational research: Tracing the sociomaterial*. New York: Routledge.

Fenwick, T., & Landri, P. (2012). Materialities, textures and pedagogies: Sociomaterial assemblages in education. *Pedagogy, Culture & Society, 20*(1), 1–7. doi:10.1080/14681366.2012.649421

Ferdig, R. E. (2010). *Continuous quality improvement through professional development for online K-12 instructors*. Retrieved from http://www.mivu.org/Portals/0/RPT_PD_Ferdig_Final.pdf

Festl, R., Schwarkow, M., & Quandt, T. (2013). Peer influence, internet use and cyberbullying: A comparison of different context effects among German adolescents. *Journal of Children and Media, 7*(4), 446–462. doi:10.1080/17482798.2013.781514

Fichten, C. S., Asuncion, J. V., Barile, M., Ferraro, V., & Wolforth, J. (2009). Accessibility of e-learning and computer and information technologies for students with visual impairments in postsecondary education. *Journal of Visual Impairment & Blindness, 103*(9), 543.

Fietkiewica, K. J., Lins, E., Baran, K. S., & Stock, W. G. (2016). Inter-generational comparison of social media use: Investigating the online behavior of different generational cohorts. *IEEE Computer Society, 16*, 1530–1605.

Finn, K. (2015). *Social media use by older adults.* Retrieved from http://wiserusability.com/wpfs /wp-content/uploads/2015/07/Social-Media-Use-by-Older-Adults.pdf

Fischer, G., & Scharff, E. (2000). Meta-design: design for designers. *Proceedings of the 3rd conference on Designing interactive systems: Processes, practices, methods, and techniques* (pp. 396-405). New York, NY: ACM.

Fisher, W., Piazza, C. C., Bowman, L. G., Hagopian, L. P., Owens, J. C., & Slevin, I. (1992). A comparison of two approaches for identifying reinforcers for persons with severe and profound disabilities. *Journal of Applied Behavior Analysis, 25*(2), 491–498. doi:10.1901/jaba.1992.25-491 PMID:1634435

Flay, B. R., Biglan, A., Boruch, R. F., Castro, F. G., Gottfredson, D., Kellam, S., & Ji, P. et al. (2005). Standards of evidence: Criteria for efficacy, effectiveness and dissemination. *Prevention Science, 6*(3), 151–175. doi:10.1007/s11121-005-5553-y PMID:16365954

Fletcher, D. (2006). Technology integration: Do they or don't they? A self-report survey from PreK through 5th grade professional educators. *AACE Journal, 14*(3), 207–219.

Fletcher-Watson, B., Crompton, C. J., Hutchison, M., & Lu, H. (2016). Strategies for enhancing success in digital tablet use by older adults: A pilot study. *Gerontechnology (Valkenswaard), 15*(3), 162–170. doi:10.4017/gt.2016.15.3.005.00

Florida Virtual School. (2015). *Florida Virtual School instructional evaluation plan.* Retrieved from https://flvs.net/docs/default-source/district/flvs-instructor-evaluation-plan.pdf?sfvrsn=8

Four-dimensional. (2010). *Oxford Dictionary of English* (3rd ed.). Oxford University Press.

Fox, K. F. (2012). Simulation-based learning in cardiovascular medicine: Benefits for the trainee, the trained and the patient. *Heart (British Cardiac Society), 98*(7), 527–528. doi:10.1136/heartjnl-2011-301314 PMID:22337950

Fraenkel, J., Wallen, N., & Hyun, H. (2012). *How to design and evaluate research in education* (8th ed.). New York, NY: McGraw Hill.

Franklin, C. (2007). Factors that influence elementary teachers' use of computers. *Journal of Technology and Teacher Education, 15*(2), 267–293.

Fraser, K., Peets, A., Walker, I., Tworek, J., Paget, M., Wright, B., & Mclaughlin, K. (2009). The effect of simulator training on clinical skills acquisition, retention and transfer. *Medical Education, 43*(8), 784–789. doi:10.1111/j.1365-2923.2009.03412.x PMID:19659492

Frater, G. (1998). Boys and literacy. In K. Bleach (Ed.), *Raising boys' achievement in schools.* Stoke-on-Trent, UK: Trentham Books.

Frater, G. (2000). *Securing boys' literacy.* London, UK: The Basic Skills Agency.

Frey, B. A., Kearns, L. R., & King, D. K. (2012). *Quality matters: Template for an accessibility policy for online courses.* Retrieved from http://www.qmprogram.org/template-accessibility-policy-online-courses

Frey, B. B., Schmitt, V. L., & Allen, J. P. (2012). Defining authentic classroom assessment. *Practical Assessment, Research & Evaluation, 17*(2), 1–18.

Friemel, T. N. (2014). The digital divide has grown old: Determinant of a digital divide among seniors. *New Media & Society, 18*(2), 313–331. doi:10.1177/1461444814538648

Fuad-Luke, A. (2009). *Design activism: Beautiful strangeness for a sustainable world*. London: Earthscan.

Fuhrman, S., Cohen, D., & Mosher, F. (2007). *The state of education policy research*. Mahwah, NJ: Erlbaum.

Fung Kwok Pan. Fluid vase. (2010). *Design Boom Newsletter 440071*. Retrieved from http://www.designboom.com/technology/fung-kwok-pan-fluid-vase/

Gaba, D. M. (2007). The future vision of simulation in healthcare. *Simulation in Healthcare: Journal of the Society for Simulation in Healthcare, 2*(2), 126–135. doi:10.1097/01.SIH.0000258411.38212.32 PMID:19088617

Gabbert, C. (2012, December 7). *Using Social Stories to Teach Kids with Asperger's Disorder*. Retrieved from http://www.brighthub.com/education/special/articles/29487.aspx

Gallant, J. P., Thyer, B. A., & Bailey, J. S. (1991). Using bug-in-the-ear feedback in clinical supervision: Preliminary evaluations. *Research on Social Work Practice, 1*(2), 175–187. doi:10.1177/104973159100100205

Gallistl, V. (2016). The digital divide and technology generations – European Implications from the Austrian Perspective. In *Third ISA Forum of Sociology*. ISACONF.

Gardner, R., & Reamer, D. B. (2008). Simulation in obstetrics and gynecology. *Obstetrics and Gynecology Clinics of North America, 35*(1), 97–127. doi:10.1016/j.ogc.2007.12.008 PMID:18319131

Gargiulo, R. M., & Metcalf, D. (2010). *Teaching in today's inclusive classroom: A universal design for learning approach*. Belmont, CA: Wadsworth.

Garrison, D. R., Anderson, T., & Archer, W. (2000). Critical inquiry in a text-based environment: Computer conferencing in higher education. *The Internet and Higher Education, 2*(2-3), 87–105. doi:10.1016/S1096-7516(00)00016-6

Gayle, B. M., Randall, N., Langley, L., & Preiss, R. (2013). Faculty learning processes: A model for moving from scholarly teaching to the scholarship of teaching and learning. *Teaching and Learning Inquiry: The ISSOTL Journal, 1*(1), 81–93. doi:10.20343/teachlearninqu.1.1.81

Gee, J. P. (2007). *What video games have to teach us about learning and literacy*. New York, NY: Palgrave Macmillan.

Gee, J. P. (2011). The new literacy studies. In *Social linguistics and literacies: Ideology in discourses* (pp. 63–86). London, UK: Routledge.

Gee, J. P. (2013). *The anti-education era: creating smarter students through digital learning*. Palgrave Macmillian.

Gemin, B., Pape, L., Vashaw, L., & Watson, J. (2015). *Keeping pace with K-12 digital learning*. Durango, CO: Evergreen Education Group.

Genta, M. L., Smith, P. K., Ortega, R., Brighi, A., Giasrini, A., & Thompson, F. et al.. (2012). Comparative aspects of cyberbullying in Italy, England and Spain: Findings from a DAPHNE project. In Q. Li, D. Cross, & P. K. Smith (Eds.), *Bullying goes to the global village: Research on cyberbullying from an international perspective* (pp. 15–31). Chichester, UK: Wiley-Blackwell. doi:10.1002/9781119954484.ch2

Gere, A. R. (1987). *Writing groups: History, theory, and implications*. Carbondale, IL: Southern Illinois University Press.

Germer, C. K. (2009). *The Mindful path to self-compassion*. New York, NY: The Guilford Press.

Gerontology. (2017). In *OxfordDictionaries.com*. Retrieved from http://www.oxforddictionaries.com/definition/english/gerontology

Ge, X., Huang, D., Zhang, H., & Bowers, B. (2013). Three-dimension design for mobile learning. In Z. L. Berge & L. Y. Muilenburg (Eds.), *Handbook of Mobile Learning*. New York: Routledge.

Giebelhaus, C. R. (1994). The mechanical third ear device: A student teaching supervision alternative. *Journal of Teacher Education, 45*(5), 365–373. doi:10.1177/0022487194045005009

Giedd, J. N. (2008). The teen brain: Insights from neuroimaging. *The Journal of Adolescent Health, 42*(4), 335–343. doi:10.1016/j.jadohealth.2008.01.007 PMID:18346658

GoAnimate. (2014). *Create Animated Videos for your Business*. Retrieved from https://goanimate.com/

Godzicki, L., Godzicki, N., Krofel, M., & Michaels, R. (2013). *Increasing motivation and engagement in elementary and middle cchool students through technology-supported learning environments*. Retrieved from http://eric.ed.gov/?id=ED541343

Goebert, D., Else, I., Matsu, C., Chung-Do, J., & Chang, J. Y. (2011). The impact of cyberbullying on substance use and mental health in a multiethnic sample. *Maternal and Child Health Journal, 15*(8), 1282–1286. doi:10.1007/s10995-010-0672-x PMID:20824318

Goldberg, N. (1990). *Wild mind*. New York, NY: Bantam.

Goldberg, N. (2000). *Thunder and lightning*. New York, NY: Bantam.

Gong, M., Xu, Y., & Yu, Y. (2004). An enhanced technology acceptance model for web-based learning. *Journal of Information Systems Education, 15*(4), 365–374.

Gonzalez, A., Ramirez, M. P., & Viadel, V. (2012). Attitudes of the elderly toward information and communications technologies. *Educational Gerontology, 38*(9), 585–594. doi:10.1080/03601277.2011.595314

González, N., Moll, L., & Amanti, C. (2005). *Funds of Knowledge: Theorizing Practices in Households, Communities, and Classrooms*. Lawrence Erlbaum Associates, Publishers.

Goodman, J., Brady, M. P., Duffy, M. L., Scott, J., & Pollard, N. (2008). The effects of bug-in-ear on special education teachers delivery of learn units. *Focus on Autism and Other Developmental Disabilities, 23*(4), 207–216. doi:10.1177/1088357608324713

Good, T. L., & Brophy, J. E. (1977). *Educational psychology: A realistic approach*. New York: Holt, Rinehart and Winston.

Gore, A. (2013). *The future*. New York, NY: Random House.

Gradinger, P., Strohmeier, D., & Spiel, C. (2009). Traditional bullying and cyberbullying. *The Journal of Psychology, 217*, 205–213.

Grady, J. L., Kehrer, R. G., Trusty, C. E., Entin, E. B., Entin, E. E., & Brunye, T. T. (2008). Learning nursing procedures: The influence of simulator fidelity and student gender on teaching effectiveness. *The Journal of Nursing Education, 47*(9), 403–408. doi:10.3928/01484834-20080901-09 PMID:18792707

Graves, D. H. (2001). *The energy to teach*. Portsmouth, NH: Heinemann.

Gray, C. A. (1996). *Social stories and comic strip conversations: unique methods to improve social understanding* [Videotape]. Arlington, TX: Future Horizons.

Gray, C. A. (2000). *Writing social stories with Carol Gray – workbook for video*. Arlington, TX: Future Horizons.

Gray, C. A., & Garand, J. D. (1993). Social stories: Improving responses of students with autism with accurate social information. *Focus on Autism and Other Developmental Disabilities, 8*(1), 1–10. doi:10.1177/108835769300800101

Green, C., Rollyson, J., Passante, S., & Reid, D. (2002). Maintaining proficient supervisor performance with direct support personnel: An analysis of two management approaches. *Journal of Applied Behavior Analysis*, *35*(2), 205–208. doi:10.1901/jaba.2002.35-205 PMID:12102142

Greenfield, A. (2006). *Everyware: The dawning age of ubiquitous computing*. Berkeley, CA: New Riders.

Greenfield, P. M. (2009). Technology and information education: What is taught, what is learned. *Science*, *323*(5910), 69–71. doi:10.1126/science.1167190 PMID:19119220

Greenwood, C. R., Delaquadri, J., & Hall, R. V. (1984). Opportunity to respond and student academic performance. In Behavior analysis in education (pp. 58-88). Columbus, OH: Charles E. Merrill Co.

Greenwood, C. R., Delaquadri, J. C., & Hall, R. V. (1989). Longitudinal effects of classwide peer tutoring. *Journal of Educational Psychology*, *81*(3), 371–383. doi:10.1037/0022-0663.81.3.371

Greer, R. D. (1994b). The measure of a teacher. In R. Gardner III, D. M. Sainata, 1. O. Cooper, T. E. Heron, W. L. Heward, J. Eschelman, & T. A. Grossi, (Eds.), Behavior analysis in education: Focus on measurably superior instruction (pp. 325-335). Pacific Grove, CA: Brooks Cole.

Greer, R. D. (1991). The teacher as strategic scientist: A solution to our educational crisis? *Behavior and Social Issues*, *1*(2), 25–41. doi:10.5210/bsi.v1i2.165

Greer, R. D. (1994a). A systems analysis of the behaviors of schooling. *Journal of Behavioral Education*, *4*(3), 255–264. doi:10.1007/BF01531981

Greer, R. D. (2002). *Designing teaching strategies: An applied behavior analysis systems approach*. San Diego, CA: Academic Press.

Greer, R. D., & Keohane, D. D. (2005). The evolutions of verbal behavior in children. *Behavioral Development Bulletin*, *1*(1), 31–47. doi:10.1037/h0100559

Greer, R. D., Keohane, D., & Healy, O. (2002). Quality and comprehensive applications of behavior analysis to schooling. *Behavior Analyst Today*, *3*(2), 120–132. doi:10.1037/h0099977

Greer, R. D., McCorkle, N. P., & Williams, G. (1989). A sustained analysis of the behaviors of schooling. *Behavioral Residential Treatment*, *4*, 113–141.

Greer, R. D., & McDonough, S. H. (1999). Is the learn unit a fundamental measure of pedagogy? *The Behavior Analyst*, *22*(1), 5–16. PMID:22478317

Grigg, D. W. (2012). Definitional constructs of cyberbullying and cyber aggression from a triangulatory overview: A preliminary study into elements. *Journal of Aggression, Conflict and Peace Research*, *4*(4), 202–215. doi:10.1108/17596591211270699

Gruwell, E., & the The Freedom Writers. (2009). The Freedom Writers diary (2nd Ed.). New York, NY: Broadway.

Guernsey, L., & Levine, M. (2014). Pioneering literacy in the digital age. In Technology and digital media in the early years: Tools for teaching and learning (pp. 104-114). New York, NY: Routledge.

Gulikers, J. M., Bastiaens, T. J., & Kirschner, P. A. (2004). A five dimensional framework for authentic assessment. *Educational Technology Research and Development*, *52*(3), 67–86. doi:10.1007/BF02504676

Gulikers, J. T., Kester, L., Kirschner, P. A., & Bastiaens, T. J. (2008). The effect of practical experience on perceptions of assessment authenticity, study approach, and learning outcomes. *Learning and Instruction*, *18*(2), 172–186. doi:10.1016/j.learninstruc.2007.02.012

Gurung, R. A. R., Chick, N. L., & Haynie, A. (2009). *Exploring signature pedagogies: Approaches to teaching disciplinary habits of mind.* Sterling, VA: Stylus Publishing.

Guskey, T. (2008). Mastery Learning. In 21st Century Education: A Reference Handbook. Thousand Oaks, CA: Sage Publications. doi:10.4135/9781412964012.n21

Guzzetti, B., & Gamboa, M. (2005). Online journaling: The informal writings of two adolescent girls. *Research in the Teaching of English, 40*(2), 168–206.

Hackett, S., & Parmanto, B. (2005). A longitudinal evaluation of accessibility: Higher education web sites. *Internet Research, 15*(3), 281–294. doi:10.1108/10662240510602690

Hall, R. F., & Barker, B. O. (1995). Case studies in the current use of technology in education. *Rural Research Report, 6*(10). Retrieved from http://files.eric.ed.gov/fulltext/ED391619.pdf

Hall, T. (2002). *Differentiated Instruction.* Retrieved from http://www.cast.org/publications/ncac/ncac_diffinstruc.html

Hall, G. E., & Hord, S. M. (2001). *Implementing change: Patterns, principles, and potholes* (2nd ed.). Boston, MA: Pearson.

Hansen, M. B. N. (2006). *Bodies in Code: Interfaces with Digital Media.* New York, NY: Routledge Taylor and Francis Group.

Harasim, L. (2000). Shift happens: Online education as a new paradigm in learning. *The Internet and Higher Education, 3*(1), 41–61. doi:10.1016/S1096-7516(00)00032-4

Harasim, L. M. (Ed.). (1995). *Learning Networks: A Field Guide to Teaching and Learning Online.* MIT press.

Hare, S., Howard, E., & Pope, M. (2002). Technology integration: Closing the gap between what preservice teachers are taught to do and what they can do. *Journal of Technology and Teacher Education, 10*(2), 191–203.

Harris, J., Mishra, P., & Koehler, M. (2009). Teachers technological pedagogical content knowledge and learning activity types: Curriculum-based technology integration reframed. *Journal of Research on Technology in Education, 41*(4), 393–416. doi:10.1080/15391523.2009.10782536

Harrison, A., Wheeler, P., & Whitehead, C. (2004). *The distributed workplace: Sustainable work environment.* New York, NY: Spoon Press.

Harrison, M. D. (2002). *Narrative based evaluation.* New York, NY: Peter Lang Publishing.

Hatala, R., Issenberg, S. B., Kassen, B., Cole, G., Bacchus, C. M., & Scalese, R. J. (2008). Assessing cardiac physical examination skills using simulation technology and real patients: A comparison study. *Medical Education, 42*(6), 628–636. doi:10.1111/j.1365-2923.2007.02953.x PMID:18221269

Hattie, J., & Timperley, J. (2007). The Power of Feedback. *Review of Educational Research, 77*(1), 81–112. doi:10.3102/003465430298487

Hauber, R. P., Cormier, E., & White, J. (2010). An exploration of the relationship between knowledge and performance-related variables in high-fidelity simulation: Designing instruction that promotes expertise in practice. *Nursing Education Perspectives, 31*(4), 242–246. PMID:20882866

Hawken, P., Lovins, A., & Lovins, L. H. (2000). *Natural capitalism: The next industrial revolution.* London: Earthscan.

Headrick, D. (2015). 4D printing transforms product design. *Research-Technology Management, 58*(2), 7–8.

Heaggans, R. C. (2012). The 60's are the new 20's: Teaching older adults technology. *SRATE Journal, 21*(2), 1-8. Retrieved from http://files.eric.ed.gov/fulltext/EJ990630.pdf

Healy, J. M. (1999). *Failure to connect: How computers affect our children's minds--for better and worse.* New York, NY: Simon and Schuster.

Heard, G. (1995). *Writing toward home.* Portsmouth, NH: Heinemann.

Heard, G. (1999). *Awakening the heart.* Portsmouth, NH: Heinemann.

Heimann, M., Nelson, K. E., Tjus, T., & Gillberg, C. (1995). Increasing reading and communication skills in children with autism through an interactive multimedia computer program. *Journal of Autism and Developmental Disorders, 25*(5), 459–480. doi:10.1007/BF02178294 PMID:8567593

Hensel, D., & Stanley, L. (2014). Group simulation for authentic assessment in a maternal-child lecture course. *Journal of the Scholarship of Teaching and Learning, 14*(2), 61–70. doi:10.14434/josotl.v14i2.4081

Herman, N. J., & Reynolds, L. T. (Eds.). (1994). *Symbolic Interaction: An Introduction to Social Psychology.* Dix Hills, NY: General Hall, Inc.

Hermans, H. (2004). Introduction: The Dialogical self in a global and digital age. *An International Journal of Theory and Research, 4*(4), 297–320.

Hermans, R., Tondeur, J., Van Braak, J., & Valcke, M. (2008). The impact of primary school teachers educational beliefs on classroom use of computer. *Computers & Education, 51*(4), 1499–1509. doi:10.1016/j.compedu.2008.02.001

Hernandez-Ramos, P. (2005). If not here, where? Understanding teachers use of technology in Silicon Valley schools. *Journal of Research on Technology in Education, 38*(1), 39–64. doi:10.1080/15391523.2005.10782449

Herzog, B., Wilson, G., & Rideout, N. (2010). Ageing independently: A Chapel Hill perspective. *North Carolina Medical Journal, 71*(2), 173–176. Retrieved from http://classic.ncmedicaljournal.com/wp-content/uploads/NCMJ/Mar-Apr-10/Herzog.pdf PMID:20552774

Heyward, V. (n.d.). *Using technology to promote physical activity.* Retrieved from http://www.humankinetics.com/excerpts/excerpts/using-technology-to-promote-physical-activity

Hill, W. F. (1977). *Learning: A Survey of Psychological Interpretations.* New York, NY: Thomas Y. Crowell Company.

Hinduja, S., & Patchin, J. W. (2007). Offline consequences of online victimization. *Journal of School Violence, 6*(3), 89–112. doi:10.1300/J202v06n03_06

Hinduja, S., & Patchin, J. W. (2008). Cyberbullying: An exploratory analysis of factors related to offending and victimization. *Deviant Behavior, 29*(2), 129–156. doi:10.1080/01639620701457816

Hinduja, S., & Patchin, J. W. (2010). Bullying, cyberbullying, and suicide. *Archives of Suicide Research, 14*(3), 206–221. doi:10.1080/13811118.2010.494133 PMID:20658375

Hinduja, S., & Patchin, J. W. (2012). Cyberbullying: Neither and epidemic nor a rarity. *European Journal of Developmental Psychology, 9*(5), 539–543. doi:10.1080/17405629.2012.706448

Hinduja, S., & Patchin, J. W. (2013). Social influences on cyberbullying behaviors among middle and high school students. *Journal of Youth and Adolescence, 42*(5), 711–722. doi:10.1007/s10964-012-9902-4 PMID:23296318

Hoadley, T. (2009). Learning advanced life support: A comparison study of the effects of low- and high-fidelity simulation. *Nursing Education Perspectives, 30*(2), 91–95. PMID:19476072

Hokoda, A., Lu, H. A., & Angeles, M. (2006). School bullying in Taiwanese adolescents. *Journal of Emotional Abuse, 6*(4), 69–90. doi:10.1300/J135v06n04_04

Holman, D. (2003). *The new workplace: A guide to the human impact of modern working practices.* Hoboken, NJ: Wiley.

Home Instead. (2017). *5 benefits of technology to share with seniors and their caregivers.* Retrieved from http://www.caregiverstress.com/geriatric-professional-resources/5-benefits-of-technology-to-share-with-seniors-and-their-caregivers/

Honeycutt, L. (2001). Comparing e-mail and synchronous conferencing in online peer response. *Written Communication, 18*(1), 26–60. doi:10.1177/0741088301018001002

Hope, A., Garside, J., & Prescott, S. (2011). Rethinking theory and practice: Pre-registration student nurses experiences of simulation teaching and learning in the acquisition of clinical skills in preparation for practice. *Nurse Education Today, 31*(7), 711–715. doi:10.1016/j.nedt.2010.12.011 PMID:21237536

Hopkins, R. L. (1994). *Narrative schooling: Experiential learning and the transformation of American education.* New York: Teachers College Press.

Horner, R. H., Carr, E. G., Halle, J., McGee, G., Odom, S., & Wolery, M. (2005). The use of single subject research to identify evidence-based practice in special education. *Exceptional Children, 71*(2), 165–179. doi:10.1177/001440290507100203

Horrigan, J. B. (2016). *Lifelong learning and technology.* Retrieved from http://www.leadinglearning.com/podcast-episode-34-lifelong-learning-and-technology-john-horrigan/

Hsin, C.-T., Li, M.-C., & Tsai, C.-C. (2014). The Influence of Young Children's Use of Technology on Their Learning: A Review. *Journal of Educational Technology & Society, 17*(4), 85–99.

Hsu, Y.-L., & Bai, D. L. (2016). The future of Gerontechnology: Proposals from the new editor-in-chief. *Gerontechnology (Valkenswaard), 15*(3), 125–129. doi:10.4017/gt.2016.15.3.001.00

Huang, Y., & Chou, C. (2010). An analysis of multiple factors of cyberbullying among junior high school students in Taiwan. *Computers in Human Behavior, 26*(6), 1581–1590. doi:10.1016/j.chb.2010.06.005

Huber, L., & Watson, C. (2014). Technology: Education and training needs of older adults. *Educational Gerontology, 40*(1), 16–25. doi:10.1080/03601277.2013.768064

Hughes, J. E. (2005). The role of teacher knowledge and learning experiences in forming technology-integrated pedagogy. *Journal of Technology and Teacher Education, 13*(2), 377–402.

Hunt-Barron, S., Tracy, K. N., Howell, E., & Kaminski, R. (2015). Obstacles to enhancing professional development with digital tools in rural landscapes. *Journal of Research in Rural Education (Online), 30*(2), 1–14.

Hunt, D. (1980). 'Bug-in-ear' technique for teaching interview skills. *Journal of Medical Education, 11*, 964–966. PMID:7441683

Hunter, J. (2015). *Technology integration and high possibility classrooms: Building from TPACK.* New York: Routledge.

Hu, S. J. (2013). Evolving paradigms of manufacturing: From mass production to mass customization and personalization. *Procedia CIRP, 7*, 3–8. doi:10.1016/j.procir.2013.05.002

Hutchison, A. C., & Reinking, D. (2011). Teachers' perceptions of integrating information and communication technologies into literacy instruction: A national survey in the U. S. *Reading Research Quarterly, 46*(4), 312–333.

Hutchison, A., Beschorner, B., & Schmidt-Crawford, D. (2012). Exploring the use of the Ipad for literacy learning. *The Reading Teacher, 66*(1), 15–23. doi:10.1002/TRTR.01090

Huyler, D., & Ciocca, D. (2016). Baby Boomers: The use of technology to support learning. *Proceedings from the 15th Annual South Florida Education Research Conference.* Miami, FL: Florida International University.

Hwang, G., & Tsai, C. (2011). Research trends in mobile and ubiquitous learning: A review of publications in selected journals from 2001 to 2010. *British Journal of Educational Technology, 42*(1).

iLynn: College reimagined. (n. d.). Retrieved June 28, 2016 from http://www.lynn.edu/ilynn

Inan, F. A., & Lowther, D. L. (2010). Factors affecting technology integration in K-12 classrooms: A path model. *Educational Technology Research and Development, 58*(2), 137–154. doi:10.1007/s11423-009-9132-y

Individuals with Disabilities Education Act, 20 U.S.C. § 1400 (2004). (n.d.). Retrieved http://idea.ed.gov/download/statute.html

Ingersoll, R. A., & Perda, D. (2006). *What the data tell us about shortages of mathematics and science teachers.* Paper presented at the NCTAF Symposium on the Scope and Consequences of K12 Science and Mathematics Teacher Turnover. Retrieved from: http://www.ucdoer.ie/index.php/Education_Theory/Constructivism_and_Social_Constructivism_in_the_Classroom

Ingham, P., & Greer, R. D. (1992). Changes in student and teacher responses in observed and generalized settings as a function of supervisor observations. *Journal of Applied Behavior Analysis, 25*(1), 153–164. doi:10.1901/jaba.1992.25-153 PMID:1533855

International Association for K-12 Online Learning. (2011a). *The online learning definitions project.* Retrieved from http://www.inacol.org/resource/the-online-learning-definitions-project/

International Association for K-12 Online Learning. (2011b). *iNACOL national standards for quality online teaching (v2).* Retrieved from http://www.inacol.org/resource/inacol-national-standards-for-quality-online-teaching-v2/

Issenberg, S. B., McGaghie, W. C., Gordon, D. L., Symes, S., Petrusa, E. R., Hart, I. R., & Harden, R. M. (2002). Effectiveness of a cardiology review course for internal medicine residents using simulation technology and deliberate practice. *Teaching and Learning in Medicine, 14*(4), 223–228. doi:10.1207/S15328015TLM1404_4 PMID:12395483

Issenberg, S. B., McGaghie, W. C., Petrusa, E. R., Gordon, D. L., & Scalese, R. J. (2005). Features and uses of high-fidelity medical simulations that lead to effective learning: A BEME systematic review. *Medical Teacher, 27*(1), 10–28. doi:10.1080/01421590500046924 PMID:16147767

Issenberg, S. B., & Scalese, R. J. (2008). Simulation in health care education. *Perspectives in Biology and Medicine, 51*(1), 31–46. doi:10.1353/pbm.2008.0004 PMID:18192764

Iwarsson, S., & Stahl, A. (2003). Accessibility, usability and universal design: Positioning and definition of concepts describing person-environment relationships. *Disability and Rehabilitation, 25*(2), 57–66. PMID:12554380

Iwata, B. A., Dorsey, M. F., Slifer, K. J., Bauman, K. E., & Richman, G. S. (1994). Toward a functional analysis of self-injury. *Journal of Applied Behavior Analysis, 27*(2), 197–209. doi:10.1901/jaba.1994.27-197 PMID:8063622

Iwata, B. A., Pace, G. M., Dorsey, M. F., Zarcone, J. R., Vollmer, T. R., Smith, R. G., & Willis, K. D. et al. (1994). The functions of self-injurious behavior: An experimental-epidemiological analysis. *Journal of Applied Behavior Analysis, 27*(2), 215–240. doi:10.1901/jaba.1994.27-215 PMID:8063623

Jang, H., Song, J., & Kim, R. (2014). Does the offline bully-victimization influence cyberbullying behavior among youths? Application of general strain theory. *Computers in Human Behavior, 31*, 85–93. doi:10.1016/j.chb.2013.10.007

Jarvis, P., Holford, J., & Griffin, C. (2003). *The theory & practice of learning.* Sterling, VA: Kogan Page Ltd.

Jeffries, P. R. (Ed.). (2012). *Simulation in nursing education: From conceptualization to evaluation.* New York, NY: National League for Nursing.

Jeffs, T. (2010). Assistive technologies and innovative learning tool. In R. M. Gargiulo & D. Metcalf (Eds.), *Teaching in today's inclusive classroom: A universal design for learning approach* (pp. 153–177). Belmont, CA: Wadsworth.

Jenkins, H., Clinton, K., Purushotma, R., Robinson, A., & Weigel, M. (2006). *Confronting the challenges of participatory culture: Media education for the 21st century*. White Paper. MacArthur Foundation.

Jennings, D., Surgenor, P., & McMahon, T. (2013). *Education theory/constructivism and social constructivism in the classroom*. Open Educational Resources of University College Dublin Teaching and Learning.

Jensen, E. (2000). *Brain-based learning*. San Diego, CA: The Brain Store.

Johnson, L., Adams Becker, S., Estrada, V., & Freeman, A. (2015). *NMC Horizon Report: 2015 K-12 Edition*. Austin, TX: The New Media Consortium.

Joinson, A. (1998). Causes and implications of behavior on the Internet. In J. Gackenbach (Ed.), *Psychology and the Internet: Intrapersonal, interpersonal, and transpersonal implications* (pp. 43–60). San Diego, CA: Academic Press.

Kahan, D. (2002). The effects of bug-in-the-ear device on intralesson communication between a student teacher and a cooperating teacher. *Journal of Teaching in Physical Education*, *22*(1), 86–104. doi:10.1123/jtpe.22.1.86

Kamps, D. M., Barbetta, P. M., Leonard, B. R., & Delaquadri, J. (1994). Classwide peer tutoring: An integration strategy to improve reading skills and promote peer interactions among students with autism and general education peers. *Journal of Applied Behavior Analysis*, *27*(1), 49–61. doi:10.1901/jaba.1994.27-49 PMID:8188563

Karadag, R., & Yasar, S. (2010). Effects of differentiated instruction on students attitudes towards Turkish courses: An action research. *Procedia: Social and Behavioral Sciences*, *9*, 1394–1399. doi:10.1016/j.sbspro.2010.12.340

Karol, E. (2016). Tangible and intangible elements of design for well-being in the home. *Gerontechnology (Valkenswaard)*, *15*(4), 227–232. doi:10.4017/gt.2016.15.4.007.00

Kaufman, D. M., & Mann, K. V. (2014). Teaching and learning in medical education: How theory can inform practice. In T. Swanwick (Ed.), *Understanding medical education: Evidence, theory, and practice* (2nd ed.; pp. 7–29). Chichester, UK: John Wiley & Sons, Ltd.

Kearney, M., Schuck, S., Burden, K., & Aubusson, P. (2012). Viewing mobile learning from a pedagogical perspective. *Research in Learning Technology*, *20*.

Keengwe, J., & Kidd, T. T. (2010). Towards best practices in online learning and teaching in higher education. *Journal of Online Learning and Teaching*, *6*(2), 533.

Keh, C. L. (1990). Feedback in the writing process: A model and methods for implementation. *ELT Journal*, *44*(4), 294–304. doi:10.1093/elt/44.4.294

Keller, F. S. (1968). Good-bye, teacher.... *Journal of Applied Behavior Analysis*, *1*(1), 79–89. doi:10.1901/jaba.1968.1-79 PMID:16795164

Kelly, G. J., & Green, J. (1998). The social nature of knowing: Toward a sociocultural perspective on conceptual change and knowledge construction. In B. J. Guzzetti & C. R. Hynd (Eds.), *Perspectives on conceptual change: Multiple ways to understand knowing and learning in a complex world* (pp. 145–181). New York: Routledge.

Kelly, K. (2010). *What technology wants*. New York, NY: Penguin Group.

Kennewell, S. (2006, November). *Reflections on the interactive whiteboard phenomenon: A synthesis of research from the UK*. Paper presented at the AARE 2006 International Education Research Conference. Retrieved from http:www.aare.edu.au/06pap/ken06138.pdf

Kenny, D. T. (1980). Direct instruction: An overview of theory and practice. *Journal of the Association of Special Education Teachers, 15*, 12–17.

Keohane, D. D., & Greer, R. D. (2005). Teachers use of a verbally governed algorithm and student learning. *International Journal of Behavioral and Consultation Therapy, 1*(3), 252–271. doi:10.1037/h0100749

Ker, J., & Bradley, P. (2014). Simulation in medical education. In T. Swanwick (Ed.), *Understanding medical education: Evidence, theory, and practice* (2nd ed.; pp. 175–192). Chichester, UK: John Wiley & Sons, Ltd.

Khattri, N., Riley, K. W., & Kane, M. B. (1997). *Students at risk in poor, rural areas: A review of the research.* Retrieved from http://eric.ed.gov/?id=ED461442

Kiili, C., Laurinen, L., & Marttunen, M. (2008). Students evaluating Internet sources: From versatile evaluators to uncritical readers. *Journal of Educational Computing Research, 39*(1), 75–95. doi:10.2190/EC.39.1.e

Kim, M., Blair, K. C., & Lim, K. (2014). Using tablet assisted social stories™ to improve classroom behavior for adolescents with intellectual disabilities. *Research in Developmental Disabilities, 35*(9), 2241–2251. doi:10.1016/j. ridd.2014.05.011 PMID:24927518

Kim, Y. S., Al Otaiba, S., Wanzek, J., & Gatlin, B. (2015). Toward an understanding of dimensions, predictors, and the gender gap in written composition. *Journal of Educational Psychology, 107*(1), 79–95. doi:10.1037/a0037210 PMID:25937667

Kindermusik. (2014, November 4). *Repeat After Me: Kids Learn from Repetition.* Retrieved from https://www.kindermusik.com/mindsonmusic/benefits-of-music/repeat-after-me-kids-learn-from-repetition/

King, W. R., & He, J. (2006). A meta-analysis of the technology acceptance model. *Information & Management, 43*(6), 740–755. doi:10.1016/j.im.2006.05.003

Kirchen, D. J. (2011). *Making and taking virtual field trips in pre-K and the primary grades.* Retrieved from http://www.naeyc.org/yc/files/yc/file/201111/Kirchen_Virtual_Field_Trips_Online 1111.pdf

Kiresuk, T. J., & Sherman, R. E. (1968). Goal attainment scaling: A general method for evaluating comprehensive community mental health programs. *Community Mental Health Journal, 4*(6), 443–453. doi:10.1007/BF01530764 PMID:24185570

Kiresuk, T. J., Smith, A., & Cardillo, J. E. (1994). *Goal attainment scaling: Applications, theory and measurement.* Hillsdale, NJ: Lawrence Erlbaum Associates.

Klanten, R., Ehmann, S., & Hanschke, V. (2011). *A touch of code: Interactive installations and experiences.* Berlin, Germany: Gestalten.

Knott, J. L. (2015). *Online teaching and faculty learning: The role of hypermedia in online course design.* Retrieved from ProQuest Digital Dissertations. (AAT 3688361)

Knowles, M. (1975). *Self-directed learning: A guide for learners and teachers.* Cambridge, UK: Prentice Hall.

Knowles, M. S. (1984). *The adult learner: A neglected species* (3rd ed.). Houston, TX: Gulf Pub. Co., Book Division.

Kochenderfer-Ladd, B., & Pelletier, M. (2008). Teachers views and beliefs about bullying: Influences on classroom management strategies and students coping with peer victimization. *Journal of School Psychology, 46*(4), 431–453. doi:10.1016/j.jsp.2007.07.005 PMID:19083367

Kokina, A., & Kern, L. (2010). Social story™ interventions for students with autism spectrum disorders: A meta-analysis. *Journal of Autism and Developmental Disorders, 40*(7), 812–826. doi:10.1007/s10803-009-0931-0 PMID:20054628

Kolb, D. A., Boyatzis, R. E., & Mainemelis, C. (2000). Experiential Learning Theory: Previous Research and New Directions. In Perspectives on cognitive, learning, and thinking styles. Lawrence Erlbaum.

Kolb, D. A. (1984). *Experiential learning: Experience as the source of learning and development.* Prentice-Hall.

Koole, M. (2009). A model for framing mobile learning. In M. Ally (Ed.), *Mobile Learning: Transforming the Delivery Of Education And Training.* Edmonton: Athabasca University Governing Council.

Korner, I. N., & Brown, W. H. (1952). The mechanical third ear. *Journal of Consulting Psychology, 16*(1), 81–84. doi:10.1037/h0061630 PMID:14907954

Kowalski, R. M., & Limber, S. P. (2007). Electronic bullying among middle school students. *The Journal of Adolescent Health, 41*(6), 22–30. doi:10.1016/j.jadohealth.2007.08.017 PMID:18047942

Kramer, J. (2011). Why distributed teams are making your traditional office obsolete. *Fullstack.* Retrieved from http://gofullstack.com/why-distributed-teams-are-making-your-traditional-office- obsolete

Kratochwill, T. R., Hitchcock, J., Horner, R. H., Levin, J. R., Odom, S. L., Rindskopf, D. M., & Shadish, W. R. (2013). Single-case intervention research design standards. *Remedial and Special Education, 34*(1), 26–38. doi:10.1177/0741932512452794

Kretlow, A., & Bartholomew, C. (2010). Using coaching to improve the fidelity of evidence-based practices: A review of studies. *Teacher Education and Special Education, 33*(4), 279–299. doi:10.1177/0888406410371643

Kueider, A. M., Parisi, J. M., Gross, A. L., & Robok, G. W. (2012). Computerized cognitive training with older adults: A systematic review. *PLoS ONE, 7*(7), e40588. doi:10.1371/journal.pone.0040588 PMID:22792378

Kukulska-Hulme, A., & Traxler, J. J. (Eds.). (2005). Mobile learning: A handbook for educators and trainers. New York: Routledge.

Kuniavsky, M. (2010). *Smart things: Ubiquitous computing user experience design.* Burlington, MA: Morgan Haufmann.

Kurti, R. S., Kurti, D. L., & Fleming, L. (2014). The philosophy of educational makerspaces: Part 1 of making an educational makerspace. *Teacher Librarian, 41*, 8.

Kwan, G. C. E., & Skoric, M. M. (2013). Facebook bullying: An extension of battles in school. *Computers in Human Behavior, 29*(1), 16–25. doi:10.1016/j.chb.2012.07.014

Kymes, A., & Ray, B. (2012). Preparing school librarians in rural areas through distance education and communities of practice. *School Libraries Worldwide, 18*(2), 35–40.

Laftman, S. B., Modin, B., & Ostberg, V. (2013). Cyberbullying and subjective health: A large-scale study of students in Stockholm, Sweden. *Children and Youth Services Review, 35*(1), 112–119. doi:10.1016/j.childyouth.2012.10.020

Lai, K., & Hong, K. (2015). Technology use and learning characteristics of students in higher education: Do generational differences exist? *British Journal of Educational Technology, 46*(4), 725–739. doi:10.1111/bjet.12161

Lambert, J. (2010). *The Digital Storytelling Cookbook.* Digital Diner Press.

Lamm, N., & Greer, R. D. (1991). A systematic replication of CABAS. *Journal of Behavioral Education, 1*, 427–444. doi:10.1007/BF00946776

Lamott, A. (1994). *Bird by bird.* New York: Anchor Books.

Lampit, A., Hallock, H., & Valenzuela, M. (2014). Computerized cognitive training in cognitively healthy older adults: A systematic review and meta-analysis of effect modifiers. *PLoS ONE, 11*(11), e1001756. PMID:25405755

Lankshear, C., Knobel, M., & Curran, C. (2012). Conceptualizing and researching "new literacies". The Encyclopedia of Applied Linguistics. doi:10.1002/9781405198431

Lankshear, C., & Knobel, M. (2003). New technologies in early childhood literacy research: A review of research. *Journal of Early Childhood Literacy*, *3*(1), 59–82. doi:10.1177/14687984030031003

Lankshear, C., & Knobel, M. (2006). *New literacies: Everyday practices and cla ssroom learning* (2nd ed.). New York, NY: Open University Press.

Larreamendy-Joerns, J., & Leinhardt, G. (2006). Going the distance with online education. *Review of Educational Research*, *76*(4), 567–605. doi:10.3102/00346543076004567

Larson, J. (2005). Seasons of love [Recorded by the cast of Rent]. On Rent: Original motion picture soundtrack [CD]. Burbank, CA: Warner Brothers Records.

Laschinger, S., Medves, J., Pulling, C., McGraw, D. R., Waytuck, B., Harrison, M. B., & Gambeta, K. (2008). Effectiveness of simulation on health profession students' knowledge, skills, confidence and satisfaction. *International Journal of Evidence-Based Healthcare*, *6*(3), 278–302. PMID:21631826

Laschke, M., Hassenzahl, M., & Diefenbach, S. (2011). *Things with attitude: Transformational products*. Presented at the Create 11 Conference, Shoreditch House, London, UK. Retrieved from http://static1.squarespace.com/static/52722face4b02a66778dc9d0/t/53318711e4b09837d5a328f8/1395754769468/Laschke%2C+Hassenzahl%2C+Diefenbach+-+Things+with+attitude+Transformational+Products+-+2011.pdf

Latour, B. (1993). *We Have Never Been Modern* (C. Porter, Trans.). Cambridge, MA: Harvard University Press.

Lattal, K. A. (2008). JEAB at 50: Coevolution of research and technology. *Journal of the Experimental Analysis of Behavior*, *89*(1), 129–135. doi:10.1901/jeab.2008.89-129 PMID:18338681

Lautenschlager, N. T., Cox, K., & Cyarto, E. V. (2012). The influence of exercise on brain aging and dementia. *Biochimica et Biophysica Acta*, *1822*(3), 474–481. doi:10.1016/j.bbadis.2011.07.010 PMID:21810472

Lave, J., & Wenger, E. (1991). *Situated learning: Legitimate peripheral participation*. New York: Cambridge University Press. doi:10.1017/CBO9780511815355

Lavranos, G., Koliaki, C., Briasoulis, A., Nikolaou, A., & Stefanadis, C. (2013). Effectiveness of current teaching methods in cardiology: The SKILLS (medical students knowledge integration of lower level clinical skills) study. *Hippokratia Medical Journal*, *17*(1), 34–37. PMID:23935341

Lawrence-Brown, D. (2004). Differentiated instruction: Inclusive strategies for standards-based learning that benefit the whole class. *American Secondary Education*, *32*(2), 34.

Layng, T. V., & Twyman, J. S. (2013). Education + technology + innovation = learning? In M. Murphy, S. Redding, & J. Twyman (Eds.), *Handbook on innovations in learning* (pp. 135–150). Philadelphia, PA: Center on Innovations in Learning, Temple University. Retrieved from http://www.centeril.org

Lazuras, L., Barkoukis, V., Ourda, D., & Tsorbatzoudis, H. (2013). A process model of cyberbullying in adolescence. *Computers in Human Behavior*, *29*(3), 881–887. doi:10.1016/j.chb.2012.12.015

Lee, M. (2010). Interactive whiteboards and schooling: The context. *Technology, Pedagogy and Education*, *19*(2), 133–141. doi:10.1080/1475939X.2010.491215

Lee, M., & Winzenried, A. (2006). Interactive whiteboards: Achieving total teacher usage. *Australian Educational Leader*, *28*(3), 22–25.

Lenhart, A. (2015). *Teens, social media & technology overview 2015*. Retrieved from: http://www.pewinternet.org/2015/04/09/teens-social-media-technology-2015/

Leonard, D. C. (2002). *Learning theories, A to Z*. Westport, CT: Oryx Press.

Leu, D. J. Jr, Kinzer, C. K., Coiro, J., & Cammack, D. (2004). Toward a theory of new literacies emerging from the Internet and other information and communication technologies. In R. B. Ruddell & N. Unrau (Eds.), *Theoretical models and processes of reading* (5th ed.; pp. 1568–1611). Newark, DE: International Reading Association.

Leu, D. J., OByrne, W. I., Zawilinski, L., McVerry, J. G., & Everett-Cocapardo, H. (2009). Expanding the new literacies conversation. *Educational Researcher*, *38*(4), 264–269. doi:10.3102/0013189X09336676

Levene, J., & Seabury, H. (2015). Evaluation of mobile learning: Current research and implications for instructional designers. *TechTrends*, *59*(6), 46–52. doi:10.1007/s11528-015-0904-4

Lewin, K. (1951). *Field Theory in Social Sciences*. New York, NY: Harper & Row.

Lewis, K., Yoder, D., Riley, E., So, Y., & Yusufali, S. (2007). Accessibility of instructional Web sites in higher education. *EDUCAUSE Quarterly*, *30*(3), 29.

Lewis, W., Agarwal, R., & Sambamurthy, V. (2003). Sources of influence on beliefs about information technology use: An Empirical study of knowledge workers. *Management Information Systems Quarterly*, *27*(4), 657–678.

Liang, H., & Xue, Y. (2009, March). Avoidance of information technology threats: A theoretical perspective. *Management Information Systems Quarterly*, *33*(1), 71–90.

Lill, S. (2015). Depression in older adults in primary care: An integrative approach to care. *Journal of Holistic Nursing*, *33*(3), 260–268. doi:10.1177/0898010115569350 PMID:25673577

Lindsley, O. R. (1990). Precision teaching: By teachers for children. *Teaching Exceptional Children*, *22*(3), 10–15. doi:10.1177/004005999002200302

Lindsley, O. R. (1991). Precision teachings unique legacy from B. F. Skinner. *Journal of Behavioral Education*, *1*(2), 253–266. doi:10.1007/BF00957007

Lin, Y., & Lee, P. (2014). Informal learning: Theory and applied. *International Journal of Business and Commerce*, *3*(5), 127–134.

Li, Q. (2007). Bullying in the new playground: Research into cyberbullying and cybervictimization. *Australasian Journal of Educational Technology*, *23*(4), 435–454. doi:10.14742/ajet.1245

Li, Q. (2008). A cross-cultural comparison of adolescents experience related to cyberbullying. *Educational Research*, *50*(3), 223–234. doi:10.1080/00131880802309333

Liyanagunawardena, T. R., & Williams, S. A. (2016). Elderly learners and massive open online courses: A review. *Interactive Journal of Medical Research*, *5*(1), e1. doi:10.2196/ijmr.4937 PMID:26742809

Locke, G., Ableidinger, J., Hassel, B. C., & Barrett, S. K. (2014). *Virtual schools: Assessing progress and accountability: Final report of study findings*. Retrieved from https://www.charterschoolcenter.org/sites/default/files/Virtual%20Schools%20Accountability%20Report.pdf

Loomis, J. W. (2008). *Staying in the game: providing social opportunities for children and adolescents with autism spectrum disorder and other developmental disabilities*. Autism Asperger Publishing Company.

Loy, J. (2008). Strategies for teaching sustainable design practice with product design students. *Proceedings of E&PDE 2008, the 10th International Engineering and Product Design Education Conference* (pp. 491-496). Design Society.

Loy, J., Canning, S., & Little, C. (2015, June-July). *Digital industrial design*. Paper presented at the International Design Technology Conference, DesTech2015, Geelong, Australia.

Loy, J., Canning, S., & Haskell, N. (2016). 3D printing sociocultural sustainability. In S. S. Muthu & M. M. Savalani (Eds.), *Handbook of sustainability in additive manufacturing, environmental footprints and eco-design of products and processes* (pp. 145–168). New York, NY: Springer. doi:10.1007/978-981-10-0549-7_7

Luijkx, K., Peek, S., & Wouters, E. (2015). Grandma, you should do it – its cool Older adults and the role of family members in their acceptance of technology. *International Journal of Environmental Research and Public Health*, *12*(12), 15470–15485. doi:10.3390/ijerph121214999 PMID:26690188

Mac an Ghaill, M. (1994). *The making of men*. Buckingham, UK: Oxford University Press.

MacArthur, C. A. (1998). Word processing with speech synthesis and word prediction: Effects on the dialogue journal writing of students with learning disabilities. *Learning Disability Quarterly*, *21*(2), 151–166. doi:10.2307/1511342

MacArthur, C. A., Graham, S., Haynes, J. B., & DeLaPaz, S. (1996). Spelling checkers and students with learning disabilities: Performance comparisons and impact on spelling. *The Journal of Special Education*, *30*(1), 35–57. doi:10.1177/002246699603000103

Machackova, H., Dedkova, L., & Mezulanikova, K. (2015). Brief report: The bystander effect in cyberbullying incidents. *Journal of Adolescence*, *43*, 96–99. doi:10.1016/j.adolescence.2015.05.010 PMID:26070168

Machackova, H., Dedkova, L., Sevcikova, A., & Cerna, A. (2013). Bystanders support of cyberbullied schoolmates. *Journal of Community & Applied Social Psychology*, *23*(1), 25–36. doi:10.1002/casp.2135

Mahmood, A., Yamamoto, T., Lee, M., & Steggell, C. (2008). Perceptions and use of Gerontechnology: Implications for aging in place. *Journal of Housing for the Elderly*, *22*(1-2), 104–126. doi:10.1080/02763890802097144

Major, C. H. (2010). Do virtual professor's dream of electric students? University faculty experiences with online distance education. *Teachers College Record*, *112*(8), 2154–2208.

Makepeace, J. (1995). *Makepeace: Spirit of adventure in craft and design*. London: Octopus.

Mallinen, S. (2001). Teacher effectiveness and online learning. In J. Stephenson (Ed.), *Teaching & learning online: Pedagogies for new technologies* (pp. 139–149). London, UK: Kogan Page.

Malott, R. W., Malott, M. E., & Trojan, B. (1999). *Elementary Principles of Behavior* (4th ed.). Pearson Education.

Mandasari, V. (2012). *Learning social skills with 2D animated social stories for children with autism spectrum disorders* (Master's thesis). Kuching, Sarawak: Swinburne University of Technology.

Mardis, M., ElBasri, T., Norton, S., & Newsum, J. (2012). The digital lives of U.S. teachers: A research synthesis and trends to watch. *School Libraries Worldwide*, *18*(1), 70–86.

Marsick, V., & Volpe, M. (1999). The nature and need for informal learning. *Advances in Developing Human Resources*, *1*(1), 1–10. doi:10.1177/152342239900100302

Martin, F., & Ertzberger, J. (2013). Here and now mobile learning: An experimental study on the use of mobile technology. *Computers & Education*, *68*, 76–85. doi:10.1016/j.compedu.2013.04.021

Marzano, R. J. (2007). *The art and science of teaching: A comprehensive framework for effective instruction.* Alexandria, VA: Association for Supervision and Curriculum Development.

Masedu, F., Mazza, M., Di Giovanni, C., Calvarese, A., Tiberti, S., Sconci, V., & Valenti, M. (2014). Facebook, quality of life, and mental outcomes in post-disaster urban environments: The L'Auila Earthquake experience. *Front Public Health, 22*(286), 1–6. PMID:25566527

Mason, K. (2008). Cyberbullying: A preliminary assessment for school personnel. *Psychology in the Schools, 45*(4), 323–348. doi:10.1002/pits.20301

Massachusetts Institute of Technology. (2015). *MIT App Inventor.* Retrieved from http://appinventor.mit.edu/explore/

Mathews, J., & Guarino, A. (2000). Predicting teacher computer use: A path analysis. *International Journal of Instructional Media, 27*(4), 385–392.

Matthew, K. I. (1995). *A comparison of the influence of CD- ROM interactive storybooks and traditional print storybooks on reading comprehension and attitude* (Doctoral dissertation). Available from ProQuest Dissertations and Theses database. (UMI No. 9542610)

Maxwell, J. A. (1996). *Qualitative research design: An interactive approach.* Thousand Oaks, CA: Sage Publications.

Maynard, T. (2002). *Boys and literacy: Exploring the issues.* Routledge.

McAdamis, S. (2001). Teachers tailor their instruction to meet a variety of student needs. *Journal of Staff Development, 22*(2), 1–5.

McDonough, C. C. (2016). The effect of ageism on the digital divide among older adults. *Journal of Gerontology & Geriatric Medicine, 2*(008), 1–7.

McDrury, J., & Alterio, M. (2003). *Learning through storytelling in higher education: Using reflection & experience to improve learning.* London: Kogan Page.

McEwan, H., & Egan, K. (1995). *Narrative in teaching, learning, and research.* New York: Teachers College Press.

McEwen, A., & Cassimally, H. (2013). *Designing the Internet of Things.* Oxford, UK: John Wiley & Sons.

McGaghie, W. C. (1999). Simulation in professional competence assessment: Basic considerations. In A. Tekian, C. H., McGuire, & W. C. McGaghie (Eds.), Innovative simulations for assessing professional competence (pp. 28-50). Chicago, IL: Department of Medical Education, University of Illinois at Chicago.

McGaghie, W. C., Issenberg, S. B., Retrusa, E. R., & Scalese, R. J. (2010). A critical review of simulation-based medical education research: 20032009. *Medical Education, 44*(1), 50–63. doi:10.1111/j.1365-2923.2009.03547.x PMID:20078756

McGrath, H., & Francey, S. (1991). *Friendly kids, friendly classrooms: teaching social skills and confidence in the classroom* (1st ed.). Melbourne: Pearson Australia.

McKenna, K. Y. A., & Bargh, J. A. (2000). Plan 9 from cyberspace: The implications of the internet for personality and social psychology. *Personality and Social Psychology Review, 4*(1), 57–75. doi:10.1207/S15327957PSPR0401_6

McKimm, J., & Forrest, K. (2013). Essential simulation in clinical education. In S. Edgar, K. Forrest, & J. McKimm (Eds.), *Essential simulation in clinical education* (pp. 1–10). Chichester, UK: Wiley-Blackwell. doi:10.1002/9781118748039.ch1

McKinney, J., Cook, D. A., Wood, D., & Hatala, R. (2013). Simulation-based training for cardiac auscultation skills: Systematic review and meta-analysis. *Journal of General Internal Medicine, 28*(2), 283–291. doi:10.1007/s11606-012-2198-y PMID:22968795

McLeod, S. A. (2016). *Maslow's hierarchy of needs*. Retrieved from www.simplypsychology.org/maslow.html

McManis, L. D., & Gunnewig, S. B. (2012). Finding the education in educational technology with early learners. *Young Children, 67*, 14–24.

McQuade, C. S., Colt, P. J., & Meyer, B. N. (2009). *Cyber bullying: Protecting kids and adults from online bullies*. Westport, CT: Praeger.

Mead, S. (2006). *The truth about boys and girls*. Washington, DC: Education Sector.

Meagher, M. (2014). Responsive architecture and the problem of obsolescence. *International Journal of Architectural Research, 8*(3), 95–104.

Means, B., Toyama, Y., Murphy, R., Bakia, M., & Jones, K. (2009). *Evaluation of evidence based practices in online learning: A meta-analysis and review of online learning studies*. Retrieved from https://www2.ed.gov/rschstat/eval/tech/evidence-based-practices/finalreport.pdf

Means, B. (2008). Technology's role in curriculum and instruction. In F. M. Connelly, M. F. He, & J. Phillion (Eds.), *The Sage handbook of curriculum and instruction* (pp. 123–144). Los Angeles, CA: Sage Publications. doi:10.4135/9781412976572.n7

Means, B., Toyama, Y., Murphy, R., Bakia, M., & Jones, K. (2009). *Evaluation of evidence-based practices in online learning: A meta-analysis and review of online learning studies*. US Department of Education.

Means, B., Toyama, Y., Murphy, R., Bakia, M., & Jones, K. (2009). *Evaluation of evidence-based practices in online learning: Meta-analysis and review of online learning studies*. US Department of Education.

Mears, T. (2015). *10 essential tech tools for older adults*. Retrieved from http://money.usnews .com/money/retirement/articles/2015/11/16/10-essential-tech-tools-for-older-adults

Melenhorst, A.-S., Rogers, W. A., & Caylor, E. C. (2001). The use of communication technologies by older adults: Exploring the benefits from the user's perspective. *Proceedings from the Human Factors and Ergonomics Society 45th Annual Meeting*, 221-225.

Mental Health America of Illinois. (n.d.). *Depression in later life*. Retrieved from www.mhai.org/Depression_Lter_in_Life.pdf

Meraz-Lewis, R. B. (2011). *The lived worlds and life experiences of residents in university linked retirement communities: A qualitative approach* (Doctoral Dissertation). Retrieved from the Eastern Michigan University DigitalCommons. Retrieved from http://commons.emich.edu/cgi/viewcontent.cgi?article=1790&context=theses

Merriam, S. B., Caffarella, R. S. & NetLibrary, I. (1999). *Learning in adulthood a comprehensive guide* (2nd ed.). San Francisco: Jossey-Bass Publishers.

MET Project. (2010). *Working with teachers to develop fair and reliable measures of effective teaching*. Retrieved from https://docs.gatesfoundation.org/Documents/met-framing-paper.pdf

MET Project. (2013). *Ensuring fair and reliable measures of effective teaching: Culminating findings for the MET project's three-year study*. Retrieved from http://www.edweek.org/media/17teach-met1.pdf

Meyer, A., & Rose, D. H. (2005). The future is in the margins: The role of technology and disability in educational reform. In D. H. Rose, A. Meyer, & C. Hitchcock (Eds.), *The universally designed classroom: Accessible curriculum and digital technologies* (pp. 13–35). Cambridge, MA: Harvard Education Press.

Meyer, G. R., Sulzer-Azaroff, B., & Wallace, M. (2011). *Behavior analysis for lasting change*. New York: Sloan Publishing.

Michael, M., Abboudi, H., Ker, J., Khan, M., Dasgupta, P., & Ahmed, K. (2014). Performance of technology-driven simulators for medical students–a systematic review. *The Journal of Surgical Research*, *192*(2), 531–543. doi:10.1016/j.jss.2014.06.043 PMID:25234749

Mifsud, L. (2014). Mobile learning and the socio-materiality of classroom practices. *Learning, Media and Technology*, *39*(1), 142–149. doi:10.1080/17439884.2013.817420

Millard, E. (1997). Differently literate: Gender identity and the construction of the developing reader. *Gender and Education*, *9*(1), 31–48. doi:10.1080/09540259721439

Miller, L. (2015). *The perceived impact of technology-based informal learning on membership organizations* (Order No. 10154967). Available from ProQuest Dissertations & Theses Global. (1818521179)

Miller, L. C. (2012). Situating the rural teacher labor market in the broader context: A descriptive analysis of the market dynamics in New York State. *Journal of Research in Rural Education (Online)*, *27*(13), 1–31.

Millet, J. A. (2012). *Virtual learning in K-12 education: Successful instructional practices and school strategies* (Doctoral dissertation). Available from ProQuest Dissertations and Theses database. (UMI No. 3497822)

Miner, C. (2014). Preparing children on the range. *Language Magazine*, *14*(4), 20–22.

Mishra, P., & Koehler, M. (2006). Technological pedagogical content knowledge: A framework for teacher knowledge. *Teachers College Record*, *108*(6), 1017–1054. doi:10.1111/j.1467-9620.2006.00684.x

MIT Media Lab. (2016). *Scratch*. Retrieved from https://scratch.mit.edu/

Mitchell, K. J., Ybarra, M., & Finkelhor, D. (2007). The relative importance of online victimization in understanding depression, delinquency, and substance use. *Child Maltreatment*, *12*(4), 314–324. doi:10.1177/1077559507305996 PMID:17954938

Mitchell, S. (2002). *Technogenesis*. New York, NY: Penguin Publishing.

Mobile Learning at ACU. (n.d.). Retrieved June 28, 2016 from http://www.acu.edu/technology/mobilelearning/

Mollenkopf, H. (2016). Societal aspects and individual preconditions of technological development. *Gerontechnology (Valkenswaard)*, *15*(4), 216–226. doi:10.4017/gt.2016.15.4.011.00

Molnar, A. (Ed.). (2014). *Virtual schools in the U.S. 2014: Politics, performance, policy, and research evidence*. Retrieved from http://nepc.colorado.edu/files/virtual-2014-all-final.pdf

Moore, M. (1993). Theory of transactional distance. In D. Keegan (Ed.), *Theoretical Principles of Distance Education*. New York: Routledge.

More, C. (2008). Digital stories targeting social skills for children with disabilities: Multidimensional learning. *Intervention in School and Clinic*, *43*(3), 168–177. doi:10.1177/1053451207312919

Morgenroth, L., & Hanley, M. (2015). On campus and in the community: How higher education can inform seniors housing models. *Seniors Housing & Care Journal*, *23*(1), 70–75.

Morin, A. (2014). *At a glance: 8 key executive functions*. Retrieved from https://www.understood.org/en/learning-attention-issues/child-learning-disabilities/executive-functioning-issues/key-executive-functioning-skills-explained

Morrisett, L. (2001). Foreword. In B. M. Compaine (Ed.), *The digital divide: Facing a crisis or creating a myth?* (pp. ix–x). Cambridge, MA: MIT Press.

Morrison, D. (2010). Social media opens social world to elderly, disable. *Wilmington Star News*. Retrieved from http://www.starnewonline.com/article/20100126/articles/10012956>

Moss, B. J., Nicolas, M., & Highberg, N. P. (2004). *Writing groups inside and outside the classroom*. Mahwah, NJ: Lawrence Erlbaum Associates.

Mossberger, K., Tolbert, C., & Stansbury, M. (2003). *Virtual inequality: Beyond the digital divide*. Washington, DC: Georgetown University Press.

Mouttapa, M., Valente, T., Gallagher, P., Rohrbach, L. A., & Unger, J. B. (2004). Social network predictor of bullying and victimization. *Adolescence*, *39*, 315–335. PMID:15563041

Moyle, W., Beattie, E., Jones, C., Klein, B., Cook, G., & Gray, C. (2013). Exploring the effect of companion robots on emotional expression. *Journal of Gerontological Nursing*, *39*(5), 46–53. doi:10.3928/00989134-20130313-03 PMID:23506125

Mueller, J., Wood, E., Willoughby, T., Ross, C., & Specht, J. (2008). Identifying discriminating variables between teachers who fully integrate computers and teachers with limited integration. *Computers & Education*, *51*(4), 1523–1537. doi:10.1016/j.compedu.2008.02.003

Nagode, M., & Dolnicar, V. (2010). Assistive technology for older people and its potential for intergenerational cooperation. *Teorija in Praksa*, *47*(6), 1278–1294.

National Alliance for Research on Schizophrenia and Depression. (n.d.). *Late life depression*. Retrieved from https://bbrfoundation.org/userFiles/facts.latelifedep.pdf

National Autistic Society. (2014). *Autism facts and history*. Retrieved from http://www.autism.org.uk/about/what-is/myths-facts-stats.aspx

National Center for Education Statistics. (2011). *Digest of education statistics, 2010*. Retrieved from http://nces.ed.gov/pubsearch/pubsinfo.asp?pubid=2011015

National Center on Education and the Economy. (2007). *Tough choices or tough times: Executive summary*. Retrieved from http://www.skillscommission.org/pdf/exec_sum/ToughChoices_EXECSUM.pdf

National Center on Universal Design for Learning. (2014). Universal Design for Learning Guidelines. *CAST, Inc.* Retrieved from http://www.udlcenter.org/aboutudl/udlguidelines_theorypractice

National Institute of Mental Health. (2014). *Autism Spectrum Disorders*. Retrieved from http://www.nimh.nih.gov/health/topics/autism-spectrum-disorders-pervasive-developmental-disorders/index.shtml?utm_source=rss_readers&utm_medium=rss&utm_campaign=rss_full

National Research Council. (2000). *How people learn: Brain, mind, experience, and school*. Washington, DC: National Academy Press.

Neff, K. (2011). *Self compassion: The proven power of being kind to yourself*. New York, NY: HarperCollins.

Nef, T., Ganea, R. L., Muri, R. M., & Mosimann, U. P. (2013). Social networking sites and older users: A systematic review. *International Psychogeriatrics*, *25*(7), 1041–1053. doi:10.1017/S1041610213000355 PMID:23552297

Neumann, A. (2009). *Professing to learn: Creating tenured lives and careers in the American research university (No. 475)*. JHU Press.

Newman, L., Wagner, M., Knokey, A.-M., Marder, C., Nagle, K., Shaver, D., & Wei, X. (2011). *The post-high school outcomes of young adults with disabilities up to 8 Years after high school: A Report from the National Longitudinal Transition Study-2 (NLTS2)*. NCSER 2011-3005. National Center for Special Education Research. Retrieved from http://eric.ed.gov/?id=ED524044

Newmann, F., Brandt, R., & Wiggins, G. (1998). An exchange of views on semantics, psychometrics, and assessment reform: A close look at 'authentic' assessments. *Educational Researcher, 27*(6), 19–22.

Nikiforou, M., Georgiou, S. N., & Stavrinides, P. (2013). Attachment to parents and peers as predictors of bullying and victimization. *Journal of Criminology, 2013*, 1–9. doi:10.1155/2013/484871

Noble, C., & Bradford, W. (2000). *Getting it right for boys...and girls*. London, UK: Routledge.

Norris, C., Sullivan, T., Poirot, J., & Soloway, E. (2003). No access, no use, no impact: Snapshot surveys of educational technology in K-12. *Journal of Research on Technology in Education, 36*(1), 15–27. doi:10.1080/15391523.2003.10782400

Novak, J. (2015). *Drawing the pen: From physical to digital and back again*. Presented at the Drawing International Brisbane Conference, Brisbane, Australia. Retrieved from http://static1.squarespace.com/static/55779bbce4b004acf1e1479d/t/56aef970b6aa60cdf1c253d6/1454307702608/JAMES+XXXX_DRAWING+THE+PEN_DIB2015.pdf

Nowak, P. (2015). *Humans 3.0: the upgrading of the species*. London: Harper Collins.

Nussbaum-Beach, S., & Hall, L. R. (2012). *The connected learner: Learning and leading in a digital age*. Bloomington, IN: Solution Tree Press.

O'Dwyer, L., Russell, M., & Bebell, D. (2004). Identifying teacher, school and district characteristics associated with elementary teachers' use of technology: A multilevel perspective. *Education Policy Analysis Archives, 12*(48). Retrieved from http://epaa.asu.edu/epaa/v12n48

Oberst, J., & Sanders, S. (2016). Realizing Intelligent Robotics. In Brain-Inspired intelligent robotics: The Intersection of robotics and neuroscience. Beijing, China: Chinese Academy of Sciences.

Oermann, M., Kardong-Edgren, S., Odom-Maryon, T., Hallmark, B. F., Hurd, D., Rogers, N., & Smart, D. A. et al. (2011). Deliberate practice of motor skills in nursing education: CPR as exemplar. *Nursing Education Perspectives, 32*(5), 311–315. doi:10.5480/1536-5026-32.5.311 PMID:22029243

Ohler, J. (2013). *Digital storytelling in the classroom: New media pathways to literacy, learning, and creativity*. Thousand Oaks, CA: Corwin Press. doi:10.4135/9781452277479

Okeechobee County School District. (2016). *Technology: District classroom plan, mission, & vision*. Retrieved July 6, 2016, from http://www.okee.k12.fl.us/technology

Olenik Shemesh, D., Heiman, T., & Pieschl, S. (2011). *Adolescents' cyberbullying: Moods, loneliness and social support*. Oral presentation at the 32nd International Conference of the Stress and Anxiety Research Society (STAR), Munster, Germany.

Oliver, P., & Brady, M. P. (2014). Effects of covert audio coaching on parents interactions with young children with autism. *Behavior Analysis in Practice, 7*(2), 112–116. doi:10.1007/s40617-014-0015-2 PMID:27547702

Olweus, D. (1993). *Bullying at school. What we know and what we can do*. Malden, MA: Blackwell Publishing.

Omari, M., & Standen, P. (2000). Selection for telework. In K. Daniels, D. Lamnf, & P. Standen (Eds.), Managing Telework: Perspectives from Human Resource Management and Work Psychology. London: Thomson Learning.

ONeill, T. A. A., Hambley, L. H., & Bercovich, A. (2014). Prediction of cyberslacking when employees are working away. *Computers in Human Behavior*, *34*, 291–298. doi:10.1016/j.chb.2014.02.015

ONeill, T. A., Hambley, L. A., & Chatellier, G. S. (2014). Cyberslacking, engagement, and personality in distributed environments. *Computers in Human Behavior*, *40*, 152–160. doi:10.1016/j.chb.2014.08.005

ONeill, T. A., Hambley, L. A., Greidanus, N. S., MacDonnell, R., & Kline, T. J. B. (2009). Predicting teleworker success: An exploration of personality, motivational, situational, and job characteristics. *New Technology, Work and Employment*, *24*(2), 144–162. doi:10.1111/j.1468-005X.2009.00225.x

Ordonez, T. N., Yassuda, M. S., & Cachioni, M. (2010). Elderly online: Effects of a digital inclusion program in cognitive performance. *Archives of Gerontology and Geriatrics*, *53*(2), 216–219. doi:10.1016/j.archger.2010.11.007 PMID:21131070

Oren, T., & Ogletree, B. T. (2000). Program evaluation in classrooms for students with autism: Student outcomes and program processes. *Focus on Autism and Other Developmental Disabilities*, *15*(3), 170–175. doi:10.1177/108835760001500308

Orlov, L. M. (n.d.). *An elder care industry veteran offers her picks for must-have aging-in-place technology.* Retrieved from http://www.homecaremag.com/top-10-technology-devices-seniors

Ortberg, J. (2014). *Soul keeping.* Grand Rapids, MI: Zondervan.

Ortman, J. M., Velkoff, V. A., & Hogan, H. (2014). *An aging nation: The older population in the United States: Population estimates and projections.* Washington, DC: United States Department of Commerce.

Ostroff, W. L. (2016). *Cultivating curiosity in K-12 classrooms: How to promote and sustain deep learning.* Alexandria, VA: ASCD.

Owston, R. (2009). Digital immersion, teacher learning and games. *Educational Researcher*, *38*(4), 270–273. doi:10.3102/0013189X09336673

Ozdemir, D., & Loose, R. (2014). Implementation of a quality assurance review system for the scalable development of online courses. *Online Journal of Distance Learning Administration*, *17*(1), n1.

Pace, G. M., Ivancic, M. T., Edwards, G. L., Iwata, B. A., & Page, T. J. (1985). Assessment of stimulus preference and reinforcer value with profoundly retarded individuals. *Journal of Applied Behavior Analysis*, *18*(3), 249–255. doi:10.1901/jaba.1985.18-249 PMID:4044458

Pachler, N., Bachmair, B., & Cook, J. (2010). *Mobile learning: Structures, agency, practices.* New York: Springer. doi:10.1007/978-1-4419-0585-7

Pachler, N., Bachmair, B., & Cook, J. (2013). Sociocultural ecological framework for m-learning. In Z. L. Berge & L. Y. Muilenburg (Eds.), *Handbook of Mobile Learning.* New York: Routledge.

Pajares, F. (2003). Self-efficacy beliefs, motivation, and achievement in writing: A review of the literature. *Reading & Writing Quarterly*, *19*(2), 139–158. doi:10.1080/10573560308222

Palloff, R. M., & Pratt, K. (1999). *Building learning communities in cyberspace: Effective strategies for the online classroom.* San Francisco, CA: Jossey-Bass.

Palmer, P. J. (1998). *The Courage To Teach: Exploring the Inner Landscape of a Teacher's Life.* San Francisco, CA: Jossey-Bass.

Papworth, L. (2015). *The internet of things: 11 experts on business opportunities.* Retrieved from http://arkenea.com/blog/internet-of-things-business-opportunities/

Parametric Parts. (2016). Retrieved from http://www.parametricparts.com/

Park, Y. (2011). A pedagogical framework for mobile learning: Categorizing educational applications of mobile technologies into four types. *International Review of Research in Open and Distance Learning, 12*(2), 78–102. doi:10.19173/irrodl.v12i2.791

Parry, E., & Urwin, P. (2011). Generational differences in work values: A review of theory and evidence. *International Journal of Management Reviews, 13*(1), 79–96. doi:10.1111/j.1468-2370.2010.00285.x

Patchin, J. W., & Hinduja, S. (2006). Bullies move beyond the schoolyard: A preliminary look at cyberbullying. *Youth Violence and Juvenile Justice, 4*(2), 148–169. doi:10.1177/1541204006286288

Patrick, S. (2012). Forward. In K. Rice (Ed.), *Making the move to K-12 online teaching: Research-based strategies and practices* (pp. ix–xi). Boston, MA: Pearson.

Pavlov, I. P. (1927). *Conditioned reflexes: An investigation of the physiological activity of the cerebral cortex.* Oxford University Press. Retrieved from http://search.alexanderstreet.com.ezproxy.fau.edu/view/work/bibliographic_entity%7Cbibliographic_details%7C2300567#page/3/mode/1/chapter/bibliographic_entity%7Cdocument%7C2300571

Peels, D. A., de Vries, H., Bolman, C., Golsteign, R. H. J., van Stralen, M. M., Mudde, A. N., & Lechner, L. (2013). Differences in the use and appreciate of a web-based or printed computer-tailored physical activity intervention for people aged over 50 years. *Health Education Research, 28*(4), 715–731. doi:10.1093/her/cyt065 PMID:23784076

Pei, E. (2014). 4D printing: Revolution or fad? *Assembly Automation, 34*(2), 123–127. doi:10.1108/AA-02-2014-014

Pekari, J. (2011). *Reshaping Lutheran education: A systems perspective* (Doctoral dissertation). Available from ProQuest Dissertations and Theses database. (UMI No. 3459161)

Pennebaker, J. W. (1997). *Opening up: the healing power of expressing emotions.* New York, NY: The Guilford Press.

Pennebaker, J. W., & Smyth, J. M. (2016). *Opening up by writing it down.* New York, NY: The Guilford Press.

Pennypacker, H. S., Gutierrez, A., & Lindsley, O. R. (2003). *Handbook of the Standard Celeration Chart (deluxe edition).* Cambridge, MA: Cambridge Center for Behavioral Studies.

Penny, V. (1998). Raising boys' achievement in English. In K. Bleach (Ed.), *Raising boys' achievement in schools.* Stoke-on-Trent, UK: Trentham Books.

Perlini, S., Salinaro, F., Santalucia, P., & Musca, F. (2014). Simulation-guided cardiac auscultation improves medical students clinical skills: The Pavia pilot experience. *Internal and Emergency Medicine, 9*(2), 165–172. doi:10.1007/s11739-012-0811-z PMID:22767224

Perren, S., Dooley, J., Shaw, T., & Cross, D. (2010). Bullying in school and cyberspace: Associations with depressive symptoms in Swiss and Australian adolescents. *Child and Adolescent Psychiatry and Mental Health, 4*(1), 1–10. doi:10.1186/1753-2000-4-28 PMID:21092266

Petrova, M. (2014). Educating designers from Generation Y: Challenges and alternatives. In *DS 78: Proceedings of the 16th International conference on Engineering and Product Design Education (E&PDE14), Design Education and Human Technology Relations* (pp. 524-529). New York, NY: ACM.

Philips Hue. (n.d.). Retrieved from http://www2.meethue.com/en-au/

Phipps, S. T. A., Prieto, L. C., & Ndinguri, E. N. (2013). Teaching an old dog new tricks: Investigating how age, ability, and self-efficacy influence intentions to learn and learning among participants in adult education. *Academy of Educational Leadership, 17*(1), 13–25.

Piaget, J. (1952). *The Origins of Intelligence in Children.* New York, NY: International University Press. doi:10.1037/11494-000

Piazza, C. C., Fisher, W. W., Hagopian, L. P., Bowman, L. G., & Toole, L. (1996). Using a choice assessment to predict reinforcer effectiveness. *Journal of Applied Behavior Analysis, 29*(1), 1–9. doi:10.1901/jaba.1996.29-1 PMID:8881340

Picciano, A. G., & Seaman, J. (2007). K-12 online learning: A survey of U.S. school district administrators. *Journal of Asynchronous Learning Networks, 11*(3), 11.

Picciano, A. G., Seaman, J., Shea, P., & Swan, K.Sloan Foundation. (2012). Examining the extent and nature of online learning in American K-12 education: The research initiatives of the Alfred P. Sloan foundation. *The Internet and Higher Education, 15*(2), 127–135. doi:10.1016/j.iheduc.2011.07.004

Picciano, A. G., & Seaman, J.Sloan Consortium. (2009). *K-12 online learning: A 2008 follow-up of the survey of U.S. school district administrators.* Sloan Consortium.

Pickering, J. (1997). *Raising boys' achievement.* Stafford, UK: Network Education Press Ltd.

Pink, D. H. (2006). *A Whole New Mind.* New York: Riverhead Books.

Pipher, M. (2006). *Writing to change the world.* New York, NY: Riverhead.

Ploessl, D. M., & Rock, M. L. (2014). eCoaching: The effects on co-teachers planning and instruction. *Teacher Education and Special Education, 37*(3), 191–215. doi:10.1177/0888406414525049

Poggio, T. (2016). *Deep learning: Mathematics and neuroscience. In Brain-Inspired intelligent robotics: The Intersection of robotics and Neuroscience* (pp. 9–12). Beijing, China: Chinese Academy of Sciences.

Pointdexter, K., Hagler, D., & Lindell, D. (2015). Designing authentic assessment. *Strategies for Nurse Educators, 40*(1), 36–40. doi:10.1097/NNE.0000000000000091 PMID:25358115

Pokémon Go. (n.d.). Retrieved from http://www.pokemongo.com/

Poore, J. A., Cullen, D. L., & Schaar, G. L. (2014). Simulation-based interprofessional education guided by Kolbs experiential learning theory. *Clinical Simulation in Nursing, 10*(5), e241–e247. doi:10.1016/j.ecns.2014.01.004

Pornari, C. D., & Wood, J. (2010). Peer and cyber aggression in secondary school students: The role of moral disengagement, hostile attribution bias, and outcome expectancies. *Aggressive Behavior, 36*(2), 81–94. doi:10.1002/ab.20336 PMID:20035548

Poulin, R. (2013). *Managing online education 2013: Practices in ensuring quality.* WICHE Cooperative for Educational Technologies.

Powell, R. (2012). The future of human evolution. *The British Journal for the Philosophy of Science, 63*(1), 145–175. doi:10.1093/bjps/axr027

Powers, J. R. (2014). *Lutheran school teachers' instructional usages of the interactive whiteboard* (Doctoral dissertation). Florida Atlantic University, Boca Raton, FL.

Prensky, M. (2010). Teaching digital natives: Partnering for real learning. Thousand Oaks, CA: Corwin.

Prensky, M. (2001). Digital natives, digital immigrants. *On the Horizon, 9*(5), 1–6. doi:10.1108/10748120110424816

Prensky, M. (2010). *Reaching digital natives: Partnering for real learning.* Thousand Oaks, CA: Corwin.

Pstross, M., Corrigan, T., Knopf, R. C., Sung, H., Talmage, C. A., Conroy, C., & Fowley, C. (2016). The benefits of intergenerational learning in higher education: Lessons learned from two age friendly university programs. *Innovation Higher Education,* 1-15.

Puentedura, R. (2014). *SAMR: A contextualized introduction.* Retrieved May 3, 2016, from http://hippasus.com/rrpweblog

Purcell, K., Heaps, A., Buchanan, J., & Friedrich, L. (2013a). How teachers are using technology at home and in their classrooms. Washington, DC: Pew Research Center's Internet & American Life Project; Retrieved from http://www.pewinternet.org

Purcell, K., Heaps, A., Buchanan, J., & Friedrich, L. (2013b). The impact of digital tools on student writing and how writing is taught in schools. Washington, DC: Pew Research Center's Internet & American Life Project. Retrieved from http://www.pewinternet.org

Quality Matters. (2013). *Quality matters program.* Retrieved from https://www.qualitymatters.org/

Quinn, C. N. (2011). *Designing mLearning: Tapping into the mobile revolution for organizational performance.* San Francisco: Pfeiffer.

Quinn, C. N. (2011). *The mobile academy: mLearning for higher education.* San Francisco: Jossey-Bass.

Radwin, D., Wine, J., Siegel, P., & Bryan, M. (2013). *2011-12 National Postsecondary Student Aid Study (NPSAS: 12): Student Financial Aid Estimates for 2011-12. First Look. NCES 2013-165.* National Center for Education Statistics.

Ramey, D., Lydon, S., Healy, O., McCoy, A., Holloway, J., & Mulhern, T. (2016). A systematic review of the effectiveness of precision teaching for individuals with developmental disabilities. *Journal of Autism and Developmental Disorders, 3*(3), 179–195. doi:10.1007/s40489-016-0075-z

Rankin, L. (2013). *Mind over medicine.* Carlsbad, CA: Hay House.

Rankin, L. (2015). *The fear cure.* Carlsbad, CA: Hay House.

Rau, P., Gao, Q., & Ding, Y. (2008). Relationship between the level of intimacy and lurking in online social network services. *Computers in Human Behavior, 24*(6), 2757–2770. doi:10.1016/j.chb.2008.04.001

Reedy, G. B. (2008). PowerPoint, interactive whiteboards, and the visual culture of technology in schools. *Technology, Pedagogy and Education, 17*(2), 143–162. doi:10.1080/14759390802098623

Reinhart, J. M., Thomas, E., & Toriskie, J. M. (2011). K-12 teachers: Technology and the second level digital divide. *Journal of Instructional Psychology, 38*(3 & 4), 181–193.

Ren, P., Chen, B., Yuan, Z., & Zheng, N. (2016). Toward robust visual cognition through brain-inspired computing. In Brain-Inspired intelligent robotics: The Intersection of robotics and neuroscience. Beijing, China: Chinese Academy of Sciences.

Renishaw. (2014, February 2). *First metal 3D printed bicycle frame manufactured by Renishaw for Empire Cycles.* Retrieved from http://www.renishaw.com/en/first-metal-3d-printed-bicycle-frame-manufactured-by-renishaw-for-empire-cycles--24154

Research Autism. (2015). *Causes of Autism.* Retrieved from http://researchautism.net/autism/causes-of-autism

Reynhout, G., & Carter, M. (2006). Social stories™ for children with disabilities. *Journal of Autism and Developmental Disorders, 36*(4), 445–469. doi:10.1007/s10803-006-0086-1 PMID:16755384

Reynolds, B. W. (2015). 76 virtual companies and distributed teams. *FLexjobs*. Retrieved from https://www.flexjobs.com/blog/post/76-virtual- companies-and-distributed-teams/

Reznick, R. K., & MacRae, H. (2006). Teaching surgical skills-changes in the wind. *The New England Journal of Medicine*, *355*(25), 2664–2669. doi:10.1056/NEJMra054785 PMID:17182991

Rice, K. (2012). *Making the move to K-12 online teaching: Research-based strategies and practices*. Boston, MA: Pearson.

Richards, J. M. (2004, August). The cognitive consequences of concealing feelings. *Psychological Science*, *13*(4), 131–134.

Rideout, V. J., Roberts, D. F., & Foehr, U. G. (2005). *Generation M: Media in the lives of 8-18-year-olds: Executive summary*. Menlo Park, CA: Henry J. Kaiser Family Foundation.

Riel, M. M., & Levin, J. A. (1990). Building electronic communities: Success and failure in computer networking. *Instructional Science*, *19*(2), 145–169. doi:10.1007/BF00120700

Rivera, J., & Meulen, R. (2014, March 19). *Gartner says the internet of things will transform the data center*. Retrieved July 26, 2016, from http://www.gartner.com/newsroom/id/2684616

Robbins, J. K., Layng, T. V. J., & Jackson, P. J. (1995). *Fluent thinking skills*. Seattle, WA: Robbins/Layng & Associates.

Robin, B. (2006). The Educational Uses of Digital Storytelling. In *Proceedings of Society for Information Technology & Teacher Education International Conference 2006* (pp. 709-716). Chesapeake, VA: AACE. Retrieved April 20, 2010 from http://www.editlib.org/p/22129

Robins, J. (2014). *What is a Distributed Company?* Lullabot. Retrieved from https://www.lullabot.com/articles/what-is-a-distributed-company.

Rock, M. L., Schumacker, R. E., Gregg, M., Howard, P. W., Gable, R. A., & Zigmond, N. (2014). How are they now? Longer term effects of eCoaching through online bug-in-ear technology. *Teacher Education and Special Education*, *37*(2), 161–181. doi:10.1177/0888406414525048

Rock, M., Gregg, M., Gable, R., Zigmond, N., Blanks, B., Howard, P., & Bullock, L. (2012). Time after time online: An extended study of virtual coaching during distant clinical practice. *Journal of Technology and Teacher Education*, *20*(3), 277–304.

Rock, M., Gregg, M., Thead, B., Acker, S., Gable, R., & Zigmond, N. (2009). Can you hear me? Evaluation of an online wireless technology to provide real-time feedback to special education teachers-in-training. *Teacher Education and Special Education*, *32*, 64–82. doi:10.1177/0888406408330872

Rogers, L. A., & Graham, S. (2008). A meta-analysis of single subject design writing intervention research. *Journal of Educational Psychology*, *100*(4), 879–906. doi:10.1037/0022-0663.100.4.879

Romano, T. (2000). *Blending genre, altering style*. Portsmouth, NH: Heinemann.

Romano, T. (2004). *Crafting authentic voice*. Portsmouth, NH: Heinemann.

Roper, K. A., & Kim, J. H. (2007). Successful distributed work arrangements: A developmental approach. *Journal of Facilities Management*, *5*(2), 103–114. doi:10.1108/14725960710751852

Roscoe, E., Iwata, B. A., & Kahng, S. W. (1999). Relative versus absolute reinforcement effects: Implications for preference assessments. *Journal of Applied Behavior Analysis*, *32*(4), 479–493. doi:10.1901/jaba.1999.32-479 PMID:10641302

Roscorla, T. (2016). *Where the internet of things could take society by 2025*. Retrieved from http://www.centerdigitaled.com/news/Where-the-Internet-of-Things-Could-Take-Society-by-2025-.html

Rosen, K. R. (2008). The history of medical simulation. *Journal of Critical Care*, *23*(2), 157–166. doi:10.1016/j. jcrc.2007.12.004 PMID:18538206

Rosen, L. D. (2007). *Me, Myspace, and I: Parenting the Net Generation*. New York: Palgrave Macmillan.

Rosen, L. D. (2011). Teaching the iGeneration. *Educational Leadership*, *68*(5), 10–15. Retrieved from http://www.ascd. org/publications/educational-leadership/feb11/vol68/num05/Teaching-the-iGeneration.aspx

Ross, D. E., Singer-Dudek, J., & Greer, R. D. (2005). The teacher performance rate and accuracy scale (TPRA): Training as evaluation. *Education and Training in Developmental Disabilities*, 411–423.

Rowland, C., Goodman, E., Charlier, M., Light, A., & Lui, A. (2015). *Designing connected products: UX for the consumer internet of things*. Sebastopol, CA: O'Reilly.

Royal College of Psychiatry. (2017). *Depression in older adults*. Retrieved from http://www.rcpsych.ac.uk/healthadvice/ problemsdisorders/depressioninolderadults.aspx

Ruble, L., McGrew, J. H., & Toland, M. D. (2012). Goal attainment scaling as an outcome measure in randomized controlled trials of psychosocial interventions in autism. *Journal of Autism and Developmental Disorders*, *42*(9), 1974–1983. doi:10.1007/s10803-012-1446-7 PMID:22271197

Ruggiero, D., & Mong, C. J. (2015). The teacher technology integration experience: Practice and reflection in the classroom. *Journal of Information Technology Education: Research*, *14*(24), 161–178.

Russell, G. (2004). Virtual schools: A critical view. In C. Cavanaugh (Ed.), *Development and management of virtual schools: Issues and trends* (pp. 1–25). Hershey, PA: Information Science Pub. doi:10.4018/978-1-59140-154-4.ch001

Rutter, M., Caspi, A., Fergusson, D. M., Horwood, L. J., Goodman, R., Maughan, B., & Carroll, J. (2004). Gender differences in reading difficulties: Findings from four epidemiology studies. *Journal of the American Medical Association*, *291*, 2007–2012. doi:10.1001/jama.291.16.2007 PMID:15113820

Rycroft-Malone, J., Seers, K., Titchen, A., Harvey, G., Kitson, A., & McCormack, B. (2004). What counts as evidence in evidence-based practice? *Journal of Advanced Nursing*, *47*(1), 81–90. doi:10.1111/j.1365-2648.2004.03068.x PMID:15186471

Sackmann, R., & Winkler, I. (2013). Technology generations revisited: The Internet generation. *Geronotechnology*, *11*(4), 493–503.

Saffo, P. (2014, March). *Elon Pew future of the internet survey report: 2025 and the internet of things*. Retrieved from http://www.elon.edu/eweb/imagining/surveys/2014_survey/2025_Internet_of_Things.xhtml

Sahin, M. (2010). Teachers perceptions of bullying in high schools: A Turkish study. *Social Behavior and Personality*, *38*(1), 127–142. doi:10.2224/sbp.2010.38.1.127

Sanchez-Gordon, S., & Lujan-Mora, S. (2016). How could MOOCs become accessible? The case of edX and the future of online learning. *Journal of Universal Computer Science*, *22*(1), 55–81.

Sanchez, M., & Kaplan, M. (2014). Intergenerational learning in higher education: Making the case for multigenerational classrooms. *Educational Gerontology*, *40*(7), 473–485. doi:10.1080/03601277.2013.844039

Sanchez-Vives, M., & Slater, M. (2005, April). From presence to consciousness through virtual reality. *Nature Reviews. Neuroscience*, *6*(4), 332–339. doi:10.1038/nrn1651 PMID:15803164

Sandberg, S. (2013). *Lean in*. New York, NY: Alfred A. Knopf.

Sandholtz, J. H., Ringstaff, C., & Dwyer, D. C. (1997). *Teaching with technology: Creating student-centered classrooms.* New York, NY: Teachers College Press.

Sanrattana, U., Maneerat, T., & Srevisate, K. (2014). Social skills deficits of students with autism in inclusive schools. *Procedia: Social and Behavioral Sciences, 116,* 509–512. doi:10.1016/j.sbspro.2014.01.249

Sansosti, F. J., & Powell-Smith, K. A. (2008). Using computer-presented social stories and video models to increase the social communication skills of children with high-functioning autism spectrum disorders. *Journal of Positive Behavior Interventions, 10*(3), 162–178. doi:10.1177/1098300708316259

Sansosti, F. J., Powell-Smith, K. A., & Kincaid, D. (2004). A research synthesis of social story interventions for children with autism spectrum disorders. *Focus on Autism and Other Developmental Disabilities, 19*(4), 194–204. doi:10.1177/10883576040190040101

Sarokoff, R. A., & Sturmey, P. (2004). The effects of behavioral skills training on staff implementation of discrete-trial teaching. *Journal of Applied Behavior Analysis, 37*(4), 535–538. doi:10.1901/jaba.2004.37-535 PMID:15669415

Schank, R. (1990). *Tell me a story: Narrative and intelligence.* Evanston, IL: Northwestern University Press.

Scheeler, M. C., Bruno, K., Grubb, E., & Seavey, T. L. (2009). Generalizing teaching techniques from university to K-12 classrooms: Teaching preservice teachers to use what they learn. *Journal of Behavioral Education, 18*(3), 189–210. doi:10.1007/s10864-009-9088-3

Scheeler, M. C., Macluckie, M., & Albright, K. (2010b). Effects of immediate feedback delivered by peer tutors on the oral presentation skills of adolescents with learning disabilities. *Remedial and Special Education, 31*(2), 77–86. doi:10.1177/0741932508327458

Scheeler, M. C., McAfee, J. K., Ruhl, K. L., & Lee, D. L. (2006). Effects of corrective feedback delivered via wireless technology on preservice teacher performance and student behavior. *Teacher Education and Special Education, 29*(1), 12–25. doi:10.1177/088840640602900103

Scheeler, M., Congdon, M., & Stansbery, S. (2010a). Providing immediate feedback to co-teachers through bug-in-ear technology: An effective method of peer coaching in inclusion classrooms. *Teacher Education and Special Education, 33*(1), 83–96. doi:10.1177/0888406409357013

Scheeler, M., & Lee, D. (2002). Using technology to deliver immediate corrective feedback to preservice teachers. *Journal of Behavioral Education, 11*(4), 231–241. doi:10.1023/A:1021158805714

Scheeler, M., McKinnon, K., & Stout, J. (2012). Effects of immediate feedback delivered via webcam and bug-in-ear technology on preservice teacher performance. *Teacher Education and Special Education, 35*(1), 77–90. doi:10.1177/0888406411401919

Scheutz, M. (2011). *The inherent dangers of unidirectional emotional bonds between humans and social robots. In Robot ethics: The ethical and social implications of robotics* (pp. 205–221). Cambridge, MA: The MIT Press.

Schlosser, L. A., & Simonson, M. R. (2006). *Distance education: Definition and glossary of terms.* Greenwich, CT: IAP.

Schmetzke, A. (2001). Online distance education: "Anytime, anywhere" but not for everyone. Information. *Technology and Disability, 7*(2), 1–23.

Schmidt, B. (2014). *The practice.* Deerfield Beach, FL: Health Communications, Inc.

Schmidt, D., Baran, E., Thompson, A., Mishra, P., Koehler, M., & Shin, T. (2009). Technological pedagogical content knowledge (TPACK): The development and validation of an assessment instrument for preservice teachers. *Journal of Research on Technology in Education, 42*(2), 123–149. doi:10.1080/15391523.2009.10782544

Schneider, N., & Goldstein, H. (2010). Using social stories and visual schedules to improve socially appropriate behaviors in children with autism. *Journal of Positive Behavior Interventions, 12*(3), 149–160. doi:10.1177/1098300709334198

Schoenholtz-Read, J., & Rudestam, K. E. (2002). *Handbook of online learning: Innovations in higher education and corporate training*. Thousand Oaks, CA: Sage.

Schunk, D. (2004). *Learning theories: An educational perspective* (4th ed.). Upper Saddle River, NJ: Pearson Education, Inc.

Scurlock, M. (2008). *Using social stories with children with Asperger syndrome* (Master's thesis). Athens, OH: Ohio University.

Seamster, C. L. (2016). *Approaching Authentic Assessment: Using Virtual School Teachers' Expertise to Develop an Understanding of Full Time K-8 Virtual School Teacher Practices* (Doctoral dissertation). Retrieved from ProQuest Dissertations and Theses database.

Selinske, J., Greer, R. D., & Lodhi, S. (1991). A functional analysis of the Comprehensive Application of Behavior Analysis to Schooling. *Journal of Applied Behavior Analysis, 13*, 645–654. PMID:1829071

Senge, P. (1990). *The fifth discipline*. New York, NY: Doubleday/Currency Publishing.

Senge, P. M. (1994). *The fifth discipline: The art & practice of the learning organization* (1st ed.). New York: Doubleday Business.

Setzer, J. C., & Lewis, L. (2005). *Distance Education Courses for Public Elementary and Secondary School Students. 2002-Tab. NCES 2005-010*. US Department of Education.

Sevcikova, A., Machackova, H., Wright, M. F., Dedkova, L., & Cerna, A. (2015). Social support seeking in relation to parental attachment and peer relationships among victims of cyberbullying. *Australian Journal of Guidance & Counselling, 15*, 1–13. doi:10.1017/jgc.2015.1

Shapka, J. D., & Law, D. M. (2013). Does one size fit all? Ethnic differences in parenting behaviors and motivations for adolescent engagement in cyberbullying. *Journal of Youth and Adolescence, 42*(5), 723–738. doi:10.1007/s10964-013-9928-2 PMID:23479327

Shariff, S., & Hoff, D. L. (2007). Cyber bullying: Clarifying legal boundaries for school supervision in cyberspace. *International Journal of Cyber Criminology, 1*, 76–118.

Sharp, C. (2000). *A writer's workshop*. New York: St. Martin's Press.

Sherer, M. (2011). Transforming education with technology: A conversation with Karen Cator. *Educational Leadership, 68*(5), 16–21.

Sherman, J. G., Raskin, R. S., & Semb, G. B. (1982). *The personalized systems of instruction: 48 seminal papers*. Lawrence, KS: TRI.

Sherman, R. O. (2016). Leading a multigenerational nursing workforce: Issues, challenges, and strategies. *Online Journal of Issues in Nursing, 11*(2), 3–7. Retrieved from http://www.medscape.com/viewarticle/536480_2 PMID:17201577

Shin, L. (2016). At these 125 companies, all or most employees work remotely. *Forbes*. Retrieved from http://www.forbes.com/sites/laurashin/2016/03/31/at-these-125-companies-all-or-most-employees-work-remotely/#7ebf93554d94

Shinnick, M. A., Woo, M., & Evangelista, L. S. (2012). Predictors of knowledge gains using simulation in the education of prelicensure nursing students. *Journal of Professional Nursing, 28*(1), 41–47. doi:10.1016/j.profnurs.2011.06.006 PMID:22261604

Shore, S., & Rastelli, L. G. (2006). *Understanding Autism for Dummies* (1st ed.). For Dummies.

Shrader, S., Wu, M., Owens, D., & Santa Ana, K. (2016). Massive open online courses (MOOCs): Participant activity, demographics, and satisfaction. *Online Learning, 20*(2), 171–188. doi:10.24059/olj.v20i2.596

Shrestha, A., Anderson, A., & Moore, D. W. (2013). Using point-of-view video modeling and forward chaining to teach a functional self-help skill to a child with autism. *Journal of Behavioral Education, 22*(2), 157–167. doi:10.1007/s10864-012-9165-x

Shugrina, M., Shamir, A., & Matusik, W. (2015). *Fab forms: Customizable objects for fabrication with validity and geometry caching.* Paper presented at the ACM Siggraph 2015, Los Angeles, CA. Retrieved from http://cfg.mit.edu/content/fab-forms-customizable-objects-fabrication-validity-and-geometry-caching

Shukla-Mehta, S., Miller, T., & Callahan, K. J. (2010). Evaluating the effectiveness of video instruction on social and communication skills training for children with autism spectrum disorders: A review of the literature. *Focus on Autism and Other Developmental Disabilities, 25*(1), 23–26. doi:10.1177/1088357609352901

Shulman, L. S. (1986). Those who understand: Knowledge growth in teaching. *Educational Researcher, 15*(2), 4–14. doi:10.3102/0013189X015002004

Shulman, L. S. (2005). Signature pedagogies in the professions. *Daedalus, 134*(3), 52–59. doi:10.1162/0011526054622015

Sidman, M., & Tailby, W. (1982). Conditional discrimination vs. matching to sample: An expansion of the testing paradigm. *Journal of the Experimental Analysis of Behavior, 37*(1), 5–22. doi:10.1901/jeab.1982.37-5 PMID:7057129

Sijtsema, J. J., Ashwin, R. J., Simona, C. S., & Gina, G. (2014). Friendship selection and influence in bullying and defending. *Effects of moral disengagement. Developmental Psychology, 50*(8), 2093–2104. doi:10.1037/a0037145 PMID:24911569

Simonson, M. R., Smaldino, S., & Zvacek, S. (2015). *Teaching and learning at a distance: Foundations of distance education.* Charlotte, NC: Information Age Publishing.

Simpson, A., Langone, J., & Ayres, K. M. (2004). Embedded video and computer based instruction to improve social skills for students with autism. *Education and Training in Developmental Disabilities, 39*(3), 240–252.

Singer-Dudek, J., Speckman, J., & Nuzullo, R. (2010). A comparative analysis of the CABAS® model of education at the Fred S. Keller School: A twenty-year review. *Behavior Analyst Today, 11*(4), 253–265. doi:10.1037/h0100705

Sjurso, I. R., Fandream, H., & Roland, E. (2016). Emotional problems in traditional and cyber victimization. *Journal of School Violence, 15*(1), 114–131. doi:10.1080/15388220.2014.996718

Skinner, B. F. (1938). *The Behavior of Organisms: An Experimental Analysis.* Acton, MA: Copley Publishing Group.

Skinner, B. F. (1953). *Science and human behavior.* New York: Pearson Education, Inc.

Skinner, B. F. (1957). *Verbal Behavior.* Prentice Hall. doi:10.1037/11256-000

Skinner, B. F. (1968). *The technology of teaching.* New York, NY: Meredith Corporation Appleton-Century-Crofts Educational Division.

Skinner, B. F. (1968). *The Technology of Teaching.* New York: Appleton-Century-Crofts.

Sladeczek, I. E., Elliott, S. N., Kratochwill, T. R., Robertson-Mjaanes, S., & Stoiber, K. C. (2001). Application of goal attainment scaling to a conjoint behavioral consultation case. *Journal of Educational & Psychological Consultation*, *12*(1), 45–58. doi:10.1207/S1532768XJEPC1201_03

Smith, A. (2011). Why Americans use social media. *PewResearchCenter Internet, Science & Tech*. Retrieved from http://www.pewinternet.org/2011/11/15/why-americans-use-social-media/

Smith, A. (2013). *Smartphone ownership 2013*. Retrieved from http://www.pewinternet.org/2013/06/05/smartphone-ownership-2013/

Smith, A. (2015). *How rural schools can support successful STEM programs*. Retrieved from https://www.noodle.com/articles/heres-how-these-rural-schools-offer-top-notch-stem-courses151

Smith, A. (1996). *Accelerated learning in the classroom*. Stafford, UK: Network Education Press Ltd.

Smith, P. K., Del Barrio, C., & Tokunaga, R. S. (2013). Definitions of bullying and cyberbullying: How useful are the terms? In S. Bauman, D. Cross, & J. Walker (Eds.), *Principles of cyberbullying research: Definitions, measures, methodology* (pp. 26–40). New York, NY: Routledge.

Smith, P. K., Mahdavi, J., Carvalho, M., Fisher, S., Russell, S., & Tippett, N. (2008). Cyberbullying: Its nature and impact in secondary school pupils. *Journal of Child Psychology and Psychiatry, and Allied Disciplines*, *49*(4), 376–385. doi:10.1111/j.1469-7610.2007.01846.x PMID:18363945

Smith, R., Gray, J., Raymond, J., Catling-Paull, C., & Homer, C. (2012). Simulated learning activities: Improving midwifery students understanding of reflective practice. *Clinical Simulation in Nursing*, *8*(9), e451–e457. doi:10.1016/j.ecns.2011.04.007

Smith, T. (2001). Discrete trial training in the treatment of autism. *Focus on Autism and Other Developmental Disabilities*, *16*(2), 286–292. doi:10.1177/108835760101600204

Snider, S., & Foster, J. M. (2000). Stepping stones for linking, learning, and moving toward electronic literacy: Integrating emerging technology in an author study project. *Computers in the Schools*, *16*(2), 91–108. doi:10.1300/J025v16n02_09

Sokal, L., & Katz, H. (2008). Effects of technology and male teachers on boys reading. *Australian Journal of Education*, *52*(1), 81–94. doi:10.1177/000494410805200106

Sopko, K. M. (2009). Universal design for learning: Policy challenges and recommendations. In D. T. Gordon, J. A. Gravel, & L. A. Schifter (Eds.), *A policy reader in universal design for learning* (pp. 93–107). Cambridge, MA: Harvard Education Press.

Sorcinelli, M., Austin, A., Eddy, P., & Beach, A. L. (2006). *Creating the future of faculty development: learning from the past, understanding the present*. Boston, MA: Anker Publishing Co.

Sørensen, E. (2009). *Materiality of learning, technology and knowledge in educational practice*. New York: Cambridge University Press. doi:10.1017/CBO9780511576362

Sourander, A., Brunstein, A., Ikonen, M., Lindroos, J., Luntamo, T., Koskelainen, M., & Helenius, H. et al. (2010). Psychosocial risk factors associated with cyberbullying among adolescents: A population-based study. *Archives of General Psychiatry*, *67*(7), 720–728. doi:10.1001/archgenpsychiatry.2010.79 PMID:20603453

Southern Regional Education Board. (2003). *Essential principles of high-quality online teaching: Guideline for evaluating K-12 online teachers*. Retrieved from http://info.sreb.org/programs/edtech/pubs/PDF/Essential_Principles.pdf

Sparke, P. (1987). *Design in context*. London: Quarto Books.

Sparrow, P., & Omereen, V. (2000). Teleworking and psychological contract: a new division of labour. In K. Daniels, D. Lamnf, & P. Standen (Eds.), Managing Telework: Perspectives from Human Resource Management and Work Psychology. London: Thomson Learning.

Sparrow, B., Liu, J., & Wegner, D. M. (2011). Google effects on memory: Cognitive consequences of having information at our fingertips. *Science, 333*(6043), 776–778. doi:10.1126/science.1207745 PMID:21764755

Spatz, E. S., LeFrancois, D., & Ostfeld, R. J. (2011). Developing cardiac auscultation skills among physician trainees. *International Journal of Cardiology, 152*(3), 391–392. doi:10.1016/j.ijcard.2011.08.027 PMID:21917333

Spillane, J. P. (2004). *Standards deviation: How schools misunderstand education policy.* Cambridge, MA: Harvard University Press.

St Clair, A. (2016). Critical thinking, wisdom and paying homage to the human experience. *Voices, 42*(1/2), 41-43.

Stahl, S. (2008). Transforming the textbook to improve learning. In D. H. Rose & A. Meyer (Eds.), *A practical reader in universal design for learning* (pp. 103–132). Cambridge, MA: Harvard Education Press.

Steege, M. W., & Watson, T. S. (2009). *Conducting School-Based functional behavioral assessment: A practitioner's guide.* New York: The Guilford Press.

Sterling, B. (2005). *Shaping things.* Cambridge, MA: MIT Press.

Stern, J. (1994). *The condition of education in rural schools.* U.S. Department of Education: Office of Educational Research and Improvement. Retrieved from http://eric.ed.gov/?id=ED371935

Stoll, L. C., & Block, R. Jr. (2015). Intersectionality and cyberbullying: A study of cybervictimization in a Midwestern high school. *Computers in Human Behavior, 52*, 387–391. doi:10.1016/j.chb.2015.06.010

Street, B. (2003). Current issues in comparative education. New York, NY: Teachers College, Columbia University.

Strohmeier, D., Aoyama, I., Gradinger, P., & Toda, Y. (2013). Cybervictimization and cyberaggression in Eastern and Western countries: Challenges of constructing a cross-cultural appropriate scale. In S. Bauman, D. Cross, & J. L. Walker (Eds.), *Principles of cyberbullying research: Definitions, measures, and methodology* (pp. 202–221). New York: Routledge.

Suler, J. (2004). The online disinhibition effect. *Cyberpsychology & Behavior, 7*(3), 321–326. doi:10.1089/1094931041291295 PMID:15257832

Sung, Y., Chang, K., & Liu, T. (2016, March). The effects of integrating mobile devices with teaching and learning on students learning performance: A meta-analysis and research synthesis. *Computers & Education, 94*, 252–275. doi:10.1016/j.compedu.2015.11.008

Sutherland-Smith, W. (2002). Weaving the literacy web: Changes in reading from page to screen. *The Reading Teacher, 55*(7), 662–669.

Sutton, B., & Basiel, A. S. (2014) *Teaching and learning online: New models of learning for a connected world* (Vol. 2). New York: NY: Routledge, Taylor & Francis Group. Retrieved from http://site.ebrary.com/lib/floridaatlantic/reader.action?docID=10752675

Szondy, D. (2016, March 9). BMW looks to the future with shape-shifting. *Vision Next 100 Concept.* Retrieved from http://www.gizmag.com/bmw-group-vision--next-100-concept/42194/

Taipale, V. T. (2014). Global trends, policies and Gerontechnology. *Gerontechnology (Valkenswaard), 12*(4), 187–193. doi:10.4017/gt.2014.12.4.001.00

Tam, M. (2014, November 02). A distinctive theory of teaching and learning for older learners: Why and why not? *International Journal of Lifelong Education, 33*(6), 811–820. doi:10.1080/02601370.2014.972998

Tangen, D., & Campbell, M. (2010). Cyberbullying prevention: One primary schools approach. *Australian Journal of Guidance & Counselling, 20*(02), 225–234. doi:10.1375/ajgc.20.2.225

Tang, J. J., Tun, J. K., Kneebone, R. L., & Bello, F. (2013). Distributed simulation. In K. Forrest, J. McKimm, & S. Edgar (Eds.), *Essential simulation in clinical education* (pp. 196–212). Chichester, UK: John Wiley & Sons, Ltd. doi:10.1002/9781118748039.ch11

Taylor, W. D. (2014). Depression in the elderly. *The New England Journal of Medicine, 371*, 1222–1236. PMID:25251617

Technology. (2017). In *OxfordDictionaries.com*. Retrieved from http://www.oxforddictionaries .com/definition/english/technology

Technology. (n.d.). In *Merriam-Webster*. Retrieved June 23, 2016, from http://www.merriam-webster.com/dictionary/technology

Teh, J., & Curran, M. (2016). *Nonvisual desktop access*. Retrieved from http://www.nvaccess.org/

Tett, R. P., & Burnett, D. D. (2003). A personality trait-based interactionist model of job performance. *The Journal of Applied Psychology, 88*(3), 500–517. doi:10.1037/0021-9010.88.3.500 PMID:12814298

The Center for Universal Design. (2016). *Universal design principles*. Retrieved from https://www.ncsu.edu/ncsu/design/cud/about_ud/udprinciplestext.htm

The National Center on Disability and Access to Education. (2016). *Cheatsheets*. Retrieved from http://ncdae.org/resources/cheatsheets/

The Online Mom. (2017). *7 technologies that can help keep the elderly safe*. Retrieved from http://www.theonlinemom.com/7-technologies-that-can-help-keep-the-elderly-safe/

The White House. (2010). *Race to the Top*. Retrieved from https://www.whitehouse.gov/issues/education/k-12/race-to-the-top

Tibbits, S. (2014). 4D printing: Multi-material shape change. *Architectural Design, 84*(1), 116–121. doi:10.1002/ad.1710

Tieso, C. (2005). The effects of grouping practices and curricular adjustments on achievement. *Journal for the Education of the Gifted, 29*(1), 60–89. doi:10.1177/016235320502900104

Tiffen, J., Corbridge, S., Shen, B. C., & Robinson, P. (2011). Patient simulator for teaching heart and lung assessment skills to advanced practice nursing students. *Clinical Simulation in Nursing, 7*(3), e91–e97. doi:10.1016/j.ecns.2009.10.003

Tindle, H. (2013). *Up: How positive outlook can transform our health and aging*. New York, NY: Hudson Street Press.

Toledano, S., Werch, B. L., & Wiens, B. A. (2015). Domain-specific self-concept in relation to traditional and cyber peer aggression. *Journal of School Violence, 14*(4), 405–423. doi:10.1080/15388220.2014.935386

Tomlinson, C. A. (2001). *How to Differentiate Instruction in Mixed-Ability Classrooms* (2nd ed.). Alexandria, VA: Association for Supervision & Curriculum Development.

Tomlinson, C. A., & Susan, D. A. (2000). *Leadership for differentiating schools & classrooms* (1st ed.). Alexandria, VA: Association for Supervision & Curriculum Development.

Totura, C. M. W., MacKinnon-Lewis, C., Gesten, E. L., Gadd, R., Divine, K. P., Dunham, S., & Kamboukos, D. (2009). Bullying and victimization among boys and girls in middle school: The influence of perceived family and school contexts. *The Journal of Early Adolescence*, *29*(4), 571–609. doi:10.1177/0272431608324190

Traxler, J. (2009). Current state of mobile learning. In M. Ally (Ed.), *Mobile Learning Transforming the Delivery of Education and Training*. Edmonton: Athabasca University Press.

Tregaskis, O., & Daniels, K. (2000). Organizational Learning. In K. Daniels, D. Lamnf, & P. Standen (Eds.), Managing Telework: Perspectives from Human Resource Management and Work Psychology. London: Thomson Learning.

Tseng, M. M., Jiao, R. J., & Wang, C. (2010). Design for mass personalization. *CIRP Annals: Manufacturing Technology*, *59*(1), 175–178. doi:10.1016/j.cirp.2010.03.097

Turner-Stokes, L. (2009). Goal attainment scaling (GAS) in rehabilitation: A practical guide. *Clinical Rehabilitation*, *23*(4), 362–370. doi:10.1177/0269215508101742 PMID:19179355

Tweddle, S. (1997). A retrospective: Fifteen years of computers in English. *English Education*, *31*(2), 5–13. doi:10.1111/j.1754-8845.1997.tb00120.x

U. S. Department of Education. (2016). *Future ready learning: Reimagining the role of technology in education*. Office of Educational Technology. Retrieved from http://tech.ed.gov

U.S. Census Bureau. (2015). *2010 Census urban and rural classification and urban Area criteria*. Retrieved from https://www.census.gov/geo/reference/ua/urban-rural-2010.html

U.S. Department of Education (U.S. D.O.E), Office of Special Education Programs. (2004). *National Instructional Materials Accessibility Standards (NIMAS). Individuals with Disabilities Act 2004*. Retrieved from http://idea.ed.gov/explore/view/p/%2Croot%2Cdynamic%2CTopicalBrief%2C12%2C

U.S. Department of Education, Office of Educational Technology. (2016). *Future Ready Learning: Reimagining the Role of Technology in Education*. Retrieved from http://tech.ed.gov/netp/introduction/

U.S. Department of Education. (1993). *Goals 2000, educate America: Building capacity: Higher education and Goals 2000*. Washington, DC: U.S. Dept. of Education.

Umemuro, H. (2004). Computer attitudes, cognitive abilities, and technology usage among older Japanese adults. *Gerontechnology Journal, 3*(2), 64-76. Retrieved from http://journal .gerontechnology.org/archives/340-342-1-PB.pdf

United States Access Board. (2016). *Section 508 standards*. Retrieved from https://www.access-board.gov/guidelines-and-standards/communications-and-it/about-the-section-508-standards/section-508-standards

United States Department of Justice. (2016). *2010 ADA regulations*. Retrieved from https://www.ada.gov/2010_regs.htm

University of Exeter. (2014). Training elderly in social media improves well-being, combats isolation. *ScienceDaily*. Retrieved from www.sciencedaily.com/releases/2014/12/141212111649.htm

Usinger, J., Ewing-Taylor, J., & Thornton, B. (2016, March). Technology Integration in Rural Districts: A Study in Differences. In *Society for Information Technology & Teacher Education International Conference* (Vol. 2016, No. 1, pp. 1155-1158). Academic Press.

Utah Office of Education. (2016). *UPSTART program evaluation: Year 6 program results*. Retrieved from http://www.schools.utah.gov/CURR/preschoolkindergarten/UPSTART/2016Summary.aspx

Van Braak, J., Tondeur, J., & Valcke, M. (2004). Explaining different types of computer use among primary school teachers. *European Journal of Psychology of Education*, *19*(4), 407–422. doi:10.1007/BF03173218 van Bronswijk, J. E. M. A., Bouma, H., Fozard, J. L., Kearns, W. D., Davison, G. C., & Tuan, P.-C. (2009). Defining Gerontechnology for R & D purposes. *Gerontechnology (Valkenswaard)*, *8*(1), 3–10.

Van Volkom, M., Stapley, J. C., & Amaturo, V. (2014). Revisiting the digital divide: Generational differences in technology use in everyday life. *North American Journal of Psychology*, *16*(3), 557–574.

VanDerHeyden, A. M., Witt, J. C., & Gilbertson, D. (2007). A multi-year evaluation of the effects of a response to intervention (RTI) model on identification of children for special education. *Journal of School Psychology*, *45*(2), 225–256. doi:10.1016/j.jsp.2006.11.004

Vannatta, R. A., & Fordham, N. (2004). Teacher dispositions as predictors of classroom technology use. *Journal of Research on Technology in Education*, *36*(3), 253–271. doi:10.1080/15391523.2004.10782415

Vavoula, G., & Sharples, M. (2009). Meeting the challenges in evaluating mobile learning: A 3-level evaluation framework. *International Journal of Mobile and Blended Learning*, *1*(2), 54–75. doi:10.4018/jmbl.2009040104

Venkatesh, V., Morris, M., Davis, G., & Davis, F. (2003). User acceptance of information technology: Toward a unified view. *Management Information Systems Quarterly*, *27*(3), 425–478.

Vermeylen, L., & McLean, S. (2014). Does age matter? Informal learning practices of younger and older adults. *The Canadian Journal for the Study of Adult Education*, *26*(1), 19–34.

Vicker, B. (1998). Behavioral issues and the use of social stories. *The Reporter*, *3*(2), 13–14.

Villalón, R., Mateos, M., & Cuevas, I. (2015). High school boys and girls writing conceptions and writing self-efficacy beliefs: What is their role in writing performance? *Educational Psychology*, *35*(6), 653–674. doi:10.1080/01443410.2013.836157

Vroman, K. G., Arthanat, S., & Lysack, C. (2014). Who over 65 is online? Older adults dispositions towards information communication technology. *Computers in Human Behavior*, *43*, 156–166. doi:10.1016/j.chb.2014.10.018

Vygotsky, L. (1986). *Thought and language*. Cambridge, MA: MIT Press.

Vygotsky, L. S., & Cole, M. (1978). *Mind in society: The development of higher psychological processes*. Cambridge, MA: Harvard University Press.

Vygotsky, L. S., Davidov, V., & Silverman, R. J. (1997). *Educational psychology*. Boca Raton, FL: St. Lucie Press.

W3C. (2008). *Web Content Accessibility Guidelines (WCAG) 2.0*. Retrieved from http://www.w3.org/TR/WCAG20/

Waddington, E. M., & Reed, P. (2009). The impact of using the Preschool Inventory of Repertoires for Kindergarten (PIRK) on school outcomes for children with Autistic Spectrum Disorders. *Research in Autism Spectrum Disorders*, *3*(3), 809–827. doi:10.1016/j.rasd.2009.03.002

Wade, A., & Beran, T. (2011). Cyberbullying: The new era of bullying. *Canadian Journal of School Psychology*, *26*(1), 44–61. doi:10.1177/0829573510396318

Walker, S. (2006). *Sustainable by design: Explorations in theory and practice*. London: Earthscan.

Wallin, J. M. (n.d.). *An introduction to social stories*. Retrieved from http://www.polyxo.com/socialstories/introduction.html

Warschauer, M., Zheng, B., Niiya, M., Cotten, S., & Farkas, G. (2014). Balancing the one-to-one equation: Equity and access in three laptop programs. *Equity & Excellence in Education*, *47*(1), 46–62. doi:10.1080/10665684.2014.866871

Washburn, K. P. (2006). *The effects of a social story intervention on social skills acquisition in adolescents with Asperger's syndrome* (Doctoral dissertation). University of Florida.

Watson, D. (2006). Understanding the relationship between ICT and education means exploring innovation and change. *Education and Information Technologies, 11*(3-4), 199–216. doi:10.1007/s10639-006-9016-2

Watson, J., Murin, A., Vashaw, L., Gemin, B., & Rapp, C. (2013). *Keeping pace with K-12 online and blended learning.* Durango, CO: Evergreen Education Group.

Wayne, D. B., Butter, J., Siddall, V. J., Fudala, M. J., Wade, L. D., Feinglass, J., & McGaghie, W. C. (2006). Mastery learning of advanced cardiac life support skills by internal medicine residents using simulation technology and deliberate practice. *Journal of General Internal Medicine, 21*(3), 251–256. doi:10.1111/j.1525-1497.2006.00341.x PMID:16637824

Wayne, D. B., & McGaghie, W. C. (2013). Skill retention after simulation-based education. *Journal of Graduate Medical Education, 5*(1), 165. doi:10.4300/1949-8357-5.1.165 PMID:24404250

WebAIM. (2015a). *Testing web content for accessibility.* Retrieved from http://webaim.org/resources/evalquickref/

WebAIM. (2015b). *WAVE (Version 1.0.1).* Retrieved from http://wave.webaim.org/

WebAIM. (2016). *Web accessibility principles.* Retrieved January 29, 2016, from http://webaim.org/resources/quickref/

Wehman, P. (2012). Supported employment: What is it? *Journal of Vocational Rehabilitation, 37,* 139–142.

Weimer, M. (2002). *Learner-centered teaching: Five key changes to practice.* San Francisco, CA: Jossey Bass.

Weiser, M. (1991). The computer for the 21st century. *Scientific American, 265*(3), 94–110. doi:10.1038/scientificamerican0991-94 PMID:1675486

Welch, N. (1997). *Getting restless.* Portsmouth, NH: Heinemann.

Welch, S. (2009). *10-10-10.* New York, NY: Scribner.

Wellman, N. S. (2010). Aging at home: More research on nutrition and independence, please. *The American Journal of Clinical Nutrition, 91*(5), 1151–1152. doi:10.3945/ajcn.2010.29527 PMID:20335549

Wells, J. G. (2007). Key design factors in durable instructional technology professional development. *Journal of Technology and Teacher Education, 15*(1), 101–122.

Wenger, E. (1998). *Communities of practice: Learning, meaning, and identity.* Cambridge, UK: Cambridge University Press. doi:10.1017/CBO9780511803932

Wentz, B., Jaeger, P. T., & Lazar, J. (2011). Retrofitting accessibility: The legal inequality of after-the-fact online access for persons with disabilities in the United States. *First Monday, 16*(11). doi:10.5210/fm.v16i11.3666

Wertsch, J. V. (1991). *Voices of the mind: A sociocultural approach to mediated action.* Cambridge, MA: Harvard University Press.

What is School-Wide Positive Behavior Support? (2009, March). *School-wide Positive Behavior Support (SWPBS).* Retrieved from http://swpbs.org/schoolwide/Training/files/Kansas_School-Wide_Positive_Behavior_Support_Newsletter.pdf

White, O. R., & Haring, N. G. (1976). *Exceptional teaching: A multi-media approach.* Columbus, OH: Merrill.

Wiberg, M. (2005). *The Interaction society: Practice, theories and supportive technologies.* Hershey, PA: Information Science Publishing. doi:10.4018/978-1-59140-530-6

Wiggins, G. (1989). Teaching to the (authentic) test. *Educational Leadership, 46*(7), 41–47.

Wiggins, G. (1998). *Educative assessment: Designing assessments to inform and improve student performance.* San Francisco, CA: Jossey-Bass.

Wiggins, G., & McTighe, J. (2007). *School by design: Mission, action, and achievement.* Alexandria, VA: Association for Supervision & Curriculum Development.

William, K., & Kemper, S. (2010). Exploring intervention to reduce cognitive decline in aging. *Journal of Psychosocial Nursing and Mental Health Services, 48*(5), 42–551. doi:10.3928/02793695-20100331-03 PMID:20415290

Williams, K. R., & Guerra, N. G. (2007). Prevalence and predictors of internet bullying. *The Journal of Adolescent Health, 41*(6), S14–S21. doi:10.1016/j.jadohealth.2007.08.018 PMID:18047941

Wilson, B. (1996). *Constructivist learning environments.* Englewood Cliffs, NJ: Educational Technologies Publication.

Wilson, K. P. (2013). Incorporating video modeling into a school-based intervention for students with autism spectrum disorders. *Language, Speech, and Hearing Services in Schools, 44*(1), 105–117. doi:10.1044/0161-1461(2012/11-0098) PMID:23087158

Wilson, K. P. (2013). Teaching social-communication skills to preschoolers with autism: Efficacy of video versus in vivo modeling in the classroom. *Journal of Autism and Developmental Disorders, 43*(8), 1819–1831. doi:10.1007/s10803-012-1731-5 PMID:23224593

Winzenried, A., Dalgarno, B., & Tinkler, J. (2010). The interactive whiteboard: A transitional technology supporting diverse teaching practices. *Australasian Journal of Educational Technology, 26*(4), 534–552. doi:10.14742/ajet.1071

Witherspoon, G. (1977). *Language and art in the Navajo universe.* Ann Arbor, MI: University of Michigan Press. doi:10.3998/mpub.9705

Witte, S. (2009). "Twitterdee, twitterdumb": Teaching in the time of technology, tweets, and trespassing. *California English, 15*(1), 23–25.

Wolfe, E. W., Bolton, S., Feltovich, B., & Niday, D. M. (1996). The influence of student experience with word processors on the quality of essays written for a direct writing assessment. *Assessing Writing, 3*(2), 123–147. doi:10.1016/S1075-2935(96)90010-0

Wolfson, N. E., Cavanagh, T. M., & Kraiger, K. (2014). Older adults and technology-based instruction: Optimizing learning outcomes and transfer. *Academy of Management Learning & Education, 13*(1), 25–44. doi:10.5465/amle.2012.0056

Wollscheid, S., Sjaastad, J., & Tømte, C. (2016). The impact of digital devices vs. Pen (cil) and paper on primary school students writing skills–A research review. *Computers & Education, 95*, 19–35. doi:10.1016/j.compedu.2015.12.001

Wong, D. S., Chan, H. C. O., & Cheng, C. H. (2014). Cyberbullying perpetration and victimization among adolescents in Hong Kong. *Children and Youth Services Review, 36*, 133–140. doi:10.1016/j.childyouth.2013.11.006

Woodill, G. (2010). *The mobile learning edge: Tools and technologies for developing your teams.* New York: McGraw-Hill.

Wood, M. (2011). Collaborative lab reports with Google Docs. *The Physics Teacher, 49*(3), 158–159. doi:10.1119/1.3555501

Woods, B., & Clare, L. (2008). *Handbook of the psychology of ageing* (2nd ed.). Hoboken, NJ: John Wiley and Sons.

Woolrych, R. (2016). Ageing and technology: Creating environments to support an ageing society. *1st Brazilian Congress of Gerontechnology, 15*(2), 66-70. doi:10.4017/gt.2016.15.2.005.00

Wozney, L., Venkatesh, V., & Abrami, P. C. (2006). Implementing computer technologies: Teachers' perceptions and practices. *Journal of Technology and Teacher Education, 14*(1), 173–207.

Wright, M. F. (2015). Cyber victimization and adjustment difficulties: The mediation of Chinese and American adolescents' digital technology usage. *CyberPsychology: Journal of Psychosocial Research in Cyberspace, 1*(1), article 1. Retrieved from: http://cyberpsychology.eu/view.php?cisloclanku=2015051102&article=1

Wright, M. F. (2013). The relationship between young adults beliefs about anonymity and subsequent cyber aggression. *Cyberpsychology, Behavior, and Social Networking, 16*(12), 858–862. doi:10.1089/cyber.2013.0009 PMID:23849002

Wright, M. F. (2014a). Cyber victimization and perceived stress: Linkages to late adolescents' cyber aggression and psychological functioning. *Youth & Society*.

Wright, M. F. (2014b). Predictors of anonymous cyber aggression: The role of adolescents beliefs about anonymity, aggression, and the permanency of digital content. *Cyberpsychology, Behavior, and Social Networking, 17*(7), 431–438. doi:10.1089/cyber.2013.0457 PMID:24724731

Wright, M. F. (2014c). Longitudinal investigation of the associations between adolescents popularity and cyber social behaviors. *Journal of School Violence, 13*(3), 291–314. doi:10.1080/15388220.2013.849201

Wright, M. F. (in press). Adolescents' cyber aggression perpetration and cyber victimization: The longitudinal associations with school functioning. *Social Psychology of Education*.

Wright, M. F., Kamble, S., Lei, K., Li, Z., Aoyama, I., & Shruti, S. (2015). Peer attachment and cyberbullying involvement among Chinese, Indian, and Japanese adolescents. *Societies, 5*(2), 339–353. doi:10.3390/soc5020339

Wright, M. F., & Li, Y. (2012). Kicking the digital dog: A longitudinal investigation of young adults victimization and cyber-displaced aggression. *Cyberpsychology, Behavior, and Social Networking, 15*(9), 448–454. doi:10.1089/cyber.2012.0061 PMID:22974350

Wright, M. F., & Li, Y. (2013a). Normative beliefs about aggression and cyber aggression among young adults: A longitudinal investigation. *Aggressive Behavior, 39*(3), 161–170. doi:10.1002/ab.21470 PMID:23440595

Wright, M. F., & Li, Y. (2013b). The association between cyber victimization and subsequent cyber aggression: The moderating effect of peer rejection. *Journal of Youth and Adolescence, 42*(5), 662–674. doi:10.1007/s10964-012-9903-3 PMID:23299177

Wu, W. H., Wu, Y. C., Chen, C. Y., Kao, H. Y., Lin, C. H., & Huang, S. H. (2012). Review of trends from mobile learning studies: A meta-analysis. *Computers & Education, 59*(2), 817–827. doi:10.1016/j.compedu.2012.03.016

Yao, L., Ou, J., Cheng, C.-Y., Steiner, H., Wang, W., Wang, G., & Ishii, H. (2015). bioLogic: Natto cells as nanoactuators for shape changing interfaces. In *Proceedings of the 33rd Annual ACM Conference on Human Factors in Computing Systems* (pp. 1-10). New York, NY: ACM. doi:10.1145/2702123.2702611

Ybarra, M. L., Diener-West, M., & Leaf, P. (2007). Examining the overlap in internet harassment and school bullying: Implications for school intervention. *The Journal of Adolescent Health, 1*(6), 42–50. doi:10.1016/j.jadohealth.2007.09.004 PMID:18047944

Ybarra, M. L., & Mitchell, K. J. (2004). Online aggressor/targets, aggressors, and targets: A comparison of associated youth characteristics. *Journal of Child Psychology and Psychiatry, and Allied Disciplines, 45*(7), 1308–1316. doi:10.1111/j.1469-7610.2004.00328.x PMID:15335350

Yettick, H., Baker, R., Wickersham, M., & Hupfeld, K. (2014). Rural districts left behind? Rural districts and the challenges of administering the Elementary and Secondary Education Act. *Journal of Research in Rural Education (Online), 29*(13), 1–15.

Yilmaz, K. (2011). The cognitive perspective on learning: Its theoretical underpinnings and implications for classroom practices. *The Clearing House: A Journal of Educational Strategies, Issues and Ideas, 84*(5), 204–212. doi:10.1080/00098655.2011.568989

Yin, R. (2009). *Case study research: Design and methods* (5th ed.). Thousand Oaks, CA: Sage Publications.

Yousef, W. S. M., & Bellamy, A. (2015). The impact of cyberbullying on the self-esteem and academic functioning of Arab American middle and high school students. *Electronic Journal of Research in Educational Psychology, 23*(3), 463–482.

Yu, R. P., Ellison, N. B., McCammon, R. J., & Langa, K. M. (2016). Mapping the two levels of digital divide: Internet access and social network site adoption among older adults in the USA. *Information Communication and Society, 19*(1), 1445–1464. doi:10.1080/1369118X.2015.1109695

Zaval, L., Ye, L., Johnson, E. J., & Webber, E. U. (2015). Complementary contributions of fluid and crystallized intelligence to decision making across the life span. *Aging and Decision Making: Empirical and Applied Perspectives*, 149-168.

Zawilinski, L. (2009). HOT blogging: A framework for blogging to promote higher order thinking. *The Reading Teacher, 62*(8), 650–661. doi:10.1598/RT.62.8.3

Zhang, B., Shi, L., & Song, S. (2016). Creating more intelligent robots through brain-inspired computer. In Brain-Inspired intelligent robotics: The Intersection of robotics and neuroscience. Beijing, China: Chinese Academy of Sciences.

Zhang, F., & Kaufman, D. (2016). Cognitive benefits of older adults digital gameplay: A critical review. *Gerontechnology (Valkenswaard), 15*(1), 3–16. doi:10.4017/gt.2016.15.1.002.00

Zheng, B., Lawrence, J., Warschauer, M., & Lin, C. H. (2015). Middle school students writing and feedback in a cloud-based classroom environment. *Technology. Knowledge and Learning, 20*(2), 201–229. doi:10.1007/s10758-014-9239-z

Zhou, Z., Tang, H., Tian, Y., Wei, H., Zhang, F., & Morrison, C. M. (2013). Cyberbullying and its risk factors among Chinese high school students. *School Psychology International, 34*(6), 630–647. doi:10.1177/0143034313479692

About the Contributors

Valerie Bryan is Professor in Educational Leadership in Adult Education at Florida Atlantic University. She has received a variety of awards and other recognitions: Eminent Scholar in Community Education, 2011; recipient of FAU Graduate Mentor Award, 2011; 2009 MacAWARD Exceptional Faculty for College of Education, 2009; FAU College of Education Distinguished Teacher of the Year, 2009; recipient of FAU's President's Award, 2006-2007; FAU College of Education's Distinguished Teacher of the Year, 2006; FAU College of Education Teacher of the Year, 2005-2006; recipient of Clemson University's President's Award, 1993; North Carolina's Individual of the Year, 1984. Recognized as webmaster of One of Top Ten US Literacy Internet sites, 1998. Served as President for College of Education Faculty Assembly, 2005-2006; President of National Fitness Coalition; President of North Carolina Recreation and Park Society; State President of Delta Kappa Gamma. Recognized for several distinctions on a variety of Who's Who list. At Florida Atlantic University, she teaches courses in management, adult learning, administration, aging, integration of technology, and a host of other subjects, online, in stand-up-mode, and on several platforms. She is active in research that embraces virtual learning communities, enhanced staff productivity using a varying of technology-based tools, and the role of successful aging. Valerie is active in the integration of technology in practice, as a doctoral chair, and in her research/grant-writing of over $1.8 M (at FAU alone) for numerous populations including senior adults, individuals with literacy or language deficiencies, career and vocational trainees, graduate students, and community-based collaboratives including recreation and leisure services and after-school programs. She has served as author/co-author of textbooks, book chapters, refereed publications at the international and national levels, state journal articles, extensive documents, host of grants, manuals and catalogs, and conducted over 250 refereed/non-refereed presentations at regional, state, national, and international conferences. In addition, she has chaired or served as committee member for 53 doctoral dissertations to completion and currently chairs 39 doctoral committees.

Ann Musgrove is an Assistant Professor in the Department of Teaching & Learning at Florida Atlantic University where she teaches instructional technology at the undergraduate and graduate level. She has an Online Teaching Certificate (OTC) from the Online Learning Consortium, she facilitates and designs workshops in their OTC program. Ann has 2 courses national recognized by Quality Matters (QM), where she is a master course reviewer and facilitator of applying the QM rubric, the peer review certification workshop and teaching online an introduction to online delivery. She helped set up FAU's center for eLearning and served as an Instructional Designer and Coordinator. Dr. Musgrove's administrative experiences include 5 years as the director of a Federal Title V cooperative grant between Broward College and the FAU Broward campus to create a learner centered pathway for teacher education students. This grant helped create the first baccalaureate program at Broward College in Teacher Education. Her research interests include best practices in online learning and cognitive styles. http://www.annmusgrove.com.

Jillian R. Powers is an Assistant Professor at Florida Atlantic University (FAU) in the College of Education in the department of Teaching and Learning. Dr. Powers teaches undergraduate and graduate courses in instructional technology and design for educators and business trainers. Her research focuses on teachers' adoption and integration of technology into classroom practices and ways in which technology shapes the teaching and learning process. Dr. Powers earned her Ph.D. in Curriculum and Instruction with a specialization in Instructional Technology from FAU in May 2014. She has previously worked as an Instructional Designer at the Institute of Excellence in Early Care and Education at Palm Beach State College and as a computer teacher in various PreK-8 schools. In these roles, she has designed and facilitated numerous technology trainings for in-service educators.

* * *

Phylise Banner is an online teaching and learning consultant with extensive experience in planning, designing, developing, delivering, and evaluating online courses, programs, and faculty development initiatives. Her work focuses on aligning institution-wide approaches to program, course, and professional development with teaching and learning effective practices and the Community of Inquiry framework. As an online learning evangelist, she actively seeks out opportunities to experiment with emerging technologies in order to best serve faculty and students, and to create communities of lifelong learners. She is featured regularly at regional, national and international conferences, speaking on the topics of online teaching and learning, faculty development, instructional strategy, experience design, social media, information visualization and GIS technologies. She also teaches Digital Storytelling online for SUNY Polytechnic Institute, and in person for the Academy for Lifelong Learning at Empire State College. She is an Adobe Education Leader, STC Fellow, performance storyteller, avid angler, aviation enthusiast, and currently training to be a private pilot. She is also the proud owner of a 1967 Amphicar.

Jennifer Bird teaches reading and writing classes for current and future teachers at Florida Atlantic University in Boca Raton, Florida. She received her Bachelor of Science in Education in Secondary English Education, Master of Education in Secondary English Education, and Doctor of Philosophy degrees from Miami University in Oxford, Ohio and her health coach certification from Duke University Integrative Medicine in Durham, North Carolina. Her research in writing and healing led to the publication of her book Innovative Collaborative Practice and Reflection in Patient Education (2015).

Michael P. Brady is Professor and Chair of the Department of Exceptional Student Education at Florida Atlantic University. His research interests include instructional procedures and coaching for teachers, behavioral teaching strategies for people with developmental disabilities, and policies that affect teacher preparation.

Melody Buckner is the Director of Digital Learning and Online Education at the University of Arizona where she oversees instructional design, graphic design, video production and quality assurance for the UA Online Campus. She also hold a faculty affiliation with at the University of Arizona in Col-

514

lege of Education within the Department of Teaching, Learning and Sociocultural Studies. She came to UA eight years ago as an Instructional Designer to help faculty create online courses that reach out and engage students in an online UA experience. Before coming to the University, she served as an Instructional Designer in Professional Development and as an adjunct faculty for Pima Community College. Her educational background includes, a Bachelor of Science from the College of Architecture at Arizona State University and a Masters in Educational Technology at Northern Arizona University. She recently graduated with a Ph.D. in Teaching, Learning and Sociocultural Studies at the University of Arizona. Her informal education consists of living in over 40 different places including several countries in Europe.

Benjamin Deaton is the Dean of the Center for Innovation and Digital Learning at Anderson University (SC) and founding Director of the South Carolina Center of Excellence for Mobile Learning. He holds a PhD in Instructional Technology from the University of Georgia, a MS in Computer Science from Clemson University, and a BS in Computer Science and Mathematics from Carson-Newman College. His work and research are focused on instructional design, mobile learning, online and blended learning, and emerging technologies.

Cynthia C. M. Deaton is an Associate Professor of Science Education at Clemson University. She teaches science methods and qualitative research courses. Her research interests include professional development, integrating technology for inquiry-based science, science teacher beliefs, and reflective practice.

Pamela A. Duffy is an assistant professor in the Department of Public Health, College of Health Sciences, at Des Moines University where she teaches about the U.S. health care system, global health foundations, policies, and partnerships for the Master of Public Health and Master of Health Care Administration programs. Dr. Duffy is known for her academic research and service in the areas of health disparities and addressing barriers to health care access for underserved populations. Her current projects are related to health care delivery for immigrant and refugee populations in the Midwest, community health measurement, and interprofessional education. She received her PhD in Education from Iowa State University in 2008, with a minor in Gerontology.

Maricris Eleno-Orama earned her Bachelor of Science and Bachelor of Arts in Environmental Engineering at Oregon State University; her Master of Science in Engineering - Civil/Water Resources at the University of Washington; and her Doctorate in Education - Organizational Leadership at Nova Southeastern University. She is a licensed Professional Environmental Engineer in Washington State. Her dissertation topic was on institutional, familial, and cultural factors affecting retention and academic success of Southeast Asian and Pacific Islander American students in college-level science, technology, engineering, and mathematics (STEM) education. In her present role as an adjunct faculty at Tacoma Community College and Western Oklahoma State College, she instructs several web-based and on-site introduction to engineering and physical science courses.

Lisa Finnegan is an Assistant Professor at Florida Atlantic University. Her research interests are universal design for learning, teacher preparation with a focus on instructional practices and classroom management, promoting inclusive practices for students with disabilities who are also English Learners as well as students with disabilities in Science and Mathematics classes for potential STEM careers. She has taught in both general education inclusive and special education classrooms with students in Grades K-8, as well as, supported K-12 teachers in curriculum & instruction.

Edwiygh Franck, Ph.D., President & CEO The Greatest You Yet!, is a senior talent development specialist, a online college professor at Southern New Hampshire University teaching Human and Organizational Behavior and a professional development consultant. She earned her doctorate degree in Educational Leadership with a concentration in Adult and Community Education at Florida Atlantic University, her Master's Degree in Education for Curriculum, Instruction and Technology from Nova Southeastern University, and her Bachelor's degree in Business Administration and Computer Information Systems from the University of Miami. She has over ten years of experience as a professional consultant and her passion is organizational development through performance management, talent review and leadership development. She has over 20 years of experience in the education, not-for-profit, and corporate arenas.

Eva Frank, originally from Germany, moved to the US in 1994 with her parents and brother. In 2003, her parents returned to Germany but she stayed in the US and pursued her goal of completing her bachelors in Athletic Training. In 2007, she graduated from Valdosta State University in Georgia after completing a capstone internship at Mississippi State University. She later became an FIU alumna in 2009 when she graduated with her masters in Physical Education. In 2016, she graduated from Florida Atlantic University with her Ph.D. in Curriculum and Instruction.

David Goodrich joined Michigan State University in 2012 as a Learning Experience Designer where he works to leverage effective active learning strategies while using emerging technologies. Dave collaborates with faculty to develop new courses, redesign existing courses, and consult on instructional learning object projects. He also enjoys facilitating faculty workshops and being a guest instructor from time to time for MSU's College of Education. Dave began as an Instructional Designer in the Office of Academic Technology Spring Arbor University in 2008 where he was elected the Faculty Representative for the Staff-Administration Personnel Association. Before this, he was a high school science and physical education teacher. He has a Masters degree in Education specializing in Instructional Design for Online Learning from Capella University. Dave is a musician and an amateur photographer. He enjoys being active outdoors in his spare time. Dave and his wife live in Jackson, Michigan and have three boys. Stop by anytime to his office in Wills House and he will brew you a cup of joe.

Angela Gunder serves as Associate Director of Digital Learning and Instructional Design for The University of Arizona, supporting the design and development of fully-online programs for UA Online. Angela came into instructional design rather circuitously, helming large-scale site designs as webmaster for The City College of New York, the honors college at ASU, and Northern Virginia Community College. Her over fifteen-year career as a designer for higher education informs her instructional design practice, where she leverages her expertise in usability, visual communication, programming, and standards-based online learning. Angela holds a B.S. in Computer Science and Fine Art from Fordham University, and a M.Ed. in Education Technology from Arizona State University. She is an Associate Editor for the Teacher Education Board of MERLOT, and a Quality Matters certified peer reviewer and online facilitator. Her research and pedagogical interests include the design and facilitation of innovation makerspaces, open educational resources, and emerging technology for second language acquisition. More specifically, her work examines effective practices for andragogy in the development of online learning environments. A voracious culinary nerd, Angela spends her free time composing, cooking and photographing original recipes for her food blog.

Josh Herron is the director of the online campus at Limestone College (SC). His background includes being a faculty member, faculty developer, and academic administrator. His research and teaching interests are in writing, communication, and new media.

Amoy Hugh-Pennie earned her Ph.D. at Columbia University Graduate School of Arts and Sciences in Special Education and Behavior Disorders graduating Cum Laude. She holds an M.A. and M.Ed. in Special Education, Curriculum Development and Instructional Design from Teachers' College, Columbia University and earned her BS in Psychology at Florida Atlantic University in Boca Raton, Florida. Dr. Hugh-Pennie has been the Director of Education at Special Education schools in the United States and Assistant Professor in Departments for Education and Educational Psychology at Mercy College (New York), Brock University and the University of Western Ontario (Canada). She is a certified Special Education Teacher (K-12) in the US and Canada. As the Director of Inclusive Education at The Harbour School in Hong Kong she is responsible for both Learning Support and Learning Extension (i.e. Gifted) services. Dr. Hugh-Pennie is an Internationally Board Certified Behavior Analyst and current President of the Hong Kong Association for Behavior Analysis. Dr Hugh-Pennie is dedicated to disseminating information about the effective use of applied behavior analysis in education and to this end she has worked as a Program Coordinator with the Association for Behavior Analysis International (ABAI) to bring lecturers from within and outside of the field of Behavior Analysis to discuss topics related to Teaching Behavior Analysis.

Jessica Knott is the Learning Design Manager for IT Services Teaching and Learning Technology at Michigan State University. She guides a team that helps faculty, staff, and academic programs effectively integrate technology into their teaching and research through consultations, demonstrations, workshops, and hands-on development. She has worked in information technology since 1998, spanning the private and academic sectors.

Bee Theng Lau is an Associate Professor in the faculty of Engineering, Computing and Science at Swinburne University of Technology, Sarawak Campus, Malaysia. She completed her PhD in 2006. Her research interests are mainly on assistive and alternative technologies utilizing ICT for learning and assisting people with special needs. She has edited two books and published various articles in peer reviewed journals, edited books and conference proceedings. In addition, she has successfully supervised/co-supervised five Master of Science by research students to completion. She coordinated and completed a few research projects on assistive technologies for special children such as facial expression recognition based communication, social skills acquisition with animations and challenging behavior recognition/monitoring.

Gabrielle Lee is an assistant professor in the Department of Counseling, Educational Psychology, and Special Education at Michigan State University. She earned her Ph.D.in Applied Behavior Analysis from Columbia University and an Ed. M in Counseling Psychology from Rutgers University. She is a licensed doctoral-level clinical psychologist and board certified behavior analyst (BCBA-D). Her research primarily focuses on early intervention for children with autism spectrum disorders.

Jessica Lowe is an elementary school teacher at Seminole Elementary School in Okeechobee, Florida. Mrs. Lowe has been teaching for 7 years in Okeechobee County and currently teaches first grade. Her research focuses on the integration of technology use in rural school districts and how technology effects learning for students and teachers in rural communities. Mrs. Lowe earned her Bachelor's Degree in Elementary Education from FAU in December 2009. She is currently completing her Master's Degree in Instructional Technology at FAU. Mrs. Lowe has presented many technology trainings through district professional development sessions as well as at school level sessions. She currently holds a position on her school leadership team as the Team Leader for Instructional Technology and is utilized for technology trainings and assistance as needed.

Jennifer Loy is Professor of Integrated Product Design at the University of Technology Sydney. She has a PhD in Industrial Design. Loy's background is in design for manufacturing, with a focus on advanced manufacturing, particularly digital technologies. Her research is on the impact of 3D printing and associated digital technologies on design and human development across disciplines, for product service systems to humanitarian logistics, medical devices to fashion design.

Nicole Luke completed her PhD degree in Applied Behavior Analysis at Columbia University. Her professional career has included consulting, coaching, and teaching in both clinical and management roles in educational settings. Her research interests include: verbal behaviour, verbal developmental theory, behavioural cusps and capabilities, and teaching as a strategic science.

Robbie K. Melton, Ph.D. is the Associate Vice Chancellor of Mobilization Emerging Technology for Tennessee Board of Regents. Melton serves as the chief system level administrator to oversee the system's mission and initiatives for the Strategic Mobilization Planning and Business Models, Mobilization Quality Assurances, Faculty and Student Use of Mobile Devices related to teaching, learning, training, and workforce development, and the coordination of research, product testing, pilots and security safety networks. She has published and presented around the nation on the impact and value of mobilization for education and the workforce and has acquired a new distinction as an "App-ologist" due to her study of the pedagogy and best teaching practices with mobilization, quality standards for the utilization of mobile apps, and for her creation of the Mobile App Education and Workforce Resource Center (50,000 + Apps that have been aligned with over ninety-five subject areas from Pre-K to Ph.D., including workforce careers, professional development and lifelong learning, according to one's mobile device of choice). Melton is the winner of numerous awards; the latest being the 2016 Online Learning Consortium Fellow, 2016 Richard Jonsen Educational Technologies top honor for her lifetime work in educational technology, 2015 MERLOT Leadership Visionary Award, CDE Top 30 2014 Technologists, Transformers and Trailblazers, 2013 Apple Distinguished Educator, 2012, Technology WOW Award, 2013 eAfrica Innovator Education Award.

Lori Miller-Rososhansky received her PhD from Florida Atlantic University in Educational Leadership & Research Methodology; her Masters of Science in Non-Profit Management from Worcester State College; her Bachelor of Arts in English from Boston University. She is a Certified Professional in Learning and Performance (CPLP) as well as a certified trainer for both Touchpoints and Bridges Out of Poverty. She is currently the Learning & Development Officer for Children's Services Council of Palm Beach County, Florida.

Jessica S. Mitchell has earned an Ed.D. in Instruction and Curriculum Leadership from the University of Memphis with a qualitative research endorsement in educational studies. Her research interests include digital literacies and social experiences of teaching and learning with technology. She has over ten years of teaching experience with five years of teaching experience in online contexts. She is currently an Assistant Professor in Secondary Education at the University of North Alabama.

James Novak is a doctoral candidate, lecturer and industrial designer at Griffith University, Australia. His research is currently looking into the opportunity for smart products to physically evolve throughout their use, in particular for the sports and health industries where the relationship between humans and products is heavily intertwined and always unique. He has previously won the Dick Aubin Distinguished Paper Award for his 3D printed bicycle, which has continued to be exhibited around the world, and been recognised as a leader in the field of 3D printing by his appointment as a Digital Champion by Advance Queensland.

Devrim Ozdemir is an experienced scholar in the field of instructional design and technology. He has experience in higher education for more than a decade. His work revolves around designing and developing efficient instructional systems and strategies which will bring the most quality with least resources. He has worked in many different settings as an academic technology support coordinator, education technology lab manager, IT support, instructional designer, director of language technologies, and instructional design coordinator. He has acted both as a leader and also a team member in many projects. His work gradually evolved over the years. He has technical, pedagogical, and administrative knowledge. He is a quick learner of emerging instructional technologies and a follower of innovative learning strategies. He is also up-to-date with changing higher education policies.

Vanessa Preast is an experienced instructional designer, trainer and researcher with a veterinary background who is dedicated to using skills in analysis, design, development, evaluation, and problem solving to improve performance, digital accessibility, learning, effectiveness, and safety within organizations and the community.

Kathleen M. Randolph is a doctoral candidate in special education at Florida Atlantic University. Her dissertation, *The Impact of iCoaching on Teacher Delivered Opportunities to Respond*, concluded that using iPods to coach teachers coupled with a teacher preparation session increased opportunities to respond for students in the teachers' classrooms. Kathleen spent more than ten years teaching in a variety of special education settings as an administrator in Pennsylvania. She is a Kaleidoscope Representative for the Teacher Education Division of the Council for Exceptional Children, and is also a board member on of the Florida Council for Exceptional Children. Her research interests are teacher preparation, positive behavioral teaching strategies, and teacher coaching with modern technology.

David B. Ross has many years of experience in adult education, leadership, ethics, policy and curriculum development, classroom instruction, and research. In his present role as an Associate Professor at the Abraham S. Fischler College of Education, Nova Southeastern University, he teaches doctoral level courses in educational, instructional, and organizational leadership as well as higher education to prepare today's practitioners who will assume leadership positions in any profession for current and future challenges. His courses focus on current trends and issues that impact society on both the national and global level. Learning from many perspectives and philosophies from mentors while attending Northern Illinois University, the University of Alabama, and Florida Atlantic University, has assisted him in guiding students in the learning process. Dr. Ross earned his Doctorate in Educational Leadership, with an emphasis in Leadership, Research, Curriculum, and Adult Education; and a Master of Justice Policy Management with a Professional Certificate in Public Administration at Florida Atlantic University. He earned his Bachelor of Science Degree in Computer Science at Northern Illinois University. Dr. Ross regularly speaks at conferences and provides consultation and training in the areas of leadership, policy issues, team building, professional development, academic writing, education, and behavior management. He has written articles on leadership, power, narcissism, organizational stress, academic integrity, plagiarism and fraud, policy development, professional development, and areas of homeland security. Dr. Ross is a dissertation chair and committee member of various methodologies: quantitative, qualitative, and mixed methods. In addition, he is a reviewer for the university's Institutional Review Board. Dr. Ross was named Professor of the Year 2015-2016 for the Abraham S. Fischler College of Education.

Christina Seamster is a passionate researcher in the field of virtual education. Dr. Seamster was previously an Assistant Principal for a state-wide virtual school. Her research focuses on evaluating virtual school teacher effectiveness, virtual school teacher pedagogy and the impact of teachers' instructional practices on student achievement. Dr. Seamster earned her Ph.D. in Curriculum and Instruction with a specialization in Instructional Technology from Florida Atlantic University in 2016.

Clark Shah-Nelson has developed, designed, taught, coordinated, and managed distance, online, and blended learning programs. Currently he serves as the Assistant Dean of Instructional Design and Technology with the University of Maryland School of Social Work in Baltimore. Previously, he led the team of instructional designers in the Center for Teaching and Learning at the Johns Hopkins Bloomberg School of Public Health, managed the online education business unit at the State University of New York at Delhi, developed and taught online German courses for Colorado Online Learning, and helped establish the Denver Public Schools Distance Learning Network.

Frank Tomsic is the Director of the McCormick Educational Technology Center at Rush University. He was the inaugural Director of Online Teaching and Learning at the Illinois Mathematics and Science Academy, as well as the inaugural Director of Distance Education at Northwestern University School of Continuing Studies. A former teacher and corporate trainer, he earned his B.A. in teaching from the University of Illinois at Urbana-Champaign where he studied language acquisition theory. He earned his M.S. in computing technology in education from Nova-Southeastern University where he focused on online learning environments. He also previously directed technology programs in both corporate and education environments, and is an active member of the Online Learning Consortium, iNACOL, and the eLearning Guild.

Elizabeth Vultaggio Salah has been teaching at the elementary school level for 28 years, all of which have been in Title 1 Schools. Dr. Salah earned her Bachelor of Arts from Florida Atlantic University, her Master of Teaching and Learning from Nova Southeastern University, and her doctorate from Nova Southeastern University. The degrees encompass concentrations in Elementary Education, Reading, Special Education, and Autism. Her dissertation topic was on the Effects of Interactive Read-Aloud and Literature Discussion on Reading Comprehension for First-Grade Students With Language Impairments in a Title 1 School. Dr. Salah was selected as the recipient of the Dr. Charles L. Faires Dissertation of Distinction Award for her research on reading comprehension for first-grade language impaired students. For the past four years, Dr. Salah has taught first-grade in an inclusive setting and is currently teaching Voluntary Prekindergarten Inclusion. She holds a Florida Certification in Elementary Education (Grades 1-6), Exceptional Student Education (K-12), Prekindergarten/Primary Education (age 3-Grade 3), Primary Education (Grades K-3), English for Speakers of Other Languages (ESOL) Endorsement, Reading Endorsement, and Autism Endorsement. For the past four years, Dr. Salah has been active in the autism community by volunteering her time to numerous events, such as Surfers for Autism, WalkAbout Autism, and Walk Now for Autism Speaks. During her undergraduate education, Dr. Salah traveled to Germany, Italy, and India to conduct research on the education systems in these countries, and compared them to the U.S. educational system. Currently, Dr. Salah is teaching master level courses at Grand Canyon University, Arizona. She also oversees her students' field experience/practicum hours.

Ko Min Win is a post-graduate student from Swinburne University of Technology, Sarawak Campus, Malaysia. He completed his Bachelor of Information and Communication Technology (BICT) and Master of Science (MSc) at Swinburne University of Technology in 2014 and 2016 respectively. He has keen interest in Autism Spectrum Disorder, Special Education, Web Technology and Assisted Technology. His research focuses on integration of Differentiated Instruction and Information Technology into Social Story approach to boost its effectiveness in social skill acquisition by children who are diagnosed with Autism Spectrum Disorder. He has recently presented a paper at the International Conference on Knowledge and Education Technology 2015 (ICKET 2015) which was later published in Journal of Advances in Environmental Biology (AEB).

Michelle F. Wright is a Research Associate at the Pennsylvania State University. Her research interests include the contextual factors, such as familial and cultural, which influence children's and adolescents' aggression and victimization as well as their pursuit, maintenance, and achievement of peer status. She also has an interest in peer rejection and unpopularity and how such statuses relate to insecurity with one's peer standing, aggression, and victimization. Her current research focuses on designing and implementing technology-assisted interventions.

Index

1:1 Computing 204
21st Century Learning 2, 159, 252

A

Accessibility 31, 57, 62, 101, 135, 187, 205, 224, 226, 239, 250, 258-266, 269-278, 280, 324
Accessibility Professional (AP) 263, 280
Actional Immersion 451-452, 460
Active Learning 4-6, 9, 13, 19-20, 25, 103, 108, 171, 336
Additive Manufacturing 404, 406, 411-412, 426
Additive Manufacturing (3D Printing) 411, 426
Adolescent 384
Aging in Place 208, 211, 213-214, 226, 233
Allied Health Professional 182
and Mathematics Education 204
Animation 304, 307, 309, 314, 323-324
Anonymity 374-375, 384
Anxiety 206, 221, 369, 373, 384, 389-393, 399, 401, 444-445, 450
Applied Behavior Analysis 330, 333-334, 336-338, 341, 351
Assessment Practices 43, 45, 50, 61, 64, 274
Assistive Technology 208, 222, 253, 265
Association for Talent Development (ATD) 33, 36, 41
Athletic Trainer 182
Authentic Assessment 45, 165, 175-177, 182
Autism 292-293, 300-301, 304, 329-330, 337, 339
Autism Spectrum Disorders 292-293, 301, 329-330

B

Baby Boomers 35, 205, 233
Baseline 309, 311, 329, 355
Behavior Chaining 352, 359
Behavior Intention 134
Behavior Intention (BI) 134
Blended 4-5, 66, 154, 192, 197, 199, 204, 252
Brain Inspired Digital Technology 458, 460

Brain-based Learning 238, 256
Bug-in-Ear 281-282, 284, 286, 299
Bug-in-Ear (BIE) 284, 286, 299
Bullying 364-366, 368-369, 371, 373, 375, 384

C

Cardiac Auscultation 175, 182
Centennials (GenZ 233
Centrality of Belief 460
Centrality of Beliefs 450, 454-455, 460
Children 24, 69, 73, 82, 185-188, 190, 195, 200, 210, 221, 245, 249, 251, 293, 300-307, 309, 311, 315, 323-325, 329, 331-332, 335, 337, 339, 346, 369-371, 374-375, 384
Coaching with Technology 283, 286, 295-296
Collectivism 384
College of Education 47, 50
Communication 11, 35, 48, 57, 68-69, 72, 74, 79, 93, 136, 152, 159, 169, 188, 191, 193, 206, 208-210, 212-216, 220, 226, 233, 281-282, 290, 295, 300-302, 304, 324, 329, 334, 337, 365, 374, 406-407, 428, 432, 434-444, 446, 448, 452, 455-457
Community of Inquiry 11, 14, 21, 92
Community of Practice (CoP) 41
Competence 77, 145, 167, 170, 174, 176, 182, 218
Concept of Self 456, 460
Connected Learner 256
Connected learners 246, 249
Connected Teacher 256
Constructivism 2-3, 42, 44-45, 48-49, 62, 64, 94
Context Awareness 10, 17
Continuous Medical Education 163
Continuous Professional Education 163, 174, 182
Core-Based Statistical Areas 204
Course Instructor 258, 260, 262-263, 280
Covert Audio Coaching 281-282, 286, 289, 294-295, 299
Covert Audio Coaching (CAC) 286, 299

Culture 4, 14, 16, 24-25, 45, 49, 54, 65, 87, 101, 105, 114, 136-137, 153, 219, 225, 242, 247, 263, 276-277, 305, 331, 395, 413, 428, 431, 434, 439-440, 443, 445-446, 457

Cyberbullying 364-376, 384

D

Design Thinking 6, 414

Differentiated animated social story 315-316, 320-321, 329

Differentiated Instruction 301, 305-307, 309, 324-325, 329

Differentiation 226, 305-306, 308, 311, 315

Digital Accessibility 260, 263, 280

Digital Citizenship 86, 246

Digital Divide 110, 135-136, 159, 219-220, 250-252, 256

Digital Literacy 20, 64, 152, 159, 187, 207, 226, 245, 374

Digital Native 236, 245-253, 256

Digital Natives 44, 64, 185, 233, 236, 244-253

Digital Reflections 17-18

Digital Skills Divide 159

Digital Space 153, 449-450, 456-457, 460

Digital Storytelling 43-45, 47-50, 52-62, 64

Digital User Divide 252, 256

Disability 207, 250, 259-261, 265, 280

Discrete Trail Training 352

Distance Education 66-69, 73, 78, 80, 82, 93, 184, 195-200

E

Educational Technology 6, 23-24, 90-91, 94, 189, 192, 246, 331, 353

EduGadgets 9, 17

Electronics 64, 88, 407, 412, 415, 418, 421

Email 78, 136, 143, 214-215, 299, 364, 369, 385-390, 395, 429, 442

Emerging Technology 9, 14, 17-18

Empathy 302, 369, 374, 384, 440

Employment Coaching 282-283, 286, 299

Engagement 14-15, 25, 33, 52, 70, 73, 92, 95, 99, 102, 104, 116, 137, 140, 152-153, 191, 195, 207, 210, 215, 224-225, 239, 242, 246, 248, 256, 291, 304, 408, 410, 419, 432, 435, 437, 444, 449, 452

Exogenous Technology 331, 336-338, 346, 351

Experiential Learning 9, 46, 49, 61, 64, 172, 206

Exploratory Installation 1-2, 13-16, 18-19

Externalizing Difficulties 369, 373, 384

F

FaceTime 23, 215, 295, 299

Faculty Development 7, 15, 97-98, 100, 130, 259

Fidelity 71-73, 82, 165-168, 170, 172, 175, 182, 283

Flipped classroom 103, 108

Formal Learning 6, 35, 38, 40-41

Full Time Online Students 86

Full Time Virtual School Teacher 86

G

Generalized animated social story 329

Generation X 35, 233

Generation Y (Gen Y) 426

Gerontechnology 205, 207-209, 214, 217, 226-227, 233

Green Screen Booth 18

H

Hacking 21, 368

Heart Maps 396, 401

Human-Centered 403-404, 406-407, 410, 413, 416, 421-422

Human-Centred Design 426

Hybrid 166, 197, 204, 418

I

iCoaching 295, 299

iGeneration 236, 244-246, 256

Immediate Feedback 170, 174, 281-284, 286, 289-292, 294, 299, 333

Independence 10, 205, 207-214, 225, 227, 233, 258, 305

Individualism 233, 384

Industrial Design 411-412, 426

Informal Learning 6, 14-15, 33, 35-42, 94, 201

Inservice Teachers 283, 299

Instant Messaging 71, 364, 366, 369, 434-435, 442

Instructional Design 5, 20-21, 34, 90, 94-95, 100, 108, 153, 170, 172, 258, 263, 280

Instructional Design Coordinator 258, 263, 280

Instructional IWB Usage (IU) 134

Interactive Whiteboard (IWB) 109-110, 112, 134

Internet of Things (IoT) 9, 17-18, 409, 426

Intervention 6, 50, 175, 177, 182, 281-282, 290-293, 300-301, 303-309, 311, 314-316, 320-321, 323-324, 329, 332-333, 338, 342, 351-355, 360-361, 376, 411

Intra-Organizational 434-435, 448

iPod 96, 299

J

Journal Writing 54, 395, 401

K

K-12 23, 66-83, 103, 139, 185, 189-190, 192-193, 195-196, 198-200, 252, 299

L

Language 4, 13, 16, 24-25, 35, 40, 45-46, 49, 58, 69, 72, 77, 91, 99, 143, 148, 185, 222, 242, 272, 286, 304, 335, 343-344, 387, 413, 455
Learn Unit 339, 341-342, 345
Learning 1-6, 9, 11-16, 18-26, 28-29, 33-50, 52-58, 60-62, 64, 66-74, 76-81, 83, 86-91, 93-103, 105, 108-109, 112, 114, 122, 136-137, 149-150, 154, 159, 162-167, 169-177, 182, 184-192, 194-201, 204-208, 219-226, 235-253, 256-257, 259-262, 272, 275, 277, 280, 283, 291, 293, 300-302, 305-308, 323-325, 331-333, 335-337, 339, 341-346, 351-357, 360-361, 371, 374, 404, 407, 409, 422, 427, 436-437, 439-441, 451-452, 456, 458, 460
Learning Coach 72, 86
Learning Management System 56, 71-73, 86, 191, 196, 204, 259, 280
Learning Management System (LMS) 86, 191, 204, 259
Learning Organization 33, 41
Learning Outcomes 9, 35, 42-45, 47-50, 52-53, 57-58, 62, 64, 73, 109, 174, 198, 305, 307
Learning Theories 2, 16, 95, 154, 237-238, 256
Life-Care Retirement Communities 234
Live Demo Space 18
Live Lesson 72, 86
Loneliness 211, 213, 215, 369, 373, 384, 391
Lutheran Church Missouri Synod 109-110, 117
Lutheran School Teacher 134

M

Makerspace 1-5, 18, 252
Makerspaces 3, 101, 252
Medical Professionals 164, 217, 392, 401
Membership Organization 33-34, 36, 41
Millennials 35, 205, 234
Mobile Learning 87-100, 102-103, 105, 108
Modeling 6, 16, 33, 101, 112, 283, 304, 334, 341, 345, 352, 356-357, 360, 406, 418-419
Multigenre Writing 387, 401
Multiple Literacies 188, 245, 256

N

Narrative Inquiry 386, 402
New Literacies Theory 136, 159
Non-formal Learning 42
Normative Belief 384

O

Online 2, 4-5, 12-13, 19, 22-23, 25, 29, 33, 35-36, 38, 42, 66-82, 86, 88, 104, 136-137, 139, 142, 145, 168, 191-192, 195-201, 204, 212-213, 215-217, 222-224, 244-246, 258-266, 270, 273-278, 291, 331, 365-366, 369-376, 407, 427, 429, 435-436, 440-441, 448
Online Education 81, 168, 198-199, 258-262, 266, 273-274, 276-278
Ontogenetic 404, 406, 421, 426
Operant Conditioning 334, 352-353, 355-356, 359-360

P

Parent 72, 195-196, 217, 245, 341, 359
Parental Mediation and Monitoring 384
Parenting Style 384
Partnering Pedagogy 246, 256
Pedagogy 2-4, 11, 14, 16, 19, 21, 23, 46-47, 66-67, 70, 75, 80, 82, 89, 91, 93-95, 100, 129, 192, 246, 256, 331, 356
Peer 4-5, 28, 52, 56, 100, 137, 149, 152-154, 194, 242, 263, 276, 290-291, 336, 369-370, 372, 375, 384
Peer attachment 369, 372, 384
Peer Contagion 384
Perceived Ease of Use 109, 111-112, 119, 121-122, 124-126, 128-130, 134, 454
Perceived Ease of Use (PEOU) 109, 111, 129, 134
Perceived Usefulness 109, 111-112, 119, 121-122, 124-125, 127-130, 134, 223, 454
Perceived Usefulness (PU) 109, 111, 129, 134
Personality 5, 237, 402, 420, 434, 436-437, 446, 448
Preschool 186, 188, 199-200, 339, 358
Preservice Teachers 289-291, 299
Professional Development 1, 4, 6, 11, 15-16, 20-22, 25, 33, 76-77, 81, 96, 98-102, 105, 115-116, 122-123, 125, 130, 190-194, 196, 201, 240, 277, 281-286, 292-296, 299, 343
Provictim Attitudes 384

Q

Quality of Life 205-207, 209-215, 217-218, 226-227, 234, 393

R

Reading 71, 90, 136, 142-143, 148-151, 186, 214, 224, 241, 245, 250, 264, 285, 290, 303-306, 314, 323, 332, 335-336, 345, 355, 388, 390-391, 393-394, 398

Relationships 72, 75, 91, 109, 130, 137, 143, 208, 210, 212-213, 215, 219, 221-222, 233, 246-247, 252, 263, 273, 275, 353, 362, 368, 370, 403-404, 412, 416, 419-420, 448-450, 455, 460

Response to Intervention 332-333, 352, 355

Rostered Lutheran School Teacher 134

Rural 68-69, 116, 159, 184-201, 204

S

Science, Technology, Engineering, and Mathematics Education 204

Self-Directed 2, 35-36, 41-42, 432, 437, 448

Self-directed Learning 35-36, 42

Self-Efficacy 135-138, 152, 154, 159, 213, 237, 454

Self-Motivation 446, 448

Shaping 111, 184, 195, 198, 325, 337, 345, 352, 357-358

Silent Generation 205, 234

Simulation-based Instruction 164, 166, 171

Simulation-Based Learning 163, 165, 171-172, 182

Situated learning 49, 94, 108, 450, 452

Social Exclusion 366, 384

Social Networking Site 220

Social skills 215, 300-302, 305, 309, 311, 315, 320-321, 323, 325, 329, 369, 374, 448

Social story 300-305, 307-309, 311-312, 314-316, 320-321, 323, 329

Social Story App (SSA) 308, 329

Socialization 205, 211, 215-216, 225, 301, 354, 434, 440, 446, 448

Sociocultural Learning Theory 159

Socio-materiality 90, 108

Stasis 404, 426

Story Sharing 402

Stress 52, 226, 369, 385-387, 390-396, 399, 401-402, 414, 433, 439, 445

Student-Centered Instructional IWB Usage (SCIU) 134

Student-Centered Instructional Usage 109, 118-119, 121, 124-126, 128-130

Study Abroad 43-44, 48, 50, 52, 55-58, 60-62, 65

Sustainability 95, 98, 262, 406, 408-412, 418-419, 421-422, 430-431, 445

Symbolic Immersion 453, 460

Systems 39, 70, 76, 89, 110-112, 136, 152, 168, 189-190, 195, 199, 209, 214-218, 237, 258, 262, 271, 280-282, 284, 295-296, 309, 337, 339, 341, 403-406, 409-410, 412-413, 416-417, 419-422, 429, 439-440, 445-446

T

Task Analysis 283, 352, 357, 359

Teacher as Strategic Scientist 342, 359

Teacher Preparation 99, 239, 285, 296

Teacher-Centered Instructional IWB Usage (TCIU) 134

Teacher-Centered Instructional Usage 109, 118-119, 121, 124-125, 127-130

Teaching 1-2, 4, 6, 9, 11, 13-16, 18-21, 23, 25, 44, 46-47, 60-62, 66-71, 74-82, 87-88, 91-93, 97-103, 105, 108-110, 113-114, 116, 122, 130, 149, 163, 167, 170-174, 176, 184, 188, 190-196, 235-240, 242-246, 248-253, 275-276, 283, 289-292, 302, 305, 308, 324, 329-339, 341-346, 352-353, 355-357, 359-360, 399

Teaching learning process 239, 246

Teaching-Learning Process (TLP) 235, 256

Technogenesis 449, 460

Technological 1, 14, 20, 33, 44, 75, 80, 91, 94-95, 98, 100, 109-110, 113-114, 121-122, 125-126, 129, 166, 189, 191-192, 195, 205-209, 214, 218, 221-222, 226, 233, 238, 250, 252-253, 273, 281-282, 293, 331, 361, 370, 385, 388, 399, 404-405, 407, 409, 411, 414, 419-420, 422, 429, 431, 433, 435-436, 438, 445, 450-451, 456, 460

Technology Rich Environments 257

Technology Test Kitchen 1-2, 4-5, 11, 14-15, 17-25

Technology-based 42, 138

Technology-based or Online Informal Learning 42

Technology-rich learning environments 235

Teleworker 448

Three-term Contingency 290-291, 334, 352-356

Traditional 5, 14-15, 44-45, 47, 52, 58, 60-62, 64-69, 71-72, 74, 76, 78, 82, 86, 89, 93-94, 103, 109, 136, 138, 140, 153-154, 165, 170-171, 174-175, 186, 197-198, 204, 218-219, 224-225, 234, 237, 239, 245, 258, 280, 283-285, 289, 291, 300, 364-366, 368-369, 371, 373, 375, 384, 403, 410, 421, 427-429, 434, 436-440, 442, 446, 451, 455-456

Traditional Face-To-Face Bullying 364-366, 368-369, 371, 373, 375, 384

Traditional Storytelling Techniques 44, 64-65
Training 2, 11, 15, 23, 25, 34-35, 39, 41, 57, 97, 99, 111, 115, 122, 139, 164, 166, 168, 171, 174, 190-191, 194, 204, 207, 212, 214-215, 217, 221-223, 226, 261-263, 274-277, 283, 292, 299, 302, 305, 307, 309, 330, 334, 337-339, 341, 343-344, 346, 352, 356, 360, 362, 371-372, 436-440, 446
Transactional Distance 93, 95, 108
Transformative Learning 42, 49, 61
Transformative Learning Process 42

U

Ubiquitous Computing 403-404, 409-411, 413-416, 420-421, 426
Ubiquitous Learning 108
Universal Design 235, 238-243, 251, 257, 261-263, 277, 280
Universal Design for Learning 235, 238-243, 251, 257, 262
Universal Design of Instruction 280
University of Arizona 20
Urgent vs. Important 398, 402

Usability 56-57, 92, 95, 258-259, 261-262, 265-266, 269-270, 273-277, 280, 308, 324

V

Virtual Hrig 457, 460
Virtual Teams 434-435, 446, 448

W

WCAG 259, 261-263, 266, 269
Web 2.0 tool 244, 257
Web Facilitated 204
writing 7, 29, 44, 48, 50, 54-55, 60, 69, 100, 135-154, 161, 204, 226, 241, 244, 303, 355, 361, 386-390, 393-396, 399, 401-402, 418, 448, 450
Writing as Healing 393-394, 402
Writing Voice 388, 390, 393-394, 402

Y

Youth 136, 375

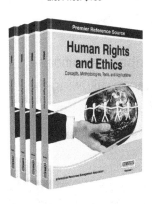
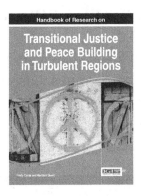
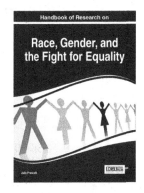

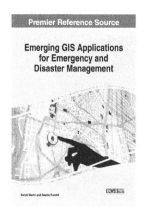
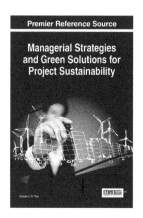

Become an IRMA Member

Members of the **Information Resources Management Association (IRMA)** understand the importance of community within their field of study. The Information Resources Management Association is an ideal venue through which professionals, students, and academicians can convene and share the latest industry innovations and scholarly research that is changing the field of information science and technology. Become a member today and enjoy the benefits of membership as well as the opportunity to collaborate and network with fellow experts in the field.

IRMA Membership Benefits:

- **One FREE Journal Subscription**

- **30% Off Additional Journal Subscriptions**

- **20% Off Book Purchases**

- Updates on the latest events and research on Information Resources Management through the IRMA-L listserv.

- Updates on new open access and downloadable content added to Research IRM.

- A copy of the Information Technology Management Newsletter twice a year.

- A certificate of membership.

IRMA Membership $195

Scan code or visit **irma-international.org** and begin by selecting your free journal subscription.

Membership is good for one full year.

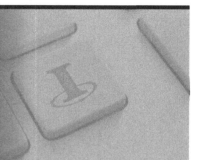

Printed in the United States
By Bookmasters